Following the Fairways

F.P. Hopkins 'THE TEE SHOT' *Courtesy of:* ***Burlington Gallery***

Back cover Robert Turnbull 'GLENEAGLES KING'S COURSE' *— Courtesy of:* ***KWP Fine Art***

Front cover Robert Turnbull 'TROON' *— Courtesy of:* ***KWP Fine Art***

KENSINGTON WEST PRODUCTIONS
LONDON
ENGLAND

ACKNOWLEDGEMENTS

ROBERT WADE 'The Eighteenth, St. Andrews' *ROSENSTIEL'S*

There have been all manner of hands that have guided the production of this, our updated, revised, improved and third edition of 'Following the Fairways'. We have published this time in our endeavour to produce what we believe is a really fun, useful, colourful guide to the golf courses of the British Isles.

We acknowledge the kind and generous advice of many golf professionals, secretaries and enthusiasts from all parts of Britain and Ireland.

In our endeavours to illustrate the book, we have been kindly assisted by the Burlington Gallery, Sarah Baddiel and other passionate golf collectors. The colour work is all credited and we are most grateful to the descendants of Harry Rountree for kindly allowing us permission to use his works.

We acknowledge also the assistance of people who have helped us in selecting hotels, restaurants and pubs around the country. We hope you enjoy your investigations.

We hope you appreciate the front and back cover which we are privileged to include in this year's book. We are also hoping to publish limited edition prints of these spectacular originals. Do please telephone if you would like further details.

I would also like to thank the staff at Kensington West for their hard work and perseverance in their tremendous effort to meet our deadlines and publish before the delights of this year's Ryder Cup. I would like to thank also the vast number of advisors who helped us and also the fantastic typists who once again put together all the facts, figures and fairways collated in this book. Jo, Camilla, Amelia, Anne, Jilly, Alice and I am bound to have forgotten someone. We hit the deadline and that was a great effort, because it means at last I can go and play a round of golf!

Finally, as publisher, I would like to thank the editor for his tremendous efforts in providing such distinguished copy. I would like to thank all the companies who helped with our production for their accomplished work.

KENSINGTON WEST PRODUCTIONS
Garretts Building, Cathles Road, London SW12 9LD
Tel: 01-675 6733

Edited by:

NICK EDMUND

Consultant Editors:

LOUISE SPELLER, TIM STOW, MATTHEW SMITH, JULIAN WEST, JAMES PORTER

Reproduction, printing and binding:

KENSINGTON WEST PRODUCTIONS, UNIVERSAL COLOUR AND NORDICA

Typesetting:

WANDSWORTH TYPESETTING LTD.
205A St. John's Hill, London SW11 1TH

FORMAL BITS

FOREWORD

During my lifetime I have seen a remarkable growth in the popularity of golf. This has inevitably led to a great increase in the number of golf courses. Personally I have been lucky enough to play on many courses, old and new, links by the sea, heathland and park courses inland. Like many golfers I have very happy memories of these visits and indeed of the hotels closely associated with the courses. Following the Fairways will remind me of them. I still share also the enjoyment of those who look forward to playing on a course for the first time. Again this book will inspire us all to such new visits and the map of golf courses will be especially valuable. Lastly, I have a non-golfing wife who has stoically borne her role as a golf widow for over 40 years. I welcome Fairways' suggestion of suitable visits for her.

For all these reasons I welcome the publication of Following the Fairways and wish it every success.

The Rt. Hon. Viscount Whitelaw, C.H., M.C.
HOUSE OF LORDS

CONTENTS

THE OPENING STROKES

CHOICE GOLF

ENGLAND

WALES

SCOTLAND

IRELAND

CHAMPIONSHIP GOLF

COMPLETE GOLF

CONTENTS

ENGLAND

WALES

SCOTLAND

IRELAND

JOHN LAVERY "North Berwick"

THE MACHRIE HOTEL

The Machrie Hotel enjoys a superb position on the enchanting Isle of Islay, the most southerly island of the Hebrides. It is verypeaceful, providing an ideal escape for those seeking a holiday in totally tranquil surroundings. Islay is famous for its malt whiskies and the industry still thrives here although there are now only half a dozen distilleries left on the island. Visitors can spend an enjoyable day going round one of them. The Hotel is a marvellously relaxing place to stay. The proprietors are Murdo and Kathleen Macpherson. Mr Macpherson's grandfather was in the same line of business, so all guests can be sure they will be very comfortable indeed.

In the cocktail bar visitors have the chance of trying eighty different malt whiskies before enjoying a superb dinner in the Byre Restaurant, once the old byre of the farm, which concentrates on using local produce such as fish and game and serves sumptious shellfish. Conference facilities are also available at The Machrie.

The hotel has a large number of extremely comfortable bedrooms, with private bathroom, television, radio, tea and coffee making facilities and hairdryer.

For those who like to come and go as they please, fifteen de luxe self-contained cottage suites have been created, complementing the hotel's facilities. Each suite is well appointed with independent central heating, full bathroom and shower, colour television and kitchen. Each cottage has been furnished to an exceptionally high standard.

The hotel is alongside the 18-hole golf course and golf is free for those staying at the hotel. However, golf is not the only enjoyable sport on offer. There is also clay pigeon shooting, and a stretch of river for guests to try casting a fly for salmon or trout, which Mr Cassidy the chef will be only too pleased to cook. Windsurfing, tennis and riding are available nearby.

The Machrie Hotel
Port Ellen
Isle of Islay
Argyll PA42 7AN
Tel: (0496) 2310

H.SANDHAM 'The Club's the Thing' *BURLINGTON GALLERY*

Inverness
Highland & Grampian
Aberdeen
Perth
Fife
Edinburgh
Lothian
Glasgow
Strathclyde
Dumfries & Galloway & Borders
Newcastle-upon-Tyne
Carlisle
Cumbria, Durham, Cleveland, Tyne & Wear & Northumberland
N. Ireland
Eire
North Yorkshire & Humberside
York
Lancashire, Merseyside, Gtr. Manchester & I.O.M.
South & West Yorkshire
Leeds
Hull
Manchester
Liverpool
Cheshire
Notts & Derbys
Lincolnshire
Gwynedd & Clwyd
Staffs & Shropshire
Northants & Leics
Norwich
Birmingham
Warwicks & West Midlands
Cambridgeshire, Suffolk & Norfolk
Dyfed, Powys, Gwent & Glamorgan
Hereford & Worcs & Gloucs
Herts, Beds & Essex
Bucks & Oxon
Swansea
Gtr. London
London
Cardiff
Berks
Somerset, Avon, Dorset & Wilts
Hampshire & Channel Islands
Surrey
Kent
Sussex
Southampton
Portsmouth
Devon
Exeter
Cornwall
Plymouth
Penzance

Following the Fairways

BURLINGTON GALLERY

As long as sports and games have been played, so their depiction in words and pictures has been popular. Through changes of taste, the image of sports, games and all things English has developed. Established in 1980, Burlington Gallery has built up a reputation for its specialisation in all sporting art forms.

Over recent years, the Gallery has held annual British Sports and Games Exhibitions which have been greatly enjoyed and are most successful. Further Sports Exhibitions are in the planning stage. Catering for all manner of sporting diversions, the stock tends to concentrate on the more specialised areas of collecting, whilst maintaining fine examples of the traditional field sports of hunting, shooting and fishing.

Pictorial depiction is the chief area of collection, but all these sports and games has encouraged other craftsmen as well. Ceramic makers, metal workers, carpenters and needleworkers have all contributed to the history of golf, tennis, cricket, rugby and the like. Examples of these works are greatly sought after and often are collection pieces in their own right.

Many examples of this can be seen in Burlington Gallery, also with their colleagues Burlington Paintings. The Gallery holds the best examples of oil paintings and watercolours available. Over the past couple of years, the Gallery has held two superb Cricket Exhibitions, with exhibits ranging from fine oils and watercolours, through some of the rarest and finest of engravings, to stunning items in ceramic and metal, jewellery and glass.

The Gallery will always be happy to keep you informed as to its plans and the availability of catalogues in advance notice of Exhibitions.

All those areas of collecting sporting memorabilia have proved to be a great investment. There is no doubt that this will continue — the supply cannot increase while the demand continues to grow. It is also becoming increasingly difficult to find these items in good condition. Items may be so rare they are accepted in any condition.

In addition to the specialised areas of stock, the Gallery always has a fine selection of London scenes and other views, caricatures, marine and decorative engravings. Burlington Paintings has excellent examples of Nineteenth and early Twentieth Century oils and watercolours.

The Gallery is open 9.30-5.30 weekdays and 10-12 Saturdays.

Burlington Gallery,
10 Burlington Gardens,
London W1X 1LG
Tel: 01-734 9228

INTRODUCTION

The third edition is, we hope ,more complete, more colourful and more helpful than ever before. We have updated green fees, telephone numbers, prices and added to our ideas for cheaper places to stay, such as holiday cottages. We have also endeavoured to consider the plight of the non-golfer, who so faithfully endures, as loved ones play the game of golf.

We have focussed on all areas of the British Isles and where sensible, we have merged some counties. Naturally, there are a number of golf courses here that are quite difficult to play, and it is always courteous and sensible to phone in advance wherever you are playing. We have therefore listed all the country's clubs and their telephone numbers for easy reference in this area. Our Championship Golf features are dedicated to a study of the finest links, parkland and heathland courses in the British Isles. With details of the history, as well as the amenities and playing requirements, we hope we will inspire you to venture out and play on these illustrious, often gorgeous, and sometimes quite fearsome fairways. Our Choice Golf generally tries to focus in on other good courses in the county. This is by no means a complete list, and on occasions, we have omitted courses who really do not want to welcome visitors. These are, I am happy to report, few and far between. If you feel we have made glaring omissions or errors, we would of course, be delighted to hear from you. Many of the country's courses are situated beside built up areas. They are often difficult to play but in Cornwall, North Scotland, Wales and Northumberland to name but four regions, golf courses are sometimes rather better and definitely less often played. We hope that you will therefore use the multitude of hotels for your trips when visiting these more tranquil parts. In our holdiay and hotel ideas, we have tried to cater for all pockets and once again, we recommend you have brochures sent to you in advance to give yourself a better feel of what the hotel really has to offer. Our list is a very personal one and has been compiled with the help of many people and once again, if you have any comments, please write to us.

The ever increasing interest golfers have in fine art is astounding. We hope we have provided a good range from some fine collections to illustrate a taste of this valuable commodity.

People are taking up golf in ever increasing numbers, the game of all nationalities, all ages and both sexes. Whichever classification you happen to fall into, we very much hope you enjoy this product and wish you well 'following the fairways' in the 1990's.

ALLEN STEWART 'The Honourable Company of Edinburgh Golfers' *BURLINGTON GALLERY*

CORNWALL

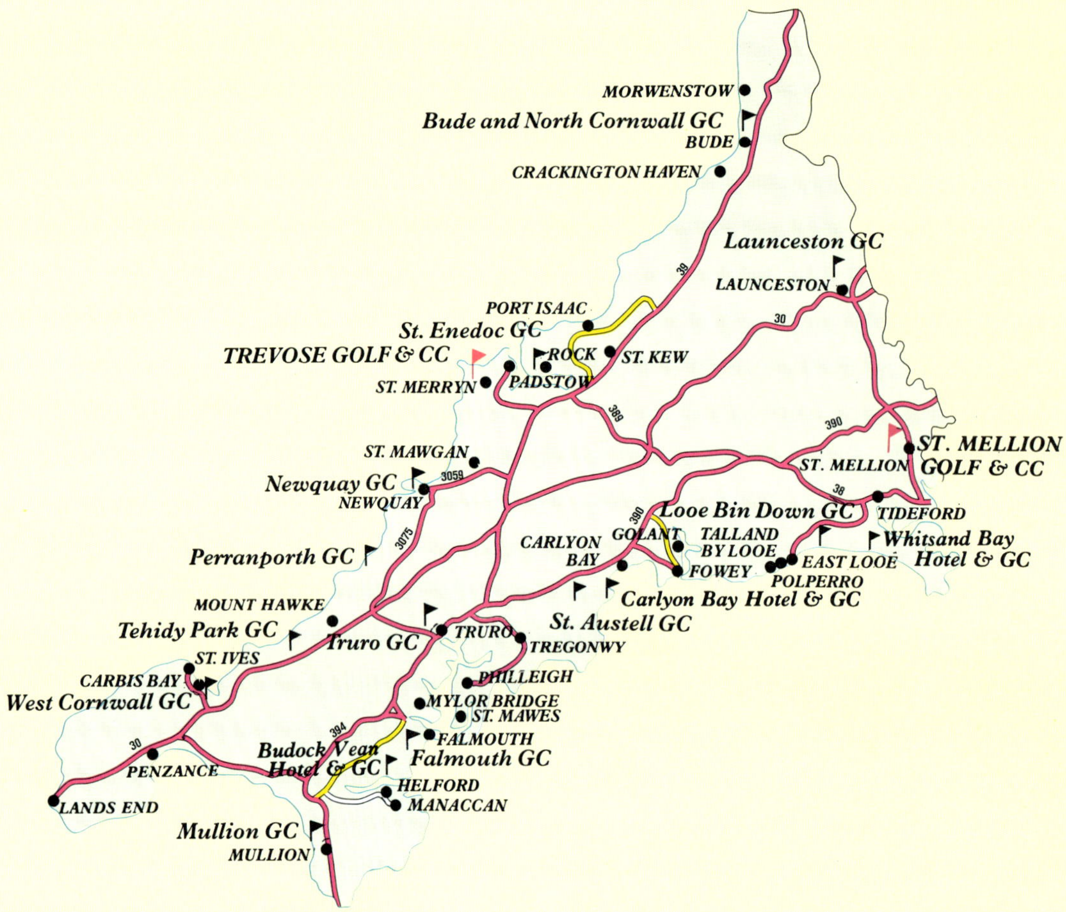

P.H.P *"Golfer and Caddy"* BURLINGTON GALLERY

CORNWALL

CHOICE GOLF

'Brandy for the Parson, Baccy for the Clerk' – **Cornwall** is the land of the smuggler's cove. It is also the land of King Arthur and the Knights of the Round Table – a land of legends. To cross the Tamar is to enter foreign soil: for centuries the Cornish Celts had more in common with the Welsh and the French Bretons than the ever-invading Anglo-Saxons. Well, the Anglo-Saxons still invade but nowadays in a more peaceful manner: 'grockles' they are called in Cornwall and they come in search of sun, sand and sea. But there is also a fairly recent addition, a sub-species commonly known as the 'golfing-grockle' who comes to Cornwall to seek out some of the finest golfing country in the Kingdom.

If one commences an imaginary tour by crossing the Tamar at Plymouth, **St Mellion Golf and Country Club** has surely to be the first port of call.

Heading westwards the wonderfully named **Looe Bin Down** Golf Club is situated on high ground to the north of Looe. An 18 hole moorland course it lies somewhat at the mercy of the elements and can get exceptionally windy. Closeby at Portwinkle the **Whitsand Bay Hotel (0503) 30276** is an ideal place to break a journey with an 18 hole golf course (belonging to the hotel), stretching out along the cliffs and looking down over the Whitsand Bay.

The area around Looe abounds with good hotels and restaurants with seafood not surprisingly being a speciality. In Fowey, two restaurants to consider: on the one hand **Food For Thought (072 613) 2359** – splendid seafood, and on the other the restaurant **Cordon Bleu (0702 613) 2359.** Another hotel where the visitor can enjoy a little extra walking – on the cliffs as on the fairways is at Talland-on-Looe; **The Talland Bay Hotel (0503) 72667** provides a good base. **The Kitchen (0503) 72780** is another excellent restaurant in Polperro. Finally at Galant, **The Cormorant Hotel (072 683) 3426** is relaxing and enjoys a wonderful setting.

We'll now, if you'll pardon the expression, leave the Looe area and set sail for St Austell. On route we note **The Pandora**, a charming thatched pub in Mylor Bridge and **The Roseland Inn** – good snacks and another attractive setting.

St. Austell provides a twin attraction for golfers: the redoubtable **Carlyon Bay** and the **St. Austell Golf Club**. The St. Austell course is situated on the western edge of the town off the **A390**. Rather shorter than Carlyon Bay but with an ample spread of gorse and numerous bunkers, it possesses plenty of challenges and attractions of its own. The Club welcomes visitors although prior telephoning is essential.

Carlyon Bay is surely one of Britains best loved 'Hotel courses'. Not a Turnberry or a Gleneagles perhaps, but very pleasing. The course has been owned by the Hotel since 1929. In its early days the glorious setting attracted the **Duke of Windsor**, probably the keenest of all 'golfing Royals' while **Winston Churchill** also spent a few of his finest hours at Carylon Bay.

St. Austell is a pleasant place to spend a day or two and golfers of course may decide to stay at **Carlyon Bay Hotel** itself **(072 681) 2304** – obviously convenient and four-star comfort as well. As a first rate alternative though, **Boscundle Manor (071 681) 3557** at Tregrehan is highly recommended. The food alone is worth a trip. Back in Carlyon Bay, the **Porth Avallen Hotel (072 681) 2802** has a restful atmosphere.

Falmouth – a glorious harbour and seagulls aplenty. More golf awaits. Like St. Austell, there are two sets of fairways on which to exercise the swing (and maybe burn off all these extra calories!); they are to be found at the **Falmouth Golf Club**, south west of the town (fine views over Falmouth Bay) and at **Budock Vean Hotel**. This latter course is most enjoyable. Only nine holes but plenty of challenges and exceptionally well-kept.

For hotels, **Budock Vean (0326) 250288** takes pride of place (more good food!) but others to note include **The Crill House (0326) 312994** and **The Hotel St Michael's (0326) 312707)**. The opening words of "The Wind in the Willows' were written at **The Greenbank (0326) 312440**, clearly an inspiring place, while **The Penmere Manor (0326) 314545** also has much to commend it. Two final thoughts in this area are **The Idle Rocks (0326) 270771** at St Mawes on the Roseland peninsula and the **Meudon Hotel (0326) 250541** in Falmouth.

Still heading down the coast, the course at **Mullion** is one of the short but sweet brigade. Seven miles south of Helston it can lay claim to being the most southerly on the British mainland. Nestling around the cliff edges overlooking some particularly inviting sands and with distant views towards St Michael's Mount, Mullion typifies the charm of Cornish holiday golf.

With green fees costing probably no more than **£8** and the particularly spectacular scenery of the Lizzard area, it's another good spot to spend a few days. In Mullion itself, or perhaps more precisely, Mullion Cove, **Henscath House (0326) 240537** is perfect for the golf course. Overlooking Polurrion Cove, **The Polurrion Hotel (0326) 240421** is another comfortable place to rest the golf clubs. Nearby in Manaccan, **The New Inn** offers a fine array of fish, lobsters and oysters and in Helford **The Shipwrights Arms** overlooking the estuary offers excellent crab among other delights (fine ales here too). A strong mention also for the **The Riverside (032 623) 443** where there is some good accommodation and outstanding cuisine.

The **West Cornwall Golf Club** lies just beyond St Ives at Lelant. A beautiful and very natural links it was laid out almost a hundred years ago by the then Vicar of Lelant. One of the most popular courses in Cornwall it is probably a good idea to telephone the Club before setting off, but generally visitors (with handicaps) are welcome, fees being about **£9** for a round.

In St Ives two hotels to note are **The Tregenna Castle (0736) 795 254** – good leisure facilities and **The Garrack (0736) 796199** – ideal for the nearby cliffs and beaches as well as the golf course. Slightly further afield at Carbis Bay the **The Boskerris Hotel (0736) 795295** is particularly friendly and provides comfortable accommodation.Passing numerous derelict tin and copper mines the inland course at **Tehidy Park** is soon reached. Located between Camborne and Portreath it presents a considerable contrast to the golf at Lelant: here we are amidst the pine trees, rhododendrons and bluebells – hopefullly not right amidst them! Getting back to the coast **Perranporth** and **Newquay** look closer on the map than they are by road. Both are links courses offering outstanding sea views. Situated on higher ground a game at Perranporth in 1989 was priced **£7** midweek, **£10** at weekends, while at Newquay (with its 100 bunkers) fees were **£10** during the week and **£12** at weekends.

In Newquay, where the crash of the Atlantic waves offers a surfers paradise there are several welcoming establishments. **The Atlantic Hotel (06387) 2244** is an ideal holiday base, as is **The Hotel Bristol (063787) 5181**. Connoisseurs of the public house might care to visit **The Falcon** at Mawgan. Golfers at Tehidy might note the **Tregarthan Country Cottage** at Mount Hawke – quite small but friendly and good value.

Further along the coast lie two marvellous golfing challenges –

CORNWALL

CHOICE GOLF

St Enodoc at Rock and **Trevose** at Constantine Bay. They are often considered as a pair although in fact they are quite different. Trevose (also featured later) is the longer course and much more open and it doesn't possess the massive sandhills that are the feature of St Enodoc links. The 6th hole at the latter, has the famous '**Himalayas**',thought to be the highest sandhill on any course in Britain. Visitors to St Enodoc must possess proof of handicap, though there are no general restrictions on time of play. The fees are about **£12**.

The two most convenient places for the golfing gourmet are at Trevose, the splendid **Treglos Hotel (0841) 520727** and for St Enodoc, **The St Enodoc Hotel (020886) 3216** in Rock. An early start can also be made from **Crackington Manor (08403) 397** at Crackington Haven and from **The Castle Rock Hotel** at Port Isaac **(0208) 880300**. This delightful fishing village also houses the 17th Century **Port Gaverne Inn (0208) 880244** – tremendous food and a charming atmosphere. Slightly further afield in St Kew, the **St Kew Inn** is well worth noting.

Our coastal tour ends appropriately at Bude – a pleasant seaside resort with a very good golf links situated almost in the town centre. Renowned for its excellent greens, the **Bude and North Cornwall Golf Club**, like Lelant, is approaching its centenary. Once described somewhat tongue-in-cheek as the 'gateway to Cornwall' the town has an impressive array of hotels. **The Burn Court Hotel (0288) 2872** is as comfortable as any and has the advantage of overlooking the golf course. One other popular spot for golfers is **The Camelot (0288) 2361**. In Morwenstow, a fine old pub **The Bush** is well worth visiting for the breathtaking clifftop views. A quick mention here also for another way of enjoying a Cornish golfing holiday: **Classic Cottages from the West Country (032 622) 755** offer a superb array of self-catering cottages, as do **Summer Cottages**, who can be contacted on **(0305) 67545**.

The golf course at Tehidy was mentioned on our little tour, but two other inland courses merit attention: the first is **Truro**, a shortish, pleasant parkland course, close to the lovely cathedral,fees **£9-£12** and the second is at **Launceston (fees £8)** one of the best courses in the county.

The White Hart coaching inn is an admirable base to explore the countryside around Launceston; however, the golf course itself is where the best views can be enjoyed. Located on high ground, to the west stretches Bodmin Moor – bogs and mystery and to the east, Dartmoor, bogs and even more mystery.

'Fore, out of the way, my Lord'

ST. MORITZ HOTEL

The St Moritz Hotel (reached via the B3314 from Wadebridge) stands in 3 acres of attractive grounds overlooking the Camel Estuary. The Hotel offers 46 bedrooms, all having the luxuries necessary to make your stay a memorable one.

The hotel dining room is called Laureates after Sir John Betjeman, who loved this part of Cornwall. Brad Trethewey and his team take great interest and care in the preparation of English and Continental cuisine, changing the menus regularly to take advantage of the local seafood and garden produce.

The St Enodoc Golf Club is ideally situated only half a mile away, with the pretty little church, made famous by Sir John Betjeman, right in the middle of the course. Offering a choice of two 18-hole courses, the old course is the venue for the 1989 England Amateur Team Championship and gives a challenge to the most accomplished of players. The new course offers a less demanding and undulating challenge for those not so well accomplished. Trevose Golf and Country Club with its 18-hole championship course and short 9-hole course is just across the estuary near the pretty little fishing town of Padstow.

St Moritz Hotel,
Trebetherick,
Nr Wadebridge,
Cornwall, PL27 6SD.
Tel: (020 886) 2242

ATLANTIC

The Atlantic Hotel is a three star hotel with five star standards and facilities.

The hotel is set in 11 acres of natural Headland and is in the unique position of having the sea on all four sides. It follows therefore that every room has a breathtaking sea view with some rooms also incorporating Newquay Golf Course in their panorama.

All bedrooms have been totally refurbished to five star standards and have fully tiled en-suite bathrooms with showers, some also having bidets. Each room has a colour television, video recorder, (video films being on hire at reception), trouser press, direct dial telephone, radio, hairdryer, mini fridge, tea and coffee making facilities with complimentary supplies.

The Hotel has a superb standard of cuisine. The wine list is extensive, the menus well balanced and the food excellent, being Egon Ronay recommended.

The sporting facilities are the best in Newquay, probably in Cornwall, and consist of indoor and outdoor heated swimming pools for both adults and children, 2 jacuzzis, 2 tennis courts, 2 squash courts, a 9-hole putting green, shuffle-board court, newly fitted gym, 2 full size saunas, steam bath, newly equipped snooker room with full size table and 2 pool tables. A badminton court is proposed for 1990.

The hotel has entertainment nightly during the summer season and most nights during the winter. The resident pianist entertains in the Cocktail Bar before dinner, and in the Dining Room during the evening meal. The Atlantic Hotel has its own pub and nightclub in the grounds but not within earshot of the main hotel. Separate entertainment is available every night.

Special reduced green fee rates of 40% discount have been arranged at Newquay golf Course for Atlantic Hotel guests, and the Club House and first tee are just a short walk from the Hotel.

The car park is suitable for up to 120 cars.

Atlantic Hotel
Dane Road
Newquay
Cornwall
TR7 1EN
Tel: (0637) 872244
Fax: (0637) 874108

BUDOCK VEAN

The Budock Vean Golf and Country House Hotel is set on the site of a small celtic monastery dedicated to the Breton Saint – St Budock – from whom the hotel takes its name.

The hotel's beautiful location on the banks of the Helford River makes it an ideal choice for anyone with an interest in water sports or sailing today. But the importance of this river in historic trading terms meant that a succession of Lords, and the one time Bishop of Exeter, sought the site for its rich income derived from river tariffs.

To suit these gentlemen's tastes a fine country manor was built on the site, and it is from this that The Budock Vean Golf and Country House Hotel has inherited its unique country house atmosphere, with surroundings which encourage leisured relaxation.

Experienced hoteliers Ted and Barbara Barlow, of The Treglos Hotel and Bud and Joan Start, formerly of The Windsor Hotel, took over joint ownership of The Buddock Vean Golf and Country House Hotel some few years ago. Their own well established and successful hotels are already popular with golfers, and Budock Vean has blossomed under their ownership and personal supervision.

During the past four years major refurbishment has been in progress to both the public rooms and bedrooms, to raise the standard to that which one would expect. The hotel's sporting facilities are extensive – set in 65 acres of sub-tropical grounds which bear witness to the mild climate enjoyed in this region. There is a private golf course, championship standard all weather tennis courts, and a superb indoor pool.

The golf course is particularly attractive, being a 9 hole parkland course that has double tees running 18 holes, which are deceptively challenging. The course has its own resident professional, who provides all the usual services as well as organising tournaments and competitions, and will advise on facilities at other fine Cornish courses. The hotel welcomes golf enquiries from groups, clubs, societies or individuals alike, and is confident it can offer golfing packages to suit all requirements.

Inside the hotel, accommodation is of a most superior standard – all 53 bedrooms being provided with full private facilities, and with all the extras you would expect from a hotel of such high calibre. There are charming English country style lounges, a popular conservatory and a sophisticated cocktail bar, all enjoying magnificent views.

The highly recommended restaurant serves an extensive selection of classic menu choices; the chef's excellent cuisine uses fresh local produce at all times and is tailored to suit a range of tastes.

The hotel has laid down a fine wine cellar – the wide selection offered will gratify the connoisseur, as well as providing well chosen table wines.

The Budock Vean Golf and Country House Hotel welcomes non residents also, and all guests to the hotel can be guaranteed care and attention at all times, while enjoying the hotel's elegant and relaxing atmosphere.

The Budock Vean Golf and Country House Hotel, Mawnan Smith, Falmouth, Cornwall, TR11 5LG. Tel: (0326) 250288

The Budock Vean Golf and Country House Hotel,
Mawnan Smith,
Falmouth,
Cornwall TR11 5LG
Tel: (0326) 250288

TREGLOS

The Treglos Hotel offers a totally relaxed and informal atmosphere, but at the same time promises good service amidst pleasant surroundings. The owner/managers Ted and Barbara Barlow have been at the hotel for 25 years, and are dedicated to providing excellent service for their guests, many of whom return year after year. The country house offers 44 comfortable bedrooms and most of these enjoy splendid views over Constantine Bay. The rooms have character as well as modern comforts and these combine to make life easy.

One of the major attributes of the house is the excellent leisure facilities. A charming indoor pool and jacuzzi are ideal for relaxing after enjoying what must be the most appealing of the hotel's attributes – Trevose Golf Course itself.

After a swim or a round of golf, it is likely that you will wish to enjoy some 'fully fledged' cooking. The hotel is proud of its excellent cuisine and its pleasantly informal dining room and bars. Log fires and comfortable sofas make further leisure easy and a promising location for conversation about today's golf or perhaps more importantly, tomorrow's round.

AA *** RAC

Recommended by Egon Ronay, Ashley Courtenay, Johansen's, Signpost

Treglos Hotel
Constantine Bay
Nr. Padstow
Cornwall
(0841) 520727

TREVOSE
CHAMPIONSHIP GOLF

To some, mention of the north coast of Cornwall will invoke thoughts of golden sandy beaches and cool, inviting seas. For others it may conjure up images of romantic coves, wild, spectacular cliffs and incessant crashing waves. Either way the place has a certain magic; after all it was here that King Arthur is said to have met Merlin. Such is the setting of the **Trevose Golf and Country Club**.

Located near the quaint little fishing port of **Padstow**, Trevose is an ideal spot for a golfing holiday – or any kind of holiday come to that, but those who haven't made space in the boot for the golf clubs are missing out on something rather special. The Club boasts a splendid 18 hole Championship course plus an adjacent 9 hole-short course which is presently being expanded to accommodate 18 holes.

A gentleman by the name of **Dr Williams** founded the Trevose Golf Club a little over sixty years ago. Today all administrative matters are in the capable hands of **Messrs P. Gammon** and **A.I.D. Savage**. Both can be contacted by telephone on **(0841) 520208**. The Club's professional **Gary Alliss**, can be reached on **(0841) 520261**. Not surprisingly the course (or courses) are at their busiest during the summer months, but whatever the time of year **visitors** looking for a game would be wise to make a quick telephone call before setting off. Visitors should find the Club very accommodating. **Societies** are also welcomed at Trevose, those organising should address written applications to the Secretary at **Trevose Golf and Country Club, Constantine Bay, Padstow, Cornwall**. Proof of handicap is required to play on the Championship course.

The 1989 **green fee** varies according to the time of year with major reductions available to those wishing to obtain temporary membership of the Club. From November to mid-March a day's golf on the 18 hole course can be purchased for **£10**. From mid-March to the end of May, plus the month of October, the green fee is **£13** per day, whilst between June and September (inclusive) the same is priced at **£15**. The green fee for a day's golf on the 9 hole course is set at **£4** during the winter months with **£6** payable at all other times. **Junior** golfers can obtain **50% reductions** on all the above rates. Finally as an example of temporary membership, a fortnight's golf on the Championship course during the peak summer period can be obtained for **£85** per person.

Whereas the image of north Cornwall is perhaps a romantic one, the same could hardly be said of the actual journey to get there. Travelling to the West Country, however, is not the painful slog it once was. The roads have been improved and – whisper it quietly – they don't seem as congested as a few years ago. Presumably it's an indirect result of the growing annual pilgramage to Spain – Benidorm rather than Bude – Torremolinos instead of Torquay. Anyway, I am reliably informed that in addition to the improved roads there are now four flights daily from Heathrow to nearby **Newquay Airport** (six miles from the Golf Club). Motorists will normally head for **Bodmin** (via the **A30** from Exeter or the **A38** from Plymouth). From Bodmin the **A389** should be taken towards Padstow. The Club is about four miles West of Padstow off the **B3276**. Finally those approaching from the St Austell area may find the **B3274** helpful.

From the Championship tees the 18 hole course measures **6608** yards (par 70, s.s.s. 72). The forward tees reduce the length by about 150 yards, while the ladies play over **5713** yards, **par 73**. The course can be described as a golf links though the visitor need not distress himself with fears of having to carry massive sandhills, and as a rule the rough is kept fairly short. The latter should ensure that the golfer spends more time admiring the scenery than searching for his golf ball. A word about the views: they are indeed tremendous, particularly those across **Booby's Bay**.

The wind at Trevose can often play a decisive role and prevent low scoring (no one, at least at the time of writing, has bettered **68**). There are a great number of well-positioned bunkers and a stream meanders through much of the course. Trevose provides a good test for any standard of golfer.

The Clubhouse with its prime situation overlooking the course offers a whole range of first class facilities. There is a large comfortable Bar and a Dining Room which can cater for over a hundred people. Breakfast, lunches and dinners are served daily in the Dining Room and in addition light snacks can be obtained at all times. For children a separate games room is provided. Swimming and tennis are also all very much a part of the Country Club scene – what's more, there's even a trendy boutique!

There is an unmistakably relaxed, holiday flavour about Trevose. The atmosphere is perhaps best epitomised by the story of four lady Members involved in a foursome game: apparently when playing the short 16th they arrived at the green only to discover that they had been so busy chattering not one of them had remembered to tee off....so much for women 'drivers'!

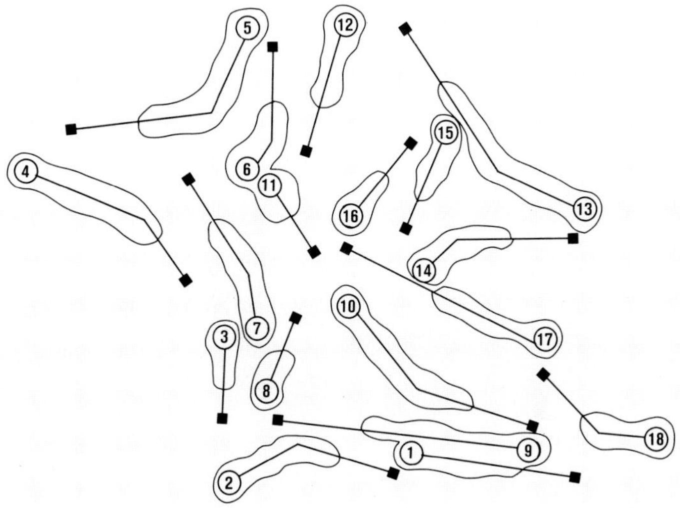

Hole	Yards	Par	Hole	Yards	Par
1	443	4	10	467	4
2	386	4	11	199	3
3	166	3	12	448	4
4	500	5	13	507	5
5	461	4	14	317	4
6	323	4	15	327	4
7	428	4	16	225	3
8	156	3	17	388	4
9	451	4	18	416	4
Out	3,314	35	In	3,294	35
			Out	3,314	35
			TOTALS	6,608	70

ST. MELLION
CHAMPIONSHIP GOLF

I wonder what the golfing critics would have said if a few years ago, someone had suggested that the Ryder Cup would one day be staged in Cornwall? 'Go tell it to the pixies', I should imagine. The extraordinary happenings at **St. Mellion** of late have made this not just a possibility but a strong probability.

St. Mellion is the brainchild of farming brothers **Martin** and **Hermon Bond**. What made thesse charming people turn from profitable pig and potato farming to golf course building remains something of a mystery; what is certain, however, is that their success has been nothing short of phenomenal.

The St. Mellion story really has two parts to it. Act One commenced a little over ten years ago when the Bonds first decided to create a golfcourse. In short, their idea met with resounding triumph and a first class championship course was constructed. Within a few years, tournament golf came to Cornwall (T.V. cameras and all) for the first time. Ambition swelled and Act Two was conceived: 'Let's build the best course in Europe' (well, why not!). An additional two hundred acres of adjoining woodland was purchased from the Duchy of Cornwall and a approach was made to none other than the great man himself, **Jack Nicklaus**. Negotiations followed and Nicklaus came over to inspect the new land. His initial thought was that the land was far too hilly and narrow – an impossible task. But of course, like the Bond brothers, Jack could never resist a challenge.

Plans were drawn up and at least on paper the object was a simple one, to build in Jack's words, 'Potentially the world's greatest galleried golf course.' Let us just say that the construction team put in a few good hours! The end result is now ready for all the world to see. By any standards, it is quite simply magnificent. Some have described it as an 'Augusta in Cornwall'; perhaps the best idea is to go and judge for yourself- you'll be made most welcome.

The **Golf Manager** at St. Mellion is the very helpful **Mr. David Webb**. He can be contacted by telephone on **(0579) 50101**. Any written correspondence should be addressed to **The Golf Manager, St. Mellion Golf and Country Club, St. Mellion, Saltash, Cornwall, PL12 6SD**. While there is an understandable wish to play the **Nicklaus Course**, we shouldn't forget that there are two fine courses at St. Mellion. When the Nicklaus course was being built, certain changes to the old Championship course (now known as the **'Old'** were necessary. However, it remains a worthy test of golf and is certainly a long way from your average 'holiday course'. **Visitors** (with handicaps) are welcome to play either course between Mondays and Fridays, and teeing times can be booked through the starter also on **(0579) 50101.**

The **green fee** to play over the **Nicklaus Course** was set at **£30** in 1989. On the **Old Course** the cost of a game is **£14**. For junior golfers, the rates are normally half. By way of final introduction, the professional at St. Mellion is **Tony Moore**.

Although it nestles deep in the Cornish countryside, St. Mellion is easily accessible from all directions. Travelling from afar most will come via Plymouth which is situated eight miles to the south east. Plymouth is linked to Exeter by the **A38** and Exeter in turn to Bristol by the **M5**. On reaching Plymouth the A38 should be followed to Liskeard from where St. Mellion is signposted.

From the Championship tees the **Nicklaus Course** can be stretched to a little over 7000 yards making it a formidable challenge. From the Medal tees it is still a very testing **6626** yards, par **72**. The **Old Course** is a more friendly **5927** yards, par**70**.

One of the many features of the Nicklaus Course is the superb greens, this despite their youth. They were laid to the American specification of a sand/peat mixture and surface flooding will never be a problem. They are slick and more importantly, very true.

As to which are the great holes on the course, the quick answer is all 18 of them. It's probably not too far from the truth. A few, however, do stand out and they exude the Nicklaus approach. The **3rd** is an excellent hole – miss the fairway to the right and you can be facing a desperate uphill shot over a ravine to a heavily protected green. On the **5th**, the drive is across a lake and thereafter the fairway sweeps around to the left towards the green which has a stream running in front of it. And so it goes on, but note especially the **11th** and **12th** which have been likened to Augusta's 12th and 13th – more streams, more lakes and some lovely splashes of colour – thrilling stuff!

It is perhaps only right to leave the last few words to the 'Golden Bear'. This is what Nicklaus had to say when he first viewed the course on its completion: 'I knew it was going to be good, but not this good – it's everything I'd hoped for and more ..... it's got such balance and such beautiful lines ..... there is no doubt that this course can stage a world-class tournament ..... like the Ryder Cup'. Hint taken.

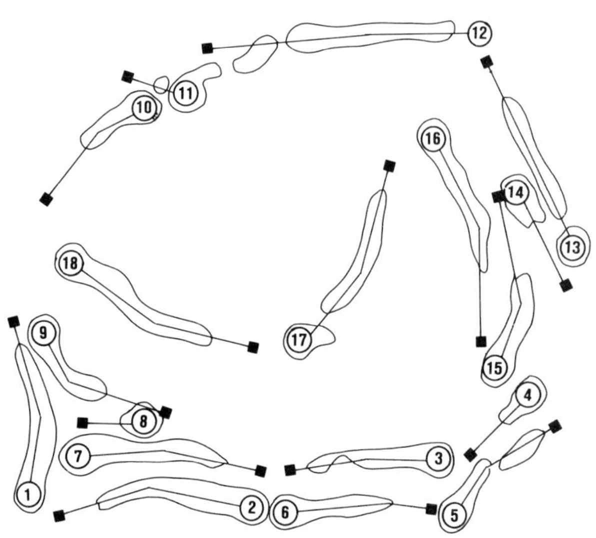

Nicklaus Course

Hole	Yards	Par	Hole	Yards	Par
1	400	4	10	410	4
2	518	5	11	181	3
3	356	4	12	525	5
4	175	3	13	361	4
5	315	4	14	158	3
6	420	4	15	411	4
7	480	5	16	520	5
8	135	3	17	426	4
9	375	4	18	460	4
Out	3,174	36	In	3,452	36
			Out	3,174	36
			TOTALS	6,626	72

CARLYON BAY
CHAMPIONSHIP GOLF

Staring out of a window from inside an office in Central London, distracted by the rain cascading down, Carlyon Bay and the Cornish Riviera seem a million light years away. Thumbing through a glossy brochure I see a luxury 4-star Hotel and a Championship golf course stretching out along the cliff tops with views across the St Austell Bay and down to miles of golden sands. At least three distinct beaches are overlooked by the course – one of them frequented by naturists! – think I'll get a cup of coffee.....

Built in 1925 as a private enterprise, the course has been owned by the Hotel since 1929. In its early days the glorious setting attracted the **Duke of Windsor**, probably the keenest of all 'golfing Royals' while **Winston Churchill** too spent a few of his finest hours at Carlyon Bay.

Considerable changes have occurred during the past decade or so. In 1978 golf architect **Hamilton Stutt** was commissioned to make alterations to various parts of the course and in the early '80's the Hotel came under new ownership. A greater emphasis has since been placed on the quality of the golf offered and the appointment of a Course Manager, **Mr Brian Summers**, was made with this view in mind.

Golfers visiting this part of the world are sure to receive a warm welcome at Carlyon Bay and there is no pre-requisite of providing a handicap certificate. The only restriction as such on times of play is that those wishing to tee-off between 8.30am and 12 noon must reserve their starting times at the pro-shop. **Nigel Sears** is the Club's professional, he may be contacted on **(072681) 4228**. The **green fees** for **1989** were set at **£12.50** for a full day's golf during the week, with **£14.50** payable at weekends and Bank Holidays. Visitors may wish to note that the Club stages a number of open competitions throughout the year, details of which can be obtained by writing to Mr Summers at **The Carlyon Bay Hotel Golf Club, Carlyon Bay, St Austell, Cornwall.** Mr Summers can be reached by telephone on **(072681) 4228**.

The Cornish Riviera is not of course a million light years from London – it's about 250 miles away and with the now regular flights to nearby **St Mawgan Airport**, Carlyon Bay can be reached in a very short time. For those travelling by more conventional methods, St Austell is the town to head for. The West Country is served by motorway as far as **Exeter (M5)** and thereafter the **A38** links Exeter with **Plymouth**. The A38 should in fact be followed to just beyond **Liskeard** from where the **A390** can be picked up. Carlyon Bay is well sign-posted from St Austell. From the West the **A390** approaches via **Truro** while those coming from the **Newquay** region should travel on the **A3058**. Finally St Austell railway station is only a few yards from the course.

From the back tees – always in play during the summer months – the course stretches to **6463** yards, par **72** (sss **71**). For the ladies, from the red tees, the course measures **5684** yards and is a par **75. Neil Coles** holds the course record at 65. Carlyon Bay is the perfect length really for holiday golf: long enough to be challenging and with enough hazards to set you thinking, but hopefully not so difficult as to make the cliffs a tempting jettison point for clubs, trolleys etc. – besides, there are a number of disused mine shafts on the course – part of it having been built on old copper mine workings. But seriously golf at Carlyon Bay should always be an enjoyable experience and the course is maintained in excellent condition throughout the year. Furthermore, whatever the standard of your game the quality of the views can never be disputed. On a warm day with the sun reflecting off St Austell Bay this is truly an idyllic spot.

The most testing holes on the front nine are probably the **2nd** – a very long par 4 with the Paddington to Penzance railway line running along the left and the cliffs to the right – and the uphill **6th** where the green overlooks Polgaver naturist beach – always an excuse for three-putting! After the spectacular **10th** the holes move away from the cliff edges and turn back towards the Clubhouse. Carlyon Bay possesses a first-class and four star 19th with extensive facilities. A catering service is provided throughout the day and there is a Bar, Lounge and Dining Room – all of which again offer tremendous views.

.....Well, back in London the coffee's gone cold and I'm afraid the rain is still coming down in floods – but at least I know where I'm going for my 'hols this year!

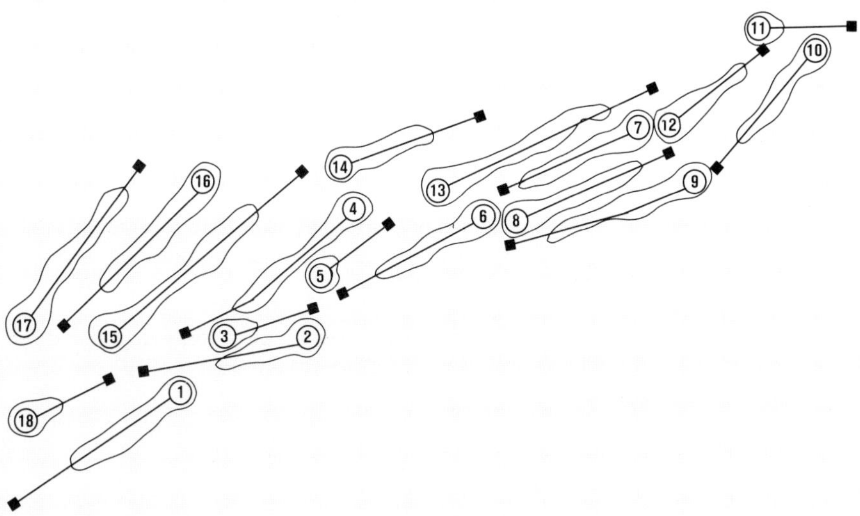

Hole	Yards	Par	Hole	Yards	Par
1	383	4	10	500	5
2	459	4	11	148	3
3	202	3	12	350	4
4	512	5	13	516	5
5	130	3	14	333	4
6	358	4	15	528	5
7	361	4	16	400	4
8	372	4	17	385	4
9	338	4	18	188	3
Out	3,115	35	In	3,348	37
			Out	3,115	35
			TOTALS	6,463	72

CORNWALL
COMPLETE GOLF

CORNWALL

Bude and North Cornwall G.C.
(18) 6202 yards
Burnview, Bude
(0288) 2006

Budock Vean Hotel G.C.
(9) 5222 yards
Mawnan Smith, Falmouth
(0326) 250288

Carlyon Bay Hotel G.C.
(18) 6463 yards
Carlyon Bay, St. Austell
(072681) 4228

Falmouth G.C.
(18) 5581 yards
Swanpool Road, Falmouth
(0326) 40525

Isles of Scilly G.C.
(9) 5974 yards
St. Mary's, Isles of Scilly
(0720) 22692

Launceston G.C.
(18) 6409 yards
St. Stephen, Launceston
(0566) 3442

Looe Bin Down G.C.
(18) 5875 yards
Widegates, Looe
(05034) 247

Mullion G.C.
(18) 5616 yards
Curry, Helston
(0326) 240685

Newquay G.C.
(18) 6140 yards
Tower Road, Newquay
(0637) 874354

Perranporth G.C.
(18) 6208 yards
Budnick Hill, Perranporth
(0872) 573701

Praa Sands G.C.
(9) 4036 yards
Germoe Cross, Penzance
(0736) 763445

St. Austell G.C.
(18) 5875 yards
Tregongeeves Lane, St. Austell
(0726) 74756

St. Enodoc G.C.
(18) 6188 yards
(18) 4151 yards
Rock, Wadebridge
(020886) 3216

St. Mellion G. & C.C.
(18) 6626 yards
(18) 5927 yards
St. Mellion, Saltash
(0579) 50101

Tehidy Park G.C.
(18) 6222 yards
Camborne
(0209) 842208

Trevose G. & C.C.
(18) 6608 yards
(9) 1367 yards
Constantine Bay, Padstow
(0841) 520208

Truro G.C.
(18) 5347 yards
Treliske, Truro
(0872) 72640

West Cornwall G.C.
(18) 6070 yards
Lelant, St. Ives
(0736) 753401

Whitsand Bay Hotel G.C.
(18) 5512 yards
Portwrinkle, Torpoint
(0503) 30470

CLOWANCE

Clowance Estate

A-frame timber design lodges in Canadian douglas fir set amongst the trees

Within one hour's drive of no less than ten of Cornwall's finest golf courses, Clowance House is one of the finest timeshare developments to be found anywhere in the world. But that's not all. Clowance offers exceptional facilities for the whole family. Acres of woodlands, 4 acre trout lake, tennis courts, squash courts, indoor swimming pool, jacuzzi and sauna will ensure that there are no golf widows on the estate, and that the children are well catered for. And what better way to guarantee these superb facilities every year but to purchase a timeshare holiday?

For a once only payment, a family can become part owners in this superb development set in the heart of the West Country. Buying a timeshare at Clowance entitles you to the use of one of the luxuriously furnished A-frame lodges set amongst the trees, for one or more weeks per year for a full 80 year period.

Just in case you have received a false impression of timeshare from the newspaper reports about the excesses of a very small segment of the industry, Clowance offers you a full guarantee of no high pressure selling and a seven day cooling off period.

The selection of courses for the golf enthusiast to test their handicaps on is numerous. From links courses such as Newquay, Perranporth and West Cornwall Golf Clubs to Tehidy Park, Tregenna Castle and Truro Golf Courses set in the beautiful parkland and countryside of Cornwall, all handicap levels are catered for. And an exclusive arrangement between Clowance and Tregenna Castle, a par 58, 18 hole course with panoramic views overlooking St Ives and the Cornish coastline, allows owners of Clowance holiday homes an extremely attractive day rate green fee.

Timeshare at Clowance gives owners more than just a holiday home. All the lodges are built to A-frame timber design in Canadian douglas fir, and offer a degree of space, warmth and relaxation that has to be felt to be fully appreciated; they fit neatly into their surroundings, hidden in natural clearings and are positioned to enjoy the magnificent views of the Estate.

Whatever its size, each lodge is furnished and equipped to lavish standards, with no expense spared. The emphasis is very much on design and luxury with leather-upholstered lounges, remote controlled colour television, stereo, video recorder and each lodge having its own individual decor. There's a barbecue on every terrace and a drying room that cuts out the bother of damp holiday clothes. Superbly-equipped kitchens with every imaginable labour-saving device to plan the simplest picnic to the most elaborate banquet; kids' hideaway bedrooms and sauna suites are all geared to the pursuit of luxury.

There's no time like a holiday and no place like Clowance. Timesharing at Clowance means you are buying a timeshare you can trust. Not only is it a five-star member of the Interval International Exchange organisation – enabling you to take a holiday in any one of over 600 worldwide resorts, it is also a founder member of the Timeshare Developers Association. This means that all the legal and financial paperwork of the property has been scrutinised by a panel of independent lawyers; that an owners' association and management arrangements have been formally established; and that as owners you also have ultimate control over the annual management charges. This is Clowance and its beauty is there for you to enjoy.

Clowance Estate,
Praze-en-Beeble,
Camborne, Cornwall.
Tel: (0209) 831111
Freephone: 0800 373961

DEVON

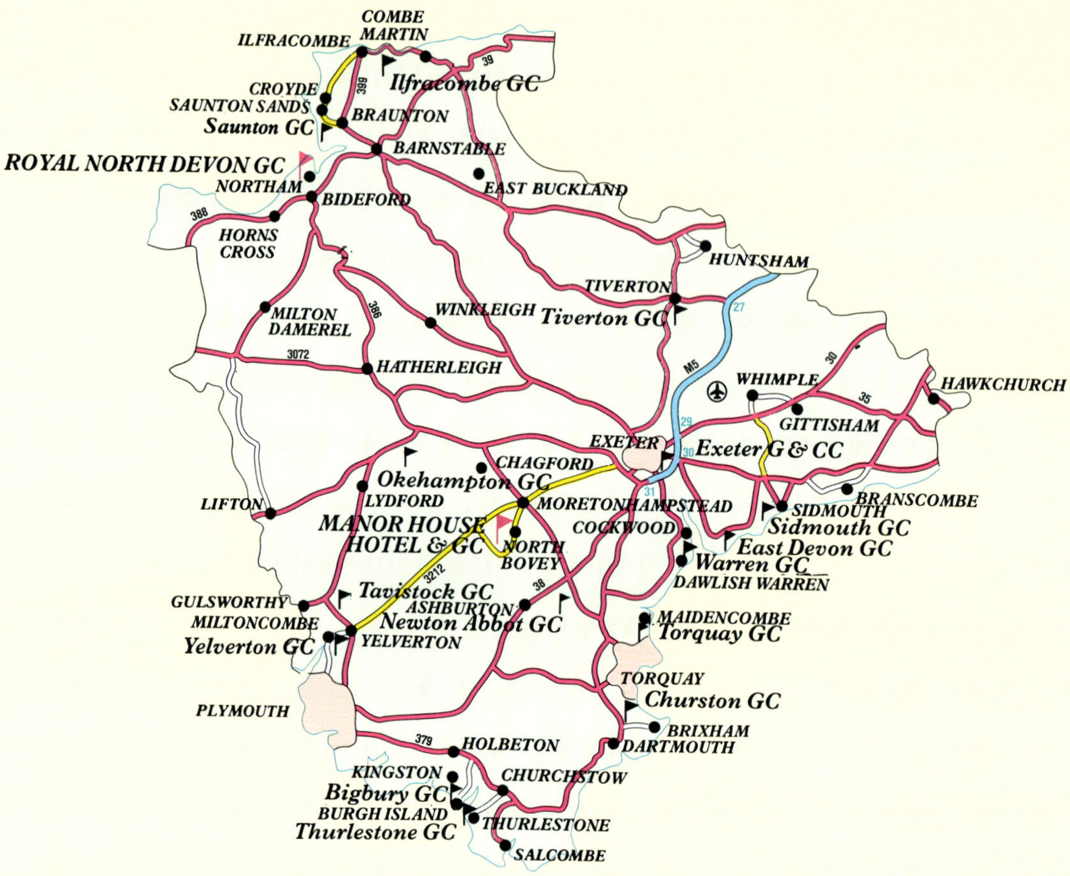

"Clear Fairways" BURLINGTON GALLERY

DEVON
CHOICE GOLF

'Glorious Devon' they call it – beaches to the north, beaches to the south and Dartmoor in the middle. Well, amidst all the glory are some thirty golf courses, the majority of which lie either directly on the coast or within a mile or so of it. The two most widely known and indeed the two Championship courses are both located to the north of the county: **Royal North Devon** (or Westward Ho! as it is commonly known) and **Saunton**. The greater number of courses, however, are on the southern coast, or to put it another way, while North Devon may have the cream, most of the tees are to be found in the south.

Firstly though, what about golf in the middle? The beautiful setting of the **Manor House Golf Course** at Moretonhampstead (see feature page) is known to many. However, it is not the sole course within Dartmoor; **Okehampton** is a moorland type course and whilst not overly long, has a number of interesting holes. Visitors are welcome at all times, fees being approximately **£7** per day. Well away from Dartmoor, but still fairly centrally located is the parkland course at **Tiverton**, easily reached from the **M5** (junction **27**). Tiverton also welcomes visitors throughout the week, but pre-booking is essential. The cost of a day's golf here is priced at about **£9** or **£12** at weekends.

With its many Tudor buildings and impressive Cathedral, Exeter makes an attractive county town. Golfwise, the city has an 18 hole course at Countess Wear, south of the town off the **A377**. A fairly short parkland course, it is renowned for its beautifully maintained greens. The fees at **Exeter** Golf Club are **£12** per day.

There are many outstanding places in which to spend a night or two when visiting this part of the world. Exeter is a likely base and here the **Royal Clarence Hotel (0392) 58464** is extremely comfortable and enjoys a splendid position overlooking the Cathedral Square. Also in the city, **The White Hart (0392) 79897** is a delightful old inn with good accommodation. One of the best known pubs in Exeter is **The Ship** on St Martins Lane – ideal unless you're over six foot tall!

On Dartmoor, the impressive **Manor House Hotel (0647) 40355** at Moretonhampstead is where many golfers will choose to hang up their spikes, but a number of splendid alternatives are at hand. Chagford offers the exceptional **Gidleigh Park (06473) 2367** and the **Mill End Hotel (06473) 2282**, and in nearby Frenchbeer, **Teignworthy House (06473) 3355** is marvellously relaxing and very good value.

Towards Okehampton in Lydford, **Lydford House Hotel (082282) 347** is pleasant as is **The Castle (082282) 242**, while in Tiverton, **Henderson's (0884) 254256** is an excellent restaurant. Whilst we are in the area, a visit to Huntsham is also in order: **Huntsham Court (039 86) 210** is a rambling Gothic Hotel, with off-beat touches such as pre-war wirelesses in the bedrooms and a bar where guests are encouraged to help themselves! After a game at Manor House, two pubs to note are **The White Hart** in Moretonhampstead and **The Ring of Bells** in North Bovey.

Suitably refreshed, more golf awaits along Devon's southern coast. To the east side of the River Exe and not too great a distance from Exeter are the courses at **Sidmouth** and Budleigh Salterton (**East Devon**). Both are on fairly high ground providing panoramic views out to sea. Sidmouth is perhaps more of a cliff top course with 'springy' turf, while East Devon is of the downland variety with much heather and gorse. Green fees at Sidmouth are around the **£8** per day mark, East Devon being a little more expensive.

To the west of the Exe Estuary, the friendly **Warren Golf Club** at Dawlish offers the only true links golf in South Devon. This is a much improved course with an interesting finishing hole that will have the wayward hitter threatening both the Members in the Clubhouse and/or quite possibly the passengers on a passing London to Penzance 125. Visitors are welcome at Dawlish seven days per week, and green fees are about **£8.50** A fairly near neighbour of 'The Warren' is **Teignmouth Golf Club**. It may be near, but Teignmouth offers a totally different challenge, being situated some 900 feet above sea level on Haldon Moor. Teignmouth can become shrouded in fog during the winter, but when it is clear, it's a very pleasant course and most attractive too.

On their way to the south coast, many may have sped past Gittisham – a mistake, for **Combe House (0404) 2756** provides great elegance and style. In Sidmouth, **The Riviera (0395) 515201** is grand, **The Torbay Hotel (0395) 513456** good value, while for a family holiday, **The Westcliff (0395) 513252** may be the best choice. Just east of Sidmouth, **The Masons Arms** at Branscombe **(029780) 300** is perfect for a relaxing dinner and a stopover if required. Travelling between Exeter and Dawlish, **The Swans Nest** in Exminster is a welcoming pub (very good food here) and in Dawlish Warren, most convenient for the golf links is **The Langstone Cliff Hotel (0626) 865155** (just roll down the hill and you're almost there).

The three handiest courses for those holidaying in the Torbay area are probably **Churston, Torquay** and **Newton Abbot**. Churston, located three miles from Paignton is a spectacular cliff top course at which visitors are welcome at all times. Visitors are similarly welcome at Torquay Golf Club which is located just north of Torquay on the **A379**. The abundant heather, woods and a meandering brook are likely to pose the most challenges here. Green fees at each are approximately **£10** per day.

One of the most pleasant places to stay in this area is **The Orestone Manor House (0803) 38098** in Maidencombe – handy for Torquay without being too much in the middle of things. In Torquay itself, there are numerous fine hotels – the grandest is the **Imperial (0803) 24301**, which offers all manner of splendid facilities but charges for it! **The Palace Hotel (0803) 22271** is less costly, but courtesy still prevails. Perhaps the best value to be found is at **Homers Hotel (0803) 213456** with its splendid restaurant.

Another popular resort can be found in Brixham. **The Quayside Hotel (08045) 55751** is charming and the town retains a much quieter atmosphere than its neighbour across the bay. In Dartmouth, two restaurants merit special comment: **The Cherub Dining Rooms (08043) 2571** has delicious seafood as a speciality, whilst cooking of the highest quality is also to be found at **The Carved Angel (08043) 2465.** Finally, a strong recommendation is **The Holne Chase Hotel (03643) 471** in Ashburton – a glorious setting with a restaurant to match.

Heading further down the coast, the picturesque village of **Thurlestone** has one of the most popular courses in Devon. It is a quite superb cliff top course with several far-reaching views along the coast. Being so popular, it is important to telephone in advance; fees are around the **£12** mark. **Bigbury** lies a short distance from Thurlestone – approximately 300 yards shorter at around 6000 yards, it is nevertheless equally attractive and looks across to Burgh Island, a favourite (or an ex-favourite) haunt of smugglers. Both Thurlestone and Bigbury can be reached from Plymouth via the **A379**, or from the Torbay region via the **A381**.

DEVON
CHOICE GOLF

The Thurlestone Hotel (0548) 560382 is a perfect base not only for playing the two nearby courses, but also for exploring what is a delightful part of Devon. For lovers of the country mansion, Holbeton offers **The Alston House Hotel (075 530) 259,** but if a good pub is sought **The Pilchard** on Burgh Island is one of the best – but beware the tide!

Golfers in Plymouth have probably been noting with interest the recent developments at nearby St. Mellion, just over the border in Cornwall. However a little nearer to the gret seafaring city, **Yelverton** is one definitely not to be missed. Yelverton lies midway between Plymouth and Tavistock on the **A386** and is very much a moorland type course(Dartmoor begins here) and very attractive too, with much gorse and heather. No shortage of ponies either! The best times for a visit are weekday afternoons, fees being **£8** midweek, **£10** at weekends.

Tavistock is also nearby. It is perhaps not as challenging as Yelverton, but worth a visit all the same. **The Moorland Links Hotel (0822) 852245** at Yelverton is pretty self explanatory and for a place to celebrate one's birdie at the eighteenth, **The Who'd of Thought It** at Milton Combe sounds appropriate – it really is an excellent pub and serves outstandingly good value lunches.

From Plymouth the north coast of Devon is about an hour and a quarter drive; from Exeter a little less. Unless there is some urgency a leisurely drive is recommended – this isn't London (fortunately) and the scenery is truly spectacular. A few suggestions for breaking the journey include Milton Damerel, where **The Woodford Bridge (040926) 481** is a first rate hotel, Hatherleigh for the handsome **George Hotel (0837) 810454** and Winkleigh, where the **Kings Arms** is a splendid pub.

North Devon can lay claim to having the oldest Golf Club in England, the **Royal North Devon Club** at Westward Ho! founded in 1864; it can also claim to have seen the lowest known score for eighteen holes of golf. In 1936 the Woolacombe Bay professional recorded a 55 on his home course – 29 out and 26 back, including a hole in one at the last! As this took place on the 1st January, one cannot help wondering quite what he did the night before! Unfortunately, there is no longer a course at Woolacombe, but there is one at nearby **Ilfracombe** (and has been for nearly 100 years). Situated several hundred feet above sea level, it offers many outstanding views of the North Devon coastline. There is an interesing selection of par three holes, one of which measures a mere 81 yards. Visitors are always at Ilfracombe, the cost of a day's golf being **£9**.

Although on the map **Saunton** and Westward Ho! appear to be very neighbourly, travelling from one to another is in fact a 20 mile trip via Barnstaple. Both deserve more than a fleeting visit and are featured ahead; Westward Ho! is a place for pilgrimage, but Saunton arguably provides the more modern championship challenge. There are two fine courses at Saunton, The East (which is a championship course) and the shorter West. Large sandhills dominate both courses, and when the wind blows .....

Should one choose not to sleep among the dunes, here are a few ideas for the 19th – in **Saunton Sands (0271) 890212**, the hotel of the same name is enormously popular with golfers. The **Preston House Hotel (0271) 890472** is also nearby and is very comfortable. At Fairy Cross, near Bideford, the **Portledge Hotel (02375) 262** is an inspiring place for the lover of peace and quiet, while in Northam the **Durrant House Hotel (02372) 72361** is great for recuperating after a day's activities at Westward Ho! More? Well, there are many: in Westward Ho! **Culloden House (02372) 79421** is small but friendly; Ilfracombe offers the **Lee Bay Hotel (0271) 63503**, set in a delightful craggy cove and at Combe Martin, the relaxing **Coulsworthy Country House (027188) 2463** is found. Then there is **The Penhaven Country House (02375) 711**, a lovely old rectory transformed into a hotel, a gem to be discovered at Parkham near Bideford.

Among a number of good eating places in the area are the **Hoops Inn** in Horns Cross, and **Gray's Country Restaurant (0271) 812809)** in Knowle. As we end this golfing tour, a few thoughts for those who would prefer to cater for themselves in one of the many pretty cottages that abound in Devon; **Classic Cottages from the West Country (032 622) 755)** are worth contacting, as are **Country Holidays** on **(0282) 445566**.

A final thought as we leave Saunton – should it actually happen and you do get stranded in the dunes, the chances are you will wake up to a glorious sunrise. Let's hope the golf is equally spectacular.

MAJOR HOPKINS 'Ladies golf at Westward Ho!' *BURLINGTON GALLERY*

THE WESTCLIFF HOTEL

Westcliff Hotel

Surrounded by superb golfing country, and with the additional attractions of Devon's lanes and moors nearby, The Westcliff Hotel offers its guests an ideal base for exploring this beautiful part of Britain.

Just as Sidmouth is the jewel of East Devon, so is Westcliff the jewel of Sidmouth. Situated in beautiful, spacious grounds facing South and enjoying spectacular coastal views over Lyme Bay Westcliff is the closest hotel to the much admired Connaught Gardens, Golf Club and Western Beach, yet still within an easy stroll along the Esplanade to the town centre.

Outdoor facilities include a putting green, mini tennis, croquet, a heated pool and ample free car parking. Indoors, elegantly refurbished lounges, restaurant and cocktail bar, all with magnificent sea views, await you. All 40 bedrooms have private facilities, are fitted to a high standard and most have sea views. Indoor facilities include a games room, pool or snooker, jacuzzi, solarium, exercise room, and lift to all floors. A new full colour brochure is available on request. The Westcliff is privately owned and family run.

The Westcliff is an Ashley Courtenay Recommended Hotel.

Westcliff Hotel,
Manor Road,
Sidmouth,
Devon, EX10 8RU.
Tel: (0395) 513252

QUEENS HOTEL

The Queens Hotel is ideally situated in the market town of Newton Abbot in central Devon. Its location makes it the perfect place for West country racegoers and tourists alike to stay.

The attractive hotel restaurant offers table d'hote and a la carte menus to choose from and you can be sure of some traditional Devonian cooking at The Queens Hotel. There is an extensive wine list to complement your food and if you are able to stay overnight you can choose from a continental or full English breakfast, which will give you a good start to your day's sightseeing or racing.

There is so much to see and do in this part of Devon. You might like to visit the coastal towns of Torbay, Shaldon, Torquay, Teignmouth, Paignton or Babbacombe, all of which are half an hour or less away. And remember, the records of sunshine in South Devon are the highest in the country throughout the year – there are even palm trees in the area!

You could take a peaceful stroll in Dartmoor's National Park which is still wild and unspoilt, but beware the sinister Princetown prison! If this does not take your fancy, why not visit the cathedral city of Exeter, which is also home of the Maritime Museum and many other historical buildings. And when you are tired of sight-seeing, there are many interesting shops to browse around.

If you are a racegoer, Newton Abbot racecourse is close and the Devon & Exeter racecourse at Haldon is only a short drive away. Whatever you decide, The Queens Hotel makes the ideal place to stay, with its comfortable accommodation, relaxing atmosphere and friendly staff.

Queens Hotel,
Queen Street,
Newton Abbot,
Devon TQ12 2EZ.

Tel: (0626) 63133

SAUNTON
CHAMPIONSHIP GOLF

At a time when the likes of **John H Taylor** and **Horace Hutchinson** were striding the windswept fairways on **Northam Burrows**, across the Taw Estuary on the **Braunton Burrows** other men were busy trapping rabbits. It took more than thirty years for matters to be put right.

Saunton Golf Club was founded in **1897**. In common with many great Clubs, Saunton's beginnings were rather modest. At first there were only nine holes and the original Clubhouse was a single room next to the local Post Office. Although the course was extended to 18 holes before the First World War (and a new Clubhouse acquired) it wasn't until after the War that Saunton's reputation really gained momentum. Chiefly reponsible for this was golf architect **Herbert Fowler**, who having reshaped Westward Ho! performed a similar task at Saunton.

In **1932** the course was selected to stage the **British Ladies Championship** and this was followed by the **English Amateur Championship** of **1937**. Unfortunately the links didn't fare too well during the Second War as it was considered the perfect place for a Battle School and concrete and barbed wire covered the fairways. Reconstruction didn't begin until **1951, C.K. Cotton** this time directing matters. Once restored the course quickly re-established itself as one of Britain's leading Championship links. In the early seventies a second 18 holes were added and today the two are known as the East (the former 'Old Course') and the West course.

In charge of all administrative matters at Saunton is the Club's secretary, **Mr. W.E. Geddes**. Mr. Geddes may be contacted by telephone on **(0271) 812436**. The Professional, **Mr. J.A. McGhee** can be contacted on **(0271) 812013**. Other than being able to provide proof of handicap there are no general restrictions on visitors – however prior telephoning is strongly recommended. Golfing **Societies** are equally welcome at Saunton; those wishing to make written applications to the Club should address correspondence to the Secretary at **The Saunton Golf Club, Saunton, Braunton, Devon**.

The **green fees** for **1989** were set at **£15** per day to play over either the Championship **East Course** or the **West Course**, with a slight increase to **£17** on Saturdays and Sundays. Juniors are offered a fifty per cent reduction on each.

Although on the map Saunton and Westward Ho! appear to be very neighbourly, travelling from one to another is in fact about a 20 mile trip via Barnstaple. The Club's precise location is off the **B3231** south of Saunton village. The **B3231** can be picked up at Braunton, with Braunton in turn being joined to **Ilfracombe** in the north and **Barnstaple** to the south by the **A361**. Those travelling from further afield should aim for Barnstaple. The town can be reached from **Exeter** by the **A377** and from **Taunton** by the **A61**, while for those approaching from the north of Cornwall the **A39** is likely to prove of most assistance.

At **6703** yards, par **71** (s.s.s.**73**) from the Championship tees, the **East Course** is nearly 400 yards longer than the **West** (**6322** yards par **70**). Both, however, provide a fairly stiff challenge with large sandhills being the dominant feature on each course. Much work has recently been done on the West course; the greens have been totally dug up and relaid – now an excellent test of golf.

The East Course could hardly be described as one of those that breaks you in gently: the first four holes all measure over 400 yards. Of the first twelve holes ten are par fours but perhaps the best on the course is the **16th** which demands a tee shot over a vast sandhill with a second needing to be carried over a deep bunker in front of the green. The course record on the East Course stands at a particularly high **70**.

Since its reopening in 1951 Saunton has hosted several important Championships, both professional and amateur. Twice the **English Open Amateur Stroke Play Championship** has been played on the East Course and in 1966 the **PGA Championship** was held at Saunton. **The St Andrews Trophy** was also played here in 1984, when the British side defeated the Continent and 1992 will see the **English Ladies Matchplay** staged here.

As for its 19th, the Clubhouse at Saunton has recently been completely refurbished and is most impressive. Full catering is offered throughout the week and in a similar vein to Westward Ho! the atmosphere is most relaxing and informal.

On more than one occasion I have read that if Saunton had a different geography it would be an Open Championship course. Maybe I'm missing the point, but I've never fully appreciated the 'geography argument'. If it's a question of remoteness, surely North Devon is no more remote than certain parts of the east and west coasts of Scotland. Attendance figures? Such is the popularity of golf in modern times it seems most unlikely that the crowds wouldn't flock to the area. North Devon abounds with places to stay, and after all, what better place for a week's holiday in July?

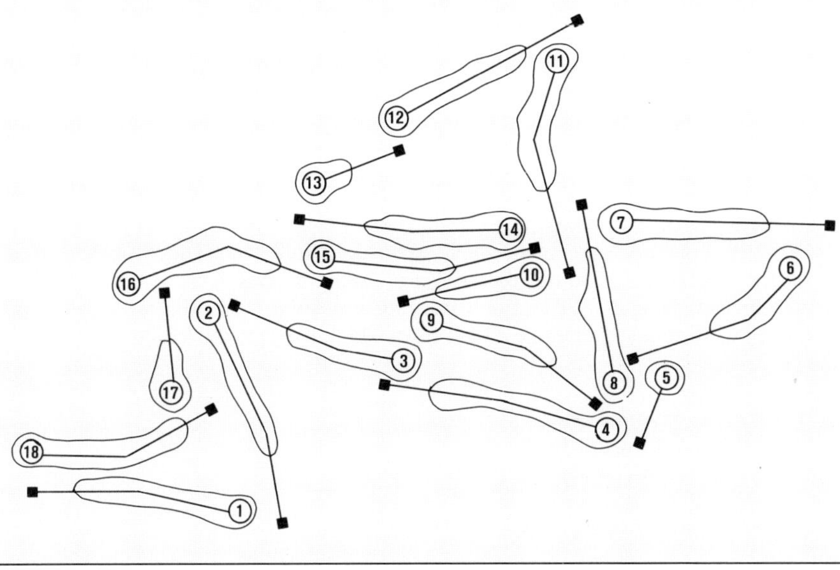

East Course

Hole	Yards	Par	Hole	Yards	Par
1	470	4	10	337	4
2	476	5	11	362	4
3	402	4	12	418	4
4	444	4	13	136	3
5	112	3	14	461	4
6	370	4	15	485	5
7	428	4	16	430	4
8	380	4	17	202	3
9	382	4	18	408	4
Out	3,464	36	In	3,239	35
			Out	3,464	36
			TOTALS	6,703	71

TEIGNWORTHY

Imagine, less than three hours from London, an oasis of serenity where luxury and the finest in food and comfort co-habit with some of the most spectacular countryside England has to offer. It's only half an hour's drive from Exeter or Newton Abbot.

Nestled among the folding green edges of Dartmoor National Park in the tiny hamlet of Frenchbeer, Teignworthy is just two and a half miles from the pretty town of Chagford. A skilful blending of quality and attention to detail, combines to create the unique ambience of Teignworthy, one of the finest country house hotels in England with an international reputation for food, wine and caring.

The oak-panelled hall, shallow staircase and huge granite fireplaces are notable features of this house, which is maintained and furnished with subtlety and respect. Comfort too has the highest priority and there is full central heating throughout. Six delightful and individual bedrooms are in the main house and three are in the converted hayloft, with a private sitting room overlooking the courtyard. All the bedrooms have an en-suite bathroom, telephone, colour television, king or queen sized bed and command a magnificent view along the South Teign valley and out over the brooding moors.

The food and wine rank among the finest in the West country. The menu changes daily and truly encapsulates the freshness and vitality of the surroundings using the finest, fresh local produce. Chef David Woolfall makes skilful and imaginative use of raw materials selected from a network of local suppliers, who share a common concern for the tradition and quality that is the heart of 'real food'.

Teignworthy has a recently re-surfaced, grass tennis court and walled croquet lawn. There is golf at nearby Mortonhampstead, horse riding on the moor and excellent fishing on the Dart and Teign rivers and at Fernworthy reservoir. Both the north and south coasts of Devon with spectacular cliffs or long sandy beaches are a short drive away.

John and Gillian Newell bought this delightful house from the original owners in 1978 and quickly built up an excellent reputation and enthusiastic following. They like their guests to feel that they are visiting friends in the country. Certainly the uniquely relaxing atmosphere that Teignworthy offers is the finest base from which to enjoy the beauty of Dartmoor.

Teignworthy,
Frenchbeer,
Chagford,
Devon.
Tel (06473) 3355

MANOR HOUSE
CHAMPIONSHIP GOLF

Dartmoor may seem an unlikely setting for one of Britain's finest golfing gems, but the **Manor House Hotel** course near Moretonhampstead is nothing less than that. Within howling distance of the Baskerville legends, it lies beneath a backdrop of granite tors and rolling hills.

Manor House itself is a vast and impressive Jacobean-style mansion, built between the Wars as a home for the **W.H. Smith family.** The golf course dominates the grounds of what is now a privately owned hotel and country club. Indeed, immediately on entering the gates, the driveway will take you alongside the 13th and 14th fairways. However, it is only on reaching the mansion ('clubhouse' somehow doesn't seem appropriate) that the full beauty of the surroundings can be appreciated. From here the view out across the course is quite simply stunning, and the bracing moorland air should inject a sense of joie de vivre into even the most wretched of souls!

One gentleman who certainly isn't a wretched soul is **Mr. Richard Lewis.** As **Golf Manager** he effectively runs the administrative side of things and all correspondence relating to golfing matters should be addressed to him at **The Manor House Hotel Golf and Country Club, Moretonhampstead, Devon.** Mr. Lewis is also the resident PGA professional, and can be reached by telephone on **(0647) 40355.** Golfers wishing to visit the course are always made very welcome and are permitted to play on any day of the week. During the summer months it is essential to book a starting time and although at most times the course is pleasantly uncrowded, a quick telephone call to check for any tee reservations is always advisable – Manor House is not surprisingly a popular meeting place for golfing societies.

In **1989** the **green fee** payable was **£12** per round or **£15** for a full day, with half-rates for **juniors**. Unless it is impossible for some reason, a day ticket is strongly recommended and if the prospect of 36 holes is a little daunting one could always consider the merits of hiring one of the electric-powered buggies that line up outside the pro-shop – who says Devon doesn't move with the times?

Whilst Moretonhampstead may look somewhat remote on the map, (the Hotel is 2 miles west of the town) the splendid scenery of these parts should make the journey a particularly pleasant one. The **B3212** is the most direct as well as the most scenic route from **Exeter** – a distance of approximately 14 miles. The Club's entrance is immediately off this road and cannot be missed. Persons approaching from the **Plymouth** region may also find the **B3212** helpful, while those travelling from further west and from the Torbay area will probably need to use the **A30/A38.**

At **6016** yards the course in not particularly long by modern standards – refreshingly so, some might say – nevertheless the par of **69** is a fairly strict one and there is only one five on the card. (From the ladies tees the course measures **5010** yards, par **70**).

To be frank though, length is really one of the last things the golfer should be concerned about when he comes to tackle this course – the sight from the elevated first tee should make this abundantly clear. The trout-filled **River Bovey** meanders its way through the centre of the course and is the dominant feature on the first seven holes. It takes a 'Sevvy' type to try and carry it on the **1st**; it runs immediately in front of the green on the dog-leg **2nd** and all the way along the right hand side of the narrow **3rd**. This tricky par three, with its overhanging trees to the left is surely one of the finest short holes in the country. At the back of the green, and circling round to the left, lie a profusion of rhododendrons and azaleas which in early summer burst into a kaleidoscope of colour: pinks and purples, yellows, reds, vivid blue and peach colours – as someone aptly remarked on seeing it, 'Augusta comes to Devon'!

The **4th** hole is the par five, and a genuine one at that with the river having to be carried from the tee, trouble all the way down the left and a raised green. The river crosses again in front of the **5th** green and reappears on the **7th**, where it twice cuts across the fairway. If you can reach the **8th** tee without having once gotten wet you're a better man than most! The 8th itself is fairly unspectacular but the **9th**, after a steep climb to the tee, gives you a chance to open the shoulders as you drive across a deep valley. Two fairly difficult par threes sandwich the **11th**, the longest par four on the course. The **13th** and **14th** are what television commentators might describe as 'potential birdie holes', but the closing stretch is quite tough, particularly the challenging **18th** with its acutely angled fairway and blind second. As you walk off the final green and sound the iron bell to signal 'all clear' you should be left in no doubt that you've played a very special golf course.

The **Hotel** acts as a rather grand 19th. An excellent and very full range of catering is offered with additional light snacks being available throughout the day. The balcony terrace, with its extensive views over the course and surrounding Hotel gardens is a must on a warm day .... imagine sitting out there on a bright and clear day in June, with just a hint of breeze and a cool drink in your hand .... joie de vivre? I should say so!

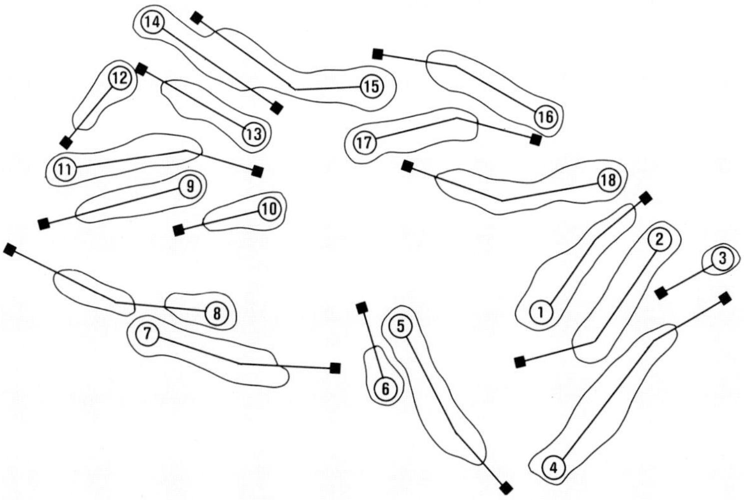

Hole	Yards	Par	Hole	Yards	Par
1	293	4	10	172	3
2	375	4	11	450	4
3	151	3	12	207	3
4	517	5	13	320	4
5	403	4	14	279	4
6	156	3	15	385	4
7	384	4	16	337	4
8	399	4	17	379	4
9	400	4	18	409	4
Out	3,078	35	In	2,938	34
			Out	3,078	35
			TOTALS	6,016	69

ROYAL NORTH DEVON

CHAMPIONSHIP GOLF

To the best of my knowledge **Ben Crenshaw** has never visited **Royal North Devon**. If true more's the pity for here is a Club truly steeped in the history of the game. **Westward Ho!**, as it is commonly known, was the first English links course and being founded in **1864** the Royal North Devon Golf Club lays claim to being the oldest English Club still playing over its original land. Furthermore it boasts the oldest Ladies Golf Club in the world, the **Westward Ho! Ladies Golf Club** which was established in **1868**.

Originally designed by **Tom Morris** and reconstructed by **Herbert Fowler** the 18 holes are situated on **Northam Burrows**. The Burrows is a vast, exposed and relatively flat area of common land-which stretches along the coast a couple of miles north of Bideford between Westward Ho! and Appledore.

Several of Britain's historic courses, particularly those in Scotland, have fascinating ties with common land and associated local rights which have existed since 'time immemorial', but whilst the inhabitants of **St Andrews** no longer use their hallowed turf for practising archery upon, nor put their washing out to dry on the banks of the Swilcan Burn, the locals of Northam village still graze their sheep and horses on the Burrows. There can surely be no other Championship course in the world where you can have teed up on the first, taken a few steps backward to survey the drive ahead only to see a sheep wander up and peer inquisitively at your ball!

Seriously, golf at Westward Ho! is a rich experience and definitely one to be recommended, few Golf Clubs are prepared to go quite so far out of their way to accommodate visitors and to offer such a warm welcome. Indeed the Club stages several open competitions during the summer months. Presently responsible for continuing the tradition of friendliness is the **Secretary, John Davies**. Mr. Davies can be contacted via **The Royal North Devon Golf Club, Golf Links Road, WestwardHo! Bideford, Devon. Tel (02372) 73817.**

Persons considering a trip to the Club may find it advisable to telephone first in order to check if any tee reservations have been made. Fine weather can make the course particularly popular during the holiday season. **Societies** are also welcomed and bookings can be arranged with the Secretary. In 1989 a **green fee** of **£12** entitled the **visitor** to either a single round or a full day's golf. The same could be purchased at weekends for **£14**. For **juniors** the green fee was a mere **£3** – excellent value. The Club's professional is **Graham Johnston** and he can be reached by telephone on **(02372) 77598**.

The course can be approached from both East and West via the **A39**, although travellers from the West may be able to avoid the busy town of Bideford by joining the **B3236** near Abbotsham. Visitors travelling from the Dartmoor region should take the **A386** road which runs from Okehampton to Bideford whilst those fromExeter should follow the **A377** to Barnstaple, thereafter joiningthe A39 as above.

From the medal tees the course measures **6449** yards (the Championship course is some 200 yards longer) and is divided into two fairly equal halves. Westward Ho! has a traditional 'out and back' layout and there are some panoramic views across Bideford Bay, especially from the 6th tee where on a clear day the Isle of Lundy can be seen. In theory the links receives a degree of protection from the elements from a large bank of shingle which separates the Burrows from the beach. I say 'in theory' for this is surely one of Britain's most windswept courses. However, the wind is not the only factor that can make scoring extremely difficult. There are numerous ditches and hidden potbunkers and then of course there are the **Great Sea Rushes.** To the uninitiated a word of caution – these giant marshland reeds, unique to Westward Ho!, can literally impale golf balls, so do as the sheep do – stay clear!

Westward Ho! is not only known for its golf course; it has literary fame as well. The village was founded a year before the Golf Club and was named after **Charles Kingsley's** adventure novel about Elizabethan seafarers. A decade or so later **Rudyard Kipling** attended the local college and remembered his days there in 'Stalky and Co'. There is no record to suggest that Mr. Kipling was 'an exceedingly good' golfer but whilst he was studying, a young boy from Northam was out on the course caddying for sixpence a round. The boy was destined to become Open Champion on five occasions. **John H. Taylor** learnt his golf at Westward Ho! and his great affection for the Club remained throughout his long life. In 1957 the Club elected him their President.

In addition to a friendly and unpretentious atmosphere, the Clubhouse offers some excellent catering. It also houses the Club's own **museum**. It is most interesting and contains a great variety of golfing memorabilia, ranging from one of Tom Watson's gloves to some priceless art.

For the golfer who has confined himself to playing on gentle heathland fairways, sheltered from any wind by tall trees, a visit to Westward Ho! would probably create quite a shock to the system. But clearly, for those with even a moderate interest in the history of the game and of course who are not afraid of a stiff challenge, Westward Ho! is a golfing must.

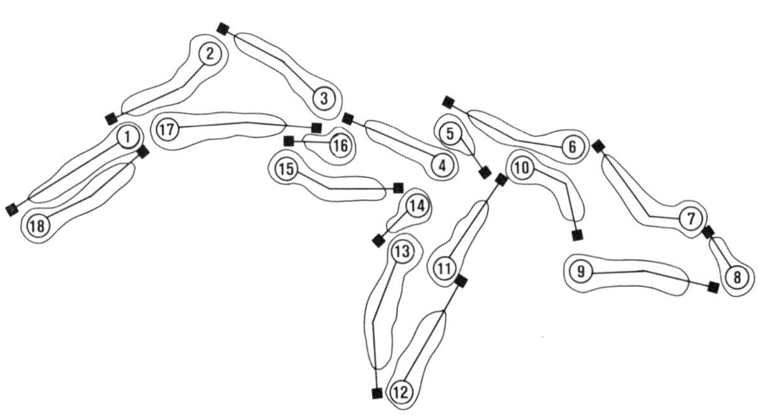

Hole	Yards	Par	Hole	Yards	Par
1	478	5	10	376	4
2	410	4	11	368	4
3	425	4	12	425	4
4	354	4	13	440	4
5	137	3	14	201	3
6	410	4	15	434	4
7	395	4	16	145	3
8	197	3	17	554	5
9	479	5	18	416	4
Out	3,285	36	In	3,359	35
			Out	3,285	36
			TOTALS	6,644	71

DEVON
COMPLETE GOLF

DEVON

Axe Cliff G.C.
(018) 4998 yds
Seaton
(0297) 20499

Bigbury G.C.
(18) 6038 yds
Bigbury-on-Sea, Kingsbridge
(054881) 557

Chulmleigh G.C.
(18) 1440 yds
Leigh Road, Chulmleigh
(0769) 80519

Churston G.C.
(18) 6201 yds
Churston, Brixham
(0803) 842751

Downes Credition G.C.
(18) 6003 yds
Hookway, Credition
(03632) 3025

East Devon G.C.
(18) 6214 yds
Northview Road, Budleigh,
Salterton
(03954) 3370

Elfordleigh Hotel G. & C.C.
(9) 5609 yds
Plympton, Plymouth
(0752) 336428

Exeter G. & C.C.
(18) 5702 yds
Countess Wear, Exeter
(039287) 4139

Great Torrington G.C.
(9) 4418 yds
Weare Trees, Torrington
(02372) 72792

Holsworthy G.C.
(18) 5935 yds
Kilatree, Holsworthy
(0409) 253177

Honiton G.C.
(18) 5236 yds
(18) 5900 yds
Midlehills, Honiton
(0404) 44422

Ilfracombe G.C.
(18) 6227 yds
HeleBay, Ilfracombe
(0271) 62176

Manor House Hotel G. & C.C.
(18) 6016 yds
Princetown Road,
Moretonhampstead
(0647) 40355

Newton Abbot (Stover) G.C.
(18) 5724 yds
Bovey Road, Newton Abbot
(0626) 2460

Okehampton G.C.
(18) 5307 yds
Okehampton
(0626) 52460

Royal North Devon G.C.
(18) 6449 yds
Westward Ho!, Bideford
(02372) 73817

Saunton G.C.
(18) 6703 yds (East)
(18) 6322 yds (West)
Saunton, Braunton
(0271) 812436

Sidmouth G.C.
(18) 5188 yds
Cotmaton Road, Sidmouth
(0395) 3451

Staddon Heights G.C.
(18) 5861 yds
Plystock, Plymouth
(0752) 402475

Tavistock G.C.
(18) 6250 yds
Down Road, Tavistock
(0822) 612049

Teignmouth G.C.
(18) 6142 yds
Exeter Road, Teignmouth
(06267) 4194

Thurslestone G.C.
(18) 6337 yds
Thurlestone, Kingsbridge
(0548) 560405

Tiverton G.C.
(18) 6227 yds
Post Hill, Tiverton
(0884) 252187

Torquay G.C.
(18) 6251 yds
Petitor Road, St Marychurch,
Torquay
(0803) 37471

Warren G.C.
(18) 5968 yds
Dawlish Warren
(0626) 862255

Wrangaton G.C.
(9) 5790 yds
Wrangaton, South Brent
(03647) 3229

Yelverton G.C.
(18) 6288 yds
Golflinks Rd, Yelverton
(0822) 852824

'The Royal North Devon Golf Club 1893'

SOMERSET, AVON, DORSET & WILTSHIRE

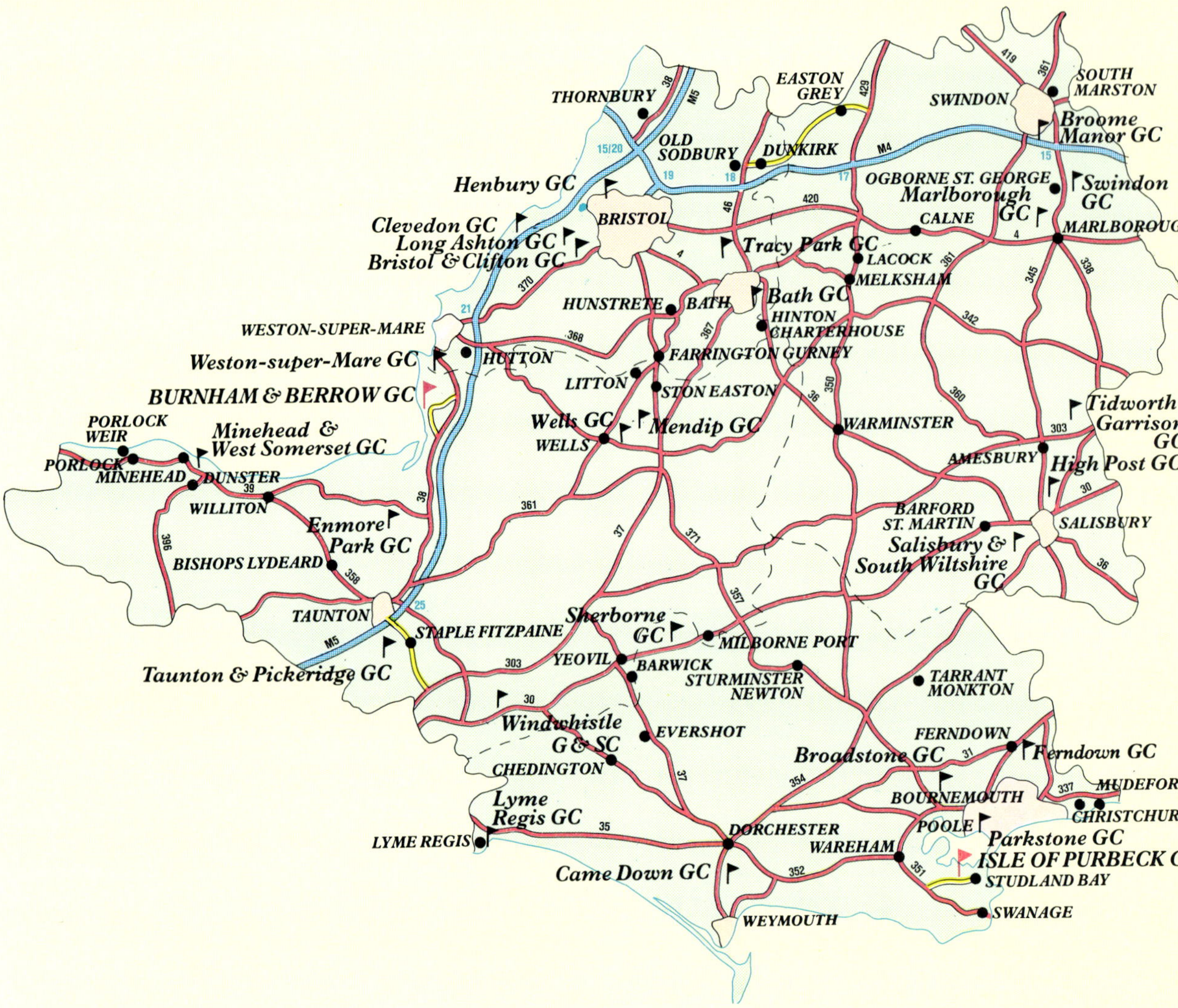

H. ROUNTREE ***"Queens Park"*** *SARAH BADDIEL'S BOOK GALLERY*

SOMERSET, AVON, DORSET & WILTSHIRE
CHOICE GOLF

From the wild beauty of Exmoor to the mystery of Stonehenge, the Quantocks and the Mendips, Lyme Regis and Bath, Avebury, Chesil Beach and Lulworth Cove. The West Country offers so much; no wonder those of us who do not live there are more than a little envious.

The golf too can be equally spectacular. There may not be a Wentworth or a St. Georges here but the region offers a considerable variety and there is certainly no shortage of challenge. There is a Championship links at Burnham and Berrow and a magnificent cliff top course at the Isle of Purbeck. Excellent downland golf can be enjoyed at Long Ashton and Bath while Bournemouth offers some majestic heathland and parkland type courses. We shall tee off in Somerset.

SOMERSET

Burnham and Berrow (featured ahead) is without doubt the finest course in the area and the place where **J.H. Taylor** wielded his famous mashie to great effect. The two holiday towns of **Minehead** and **Weston-Super-Mare** house the region's other two links courses. The **Minehead and West Somerset Golf Club** has more than a hundred years of history – it therefore remembers the quieter days in the years 'Before Butlins'. A fairly flat and windy course, it is situated on the eastern side of the town. Visitors are welcome at all times, though during the peak season a quick telephone call to the Club is advisable. The same can be said of **Weston** – a slightly longer, well-maintained course, located just off the main **A370** Bristol road. Fees at Weston are about **£9**, at Minehead a little less.

After a days golf at Burnham visitors can stay in the Club's new Dormy House. However, if a hotel is desired, Weston has a number of alternatives, perhaps the best is **The Grand Atlantic (0934) 26543** right on the seafront, while just outside the resort, **Hutton Court (0934) 814343** at Hutton is a magnificent 15th Century manor house. In Minehead, **The York Hotel (0643) 5154** is very handy for the course, other thoughts near here include **The Luttrell Arms (0643) 821555** in Dunster, a superb hostelry: and in Porlock Weir, **The Anchor Hotel (0643) 862753**. There are many fine pubs on Exmoor (if your thirst can wait!)

Taunton's golf course is at Corfe, the **Taunton and Pickeridge** Golf Club. It is another laid out close to the town's race track – a fairly undulating course visitors can normally play during the week. **The Taunton Castle (0823) 272671** is a super place to stay and a nearby pub of note is the **Greyhouse** at Staple Fitzpaine.

The city of **Wells** is certainly worth inspecting. The Cathedral is splendid and after a round on the Wells golf course a pleasant lunch can be enjoyed at the **Ancient Gate House (0749) 72029**. One final course to mention in the two counties is the magnificently titled **Windwhistle Golf and Squash Club** at Chard. The golf course is laid out on high ground and offers extensive views. It's also close the the famous Cricket St. Thomas Wildlife Park, where birdies and eagles abound.

AVON

Further north along this coastline the golf course at **Clevedon** stares specatacularly out across the mouth of the Severn. Clevedon is a cliff top course rather than a links. Well worth a visit, green fees are **£10** midweek, **£12** at the weekend. By travelling inland from Clevedon towards Bristol along the **B3128**, two of the city's best courses are reached before the famous Suspension Bridge. **Long Ashton** is actually immediately off the B3128, while to find **Bristol and Clifton** a left turn should be taken along the **B3129**. There is probably little to choose between the two, both being particularly attractive examples of downland golf. Visitors should be able to provide proof of handicap. Green fees are around the **£13-£16** mark. **Henbury** Golf Club is closer to the centre of Bristol, about 3 miles to the north to be precise, in the quiet suberb of Westbury-on-Trym. Henbury is a very mature parkland course with an abundance of trees making for some very attractive and challenging holes.

In most large cities the majority of centrally located hotels are modern and not particularly attractive. Bristol unfortunately is no exception. Perhaps the most stylish though is the aptly named **Grand Hotel (0272) 219645** on Broad Street. Two recommended restaurants are **Harvey's (0272) 277665** and **Les Semailles (0272) 686456** in Stoke Bishop. An excellent base to the north of the city at Thornbury is the tudor styled **Thornbury Castle (0454) 418511**.

Anyone travelling from Bristol to Bath (or vice versa) is likely to pass within a few miles of the **Tracy Park** Golf and Country Club at Wick. If possible a detour is strongly recommended. Tracy Park is a newish course, built in the mid-seventies around a 400-year old mansion which acts as a rather impressive Clubhouse. Quite a lengthy course, it receives visitors at most times although a preliminary telephone call is recommended. Green fees are **£12** midweek, **£14** at the weekend.

Everybody, they say, falls in love with Bath – the Romans did, the Georgians did and the Americans think it's 'cute'. For visiting golfers, if the 'other half' should come under the spell, the City has two attractive propositions: **Bath** Golf Glub and **Lansdown** Golf Club. The former, commonly known as **Sham Castle**, has an excellent situation high above the City and provides tremendous views over the surrounding countryside. In 1989 the fees to play at Bath were **£12** weekdays and **£14** at weekends. The club is one of the oldest in England. Lansdown occupies flatter ground adjacent to Bath Races. Visitors are welcome at all times, but as the course closes on racing days I cannot recommend an each-way double.

Staying in Bath is a sheer delight: with the Roman Baths, the Abbey, The Pump Rooms, a wealth of museums and galleries, the Royal Crescent and the Theatre Royal – there are so many attractions. The hotels in the city are amoung some of the finest in the country. **The Royal Crescent (0225) 319090** takes pride of place but **The Apsley House (0225) 336966** and **The Priory (0225) 331922** are also superb. The Hotels themselves house excellent restaurants but other popular eating places in Bath include **Popjoys (0225) 460494** and **The Clos du Roy (0225) 64357**. Only a short distance to the south of Bath, and set in the heart of some glorious countryside, are a number of other outstanding establishments. **Ston Easton Park (076 121) 631** in Ston Easton Ashton boasts a considerable reputation as does **Hunstrete House (07618) 578**. Another gem is **The Homewood Park Hotel (022 122) 3731** in Hinton Charterhouse. If a fine restaurant is required then the **Old Parsonage (0761) 52211** in Farrington Gurney is a good place to find. North of Bath the marvellously named Old Sodbury offers **The Cross Hands Hotel (0454) 313000** and Dunkirk, **The Petty France Hotel (045 423) 361.** Just outside Bath at Colerne is **Luckham Park (0225) 742777** a delightful early 18th century mansion converted into a hotel.

Tearing oneself away from Bath, more golf is found near Bridgewater. **Enmore Park**, located to the south of the town is a very pleasant medium length affair. The green fees are fairly modest at around **£10** per day and the course enjoys a delightful setting and nestles around the foothills of the Quantocks. **The White House Hotel (0984) 32306** at Wilton is very convenient for the course.

Moving from the Quantocks to the Mendips, the **Mendip Golf Club** at Gurney Slade offers possibly the most spectacular vistas of any course in the South West. From its 4th fairway, almost 1,000 feet above sea-level, on a clear day it is possible to sight the Cotswolds and the Quantocks, the Welsh Mountains and the Purbeck Hills, Glastonbury Tor and Westbury's White Horse ... need I go on? Mendip is an efficiently run Club that welcomes visitors at all times. A days golf will cost **£8** during the week and **£10** at the weekend. A good pub to note in Gurney Slade is **The George Inn**.

WILTSHIRE

There are twelve golf courses in **Wiltshire** and they are spread fairly evenly across the county. While none could be classed as genuine championship material, the majority offer a particularly enjoyable day's golf amidst some exceptionally attractive surroundings.

Beginning in the north of Wiltshire, Swindon is the county's largest town and there are two courses close at hand: **Broome Manor** and the **Swindon Golf Club**; both are situated south of the town. The latter at Ogbourne St George, despite its name, is in fact closer to Marlborough than Swindon. **Broome Manor** is a public course and as such visitors can arrange a game seven days of the week. In addition to 27 holes of rolling parkland golf there is an excellent covered driving range. **Swindon** is a downland type course, quite undulating with many extensive views. Visitors are welcome during the week and after 4pm on Sundays. Fees are about **£12**.

Swindon is the fastest growing town in the British Isles. A comfortable place to stay here is **The Wiltshire (0793) 28282** and in Blunsdon, just north of the town **Blunsdon House (0793) 721701**. The **Robin Hood Inn**, Ogbourne St George is very handy after a game at Swindon.

Marlborough Golf Club is a near neighbour of Swindon Golf Club, being situated to the north west of the town on the Marlborough Downs. Offering similarly wider ranging views (and similarly breezy!) it too welcomes visitors during the week. Weekends are naturally busier but it may still be possible to obtain a game. Fees are approximately **£9. The Sun (0762) 52081** in Marlborough offers good food in addition to reasonably priced accommodation. Also worth a visit is **The Ivy House Hotel (0672) 55333** – extremely comfortable. A pleasant drive westwards will take you to Lacock near Chippenham. Here the **Sign of The Angel** is a tremendous 15th Century Inn.

Dropping down the county, **Tidworth Garrison** is one of Wiltshire's top courses. It lies on Salisbury Plain and is owned by the Army. Green fees are about **£8**. (Note the excellent **Antrobus Arms (0980) 23163** in Amesbury).

Salisbury offers two fine challenges, to the north, **High Post** and to the south west **Salisbury and South Wilts**. Situated fairly close to Stonehenge, High Post is generally considered to be the leading course in the county. It's another downland type course, measuring 6267 yards. Arranging a game shouldn't be much of a problem and for a fee of approximaetly **£9** a good day's golf should be enjoyed. Salisbury and South Wilts offers some splendid views of Salisbury's celebrated Cathedral. One's best base in Salisbury is probably **The Rose and Crown Hotel (0722) 27908. The Old Bell Inn (0722) 27958** is an attractive alternative and for a good nearby restaurant visit **Michel's** at Barford St Martin **(0722) 742240**.

DORSET

Dorset is quite different; golf wise the county is rather 'lopsided': it has a greater number of courses, but if the south eastern corner were suddenly to be removed (one wonders by what!) the proverbial cupboard would be almost bare. The better golf courses in Dorset lie within a ten mile radius of the centre of Bournemouth. Having said that, **Sherborne** in the far north of the county is undoubtedly one of the prettiest inland courses to be found anywhere in Britain.

In Evershot, **The Summer Lodge (093 583) 666** is a fine restaurant and in Sturminster Newton stands **Plumber Manor (0258) 72507** a gorgeous country house. In the south west of the county **Lyme Regis**, famed for its fossils and more recently its French Lieutenant's Woman, has a fairly undulating 18 hole course which lies to the east of the town. Visitors are welcome weekdays and on most Sundays. The road between Lyme Regis and Weymouth provides dramatic views over Chesil Beach and passes through some of the most beautiful villages in England. The area north of Weymouth is Thomas Hardy country. Dorchester stands in the middle of it all and **Came Down Golf Club** is well worth noting when in these parts.Green fees are about **£9** during the week.

If one chooses to stay in Lyme Regis, **The Mariners (02974) 2753** may be the best bet and **The Pilot Boat** is a good pub. Beyond Weymouth our journey takes us through Wareham where **The Priory Hotel (09295) 51666** is perfectly placed for either a visit to Swanage and the Isle of Purbeck or for playing the Bournemouth courses.

Like Burnham and Berrow, The Isle of Purbeck is featured ahead but **Ferndown, Parkstone** and **Broadstone** all fall in the 'must be visited' category. They are beautiful heathland courses (Ferndown in fact has 36 holes) with much heather, gorse and pine trees and each is kept in immaculate condition. The green fees range between **£17** and **£22** and before trying to play any of the courses a quick telephone call is strongly recommended.

In addition to a game on one or more of these great courses, Bournemouth's two public courses shouldn't be overlooked. **Meyrick Park** is very good while **Queen's Park** is often described as the finest public course in England.

The Bournemouth – Poole – Swanage area abounds with hotels and restaurants. Here are just a few suggestions: In Bournemouth **The Highcliff (0202) 27702** and **The Royal Bath (0202) 25555**, are good whilst **Crusts (0202) 21430** is an excellent restaurant; in Poole, **The Mansion House (0202) 685666** and **Gullivers** restaurant **(0202) 708810**. Swanage offers **The Pines (0929) 425211** and Christchurch, **Splinters** restaurant **(0202) 48345**. Ferndown golfers can look to the comfortable **Dormy Hotel (0202) 872121** and Parkstone players can enjoy superb food at **Isabels (0202) 747885** and **The Wharehouse on the Quay**. Finally, people wishing to get away from the sea and sand, or the water hazards and bunkers should visit Tarrant Monkton. Here a converted stables house makes for a really splendid little restaurant – **Langton's (025889) 225**, and the local pub, **The Langton Arms (0202) 677238** is tremendously popular.

IVY HOUSE

The Ivy House Hotel is a luxury Georgian residence which overlooks the famous Marlborough High Street on the edge of the Marlborough Downs. Bath, Salisbury and Newbury racecourses are all easily reached from this central location.

The main building is Georgian and contains elegant lounges and a Palladian style restaurant and cocktail bar in pale pink and Wedgwood blue.

There are 30 luxurious bedrooms all equipped to the highest standards expected from discerning guests. All the bedrooms have a private bath and shower, colour T.V., in-house movies, trouser press, hairdryer and minibar; and they're all individually decorated.

Guests at the Ivy House are personally looked after by resident proprietors, David Ball and Josephine Scott and their young team of English staff.

Their genuine objective is to provide an excellence in hospitality exceeding the expectations of the guests. Their success in this area is illustrated by their file of thankyou letters from past and regular guests, and merit awards from the AA and RAC, for hospitality, bedrooms, lounges, restaurant and overall comfort.

From the Ivy House, with its country house hotel atmosphere, one can visit Stonehenge, Avebury Ring, the cities of Bath and Salisbury, numerous stately homes and also the Marlborough Downs. But return to the hotel to dine with elegance in the Garden Restaurant, specialising in English and French cuisine and using only the best fresh local produce.

The Ivy House Hotel,
Marlborough,
Wiltshire. SN8 1HJ
Tel: (0672) 55333

BURNHAM AND BERROW
CHAMPIONSHIP GOLF

I wonder how many people have travelled along the M5 between Bristol and Exeter and wondered what lay beyond the great Iron Age fort that rises out of level ground, 'like something from out of 'Close Encounters',' midway between Weston and Bridgwater. Well, many golfers will know that a short distance behind the great hill lies one of England's finest links courses.

Burnham and Berrow appeared on the golfing map in 1891 and the first professional the Club engaged was a no lesser man than **John H. Taylor**. The great man was then in fact a lad of 19 although within 3 years he was to win the Open Championship at Sandwich – the first of his five victories. John Henry thought very highly of what, until quite recently, had been a 'wild rabbit infested waste of sandhills' for he said it was here, at Burnham, that he was 'given the splendid opportunity of developing my mashie play' (as the course) 'necessitated very accurate approach play.'

The present day visitor to the North Somerset club is most unlikely to confront a gathering of wild rabbits (at least of the animal variety) nor, one assumes, will he possess a mashie amongst his armoury. However, despite a number of alterations made over the years, the towering sandhills remain by far the course's most dominant feature.

Not surprisingly Burnham and Berrow is a popular course and whatever the time of year visitors would be wise to telephone the Club before setting off. **Mrs. E.L.Sloman** is the new **Secretary** and she can be contacted on **(0278) 785760**. The Club's professional, **Nigel Blake**, can be reached on **(0278) 784545**. Persons interested in organising a Society meeting are advised to write to the Secretary, the Club's full address being, **Burnham and Berrow Golf Club, St Christopher's Way, Burnham-on-Sea, Somerset.**

Green fees for 1989 were set at **£18** for weekdays and **£20** at weekends, fees being payable at the Club House. For **juniors** the fees were half the above rates. Persons holidaying in the vicinity (Weston-Super-Mare is less than 10 miles away) might well consider the merits of a weekly ticket (**£100** in 1989) or a fortnightly ticket (**£180** in 1989). Furthermore, in addition to the 18 hole Championship Course there is also an adjacent 9 hole course situated alongside the sea. Whilst probably not quite up to the standard of the full Championship course, at **3275** yards, par **36**, it certainly represents a fine challenge and the **green fee** of **£6** would appear to be excellent value. Golf clubs can be hired from the pro- shop and in summer it may be possible to find a caddy – hopefully one well acquainted with the best paths over and around the enormous sandhills.

Approaching by car from both North and South the **M5** is the most direct route, leaving at exit **22.** Thereafter one should follow the **B3140**. The course is situated about a mile north of Burnham-on- Sea and is well signposted.

It has been written that Burnham's setting is unspectacular: in a word 'false'. Whilst it may not be Gleneagles, Somerset is never dull. From many points on the course there are superb views across the Bristol Channel and the panorama from the 12th green is quite breathtaking.

Right from the first hole the premium on accuracy becomes apparent. Anything short of a straight tee shot will leave a blind, not to mention very awkward second. At one time the layout of the course necessitated the playing of several blind shots. However today, accurate driving will largely eliminate such difficulties although on a number of holes the base of the flagstick will not be visible when playing the approach shot. Burnham's **2nd** is a good straight hole played from an elevated tee, whereas the **3rd**, at least from the back, is one of those 'bite- off-as-much-as-you-dare' holes with the fairway dog-legging sharply to the left towards a sunken punch-bowl green. From the **4th** tee there is the first view of the Bristol Channel and distant Wales as the course moves nearer the sea. There are two par 3's on the front nine, the **5th** and the **9th**, the latter surely being one of the finest short holes to be found anywhere.

On reaching the turn anyone claiming to have mastered the large sandhills may well have to eat his words after playing the **10th**: a minor mountain must be carried from the tee and there is a severe drop away to the right – be warned! If the front nine is perhaps the more interesting of the halves, the second nine is probably the more testing. The **12th** and **13th** require very precise second shots; both the short holes are exceptionally tricky and the **18th** needs a couple of mighty big hits if it is to be reached in two. A good score at Burnham certainly has to be earned, but is immensely satisfying if achieved.

Visitors should find the Clubhouse atmosphere pleasingly informal. The catering is of a high standard and is offered daily between the hours of 11 am and 6 pm. With prior notice both breakfast and dinner can be arranged. Burnham and Berrow is a friendly Club and well worth a visit. Clearly the message to all golfers who pass down the M5 oblivious to what goes on beyond the 'great hump' is quite simply, come on over!

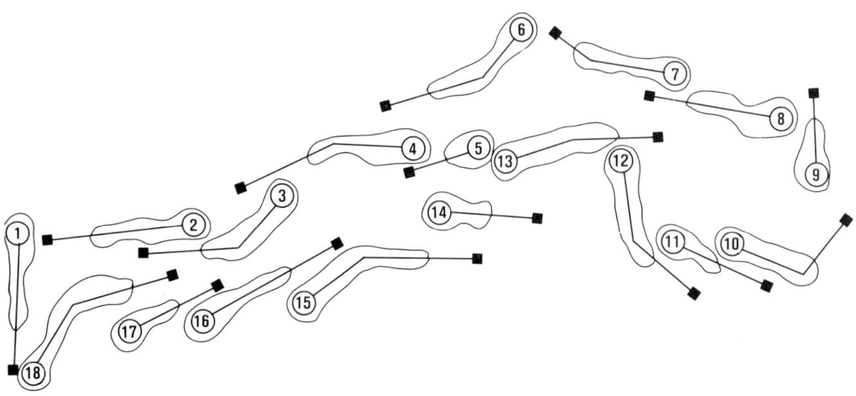

Hole	Yards	Par	Hole	Yards	Par
1	381	4	10	370	4
2	396	4	11	422	4
3	384	4	12	388	4
4	480	5	13	475	5
5	160	3	14	181	3
6	397	4	15	438	4
7	450	4	16	329	4
8	483	5	17	201	3
9	163	3	18	449	4
Out	3,294	36	In	3,253	35
			Out	3,294	36
			TOTALS	6,547	71

FERNDOWN

CHAMPIONSHIP GOLF

When it comes to beautifully manicured fairways and quick, ultra-true greens then the better American courses tend to be superior to their British counterparts. **Ferndown** is a definite exception. The fairways and greens are perhaps in the best kept condition in the whole of Britain. Someone deserves a mighty large pat on the back!

There are in fact two courses at Ferndown, the **Old** and the **New**. The Old Course was originally designed in **1912** by **Harold Hilton**, who was twice Open Champion before the turn of the century. The shorter New Course, which has nine holes but eighteen tees, has a much more recent history being designed in **1969** by **J. Hamilton-Stutt** and opened two years later.

The Secretary at Ferndown is **Mr. Hodson**, Tel **(0202) 874602**. **Visitors** to the Club are welcome on any day provided prior permission is first obtained. **Societies** are limited to Mondays, Wednesdays and Fridays and written applications should be addressed to the Secretary at **Ferndown Golf Club, 119 Links Road, Ferndown, Wimborne, Dorset, BH22 8BU**. All visitors and Society members must be prepared to produce a handicap certificate or alternatively a letter of introduction from their home Club.

To play the Old Course the **green fee** set in **1989** was **£20** during the week with **£27** payable at the weekend – this sum applies for a single round or a full day's golf. The green fee for the New Course is **£10** during the week or **£16** for weekends.

Doug Sewell, the professional at Ferndown, can be reached on **(0202) 873825**. A former Walker Cup player and very fine professional, I once read that in an Alliance Meeting at Ferndown he played the course in 60 strokes – enough said! Ferndown has indeed been very fortunate with its professionals; Percy Allis served the Club for over 25 years.

Located approximately six miles north of Bournemouth, Ferndown is quite easily reached from all directions. Motoring from the West of England the **A35** from Dorchester, which suddenly becomes the **A31** near Bere Regis passes through Ferndown very close to the Golf Club.

Approaching from the East, from London the **M3** runs to Southampton which in turn is linked to Ferndown (or Trickett's Cross to be precise) by the **A31**. The left fork should be taken at Trickett's Cross and this leads on to Golf Links Road, the course being immediately on the left. From the North the route is via Salisbury where the **A338** should be followed as far as Ringwood and thereafter the **A31** as above. Finally anyone who happens to possess their own jet may wish to note that Bournemouth has a small airport at **Hurn**, very close to the Golf Club.

The Old Course at Ferndown measures **6442** yards from the back tees, par and standard scratch both being **71**. From the forward tees the length is reduced by a little over 200 yards. The layout is essentially one of two loops, an inner loop comprising holes one to eight and the outer containing the ninth to the eighteenth.

Its fairways are of the sandy heathland type and are gently undulating throughout. The rough consists mainly of heather and together with the many pines and firs gives the course a most attractive appearance.

There are a considerable number of dog-leg holes necessitating much thought from the tee. The toughest holes on the course are possibly the **6th**, with its elevated green, the dog leg **9th** and the uphill **11th** – all fairly lengthy par fours from the back tees. One should also mention the **5th**, an excellent par 3, with the rhododendrons providing a splash of colour in the right season.

At **5,604** yards (par 70) the New Course is less demanding in terms of length but it too has its challenges and it is set in equally beautiful surroundings.

Ferndown's Clubhouse has a prime location grandly surveying the course from its elevated position. On a clear day there are views across the course to the Isle of Wight. The facilities are excellent with lunches being offered daily. Both breakfast and dinner can be arranged with prior notice. A jacket and tie should be worn in public rooms at all times.

In recent years, the Club has played host to many competitions and tournaments, such as the **Women's English Amateur Championship** in 1985 and the **Hennessy Cognac Cup**, a four man team competition, played over the Old Course in 1982 and 1984. The **Ladies European Open** visited the course in 1987, and 1989 sees the **British Ladies Open** at Ferndown. The superb condition of the course, combined with its excellent location, should ensure that Ferndown retains its considerable popularity far into the future.

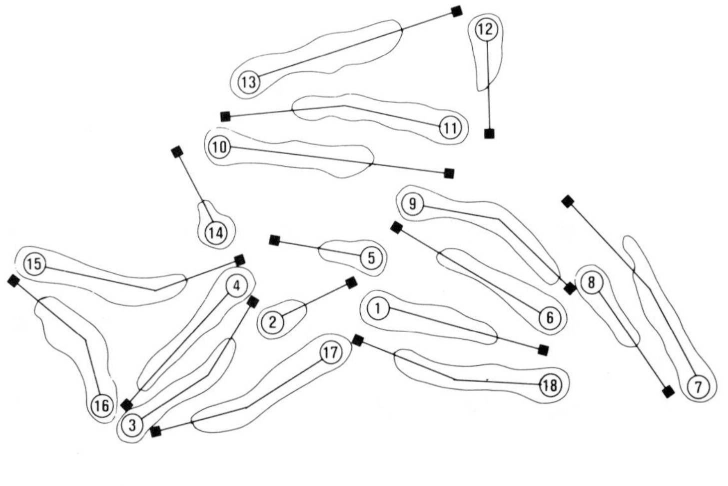

Old Course

Hole	Yards	Par	Hole	Yards	Par
1	396	4	10	485	5
2	175	3	11	438	4
3	398	4	12	186	3
4	395	4	13	488	5
5	206	3	14	152	3
6	409	4	15	398	4
7	480	5	16	305	4
8	304	4	17	397	4
9	427	4	18	403	4
Out	3,190	35	In	3,252	36
			Out	3,190	35
			TOTALS	6,442	71

ISLE OF PURBECK
CHAMPIONSHIP GOLF

Most people are a little suprised when they learn that the **Isle of Purbeck** Golf Club was founded as long ago as **1892** – a decade before Sunningdale and Walton Heath. They are probably even more surprised when they hear that **Enid Blyton** and her husband were once owners of the Club. Originally only a 9 hole course, there are now 27 holes comprising the **18 hole Purbeck Course** and an adjacent, shorter **9 hole** course, **The Dene**. In **1966**, a superb new Clubhouse was built using the local Purbeck stone and it was around this time that more and more people began to consider seriously the quality of the golf here as well as the sheer beauty of the Club's setting.

Today the Club is owned and managed by the Robinson family. **Mrs. Joan Robinson** is **Managing Director** and she can be contacted on **(0929) 44361**. All written communications should be addressed to her at **The Isle of Purbeck Golf Club, Swanage, Dorset, BH19 3AB.** The Club's Professional is **Paul Sowerby**, who can be contacted on **(0929) 44354**.

Visitors to the Isle of Purbeck are welcome to play on both courses, although those wishing to play on the Purbeck course must possess a handicap. **Green fees** for 1989 were set at **£16** per day to play on the Purbeck course, with **£18.50** payable at weekends and Bank Holidays. It should be remembered that these sums are for a full day ticket as opposed to a single round fee. Junior golfers are asked to part with **£8** for a weekday round on the Purbeck course and **£10** at weekends. The Dene course can be played for **£7.50** during the week or **£9** at the weekend, with a **£5** reduction for those teeing off after 4.30pm. Buggies are even for hire at an extra **£15** per round.

Swanage has become a very popular holiday centre and keen golfers should perhaps consider the merits of short temporary membership of the Club. In 1989, a week's golf on the Purbeck course was set at for **£86,** two weeks at **£130,** three at **£150** and four weeks at **£168**. There are reductions for joint membership and for those wishing to limit their golf to the Dene course. Visitors may also wish to note that the Club stages a limited number of open competitions during the summer. Information concerning these can be obtained from Mrs. Robinson. Golfing **Societies** are encouraged to come to the Isle of Purbeck and those organising should find the Club very accommodating; indeed, Societies may book up to two years ahead. What better place for an annual gathering?

Getting to the Isle of Purbeck may present the biggest headache. This is hardly the most accessible of Britain's golf clubs – not that the Club can be blamed for that! Anyway, the best routes are probably as follows: from the West the **A35** runs from Honiton through Dorchester and joins the **A351** at Lytchett Minster near Poole. The **A351** should be followed as far as Corfe Castle from which the **B3351** Studland road should be taken. The Club is situated just off this road. Travelling from the North the **A350** also joins the **A351** near Poole, whilst from the Bournemouth/Poole area a car ferry operates between Sandbanks and Shell Bay and avoids the drive around Poole Harbour.

Any of the aforementioned headaches should surely be dispelled on arrival at theClubhouse. The south coast possesses a number of scenic courses, but one would be very pushed to find an equal to the magnificent views provided by the Isle of Purbeck. The view from the **5th** on the Purbeck Course ('Agglestones') is particularly outstanding as you tee off from the top of an ancient Saxon burial mound. The Par 3 **11th**, 'Island', with its backdrop of pines and two tier green is also an exceptional hole.

For those who find the modern day monster courses somewhat tedious with the great emphasis they place on brute force (and ignorance?) the Purbeck Course should prove rather refreshing. From the back tees it measures **6248 yards** (par **71)** whilst from the forward tees the course is reduced to **5823 yards** (par **69)**. From the Ladies Tees the course measures **5648,** (par **73**).

On returning to the Clubhouse, the golfer should find that a full range of catering is offered and that the food and service is of a high standard. The Clubhouse has recently undergone total refurbishment, with a new bar, restaurant and showers. Breakfast can be arranged and lunch, high teas and dinner are all offered daily. A jacket and tie should be worn for dinner and Sunday Lunch. Again, some splendid views are to be had from the Clubhouse.

When in South Dorset many visitors like to take in a spot of fossil hunting. Lyme Regis and Charmouth are within easy reach, however, golfers need not look beyond the four walls of the Clubhouse – it is full of old fossils. Lest I be accused of insulting the Members, I should quickly explain: when the Clubhouse was built several fossilised dinosaur footprints and some massive ammonites were incorporated into the interior walls. It therefore follows – and golf historians please note -that to a limited extent the Isle of Purbeck could be said to possess the oldest Clubhouse in the world!

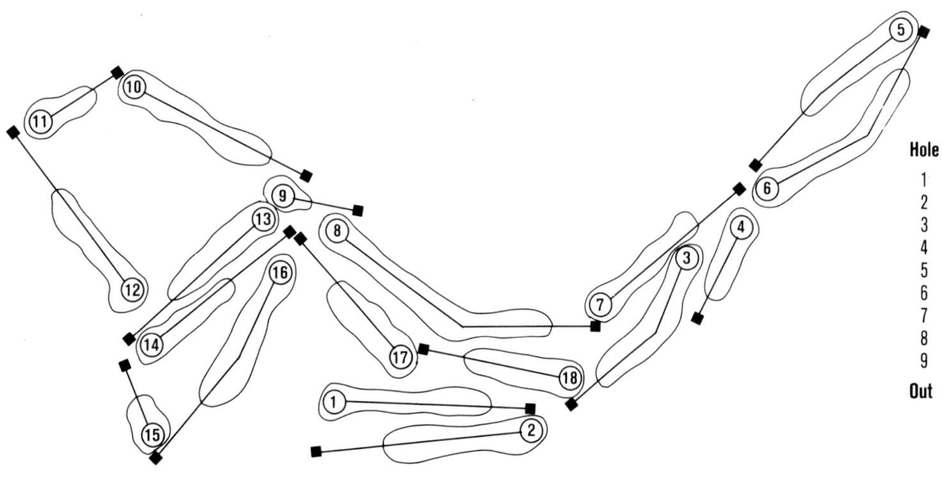

Hole	Yards	Par	Hole	Yards	Par
1	360	4	10	414	4
2	414	4	11	207	3
3	304	4	12	423	4
4	186	3	13	373	4
5	403	4	14	385	4
6	501	5	15	188	3
7	355	4	16	372	4
8	583	5	17	325	4
9	146	3	18	309	4
Out	3,252	36	In	2,996	34
			Out	3,252	36
			TOTALS	6,248	70

SOMERSET, AVON, DORSET & WILTSHIRE

COMPLETE GOLF

SOMERSET

Brean G.C.
(14) 5470 yards
Brean, Burnham-on-Sea
(027875) 467

Burnham and Berrow G.C.
(18) 6547 yards
(9) 6550 yards
St Christopher's Way,
Burnham-on-Sea
(0278) 785760

Enmore Park G.C.
(18) 6443 yards
Enmore, Bridgewater
(027687) 481

Minehead and West Somerset G.C.
(18) 6131 yards
The Warren, Minehead
(0643) 2057

Taunton and Pickeridge G.C.
(18) 5927 yards
Corfe, Taunton
(082342) 240

Vivary Park G.C.
(18) 4620 yards
Taunton
(0823) 333875

Wells G.C.
(18) 5288 yards
East Horrington Road, Wells
(0749) 72868

Windwhistle G. & S.C.
(12) 6055 yards
Cricket St. Thomas, Chard
(046030) 231

Yeovil G.C.
(18) 6139 yards
Sherborne Road, Yeovil
(0935) 22965

AVON

Bath G.C.
(18) 6369 yards
Sham Castle, North Road, Bath
(0225) 25182

Bristol and Clifton G.C.
(18) 6294 yards
Beggar Bush Lane, Failand,
Bristol
(0272) 393474

Chipping Sodbury G.C.
(18) 6912 yards
(9) 6194 yards
Chipping Sodbury
(0454) 319042

Clevedon G.C.
(18) 5835 yards
Castle Road, Clevedon
(0272) 874057

Filton G.C.
(18) 6227 yards
Golf Course Lane, Filton, Bristol
(0272) 694169

Fosseway G.C.
(9) 4148 yards
Charlton Lane, Midsomer Norton
(0761) 412214

Henbury G.C.
(18) 6039 yards
Henbury Hill, Westbury-on-Trym,
Bristol
(0272) 500044

Knowle G.C.
(18) 6016 yards
Fairway, Brislington, Bristol
(0272) 770660

Lansdown G.C.
(18) 6267 yards
Lansdown, Bath
(0225) 22138

Long Ashton G.C.
(18) 6051 yards
Long Ashton, Bristol
(0272) 392316

Mangotsfield G.C.
(18) 5297 yards
Carsons Road, Mangotsfield
(0272) 565501

Mendip G.C.
(18) 5982 yards
Gurney Slade, Bath
(0749) 840570

Saltford G.C.
(18) 6081 yards
Manor Road, Saltford
(02217) 3220

Shirehampton Park G.C.
(18) 5943 yards
Parkhill, Shirehampton, Bristol
(0272) 822083

Tracy Park G. & C.C.
(18) 6613 yards
(9) 5200 yards
Bath Road, Wick
(027582) 2251

Weston-Super-Mare G.C.
(18) 6225 yards
Uphill Road, Weston-Super-Mare
(0934) 621360

Worlebury G.C.
(18) 5945 yards
Worlebury Hill Road,
Weston-Super-Mare
(0934) 623214

DORSET

Ashley Wood G.C.
(9) 6227 yards
Wimborne Road, Blandford
(0258) 52253

Bridport & West Dorset G.C.
(18) 5246 yards
East Cliff, West Bay, Bridport
(0308) 22597

Boscombe G.C.
(18) 6505 yards
Queen's Park, Bournemouth
(0202) 36198

Broadstone G.C.
(18) 6204 yards
Wentworth Drive, Broadstone
(0202) 692595

Came Down G.C.
(18) 612: yards
Came Down, Dorchester
(030 581) 2531

Christchurch G.C.
(9) 4824 yards
Ilford Bridge, Christchurch
(0202) 473817

Ferndown G.C.
(18) 6442 yards (Old Course)
(9) 5604 yards (New Course)
119 Golf Links Road, Ferndown
(0202) 874602

Highcliffe Castle G.C.
(18) 4732 yards
107 Lymington Road,
Highcliffe-on-Sea
(04252) 72210

Isle of Purbeck G.C.
(18) 6248 yards
(9) 2022 yards
Studland, Swanage
(0929) 44361

Knighton Heath G.C.
(18) 6206 yards
Francis Avenue, West Howe,
Bournemouth
(0202) 572633

Lakey Hill G.C.
(18) 6146 yards
Hyde, Wareham
(0929) 471776

Lyme Regis G.C.
(18) 6262 yards
Timber Hill, Lyme Regis
(02974) 2963

Meyrick Park G.C.
(18) 5878 yards
Central Drive, Bournemouth
(0202) 290871

Parkstone G.C.
(18) 6250 yards
Links Road, Parkstone
(0202) 707138

Sherborne G.C.
(18) 5768 yards
Higher Clatcombe, Sherborne
(0963) 814431

Wareham G.C.
(9) 5196 yards
Sandford Road, Wareham
(09295) 54147

Weymouth G.C.
(18) 5760 yards
Links Road, Westham, Weymouth
(0305) 773981

WILTSHIRE

Brinkworth G.C.
(18) 6086 yards
9 Callows Cross, Brinkworth
Chippenham
(066641) 277

Broome Manor G.C.
(18) 6359 yards
(9) 5610 yards
Pipers Way, Swindon
(0793) 32403

Chippenham G.C.
(18) 5540 yards
Malmesbury Rd, Chippenham
(0249) 652040

High Post G.C.
(18) 6267 yards
Great Durnford, Salisbury
(0722) 73356

Kingsdown G.C.
(18) 6265 yards
Kingsdown, Corsham
(0225) 742530

Marlborough G.C.
(18) 6440 yards
The Common, Marlborough
(0672) 52147

North Wilts G.C.
(18) 6450 yards
Bishops Cannings, Devizes
(038068) 627

R.A.F. Upavon G.C.
(9) 5597 yards
R.A.F. Upavon, Pewsey
(0980) 630787

Salisbury & South Wilts G.C.
(18) 6189 yards
(9) 4848 yards
Netherhampton, Salisbury
(0722) 742645

Swindon G.C.
(18) 6226 yards
Ogbourne St. George,
Marlborough
(067284) 327

Tidworth Garrison G.C.
(18) 5990 yards
Bulford Road, Tidworth
(0980) 42321

West Wilts G.C.
(18) 5701 yards
Elm Hill, Warminster
(0985) 212702

HAMPSHIRE & THE CHANNEL ISLES

C.E. BROCK "The Putt" SOTHEBY'S

HAMPSHIRE & THE CHANNEL ISLANDS

CHOICE GOLF

Even if the Isle of Wight and the Channel Islands were taken away from this region it would still score top marks, both for the quality of the golf and the quality of the accompanying scenery. With the New Forest to the south, the Downs to the north and Winchester Cathedral standing proudly in the middle, Hampshire is arguably the fairest of all English counties. And amongst all this finery stand the likes of **Liphook, North Hants, Blackmoor** and **Brockenhurst Manor** – four of the country's leading inland courses.

Three of those four mentioned above, Liphook, North Hants and Blackmoor, lie towards the east of the county close to the boundary with Surrey. Not surprisingly they are staunch members of the 'heathland club' – silver birch and pine, fir, heather and a dash of gorse. **Liphook** is possibly the pick of the three, though it's a close thing, and both **North Hants** (at Fleet) and **Blackmoor** (off the A325 at Bordon) annually stage major amateur events – North Hants the **Hampshire Hog** and Blackmoor the **Selborne Salver**. Each measures between 6,200 and 6,300 yards and is maintained in superb condition. Visitors looking for a game on any of the three should telephone the Club in question before making any firm plans. Certain restrictions apply, particularly at weekends. Green fees at these courses are around the **£16-£20** mark.

The final mention in this area goes to one of the country's newest recruits, the **Old Thorns Golf and Country Club**, situated south of Liphook. Old Thorns is owned by a large Japanese Company and in addition to a rapidly maturing Championship standard golf course (lakes and all) the famed Japanese hospitality offers French, English and Japanese restaurants, a heated swimming pool and even a Japanese masseur!

There's no shortage of comfortable hotels in the north of Hampshire and often quite hidden in the countryside are some delightful pubs and restaurants. Pubs to ease your slumber include two first rate establishments. They are **The Crown and Cushion** in Minley and **The Chequers** in Well. Fleet dissects these two villages and **The Lismoyne Hotel (0252) 628555** is ideally located. In Passfield, **The Passfield Oak** does good food and some popular real ales, while in Grayshott, **Woods (042873) 5555** is an excellent little restaurant and it sounds perfect for golfers. In Liphook, as well as the superb **Old Thorns (0428) 724555**, the **Links Hotel (0428) 723773** is very handy for the 9th and 10th tees on the Liphook course. If you prefer curry then **Lai Quilla (0428) 722095** is recommended (and certain to add 20 yards to your drive!).

Winchester golfers, like those at Liphook, are doubly fortunate having two first class courses at hand: **Royal Winchester**, and **Hockley**, located two miles south of the City on the **A333**. Both are downland type courses where visitors should be able to arrange a game during the week, fees being approximately **£15**.

In Ampfield, south of Winchester, and Romsey, also south of the Cathedral town, two establishments catch the eye. In the former **Potters Heron (0703) 266611** is comfortable and convenient for the A31 and **The Old White Horse (0794) 512431** is a welcoming Inn located in Romsey's market place. In Winchester not too far from school and cathedral there are numerous restaurants, perhaps the best is **The Old Chesil (0962) 53177**. Also in Winchester **The Wessex Hotel (0962) 61611** is by no means cheap but particularly comfortable. North west of Winchester is Sparsholt, where one finds one of those rare exquisite English Country House Hotels, **Lainston House (0962) 63588** – ideal for people who want true luxury. In Stockbridge, **The Game Larder (0624) 810414** is excellent and **The Sherriff House (0264) 810677** also offers outstanding food and for both, do book. People coming from or returning to the west, should note Middle Wallop – more specifically – **Fifehead Manor (0264) 781565**, a delightful manor house with a good restaurant. Finally, I must point pub lovers in mid-Hampshire in the direction of Ovington where **The Bush** is excellent.

Returning to the fairways, and switching nearer to the south coast the **Rowlands Castle** parkland course occupies a peaceful setting. Visitors are welecome seven days a week though prior telephoning is advisable at the weekends. The course can play fairly long, especially from the back markers (close to 6,700 yards). While we're on the subject of length, a hundred years ago the excellent links at **Hayling Island** (green fee **£15**) is said to have measured 7,480 yards – so much for the modern-day monster courses! Today the course is less frightening but still quite a challenge and visitors are warmly received. Fees are similar to Rowlands Castle **(£15)**.

A drink is needed and two fine pubs are at hand – **The Old House at Home** (superb name) in Havant and **The Royal Oak**, Langstone, both ideally situated for Rowlands Castle. Other establishments to sample in this area of Hampshire include the truly delightful **Old House Hotel (0329) 833049** in Wickham. Trekking northwards one comes to Botley, here **Cobbett's (04892) 2068** is a fine French restaurant.

Stoneham is without doubt the pick of the courses in the Southampton area, 2 miles north of the town. The venue of the first Dunlop masters tournament back in 1946, it is quite undulating with an ample sprinkling of gorse and heather which though appealing to look at is often the curse of the wayward hitter. Subject to Club competitions, visitors are welcome throughout the week, fees in 1989 being **£12** midweek, **£14** at weekends.

Midway between Portsmouth and Southampton (**M27 junction 7) Meon Valley Golf and Country Club** is similarly good for a visit on any day of the week. A fairly new parkland course, designed by **Hamilton Stutt**, it too has an attractive setting. Golfers (with handicaps) could enjoy a game, in 1988 for **£13** during the week and for **£17** at weekends. For a nights rest the **Meon Valley Hotel (0329) 833455** is the obvious selection – both comfortable and highly convenient.

I'm afraid I know very little about William the Conqueror but I understand there are at least two things we should thank him for – one is the Domesday Book and the other is the New Forest, without doubt one of the most beautiful areas in Britain. **Brockenhurst Manor Golf Club** lies amidst the splendour, and several deer including a rare white buck frequent the surrounding woodlands. A superb heathland course, Brockenhurst welcomes visitors during the week and to a limited extentat weekends – telephoning again recommended. The cost of a day's golf in 1989 was priced at **£15**, reduced if teeing off after 4pm. A short distance from the New Forest, **Barton-on-Sea**'s exposed cliff top course is well worth a visit if in the area. Not overly long but with enough challenges and some spectacular views across to the Isle of Wight and Christchurch Bay.

A few ideas for the 19th hole, and we make a start at Lyndhurst and the **The Parkhill House Hotel (042128) 2944** – an ideal spot, a good restaurant as well. Two B's now, but before you get offended, I refer to Beaulieu and Brockenhurst. In the former case **The Montagu Arms (0590) 612324** and its fine restaurant is ideal to hang up one's clubs and in the latter a number of places should be considered. Two include **Carey's Manor (0590) 23551** a great all rounder and **The Forest Park (0590) 28844** in Brockenhurst. Further south on the A337 we arrive at Lymington. In another good hotel setting stands **The Passford House (0590) 682398** while among other things, **The Stanwell House (0590) 77123** is convenient for ferries leaving for the Isle of Wight, while **Limpets (0590) 75595** is a tasty restaurant in town. Further up the coast, westwards, one arrives in Barton-on-Sea where **The Red House Hotel (0425) 610119** is recommended. In New Milton, we find the county's (quite probably the country's) finest country house hotel, **Chewton Glen (0425) 275341** which is spectacular. (They're laying down a nine hole golf course in the grounds – marvellous!) Finally, **New Forest Cottages (0590) 79655** should be contacted if you want first-class self-catering accommodation in this area.

ISLE OF WIGHT

Across the water and the **Isle of Wight** – some good golf here with some really welcoming hotels. In Shanklin, **The Cliff Tops (0983) 863262** and **The Luccombe Hall (0983) 863082** stand out, though there are many more. Two pubs to visit include **The Fisherman's Cottage** – good food and a fine setting and **The Crab**, more seafood and a high street position. Elsewhere on the island Cowes of course is busy and fun, especially during Cowes week itself, but for our purposes Bonchurch beckons, where **The Peacock Vane (0983) 852019** is a delightful restaurant – with some rooms. Alternative accommodation can be tracked down in **The Winterbourne Hotel (0983) 852535**.

There are no fewer than seven golf courses on the Isle of Wight. Whilst **Shanklin and Sandown** is possibly the best known, and **Osborne** the most scenic, a visit to any is appealing. All courses welcome visitors and green fees tend to compare favourably with those on the mainland.

THE CHANNEL ISLANDS

If the Isle of Wight is good for golf, the Channel Islands are even better. Not that there is a proliferation of courses but there are three: **La Moye, Royal Jersey** and **Royal Guernsey** that are particularly outstanding. Unfortunately the German troops didn't share this opinion during the Islands's four year occupation: they demolished La Moye's Clubhouse and dug up the fairways at Royal Guernsey. Both have long since recovered and all three provide tremendous holiday golf. Visitors are welcome at Royal Guernsey Mondays, Tuesdays, Wednesdays and Fridays for a fee of **£8.50** per round, **£10.50** per day. The Jersey courses are a little more expensive but it may be possible to get a game at weekends. However, both being understandably popular, prior telephoning is strongly recommended.

In the Channel Isles, when it comes to hotels one is quite simply spoilt for choice. In Guernsey St Peter's Port offers a whole handful of excellent establishments, generally good value as well. **The St Pierre Park (0481) 28282** is the most luxurious, but **The Old Government House (0481) 24921** is beautifully stylish, while **The Flying Dutchman (0481) 23787** has a good restaurant to match a friendly welcome.

In Jersey, St Brelade's Bay offers the superb **Atlantic Hotel (0534) 44104** (ideal for La Moye links). Another excellent hotel here is **Hotel L'Horizon (0534) 43101**. St Helier boasts the outstanding **Grand Hotel (0534) 22301** – note especially the restaurant – and St Peter, **The Mermaid (0534) 41255**. Perhaps the best restaurant on the island is to be found at St. Saviours – **Longueville Manor (0534) 25501**. Finally in Grouville Bay where the Royal Jersey Golf Club is situated is **La Hougue Grange (0534) 51899**, a charming country house and one of those great treats where the words 'fore' and 'fare' can be combined so happily.

'Fifehead Manor, Middle Wallop'

CHEWTON GLEN

In verdant parkland on the southern edge of the New Forest stands a magnificent country house hotel. Chewton Glen and its combination of splendour, elegance and comfort affords the discerning visitor every amenity he could wish for. The public areas are beautiful decorated, such as the light, airy main sitting room looking out onto the garden and the cosy inner lounge with its marble fireplace.

Our suites and double bedrooms have bathrooms ensuite, colour television, direct dial telephone and radio. They are furnished with antiques, attractive painted furniture and luxurious fabrics.

Guests can stroll around the thirty acre grounds or play tennis, croquet, golf or alternatively bathe in the heated swimming pool or off the shingle beach. The hotel has its own nine hole golf course.

Hotel's Michelin-rosetted restaurant, offers sumptuous fare. Our distinguished modern french cooking is matched only by the quality of the service.

To find us leave the A35 on the Walkford Road and once through Walkford turn left down Chewton Farm Road.

Your stay will be a pleasant-one; we hope it will be a long one. Whether you have enjoyed a day at the races or a round of golf at one of the many nearby golf courses we know that Chewton Glen will make your day that extra bit special.

Chewton Glen, New Milton, Hampshire. Tel: (04252) 5341

Chewton Glen
New Milton
Hampshire
Tel: (04252) 5341

LA MOYE
CHAMPIONSHIP GOLF

England is part of the Channel Islands. Yes, England is part of the Channel Islands – at least this is what an islander will tell you. Apparently, the islands belonged to William, Duke of Normandy before he came over and added England to his territories.

So what of the golf in the 'mother country', the land where the great **Harry Vardon** was born? In short there are three very fine courses: Royal Guernsey, Royal Jersey and La Moye. The first two certainly offer a marvellous day's golf but the general day's consensus is that La Moye is the best of a tremendous trio. Its setting alone makes it stand out. The course is laid out two hundred and fifty feet above St. Ouen's Bay, Jersey's finest beach, on the south west of the island. From such a vantage point there are some tremendous views to be enjoyed from the course, particularly perhaps from the **4th,** where the four sister islands of Guernsey, Sark, Herm and Jetou can all be sighted. Add to this a warm climate and, of course, the Championship links itself and you can see why people want to golf here!

La Moye Golf Club was founded in **1902** by the then headmaster of the local school, one George Boomer. A course was laid out, but it didn't really take shape until James Braid added his skilful craftsmanship. Thereafter the course was more or less untouched, so to speak, until 1977 when major alterations were made, resulting in an improved and, when played from the back tees, much longer course.

The current **Secretary** at **La Moye** is **Mr. D. Lowton**; he can be contacted by telephone on **(0534) 43401** or by writing to: The **Secretary, La Moye Golf Club, La Moye, Jersey, Channel Islands.** The Club professional, **David Melville** can be reached on **(0534) 43130**.

In addition to being a superb Championship course, La Moye doubles as a very popular holiday course, in the best sense of the word, and visitors are always made very welcome. The only specific requirement is that they must be members of a recognised Golf Club. It isn't essential to book a tee time but during the summer months especially, the course can become extremely busy. Making an early start is always a good idea (whether this fits in with the holiday schedule is another matter!)

The Green Fees for 1989 were set at **£22** during the week, with **£25** during the weekend. For junior golfers a reduced fee of **£11** is payable, or **£12.50** during the weekend. A weekly ticket may well be preferred, and can be purchased for **£100** – ideal if you are into thirty six holes a day; for longer stays a fortnightly ticket is priced at **£180**.

As for finding the course, there really should be no problem: La Moye is only a mile or so from St. Brelade and just five minutes by road from Jersey's Airport. The island is such a size that it shouldn't take much more than half an hour to travel between La Moye and Royal Jersey in Grouville, though of course it depends on the traffic and on how much of Jersey you want to take in along the way.

From the Championship tees, the course can be stretched to beyond **6700** yards, as it is for the **Jersey Open**, which is played here each year. The medal tees however, are less exacting and the total yardage is **6464** yards, par **72.** No pushover certainly, and there is often a very stiff wind. From the ladies tees the course measures **5903** yards, par **74**. La Moye is a typcial links type course – large sand hills, pot bunkers, the odd blind shot, gorse bushes and punishing rough (though it's not as punishing as at some). It really is full of variety with a number of dog legs and plateau greens. Apart from the 4th and its enchanting views, many will probably remember the **8th** hole best of all: it is a lengthy par four, with the green dramatically set on the edge of the cliffs, rather like the famous **5th** hole at Portrush.

The Jersey Open is a very popular event on the European Tour, and the pros are often inspired by the surroundings and produce some very good scores, although La Moye is never torn apart. Some well known names have won in recent years, including **Sandy Lyle, Tony Jacklin, Bernard Gallacher** (twice), **Howard Clark** and **Ian Woosnam**.

In the last edition of this book, I said it was a little difficult to comment on the 19th hole, as it was in the process of being demolished! I am glad to say that a new Clubhouse has now been built, one in a series for the Club. The original one burned down, while the second one was destroyed by German soldiers during the island's war-time occupation. Let's just wish the new one the best of British luck!

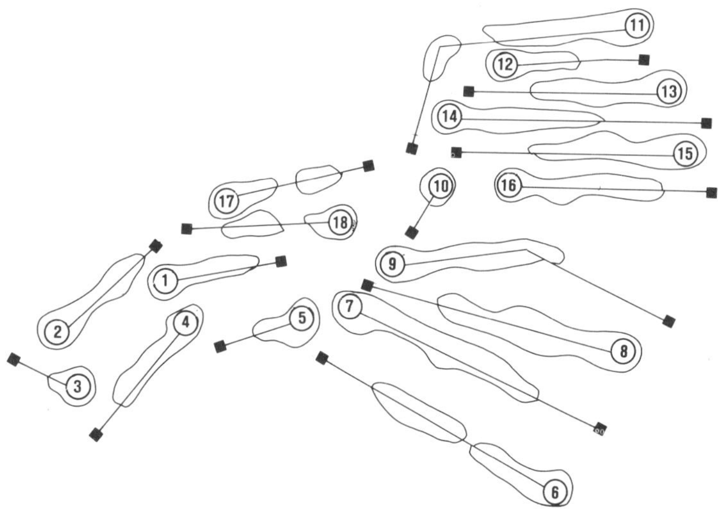

Hole	Yards	Par	Hole	Yards	Par
1	356	4	10	148	3
2	489	5	11	495	5
3	128	3	12	179	3
4	386	4	13	418	4
5	179	3	14	434	4
6	330	4	15	476	5
7	476	5	16	363	4
8	420	4	17	403	4
9	382	4	18	402	4
Out	3,146	36	In	3,318	36
			Out	3,146	36
			TOTALS	6,464	72

LIPHOOK
CHAMPIONSHIP GOLF

The counties of Surrey and Berkshire don't have a monopoly of the outstanding heathland and heather type courses in England. There is Pulborough in West Sussex and Woodhall Spa in Lincolnshire and there is also Liphook, the pride and joy of Hampshire. Now the latter part of that sentence is troubling me somewhat – Liphook's quality is undeniable – it's the 'Hampshire bit'. As a town Liphook is undoubtedly situated in Hampshire, but a great part of the golf course lies over the border in Sussex. The 13th hole, appropriately named 'Two Counties', has the golfer teeing off in Sussex and holing out in Hampshire. In exploring the quandary I telephoned the professional shop and on suggesting that the larger part lay in Hampshire I received the reply 'debatable' and furthermore the remark 'where I'm standing is Sussex'! Anyway it's a superb course wherever it is!

Liphook Golf Club was founded in **1922** and the course was designed by **A.C. Croome** and **Thomas Simpson**. The phrase, 'natural golfing land' has become something of a golfing cliche, but hopefully it can be forgiven in this instance. Being sited on gently undulating terrain with a marvellous spread of silver birch and fir trees, heather and bracken, only the sand bunkers needed to be added and this was done with the most careful of planning. Striking a balance between being sufficiently testing yet not too severe requires a fine judgement – Messrs. Croome and Simpson, if you'll pardon another expression, 'got it right to a tee'.

Persons wishing to explore the delights of Liphook must make prior arrangements with the Club's **Secretary, Major J.B. Morgan, M.B.E.** One can either telephone on **(0428) 723785** or address a written application to Major Morgan care of **Liphook Golf Club, Wheatsheaf Enclosure, Liphook, Hants, GU30 7EH.** Generally visitors must be members of recognised Golf Clubs and be in possession of a handicap of 24 or less (29 or less for ladies). Subject to the above a game can normally be arranged between Monday and Friday and on Sunday after 1pm. Golfing Societies are also received during the week, usually on Wednesdays, Thursdays and Fridays – written applications again to be addressed to the Secretary. In **1989** the **green fees** at Liphook were set at **£15** for a weekday round with **£25** payable for a full day's golf and **£25** and **£30** respectively at weekends and on Bank Holidays. Visitors and Societies should perhaps also note that two ball matches (and foursomes) are preferred; indeed Societies are not permitted to play three balls or four balls. I should also add that Liphook's professional, **Ian Large** can be contacted on **(0428) 723271**.

Travelling to Liphook from London couldn't be more direct. The **A3** London to Portsmouth road passes right through the middle of the course! Those approaching from other directions may have a little more trouble. Coming from Birmingham and the North those in a hurry might choose to use a combination of the **M1, M25** and **A3**. The more scenic route is to travel via Oxford on the **A34** leaving at Newbury and thereafter taking the **A339** to Alton and the **B3004** to Liphook (well at least it avoids London!) Motoring from the South West, Winchester is probably the best place to head for. From Winchester the **A272** should be taken to Petersfield where the **A3** can be joined.

In the era of the 7,000 yard Championship course Liphook's modest **6,207** yards may not sound particularly daunting. Par, or bogey as seems to be preferred here, is a fairly tight **70** but primarily Liphook is a 'thinking man's course' rather than a 'hitting course'. The bunkers are strategically placed and straying off the fairways can usually result in the dropping of a shot – such is the tangling nature of the heather.

Liphook is one of the few leading English courses that commences with a par 3 – Royal Lytham being another rare example. Measuring over 200 yards it is certainly a testing opener. The fourth hole is possibly the toughest on the front nine, after which the busy Portsmouth Road must be crossed. On the back nine, notable holes include the eleventh, a superb short hole with a narrow entrance to a green backed by fir trees and the thirteenth, the aforementioned 'Two Counties', where a glorious downhill drive is followed by a second over a brook.

Liphook's Clubhouse stands on high ground, giving a perfect view of the first and the eighteenth. Within, lunches are served daily between 12pm and 2pm and teas from 3.45pm to 5.30pm. Breakfasts and dinners are only available by special arrangement. A jacket and tie should be worn in the Clubhouse after 11am with the exception of the small bar.

Notwithstanding the A3 and the railway line (which also cuts through the centre of the course!), Liphook exudes an air of genuine tranquillity and charm, the equal of which is difficult to find anywhere and one that once experienced is never forgotten.

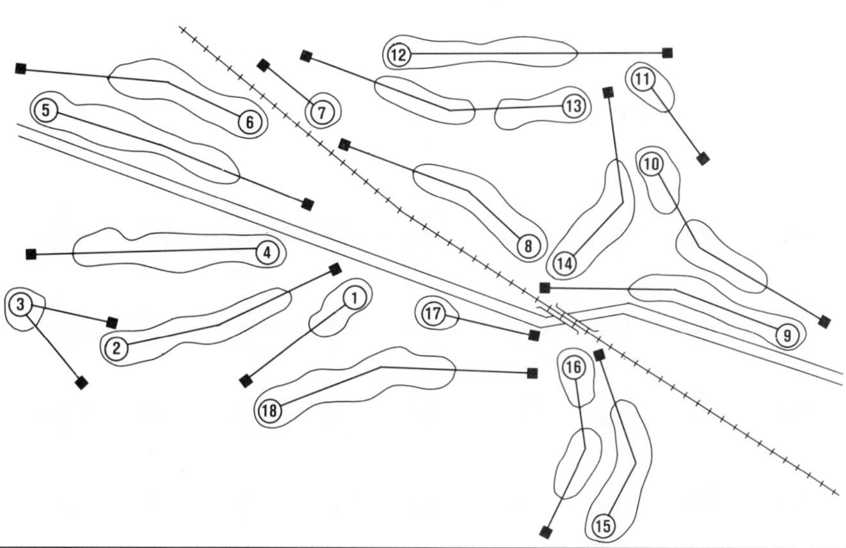

Hole	Yards	Par	Hole	Yards	Par
1	207	3	10	347	4
2	424	4	11	164	3
3	133	3	12	425	4
4	466	4	13	476	5
5	484	5	14	341	4
6	432	4	15	368	4
7	157	3	16	364	4
8	338	4	17	163	3
9	438	4	18	480	5
Out	3,079	34	In	3,128	36
			Out	3,079	34
			TOTALS	6,207	70

LAINSTON HOUSE

Built in the late seventeeth century, set in sixty-three acres of grounds and overlooking some of England's loveliest downlands, this beautiful English Manor House has been discreetly restored to provide every luxury the discerning traveller could wish for. The hotel is approached by a curving drive of about half a mile, lined with lime trees. The walls of the octagonal kitchen garden, the well-house with its original horse wheel, the dovecote and ruins of the Norman Church are all of historic interest.

The thirty-two luxurious bedrooms, all with private bathrooms, have been individually designed and tastefully furnished. Drinks are served in the club-like atmosphere of the Cedar Room which is panelled with wood taken from a magnificent Cedar Tree which fell in the grounds long ago. The Restaurant is renowned for its high standards. The service is friendly and informal, the menu creative and interesting, using the best of local produce. The individually cooked dishes are complemented by a thoughtfully compiled wine list.

The hotel is located off the A272, a mere two and a half miles from Winchester. It is convenient for Winchester and Hockley Golf Clubs and within easy reach of Broadlands, home of the late Earl Mountbatten, Wilton House, home of the Earl of Pembroke and, of course, Salisbury and Winchester Cathedrals.

Lainston House Hotel
Sparsholt
Winchester
Hants
Tel: (0962) 63588

HAMPSHIRE & THE CHANNEL ISLANDS

COMPLETE GOLF

HAMPSHIRE

Alresford G.C.
(9) 5992 yards
Cheriton Road, Alresford
(096273) 3746

Alton G.C.
(9) 5699 yards
Old Oldiham Road, Alton
(0420) 82042

Ampfield Par Three G.C.
(18) 2478 yards
Winchester Road, Ampfield
(0794) 68480

Andover G.C.
(9) 5933 yards
Winchester Road, Andover
(0264) 58040

Army G.C.
(18) 6553 yards
Laffans Road, Aldershot
(0252) 540638

Barton-on-Sea G.C.
(18) 5565 yards
Marine Drive, Barton-on-Sea
(0425) 615308

Basingstoke G.C.
(18) 6253 yards
Kempshott Park, Basingstoke
(0256) 465990

Basingstoke Hospitals G.C.
(9) 5480 yards
Aldermaston Road, Basingstoke
(0256) 20347

Bishopswood G.C.
(9) 6474 yards
Bishopswood Lane, Tadley,
Basingstoke
(07356) 5213

Blackmoor G.C.
(18) 6213 yards
Golf Lane, White Hill, Bordon
(04203) 2775

Bramshaw G.C.
(18) 6233 yards (Manor Course)
(18) 5774 yards (Forest Course)
Brook, Lyndhurst
(0703) 813433

Bramshott Hill G.C.
(18) 6223 yards
Dibden, Southampton
(0703) 845596

Brockenhurst Manor G.C.
(18) 6216 yards
Sway Road, Brockenhurst
(0590) 23332

Burley G.C.
(9) 6224 yards
Burley, Ringwood
(04253) 2431

Corhampton G.C.
(18) 6088 yards
Sheeps Pond Lane, Droxford,
Southampton
(0489) 877279

Dunwood Manor G.C.
(18) 5959 yards
Shootash Hill, Romsey
(0794) 40549

Fleming Park G.C.
(18) 4436 yards
Magpie Lane, Eastleigh
(0703) 612797

Gosport and Stokes Bay G.C.
(9) 5806 yards
Haslar, Gosport
(0705) 527941

Great Salterns G.C.
(18) 5970 yards
Eastern Road, Porstmouth
(0705) 664549

Hartley Wintney G.C.
(9) 6096 yards
London Road, Hartley Wintney
(025126) 4211

Hayling G.C.
(18) 6510 yards
Ferry Road, Hayling Island
(0705) 464446

Hockley G.C.
(18) 6260 yards
Twyford, Winchester
(0962) 713165

Leckford & Longstock G.C.
(9) 3251 yards
Leckford, Stockbridge
(0264) 810710

Lee-on-the-Solent G.C.
(18) 6022 yards
Brune Lane, Lee-on-the-Solent
(0705) 551170

Liphook G.C.
(18) 6207 yards
Wheatsheaf Enclosure, Liphook
(0428) 723785

Meon Valley Hotel G. & C.C.
(18) 6519 yards
Sandy Lane, Shedfield
(0329) 833455

New Forest G.C.
(18) 5748 yards
Lyndhurst
(042128) 2450

North Hants G.C.
(18) 6257 yards
Minley Road, Fleet
(0252) 616443

Old Thorns Hotel & G.C.
(18) 6447 yards
Longmoor Road, Liphook
(0428) 724555

Petersfield G.C.
(18) 5751 yards
Heath Road, Petersfield
(0730) 62386

Portsmouth G.C.
(18) 6259 yards
Crookhorn Lane, Woodley,
Portsmouth
(0705) 372210

Romsey G.C.
(18) 5752 yards
Nursley, Southampton
(0703) 734637

Rowlands Castle G.C.
(18) 6627 yards
Links Lane, Rowlands Castle
(070541) 2784

Royal Winchester G.C.
(18) 6218 yards
Sarum Road, Winchester
(0962) 52462

Southampton G.C.
(18) 6218 yards
(9) 2391 yards
Golf Course Road, Bassett,
Southampton
(0703) 790732

Southsea G.C.
(18) 5800 yards
Great Salterns, Portsmouth
(0705) 664549

Southwick Park G.C.
(18) 5970 yards
Pinsley Drive, Southwick
(0705) 380131

Southwood G.C.
(9) 2263 yards
Ively Road, Cove, Farnborough
(0252) 548700

Stoneham G.C.
(18) 6310 yards
Bassett, Southampton
(0703) 768151

Tylney Park G.C.
(18) 6108 yards
Rotherwick, Basingstoke
(025672) 2079

Waterlooville G.C.
(18) 6647 yards
Idsworth Road, Cowplain,
Portsmouth
(0705) 263388

ISLE OF WIGHT

Cowes G.C.
(9) 5880 yards
Crossfield Avenue, Cowes
(0983) 292303

Freshwater Bay G.C.
(18) 5628 yards
Afton Down, Freshwater Bay
(0983) 752955

Newport G.C.
(9) 5704 yards
St. George's Down, Newport
(0983) 525076

Osborne G.C.
(9) 6286 yards
Osborne, East Cowes
(0983) 295421

Ryde G.C.
(9) 5220 yards
Binstead Road, Ryde
(0983) 614809

Shanklin and Sandown G.C.
(18) 6000 yards
The Fairway, Sandown
(0983) 403217

Ventnor G.C.
(9) 5910 yards
Steephill Down Road, Ventnor
(0983) 853326

CHANNEL ISLANDS

Alderney G.C.
(9) 2528 yards
Routes des Carriers, Alderney
(048182) 2835

La Moye G.C.
(18) 6464 yards
La Moyte, St. Brelade
(0534) 43401

Royal Guernsey G.C.
(18) 6206 yards
L'Ancresse, Guernsey
(0481) 47022

Royal Jersey G.C.
(18) 6106 yards
Grouville, Jersey
(0534) 54416

St. Clements G.C.
(9) 3972 yards

EAST AND WEST SUSSEX

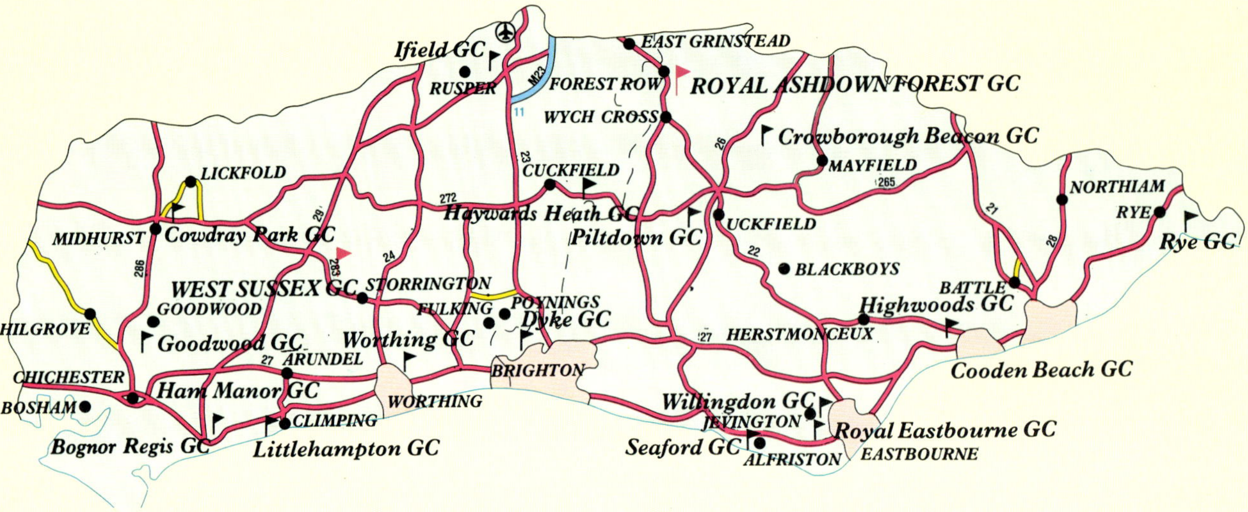

***LAWSON WOOD** "Tongue Tied"* *ROSENSTIELS*

EAST AND WEST SUSSEX

CHOICE GOLF

Sussex, where the South Downs tumble gently towards spectacular chalk cliffs or as Tennyson wrote, 'Green Sussex fading into blue'. Here is the county of downland and weald, of dramatic rollercoasting cliffs, the Seven Sisters and Beachy Head.

The situation in Sussex is superb. The golf is glorious as is the countryside all around, while at no time can you claim to be isolated – except perhaps when you visit the gorse at Ashdown Forest. West Sussex is as charming an area as one could find – the golf course of the same name is delightful and reflects the quality of some splendid country house hotels. While in Rye, the golfer must visit with a packed wallet in order to seduce a member in a local drinking haunt and thus secure that elusive thing – a round of golf at **Rye** – a more spectacular day could not be wished for.

Tempting as it is to think of Sussex as one region, there are of course two counties, East and West, and between them they possess over forty courses, many of which are outstandingly good. Golfers in these parts can count themselves pretty fortunate!

WEST SUSSEX

On a selective tour of some of the better courses in Sussex, there seems no more logical a place to commence than in the region's South West corner, and **Goodwood** – 'glorious Goodwood' to racegoers, though the golf course is in a similarly idyllic spot, nestling in the southern foothills of the South Downs. Some four miles north of Chichester on the **A286** it is in fact located just below the race course and has a magnificent 18th century clubhouse. Visitors are welcome at most times though prior arrangement is preferable. Fees are around the **£12-£15** mark.

In Goodwood itself, **Goodwood Park Hotel (0243) 775537** is an excellent place to stay and very convenient for the course, but the delights of Chichester are also close at hand. Here there are a variety of attractions including numerous antique shops and the excellent **Festival Theatre (0243) 781312. The Dolphin and Anchor (0243) 785121** opposite the cathedral near the Market Cross is most welcoming (note the fine bar snacks). **Clinch's (0243) 789915** is also a friendly place to stay, the restaurant is good and breakfast ideal before a day in the South Downs. A theatre of the open air variety can be found at Bosham as can the pleasant **Millstream Hotel (0243) 573234**.

Staying in the south west of the region **Bognor Regis** is worth a visit – a flattish but attractive parkland course and apart from the summer season, when weekends are busy, golfers are welcome at all times at a cost of **£12** per day. Note the **Royal Hotel (0243) 826222** in town as well as the many near Chichester.

The course at **Littlehampton** (green fees **£12** during the week, **£15** at weekends), lies about seven miles east of Bognor Regis off the **A259**. It is the nearest one gets to a links course in West Sussex. Always kept in first class condition, the club welcomes visitors on weekdays, though again it is wise to telephone before finalising any plans. Further along the **A259** at Angmering is the friendly club of **Ham Manor** – a parkland course with an interesting layout of two distinct loops. Well worth visiting – there are no general restrictions on times visitors can play and furthermore the food there is quite outstanding! At both courses green fees are approximately **£12-16**.

This area of West Sussex is renowned for its tremendous hotels and after a day's golf there can be no better place to visit than Arundel where **The Norfolk Arms (0903) 882101**, a Georgian Coaching Inn has welcomed travellers for over two hundred years and the tradition continues today. South of Arundel, lies Climping, here **Bailiffscourt (0903) 723511**, a 13th century replica offers superb comforts and an excellent restaurant.

As a town **Worthing** is somewhat overshadowed by neighbouring Brighton (though apparently it inspired Oscar Wilde overshadowed or not), it has one of the leading clubs in Sussex. The venue of the 1987 Sussex Amateur Championship. Worthing has two eighteen hole courses, the Lower and the Upper. Both are exceptionally fine tests of golf. Visitors are welcome although prior arrangement with the Secretary is essential. A day's golf will cost around **£10-14**. One recommendation here is **The Chatsworth Hotel (0903) 36103** – good value.

EAST SUSSEX

Moving into East Sussex and the town of Brighton, probably the best course in the area, and there are a number to choose from, is **The Dyke Golf Club**, located five miles north of the town centre. One of the more difficult courses in Sussex, it is on fairly high ground and provides some splendid views. Visitors should first telephone but are generally welcome. Green fees are similar to those at Worthing.

As arguably the most famous resort in Britain, it isn't surprising to find, literally hundreds of hotels. Among the best are the **Sheridan Hotel (0273) 23221** with its excellent sea food restaurant and **The Grand Hotel (0273) 21188**.

A short distance along the **A259** is Seaford. **The Seaford Golf Club** at East Bletchington celebrated its centenary in 1987. A fair sprinkling of gorse and hawthorn is the feature of this interesting downland course. Also worth noting is the dormy house adjacent to the course where you can stay. Visitors are able to play after 9.30 am on weekdays and after 1.00 pm at weekends. Green fees are **£15**.

Passing near to Beachy Head we arrive at Eastbourne where there are two fine courses – **Royal Eastbourne** and **Willingdon**. The former is another that celebrated its centenary in 1987. It is situated very close to the town centre with the enviable address of Paradise Drive. Fees are approximately **£10.50**. Willingdon, north of the town off the **A22**, is quite a hilly course and very tough. Its interesting design has been likened to an oyster shell with the Clubhouse as the pearl. Willingdon accepts visitors during the week. Both Clubs advise telephoning in advance. In the area around Bexhill, both **Cooden Beach** and **Highwoods** are well established courses. For visitors wishing to play the former some prior arrangement with the Secretary is essential. At Highwoods there are no general restrictions, but players should be able to provide proof of handicap. Hotels in the area are less plentiful than in Brighton but Eastbourne does offer the exceptionally fine **Lansdowne (0323) 25174**, while in Battle, **Netherfield Place (04246) 4455** is extremely elegant.

Before heading inland a quick word on **Rye**. It is unquestionaly one of the greatest links courses in Britain – in many people's opinion the equal of Deal and Sandwich. However, visitors are only permitted to play if accompanied by a Member – hence the remarks in the second paragraph. Where might such a seduction take place then? In Rye itself, **The Mermaid Inn (0797) 223065** is an historic establishment standing in a steep cobbled street, while for a cosy guest house, try **The Old Vicarage (0797) 22119**. Another charming inn nearby is **The Hayes Arms (07974) 3142** in Northiam.

EAST AND WEST SUSSEX

CHOICE GOLF

The majority of the leading courses in Sussex are located either on the coast or within a few miles of it – hardly suprising considering this is where the major towns are situated. However, inland there are a handful of exceptionally attractive courses particularly worth visiting. **Piltdown**, two miles to the west of Uckfield, is certainly one of these. Piltdown is a heathland course with a beautiful setting and, in common with Royal Ashdown Forest, has no bunkers – though there are certainly enough natural hazards to set the golfer thinking. The best days for a game here are Mondays, Wednesdays and Fridays. Green fees are about **£13**, and depend on the season.

Leaving the Piltdown Men and moving from East to West and from Uckfield to Cuckfield, **Haywards Heath** stands right in the middle of Sussex. A very good heathland course this, but the pride of West Sussex is Pulborough – **The West Sussex Golf Club**. Along with **Royal Ashdown** it is featured on a later page – suffice to say here that its reputation extends far beyond the bounds of East and West Sussex. Still in the West two more to note are in the north, and very convenient for Gatwick, the **Ifield Golf and Country Club** (visitors at weekends only), and **Cowdray Park** – very pleasant and ideal of course, should you happen to play polo as well!

Places to stay? For Cowdray, **The Spread Eagle (073081) 6911** at Midhurst – hotel and restaurant are both excellent. For Pulborough, **Little Thakeham (09066) 4416** at Storrington and **Abbingworth Hall (07983) 3836** at Thakeham – sounds confusing? Fear not, both are outstanding. Piltdown also possesses a peach – **Horsted Place (0825) 75581** near Uckfield.

Towards the north of Sussex, **Royal Ashdown Forest** (see feature page) and **Crowborough Beacon** are again two wonderfully scenic courses where the heather and gorse simply run riot. Crowborough's course is situated some 800 feet above sea level and on clear days the sea can be seen from the Clubhouse. Sir Arthur Conan Doyle would have taken in this view on many occasions for he lived very nearby and was Captain of the Golf Club in 1910. It really is the most beautiful of courses and the fee of **£10** mid-week, **£11** at the weekend represents excellent value.

The 16th century **Middle House Hotel (0435) 872146** at Mayfield is recommended for a stay near Crowborough. As for Royal Ashdown three ideas here: for convenience (and considerable comfort) **The Ashdown Forest Hotel (034282) 4866** while in East Grinstead, glorious **Gravetye Manor (0342) 810567** is pehaps unsurpassed anywhere, but note also **The Felbridge (0342) 26992**.

In the course of our brief trip no doubt several splendid hotels have been omitted, but such is life. In order to fit in more restaurants, please forgive this somewhat hasty appraisal. **Le Francais (0273) 680716** at Brighton is busy while **Byron's (0323) 20171** at Eastbourne is fishy – and good. In Rusper, **Ghyll Manor (029384) 571** provides, while in Rye, **Simmons (0797) 222026** stands by. Returning to Alfriston, we see **Moonrakers (0323) 870472** – try a Hot Sussex Smokie! In Herstmonceux, **The Sundial (0323) 832217** is French, whilst **Jevington's Monk is Hungry (03212) 2178** is outstanding. In Chichester, **Little London (0243) 07987** is fine and **Rassell's (0243) 782146** is noted for house wine. In Midhurst try **Mida (073086) 3284**, in Pulborough plump for **Stane Street Hollow** while in Poynings **Au Petit Normand (079156) 346** should answer your prayers. But for a finale to end this array, try **Manley's (09066) 2331** in Storrington – (if you can get a table!)

No trip to Sussex is complete without a visit to one of their country houses, castles or pubs. **The White Horse Inn (024359) 215** in Chilgrove has an excellent restaurant, while **The Shepherd and Dog** in Fulking and the **Lickfold Inn** at Lickfold are also worthwhile. Aside from the antiques of Chichester – Arundel, (an excellent castle to see here) and Petworth which offers the superb **Petworth House**, there is a summer of unsurpassed opera at **Glyndebourne**. In contrast, a totally flamboyant place to spend time is Brighton. The streets in the old town offer several bargains while **The Grand Pavilion** is as striking as ever. Returning to the subject of castles, then **Bodiam** in East Sussex is majestic. Any other thoughts for the player who had troubles in the groping gorse as Ashdown? Well, **Blackboys**, the pub of the same name is superb as is the **Wild Boar** in Crowborough, while **The Roebuck** in Wych Cross is nearer if your're really desperate. But perhaps the best plan is to return to Alfriston. **The Smugglers** and **The Star (0323) 870495** are great value. Sussex, in short, is a true light, both on and off the fairways.

W.DENDY SADLER 'The Stymie' *BURLINGTON GALLERY*

ROYAL ASHDOWN FOREST
CHAMPIONSHIP GOLF

In **1988 Royal Ashdown Forest** celebrated its centenary. It was on Christmas Eve just over a hundred years ago that the **Reverend A.T. Scott** teed up his ball and struck the very first shot. The course has changed very little over the years, a fact which speaks volumes for the original layout. The Club acquired the title 'Royal' during Queen Victoria's reign and long before the turn of the century had established itself as one of the finest tests of golf in southern England.

The charm of Royal Ashdown Forest lies in its setting, and of course the name gives it away. Deeply secluded in a forest of pine and silver birch it is difficult to believe that the frantic chaos, commonly called Greater London, is little more than half an hour's drive away.

Many great players have been associated with Royal Ashdown Forest over the years. The **Cantelupe Club,** the associate club connected to Royal Ashdown, included **Abe Mitchell** and **Alf Padgham** (Open Champion of 1936) among its ranks and several celebrated amateurs have improved their technique on this most challenging course.

Casual visitors are welcomed at Royal Ashdown – rather more so, it must be said, than at some of the south-east's leading courses. A recognized club handicap is, however, a requirement and it is normally advisable to telephone the Club before finalising any plans. Not suprisingly the course is very popular in the summer months.

The Club **Secretary** is **Mr. K.P.A. Mathews,** who can be contacted via the **Royal Ashdown Forest Golf Club, Forest Row, East Sussex. Tel. (034282) 2018**. Those wishing to organise a Society meeting should write to Mr. Mathews at the above address. Societies can normally be accommodated during the week, **Tuesday** being an exception. The **green fees** for **1989** were set at **£20.00** for weekdays with **£25** payable at weekends and on Bank Holidays. Visitors should note that singles and foursomes are generally preferred. Alf Padgham's son **Hector** is the **professional** at Royal Ashdown and it is he who is responsible for the course record being an alarmingly low **62**. Mr. Padgham can be reached on **(034282) 2247.**

The Club is located within Ashdown Forest, approximately 4 miles south of East Grinstead. Motoring from **London** and the **North** the **A22** is by far the most direct route. This can be joined from the **M25** at **Junction 6**. The **A22** should be followed for some 4 miles beyond East Grinstead as far as Forest Row. There one should take the **B2110** Hartfield road turning left after a quarter of a mile on to Chapel Lane where the Club can be found. Approaching from the **South** the **A22** can be joined from a number of roads north of Eastbourne.

The view generally held is that Royal Ashdown Forest is a particularly difficult course. Whilst not overly long (the course measures **6439 yards** from the medal tees), on several of the holes a fairly lengthy tee shot will be required in order to find the safety of the fairway. The ever present stream and the considerable scattering of gorse and heather create a multitude of problems for the wayward golfer – and as if they are not enough, on several of the holes the fairway is narrow and the forest will gratefully accept the result of a slice or a hook. So the message is clearly, 'hit it hard and hit it straight!'

Despite the variety of hazards of all the country's leading courses Royal Ashdown Forest must surely be unique in not possessing a single bunker. **Bernard Darwin** is doubtless not the only golfer who failed to discover this fact until the conclusion of his game; as he put it, 'It is only at the end of a round that we realise with a pleasurable shock that there is not a single hideous rampart or so much as a pot bunker'. The Club was prevented long ago by the Forestry Commission, or the then equivalent, from creating bunkers and their absence now forms part of the character of the course.

The undulating nature of the landscape produces some truly magnificent views over the Forest and whatever be the standard of his game the golfer who does not relish a return to Royal Ashdown isn't really a golfer at all.

The Clubhouse offers a very high standard of catering. A light lunch, such as a ploughman's, can be obtained whilst a full four course meal can also be arranged. During the months of November and December a full English breakfast is available – a welcome facility which many clubs would do well to copy: golfers are hungry animals and some are more than quick to claim that the missed three footer is a result of a missed breakfast!

Whether or not the Members decided in their centenary year to invite the local Reverend to come along to the course on Christmas Eve and perform the necessary ritual, Royal Ashdown Forest can confidently look forward to an interesting second century.

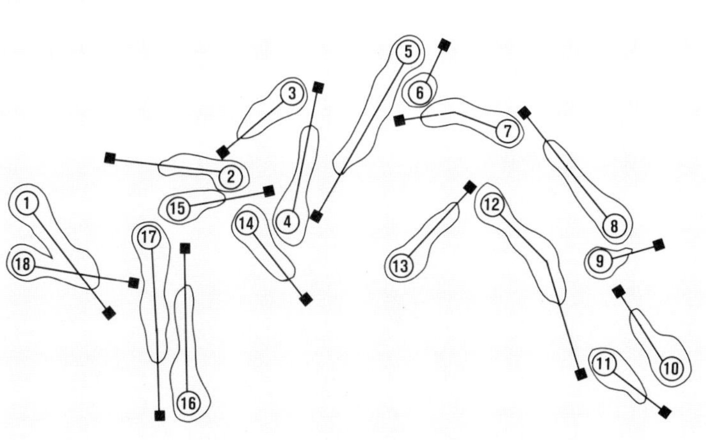

Old Course

Hole	Yards	Par	Hole	Yards	Par
1	332	4	10	485	5
2	384	4	11	249	3
3	327	4	12	558	5
4	356	4	13	367	4
5	509	5	14	200	3
6	126	3	15	310	4
7	365	4	16	407	4
8	498	5	17	472	4
9	142	3	18	352	4
Out	3,039	36	In	3,400	36
			Out	3,039	36
			TOTALS	6,439	72

WEST SUSSEX (PULBOROUGH)

CHAMPIONSHIP GOLF

'Concentrate your mind on the match until you are dormy. Then look at the surrounding scenery and expatiate on its beauties.' (A.J. Robertson)

In the opinion of many **West Sussex**, or **Pulborough** as it is commonly known, is quite simply the most beautiful course in England. The setting is the South Downs and seclusion is total. **Commander George Hillyard** founded the Club in **1930** having conceived the idea, so the story goes, as he looked out of his bathroom window one day while taking his morning shave! (His house, it should be explained, overlooked the present layout). The course was designed by **Sir Guy Campbell** and **Major C.K. Hutchinson** and opened for play in October, **1930**.

In a similar vein to Woodhall Spa in Lincolnshire, Pulborough has often been described as something of an oasis, the surrounding countryside being predominantly meadow and marshland with the course lying on sandy soil and heather running throughout. Heather naturally adds charm to any golf course but it is perhaps the magnificent spread of pines, oaks and silver birch trees that are most striking at Pulborough.

Mr. G.R. Martindale is the present Club **Secretary**; he may be contacted via the **West Sussex Club, Pulborough, West Sussex,** telephone **(07982) 2563**. Visitors are welcome, but strictly by appointment only; the same applies to golfing **Societies**. It should also be noted that three ball and four ball matches are not generally permitted – singles and foursomes being preferred. The only general restrictions on times visitors can play are before 9.30am (throughout the week) and on Tuesdays.

The **green fees** for 1989 were set at **£20** for either a single round or a day ticket during the week **(£25 at weekends).** One final introduction: **Tim Packham** is the Club's professional, and may be reached by telephone on **(07982) 2426.**

While Pulborough may enjoy a gloriously peaceful setting situated right in the heart of the glorious Sussex countryside, it could hardly be described as remote and is easily accessible from all directions. The Club's precise location is about 2 miles south of Pulborough just off the **A283** road to Storrington. The **A283** links Pulborough to the outskirts of Brighton on the south coast and to Milford (near Guildford) to the north. For those approaching from westerly directions the **A272** from Winchester is likely to prove of most assistance, joining the **A283** at Petworth approximately five miles from Pulborough. Motoring from the London area the quickest route is probably to take the **M23** towards Gatwick joining the **A264** at Crawley and travelling through Horsham. The **A264** merges into the **A29** near Billingshurst which in turn joins with Pulborough.

One of the features of Pulborough is its conspicuous absence of a par five beyond the first hole – a hole which in any event becomes a four when played from the tees of the day. At **6156** yards, s.s.s. **70**, the par of **68** is a difficult one to match. With none of the par fours being overly short there aren't any really obvious 'birdie opportunities'. Perhaps the best known hole on the course is the par three **6th**; measuring 220 yards it requires an exceptionally accurate tee shot across water to a green that has an out-of-bounds to the right and tall trees directly behind it. **Henry Longhurst**, a great admirer of Pulborough, very aptly said of the 6th, 'If ever there was an all or nothing hole, this is it.' Immediately after the potential disaster of the 6th, the **7th** requires a long uphill drive to carry over some thick heather and scrub not to mention an enormous sand bunker. The **13th** and **15th** are two more superb holes and the round finishes with a pair of testing par fours.

As for its 19th, West Sussex has a very comfortable Clubhouse offering full catering facilities including two bars. A jacket and tie should be worn in all public rooms.

Henry Longhurst is only one of a number of celebrated admirers of Pulborough and the late **Bobby Locke**, four times Open Champion considered it his favourite English course. While no major men's tournament has been played over the course (somewhat surprisingly) the Club has recently hosted both the **English Ladies Amateur Championship, Vanessa Marvin** winning in **1978** and in **1986**, and the **British Ladies Championship,** won by New Zealander **Marnie Maguire**.

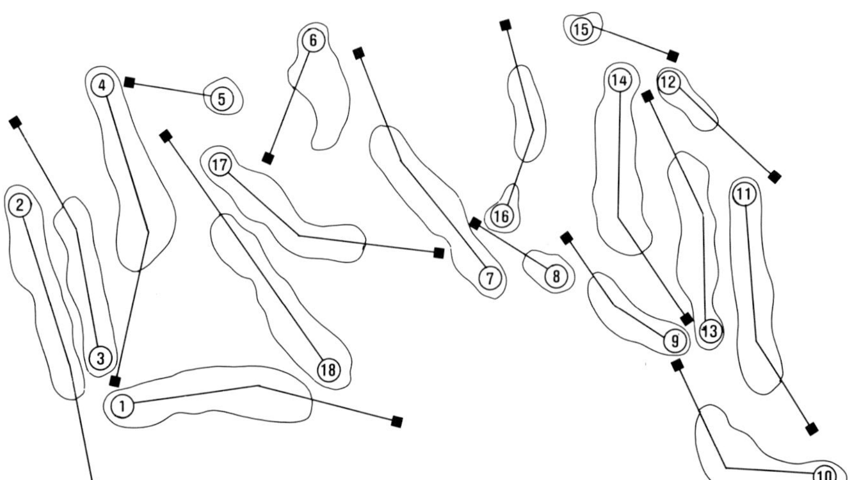

Hole	Yards	Par	Hole	Yards	Par
1	481	5	10	405	4
2	411	4	11	448	4
3	371	4	12	210	3
4	351	4	13	363	4
5	146	3	14	434	4
6	220	3	15	132	3
7	442	4	16	365	4
8	183	3	17	441	4
9	350	4	18	403	4
Out	**2,955**	**34**	**In**	**3,201**	**34**
			Out	**2,955**	**34**
			TOTALS	**6,156**	**68**

EAST AND WEST SUSSEX
COMPLETE GOLF

WEST SUSSEX

Bognor Regis G.C.
(18) 6238 yards
Downview Road, Felpham, Bognor Regis
(0243) 821929

Copthorne G.C.
(18) 6205 yards
Borers Arms Road, Copthorne
(0342) 712508

Cottesmore G.C.
(18) 6097 yards (Old)
(18) 5321 yards (New)
Buchan Hill, Crawley
(0293) 28256

Cowdray Park G.C.
(18) 6212 yards
Midhurst
(073081) 3599

Effingham Park G.C.
(9) 1749 yards
Copthorne
(0342) 716528

Goodwood G.C.
(18) 6370 yards
Goodwood, Chichester
(0243) 774968

Ham Manor G.C.
(18) 6216 yards
Angmering
(0903) 783288

Haywards Heath G.C.
(18) 6202 yards
High Beech Lane, Haywards Heath
(0444) 414457

Hill Barn G.C.
(18) 6224 yards
Hill Barn Lane, Worthing
(0903) 37301

Ifield G. & C.C.
(18) 6265 yards
Rusper Road, Ifield, Crawley
(0293) 20222

Littlehampton G.C.
(18) 6072 yards
170 Rope Walk, Littlehampton
(0903) 717170

Mannings Heath G.C.
(18) 6402 yards
Goldings Lane, Mannings Heath
(0403) 210228

Selsey G.C.
(9) 5654 yards
Golf Links Lane, Selsey
(0243) 602203

Tilgate G.C.
(18) 6359 yards
Titmus Drive, Tilgate, Crawley
(0293) 30103

West Sussex G.C.
(18) 6156 yards
Pulborough
(07982) 2563

Worthing G.C.
(18) 6519 yards (Lower)
(18) 5243 yards (Upper)
Links Road, Worthing
(0903) 60801

EAST SUSSEX

Ashdown Forest Hotel G.C.
(18) 5433 yards
Chapel Lane, Forest Row
(034 282) 4866

Brighton and Hove G.C.
(9) 5722 yards
Dyke Road, Brighton
(0273) 556482

Cooden Beach G.C.
(18-20) 6411 yards (White)
(18-20) 6099 yards (Yellow)
Cooden, Bexhill
(04243) 2040

Crowborough Beacon G.C.
(18) 6279 yards
Beacon Road, Crowborough
(08926) 61511

Dale Hill G.C.
(18) 6035 yards
Ticehurst, Wadhurst
(0580) 200112

Dyke G.C.
(18) 6557 yards
Dyke Road, Brighton
(079156) 296

Eastbourne Downs G.C.
(18) 6629 yards
East Dean Road, Eastbourne
(0323) 20827

East Brighton G.C.
(18) 6291 yards
Roedean Road, Brighton
(0273) 604838

Hastings G.C.
(18) 6073 yards
Battle Road, St. Leonards-on-Sea
(0424) 52981

Highwoods G.C.
(18) 6218 yards
Ellerslie Lane, Bexhill-on-Sea
(0424) 212625

Hollingbury Park G.C.
(18) 6415 yards
Ditching Road, Brighton
(0273) 552010

Horam Park G.C.
(9) 2600 yards
Chiddingly Road, Horam
(04353) 3477

Lewes G.C.
(18) 5951 yards
Chapel Hill, Lewes
(0273) 473245

Peacehaven G.C.
(9) 5235 yards
Brighton Road, Newhaven
(0273) 514049

Piltdown G.C.
(18) 6059 yards
Piltdown, Uckfield
(082572) 2033

Pyecombe G.C.
(18) 6201 yards
Clayton Hill, Pyecombe
(07918) 5372

Ashdown Forest Hotel and Royal Ashdown Forest new course
(18) 6439 yards
Chapel Lane, Forest Row
(034282) 2018

Royal Eastbourne G.C.
(18) 6084 yards
(9) 2147 yards
Paradise Drive, Eastbourne
(0323) 29738

Rye G.C.
(18) 6301 yards
(9) 6625 yards
(0797) 225241

Seaford G.C.
(18) 6241 yards
East Blatchington, Seaford
(0323) 892442

Seaford Head G.C.
(18) 5812 yards
Southdown Road, Seaford
(0323) 894843

Waterhall G.C.
(18) 5615 yards
Mill Road, Brighton
(0273) 508658

West Hove G.C.
(18) 6130 yards
Old Shoreham Road, Hove
(0273) 419738

Willingdon G.C.
(18) 6049 yards
Southdown Road, Eastbourne
(0323) 32383

LIONEL EDWARDS 'A Threesome' *BURLINGTON GALLERY*

KENT

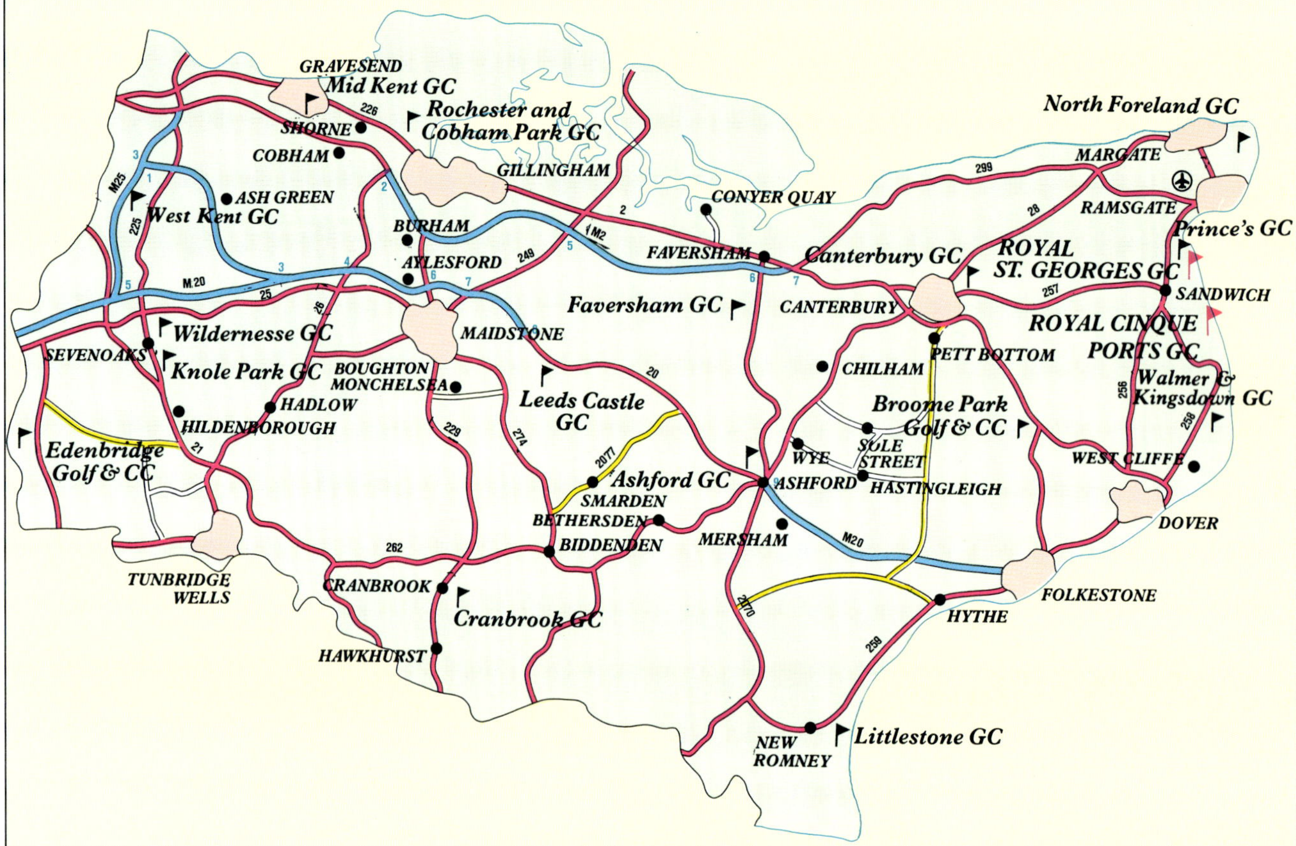

JULIAN BARROW ***"Royal St. Georges"*** ***BURLINGTON GALLERY***

KENT

CHOICE GOLF

From the mysterious and desolate lands of Romney Marsh to the famous White Ciffs of Dover. From the rich orchards of the Garden of England to the outskirts of Greater London. A county of great contrast. From the windswept links of Sandwich and Deal to the secluded Parks of Belmont and Knole, a county of great contrast.

Kent's reputation as one of the country's greatest golfing counties has been built around a three mile stretch of land lying midway between St Margaret's Bay and Pegwell Bay. Within this short distance lie three Open Championship courses **Princes (1962), Royal Cinque Ports (1909 and 1920)** and **Royal St Georges** (too numerous to list!) Kent has two other fine links courses, namely **Littlestone** and **North Foreland** but the golfer who sticks hard to the coast will be missing out on some of the most enjoyable golf Southern England has to offer.

In common with each of the counties that border Greater London many of Kent's courses are gradually finding themselves more in London than in Kent. When the Blackheath golfers left their Common and set up base at Eltham they were doubtless surrounded by the green fields of Kent. Charles Darwin's village of Orpington is now feeling the pinch but happily the **West Kent Golf Club** provides a most pleasant retreat. (Green fees **£14** per round, **£17** per day.)

Enough grousing! The ancient town of Sevenoaks is categorically in Kent and a very fortunate place too with **Wildernesse Golf Club** to the north and **Knole Park** to the south. The former is arguably the finest inland course in the country; with narrow fairways and thickly wooded, it is also one of the toughest. **Knole Park** is one of several Kentish courses that enjoy stately surroundings, being laid out in the handsome Deer Park of Lord Sackville. At both courses visitors should be able to arrange a game during the week. However, restrictions apply at weekends and as both are popular, prior telephoning is preferable.

For a stop-over in Sevenoaks **The Royal Oak Hotel (0732) 451109** is comfortable and a number of fine restaurants are close at hand; they include **La Cremaillere (0732) 851489** in Hadlow (french cooking), **The Gate Inn (0732) 832103** in Hildenborough (good sea food) and the outstanding **Thackeray's House (0892) 37558** in Tunbridge Wells. If you are short of a place to stay in Tunbridge Wells, **The Royal Wells (0892) 23414** is particularly good value.

To the north of the county, both **Mid Kent's** downland course at Gravesend and **Rochester and Cobham Park** (green fees **£14**) are handy for those travelling along the **A2**. Further along this road is the attractive town of Faversham and south of the town off the **A251** is Belmont Park, the estate of Lord Harris and the home of **Faversham Golf Club**. Here golf is played in the most tranquil of settings, particularly delightful in autumn when the fairways abound with countless strolling pheasants. Visitors are welcome during the week, fees are about **£11-£16**.

Beyond the 18th green a few ideas emerge. In Shorne, the **Inn On The Lake (047482) 3333** is a most pleasant place to stay. An alternative for pub lovers is the Dickensian **Leather Bottle (0474) 814327** in Cobham where perfectly adequate bedrooms are good value. More expensive accommodation is located near Ash Green in the alarmingly named village of Fawkham; the hotel **The Brandshatch Place (0474) 872239** offers tremendous comfort and a very good restaurant. Two pubs to note in the area are the **Golden Eagle** in Durham and the particularly pleasant and aptly named **Little Gem** in Aylesford. Over towards Faversham a fine place to rest the spikes is **The Tanyard Hotel (0622) 44705** at nearby Boughton Monchelsea. If it's quality fayre that is required, then Faversham itself houses the extremely popular **Reads (0795) 535344** (delightful French cooking).

Leaving Faversham, famous pheasants and all, we must make a pilgrimage. The **Canterbury Golf Club**, situated to the east of the cathedral town along the **A27** is well worth a visit. A much improved parkland course and one of the best in the county, a game is usually possible in midweek, the cost of a round being **£15** with **£17** entitling you to a full day's golf.

South of Canterbury (via **A2 and A260**) at Barham is the **Broome Park Golf and Country Club,** set in the grounds of a famous country house – this time a beautiful 300 year old mansion, the former home of Lord Kitchener. Visitors are usually received between Mondays and Saturdays, fees being approximately **£15** per day. A very pleasant parkland course and quite lengthy too, measuring some 6,600 yards.

Whether it's the proliferation of nearby golf courses or the Cathedral or even the glorious Kent countryside that attracts most, Canterbury deserves more than a short visit. Perhaps the leading hotel which also houses a commendable restaurant is **The County (0227) 66266**. There are eating places a-plenty in Canterbury: two superb examples include **Waterfields (0227) 450276** with its French and English provincial cooking and the **Restaurant Seventy Four (0227) 67411** which offers nouvelle style cuisine. The aforementioned glorius countryside is riddled with village pubs: two of note are **The Duck Inn** at Pett Bottom, and **The White Horse** at Chilham Castle.

Maidstone may not have the appeal of Canterbury but to the south east of this busy commuter town is one of Englands most attractive golf courses, **Leeds Castle** (green fees **£7**). The castle itself was described by Lord Conway as the most beautiful in the world and the setting really is quite idyllic. There are nine very individual holes and as it's a public course there are no real restrictions on times of play. It's popular though, so a preliminary telephone call is advisable.

The golf course at **Ashford** is pretty much in the middle of the county, and is another strongly worth noting. A heathland type course, which in itself is fairly unique to Kent and where except before 11.30am on Saturdays and Sundays, golf can be enjoyed throughout the week (**£9** Monday to Fridays, **£12** at weekends).

We're now in the heart of the Kent Downs and a variety of fine establishments beckon. **Eastwell Manor (0233) 35751** takes pride of place. Elegant and relaxing with a splendid restaurant – in fact outstanding in every way. In Wye, **The Wife of Bath (0233) 812540** is a tremendous restaurant. Note also the **Woodmans Arms Auberge** at Hastingleigh and **The Stone Green Hall Hotel and Restaurant (023372) 418** at Mersham. An ideal tavern is **The Compasses** at Side Street and for a pub with good value accommodation **The Bell** near Smarden is recommended.

Back to the fairways and a word for **Cranbrook**, a pleasant parkland course and the scene of **Bing Crosby's** last round in England. Apparently he was close to purchasing the course before his death in Spain. Green fees are set at **£9** per day midweek, **£12** at the weekends. Also in Cranbrook is one of Kent's most popular hotels, **The Kennel Holt Hotel (0580) 712032** – excellent for dinner and convenient for **Lamberhurst Golf Club**. Also recommended in the town is the **Willesley Hotel (0580) 713555**. Finally another good eating place in the area is **The Three Chimneys (0580) 291472** at Biddenden.

Switching from the rich countryside of Kent we now visit the coast. **Littlestone** is the first port of call, and it's quite a contrast, situated on the edge of the flatlands of Romney Marsh, it enjoys a somewhat remote setting. A splendid links and an Open Championship qualifying course, which doesn't deserve to be overshadowed by Kent's more illustrious trio further along the coast. 1988 was centenary year at this famous club. The current cost of green fees (weekdays only) is **£10** per round, **£12** per day.

North of the Sandwich is the **North Foreland** links at Broadstairs, also an Open qualifying course and where visitors are welcome at most times, (telephoning recommended), while to the south of Deal is **Walmer and Kingsdown**, a downland course providing views to Holland and France. Apart from weekend mornings, visitors are welcome on any day of the week, the fees in **1989** being **£10** per day midweek, **£12** at weekends.

Perhaps not surprisingly, where there is one great golf links there is often another nearby. Troon, Turnberry and Prestwick in Ayrshire, Birkdale, Lytham and Hoylake in Lancashire. Of Kent's famous three, **St Georges** and **Royal Cinque Ports** are featured ahead but **Princes** too has its admirers and it goes without saying that those wishing to admire any one of the three should contact the particular Club before setting off.

Despite the great quality of golf on offer there aren't too many places where one can put the feet up (or the golf clubs for that matter). Anyway, in Sandwich – blink and you might miss the village- **The Bell Hotel** is comfortable and convenient **(0304) 613388**; its quayside setting is pleasant and handy for **The Fisherman's Wharf Restaurant (0304) 613636**. Two pubs to note are the **Kings Arms (0304) 617330** and the **Fleur-de-Lis (0304) 611131**, St Margarets Bay, located on National Trust land is worth a look and the **Cliffe Tavern (0304) 852749** nearby is a good place to wet one's whistle and stay if you wish. As a final tip it might be a good idea to take the car on a short drive to Westcliffe, where **Wallett's Court** is supremely welcoming. As we conclude our trip midway between Dover and Folkestone another thought emerges – Hardelot, Le Touquet...

'Knole'

Whether you are a keen golfer or someone who simply enjoys the most beautiful countryside in the Garden of England, the Kennel Holt Hotel at Cranbrook must be the ideal setting to take a break. From the moment you arrive your stay will entice you into a fascinating world of Elizabethan elegance and the very best of English hospitality.

Kennel Holt was built around 1560 as an Eliabethan manor with all the splendour of spacious panelled rooms, a wealth of heavy oak beams and set in the most glorious sweeping gardens and overlooking wooded valleys, you can relax in undisturbed tranquility.

When you are ready for your first round of golf there is the choice of no less than five 18 hole courses in the immediate vicinity. With three of these courses there are arrangements for guests of Kennel Holt. So whatever your golfing aspirations, Kennel Holt will fulfil your needs.

At the end of your day on the course, return to round off the day with a sumptious dinner in the intimate restaurant laid on for you by two of the most talented young chefs in the South of England. The cuisine ranks among the best in the country. The cost of a room includes the five course dinner from a superb Cordon Bleu menu which is renewed daily. Your room, which features private facilities, telephone, colour television, clock radio, trouser press and a towel warmer, will encourage you to relax in unsurpassed luxury to prepare yourself for the golf of tomorrow.

Not only can the Kennel Holt Hotel provide you with an excellent golfing retreat, but if your time permits, you are very close to many places of interest and attractions that could divert you for hours. Right on the doorstep is the historic Tudor estate of Sissinghurst with one of the most famous gardens in the world. Other features of historic importance that are very close include: the fine moated castle and grounds at Scotney, Penhurst Place, c. 1340, full of marvellous art treasures, Winston Churchill's family home at Chartwell, and the operatic oasis of Glyndebourne. For the sporting among you, you will find within easy reach, horse riding in the South Downs, coarse, fly and sea fishing, shooting, plus a wealth of beautiful country walks.

Your hosts David and Jane Misseldine will look forward to hearing from you and will guarantee to provide you with the most personable hospitality in Kent. The Kennel Holt is an AA rated Red Star Hotel and one of Arthur Eperon's 50 British Selected Hotels. It is also recommended by Egon Ronay and Derek Johansen, and has received the RAC Blue Ribbon Award for Excellence.

Kennel Holt Hotel
Cranbrook
Kent TN17 2PT
Tel: (0580) 712032
Fax: (0580) 712931

ROYAL CINQUE PORTS (DEAL)
CHAMPIONSHIP GOLF

In the year 55 B.C. **Julius Caesar** landed on the coast near Deal. In 1920 an American invader by the name of **Walter Hagen** came to Deal to play in his first Open Championship. Both came, both saw, but neither conquered. In fact both returned from whence they came, tails firmly between legs – small wonder Deal is often considered the toughest of all England's Championship links!

The **Royal Cinque Ports Golf Club** was founded in February 1892 by **Major General J.M.Graham** whilst at lunch in Deal's Black Horse Hotel. The 18 hole course was opened in 1895 and has required very few alterations during its distinguished history. Today the gentleman responsible for the efficient organisation of the Club is the Secretary, **Mr. N.S. Phillips**. Mr. Phillips may be contacted at the **Royal Cinque Ports Golf Club, Golf Road, Deal, Kent. Tel (0304) 374007. Andrew Reynolds** is the professional. He can be reached on **(0304)374170**.

Visitors with official handicaps are welcome to play the famous links although prior booking with the Secretary is essential. As with a number of the more traditional Clubs, three and four ball matches have no standing on the course; indeed they are only permitted by arrangement with the Secretary.

In **1989** a **green fee** of **£22** entitled the visitor to a full day's golf, and persons arriving after 1 pm can obtain a **25%** reduction. The Club also offers a twilight green fee where there is a **50%** reduction for those teeing off after **5pm**. An early start in winter with a later start in summer would appear to be the best bet. Sadly, weekend bookings are no longer possible.

The golf course is situated approximately one mile north of the town. Probably the best route from **London** is to travel on the **A2/M2** as far as **Canterbury**. There one should pick up the **A257 Sandwich** road and thereafter the **A258** which takes you to **Deal**. From the South the **A258** runs from **Dover**. Also worth noting is the Deal Railway Station which is on the northern side of the town, near the pier.

Very often it is Mother Nature who provides the greatest challenge at Deal. Strong winds billowing in from the sea, capable of changing direction several times during a round can turn what appear to be modest holes into monsters. The course measures **6409** yards from the medal tees (par **70**) with the Championship tees extending the course to some **6744** yards (par **72**). The corresponding distances for the ladies are **5190** yards and **5675** yards (par **74**). The outward nine is generally considered the easier half – (**Michael Bonallack** turned in 31 during his record amateur score of 65 – a record which has stood for 23 years). Certainly the back nine is longer and Deal is renowned for its tough finish, the 16th perhaps being the most difficult hole on the course. The fairways are humpy and hillocky and well bunkered. The rough is often thick and many of the greens stand on natural plateaux. On a clear day there are some magnificent views across the course towards the English Channel and to the distant white cliffs beyond Pegwell Bay.

Two Open Championships have been held at Deal, in **1909** and in **1920**. The 1909 Championship was won by the Englishman **John H. Taylor**, his fourth victory in the event. The 1920 Open has already been referred to – the luckless Hagen in fact finished fifty third in a field of fifty four. Also entitled to feel somewhat peeved that year was **Abe Mitchell** who allowed **George Duncan** to come from thirteen strokes behind him to snatch victory. Plans to stage a third Championship at Deal in 1949 had to be abandoned when extensive flooding led to a temporary closure of the course.

The Royal Cinque Ports Club has also twice been selected to host the **Amateur Championship**, firstly in **1923** and secondly during its centenary year in **1982**. One of the annual highlights on the Club's calendar is the **Halford Hewitt Challenge Cup**, an 'Old Boys' competition played for in April.

The Members of Royal Cinque Ports are doubly fortunate. Blessed with such a fine course, they also possess an excellent Clubhouse. The facilities are first class and both the early starter and our 'twilight golfer' will be glad to find that hot and cold snacks are normally available at all times. With prior notice both breakfast and dinner can be arranged. For those just wanting a quick drink in between rounds (a stiff one may be in order!) a bar is provided.

It would not of course be fair, either to the Romans or Mr Hagen, to leave Deal without recording that both did eventually achieve their ambitions. The Romans returned a century later and conquered the Brits, and as for Walter, he didn't have to wait quite so long, for in 1922 he won the first of four Open Championships, none of which though, alas, was at Deal.

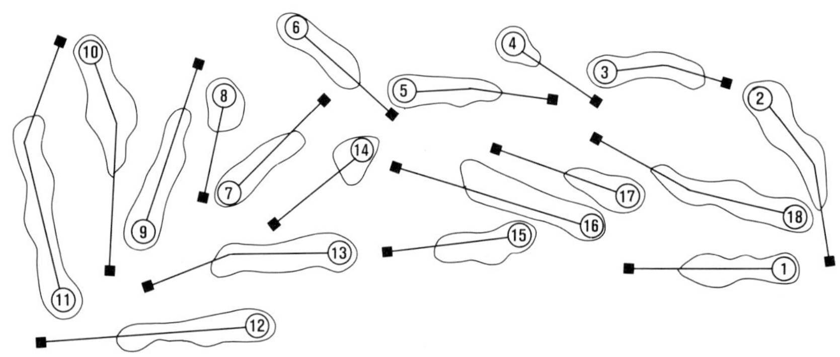

Hole	Yards	Par	Hole	Yards	Par
1	361	4	10	362	4
2	399	4	11	398	4
3	492	5	12	437	4
4	153	3	13	420	4
5	502	5	14	222	3
6	315	4	15	455	4
7	385	4	16	506	5
8	154	3	17	372	4
9	404	4	18	407	4
Out	3,165	36	In	3,579	36
			Out	3,165	36
			TOTALS	6,744	72

ROYAL ST. GEORGES

CHAMPIONSHIP GOLF

As with many of the Championship links of Britain, the golfer is at the mercy of the elements. Sandwich on a fresh, sunny morning can be veritable golfer's treat, but woe betide when the weather turns. In **1898**, the storm during the Varsity match was so severe that some team members adjourned for the day; later the same spineless warriors were dragged from the bar and ordered to resume their matches. In the worst of the storm one player took three air shots at one hole, still securing a win, due to the fact that his opponent was unable to find his ball. We wish you no such perils on your quest to tame the links of St. Georges!

The Club was founded in **1887**, rather ironically by two Scottish gentlemen, **Dr. Laidlaw Purves** and **Henry Lamb** after what can only be described as a rather eccentric venture. Like all good Scotsmen they had been bitten by the 'bug'; however, both were presently living in Victorian London which meant that their golf was more or less confined to the various commons where the game was played alongside every conceivable activity imaginable. To them golf was meant to be played on a links by the sea. Hence the pair found themselves at Bournemouth setting off in an easterly direction looking for a suitable site. Having reached the eastern shore of Kent they had drawn the proverbial blank, with patience no doubt wearing thin, 'land ahoy' Doctor Purves sights a vast stretch of duneland at Sandwich. The story is that he 'spied the land with a golfer's eye' from the tower of St Clement's Church. Quite what he was doing at the top of the tower is irrelevant – St. Georges had been located. Within seven short years the Open Championship had 'come south' and St. Georges was the first English venue.

One hundred years on **Captain R. J. Hitchen RN** is the **Secretary** at St. Georges and he can be contacted by telephone on **(0304) 613090**. All written communications should be directed to the Secretary at **The Royal St. Georges Golf Club, Sandwich, Kent CT13 9PB**. Golfers wishing to visit the course must make prior arrangements with the Secretary. As a general guide visitors are welcome between Mondays and Fridays and gentlemen must possess official handicaps of 18 or less, ladies 15 or less. Other points to note are that the 1st tee is reserved daily for Members until 9.45am and between 1.15pm and 2.15pm; however, the 10th tee is usually free in the early mornings. St. Georges is essentially a singles and foursomes Club and three ball and four ball matches are only permissible with the agreement of the Secretary.

The **green fees** for 1989 were set at **£25** per round, **£35** per day. During the months of December, January and February the **£25** fee is applicable for a full day's golf. Should there be a wish to hire golf clubs, a limited supply are for hire through the professional, **Neil Cameron,** telephone **(0304) 617380**. Finally the services of a caddie can be booked via the Caddiemaster, also on **(0304) 617380** – a week's warning is preferable.

Please excuse the awful pun but travelling to Sandwich should be a 'piece of cake.' The town is linked to Canterbury to the west by the **A257**, a distance of approximately 15 miles and to Deal, 6 miles south east of Sandwich by the **A258**. Motoring from London, the most direct route is to head for Canterbury using a combination of the **A2** and **M2** and thereafter following the **A257** as above. For those coming from the south coast Ashford is the place to head for. Ashford is joined to Canterbury by the **A28**. Sandwich can also be reached by train.

Since its first Open of **1894**, won by **John H. Taylor**, the Championship has been held at Sandwich on ten further occasions, most recently of course in 1985 when **Sandy Lyle** became the first British winner for sixteen years. The visitor will not have to tackle the course from the Championship tees but he'll still have to confront the many dunes and the awkward stances that St. Georges is so famous for. And then of course there is the ever present wind.

St. George's has seen many great happenings: **Walter Hagen** winning the Championship in **1922** and then promptly handing his winnings straight to his caddie; **Henry Cotton's** opening 67-65 in the **1934** Championship and then the **Harry Bradshaw** 'broken bottle' episode of **1949**. After a gap of 32 years the Open returned to St. Georges in **1981** when the American **Bill Rogers** won.

Having done battle with the elements the golfer will find the Clubhouse welcoming. Excellent lunches are served daily and both breakfasts and dinners can be obtained with prior arrangement. A jacket and tie should be worn in all public rooms.

The weather is not always the enemy of the golfer; indeed, Alf Padgham in the 1938 **Open**, holed out in two on the old **11th**, a distance of some 385 yards. An historic course, fair weather or foul – long may the flag of St. Georges fly!

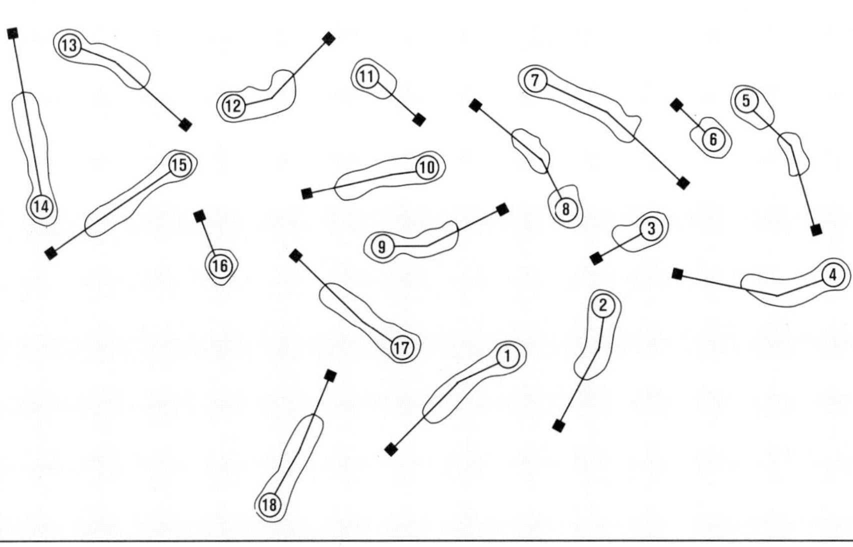

Hole	Yards	Par	Hole	Yards	Par
1	445	4	10	399	4
2	376	4	11	216	3
3	214	3	12	362	4
4	470	4	13	443	4
5	422	4	14	508	5
6	156	3	15	467	4
7	529	5	16	165	3
8	415	4	17	425	4
9	387	4	18	458	4
Out	3,414	35	In	3,443	35
			Out	3,414	35
			TOTALS	6,857	70

KENT

COMPLETE GOLF

KENT

(See also Gtr London)

Ashford G.C.
(18) 6246 yds
Sandyhurst Lane, Ashford
(0233) 22655

Barnehurst G.C.
(9) 5320 yds
Mayplace Rd, East Barnehurst
(0322) 523746

Bearsted G.C.
(18) 6253 yds
Ware St, Bearsted, Maidstone
(0622) 38198

Broome Park G. & C.C.
(18) 6606 yds
Barham, Canterbury
(0227) 831701

Canterbury G.C.
(18) 6209 yds
Scotland Hills, Canterbury
(0227) 453532

Cherry Lodge G.C.
(18) 6908 yds
Jail Lane, Biggin Hill
(0959) 72250

Chestfield G.C.
(18) 6068 yds
Chestfield, Whitstable
(022779) 2365

Cobtree Manor
(18) 5701 yds
Chatham Rd, Boxley, Maidstone
(0622) 53276

Cranbrook G.C.
(18) 6128 yds
Beneden Rd, Cranbrook
(0580) 712833

Cray Valley G.C.
(18) 6338 yds
Sandy Lane, St Paul's Cray,
Orpington
(0689) 39677

Darenth Valley G.C.
(18) 6356 yds
Station Rd, Shoreham
(09592) 2944

Dartford G.C.
(18) 5914 yds
Dartford Heath, Dartford
(0322) 26455

Deangate Ridge G.C.
(18) 6300 yds
Hoo, Rochester
(0634) 251180

Edenbridge G. & C.C.
(18) 6635 yds
Crouch House Rd, Edenbridge
(0732) 865097

Faversham G.C.
(18) 5979 yds
Belmont Park, Faversham
(079589) 561

Gillingham G.C.
(18) 5911 yds
Woodlands Rd, Gillingham
(0634) 53017

Hawkhurst G.C.
(9) 5791 yds
High St, Hawkshurst
(05805) 2396

Herne Bay G.C.
(18) 5364 yds
Eddington, Herne Bay
(0227) 373964

High Elms G.C.
(18) 6210 yds
High Elms Rd, Downe
(0689) 58175

Holtye G.C.
(9) 5289 yds
Holtye Common, Cowden,
Edenbridge
(034286) 635

Hythe Imperial G.C.
(9) 5583 yds
Princes Parade, Hythe
(0303) 67554

Kingsgate G.C.
(18) 6374 yds
Kingsgate, Broadstairs
(0843) 62140

Knole Park G.C.
(18) 6249 yds
Seal Hollow Rd, Sevenoaks
(0732) 452150

Lamberhurst G.C.
(18) 6277 yards
Church Rd, Lamberhurst
(0892) 890241

Leeds Castle G.C.
(9) 6017 yds
Leeds Castle, Maidstone
(062780) 467

Littlestone G.C.
(18) 6417 yds
St. Andrews Road, Littlestone,
New Romney
(0679) 63355

Lullingstone Park G.C.
(18) 6674 yds
(9) 2432 yds
Park Gate, Chelsfield, Orpington
(0959) 34542

Mid Kent G.C.
(18) 6206 yds
Singlewell Road, Gravesend
(0474) 68035

Nevill G.C.
(18) 6336 yds
Benhall Mill Road,
Tunbridge Wells
(0892) 25818

North Foreland G.C.
(18) 6382 yds
Convent Road, Broadstairs
(0843) 62140

Poult Wood G.C.
(18) 5569 yds
Higham Lane, Tonbridge
(0732) 364039

Prince's G.C.
(18) 6923 yds
(9) 3134 yds
Sandwich Bay, Sandwich
(0304) 61[illegible]18

Rochester & Cobham Park G.C.
(18) 6434 yds
Park Dale, Rochester
(047482) 3411

Royal Cinque Ports G.C.
(18) 6744 yds
Golf Road, Deal
(0304) 374007

Royal St. George's G.C.
(18) 6857 yds
Sandwich
(0304) 613090

Ruxley G.C.
(18) 5017 yds
St Paul's Cray, Orpington
(0689) 71490

St. Augustine's G.C.
(18) 5138 yds
Cliffsend, Ramsgate
(0843) 590333

Sene Valley G.C.
(18) 6320 yds
Sene, Folkestone
(0303) 68513

Sheerness G.C.
(18) 6500 yds
Powe Station Road, Sheerness
(0795) 662585

Sittingbourne & Milton Regis G.C.
(18) 6121 yds
Wormdale,
Newington, Sittingbourne
(0795) 842261

Tenterden G.C.
(9) 5119 yds
Woodchurch Road, Tenterden
(05806) 3987

Tudor Park G & CC.
(18) 6000 yards
Ashford Rd, Maidstone
(0622) 34334

Tunbridge Wells G.C.
(9) 4684 yds
Langton Road, Tunbridge Wells
(0892) 23034

Walmer & Kingsdown G.C.
(18) 6451 yds
Kingsdown, Deal
(0304) 373256

Westgate & Birchington G.C.
(18) 4926 yds
Domneva Road, Westgate-on-Sea
(0843) 31115

West Kent G.C.
(18) 6392 yds
Downe, Orpington
(0689) 51323

West Malling G.C.
(18) 6950 yds
Addington, Maidstone
(0732) 844785

Whitstable & Seasalter G.C.
(18) 5276 yds
Collingwood Road, Whitstable
(0227) 272020

Wildernesse G.C.
(18) 6478 yds
Seal, Sevenoaks
(0732) 61199

Woodlands Manor G.C.
(18) 5858 yds
Woodlands, Sevenoaks
(09592) 3806

Wrotham Heath G.C.
(9) 5823 yds
Comp, Sevenoaks
(0732) 884800

EASTWELL MANOR

Eastwell Manor has a long tradition of treating people regally. Queen Victoria and King Edward were frequent visitors. Prince Alfred and his wife lived here. A queen of Rumania was born here.

Today, the tradition continues. The elegant bedrooms, luxurious bathrooms and the character filled lounges, dining room and billiard room are all witness to the hotel's exceptional history.

An internationally acclaimed restaurant renowned for its haute cuisine adds to the pleasure of staying at this historic house. Fresh ingredients are used to create meals of unsurpassed quality, complemented by a thoughtfully compiled wine list.

Set in 62 acres of undulating parkland in the heart of the Kentish Downs, Eastwell Manor is peaceful and secluded. However, the historic cathedral city of Canterbury is close by and Eastwell Manor is within easy reach of both London and the ferry ports of Dover, Folkestone and Ramsgate.

There are all manner of other fun activities that guests can enjoy. Ballooning from the grounds of Eastwell Manor gives one the most envigorating view of the Kent Countryside or closer to the ground fishing on the Estate or on the river Stour can be arranged.

Kent is well known for its rolling countryside — and English wines can be sampled at Bibenden vineyards. The hotel can arrange transport if you feel the tasting may be too much. Other sports to try include riding, clay pigeon shooting in the grounds, golf — a splendid array of fine courses surround the hotel and for the airborne try handgliding or gliding.

Whichever direction you are travelling in Eastwell Manor provides a most relaxing place to stay within the garden of England.

Eastwell Manor
Eastwell Park,
Kent
TN25 4HR
Tel: (0233) 35751

SURREY

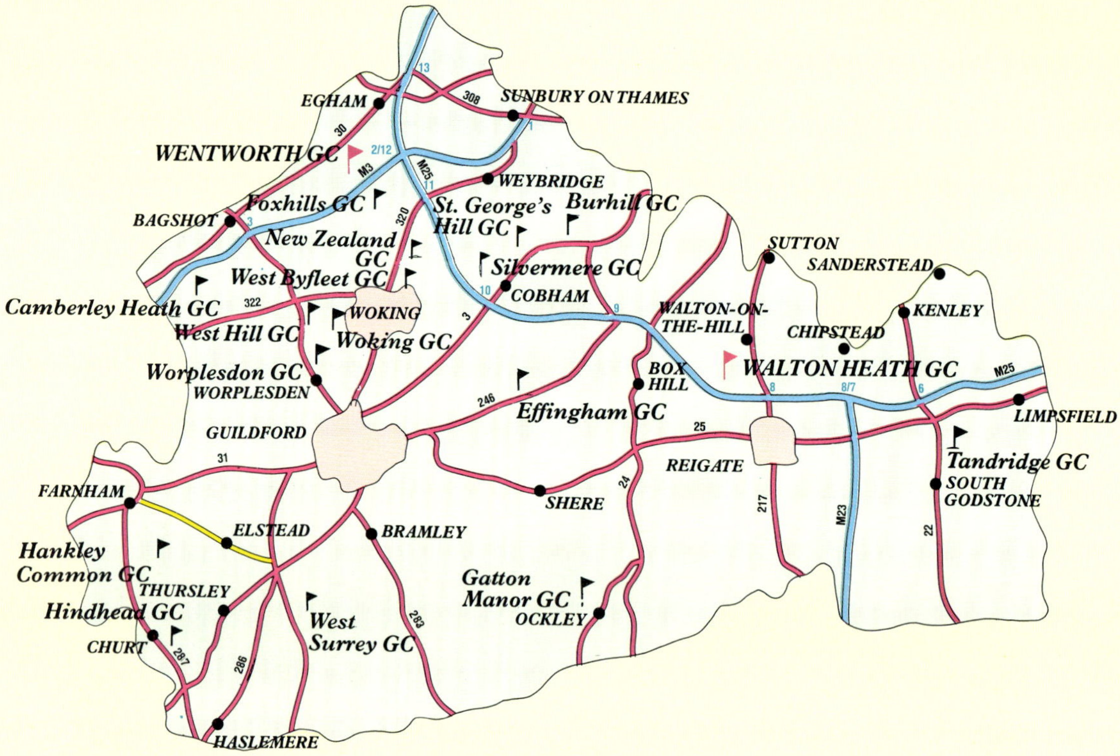

JULIAN BARROW "Walton Heath" BURLINGTON GALLERY

SURREY

CHOICE GOLF

When Providence distributed land best suited for building golf courses it wasn't done in the most democratic of spirits. Suggesting the top dozen or so courses in a county like Wiltshire is a fairly straightforward task – there aren't many more than a dozen or so to choose from. Recommending a similar number in Hampshire is, as the Americans would say, 'a different ball game', there being a number of very fine courses. Attempting the same in Surrey is nigh on impossible for in golfing terms no other county in England is so well-endowed.

Though very different in appearance it is probably safe to suggest that **Walton Heath** and **Wentworth** are the county's two leading courses. (Sunningdale of course being just over the border in Berkshire). But Walton and Wentworth (both featured on later pages) are only two of Surrey's famous 'W Club' – there's also **Worplesdon** and **Woking, West Hill, West Surrey** and **West Byfleet**.

Located on the **A32** to the west of Woking, Worplesdon, West Hill and Woking Golf Clubs lie practically next door to one another. Indeed it might be possible to devise a few dramatic 'cross-course' holes – though in view of the value of some of the properties that would have to be driven over it's perhaps not such a good idea! **West Hill** (Green fees: **£19** per day) is generally considered the most difficult of the three, the fairways at times being frighteningly narrow. **Worplesdon** (green fees **£20** per day) with its superb green is probably the most widely known (largely due to its famous annual foursomes event), while **Woking**,(**£12.50** per day) founded almost a century ago, perhaps possesses the greatest charm. Whatever their particular merits, all three are outstanding examples of the natural heathland and heather type course. Visitors are welcome at each during the week although prior telephoning is essential and proof of handicap is normally required. A full day's golf on any of the three can be enjoyed for around the **£19-20** mark. Also worth a visit is the **Fernfell Golf and Country Club** in Cranleigh.

Slightly closer to the capital and still very much in the heart of stockbroker-belt country is a second trio of courses centred around Weybridge: **St George's Hill, New Zealand** and **West Byfleet**. Once again heathland-type courses where golf is played amidst heavily wooded surroundings, the combination of pines, silver birch and purple heather, make for particularly attractive settings. **St George's Hill** is in fact one of the more undulating courses in Surrey and calls for several spectacular shots. It need hardly be said that all three courses are again very popular and one shouldn't consider arranging a game without first telephoning the Club in question.

Golf in Surrey isn't of course all heathland and heather. Just a short drive from Weybridge is the delightful parkland course at **Burhill**, situated some two miles south of Walton-on-Thames. Burhill's Clubhouse is a particularly grand affair, at one time it was the home of the Dowager Duchess of Wellington. Much less grand but to some of equal interest, is the 'Dick Turpin' cottage sited on the course and reputed to have been used by the infamous highwayman. Green fees at Burhill are priced at **£13** per round, **£20** per day. Also worth noting is a nearby public course. **Silvermere**, located midway between Byfleet and Cobham and where green fees are naturally lower – (around the **£6** mark).

Some thoughts for the 19th hole are required. Surrey is a rich county – in more ways than one. Quality golf comes in abundance, so too do the country houses, pubs, hotels and restaurants. Here are a few suggestions. In Walton-on-the-Hill, very convenient for Walton Heath is **Ebenezer Cottage (073 781) 3166** – a super restaurant. More fine fare is found at Sutton. **Partners 23 (01) 644 7743** is the place, and at Chipstead where **Dene Farm (0737) 552661** has a delightful country setting.

After a day's golf on any of the courses in the Woking area **The Wheatsheaf Hotel (04862) 73047** is a good spot to collect one's thoughts. Another well thought of hotel is the **Mayford Manor (04862) 48364** – centrally located and pleasant, as is **Oatlands Park (09328) 47242. The Cricketers (0932) 62105** on Downside Common, Cobham is a sporting little pub. Two outstanding restaurants are **La Bonne Franquette (0784)39494** in Egham and **Casa Romana (0932) 43470)** in Weybridge. Finally, two of the county's (and the country's) finest country house hotels are in this area – convenient incidentally for a trip to Wentworth – **Pennyhill Park (0276) 71774** near Bagshot, and **Great Fosters (0784) 33822** near Egham.

Generally speaking golf in Southern England and golf in America have precious little in common. However, the **Foxhills** Club at Ottershaw (off the **A320**) can make a genuine claim to have married the two successfully. A Jacobean-styled manor house run on American country club lines including an outstanding range of leisure facilities, it has two Championship length heathland type courses. Not surprisingly, Foxhills is a popular haunt for golfing societies, but it is normally possible for individual visitors to play either (or both) courses during the week, for about **£16** a round.

The country club scene may not of course appeal to all types and excellent golf, in a more sedate atmosphere, can be enjoyed at **Gatton Manor** situated in Ockley near Dorking. The 18 hole course was opened in 1969 and from its back tees can be stretched to 6906 yards. The course has a very scenic layout running through woods and alongside lakes. With the exception of Sunday mornings visitors are welcome throughout the week and green fees are good value at around **£12**. One doesn't have to look too far for a good night's rest – the Manor House is now a very relaxing hotel with golf obviously very much on the menu. Note also the **Punch Bowl** in nearby Oakwood Hill – an excellent country pub.

The rich heathland seam runs the breadth of the country and over to the west, practically straddling the three counties of Surrey, Berkshire and Hampshire, lies the superb **Camberley Heath** course, while down in the south-west corner there is yet another outstanding trio of clubs: **Hindhead, West Surrey** and **Hankley Common**.

The south-west corner of Surrey is particularly scenic. The hustle and bustle of London seems a world away – and of course in a way it is. In Bramley, **The Bramley Grange Hotel (0483) 893434** is an ideal base from which to explore the countryside. Close to the Sussex borders lies Haslemere and another fine hotel, a timbered farmhouse on this occasion, **The Lythe Hill Hotel (0428) 51251** where bedrooms in the original house have great character. People who have still not found a restaurant to visit must surely do so here for **Morels (0248) 51462** offers some simply splendid dishes in an excellent atmosphere.

Returning one more time to the fairways. West Surrey is probably best described as a heather/parkland mix and is one of the few leading courses in the country where visitors can play at weekends. However,prior telephoning is again to be recommended. **Hankley Common** was for many years a favourite of the late South African **Bobby Locke**, four times Open Champion, who once owned a house adjacent to the course. Hankley Common is widely known for its fire of ten years ago, and its spectacular 18th hole – one of the greatest closing holes in golf. A vast gulley which seems to possess magnetic powers looms in front of the green. Visitors are welcome to test their skills during the week, prior contact with the secretary being essential. Green fees are about **£16**.

WALTON HEATH

CHAMPIONSHIP GOLF

Gavrillo Princip may have pulled the trigger that ignited the Great War but our history books tell us that tension in Europe had sometime earlier reached boiling point. In their Palaces in St. Petersburg and Berlin the Czar and the Kaiser pondered the strength of their armies. Meanwhile the great statesmen of Britain were engaged in battles of a different nature......

All square as they reach the 18th green on the **Old Course** at **Walton Heath, Churchill** turns to **Lloyd-George** and says, 'Now then, I will putt you for the Premiership'.

Herbert Fowler once said, 'God builds golf links and the less man meddles the better for all concerned.' Herbert Fowler designed Walton Heath. However, before the opening of the Old Course in **May 1904**, a little meddling was called for. The glorious heathland through which the emerald fairways were cut was once covered, or nearly covered in thick heather, in parts as much as two feet thick (the Members will tell you it still is!). While many of Britain's leading Clubs took several years to establish their reputations, that of Walton Heath was assured months before the first stroke was even played; in **January 1904 James Braid** agreed to become Walton's first professional. Braid initially signed a seven year contract, his performances in the next seven Open Championships were: **2nd, 1st, 1st, 5th, 1st, 2nd and 1st**, after which he became the first ever golfer to win five Opens. Hardly surprisingly his contract was extended and so indeed began an association with the Club that was to last for nearly fifty years.

In the years immediately before the First War, Walton Heath Members included no fewer than 24 M.Ps (including Winston Churchill and Lloyd George) and 21 Members of the Lords. Another famous Walton golfer was **W.G. Grace** (who it is said compiled as many hundreds on the Heath as he did at the Oval). After the War a more 'Royal Flavour' dominated with the **Prince of Wales** becoming an Honorary Member in **1921** and **Captain** in **1935**.

Time to leap forward to the present and introduce the Club's **Secretary; Mr. Heron** is the very helpful gentleman in question. He may be contacted at **The Walton Heath Golf Club, Tadworth, Surrey (073781) 2380**. Subject to prior arrangement with the Secretary, golfers are welcome to visit Walton Heath between Mondays and Fridays. Proof of both Club Membership and an official handicap is required. The **Greenfees** for **1989** were set at **£30** for a full day's golf, with a reduced rate of **£25** available if teeing off after 11.30am. For juniors the fees were half the above rates. Golfing Societies are equally welcome, pre-booking being essential. The hire of golf clubs and the arranging of a caddy can be done through the Club's professional, **Ken MacPherson**. He may be reached by telephone on **(073781) 2152**.

Located south of London, motoring to the Club is assisted greatly by the **M25**. Those aproaching on this motorway should leave at exit **8** turning south on to the **A217**. The A217 should be followed for approximately 2 miles after which a left turn should be taken on to the **B2032**. The Golf Club is situated a mile or so along this road. Travelling from further afield, the M25 is linked to the **M23** to the South, the **M20** to the East and to the North and West by the **M3, M4** and **M1**. There are two great courses at Walton Heath, the **Old** and the **New** (the latter first appearing as nine holes in 1907 but later extended to the full 18). Lying adjacent to one another each possesses the same classical heathland characteristics – heather, bracken, gorse, pines and silver birch. The Old Course is slightly longer than the New, their respective distances being **6813** yards (par **73**) and **6659** yards (par **72**). From the ladies tees the lengths of the two are **5957** yards (par **74**) and **6005** yards (par **74**). The finishing three holes on the Old are thought by many to be the finest on any course. The **16th** is a very mild dog-leg to a raised green which slopes from left to right, with the right side of the green heavily guarded by bunkers. The par three **17th** has sand traps practically encircling the green, creating a near island effect and the **18th** requires a testing second to carry an enormous cross bunker.

Over the years Walton Heath has played host to many important tournaments. The major amateur championships have included the **English Amateur and both the Ladies English Amateur** and the **Ladies British Open Amateur Championships**. Among the professional events, twenty-two of the **PGA Match Play Championships** were staged at Walton Heath and in recent years **The Ryder Cup** of **1981** as well as three **European Open Championships**.

Walton Heath has a fine Clubhouse with an excellent restaurant and lounge. A jacket and tie should be worn in all public rooms after 11am. Lunches are served between 12pm and 2.30pm and both breakfast and dinners (minimum number 24) can be arranged with prior notice.

Understandably wherever you turn in the Clubhouse you are likely to see a reminder of the long association with James Braid. One small note sent to him from the Prince of Wales conveys a message all golfers can appreciate. It relates how the Prince came to the 18th requiring a four for a 79. After explaining how his second finished just through the green he then tells how, 'with the chance of breaking 80, I couldn't stand the nerve-strain and fluffed the chip and took two putts...' How the mighty fall!

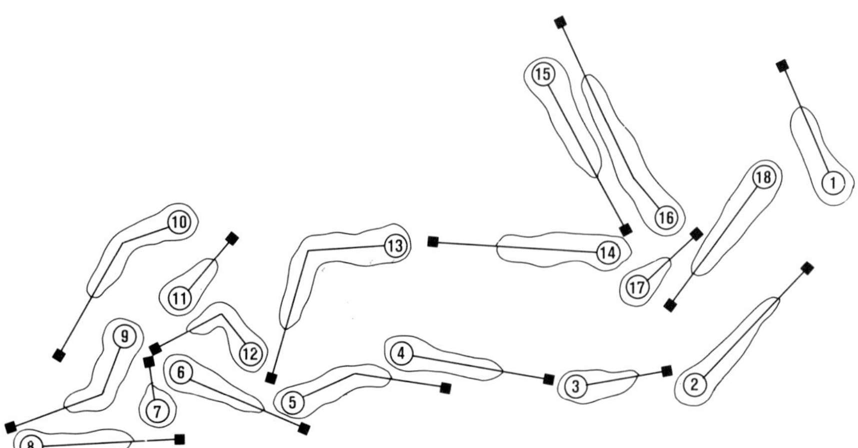

Old Course

Hole	Yards	Par	Hole	Yards	Par
1	298	4	10	395	4
2	439	4	11	189	3
3	289	4	12	371	4
4	443	4	13	507	5
5	391	4	14	517	5
6	422	4	15	404	4
7	174	3	16	510	5
8	489	5	17	181	3
9	390	4	18	404	4
Out	3,335	36	In	3,478	37
			Out	3,335	36
			TOTALS	6,813	73

WENTWORTH
CHAMPIONSHIP GOLF

It is autumn. A reddish-gold leaf scurries across the 18th green. The huge gallery is silent. Fully fifty yards away, to the right of the fairway close to the trees and in the rough is **Severiano Ballesteros.** He is one down to the legendary **Arnold Palmer** and he needs a miracle. The blade flashes, and a ball flies towards the green. It pitches, it rolls, and it drops....the eagle has landed.

A stunningly beautiful place, **Wentworth** is set in the heart of the famous Surrey heathland belt. The name first appeared on the golfing map in the mid nineteen twenties when **Harry Colt** was commissioned to design two eighteen hole courses. The **East Course** was first to open in **1924,** with the **West Course** following two years later.

Before the War it was the East Course that captured the limelight by staging the Club's first important events: in **1926** an unofficial match between British and American teams and in **1932** the first ever playing of the **Curtis Cup**. In the period since **1945** the longer West Course has grabbed most of the glory. In the 1950's came the **Ryder Cup** and the **World Cup** and in the 60's, the **World Matchplay Championship**.

The administration of the Club is presently in the very capable hands of the **Secretary, Mr. Doyle-Davison** and his staff. Mr. Doyle-Davison may be contacted via the **Wentworth Golf Club, Virginia Water, Surrey. Tel (09904) 2201**. It is essential for persons wishing to visit Wentworth that they pre-book a starting time with the Secretary. Unless accompanied by a Member, visitors are limited to playing during weekdays and must be in possession of a current handicap.

Also well-worth noting is that from Fridays to Mondays inclusive a system of course allocation is operated. One of the courses is designated for two balls or foursomes with the other for three ball or four ball matches. **Society** days at Wentworth are usually Tuesdays, Wednesdays and Thursdays, with Mondays and Fridays subject to availability.

In **1989**, green fees were set at **£69** for the West course and **£46** for the East course. If you are lucky enough to play with a Member, you can play for **£20** during the week of **£25** during the weekend. It is usual for the green fee to be half the normal rate during the winter months. The Club has excellent practice facilities and both electric trolleys and sets of clubs can be hired from the professional shop. **Bernard Gallacher**, the Scottish Ryder Cup player, is the professional at Wentworth. He can be reached on **(09904) 3353**.

Travelling to Wentworth ought not to present too many difficulties, the area being well served by major roads. The entrance to the Wentworth Estate is on the main **A30** road, some two miles west of Staines. The **M3, M4** and **M25** all pass close to the course making access easy from any direction. Finally **Heathrow Airport** is no more than twenty minutes drive away.

Wentworth's West Course, or **'Burma Road'** as it has become commonly known, is one of Britain's longest (and most difficult) inland courses. From the back tees it stretches to a formidable **6945** yards with a par of **72**, while from the forward yellow tees it is still a very testing **6675** yards. Even from the ladies tees the Course measures a shade over **6000** yards! The East Course is considerably shorter, being **6176** yards from the back markers. However, the par is a tough **68** with five of the par fours measuring over 420 yards. Apart from their length the two courses differ slightly in general appearance; as the Club's previous Secretary put it, 'The West Course is mainly wooded with some heather while the East Course is mainly heather with some woods.'!

In 1988 the **Volvo** sponsored **P.G.A.** Championship was held at Wentworth, victory in this instance going to **Ian Woosnam** who compiled an impressive aggregate of 274. Few, however, would dispute that the word 'Wentworth' instantly invokes thoughts of early Autumn – Wentworth in all its glory – the setting of course for the World Matchplay Championship. First held in 1964, when matchplay events were few and far between, the Championship immediately caught the imagination of the public. People to this day talk of **Gary Player's** incredible comeback against **Tony Lema** in the semi-final of 1965 when he was seven down with seventeen to play. The South African won that year as he did on four further occasions. There was also **Isao Aoki's** hole in one at the 2nd during the 1979 Championship – his reward for five seconds of work being a £55,000 luxury summer house! In more recent years **Severiano Ballesteros** and **Greg Norman** have dominated the event sharing the titles in the years between 1980 and 1986, Norman winning three times, Ballesteros four. 1988 saw the exciting contest between **Sandy Lyle** and **Nick Faldo**, in which Faldo was finally pipped at the post.

It is perhaps not too surprising that 'El Gran Senor' – Ballesteros, should feel so at home at Wentworth – the elegant Clubhouse was once the home of a Spanish Countess. The more mortal golfer may wish to note that beyond the castle-like exterior some excellent catering is provided. Although breakfasts are not offered, dinners can be arranged for parties of 25 or more. In fact Wentworth's 19th (or should one say 37th?) provides an admirable compliment to the quality of the golf – and that is saying something!

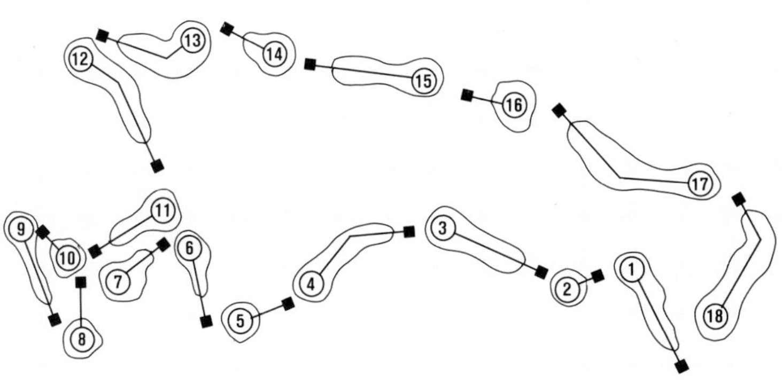

West Course

Hole	Yards	Par	Hole	Yards	Par
1	471	4	10	186	3
2	155	3	11	376	4
3	452	4	12	483	5
4	501	5	13	441	4
5	191	3	14	179	3
6	344	4	15	466	4
7	399	4	16	380	4
8	398	4	17	571	5
9	450	4	18	502	5
Out	3,361	35	In	3,584	37
			Out	3,361	35
			TOTALS	6,945	72

FERNFELL

Fernfell Golf and Country Club is located just out of Cranleigh. Guildford is 8 miles away and travelling from London is a straightforward journey on the A3 to Guildford and the A281 to Cranleigh.

Turning into the drive, one's eye is immediately drawn to the view across the parkland 18 hole course to the surrounding woodland. The drive winds up to the Club House, a 400 year old Sussex barn which we are told must be one of the most impressive club houses in the country.

During the summer the interior is light and airy. When the nights draw in, the beams, huge log fire and leaded windows combine to create a warm and welcoming atmosphere. The snooker table is an added point to remembers. Members, golf societies, green fee players and those attending company golf days all comment on the catering and the efficient friendly staff.

The 18 hole, 5236 yards, par 69 course is interspersed with fine specimen trees, white sanded bunkers and a picturesque stream runs through the course to challenge the golfer. The holes that linger in the memory are the 1st, 13th and 16th. The 1st is a par 3 from an elevated tee across the stream which runs in front of an elevated green. Elevation and elation are the key words here.

There is woodland both on the course and surrounding it, which abounds with wild life. A past golf captain who has written papers on various aspects of ornithology, has counted 72 species of birds, amongst which the mandarin dune, woodpigeon, tawny owl and green woodpecker are worth mentioning. During the spring, vast splashes of blue appear when the bluebells open. The Club House, the course and the Surrey countryside, make an exceptional golfing day. Company golf day organisers and golf societies should make particular note of Fernfell and its easy access from London.

The golf professional can organise golf clinics and make video recordings of parts of a golf day. Three en tout cas hard tennis courts and an open air swimming pool are all part of the facilities. Both ladies and gents changing rooms contain saunas.

Fernfell is one of three group golf courses, the other two are Murrayshall and Westerwood. Murrayshall is at Scone, Perthshire and also boasts a country house hotel which won restaurant of the year and Scottish chef of the year 1989. Westerwood, which opened in May is a Seve Ballesteros, Dave Thomas designed course at Cumbernauld, near Glasgow. A 57 bedroom hotel is currently under construction there. For details of these courses, please refer to their entries in this guide.

Corporate golf packages are offered at all three courses with the opportunity to place your company name and logo on a tee and book the course for your company golf day.

Come to a Fernfell welcome and a good day's golf.

Fernfell Golf and Country Club
Barhatch Lane
Cranleigh
Surrey
Tel: (0483) 276626

SURREY
COMPLETE GOLF

SURREY
(See also Gtr London)

Betchworth Park G.C.
(18) 6242 yards
Reigate Road, Dorking
(0306) 882052

Bramley G.C.
(18) 5910 yards
Godden Hill, Bramley
(0483) 892696

Burhill G.C.
(18) 6224 yards
Walton-on-Thames
(0932) 227345

Camberley Heath G.C.
(18) 6402 yards
Golf Drive, Camberley
(0276) 23258

Chipstead G.C.
(18) 5454 yards
How Lane, Coulsdon
(07375) 55781

Crondall G.C.
(9) 6000 yards
Oak Park, Heath Lane, Crondall
(0252) 850880

Dorking G.C.
(9) 5120 yards
Chart Park, Dorking
(0306) 886917

Drift G.C.
(18) 6404 yards
The Drift, East Horsley
(04865) 4641

Effingham G.C.
(18) 6488 yards
Guildford Road, Effingham
(0372) 52203

Epsom G.C.
(18) 5725 yards
Longdown Lane, Epsom
(03727) 21666

Farnham G.C.
(18) 6313 yards
The Sands, Farnham
(02518) 2109

Foxhills G.C.
(18) 6658 yards
(18) 6406 yards
Stonehill Road, Ottershaw
(093287) 2050

Gatton Manor Hotel & G.C.
(18) 6902 yards
Ockley, Dorking
(030679) 555

Guildford G.C.
(18) 6080 yards
High Path Road,
Merrow, Guildford
(0483) 63941

Hankley Common G.C.
(18) 6403 yards
Tilford, Farnham
(025125) 2493

Hindhead G.C.
(18) 6357 yards
Churt Road, Hindhead
(042873) 4614

Hoebridge G.C.
(18) 6587 yards
Old Woking Road, Old Woking
(04862) 22611

Kingswood G.C.
(18) 6821 yards
Sandy Lane, Kingswood
(0737) 832188

Laleham G.C.
(18) 6203 yards
Laleham Reach, Chertsey
(09328) 64211

Leatherhead G.C.
(18) 6069 yards
Kingston Road, Leatherhead
(037284) 3966

Limpsfield Chart G.C.
(9) 5718 yards
Limpsfield, Oxted
(088388) 2106

Mannings Heath G.C.
(18) 6404 yards
Goldings Lane, Mannings
Heath
(0403) 210228

Moor Place G.C.
(9) 3512 yards
Portsmouth Rd, Esher
(0372) 63533

New Zealand G.C.
(18) 6012 yards
Woodham Lane,
Woodham, Weybridge
(09323) 42891

North Downs G.C.
(18) 5787 yards
Northdown Road, Woldingham
(088385) 2057

Puttenham G.C.
(18) 5367 yards
Puttenham (near Guildford)
(0483) 810498

R.A.C. Country Club
(18) 6672 yards
(18) 5520 yards
Woodcote Park, Epsom
(03722) 76311

Redhill & Reigate G.C.
(18) 5193 yards
Pendleton Road, Redhill
(07372) 240777

Reigate Heath G.C.
(9) 5554 yards
Reigate Heath, Reigate
(07372) 42610

St. George's Hill G.C.
(18) 6492 yards
(9) 2360 yards
St George's Hill, Weybridge
(0932) 847758

Sandown Park G.C.
(9) 5658 yards
Moor Lane, Esher
(0372) 63340

Shillingle Park G.C.
(9) 2500 yards
Chiddingfold, Godalming
(0428) 53237

Silvermere G.C.
(18) 6608 yards
Redhill Road, Cobham
(0932) 57275

Tandridge G.C.
(18) 6260 yards
Oxted
(08833) 2274

Tyrell's Wood G.C.
(18) 6219 yards
Tyrell's Wood, Leatherhead
(0372) 376025

Walton Heath G.C.
(18) 6813 yards (Old)
(18) 6659 yards (New)
Tadworth
(073781) 2380

Wentworth G.C.
(18) 6945 yards (West)
(18) 6176 yards (East)
Virginia Water
(09904) 2201

West Byfleet G.C.
(18) 6211 yards
Sheerwater Road, West Byfleet
(09323) 43433

West Hill G.C.
(18) 6307 yards
Bagshot Road, Brookwood
(04867) 4365

West Surrey G.C.
(18) 6247 yards
Enton Green, Godalming
(04868) 21275

Windlemere G.C.
(9) 5346 yards
Windlesham Road,
West End, Woking
(09905) 8727

Woking G.C.
(18) 6322 yards
Pond Road, Hook Heath, Woking
(04862) 60053

Worplesdon G.C.
(18) 6422 yards
Heath House Road, Woking
(04867) 2277

SHORTSPOON 'The Putt' *BURLINGTON GALLERY*

GREATER LONDON

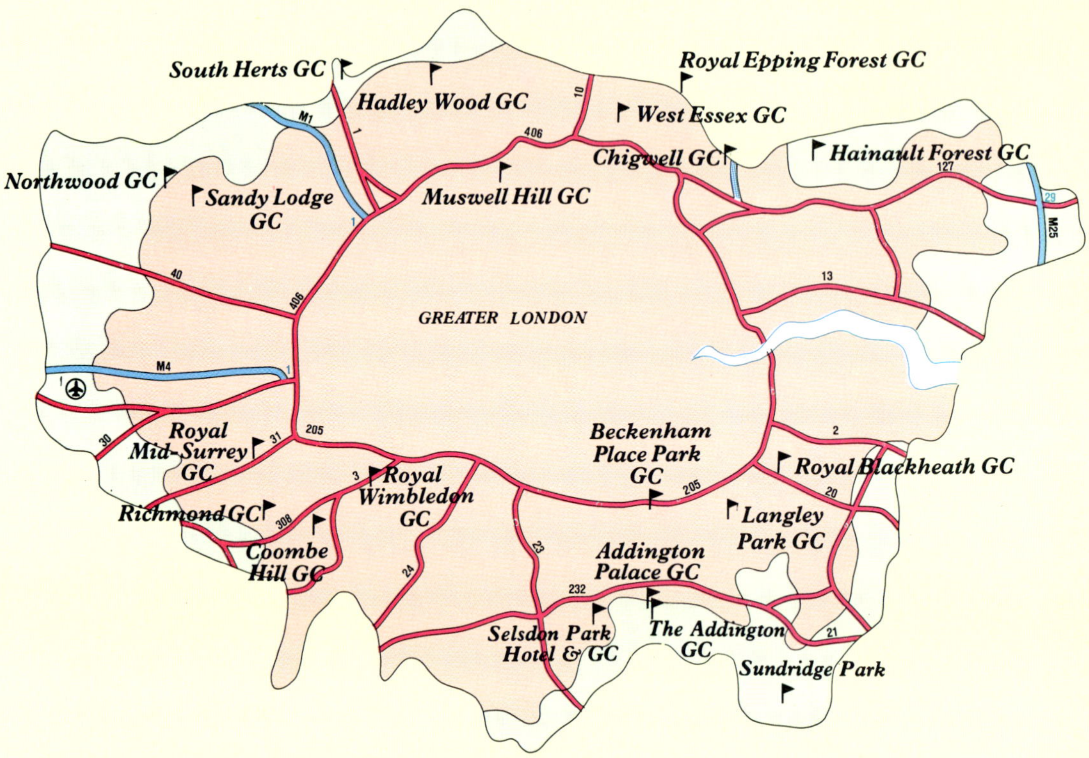

AFTER L.F. ABBOTT ***"Blackheath"*** *BURLINGTON GALLERY*

GREATER LONDON
CHOICE GOLF

Records suggest that golf was first played in England in **1608**; the venue was **Blackheath Common** in London but the participants were Scottish not English. **James I** (James VI of Scotland) and his courtiers are generally credited with bringing the game south of the border. The exact date that the English caught 'the bug' is unclear, certainly in the 18th Century it was still pretty much an alien pastime – in his first English dictionary compiled in 1755 **Dr Samuel Johnson** described golf as, 'a game played with a ball and a club or bat'.

During its formative years golf in London was largely confined to the public commons such as those at Blackheath, Clapham, Chingford and Tooting Bec, the golfers having to share their rather crudely laid-out courses with 'nurse-maids, dogs, horses and stubborn old ladies and gentlemen'.

Not surprisingly when the first Golf Clubs started to form the tendency was to retreat from the public stage. The **Royal Blackheath Golf Club**, (green fees **£25**) fittingly enough the first English Club to be founded (it dates from 1787) eventually moved from the common and now plays on a private course at Eltham. Golf is no longer played (or at least shouldn't be!) on the commons at Clapham and Tooting Bec. However, golf does survive on those at Wimbledon and Chingford, the latter being the home of **Royal Epping Forest** and where golfers are still required to wear red coats in order that they are distinguishable from other users of the common.

The majority of 'London Clubs' are for obvious reasons set in deepest suburbia and with many it is often far from clear as to whether they fall within Greater London or not. In anyone's book **Muswell Hill** is in London, which for present purposes is just as well because it's an excellent course. Measuring close to 6,500 yards, and quite undulating, it represents a fairly stiff test. Visitors can normally arrange a game here between Mondays and Fridays, green fees being approximately **£13.50**.

A cluster of good courses lie to the north west of the capital. Near neighbours of one another are **Northwood** (green fees **£11.50**) and **Sandy Lodge** (green fees **£12**). The latter could be said to be 'Sandy by name, sandy by nature'- a heathland course but it can play more like a golf links at times. Anyway, it's certainly an exceptionally fine course and hosts many top class events. Northwood is full of character: in parts parkland, in parts heathland with an exceptionally good back nine.

The other side of the M1 one finds **South Herts** and **Hadley Wood**. South Herts is somewhat tucked away in Totteridge but well worth finding. The Club can boast having had both **Henry Cotton** and **Dai Rees** among its past professionals. Hadley Wood, near Barnet is a very beautiful course, with lovely tree-lined fairways. The Clubhouse is very elegant too. At each of the four above-mentioned courses green fees are around the **£15** mark and although visitors are generally welcome, prior telephoning is advisable – London Clubs are busy!Over towards Essex, **Royal Epping Forest** has been mentioned (prior telephoning is recommended). Also within Epping Forest itself, **West Essex** is a fine parkland course (where again visitors are welcomed on weekdays) and there are two excellent public courses at **Hainault Forest**.

Before looking at golf in the south of the metroplis a word on some of London's better hotels. Finding real value isn't easy-local knowledge helps and it may be a case of rub of the green. The following appraisal is dedicated to the American and Japanese visitor – and to any of us who have a generous expense account!

In Park Lane, **The Inn on the Park 01-499 0888** is quite excellent and its restaurant, **The Four Seasons** is outstanding. Luxury of the highest order is also offered in **The Dorchester 01-629 8888** as it proudly overlooks Hyde Park (alas no golf). **The Grill Room** and **The Terrace** are both restaurants of distinction, the Walton Heath and Wentworth of the culinary circuit. The international class of the **Ritz 01-493 8181** is obvious- one can quite simply sniff the style. Nearby, **Browns 01-493 6028** is contrastingly English and justifiably proud of it. A few more? Well how about **The Savoy 01-836 4343**, note the delightful settings of its restaurants **The Grill Room and The River Restaurant**. Another member of the Savoy group is **Claridges 01-629 8860**, traditional but extremely popular among the lunching fraternity of the city's businessmen.

For people not wishing to stay in Central London these hotels may be of some help: in Hadley Wood **The West Lodge Park 01-440 8311** is a superb 19th Century mansion – very convenient for the many courses of South Hertfordshire. A galleried hall is one of the features of **The Mansion House at Grim's Dyke 01-954 4227**. The former home of W.S.Gilbert this hotel is located in Harrow Weald – ideal for playing (or speculating) at Moor Park.

Among the city's leading restaurants are the Roux Brothers **Le Gavroche (01-408 0881)** and **Rue St Jacques (01-637 0222)** (very French), and the Hungarian **Gay Hussar (01-437 0973).** For lovers of seafood try **Le Suquet (01-581 1785)** or **La Croisette (01-373 3694)**. A little less expensive than London's top restaurants but still very good are **Gavvers (01-730 598)** (French), **Simpsons (01-836 9112)** (exceedingly English) and **Leith's (01-229 4481)** which sounds perfect for golf historians. Enough feeding – back to the fairways.

Those looking for a game in south west London might consider looking in the Wimbledon area where there are several Clubs; **Royal Wimbledon** is just about the best course in London but golfers should definitely telephone before making any fixed plans. It may be easier to arrange a game (at least during the week) at the **London Scottish Club**, located two miles from Wimbledon railway station. A little further out at Richmond, games can be enjoyed at **Royal Mid Surrey** (green fees **£15**) and at **Richmond Golf Club** with its surperb Georgian Clubhouse. A mention must be made here of **Cannizaro House (01-879 1464)**, a truly excellent hotel on Wimbledon Common, which is perfect for the London and Surrey golfer, or indeed any golfer!

Due south of London the Croydon area is another that is thick with Clubs. **Addington** is generally consider the best, a lovely heathlandcourse (fees approximately **£14**), but **Addington Palace** is also well thought of, as indeed is **Croham Hurst** (green fees **£14**). To make up a four, especially if one requires a base, **Selsdon Park** must be the selection. A delightful parkland course set around the Selsdon escarpment. Seldson Park is very popular with societies and with prior booking visitors are welcome throughout the week, fees for a day's golf being **£17**, visitors welcome Mondays to Fridays.

Elsewhere in the south east there is a particularly attractive public course at **Beckenham Place Park** (cheap green fees) and a final mention of course for **Royal Blackheath**. The Club has a great sense of history and the course is full of character. The 18th heathland course (fees approximately **£14**), but **Addington** hedge to the green. In some ways it's unfortunate that the Club ever had to leave its famous common. Blackheath village is full of charm – but then the author of this tome may just be a little biased!

CANNIZARO HOUSE

London's first Country House Hotel has now been operating for over two years, and in this time the hotel has established a reputation for offering the highest standards of service, cuisine and comfort.

Cannizaro House enjoys a wonderfully peaceful setting overlooking Wimbledon Common at the front and the sweeping lawns and woods of Cannizaro Park's 34 acres to the rear, and yet it is only a few miles from all the amenities of Central London. Since 1727, when the known history of the house begins, it has been lived in and visited by the rich and famous, including Prime Minister William Pitt, Lord Auckland, Lord Tennyson and Oscar Wilde. It was purchased in 1986 by Thistle Hotels, and since then has undergone a £3.7 million refurbishment.

Cannizaro House has 48 bedrooms, all furnished in English country house style with pretty chintzes, soft colours for the carpets, sofas and chairs, and elegant marble and brass fittings in all the ensuite bathrooms.

The public rooms are elegant and spacious while three private rooms overlooking the park are ideal for meetings, luncheons and dinners.

The 45 seat restaurant and Cannizaro House's extensive wine cellar are playing a major role in establishing the property's reputation. The style of cooking is described as 'cuisine moderne – light, imaginative and using the very best and freshest ingredients.' Impeccably presented, dishes are works of art.

Near Cannizaro House keen golfers can find the London Scottish Golf Club, Wimbledon Common Golf Club, the Royal Wimbledon Golf Club and Richmond Park Golf Club.

Luxury, elegance and peace in a country setting, yet only eight miles from Hyde Park Corner, make Cannizaro House unique among London hotels.

Cannizaro House,
West Side, Wimbledon Common,
London WIY 1PG.
Tel: 01 879 1464
Fax: 01 879 7338

GREATER LONDON
COMPLETE GOLF

GREATER LONDON
(Including Middlesex)

Addington G.C.
(18) 6242 yds
Shirley Church Road, Croydon
(01) 777 6057

Addington Court G.C.
(18) 5577 yds (Old)
(18) 5513 yds (New)
Featherbed Lane, Addington, Croydon
(01) 657 0281

Addington Palace G.C.
(18) 6410 yds
Gravel Hill, Addington, Croydon
(01) 654 3061

Arkley G.C.
(9) 6045 yds
Rowley Green Road, Barnet
(01) 449 0394

Ashford Manor G.C.
(18) 6372 yds
Fordbridge Road, Ashford
(0784) 255940

Banstead Downs G.C.
(18) 6169 yds
Burdon Lane, Belmont, Sutton
(01) 642 2284

Beckenham Place Park G.C.
(18) 5722 yds
Beckenham Hill Road, Beckenham
(01) 650 2292

Bexley Heath G.C.
(9) 5239 yds
Mount Road, Bexley Heath
(01) 303 6951

Brent Valley G.C.
(18) 5426 yds
Church Road, Hanwell W7
(01) 567 1287

Bushey G.C.
(9) 6,000 yds
High Street, Bushey
(01) 950 2215

Bush Hill Park G.C.
(18) 5809 yds
Winchmore Hill, N21
(01) 360 5738

Chigwell G.C.
(18) 6279 yds
High Road, Chigwell
(01) 500 2059

Chingford G.C.
(18) 6309 yds
158 Station Road, Chingford E4
(01) 529 5708

Chislehurst G.C.
(18) 5128 yds
Camden Place, Chislehurst
(01) 467 2782

Coombe Hill G.C.
(18) 6286 yds
Kingston Hill
(01) 942 2284

Coombe Wood G.C.
(18) 5210 yds
George Road, Kingston Hill
(01) 942 0388

Coulsdon Court G.C.
(18) 6030 yds
Coulsdon Road, Coulsdon
(01) 660 0468

Crews Hill G.C.
(18) 6208 yds
Cattlegate Road, Crews Hill, Enfield
(01) 363 6674

Croham Hurst G.C.
(18) 6274 yds
Croham Road, South Croydon
(01) 657 2075

Cuddington G.C.
(18) 6282 yds
Banstead Road, Banstead
(01) 393 0952

Dulwich & Sydenham Hill G.C.
(18) 6051 yds
College Road, SE21
(01) 693 3961

Dyrham Park G.C.
(18) 6369 yds
Galley Lane, Barnet
(01) 440 3361

Ealing G.C.
(18) 6216 yds
Perivale Lane, Greenford
(01) 997 0937

Elstree G.C.
(18) 5245 yds
Watling Street, Elstree
(01) 953 6115

Eltham Warren G.C.
(9) 5840 yds
Bexley Road, Eltham SE9
(01) 859 7909

Enfield G.C.
(18) 6137 yds
Old Park Road South, Windmill Hill, Enfield
(01) 363 3970

Finchley G.C.
(18) 6411 yds
Frith Lane, NW7
(01) 346 2436

Fulwell G.C.
(18) 6490 yds
Hampton Hill, TW12 1JX
(01) 977 2733

Greenford G.C.
(9) 4418 yds
Rockware Avenue, Greenford
(01) 578 3949

Grim's Dyke G.C.
(18) 5598 yds
Oxhey Lane, Hatch End, Pinner
(01) 428 4539

Hadley Wood G.C.
(18) 6473 yds
Beech Hill, Hadley Wood, Barnet
(01) 449 4328

Hainault Forest G.C.
(18) 5754 yds (No.1)
(18) 6445 yds (No.2)
Chigwell Row, Hainault Forest
(01) 500 2131

Hampstead G.C.
(9) 5812 yds
Winnington Road, N2
(01) 455 7089

Harefield Place
(18) 5711 yds
The Drive, Harefield Place, Uxbridge
(0895) 31169

Hartsbourne G. & C.C.
(18) 6305 yds
(9) 5432 yds
Bushey Hatch, WD2
(01) 950 1113

Haste Hill G.C.
(18) 5787 yds
The Drive, Northwood
(09274) 26485

Hendon G.C.
(18) 6241 yds
Devonshire Road, NW7
(01) 346 6023

Highgate G.C.
(18) 5964 yds
Denewood Road, Highgate N6
(01) 340 1906

Hillingdon G.C.
(9) 5469 yds
18 Dorset Way, Hillingdon
(0895) 33956

Home Park G.C.
(18) 6497 yds
Hampton Wick, Kingston
(01) 977 2423

Horsenden Hill G.C.
(9) 3236 yds
Woodland Rise, Greenford
(01) 902 4555

Hounslow Heath G.C.
(18) 5820 yds
Staines Road, Hounslow
(01) 570 5271

Ilford G.C.
(18) 5710 yds
Wanstead Park Road, Ilford
(01) 554 2930

Langley Park G.C.
(18) 6488 yds
Barnfield Wood Road, Beckenham
(01) 650 2090

Leaside G.C.
(9) 4978 yds
Picketts Lock Centre, Edmonton
(01) 803 3611

London Scottish G.C.
(18) 5486 yds
Windmill Enclosure, Wimbledon Common SW19
(01) 788 0135

Magpie Hall Lane G.C.
(9) 5538 yds
Magpie Hall Lane, Bromley
(01) 462 7014

Malden G.C.
(18) 6735 yds
Traps Lane, New Malden
(01) 942 0654

Mill Hill G.C.
(18) 6309 yds
Barnet Way, Mill Hill NW7
(01) 959 2339

Mitcham G.C.
(18) 5935 yds
Carshalton Road, Mitcham Junction
(01) 648 4197

Muswell Hill G.C.
(18) 6470 yds
Rhodes Avenue, Wood Green N22
(01) 888 1764

North Middlesex G.C.
(18) 5611 yds
Friern Barnet Lane, N20
(01) 445 1604

Northwood G.C.
(18) 6464 yds
Rickmansworth Road, Northwood
(09274) 25329

Oaks Sports Centre G.C.
(18) 5873 yds
Woodmansterne Road, Carshalton
(01) 643 8363

Old Ford Manor G.C.
(18) 6473 yds
Hadley Green, Barnet
(01) 440 9185

GREATER LONDON
COMPLETE GOLF

Perivale Park G.C.
(9) 5334 yds
Ruislip Road East, Greenford
(01) 578 1693

Pinner Hill G.C.
(18) 6293 yds
South View Road, Pinner Hill
(01) 866 0963

Purley Downs G.C.
(18) 6237 yds
Purley Downs Road, Purley
(01) 657 8347

Richmond G.C.
(18) 6020 yds
Sudbrook Park, Richmond
(01) 940 4351

Richmond Park G.C.
(18) 5971 yds
(18) 5925 yds
Richmond Park, SW15
(01) 940 3205

Roehampton G.C.
(18) 6057 yds
Roehampton Lane, SW15
(01) 876 5505

Royal Blackheath G.C.
(18) 6216 yds
Court Road, Eltham SE9
(01) 850 1795

Royal Epping Forest G.C.
(18) 6620 yds
Forest Approach, Chingford E4
(01) 529 2195

Royal Mid-Surrey G.C.
(18) 6331 yds (Outer)
(18) 5446 yds (Inner)
Old Deer Park, Richmond
(01) 940 1894

Royal Wimbledon G.C.
(18) 6300 yds
29 Camp Road, Wimbledon SW19
(01) 946 2125

Ruislip G.C.
(18) 5235 yds
Ickenham Road, Ruislip
(0895) 638835

Sandy Lodge G.C.
(18) 6340 yds
Sandy Lodge Lane, Northwood
(09274) 25429

Selsdon Park Hotel G.C.
(18) 6402 yds
Addington Road, Sanderstead
(01) 657 8811

Shirley Park G.C.
(18) 6210 yds
Addiscombe Road, Croydon
(01) 654 1143

Shooters Hill G.C.
(18) 5718 yds
Eaglesfield Road, SE18
(01) 854 6368

Shortlands G.C.
(9) 5261 yds
Meadow Road, Shortlands, Bromley
(01) 460 8828

Sidcup G.C.
(9) 5692 yds
Hurst Road, Sidcup
(01) 300 2150

South Herts G.C.
(18) 6470 yds
Links Drive, Totteridge, N20
(01) 445 2035

Stanmore G.C.
(18) 5925 yds
Gordon Ave, Stanmore
(01) 954 2599

Strawberry Hill G.C.
(9) 4762 yds
Wellesley Road, Twickenham
(01) 894 0165

Sudbury G.C.
(18) 6282 yds
Bridgewater Road, Wembley
(01) 902 3713

Sundridge Park G.C.
(18) 6410 yds (East)
(18) 6027 yds (West)
Garden Road, Bromley
(01) 460 0278

Surbiton G.C.
(18) 6211 yds
Woodstock Lane, Chessington
(01) 398 3101

Thames Ditton & Esher G.C.
(9) 5415 yds
Portsmouth Road, Esher
(01) 398 1551

Trent Park G.C.
(18) 5971 yds
Bramley Road, Southgate N14
(01) 366 7432

Twickenham G.C.
(9) 6014 yds
Staines Road, Twickenham
(01) 979 0032

Wanstead G.C.
(18) 6211 yds
Overton Drive, Wanstead E11
(01) 989 3938

West Middlesex G.C.
(18) 6242 yds
Greenford Road, Southall
(01) 574 3450

Whitewebbs G.C.
(18) 5755 yds
Clay Hill, Enfield
(01) 363 4458

Wimbledon Common G.C.
(18) 5486 yds
Camp Road, Wimbledon Common SW19
(01) 946 7571

Wimbledon Park G.C.
(18) 5465 yds
Home Park Road, Wimbledon SW19
(01) 946 1002

Woodcote Park G.C.
(18) 6624 yds
Meadow Hill, Coulsdon
(01) 668 2788

Wyke Green G.C.
(18) 6242 yds
Syon Lane, Isleworth
(01) 560 8777

CHARLES PYNE 'Wimbledon Common' *BURLINGTON GALLERY*

SELSDON PARK

Set high in the rolling hills of the Surrey countryside Selsdon Park combines the ancient virtues of hospitality and courtesy with the modern attributes of efficiency and friendliness.

The estate was purchased by the present owner's father and converted into an hotel in 1925. Additions were made during the thirties, and again in the eighties to include a modern courtyard wing and a tropical leisure complex. The hotel now has 170 bedrooms and suites and a considerable range of conference and banqueting rooms.

An outstanding asset to Selsdon Park is the 18 hole championship golf course laid out in 1929 by five-times British Open Champion, J H Taylor. Originally cut out of the thick forest which clothed this part of the Surrey Hills, the course has been extended over the years, but the layout remains substantially as it was sixty years ago. Covering 6402 yards, this course is not perhaps for the novice, although it provides a stimulating challenge to low and high handicappers alike.

A round or two on this interesting course prepares the golfer to sample the pleasures of luncheon or dinner in the Restaurant, or the more informal cuisine of the Phoenix Brasserie and Grill which is open from Monday to Friday The traditional Bar Lounge, warmed in winter by crackling logs, provides old world comfort while the contemporary atmosphere of the Phoenix Bar makes it an ideal place to sample the wide range of cocktails available.

Golfing weekends here are a delight, and there is plenty to occupy the time of a non-golfing partner. There is a heated outdoor swimming pool (open from May to September), a jogging trail, two hard tennis courts and two grass courts (floodlit as necessary), boules pitch and croquet lawn. A large billiard room containing four full sized snooker tables remains open for the use of resident guests until 1 am. Horse riding can be organised at a stables nearby. The architect-designed Leisure Complex contains a well-equipped gymnasium and squash courts, providing opportunities for vigorous exercise, while the tropical swimming pool, sunbeds, steambath, sauna and jacuzzi provide less strenuous pleasures.

Selsdon Park Hotel has an almost unbeatable combination of sporting and leisure facilities to offer the golfer and non-golfer alike, together with all the amenities of a 4-star hotel.

Selsdon Park Hotel
Sanderstead,
South Croydon,
Surrey CR2 8YA.
Tel: 01-657 8811
Fax: 01-651 6171

HERTFORDSHIRE, BEDFORDSHIRE & ESSEX

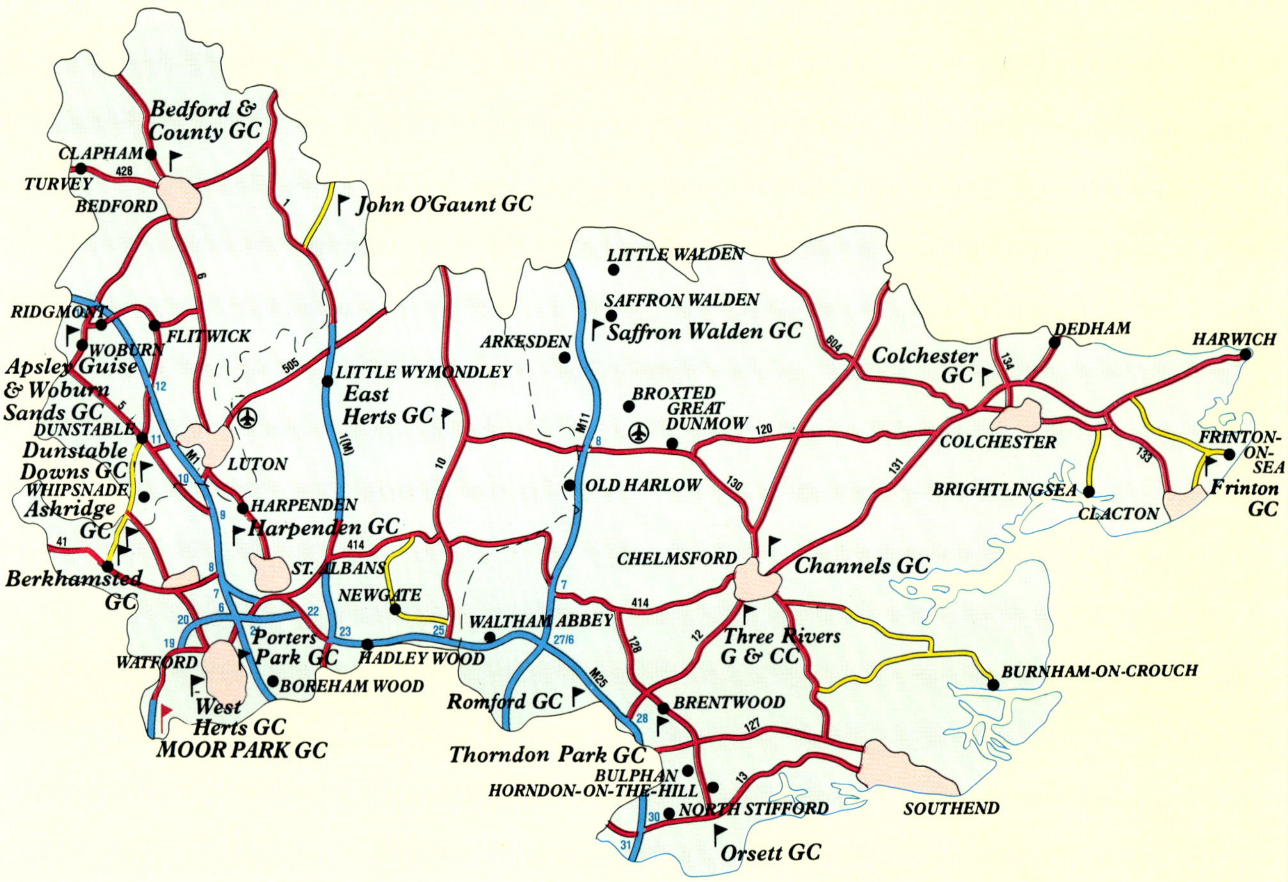

"*Putting*" *BURLINGTON GALLERY*

HERTFORDSHIRE, BEDFORDSHIRE & ESSEX

CHOICE GOLF

Unfortunately, for all too many, the first and often lasting impression of a place can be determined by the great blue ribbons that now stretch the length and breadth of the country – Britain's ever expanding motorway network. The **M1** (not to mention the **M25**) cuts through the heart of **Hertfordshire** and slices off the left ear of **Bedfordshire**. Between London and Luton it is a fearsome animal at the best of times and passing beyond these two counties one often draws a sigh of relief. The greater expanse of **Essex** fares a little better escaping with a few nasty scratches, but in all three counties the deeper realms are not as often explored as they might be, except, needless to say, by those who live there.

The golfing breed is a little more fortunate than most, in every country in Britain he, and she, can visit golf courses that are tucked away in the most secluded and tranquil of settings and Hertfordshire, Bedfordshire and Essex are certainly no exceptions to the rule.

HERTFORDSHIRE

A glance at the map tells you that **Ashridge** (green fees **£20** a day) in Hertfordshire isn't all that great a distance from London and the **M1** but it occupies a particularly peaceful spot and the approach road which runs alongside **Berkhamsted Golf Club** (Green fees **£19** a day) passes through some glorious countryside – the kind that once covered much of this part of the world. Both are delightful heathland/parkland courses. **Berkhamsted** is best known for its conspicuous absence of bunkers, though like Royal Ashdown Forest in Sussex has more than enough hazards to test any golfer, while **Ashridge** is perhaps most famed for its long association with **Henry Cotton**, for many years the Club's professional. Both courses are decidedly worth a visit though at each prior arrangement with the Secretary is essential. A day's golf is priced at approximately **£15-£20**.

In Berkhamsted, **The Swan Inn (04427) 5832** is a great little place to stay, so convenient for the delights of Ashridge and South Bedfordshire. In Whipsnade, the Zoo is excellent while the downs nearby are a good place to get rid of some energy. Hit a golf ball from the pinnacle of the Dunstable Downs and see how far it slices (second thoughts, better not you may wing a hang glider). In Dunstable's town centre **The Old Palace Lodge (0582) 62201** is well worth a visit.

BEDFORDSHIRE

Bedfordshire is much less endowed in terms of numbers of courses but in **John O'Gaunt and Dunstable Downs** it has two of the finest courses in Southern England. The former, located at Sandy was the venue for the 1966 English County Finals. A parkland course, the club welcomes visitors throughout the week: a day's golf being priced at **£14** midweek, **£20** at weekends. John O'Gaunt has an additional 18 holes, the **Carthagena** course, which though some 500 yards shorter at just under 6,000 yards is kept in similarly superb condition.

The **Dunstable Downs** course is laid out on high ground, offering remarkably extensive views – both Surrey to the south and Warwickshire to the north west can be sighted. A downland type course, visitors are received Monday to Fridays at a cost of **£15** per day.

Elswhere in the county **Aspley Guise and Woburn Sands** (the more famous Woburn Golf and Country lies over the border in Buckinghamshire, is another that provides far reaching views and at which a game can be enjoyed seven days of the week. Also of note is the **Bedford and County Golf Club** just north of the county town off the **A6**.

In Woburn some excellent hotels can be found as well as the delightful House and game reserve. The **Paris House (0252) 290692** is an outstandingly good restaurant while the **Bedford Arms (0525) 290449** is a welcoming Georgian coaching inn. **The Black Horse** and **The Bell** are good pubs to visit while if your appetite is large after a days golf visit **Crispins (052525) 516**, good value. Outside the town itself in Flitwick, the 17th Century **Flitwick Manor (0525) 712242** is very good and the restaurant is also excellent. En route to the county town the **Rose & Crown (052528) 245** in Ridgmount serves a good pint and bar snacks. In Bedford itself we call upon the services of the Moat House group – **The Bedford Moat House (0234) 55131**. For grander accommodation **The Woodlands Manor (0234) 63281** in Clapham offers a delightful hotel with a good restaurant. Finally, in the corner of Bedfordshire Turvey offers two restaurants, **The Three Fyshes (02306) 604** and **Laws (023064) 655**; some accommodation is available in the latter.

ESSEX

Although one of England's larges counties, **Essex** possesses a relatively small number of top class courses, however within that category fall **Thorndon Park** (2 miles South of Brentford) and **Orsett** (2 miles East of Grays and in the wonderfully named area of Mucking and Fobbing). Each can be reached via the **A128**. Thorndon Park, as its name suggests, is a parkland type course whereas Orsett is much more of the heathland variety with sandy subsoil. Both welcome visitors during the week, a game being priced at around **£12**.

In a similar vein to Hertfordshire a number of the county's better courses are being gradually swallowed up by Greater London, the fine parkland course at **Abridge** being one of them, now lying the 'wrong side' of the M25 (as does the famous course of **Epping Forest**). **Romford** is one that holds its Essex identity. A very attractive course and well bunkered too. Visitors are again received during the week for similar fees to Thorndon and Orsett.

Further afield both **Colchester** (the oldest town in England) and **Saffron Walden** have courses set in very pretty surroundings and for lovers of seaside golf there is a pleasant (though windy!) course at **Frinton-on-Sea**. Finally, for those visiting Chelmsford the **Channels Golf Club** with its superb Elizabethan Clubhouse can be recommended along with **The Three Rivers Golf and Country Club** nearby in Purleigh (two courses here).

Essex is blessed with many outstanding hotels and restaurants. A number of thoughts for the 19th hole emerge. Dedham presents an ideal starting point. Here we find the superb **La Talbooth (0206) 323150**. This is a monument to good food, an ideal place to celebrate. Close by, also in Dedham, **The Maison Talbooth (0206) 322367** offers stylish accommodation. This delightful village with its views of the Stour also offers the **Dedham Vale Hotel (0206) 322273** and its first class restaurant. They are also convenient for many Suffolk courses. Resisting the temptation to venture further up the Stour and discover the delights of Constable's country we arrive at the coast and Harwich – heading directly for the **The Pier (0225) 241212**, here as you may suspect the seafood is the speciality of the house. Golfers taking in the course at Frinton may wish to sample a local hotel, **The Rock Hotel (0225) 677194**. The area remains quiet and its sandy beaches and its golfcourse appeal.

HERTFORDSHIRE, BEDFORDSHIRE & ESSEX
CHOICE GOLF

Further up the coast in Brightlingsea a restaurant and a pub should be pointed out. **Jacobs (020630) 2113** is the restaurant while the **Cherry Tree** is the pub.

Brentford is our next port of call – where the **Brentwood Moat House (0277) 225252** is a really good example of this chain of hotels. Another one is locally situated in North Stifford – **The Stifford Moat House, (0375) 390909** convenient for the motorway network, but don't worry it's not a bad setting at all. An excellent pub to recommend in the area is situated at Horndon-on-the-Hill, **The Bell**.

Remaining in Essex and following the M25 to Waltham Abbey, the burial place of King Harold, also the home of a charming restaurant **Blunks (0992) 712352**. More thoughts and in Arkesden a thatched pub **The Axe & Compasses** provides good food and a cheerful hostelry. Saffron Walden offers the **Saffron Hotel (0799) 22676** – nothing grand, but extremely comfortable with a well thought of restaurant. Another Walden this time a Little one, north of Saffron; in the quiet village lies **The Crown** – good bar food. Another Essex hotel handy for a motorway, this time the M11 is **The Green Man (0279) 442521** in Old Harlow – opposite the village green the hotel totally belies the proximity of the nearby autoroute. Not that close to the golfcourses, but well worth a trip is **The Whitehall Hotel (0279) 850603** in Broxted where the restaurant is excellent.

In Great Dunmow, where the legendary Flitch trials take place, is **The Saracens Head Hotel (0371) 3901** – smallish but very pleasant. If you are rushing home and cannot spend a night in the area then dinner at **The Starr (0371) 4321** is a possibility. Incidentally for those unfamiliar with the Flitch trials, the basic idea is to test the suitability of man with woman. Not apparently a necessity for selecting one's golf partner though!

There is certainly no shortage of golf courses in **Hertfordshire**. In the 'upper realms' of the county Harpenden, convenient for those motoring along the M1, has two fine courses, **Harpenden** and **Harpenden Common**, the former at Hammonds End being perhaps the pick of the two. **East Herts** (green fees **£12** a round). near Buntingford, is also worth noting, if travelling along the **A10**. The greater concentration of courses, however, perhaps not surprisingly, is in the area just north of London. **Moor Park**, featured a few pages on, is the most widely known though nearby **Porters Park** (in the quiet of Radlett) and **West Herts** (on the edge of Watford, yet similarly peaceful) also strongly merit attention. Both Potters Park and West Herts receive visitors during the week, fees being around the **£15** mark.

It is possible to view the county's best courses from a London base. This isn't to say, however, that a number of excellent establishments can't be found beyond the city limits; in Newgate Street, **The Ponsbourne Hotel (0707) 875221** has good leisure facilities; in Hadley Wood, **The West Lodge Park** is an elegant mansion house **01-440 8311**, while Boreham Wood carries a restaurant to note – **Signor Batti's**.

The best bet if you are playing the delightful Moor Park is the **Mansion House at Grims Dyke 01-954 4227** in Harrow Weald. St Albans and Harpenden where the traffic races through, is littered with good pubs off the busy high streets. St Albans offers its superb Cathedral and the delightful **St Michael's Manor (0727) 64444** which lies in it's shadow. Harpenden's **Moat House (05827) 64111** is a little pricey but extremely well thought of. An idea for East Herts – **The Redcoats Farmhouse (0438) 729500** at Little Wymondley – very cosy.

Finally, for golfers seeking genuine excellence – a true pinnacle perhaps – **The Briggen House Hotel (027979) 2416** and its elegant restaurant at Ware should serve admirably.

'Photograph 1890 – Harold Hilton'

MOOR PARK
CHAMPIONSHIP GOLF

I don't suppose many would dispute that the Clubhouse at St Andrews is the best known 'nineteenth in the world'. However, for the title of 'most magnificent' or 'most grand' it is doubtful whether **Moor Park** can have any serious rivals. The **Moor Park Mansion** dates from the **13th century**. In its illustrious history it has been the home of earls, dukes, cardinals, archbishops and even a queen – **Catherine of Aragon** living there in the 16th century. During the last war the Mansion was requisitioned, becoming first the headquarters of the Territorial Army, then of the A.T.S. and later of the American 2nd Airborne Corps and it was from within Moor Park that preparations were made for the invasion of **Arnhem** in **1944**.

Golf first came to Moor Park in **1923, Lord Ebury** founding the Golf Club just four years after the estate had been purchased by Lord Leverhulme. **Harry Colt** was called in to design three golf courses, two of which remain with the Club, **The High** and **The West** courses, the third now being a public course **(Rickmansworth)** although it is in fact maintained by the Moor Park Club.

The Club's current **Secretary** is **Mr. John Davies**; he may be contacted by telephone on **(0923) 773146**. The professional, **Mr.E.R. Whitehead** can also be contacted at this number. **Visitors** are welcome at Moor Park between Mondays and Fridays although it is essential to telephone the Club in advance in order to book a starting time and visitors should note that proof of handicap is required. The only general restrictions during the week are on Tuesday and Thursday mornings, when both courses are reserved for members between 8.30am and 10am. Moor Park is extremely popular with Golfing Societies and up to 110 players can normally be catered for. Those organising must make prior arrangements with the Club, written applications to be addressed to **The Secretary, Moor Park Golf Club, Rickmansworth, Herts WD3 1QN**. In 1989 the **green fee** for a full day's golf was priced at **£32**, entitling the visitor to a round over both courses. For junior golfers the fees were half the normal rate.

Situated on the north western outskirts of Greater London, Moor Park is very accessible from all parts of the country. Its precise location is off the **A404** Northwood to Rickmansworth road. Those travelling from afar should find the new **M25** of great assistance with junctions **17** or **18** probably being the best points of exit. As for **rail stations**, Moor Park is the nearest at a distance of approximately three-quarters of a mile from the Golf Club (a good uphill walk mind you!). Rickmansworth is also less than two miles away.

The major Championships staged at Moor Park are all played over the **High Course**. Measuring **6713** yards (par**72**, sss**72**) it is some 900 yards longer than the **West Course**, though this at **5815** yards (par **69**, sss**68**) is certainly no 'pushover'. Both courses, it need hardly be said, are kept in superb condition.

The **High Course** begins with a fairly straightforward, slightly uphill first but the second which dog-legs to the right, is one of the toughest 'fours' of the round. Towards the middle of the front nine a sliced tee shot will send a ball into some particularly pleasant properties whose gardens border the fairways (attempting to retrieve your ball is not to be recommended!). The back nine contains three excellent short holes including the 12th (surrounded by willows and surely one of the best par threes in the country) and rather unusually the 18th.

Within two years of the Club being founded Moor Park played host to the **1925 PGA Matchplay Championship**, won by Archie Compston. Several professional tournaments have been played since, and one of the major amateur events, the **Carris Trophy**, is staged annually at Moor Park; limited to junior golfers, winners in the past have included **Sandy Lyle** and **Ken Brown**.

Perhaps the best known game of golf at Moor Park took place back in 1928. A 72 hole challenge match was played between the American **Walter Hagen**, the leading professional of the day, and the aforementioned **Archie Compston**, one of Britain's finest players. With only one hole completed of the final round the match was all over, Hagen having been defeated **18** up with **17** to play – the greatest margin of victory ever recorded. Ironically a few weeks later Hagen won his third Open Championship at **Sandwich**, finishing three strokes ahead of Compston.

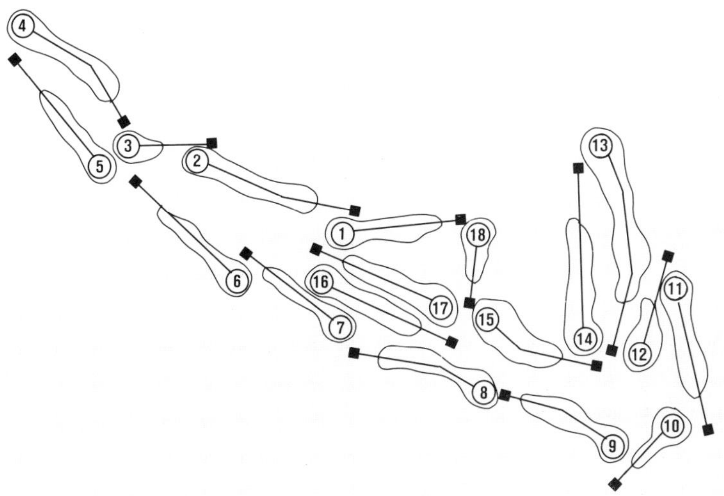

High Course

Hole	Yards	Par	Hole	Yards	Par
1	371	4	10	145	3
2	418	4	11	393	4
3	165	3	12	210	3
4	426	4	13	507	5
5	334	4	14	435	4
6	493	5	15	430	4
7	362	4	16	517	5
8	467	4	17	408	4
9	480	5	18	152	3
Out	**3,516**	**37**	**In**	**3,197**	**35**
			Out	**3,516**	**37**
			TOTALS	**6,713**	**72**

HERTFORDSHIRE, BEDFORDSHIRE & ESSEX
COMPLETE GOLF

HERTFORDSHIRE
(See Gtr. London)

Aldenham G. & C.C.
(18) 6455 yards
Radlett Road, Aldenham, Watford
(09276) 3929

Ashridge G.C.
(18) 6508 yards
Little Goddesden, Berkhamsted
(044284) 2244

Batchwood Hall G.C.
(18) 6463 yards
Batchwood Drive, St. Albans
(0727) 52101

Berkhamsted G.C.
(18) 6546 yards
The Common, Berkhamsted
(04427) 5832

Bishop's Stortford G.C.
(18) 6440 yards
Dunhow Road, Bishop's Stortford
(0279) 54715

Boxmoor G.C.
(9) 4854 yards
18 Box Lane, Hemel Hempstead
(0442) 42434

Brickendon Grange G.C.
(18) 6315 yards
Brickendon, Hertford
(099286) 258

Brookman's Park G.C.
(18) 6438 yards
Golf Club Road, Hatfield
(0707) 52487

Bushey Hall G.C.
(18) 6071 yards
Bushey Hall Drive, Bushey
(0923) 25802

Chadwell Springs G.C.
(9) 6418 yards
Hertford Road, Ware
(0920) 3647

Cheshunt Park G.C.
(18) 6608 yards
Park Lane, Cheshunt
(0992) 24009

Chorleywood G.C.
(9) 5676 yards
Common Road, Chorleywood
(09278) 2009

East Herts G.C.
(18) 6449 yards
Hammels Park, Buntingford
(0920) 821978

Harpenden G.C.
(18) 6363 yards
Hammonds End, Harpenden
(05827) 2580

Harpenden Common G.C.
(18) 5613 yards
East Common, Harpenden
(05827) 5959

Knebworth G.C.
(18) 6440 yards
Deards End Lane, Knebworth
(0438) 812752

Letchworth G.C.
(18) 6082 yards
Letchworth Lane, Letchworth
(0462) 683203

Little Hay G.C.
(18) 6610 yards
Bovingdon, Hemel Hempstead
(0442) 833798

Mid Herts G.C.
(18) 6094 yards
Gustard Wood, Wheathampstead
(058283) 2242

Moor Park G.C.
(18) 6713 yards (High)
(18) 5815 yards (West)
Moor Park, Rickmansworth
(0923) 773146

Panshangar
(18) 6538 yards
Herns Lane, Welwyn Garden City
(0707) 333350

P.L. London G.C.
(18) 6878 yards
Bedwell Park, Essendon, Hatfield
(0707) 42624

Porters Park G.C.
(18) 6313 yards
Shenley Hill, Radlett
(09276) 4127

Potters Bar G.C.
(18) 6273 yards
Darkes Lane, Potters Bar
(0707) 52020

Redbourn G.C.
(18) 6407 yards
Kingsbourne Green Lane, Redbourn
(058285) 3493

Rickmansworth G.C.
(18) 4412 yards
Moor Lane, Rickmansworth
(0923) 773163

Royston G.C.
(18) 6032 yards
Baldock Road, Royston
(0763) 42696

Stevenage G.C.
(18) 6451 yards
Aston, Stevenage
(043888) 424

Verulam G.C.
(18) 6836 yards
London Road, St. Albans
(0727) 53327

Welwyn Garden City G.C.
(18) 6200 yards
High Oaks Road, Welwyn Garden City
(0707) 325243

West Herts G.C.
(18) 6488 yards
Cassiobury Park, Watford
(0923) 36484

Whipsnade Park G.C.
(18) 6812 yards
Studham Lane, Dagnall
(044284) 2330

BEDFORDSHIRE

Aspley Guise & Woburn Sands G.C.
(18) 6115 yards
West Hill, Aspley Guise
(0908) 583596

Bedford & County G.C.
(18) 6347 yards
Green Lane, Clapham, Bedford
(0234) 52617

Bedfordshire G.C.
(18) 6172 yards
Bromham Road, Biddenham, Bedford
(0234) 61669

Cainhoe Wood G. & C.C.
(18) 6397 yards
(9) 5918 yards
Beadlow, Shefford
(0525) 60800

Dunstable Downs G.C.
(18) 6184 yards
Whipsnade Road, Dunstable
(0582) 604472

John O'Gaunt G.C.
(18) 6505 yards (John O'Gaunt)
(18) 5882 yards (Carthagena)
Sutton Park, Sandy, Biggleswade
(0767) 260360

Leighton Buzzard G.C.
(18) 5366 yards
Plantation Road, Leighton Buzzard
(0525) 373525

Millbrook G.C.
(18) 6966 yards
Millbrook, Ampthill
(0525) 712001

Mowsbury G.C.
(18) 6514 yards
Kimbolton Road, Bedford
(0234) 771042

South Beds G.C.
(18) 6342 yards
(9) 4954 yards
Warden Hill Road, Luton
(0582) 591500

Stockwood Park G.C.
(18) 5964 yards
London Road, Luton
(0582) 413704

Tilsworth G.C.
(9) 5443 yards
Dunstable Road, Tilsworth
(0525) 210721

Wyboston Lakes G.C.
(18) 5310 yards
Wyboston
(0480) 212501

ESSEX
(See also Gtr. London)

Abridge G. & C.C.
(18) 6703 yards
Stapleford Tawney, Abridge
(04028) 396

Ballards Gore G.C.
(18) 7062 yards
Gore Road, Canewdon, Rochford
(03706) 8717

Basildon G.C.
(18) 6122 yards
Clay Hill Lane, Basildon
(0268) 3849

Belfairs Park G.C.
(18) 5857 yards
Eastwood Road, Leigh-on-Sea
(0702) 525345

Belhus Park G.C.
(18) 5900 yards
Belhus Park, South Ockendon
(0708) 854260

Bentley G.C.
(18) 6766 yards
Ongar Road, Brentwood
(0277) 73179

Birch Grove G.C.
(9) 2828 yards
Layer Road, Colchester
(0206) 34276

Boyce Hill G.C.
(18) 5882 yards
Vicarage Hill, South Benfleet
(0268) 793625

Braintree G.C.
(18) 6026 yards
Kings Lane, Stisted, Braintree
(0376) 24117

Brentwood G.C.
(18) 6238 yards
King George's Playing Fields, Brentwood
(0277) 218714

Bunsay Downs G.C.
(18) 5826 yards
Woodham Walter, Maldon
(024541) 2648

Burnham-on-Crouch G.C.
(9) 5866 yards
Creeksea, Burnham-on-Crouch
(0621) 782282

Canon's Brook G.C.
(18) 6462 yards
Elizabeth Way, Harlow
(0279) 21482

Channel's G.C.
(18) 6033 yards
Belsteads Farm Lane, Little Waltham, Chelmsford
(0245) 440005

Chelmsford G.C.
(18) 5912 yards
Widford Rd, Chelmsford
(0245) 256483

Clacton G.C.
(18) 6217 yards
West Rd, Clacton-on-Sea
(0255) 421919

Colchester G.C.
(18) 6319 yards
Braiswick, Colchester
(0206) 853396

Forrester Park G.C.
(9) 5350 yards
Great Totham, Maldon
(0621) 891406

Frinton G.C.
(18) 6259 yards
Esplanade, Frinton-on-Sea
(02556) 4618

Harwich & Dovercourt G.C.
(9) 5692 yards
Parkestown Rd, Harwich
(0255) 503616

Havering G.C.
(18) 5687 yards
Lower Bedfords Rd, Romford
(0708) 22942

Maldon G.C.
(9) 6197 yards
Beeleigh Landford, Maldon
(0621) 53212

Manifolds G.C.
(18) 6450 yards
Colchester Rd, Tolleshunt D'Arcy
(0621) 860410

Maylands G.C.
(18) 6182 yards
Harold Park, Romford
(04023) 73080

HERTFORDSHIRE, BEDFORDSHIRE & ESSEX
COMPLETE GOLF

Orsett G.C.
(18) 6622 yards
Brentwood Rd, Orsett
(0375) 891352

Pipps Hill G.C.
(9) 5658 yards
Cranes Farm Rd, Basildon
(0268) 523456

Risebridge G.C.
(18) 6288 yards
Lower Bedfonts Rd, Romford
(0708) 27376

Rochford Hundred G.C.
(18) 6255 yards
Rochford Hall, Rochford
(0702) 544302

Romford G.C.
(18) 6377 yards
Gidea Park, Romford
(0708) 40986

Saffron Walden G.C.
(18) 6608 yards
Windmill Hill, Saffron, Walden
(0799) 22689

Skips G.C.
(18) 6146 yards
Tysea Hill, Stapleford Abbotts
(04023) 48234

Stoke-by-Nayland G.C.
(18) 6471 yards
(18) 6498 yards
Leavenheath, Colchester
(0206) 262836

Theydon Bois G.C.
(18) 5472 yards
Theydon Rd, Epping
(0378) 3054

Thorndon Park G.C.
(18) 6455 yards
Ingrave, Bretwood
(0277) 811666

Thorpe Hall G.C.
(18) 6259 yards
Thorpe Hall Ave, Thorpe Bay
(0702) 582205

Three Rivers G. & C.C.
(18) 6609 yds (Kings)
Stow Road, Purleigh, Chelmsford
(0621) 828631

Towerlands G.C.
(9) 5396 yards
Panfield Rd, Braintree
(0376) 26802

Upminster G.C.
(18) 5926 yards
114 Hall Lane, Upminster
(04022) 22788

Warley Park G.C.
(18) 6261 yards
(9) 3166 yards
Little Warley, Brentwood
(0277) 224891

Warren G.C.
(18) 6211 yards
Woodham Walter, Maldon
(024541) 3258

Westcliff G.C.
(18) 6609 yards
Stow Rd, Purleigh
(0621) 828631

'Golfers all'

BERKSHIRE

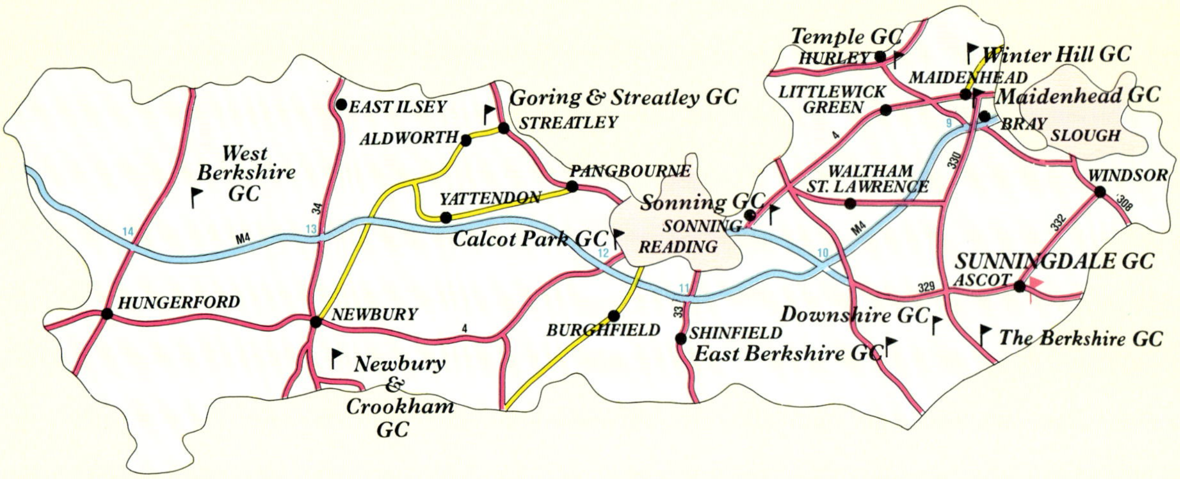

JULIAN BARROW "The Berkshire" BURLINGTON GALLERY

BERKSHIRE
CHOICE GOLF

Berkshire – or should one say 'Royal Berkshire' is often described as being cigar-shaped. Now whilst this may not say much for the present day talents of cigar-makers it does serve as a fairly rough description in as much as the County is indeed peculiarly long and thin. When it comes to surveying the County's twenty or so golf courses it is tempting to adopt another cigar analogy in that one end could be said to glow rather more brightly than the other.

To the east of the County there is a famous heathland belt and it is here that the twin pearls of **Sunningdale** and **The Berkshire** are to be found. Both Clubs possess two 18 hole courses which can stand comparison with anything that golf can offer. **Sunningdale** is featured a few pages ahead but the Berkshire should never be overlooked. Its two courses, the Red and the Blue were designed by Herbert Fowler whose other great works include Walton Heath and Saunton. They occupy **400 acres** of Crown Land over which Queen Anne's carriage used to pass en route to the hunting in Swinley Forest. The Berkshire is famed for its glorious tree-lined fairways. There is a splendid mix of mature pines, chestnuts and silver birch and both courses are kept in the most superb condition. Much of the rough consists of heather and the Berkshire provides a stern test for the wayward hitter. Visitors are welcome during the week but prior arrangement with the secretary is essential. Green fees are approximately **£14** per round, **£23** per day. **Swinley Forest** is the other outstanding heathland course in the area but as we were courteously informed, visitors are only permitted to play as guests of Members and so the stranger must look further afield for his game. Still in heather and pine country is the very attractive **East Berkshire** Course at Crowthorne. It is possible for visitors to get a game here during the week although a handicap certificate or letter of introduction from a Golf Club is required. A day's golf is likely to cost around **£18**. In close proximity is the popular **Downshire** public course. A game can be arranged for any day of the week but booking in advance is again requested. Green fees are decidedly lower than at the above mentioned courses.

Windsor is where many will choose to spend a night or two. Pride of place must go to **Oakley Court (0628) 74141**; its outstandingly comfortable rooms are complemented by splendid grounds and a delightful dining room, **The Oak Leaf**.

Elswhere in Windsor, **Sir Christopher Wren's House (07538) 61354** named after the famous Sir Christopher is excellent: there are an array of things to see in Windsor and naturally the Castle stands out, numerous pubs and some quaint restaurants are also worth visiting. In nearby Eton, antiques are the order of the day, a good wine bar in the High Street is ideal for lunch. In Ascot a number of good establishments – **The Thatched Tavern (0990) 20874** is a pleasant place to have lunch or dinner while **The Berystede Hotel (0990) 23311** is an outstanding place to stay. A good local pub is the **Slug and Lettuce** in Winkfield Row – a fine atmosphere and a charming restaurant. This area of Berkshire of course borders Surrey and we shouldn't forget its many delights. One tip is **Pennyhill Park (0726) 71774** in Bagshot – a superb hotel and very convenient for the likes of Sunningdale.

Temple's fine course can be viewed from the main **A23** Maidenhead to Henley Road. It has an interesting layout with many fine trees and lush fairways. Designed by Willie Park early this century, it was for a number of years the home of Henry Cotton. The course is always maintained in first class condition and the Club welcomes visitors with handicaps on weekdays. Fees are **£18** per day.

In Maidenhead, **Frederick's Hotel (0628) 35934** has a considerable reputation for comfort, its restaurant is also highly acclaimed while in nearby Bray, **The Waterside Inn (0628) 20691** is a quite outstanding restaurant. **The Boulters Lock Inn (0628 21291)** standing on Boulters island, is a delightful place to stay. If you are dining in Maidenhead then **Shoppenhangers Manor (0628) 23444** is a splendid French restaurant located in a charming English Manor. West of Maidenhead, Littlewich Green and the **Warrener Restaurant (062882) 2803** are very highly thought of. North of here in Hurley one finds yet another gem, **Ye Olde Bell (062882) 5881**, a very popular Norman Inn. Meandering further down the Thames other recommended Hotels included **The White Hart at Sonning (0734) 692277** which has a charming Elizabethan courtyard while also in Sonning **The French Horn (0734) 692204** is a super restaurant. In Streatley, further up the Thames, **The Swan Diplomat (0491) 873737** has a splendid riverside setting. The restaurant here is extremely good. In need of a pub? A visit to **The Bell** at Aldworth should do the trick. Another nearby local is the **Crown and Horns** at East Ilsley.

Two towns with good hotel and restaurant combinations are Pangbourne, **The Copper Inn (07357) 2244** and Yatterdon, **The Royal Oak (0635) 201325**.

On the western edge of Reading **Calcot Park** poses many interesting challenges, it can boast Guinness Book of Records fame in that one sterling fellow sprinted round the course in a motorised cart in just over 24 minutes – a more leisurely round is recommended!

Before leaving Berkshire it is worth noting one of the county's most recent additons, **West Berkshire**, situated just south of the Village of Chaddleworth. It is a splendid downland course, but not exactly one for the weak-kneed – it stretches to around the 7000 yard mark with one par five measuring well over 600 yards. (Green fees here are good value – **£6** during the week, **£10** at weekends).

THE BERKSHIRE
CHAMPIONSHIP GOLF

The residents of Ascot must number among the luckiest folk in England – at least to those who are into horseracing and golf, for right on their doorsteps lie the cream of each. They have of course three golfing pearls close at hand, Sunningdale, Wentworth and The Berkshire, the youngest of the illustrious trio.

The two eighteen hole courses of **The Berkshire**, the **'Red'** and the **'Blue'**, were designed in 1928 by **Herbert Fowler** – a master among golf architects whose other great works include Walton Heath and Saunton. They occupy some 400 acres of Crown Land over which Queen Anne's carriage used to pass en route to the hunting in Swinley Forest.

Today, both courses give the appearance of having been hewn out of a dense forest, rather in the way that the Duke and Duchess courses were created at Woburn. This, in fact, was not the case, as much clearing of the forest occurred during the First World War when the land was used for military purposes and much of the present thick woodland is of comparatively recent origin.

The Berkshire has been described as being primarily a Member's Club, this largely through the conspicuous absence of any big-time professional golf tournament. Perhaps the Club does not wish to have its tranquility stirred or its rough trampled over by hordes of excited spectators, but this does not imply that the club closes its doors to the otuside world, or makes visitors unwelcome. Indeed, the Berkshire is a busy and popular Club with a great number of Societies choosing to return year after year. For individual visitors, no less than Societies, booking with the **Secretary** is essential and **Major P.D. Clarke** is the gentleman in question. He can be contacted at the **Berkshire Golf Club, Swinley Road, Ascot, Brkshir,SL5 8AY. Tel: (0990) 21496**. It should be emphasaised that unless otherwise invited, **visitors** are only permitted to play the course during weekdays. **Green fees** for 1989 were set at **£24** for a single round with **£37** payable for a day ticket, this securing a game on both courses – something to be strongly recommended. If clubs need to be hired the professional, **Mr. K.A. MacDonald** can assist – some forewarning is advisable. He can be contacted on **(0990) 22351**.

The Berkshire can be reached easily from London. It lies just off the **A332** road between Ascot and Bagshot. The A332 can be joined from Windsor to the north and Guildford to the south, whilst motoring from Reading and the West, the **M4** should be left at junction **10** and the **A329** followed to Ascot.

The two courses are of fairly similar length – the **Red** slightly longer, measuring **6356** yards to the **Blue's 6258** yards, although the latter's par is one fewer at **71**. The Red course is perhaps the better known of the two, to some extent due to its comprising an unusual six par three, six par fours and six par fives. In any event, people probably agree that there is little to choose between the two, both in terms of beauty and in degree of difficulty.

The Berkshire is famed for its glorious tree-lined fairways. There is a splendid mix of mature pines, chestnuts and silver birch and both courses are kept in the most superb condition. Much of the rough consists of heather and the Berkshire provides a stern test for the wayward hitter.

The Club may have avoided professional tournaments, but it does play host to a number of important amateur events. The **Berkshire Trophy** is one of the annual highlights on the amateur calendar and before turning professional **Messrs. Faldo and Lyle** were both winners. It is an open event limited to three handicap players. A major ladies amateur open the **Astor Salver** is also played at the Berkshire, with a handicap limit of seven.

As for its 19th hole, the Club possesses one of the country's largest and grandest Clubhouses; furthermore, it has a reputation for providing the most stupendous roast lunches. A gentleman by the name of Sam is responsible for these veritable feasts. Well now, 18 holes on the Blue, one of 'Sam's specials' and then 18 on the Red – what better way to spend a day?

Red Course

Hole	Yards	Par	Hole	Yards	Par
1	518	5	10	187	3
2	146	3	11	338	4
3	481	5	12	328	4
4	394	4	13	484	5
5	182	3	14	436	4
6	353	4	15	477	5
7	201	3	16	221	3
8	427	4	17	529	5
9	477	5	18	177	3
Out	**3,179**	**36**	**In**	**3,177**	**36**
			Out	**3,179**	**36**
			TOTALS	**6,356**	**72**

Blue Course

Hole	Yards	Par	Hole	Yards	Par
1	217	3	10	200	3
2	340	4	11	478	5
3	477	5	12	360	4
4	152	3	13	159	3
5	316	4	14	365	4
6	481	5	15	406	4
7	363	4	16	452	4
8	405	4	17	375	4
9	310	4	18	402	4
Out	**3,061**	**36**	**In**	**3,197**	**35**
			Out	**3,061**	**36**
			TOTALS	**6,258**	**71**

SUNNINGDALE
CHAMPIONSHIP GOLF

On seeing the spectacularly beautiful 18th hole at **Killarney** during one of his visits to Ireland the late **Henry Longhurst** declared, 'What a lovely place to die'. Now whilst one rarely wishes to dwell on the subject of 'meeting our maker', golfers have been known to indulge in a considerable amount of speculation as to the type of course they might find on the arrival of such an occasion. There is a story of one heated discussion which involved, quite by chance, an Englishman, a Scotsman and an American. The latter argued with great conviction that a large number of the holes would, 'as sure as hell', resemble **Augusta,** whilst the Scotsman vehemently insisted that even the most minute deviation from the **Old Course** at **St Andrews** would constitute an act of heresy; as for the Englishman, he naturally had no doubts whatsoever that he could stroll through the Pearly Gates and meet a second **Sunningdale**.

Well perhaps the heavenly blend is a mixture of all three but in any event the gentleman in charge of the terrestrial Sunningdale is the **Secretary, Keith Almond**. Mr. Almond may be contacted on **(0990) 21681. Keith Maxwell** is the Club's resident professional and he can be reached on **(0990) 20128.**

As with neighbouring Wentworth and The Berkshire there are two eighteen hole courses, the **'Old'**, designed in 1900 by **Willie Park** and the **'New'** which was constructed by **Harry Colt** in 1922. Both are splendid, and many would say the leading examples of the famous Berkshire/Surrey heathland type course. The holes wind their way through glorious forests of conifer and pine with heather and gorse bordering each fairway. All around there are splashes of silver sand.

With its great reputation and close proximity to the capital, Sunningdale is not suprisingly very popular. Unless accompanied by a Member **visitors** are restricted to weekdays and must make prior arrangement with the Secretary. A letter of introduction is also required. All written communications should be addressed to Mr. Almond at **The Sunningdale Golf Club, Ridgemount Road, Sunningdale, Berkshire.** In **1989** the **green fee** was set at **£47**. This entitled the visitor to a full days golf, enabling a round over both courses. Sets of clubs can be hired from the professional shop should the need arise. Persons keen to organise a **Society** meeting are also advised to approach Mr. Almond via the above address. A handicap limit of 20 normally applies and the Society days are Tuesdays, Wednesdays and Thursdays.

Sunningdale is situated just off the **A30**, about 28 miles West of **London**. Motoring from the South and West the **M3**, (leaving at junction **3**) and the **M4** (junction **10**) may be of assistance, while from the North both the **A332** and the **A330** pass through nearby **Ascot**. The Club's precise location is some 300 yards from Sunningdale Railway Station.

When golfers talk of Sunningdale, invariably it is the Old Course they have in mind, this despite the fact that a large number of people consider the New to be its equal. The former has acquired such preeminence largely as a result of the many major professional and amateur tournaments that have been staged there. However the Old Course is perhaps best known for a single round of golf played by the legendary **Bobby Jones**. In qualifying for the 1926 Open Championship, which he in fact went on to win, the great man put together what has often been described as the finest 18 holes of golf ever seen. Jones' record 66 comprised twelve fours and six threes – 33 for the front nine and 33 for the back nine. More remarkably Jones played only 33 shots from tee to green and took 33 putts – as Bernard Darwin put it, 'incredible and indecent'.

In more recent years Sunningdale has repeatedly been selected to host the prestigious **Panasonic European Open**. During the 1970's the finest lady golfers assembled for the Colgate sponsored **European WPGA Championship** and in 1987 the **Walker Cup** was played at Sunningdale.

At **6341** yards **(**par **70)** the Old Course is more than three hundred yards shorter than the New **(6676** yards, par **70)**. The respective distances from the Ladies tees are **5825** yards and **5840** yards (both being par **74**). It seems somehow wrong to single out individual holes, each course possessing its own wealth of variety and charm. The views from the **5th** and **10th** tees on the Old Course are, however, particularly outstanding and the 18th also provides a spectacular closing hole as it gently dog-legs towards the green and the giant spreading oak tree, very much the symbol of Sunningdale.

Behind the famous oak tree is the Sunningdale Clubhouse. With the exception of Mondays, lunches are served daily and there are three bars. Breakfasts can be made available as can dinners to golfing parties of forty or more provided prior arrangement is made. A jacket and tie should be worn in the Dining Room.

Sunningdale's glorious setting has been described as both 'heavenly' and 'hauntingly beautiful'; certainly the golfer privileged to stroll up the final fairway on a summer's evening as the sun begins its leisurely dip can be forgiven if he amends the words of Henry Longhurst and declares 'What a lovely place to be alive!'

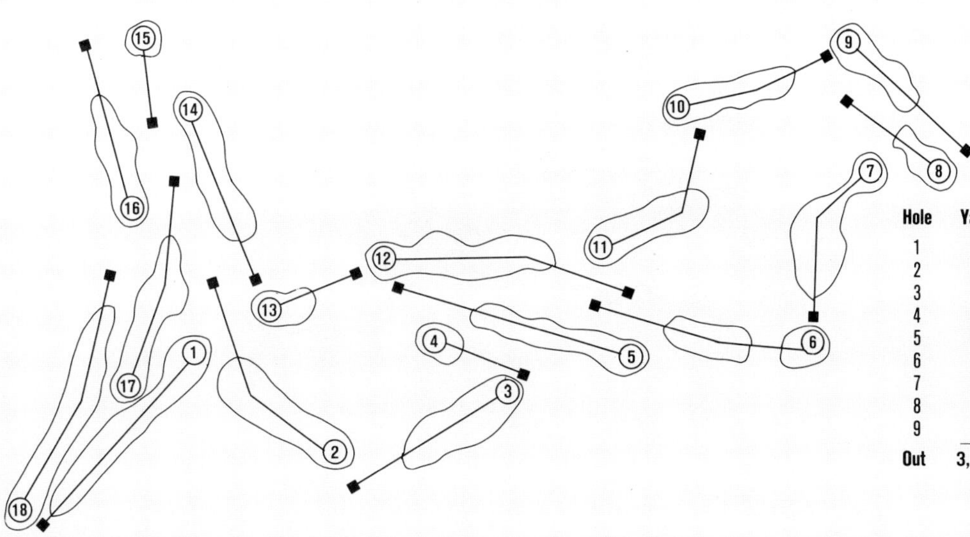

Old Course

Hole	Yards	Par	Hole	Yards	Par
1	494	5	10	463	4
2	456	4	11	299	4
3	296	4	12	423	4
4	161	3	13	178	3
5	400	4	14	477	5
6	388	4	15	226	3
7	383	4	16	423	4
8	172	3	17	421	4
9	267	4	18	414	4
Out	3,017	35	In	3,324	35
			Out	3,017	35
			TOTALS	6,341	70

BERKSHIRE
COMPLETE GOLF

BERKSHIRE

Berkshire G.C.
(18) 6356 yards (Red)
(18) 6258 yards (Blue)
Swinley Road, Ascot
(0990) 21496

Calcot Park G.C.
(18) 6283 yards
Bath Road, Calcot
(0734) 27124

Downshire G.C.
(18) 6382 yards
Easthampstead Park, Wokingham
(0344) 424066

East Berkshire G.C.
(18) 6315 yards
Ravenswood Avenue, Crowthorne
(0344) 772041

Goring &
Streatley G.C.
(18) 6255 yards
Rectory Road, Streatley-on-Thames
(0491) 873229

Hawthorn Hill G.C.
(18) 6212 yards
Drift Road, Maidenhead
(0628) 75588

Hurst G.C.
(9) 3015 yards
Davis Street, Hurst
(0734) 345143

Maidenhead G.C.
(18) 6344 yards
Shoppenhangars Road, Maidenhead
(0628) 24693

Newbury &
Crookham G.C.
(18) 5880 yards
Greenham, Newbury
(0635) 40035

Reading G.C.
(18) 6011 yards
Kidmore End Road, Reading
(0734) 472909

Royal Ascot G.C.
(18) 5653 yards
Winkfield Road, Ascot
(0990) 25175

Sonning G.C.
(18) 6310 yards
Duffield Road, Sonning-on-Thames
(0734) 693332

Sunningdale G.C.
(18) 6341 yards (Old)
(18) 6676 yards (New)
Ridgemount Road, Sunningdale
(0990) 21681

Sunningdale Ladies G.C.
(18) 3622 yards
Cross Road, Sunningdale
(0990) 20507

Swinley Forest G.C.
(18) 6001 yards
Coronation Road, South Ascot
(0990) 20197

Temple G.C.
(18) 6206 yards
Henley Road, Hurley, Miadenhead
(062882) 4795

West Berks G.C.
(18) 7053 yards
Chaddleworth, Newbury
(04882) 574

Wexham Parks G.C.
(18) 5424 yards
Wexham, Slough
(02816) 3271

Winter Hill G.C.
(18) 6432 yards
Grange Park, Cookham, Maidenhead
(06285) 27613

H. ROUNTREE 'The Penguin' *BURLINGTON GALLERY*

THE SWAN DIPLOMAT

The Swan Diplomat at Streatley nestles beneath the ancient ridgeway, in a fold of the Streatley Hills beside the River Thames. This is the Thames at its Berkshire best, as it winds through the hills, with its spectacular views and placid backwaters.

Situated in some 25 acres of grounds, including 3 acres of delightful gardens, The Swan Diplomat offers the highest standards of service and cuisine. The Riverside Restaurant is renowned for its 'a la carte' and gastronomique menus as well as its wine list. Herbs from the hotel's own garden are used, as well as organically grown vegetables, meats and fruits.

The unique character of the hotel is reflected in the Magdalen Barge, an intriguing venue for meetings and private functions. Built in the 19th century for Oxford's Magdalen College, it has been completely restored to its former glory. Guests can now sample riverborne entertainment – in traditional Oxford College style.

Each bedroom is spacious, individually designed and furnished in traditional rich mahogany. Every bedroom also has a private bathroom with a shower, a direct telephone, refreshment facilities, hair-dryers and remote controlled television.

The Reflexions Leisure Club at the hotel boasts a solarium, sauna and the latest exercise machines. Guests can even test themselves in the fitness pool against the counter-current swimming unit. For private or business functions, The Garden and Terrace Rooms are available for smaller occasions, while The Icknield Suite is available for larger presentations and meetings.

The Swan Diplomat is set amidst glorious Berkshire countryside and yet is under one hour from London. It provides an ideal base for racing at Newbury or Ascot. Keen golfers can enjoy a round or two by arrangement at quality local courses, and the charming market towns and National Trust properties nearby ensure a most pleasant stay.

Guests at The Swan are assured of good service and a warm welcome at all times.

The Swan Diplomat
Streatley on Thames,
Berkshire RG8 9HR
Tel: (0491) 873737
Fax: (0491) 872854

BUCKINGHAMSHIRE & OXFORDSHIRE

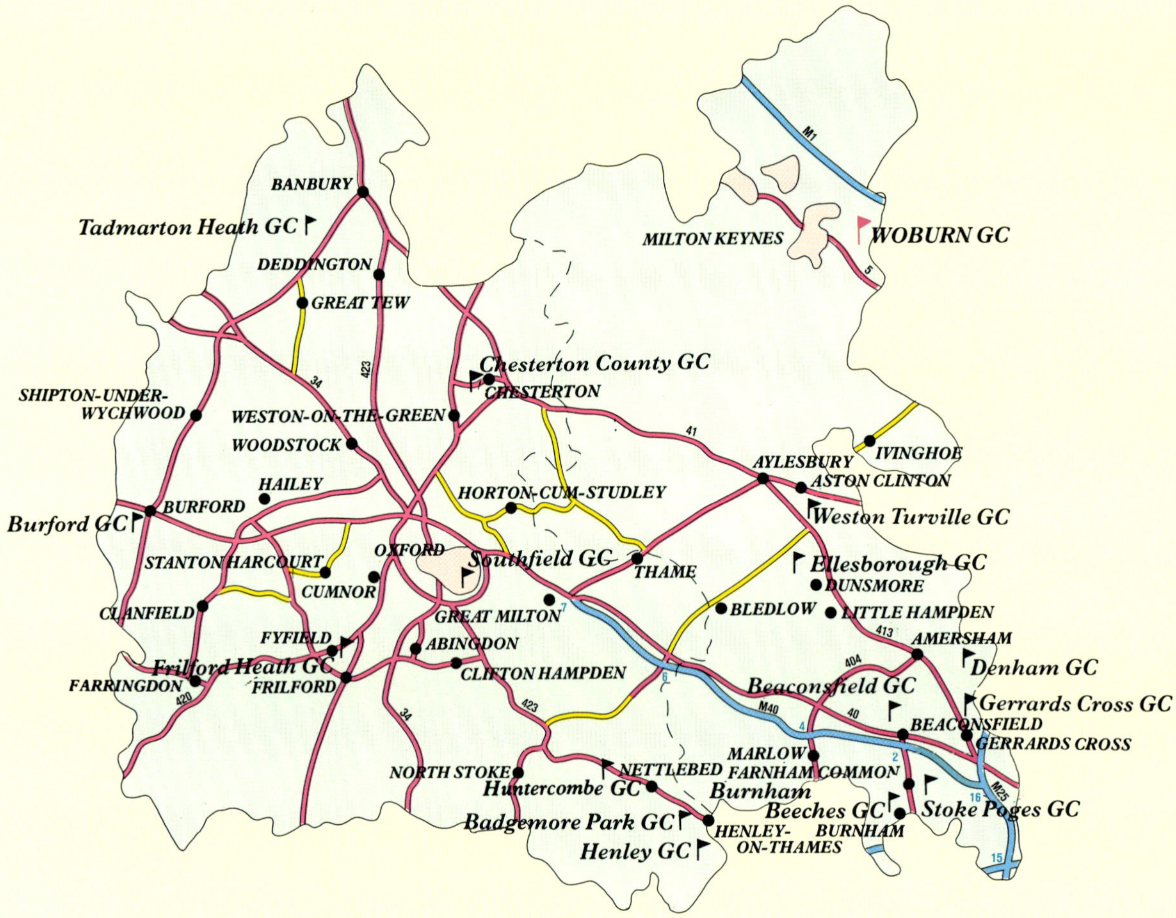

H. ROUNTREE ***"Stoke Poges"*** *SARAH BADDIEL'S BOOK GALLERY*

BUCKINGHAMSHIRE & OXFORDSHIRE

CHOICE GOLF

OXFORDSHIRE

And so to Oxfordshire. We start at **Huntercombe**, a charming Club which has enjoyed an interesting history.

In the early years of the century three rather old Daimler motor cars were used to ferry Members to and from the local station and later a thirty seater bus was acquired for the same purpose. The course itself passed through various owners – at first a property company, then an insurance company (the Norwich Union) and later **Viscount Nuffield** before finally becoming a Members Club in 1963. Situated on the edge of the Chilterns at some 700 feet above sea level there are some marvellous views accross the Oxford Plain. The green fees at Huntercombe are **£15** midweek, **£20** at the weekend.

Nearby in Henley there are two courses, the more established **Henley Golf Club** and **Badgemore Park**, a fairly new course but one that has settled down quickly. Visitors should be able to arrange a game on either course during the week, (both **£14-£15** a day).

In Henley, **The Red Lion (0491) 571261** is a commendable hotel. In Nettlebed, the **White Hart (0491) 641245** is a pleasing pub with some good value bedrooms (very handy for Huntercombe) and North Stoke offers the excellent **Springs Hotel (0491) 36687** with its first class restaurant, **The Fourways** (not Fairways).

As the Berkshire has a Red and a Blue, so **Frilford Heath** has a Red and a Green. Two exceptionally fine heathland courses, renowned for their large greens. Visitors are welcome midweek but being a popular Club prior telephoning is strongly recommended. Good food and drink can be found in nearby Fyfield at **The White Hart** and in Frilford at **Noah's Ark (0865) 391470**. A short trip to Abingdon can be recommended, here the **Upper Reaches Hotel (0235) 22311** is most welcoming.

Oxford is actually not all that far away. There are two courses either side of the town – **North Oxford** and **South Oxford**, both certainly worth a game. The latter is the home of Oxford University. **The Randolph (0865) 247481** is the pick of the Oxford hotels, and for first class restaurants, **The Cherwell Boathouse (0865) 52746** is certainly among the best. There are numerous shops (note the covered market), museums, and pubs in the town and a day in Oxford goes quickly past. Outside in Cumnor, **The Bear and Ragged Staff** serves good food while a little further afield in Stanton Harcourt **The Harcourt Arms (0865) 882192** has a tremendous atmosphere, a good restaurant, a good pint and excellent accommodation. Another fine restaurant within striking dis tance of Frilford is **The Plough** at Clanfield **(036781) 222**. A final recommendation in this area is to visit Great Milton – **Le Manoir Aux Quat' Saisons (08446) 8881** – possibly the country's finest restaurant.

Back on the fairways (suitably fed one hopes!) and in the north of Oxfordshire there is a flattish parkland course at Bicester. The **Chesterton County** Golf Club (fees are approximately **£8-£10**), and a much improved course at **Burford** (**£13**). However, the best in the north of the County is clearly **Tadmarton Heath**. At less than 6000 yards in length, it is fairly short by modern standards, but the narrow fairways and a great spread of gorse can make it a very difficult test. It also has a wonderfully remote setting. Golf can be enjoyed here between Mondays and Fridays, though advance telephoning is once again recommended.

BUCKINGHAMSHIRE

Heading into Buckinghamshire? **Woburn** stands rather alone in the far north of the county. Within a short distance of Milton Keynes, it is particularly convenient when the business meeting finishes early. It is equally convenient after a morning exploring Woburn Abbey and the famous Safari Park. The Golf and Country Cub is featured ahead, but a brief thought on where to say: in Woburn Park itself **The Paris House (0525) 290692** is highly recommended while for less expensive accommodation try the friendly **Bedford Arms (052525) 441**, a delightful coaching inn. In Apsley Guise near Woburn, the superb **Moore Place (0908) 282000** is also well worth visiting.

Heading 'down the county' **Ellesborough** is another with rather stately surroundings being sited on part of the property of Chequers. Quite a hilly course and rather testing, there are some commanding views across the Buckinghamshire countryside. The Club welcomes visitors during the week, though prior telephoning is recommended. Elsewhere in the centre of the county, there is a fairly lengthy parkland course at **Weston Turville**, south of Aylesbury. Visitors should be able to get a game here most days of the week. Also, nestling in the Chilterns is **Whiteleaf** a delightful 9-hole course.

Ideas for a 19th hole in these parts include in Ivinghoe **The Kings Head (0296) 668388** a splendid restaurant in a 17th century posting inn and two 'Bells', **The Bell (0296) 89835** in Aylesbury's market place and **The Bell (0296) 630252** in Aston Clinton (note the superb wine list here.) A couple of good pubs are **The Rising Sun** at Little Hampden and **The Fox** at Dunsmore.

It is in Southern Buckinghamshire where most of the county's better courses are to be found. **Stoke Poges** has staged many leading amateur events, not at all surprisingly, this being one of the finest parkland courses in the south of England. Several lengthy par fours are a feature of the 6700 yard layout. The Club receives visitors at weekends, although prior telephoning is essential (green fees **£15** a round).

Denham (green fees **£11** a round), is a near neighbour of Stoke Poges lying some 3 miles north of Uxbridge, and as the Club handbook will tell you 'half an hour's drive from Marble Arch'. Denham enjoys an exceptionally tranquil setting, deeply secluded amidst some glorious countryside.

In equally beautiful surroundings is the **Burnham Beeches** Golf Club, situated approximately 4 miles west of Slough. Always immaculately kept, it has some prodigiously difficult rough and staying on the fairways is to be strongly recommended. At both Burnham and Denham prior arrangement with the Secretary is preferred. Others to note in southern Buckinghamshire include **Beaconsfield** and **Gerrards Cross**, both are within fairly easy access of the capital. The cost of a game on any of the above courses tends to range between **£12-£18**, and it is probably advisable for the visitor to bring proof of handicap with him.

There are a number of comfortable hotels in the area where the dining is also up to scratch. These include **The Bell-house Hotel (0753) 887211** just outside Beaconsfield, **The Burnham Beeches Hotel (06286) 3333** a former hunting lodge – ideal for the golf course, and **The Compleat Angler Hotel (06284) 4444** at Marlow Bridge – a superb riverside setting. In Farnham Common. **Oscar's (02814) 6211** is an informal restaurant while two good pubs are **The Kings Arms** in Amersham and **The Lions** at Bledlow.

WOBURN

CHAMPIONSHIP GOLF

A magnificent Stately Home housing one of the finest art collections in the world, the largest wildlife safari park in Europe and two of the finest inland golf courses in Britain – quite a place Woburn!

The Stately Home is of course **Woburn Abbey** which since the reign of Henry V111 has been the home of the Dukes of Bedford, while the Wildlife Park and the golf courses lie within the grounds of the great estate.

In a game that prides itself on its antiquity **The Woburn Golf and Country Club** might be described as a remarkably precocious youngster. It was founded as recently as 1976 and its two courses, aptly named the **Duke's** and **Duchess**, were not opened until 1977 and 1979 respectively. In such a short period of time Woburn has acquired an enviable reputation.

In charge of all golfing matters at Woburn is **Alex Hay** whose Celtic tones are well-known to millions of television viewers. Mr. Hay acts as both Managing Director and resident professional. In the former capacity he may be contacted on **(0908) 70756** and when donning his golf professional hat Mr Hay can be reached by telephone on **(0908) 647987.**

Visitors, Societies and Company Days are all welcome from Monday to Friday at Woburn, although **prior booking** is essential. In addition visitors must be Members of recognised golf clubs and be able to provide proof of handicap. All written enquiries should be addressed to the **Managing Director, Woburn Golf and Country Club, Bow Brickhill, Milton Keynes, MK17 9LJ.** The **green fees** for **1989** were set at **55** per person per day for parties of nine and above, and **50** for parties of less than nine. This fee is inclusive of golf, coffee and lunch, and dinner can also be arranged if there are 24 people or more.

Having booked a game, travelling to Woburn ought not to present too many problems. The Club is located approximately 45 miles from London and 73 miles from Birmingham and is well-served by major roads. Both the **M1** (junction **13**) and the **A5** pass close by. For those using British Rail, **Bletchley Station**, some 4 miles away has good connections from both London and **Birmingham. Luton and Heathrow Airports** are also within fairly easy reach. The town of Woburn and the Abbey are both actually within the county of Bedfordshire while the Golf and Country Club lies a short distance over the boundary in Buckinghamshire.

Fifteen years ago if someone had suggested that a Championship Course (never mind two) could have been built on the Woburn Estate, the famous lions would probably not have been the only ones to roar. The present site was then a dense forest, with giant trees and bracken restricting vision beyond a few yards. (In fact today to gain a picture of how the whole scene looked, one has only to take a few paces off any of the fairways – even Robin Hood would have been unimpressed).

Golf architect **Charles Lawrie** was called in and plans were drawn up. The bulldozers soon arrived and from amidst the pines and the chestnuts great avenues were carved. The fairways flourished on the sandy subsoil and within two years of opening, The Duke's Course was considered fit to stage a major professional tournament. It proved a popular decision and a succession of sponsors decided to follow suit. Following its opening the Duchess matured with equal rapidity and Woburn soon possessed two precious gems.

The tournaments held at Woburn have included four **Masters Championships, the Hitachi Ladies British Open (1984)** and, in each year since 1982, **The Ford Ladies Classic**. Under the sponsorship of Dunhill, Woburn has also become something of a home for the British Masters event, which has quickly established itself as one of the most attractive fixtures in the golfing calendar.

From the back markers (or tiger tees?) the Duke's course stretches to **6883** yards (par **72**), while the Duchess measures **6616** (par **71**). The corresponding distances for the ladies are **6065** yards (par **75**) and **5831** yards (par **74**).

From their forward tees both courses are considerably reduced in length and straight hitting rather than sheer distance ought to be the chief priority – as enchanting as they may be, the woods should be avoided at all cost.

As one might expect from a modern Golf and Country Club the facilities at Woburn are excellent. The Clubhouse offers a full complement of catering, though dinners must be pre-arranged. For the sporty types there is tennis, squash and an open-air heated swimming pool. The majority of golfers, however, will probably head for one of the two Bars.....and toast the Duke and the Duchess.

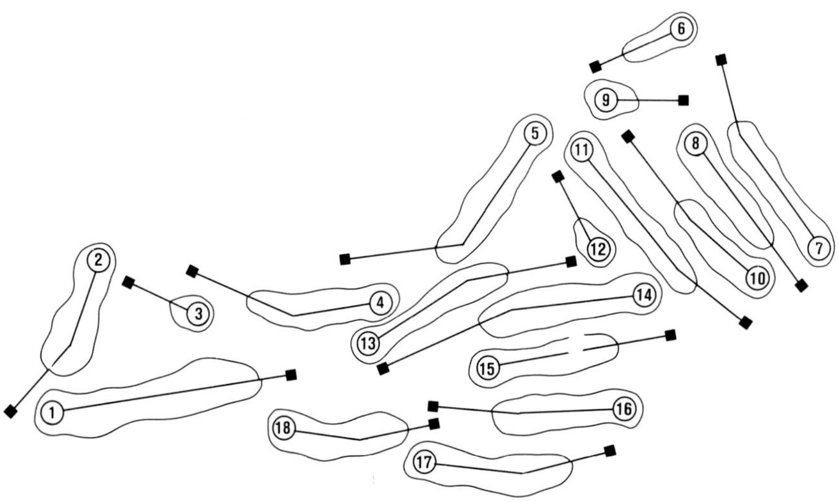

Duke's Course

Hole	Yards	Par	Hole	Yards	Par
1	514	5	10	404	4
2	385	4	11	502	5
3	134	3	12	193	3
4	395	4	13	419	4
5	510	5	14	565	5
6	207	3	15	432	4
7	464	4	16	444	4
8	409	4	17	400	4
9	177	3	18	329	4
Out	3,195	35	In	3,688	37
			Out	3,195	35
			TOTALS	6,883	72

MOORE PLACE

When Francis Moore built his elegant Georgian mansion in the tranquil Bedfordshire village of Aspley Guise in 1786 he could never have imagined it would be such a focal point for hospitality 200 years later. Thoughtfully renovated and extended, the original house now has a Victorian style conservatory restaurant, and a collection of new bedrooms which create a courtyard effect, featuring a rock garden and water cascade. The hotel's attractive day rooms – including an airy, glass roofed reception and relaxing bar-lounge – are decorated and furnished in handsome period style.

The 54 prettily decorated bedrooms all have ensuite bathrooms, direct dial telephone, colour television, tea and coffee making facilities and hairdryer.

There are 3 private function rooms in this charming Georgian house, where banquets and conferences are well provided for. The rooms are traditionally decorated, yet equipped with full audio-visual facilities.

The highly acclaimed restaurant is an outstanding success. Accomplished cooking in the modern mode can be enjoyed in the beautiful, picture windowed restaurant. Excellent cuisine is complemented by a good selection of fine wines. Moore Place is surrounded by interesting places to visit, such as the Duke of Bedford's Woburn Abbey, Dunstable Downs and Whipsnade Zoo. Woburn golf course is also nearby.

Moore Place,
Aspley Guise,
Nr Woburn, Beds MK17 8DW
Tel: (0908) 282000
Fax: (0908) 281888

HUNTERCOMBE
CHAMPIONSHIP GOLF

In all probability there are more dog legs on the course at **Huntercombe** than on any other in the British Isles. I do not however refer to an abundance of right-angled and left-angled holes, but rather to the canine breed. It is difficult to play a round at Huntercombe without coming across one of our four legged friends. Collies, labradors and gun-dogs all proudly parade the fairways, canine caddies you might say, or the wondrous hounds of Huntercombe.

Few Golf Clubs can have enjoyed as colourful a history as this charming Oxfordshire Club. Situated almost 700 feet above sea level on the edge of the Chilterns and overlooking the Oxford Plain, Huntercombe was founded in **1901. Young Willie Park** the son of the first Open Championship winner, both designed and opened the course. Park's creation met with instant approval. **Walter Travis** the great American amateur golfer said of Huntercombe: 'It is easily the best laid out links that I have ever played over anywhere,' while another commented: 'The turf on the putting greens is so excellent and the ball runs so truly that the golfer who cannot putt or learn the art of putting at Huntercombe had better resign himself to the fate of never being able to putt at all.'

In the early years of the century three rather old Daimler motor cars were used to ferry Members to and from the local station and later a thirty seater bus was acquired for the same purpose. The course itself passed through various owners – at first a property company, then an insurance company (the Norwich Union) later **Viscount Nuffield** before finally becoming a Members Club in **1963**.

Approaching a quarter of a century later the Secretary at Huntercombe is **Colonel Hutchinson**; he may be contacted by telephone on **(0491) 641207**. All written correspondence should be addressed to the Secretary at **Huntercombe Golf Club, Nuffield, Henley-on-Thames, Oxfordshire, RG9 5SL. John Draycott** is the Club's professional and he can be reached on **(0491) 641241**.

Visitors are welcome at Huntercombe after 10am during the week, but sadly cannot play the course at weekends; the cost of a day's golf in 1989 was set at **£19.50**. Golfing **Societies** are also welcome, the usual society days being Tuesdays and Thursdays. It should be added that three ball and four ball matches are discouraged with singles and foursomes strongly preferred.

The Golf Club is located approximately 7 miles from **Henley-on- Thames** and **12 miles from Reading** off the **A423**. Travelling from **London** the best route is to take the **M4** westbound leaving at exit **8** and thereafter following the Henley Road (which is in fact the **A423**). Approaching from the Midlands and the north of England the **A423** can be picked up at Oxford while those coming from the south and west of the country should head for Reading, the **A4** and **M4** assisting from the west and the **A33** helping from the south.

Huntercombe might be described as both downland and woodland in nature. When first there were very few trees making the course quite exposed and being on fairly high ground it could get rather breezy. However, many mature trees now provide shelter with a considerable spread of heather and gorse and a wide variety of wild flowers. Huntercombe is an exceptionally attractive course. From the men's tees it stretches to **6223** yards par **70** while the ladies course measures **5672** yards, par **72**. With the exception of a slope on the **3rd** hole the course is very flat, making for easy walking. Sand bunkers are few and far between though there are several grass pots and hollows. If there is one feature of the course that particularly stands out it is probably the superb greens which are always true and generally quite fast.

The 19th at Huntercombe is a splendid building built in the mid 1960s and views over much of the course can be enjoyed from the terrace. In addition to bar snacks which are available throughout the day, lunches can be prepared with prior notice and dinners may also be arranged for societies if required.

With its quiet situation on the edge of the Chilterns, Huntercombe is a delightful retreat from the nearby confusion. The mood at Huntercombe is of the kind that A.J. Balfour described when he said: 'Give me my books, my golf clubs and leisure and I would ask for nothing more'.

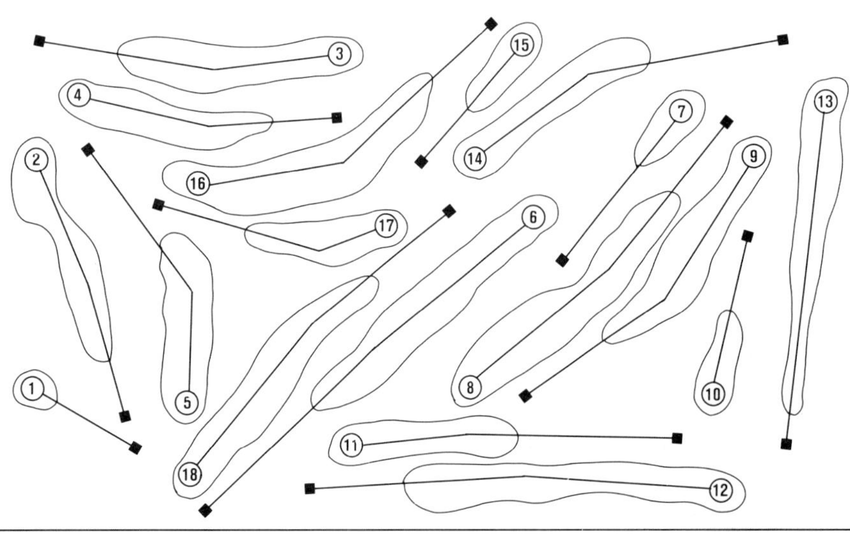

Hole	Yards	Par	Hole	Yards	Par
1	150	3	10	184	3
2	394	4	11	336	4
3	366	4	12	409	4
4	335	4	13	407	4
5	396	4	14	432	4
6	525	5	15	175	3
7	214	3	16	492	5
8	436	4	17	279	4
9	369	4	18	358	4
Out	3,185	35	In	3,072	35
			Out	3,185	35
			TOTALS	6,257	70

BUCKINGHAMSHIRE & OXFORDSHIRE
COMPLETE GOLF

BUCKINGHAMSHIRE

Abbey Hill G.C.
(18) 6193 yards
Stony Stratford, Milton Keynes
(0908) 563845

Beaconsfield G.C.
(18) 6469 yards
Seer Green, Beaconsfield
(04946) 6545

Buckingham G.C.
(18) 6082 yards
Tingewick Road, Buckingham
(0280) 815566

Burnham Beeches G.C.
(18) 6415 yards
Green Lane, Burnham
(06286) 61448

Chesham & Ley Hill G.C.
(9) 5147 yards
Ley Hill, Chesham
(0494) 784541

Chilton Forest G.C.
(9) 5724 yards
Halton, Aylesbury
(0296) 631267

Datchet G.C.
(9) 5978 yards
Buccleuch Road, Datchet
(0753) 43887

Denham G.C.
(18) 6439 yards
Tilehouse Lane, Denham
(0895) 832022

Ellesborough G.C.
(18) 6207 yards
Butler's Cross, Aylesbury
(0296) 622114

Farnham Park G.C.
(18) 5847 yards
Park Road, Stoke Poges, Slough
(06286) 61521

Flackwell Heath G.C.
(18) 6150 yards
High Wycombe
(06285) 20929

Gerrards Cross G.C.
(18) 6305 yards
Chalfont Park, Gerrards Cross
(0753) 885300

Harewood Downs G.C.
(18) 5958 yards
Cokes Lane, Chalfont St. Giles
(02404) 2184

Iver G.C.
(9) 6214 yards
Hollow Hill Lane, Iver
(0753) 655615

Little Chalfont G.C.
(9) 5852 yards
Lodge Lane, Little Chalfont
(02404) 4877

Stoke Poges G.C.
(18) 6654 yards
Park Road, Stoke Poges
(0753) 26385

Weston Turville G.C.
(13) 6782 yards
New Road, Weston Turville, Aylesbury
(0296) 24084

Whitelief G.C.
(9) 5391 yards
Whiteleaf, Whiteleaf, Aylesbury
(08444) 3097

Windmill Hill G.C.
(18) 6773 yards
Tattenhoe Lane, Bletchley, Milton Keynes
(0908) 78623

Woburn G. & C.C.
(18) 6883 yards Duke's
(18) 6616 yards Duchess
Bow Brickhill, Milton Keynes
(0908) 70756

OXFORDSHIRE

Badgemore Park G.C.
(18) 6112 yards
Henley-on-Thames
(0491) 572206

Bremhill Park G.C.
(18) 6040 yards
Shrivenham
(0793) 782946

Burford G.C.
(18) 6405 yards
Burford
(099 382) 2583

Chesterton G.C.
(18) 6496 yards
Chesterton, Bicester
(0869) 241204

Chipping Norton G.C.
(9) 6137 yards
Southcombe, Chipping Norton
(0608) 2383

Frilford Heath G.C.
(18) 6768 yards (Red)
(18) 6006 yards (Green)
Frilford Heath, Abingdon
(0865) 390428

Henley G.C.
(18) 6329 yards
Harpsden, Henley-on-Thames
(0491) 575742

Huntercombe G.C.
(18) 6257 yards
Nuffield, Henley-on-Thames
(0491) 641207

North Oxford G.C.
(18) 5805 yards
Banbury Road, Oxford
(0865) 54924

Southfield G.C.
(18) 6230 yards
Hill Top Road, Oxford
(0865) 242158

Tadmarton Heath G.C.
(18) 5917 yards
Wiggington, Banbury
(0608) 737278

'The nineteenth hole'

GLOUCESTER, HEREFORD & WORCESTER

C.E. BROCK "The Drive" SOTHEBY'S

GLOUCESTERSHIRE, HEREFORD & WORCESTER

CHOICE GOLF

A hush descends as you ponder your fist swing in Worcestershire. Apple and cherry trees are in blossom and in the distance a herd of white faced Herefords appraise your stance. Your're fortunate, for several hundred years ago the air was thick with the clatter of sword against sword but now there is peace. Crack. Straight down the fairway – the echo resounds and then dies – you're on your way.

Herefordshire, Worcestershire and **Gloucestershire** – what a lovely trio! Bordering the Principality the region is arguably the most peaceful in England. It is an area of rich pastures and cider orchards, of small market towns and sleepy villages rather than crowded cities, and encompasses the Cotswolds and the Malverns, the beautiful Wye Valley and the splendid Vale of Evesham.

HEREFORD AND WORCESTER

Herefordshire and Worcestershire are no more – at least according to the modern county boundaries – **Hereford and Worcester** it is now, no doubt a compromise to the two county towns.

Golf courses aren't exactly plentiful, but those there are tend to be very scenic, often hidden away deep in the glorious countryside. To the north west of Hereford, **Kingston** and **Herefordshire** are two typical examples. The latter is located off the **A480**. Visitors are welcome though a telephone call is advisable. Green fees are approximately **£7** per day. Kington is further towards Wales and is reputed to be the highest course in either country. Well worth a visit and where poor golf can always be blamed on the rarefied atmosphere. To the south of Hereford is another attractive course, **Belmont**, possibly the newest in the region, but one that has already gained a good reputation.

Hereford in a natural base and there are a number of good hotels. **The Green Dragon Hotel (0432) 272506** is particularly comfortable – note the many four-poster beds – and in nearby Much Birch, **The Pilgrim Hotel (0981) 540742** is a splendid former rectory. A short drive to Weobley reveals the **Red Lion (0544) 318220**, a 14th century Inn in the centre of a delightful village – very handy for **Herefordshire Golf Club**. Near the same golf course is a good pub **The Bell** at Tillington, while for Belmont, **The Butchers Arms** is recommended (some accommodation here). Finally in this area, Kington has a first class restaurant, **Penrhos Court (0544) 230720**.

Ross-on-Wye is a renowned beauty spot and the town's golf course (green fees **£10.50** week days, **£14** at weekends) lives up to the reputation. Set in the heart of the Wye Valley and surrounded by a blaze of colur, it's hard to believe that the M50 is under a mile away (junction 4). If staying a few days in the area, **The Pengethley Hotel (098987) 211** is most charming, so too **Walford House (0989) 63829** with its tremendous restaurant.

Worcester is an attractive city with a very beautiful Cathedral. Only a mile from the town centre off the **A4103** is the **Worcester Golf and Country Club**. Visitors are welcome during the week. The oldest course in the county, and probably the finest is at the appropriately named **Worcestershire Golf Club**, situated two miles south of Great Malvern There are extensive views from the course towards the Malverns, the Severn Valley and the Cotswolds. Green fees are **£11** midweek, **£12** at the weekend.

In Worcester **The Elms Hotel (0299) 896666** at Abberley is an outstanding Country House while Malvern Wells offers two excellent restaurants, **The Croque-en-Bouche (06845) 65612** and **The Cottage in the Wood (06845) 3487**. Great Malvern provides a charming 19th century coaching inn, **The Foley Arms (06845) 3397**. A final suggestion for the area is to visit Colwall Village, here the **Colwall Park Hotel (0684) 40206** is exceptionally good value.

GLOUCESTERSHIRE

Heading into Gloucestershire, I trust that when Doctor Foster went to Gloucester he wasn't a golfer. The County has very few courses and Gloucester itself didn't possess one at all until as recently as 1976. Neighbouring Cheltenham has been a little more fortunate but granted one or two exceptions, the quality of the golf in the county doesn't exactly match up to the undeniable quality of its scenery.

The county's two best known courses are probably **Cotswold Hills** and **Lilley Brook**, located to the north and south of Cheltenham respectively. Both offer commanding views of the Gloucestershire countryside, especially perhaps Lilley Brook, one of southern England's most undulating courses. Each is well worth a visit – generally possible on all days of the week although prior telephoning is advisable. A day's golf on either can be enjoyed for approximately **£8-£12**.

Cleeve Hill is Cheltenham's third 18 hole course. Situated on high ground to the north of the town it can be rather cold in winter. One anonymous person said that when visiting Cheltenham he enjoyed a game at Lilley Brook in the summer as half of him was mountain goat, and at Cleeve Hill in the winter because the other half of him was eskimo!

The Cheltenham area has many fine hotels, but perhaps the best know is the **Queen's Hotel (0242) 514724**. Two hotels in the surrounding hills are the **Hotel De La Bere (0242) 37771** in Southam and the simply splendid **Greenway (0242) 862352** which lies in Shurdington. This hotel offers an excellent welcome, a first class menu and gorgeous grounds. In Cleeve Hill, the **Malvern View Hotel (024267) 6207** is well thought of, its name self-explanatory, and a little further north in Bishop's Cleeve, **Cleeveway House (024267) 2585** has a small number of rooms and an outstanding restaurant.

Outside of Cheltenham. **Minchinhampton** has the biggest reputation. A Club of great character, it celebrated its centenary in 1989. However, the course is only about a dozen years old, the former having been laid out on common land. Perhaps most remarkable is that the Members stayed on their original site for so long. Green fees, are **£10** midweek, **£12** at the weekend. A fine place to stay is the nearby **Burleigh Court (0453) 883804**, while to the north, **The Amberley Inn** in Amberley with its fine views over Woodchester Valley has considerable charm. For a good pub visit Painswick, **The Royal Oak** – a short 18 hole course here too.

The 18 hole course at **Cirencester** is probably the nearest one gets to golf in the Cotswolds. Cirencester is certainly a pleasant enough place but to most of us the real Cotswolds are the many wonderfully named villages: Bourton-on-the-Water, Stow-on-the-Wold, Upper Slaughter and Lower Slaughter.

Gloucester's newish course lies within the grounds of **The Gloucester Hotel (0452) 25653** at Robinswood Hill. The course enjoys a pleasant setting and has matured very rapidly. The same can be said of **Tewkesbury Park Hotel's** golf course **(0684) 295405** which is laid out on the site of the famous Roses Battle of 1471. Both hotels are comfortable and their courses are open to residents and non-residents alike, although booking in advance is preferred.

The Forest of Dean is our last port of call – another beauty spot and some good golf too at the **Royal Forest of Dean Golf Club** in Coleford. Green fees are very reasonable at about **£7** per day and visitors can play throughout the week. A notable inn nearby is **The Speech House (0594) 22607**. Staying a few days in the area is recommended: the countryside is splendid and just 8 miles away lies Chepstow – and the delights of **St Pierre**.

Last but not least, **Broadway Golf Club** – the course being a mile and a half or so from 'the lovliest village in England'. It really is a beautiful part of the world and those wishing to do some exploring will find several superb hotels, any of which will make an ideal base. **The Lygon Arms (0386) 852255** in Broadway with its outstanding frontage probably takes pride of place but for excellent value the **Collin House Hotel (0386) 858354** takes some beating. Both have very fine restaurants. Before visiting the golf course a quick telephone call is recommended. Green fees are about **£12** per day. True to form there are again some marvellous views – this time looking out across that splendid Vale of Evesham.

R. M. ALEXANDER 'Over the Big Bunker' *BURLINGTON GALLERY*

COTSWOLD HOUSE

The Cotswold House is a magnificent country hotel, standing in pride of place on Chipping Camden's historic High Street, once described by Trevelyn as 'the most beautiful village street left in this island'.

The hotel dates back to the 17th century, and now belongs to Cotswold hoteliers Robert and Gill Greenstock. In their capable hands, the property has been extensively refurbished and restored to its former glory. It is now without doubt one of the finest hotels in the Cotswolds.

Ably assisted by the Manager Peter Jordan, the Greenstocks are dedicated to providing all that is best in hotel-keeping. The emphasis is on comfort, discreet friendly service and attention to detail.

Rooms throughout are elegantly furnished, with antiques and works of art complimenting the many period features. The original spiral staircase, listed as being of special architectural interest, is a visual delight. So too is the Restaurant which enjoys not only delightful views of the garden, but also an enviable reputation for its food.

In winter, open fires blaze invitingly in the lounge and sitting room, whilst in summer the willow-shaded courtyard, adjoining Greenstocks continental style Cafe-Bar, is perfect for pre-dinner drinks or al fresco eating.

Upstairs there are fifteen luxurious bedrooms. Each room is highly individual and is decorated and furnished with its own unique theme. All have private bathrooms and are equipped with direct dial telephone, radio and television.

Outside, mellow stone walls and clipped yew hedges shelter over an acre of old world garden which is ablaze with colour from spring until the first frosts of winter.

The Cotswold House Hotel is ideally situated for racing at either Cheltenham or Stratford, or for a golfing break in the area. It is also an excellent base for exploring the Cotswolds and Shakespeare country. A memorable stay is most certainly assured.

The Cotswold House Hotel and Restaurant,
Chipping Camden,
Gloucestershire, GL55 6AN
Tel: (0386) 840330
Fax: (0386) 840310

THE LYGON ARMS

For over 450 years, the picturesque village of Broadway has been the home of the Lygon Arms. Set in delightful Cotswold countryside, the Inn offers charming 'olde worlde' accommodation and combines quality of service with a warm, friendly atmosphere.

In our restaurant, the Great Hall, you can relax and enjoy fine English cuisine complemented by our extensive selection of wines. Adjacent to the Inn, Goblets Wine Bar provides the cosy setting for a delicious meal in front of a roaring fire.

Approximately 2 miles from The Lygon Arms is Broadway Golf Club, open to non-members who have a handicap. A round of golf can be arranged when you make a reservation. Alternatively, why not try our 'Golfing Break', a 2 day all inclusive programme, ideal for the individual or group.

For conferences, meetings, seminars or dinner, The Lygon Arms is the perfect venue. Our comprehensive range of facilities boast the very latest in communications technology, together with comfortable, well equipped and spacious meeting rooms.

For further information, contact:

The Lygon Arms,
High Street,
Broadway,
Worcestershire, WR12 7DU.
Tel: (0386) 852255
Fax: (0386) 858611

GLOUCESTER, HEREFORD & WORCESTER

COMPLETE GOLF

GLOUCESTERSHIRE

Cirencester G.C.
(18) 6007 yards
Cheltenham Rd, Bagendon
Cirencester
(0285) 2465

Cleeve Hill G.C.
(18) 6217 yards
Cleeve Hill, Cheltenham
(0242) 672592

Cotswold Hills G.C.
(18) 6716 yards
Ullenwood, Cheltenham
(0242) 515264

Gloucester Hotel G. & C.C.
(18) 6135 yards
Robinswood Hill, Gloucester
(0452) 411331

Lilley Brook G.C.
(18) 6226 yards
Cirencester Rd, Charltonkings,
Cheltenham
(0242) 526785

Lydney G.C.
(9) 5382 yards
Lakeside Ave, Lydney
(0594) 42614

Minchinhampton G.C.
(18) 6295 yards (Old Course)
(18) 6675 yards (New Course)
Minchinhampton, Stroud
(045383) 3866 (New)
(045383) 2642 (Old)

Painswick G.C.
(18) 4780 yards
Painswick, Stroud
(0452) 812180

Royal Forest of Dean G.C.
(18) 5519 yards
Lords Hill, Coleford
(0594) 32583

Stinchcombe Hill G.C.
(18) 5710 yards
Stinchcombe Hill, Dursley
(0453) 2015

Tewkesbury Park Hotel G.C.
(18) 6533 yards
Lincoln Green Lane, Tewkesbury
(0684) 295405

Westonbirt G.C.
(9) 4504 yards
Westonbirt, Tetbury
(0666) 242

HEREFORD & WORCESTER

Belmont G.C.
(18) 6766 yards
Belmont House, Belmont
(0432) 277445

Blackwell G.C.
(18) 6105 yards
Blackwell, Bromsgrove
(021) 445 1994

Broadway G.C.
(18) 6211 yards
Willersey Hill, Broadway
(0386) 853683

Churchill & Blakedown G.C.
(9) 5399 yards
Blakedown, Kidderminster
(0562) 700200

Droitwich G. & C.C.
(18) 6036 yards
Ford Lane, Droitwich
(0905) 774344

Evesham G.C.
(9) 6418 yards
Fladbury Cross, Pershore
(0386) 860395

Habberley G.C.
(9) 5440 yards
Habberley, Kidderminster
(0562) 745756

Herefordshire G.C.
(18) 6036 yards
Wormsley, Hereford
(0432) 71219

Kidderminster G.C.
(18) 6156 yards
Russell Road, Kidderminster
(0562) 822303

Kington G.C.
(18) 5830 yards
Bradnor Hill, Kington
(0544) 230340

Leominster G.C.
(9) 5314 yards
Ford Bridge, Leominster
(0568) 2863

Little Lakes G.C.
(9) 6204 yards
Lye Head, Bewdley
(0299) 266385

Redditch G.C.
(18) 6671 yards
Callow Hill, Redditch
(0527) 43309

Ross-on-Wye G.C.
(18) 6500 yards
Gorsley, Ross-on-Wye
(098982) 267

Tolladine G.C.
(9) 5630 yards
Tolladine Road, Worcester
(0905) 21074

Worcester G. & C.C.
(18) 5890 yards
Boughton Park, Worcester
(0905) 422555

Worcestershire G.C.
(18) 6449 yards
Wood Farm, Malvern Wells
(06845) 5992

***CHARLES CROMBIE 'The Rules of Golf – Rule 4'** ROSENSTIEL'S*

WARWICKSHIRE & THE WEST MIDLANDS

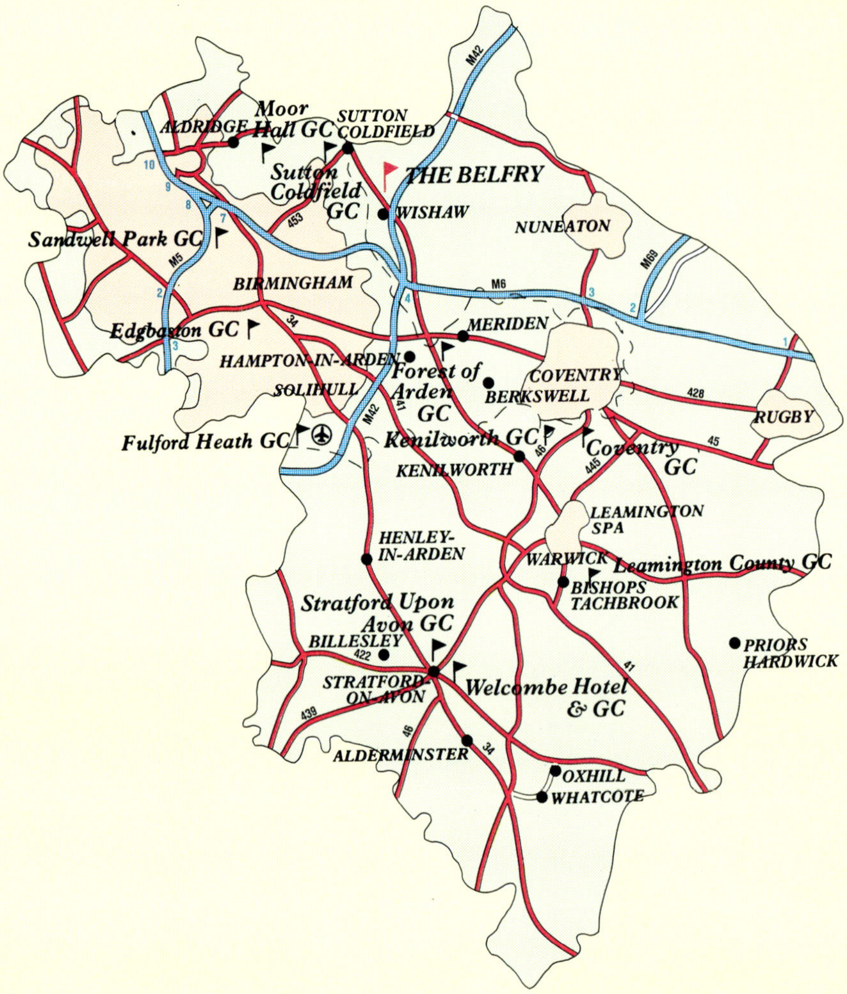

H. ROUNTREE "Serious Bridger" BURLINGTON GALLERY

WARWICKSHIRE & THE WEST MIDLANDS
CHOICE GOLF

WEST MIDLANDS

Golfers in the City of London have often been known to get frustrated at having to travel many a mile for a decent game of golf. In 1919 one obviously disgusted individual teed up at **Piccadilly Circus** and proceeded to play along **The Strand**, through **Fleet Street** and **Ludgate Hill** firing his last shot at the **Royal Exchange**. Such behaviour is, as far as I'm aware, unknown in **Birmingham** – the **Bull Ring** and the **NEC** in their admittedly shorter existence, have never been peppered with golf balls, this I suspect may be because the needs of its golfing citizens have been properly attended to.

Within a sensible distance (ie. easy access) of the town centre lie the likes of **The Belfry and Little Aston** to the North, **Fulford Heath** and **Kings Norton** to the South,and **Sandwell Park** and **Edgbaston** lying somewhere in the middle. Golfers north of Birmingham are indeed particularly fortunate for in addition to the Belfry and Little Aston there is also **Sutton Coldfield** and **Moor Hall**. With the exception of Sutton Coldfield and Fulford which are heathland, the above are all tree-lined parkland types and provide pleasant retreats from the noise and confusion of England's second largest City.

Despite its relative youth, **The Belfry** (featured on a following page) has become the area's best known golfing attraction thanks largely of course to the European **Ryder Cup** victory there in **1985**. However, **Little Aston** has long been regarded as one of Britain's finest inland courses and has staged numerous major events – both amateur and professional. At Little Aston, as indeed at all of the Birmingham Clubs mentioned, visitors are welcome between Mondays and Fridays though restrictions normally apply at weekends (The Belfry and Edgbaston being notable exceptions). Green fees are **£16** for a day's golf and at each Club prior telephoning is recommended.

Looking in and around Birmingham for places to stay a few obvious thoughts emerge. **The Belfry Hotel (0675) 70301** is most luxurious and ideal for its own two courses (as well as the plethora of golf courses in the Sutton Coldfield area). It offers practically every activity under the sun. (When does the sun ever shine in Birmingham, you ask). **Moor Hall 021 308 3751** also provides a most comfortable and convenient 19th hole – an attractive mansion this. Still in Sutton Coldfield **Penns Hall 021 351 3111** enjoys a peaceful lake-side setting while a short distance away in Aldridge is another alternative **The Fairlawns Hotel (0922) 55122.**

Solhihull is surrounded by good golf and has Birmingham on its doorstep. **The George Hotel 021 711 2121** here is a modernised coaching inn and a perfectly adequate place in which to stay. **Liaison** is a pleasant spot to have dinner **021-743 3993**. Another suburb of Birmingham, on this occasion Edgbaston, provides the restaurant **Sloans 021-455 6697**. Two pleasant and popular pubs to track down when visiting these parts include **The Bear** at Berkswell and another beast, on this occasion **The White Lion** in Hampton-in-Arden.

Staying more centrally in Birmingham, **The Albany 021-643 8171** is well thought of while close to the National Exhibiton Centre **The Birmingham Metropole 021 780 4242** is also good. Perhaps the best word for Birmingham's restaurants is cosmopolitan, a huge range can be sampled. The Albany restaurant, **The Four Seasons** is as good as most. Note also the excellent cocktail bar.

Like Birmingham, the City of Coventry has been removed from Warwickshire and now bears the West Midlands label. **Coventry Golf Club** (Green fees **£12**) enjoys a decidedly peaceful setting at Finham Park, two miles south of the City along the **A444**. The course is good enough to have recently staged the British Seniors Championship. To the north west of Coventry at Meriden, the **Forest of Arden Golf and Country Club** offers a pretty stern test, its course measuring close to 7,000 yards. Both welcome visitors in midweek, fees being approximately **£12** per day.

The major attraction in Coventry is undoubtedly the spectacular Cathedral. A fine piece of modern architecture sadly not reflected in the city's hotels – but then Coventry is no different from most, **De Vere Hotel (0203) 633733**, near the Cathedral is perhaps the best although **The Post House (0203) 402151** is also wel thought of. In Meriden **The Manor Hotel '0676) 22735** is recommended – convenient for the golf course and also for the Exhibtion Centre.

WARWICKSHIRE

Birmingham and Coventry removed, Warwickshire has been left with only a handful of courses. The county's two most popular towns (tourist wise) are unquestionably **Stratford and Warwick**. Whilst Warwick has only a nine hole course located inside its race track, Shakespeare-spotters who've sneaked the clubs into the boot will be well rewarded. There are two fine 18 hole courses in Stratford, **Stratford Golf Club** and the **Welcombe Hotel Golf Course**. The latter might be said to be particularly welcoming in that visitors can play seven days a week (telephoning advisable at weekends). Fees for a day's golf are **£12** during the week, **£15** at weekends.

The Welcombe Hotel (0789) 295252 is a beautiful mansion with good rooms and an excellent restaurant. But there are many outstanding alternatives for those spending a night or two in the Stratford area. Pride of place must go to **Billesley Manor (0789) 400888** to the west of the town: quite simply majestic – and with a superb restaurant to boot. For pubs, a short drive towards Oxhill is recommended where **The Peacock** and **The Royal Oak** (in Whatcote) will provide excellent sustenance.

Warwick has a famous castle and a good restaurant to note nearby is **Randolph's (0926) 491292. Kenilworth** also has a castle (and a pretty reasonable golf course too). Here **The Clarendon House (0926) 57668** is the place to stay and a restaurant to savour is **The Restaurant Bosquet (0926) 52463**.

Lastly we visit Leamington Spa. It may not have the attractions of Stratford or a Warwick but it does have a very fine golf course. **Leamington and County** is a hilly parkland course, situated to the south of Leamington. Visitors are welcome during the week for a fee of around **£10**. **The Lansdowne (0926) 450505** is a smallish well-priced hotel in town but if one is looking to spoil oneself – perhaps after a particularly good round – then travel to Bishops Tachbrook and **Mallory Court (0926) 30214** – superb rooms and a terrific restaurant... Bon Appetit!

THE BELFRY

CHAMPIONSHIP GOLF

To adopt lawyers' jargon, it is 'beyond any reasonable doubt' that the game of golf was invented in Scotland. A handful of golfing pioneers brought the game south and today with the exception of a few notable areas in the north, where to live is to play golf, the sport is almost as popular south of the border.

One cannot help wondering quite what those early pioneers would have made of the '**Belfry** project'.....'American-style target gowff'.. ..'and what d'ya mean man-made mounds and lakes!'.....'more than 7,000 yards did ya say?'....'Too many whiskies m'friend, you must be out o'your wee mind!'

The 'Belfry project' involved not only a plan to build a Championship course on American lines where in due course the **Ryder Cup** could be staged, but also the siting of a new headquarters for the P.G.A. **Peter Alliss** and **Dave Thomas** were given the task of designing the show piece and a very great task it was, for the land they were given was flat, uninteresting and comprised one small lake, a stream and numerous acres of potato fields.

Well, the boys didn't hang about: earth mountains were moved, the potatoes disappeared and hundreds of trees were planted – the end result in fact produced two 18 hole courses, opened in June **1977**. The feature course was named the **Brabazon**, after Lord Brabazon a former President of the P.G.A. and the shorter, easier course the **Derby**.

Right from its outset the Belfry became the centre of great controversy and some stinging criticism was levelled at the Brabazon. In particular many claimed that the place was still flat and uninteresting and that a sluggers paradise had been created. So what happened?....

In **September 1985** the Great Britain and Europe team comes to the Belfry and amidst scenes of near hysteria gives the American side a mighty good walloping to win the **Ryder Cup** for the first time in nearly thirty years...and, yes you've guessed it...'what a marvellous course!'

A unique feature of the Belfry is that it is a Club without any Members. Both courses open their doors to the general public at all times all the year round. Not surprisingly the Brabazon is particularly busy and before setting off it is best to telephone and book a starting time. The **Administration Manager, Mrs. Butler** and the **Professional, Peter McGovern** run the show efficiently. They can be contacted on **(0675) 70301**. Persons wishing to make a written enquiry should address a letter to the Administration Manager at **The Belfry, Lichfield Road, Wishaw, Sutton Coldfield, West Midlands.**

In **1989** the **green fees** payable for a round on the Brabazon course were **£23** for weekdays and **£25** for weekends. This contrasted with **£9** for a weekday round on the Derby course with **£11** payable at weekends. For the fitter among us intent on tackling the pair in a day a weekday ticket cost **£24.50**, with **£35.50** payable at weekends. For the less fit, petrol driven caddy carts may be hired from the professional shop at **£15** per round, **£20** per day. Half sets of clubs can also be hired at **£5** per round.

Situated close to the country's industrial heart there is surely no golfing complex in Britain better served by communication networks. The Belfry is one mile from the **M42** (junction **9**), five miles from the **M6**(junction **4**), nine miles from Birmingham city centre and less than ten minutes from Birmingham International Airport and the N.E.C. Railway Station. The exact positioning of the Golf Club is at the apex of the **A446** and **A4091** Lichfield-Tamworth roads.

Apart from the sheer length of the Brabazon course the many water hazards are likely to present the greatest challenge. One can only speculate as to how many thousands have attempted to emulate Messrs. **Ballesteros, Norman** and a handful of others by driving over the lake at the par 4 **10th** onto the green. What is clear though is that the majority of those thousands have failed. Of course should you decide to flex the muscles and fail then whatever you do don't put on your snorkel and flippers and go wading into the lake – or at least if you do, make sure that it's your ball you fish out! (Puzzled? – Please refer to a 1986 Law Report)

In addition to being a luxury four-star hotel with a full complement of facilities, the **Belfry Hotel** has public bars and restaurants open to the general public. If after a meal and a few drinks you're still not satisfied with your golf there's a final opportunity to put things right on the impressive floodlit covered driving range.

Mention has been made of how this American-styled extravaganza was created out of a field of potatoes; well interestingly, the American legend Sam Snead on first viewing **St. Andrews** declared that it 'looked like the kind of real estate you couldn't give away'.... obviously the message is clear – let's plough the old place up, fill the Road Hole Bunker with water, plant a few trees, create a lake out of the Valley of Sin......

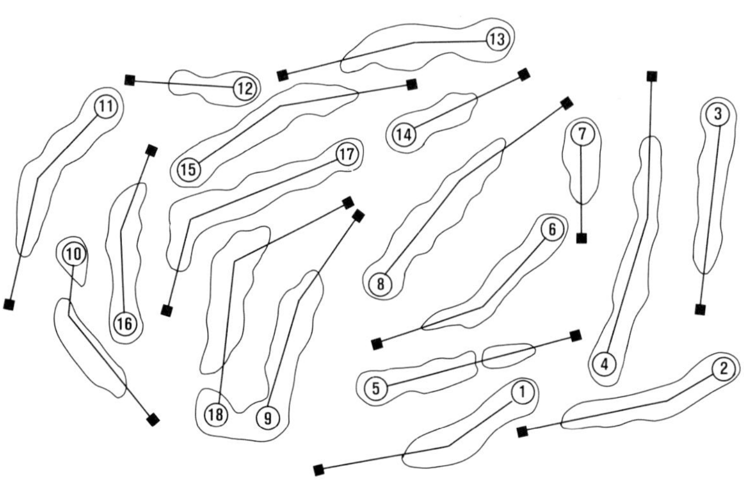

Brabazon Course

Hole	Yards	Par	Hole	Yards	Par
1	408	4	10	301	4
2	340	4	11	365	4
3	455	4	12	225	3
4	569	5	13	364	4
5	389	4	14	184	3
6	386	4	15	540	5
7	173	3	16	400	4
8	476	5	17	555	5
9	390	4	18	455	4
Out	3,586	37	In	3,389	36
			Out	3,586	37
			TOTALS	6,975	73

THE BELFRY

This beautiful country manor, set in the heart of the Warwickshire Countryside and surrounded by two top class golf courses, is now world renowned, largely due to the success of the European Team during the 1985 Ryder Cup matches, played on the famous Brabazon Course.

The Belfry is a 220 bedroomed, four star hotel with restaurants, bars, magnificent leisure club with indoor swimming pool, squash courts, saunas, etc. It has a range of Conference facilities varying in size to cater for numbers from 2 to 350 in luxurious surroundings. For those who want to dance the night away, there is the fabulous Bel-Air Nitespot.

Without doubt, the ever expanding attractions of the Belfry complex now offers the most comprehensive opportunities for anyone interested in playing golf or looking to hold a Conference with a difference. The Belfry can cater for the individual with his family, or for the Company and the organised day out, or weekend golfing and business affairs.

Millions of pounds have been poured into the complex by the owners, Greenall Whitley plc, £3,000,000 being spent prior to last year's Ryder Cup to guarantee it matched the importance of the occasion.

In the future, a further luxury development is planned, transforming an already impressive scene into a continental plaza type village, with high class shops, executive suites and extra facilities.

The Belfry
Wishaw North
Warwickshire, B76 9PR
Tel: (0675) 70301
Telex: 338848

BILLESLEY MANOR

It would be difficult to find a more appropriate venue in the heart of Shakespeare country, whatever the purpose of your visit.
Recently refurbished, oak panels and carved fireplaces blend with the more modern comforts to provide a truly welcoming atmosphere.

Whether you choose a suite, a wood panelled four-poster bedroom or a more modern room, you will enjoy a spacious bathroom, television and telephone.

The public rooms are also spacious and superbly comfortable and many have open logfires. In the restaurants, some of the finest dishes are prepared and this is reflected in the service. Billesley's cellar is exceptional and they will gladly help you select a vintage, to add the final touch to your meal!

Billesley Manor is only 3 miles from Stratford-upon-Avon, the very heart of England. It is an ideal base for visiting the theatre, Warwick Castle or exploring the many sights or Warwickshire and the Cotswolds.

Whatever your reason for visiting Billesley Manor, you will find ten centuries of history and tradition to welcome you.

Billesley Manor,
Billesley,
Nr. Stratford-upon-Avon,
Warwickshire
Tel: (0789) 763737

WARWICKSHIRE & THE WEST MIDLANDS

COMPLETE GOLF

WARWICKSHIRE

Atherstone G.C.
(18) 6239 yds
The Outwoods, Atherstone
(08277) 714579

Kenilworth G.C.
(18) 6408 yds
Crew Lane, Kenilworth
(0926) 58517

Leamington & County G.C.
(18) 6430 yds
Whitnash, Leamington Spa
(0926) 28014

Newbold Comyn G.C.
(18) 6259 yds
Newbold Terrace East,
Leamington Spa
(0926) 21157

Nuneaton G.C.
(18) 6368 yds
Whitestone, Nuneaton
(0203) 347810

Purley Chase G.C.
(18) 6604 yds
Ridge Lane, Nuneaton
(0203) 395 348

Rugby G.C.
(18) 5457 yds
Clifton Rd, Rugby
(0788) 75134

Stratford-upon-Avon G.C.
(18) 6309 yds
Tiddington Rd, Stratford
(0789) 205749

Warwick G.C.
(9) 5364 yds
The Racecourse, Warwick
(0926) 494316

Welcombe Hotel & G.C.
(18) 6202 yds
Warwick Rd, Stratford-upon-Avon
(0789) 295252

WEST MIDLANDS

The Belfry
(18) 6975 yds (Brabazon)
(18) 6082 yds (Derby)
Lichfield Rd, Wishaw,
Sutton Coldfield
(0675) 70301

Blackhill Wood G.C.
(18) 6029 yds
Bridgnorth Rd, Swindon, Dudley
(0902) 892279

Bloxwich G.C.
(18) 6286 yds
Stafford Rd, Bloxwich
(0922) 405724

Boldmere G.C.
(18) 6078 yds
Monmouth Dr, Sutton Coldfield
(021) 354 3379

Brand Hall G.C.
(18) 5813 yds
Heron Rd, Oldbury, Warley
(021) 552 2195

Calderfields G.C.
(18) 6636 yds
Aldridge Rd, Walsall
(0922) 32243

City of Coventry G.C.
(18) 6530 yds
Brandon Lane, Coventry
(0203) 54314

Cocks Moor Woods G.C.
(18) 5888 yds
Alcester Rd South, Kings Heath
Birmingham
(021) 444 3584

Copt Heath G.C.
(18) 6504 yds
Warwick Rd, Knowle, Solihull
(05645) 2650

Coventry G.C.
(18) 6613 yds
Finham Park, Coventry
(0203) 414152

Dartmouth G.C.
(9) 6060 yds
Vale St, West Bromwich
(021) 588 2131

Druids Heath G.C.
(18) 6914 yds
Stonnall Rd, Aldridge
(0922) 55595

Dudley G.C.
(18) 5715 yds
Turners Hill,
Rowley Regis, Warley
(0384) 53719

Edgbaston G.C.
(18) 6118 yds
Church Rd, Edgbast, Birmingham
(021) 454 1736

Enville G.C.
(18) 6541 yds
Highgate Common, Envilk,
Stourbridge
(0384) 872074

Forest of Arden G. & C.C.
(18) 6962 yds
Maxstone Lane,
Meriden, Coventry
(0676) 22118

Fulford Heath G.C.
(18) 6256 yds
Tanners Green Lane, Wythall,
Birmingham
(0564) 824758

Gay Hill G.C.
(18) 6532 yds
Alcester Rd,
Hollywood, Birmingham
(021) 430 8544

Grange G.C.
(9) 6002 yds
Copeswood, Coventry
(0203) 451465

Great Barr G.C.
(18) 6545 yds
Chapel Lane, Birmingham
(021) 357 1232

Hagley G.C.
(18) 6353 yds
Stourbridge
(0562) 883701

Halesowen G.C.
(18) 5673 yds
The Leasowes, Halesowen
(021) 501 3606

Handsworth G.C.
(18) 6312 yds
11 Sunningdale Close,
Handsworth, Birmingham
(021) 554 0599

Harborne G.C.
(18) 6240 yds
40 Tennal Rd, Harborne,
Birmingham
(021) 427 1728

Harborne Church Farm G.C.
(9) 4514 yds
Vicarage Rd, Harborne,
Birmingham
(021) 427 1204

Hatchford Brook G.C.
(18) 6164 yds
Coventry Rd, Sheldon,
Birmingham
(021) 743 9821

Hearsall G.C.
(18) 5951 yds
Beechwood Ave, Coventry
(0203) 713470

Hill Top G.C.
(18) 6200 yds
Park Lane, Handsworth,
Birmingham
(021) 554 4463

Himley Hall G.C.
(9) 3090 yds
Himley Hall Park, Dudley
(0902) 895207

Kings Norton G.C.
(18) 6754 yds
(9) 3290 yds
Brockhill Lane, Weatheroak,
Alvechurch
(0564) 822822

Ladbrook Park G.C.
(18) 6407 yds
Poolhead Lane, Tanworth-in-
Arden, Solihull
(05644) 2264

Little Aston G.C.
(18) 6724 yds
Streetly, Sutton Coldfield
(021) 353 2060

Maxstone Park G.C.
(18) 6437 yds
Castle Lane, Coleshill,
Birmingham
(0203) 64915

Moor Hall G.C.
(18) 6249 yds
Moor Hall Park, Sutton Coldfield
(021) 308 6130

Moseley G.C.
(18) 6227 yds
Springfield Rd, Kingsheath,
Birmingham
(021) 444 4957

North Warwickshire G.C.
(9) 6362 yds
Hampton Lane,
Meriden, Coventry
(0676) 22259

North Worcestershire G.C.
(18) 5919 yds
Northfield, Birmingham
(021) 475 1047

Olton G.C.
(18) 6229 yds
Mirfield Rd, Solihull
(021) 705 1083

Oxley Park G.C.
(18) 6153 yds
Bushbury, Wolverhampton
(0902) 25445

Penn G.C.
(18) 6449 yds
Penn Common, Wolverhampton
(0902) 341142

Pype Hayes G.C.
(18) 5811 yds
Walmley, Sutton Coldfield
(021) 351 1014

Robin Hood G.C.
(18) 6609 yds
St Bernards Rd, Solihull
(021) 706 0061

Rose Hill G.C.
(18) 6010 yds
Lickey Hills, Rednal, Birmingham
(021) 453 3159

Sandwell Park G.C.
(18) 6470 yds
Birmingham Rd, West Bromwich
(021) 553 4637

Shirley G.C.
(18) 6445 yds
Stratford Rd, Solihull
(021) 744 6001

South Staffordshire G.C.
(18) 6538 yds
Danescourt Rd, Tettenhall
Wolverhampton
(0902) 751065

Stourbridge G.C.
(18) 6178 yds
Pedmore, Stourbridge
(0384) 395566

Sutton Coldfield G.C.
(18) 6541 yds
Thornhill Rd, Sutton Coldfield
(021) 353 9633

Walmley G.C.
(18) 6340 yds
Wylde Green,
Sutton Coldfield
(021) 373 0029

Walsall G.C.
(18) 6232 yds
The Broadway, Walsall
(0922) 613512

Warley G.C.
(9) 5212 yds
Lightwood Hill, Warley
(021) 429 2440

NORTHAMPTONSHIRE & LEICESTERSHIRE

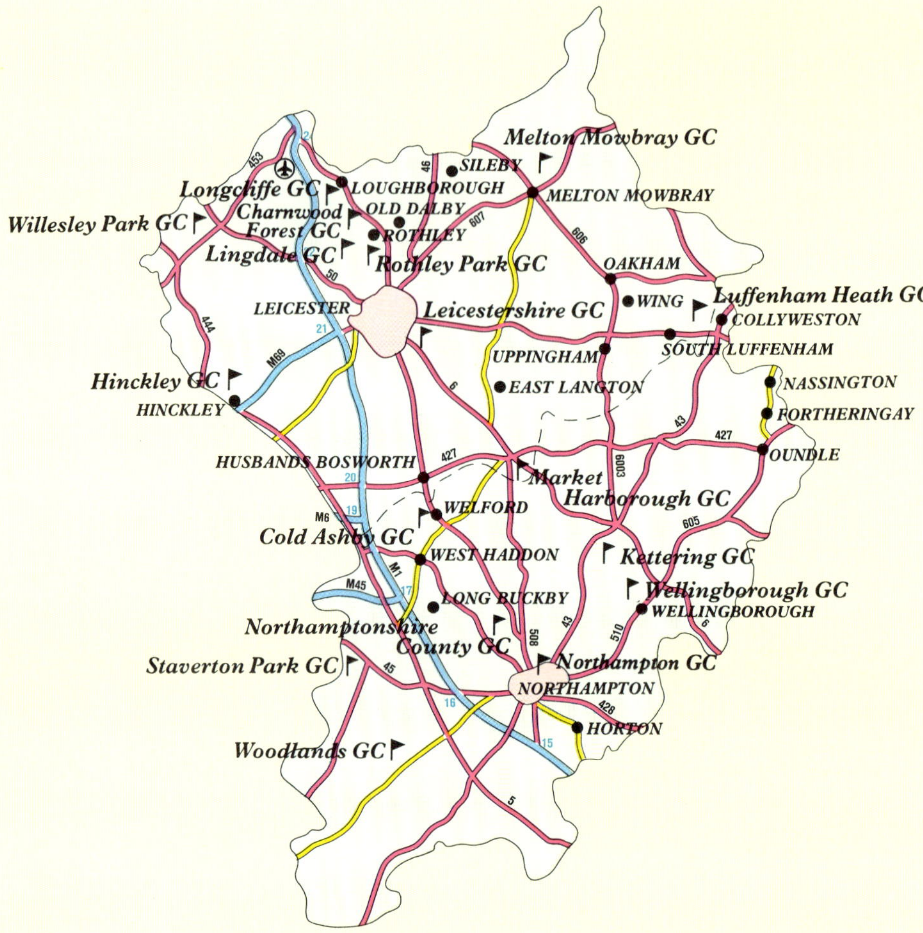

H. ROUNTREE ***"Bulldog Breed"*** *BURLINGTON GALLERY*

NORTHAMPTONSHIRE & LEICESTERSHIRE

CHOICE GOLF

LEICESTERSHIRE

Starting in **Leicestershire, Luffenham Heath** lies over to the very far east of the county within what was formerly **Rutland** and very close to the border with Lincolnshire. It is without question one of the most attractive heathland courses in England and being a conservation area something of a haven for numerous species of wildlife. Measuring 6,254 yards from the back tees (par 70) it isn't the longest of courses but then, thankfully, golf isn't always a question of how far you can belt the ball! Visitors are welcome at Luffenham Heath, green fees being approximately **£16**, however, prior arrangement with the secretary is essential.

The splendid Rutland countryside reveals many outstanding establishments. In Oakham, **Hambleton Hall (0572) 56991** is quite tremendous. If you cannot spend the night here the restaurant is equally superb. In total contrast, though very enjoyable, is **The George (0572) 56971** in Oakham's Market Square – a fine inn with good beers, snacks and some comfortable accommodation. Note that this is Ruddles country -some excellent country pubs lie in wait. **The King's Arms** in Wing is a good example and there's a nearby maze in which to discard the children before a round of golf or a pint of County. Another good pub is the **Cavalier** at Collyweston – famous for its stone. **The Boot and Shoe**, South Luffenham **(0780) 720177** is also a fine pub in which to stay or merely have a pie 'n' pint.

The town of Leicester is well served by golf courses and there are no fewer than three 18 hole municipal courses within four miles of the centre of Leicester. **Western Park** perhaps being the best of these, **Leicestershire Golf Club** is situated just 2 miles from the city centre along the **A6**. An undulating parkland course with a stream running through it, visitors should be able to get a game here most days of the week, fees are around the **£12** mark.

Rothley Park Golf Club, adjacent to 13th Century Rothley Court, is one of the county's most picturesque parkland courses and is within easy access of Leicester, lying some 7 miles to the north of the county town off the **A6**. Those looking for a game would probably do well to contact the Secretary in advance. A day's golf at Rothley is priced **£12** midweek, **£15** at the weekend.

Leicester may not be the country's most attractive city but it does have its good points. The **Haymarket Theatre** offers a variety of productions while the Art Gallery includes works by English sporting artists and if you have business in town the **Grand Hotel (0533) 55599** will prove the best selection. Outside the town at Quorn, the **Quorn Country Hotel (0509) 415050** offers style in a particularly English environment. Also convenient for the county town is the aforementioned **Rothley Court**, Rothley **(0533) 374141**.

Looking further afield, in the north of the county the ancient town of **Melton Mowbray** has a fine nine hole course sited on high ground to the north east of the town and Loughborough possesses an 18 hole heathland type course, (**Longcliffe**) which is heavily wooded with a particularly testing front nine. In the south of the county **Market Harborough**'s nine hole course offers extensive views across the surrounding countryside (green fees here are **(£6)**. North-west of Leicester, Charnwood Forest is one of the Midland's most pleasant retreats, an area where heath and woodland confront rocky craggs and granite outcrops. The village of Woodhouse Eaves lies on the eastern edge of the 'Forest' and has two extremely pleasant nine hole courses at hand, **Lingdale** and **Charnwood Forest**. Though they are less than two miles apart they offer quite different challenges. Lingdale has a parkland setting with a trout stream flowing through it, while Charnwood Forest is a heathland type course – no bunkers but several outcrops of granite around which one must navigate. Green fees at both are **£8** a day.

Hinckley is linked to the centre of Leicester by the **A47**. Hinckley's golf course is a fairly new creation, built over the original nine hole Burbage Common layout. Several lakes and much gorse have to be confronted making this potentially the toughest in the county. A final mention goes to **Willesley Park** at Ashby-de-la-Zouch. A parkland-heathland mix this and well worth a game.

Some ideas for life beyond the 18th fairway. If a pork pie and a piece of Stilton is what you're after then Melton Mowbray is an answer to your prayers – try **The George (0664) 62112** – a charming inn with comfortable rooms. In the Loughborough area **The Kings Head (0509) 23222** is popular and for two good restaurants, try **The Old Schoolhouse (050981) 3941** in Sileby and **The Cottage in the Woods (0509) 890318**, Woodhouse Eaves. **The Crown** in Old Dalby is a good pub.

NORTHAMPTONSHIRE

The **Northamptonshire County** course is situated some five miles north of Northampton at Church Brampton, and indeed is often referred to locally as 'Church Brampton'. Famed for its many testing par fours, it is a splendid heather and gorse type with a fair few undulations in its 6,500 yards. Rather like Liphook in Hampshire a railway line bisects the course. The venue in the past of the British Youths Championship visitors are welcome on most days, though being the most popular course in the county it can get busy and arrangements must be made in advance. Fees are **£15** per day. Things are certainly happening around Northampton. At **Collingtree Park** Johnny Miller recently undertook an ambitious project to produce a spectacular golf and lesure extravaganza. The town has another notable course, **Northampton**, which is renowned for its superb greens. If staying in Northampton, **The Moat House Hotel (0604) 22441** is modern, but comfortable and handy for the centre, while the **Westone Moat House (0604) 406262** is a mansion with modern additions. South of Northampton in Horton, **The Horton Inn (0258) 840252** is recommended for food and to the north in Long Buckby, **The Buckby Lion** is a good pub. Elsewhere in the county **Wellingborough** is a fairly lengthy course measuring close to 6,600 yards. Two miles east of the town it is set around the former Harrowden Hall. Quite hilly again with several lakes and mature trees visitors can play during the week. Green fees are **£12. Kettering's** course is very close to the town centre. One of the oldest clubs in the county, now approaching its centenary, it is another that welcomes visitors midweek. **Staverton Park** at Daventry and **Woodlands** close to Towcester are two of the newer courses in the county worth noting, as certainly is **Cold Ashby** located to the far north of the county (close to Naseby with superb views across the Northamptonshire Uplands.

Pleasant countryside surrounds the towns of Wellingborough and Kettering. Perhaps the best bet for accommodation in the area is **The Hind (0933) 22827** in Wellingborough. In the south of the county, **The Crossroads (0327) 40354** at Weedon and **The Saracen's Head** at Towcester are both welcoming while to the north, and convenient after a round at Cold Ashby are two notable pubs, **The Pytchley** in West Haddon and **The Elizabethan** in Welford.

HAMBLETON HALL

Hambleton Hall is set in a part of Britain whose natural advantages remain remarkably unspoilt and undiscovered, and yet it is only 100 miles north of London.

The grassy bumps and stone-built market towns may remind you of the Cotswolds but you will find fewer souvenir shops and traffic jams.

Arriving through a corridor of laurels, yews, hollies and fine cedars, you find a substantial, much gabled, stone, Victorian house. But it is inside the house that its chief glories are apparent. Facing south from its hilltop site the hotel's principal rooms have spectacular views over the gardens, the Rutland landscape and Rutland Water, a 500 acre man-made lake of surprising beauty.

The decoration and furnishings impart an immediate sense of comfort and a welcome that is immensely stylish, without a trace of stuffiness or excessive formality.

An oak-panelled hall, a cosy bar and a 'glam', spacious drawing-room lead to a magnificent dining-room. Each of these rooms seems the right size for the house party of 25-30 which the hotel's 15 bedrooms can accommodate.

Upstairs, the same attention to detail is apparent. Down pillows, Egyptian cotton sheets and the softest merino wool blankets ensure a good night's rest, while charming chintzy decorations in the English country house idiom achieve the same combination of comfort and elegance.

Hambleton is particularly well known for its food and wines. The culinary style seems to combine the presentational flair of the best modern cooking, with a fundamental respect for top ingredients and authentic flavours. Brian Baker, who took over as head chef from Nicholas Gill in 1986, uses local pike and trout, herbs and salads from the garden and the prodigious range of game available in season to help create a menu that is always unusual, without being fussy or over-complicated. The wine list won Egon Ronay's Cellar of the Year award in 1986.

Tim and Stefa Hart established Hambleton Hall in the early '80's and still play an active part, with the day to day management of the hotel in the capable hands of Jeffrey Crockett, General Manager. It is the welcome and efficient service produced by Mr. Bos and his team, as much as anything which keeps Hambleton in the front rank of British country house hotels.

Hambleton Hall,
Hambleton,
Oakham,
Rutland LE15 8TH.

Tel (0572) 756991
Telex: 342888 Hamble

NORTHAMPTONSHIRE & LEICESTERSHIRE
COMPLETE GOLF

NORTHAMPTONSHIRE

Cherwell Edge G.C.
(18) 5925 yards
Chacombe, Nr. Banbury
(0295) 711591

Cold Ashby G.C.
(18) 5898 yards
Cold Ashby
(0604) 740548

Daventry & District G.C.
(9) 5555 yards
Norton Rd, Daventry
(0327) 702829

Delapre G.C.
(18) 6293 yards
Nene Valley Way, Northampton
(0604) 64036

Kettering G.C.
(18) 6035 yards
Headlands, Kettering
(0536) 511104

Kingsthorpe G.C.
(18) 6006 yards
Kingsley Rd, Northampton
(0604) 710610

Northampton G.C.
(18) 6002 yards
Kettering Rd, Northampton
(0604) 719453

Northamptonshire County G.C.
(18) 6503 yards
Church Brampton, Northampton
(0604) 843025

Oundle G.C.
(18) 5507 yards
Oundle
(0832) 73267

Priors Hall G.C.
(18) 6677 yards
Stamford Rd, Weldon
(0536) 60756

Rushden & District G.C.
(9) 6300 yards
Kimbolton Rd, Chelveston
(0933) 312197

Staverton Park G.C.
(18) 6634 yards
Staverton, Daventry
(0327) 705911

Wellingborough G.C.
(18) 6604 yards
Harrowden Hall, Wellingborough
(0933) 677234

Woodlands G.C.
(18) 6330 yards
Farthingstone, Towcester
(032736) 291

LEICESTERSHIRE

Birstall G.C.
(18) 6203 yards
Station Rd, Birstall, Leicester
(0533) 674322

Charnwood Forest G.C.
(9) 6202 yards
Breakback Lane, Woodhouse, Eaves
(0509) 890259

Cosby G.C.
(18) 6270 yards
Chapel Lane, Cosby
(0533) 864759

Glen Gorse G.C.
(18) 6641 yards
Glen rd, Oadby, Leicester
(0533) 714159

Hinckley G.C.
(18) 6578 yards
Leicester Rd, Hinckley
(0455) 615014

Humberstone Heights G.C.
(18) 6444 yards
Gipsy Lane, Leicester
(0533) 761905

Kibworth G.C.
(18) 6282 yards
Weir Rd, Kibworth, Beauchamp
(053753) 2301

Kirby Muxloe G.C.
(18) 6303 yards
Kirby Muxloe, Leicester
(0533) 393457

Leicestershire G.C.
(18) 6312 yards
Evington Lane, Leicester
(0533) 738825

Lingdale G.C.
(9) 6114 yards
Joe Moores Lane, Woodhouse Eaves
(0509) 890035

Longcliffe G.C.
(18) 6485 yards
Snell's Nook Lane, Loughborough
(0509) 239129

Luffenham Heath G.C.
(18) 6254 yards
Kelton, Stamford
(0780) 720205

Lutterworth G.C.
(18) 5734 yards
Rugby Rd, Lutterworth
(04555) 2532

Market Harborough G.C.
(9) 6080 yards
Oxenden Rd, Market Harborough
(0858) 63684

Melton Mowbray G.C.
(9) 6168 yards
Waltham Rd, Melton Mowbray
(0664) 62118

Oadby G.C.
(18) 6228 yards
Leicester Rd, Oadby
(0533) 709052

Rothley Park G.C.
(18) 6487 yards
Westfield Lane, Rothley
(0533) 302809

R.A.F. North Luffenham
(18) 5629 yards
North Luffenham, Oakham
(0780) 720041

Rushcliffe G.C.
(18) 6057 yards
Stocking Lane, East Leake, Loughborough
(050982) 2959

Scraploft G.C.
(18) 6166 yards
Beeby Rd, Scraploft
(0533) 419000

Ullesthorpe G.C.
(18) 6048 yards
Ullesthorpe, Luttersworth
(0455) 20902

Western Park G.C.
(18) 6818 yards
Scudmore Rd, Leicester
(0533) 872339

Willesley Park G.C.
(18) 6310 yards
Tamworth Rd, Ashby-de-la-Zouch
(0530) 414596

***CHARLES CROMBIE 'The Rules of Golf'** ROSENSTIEL'S*

EAST ANGLIA

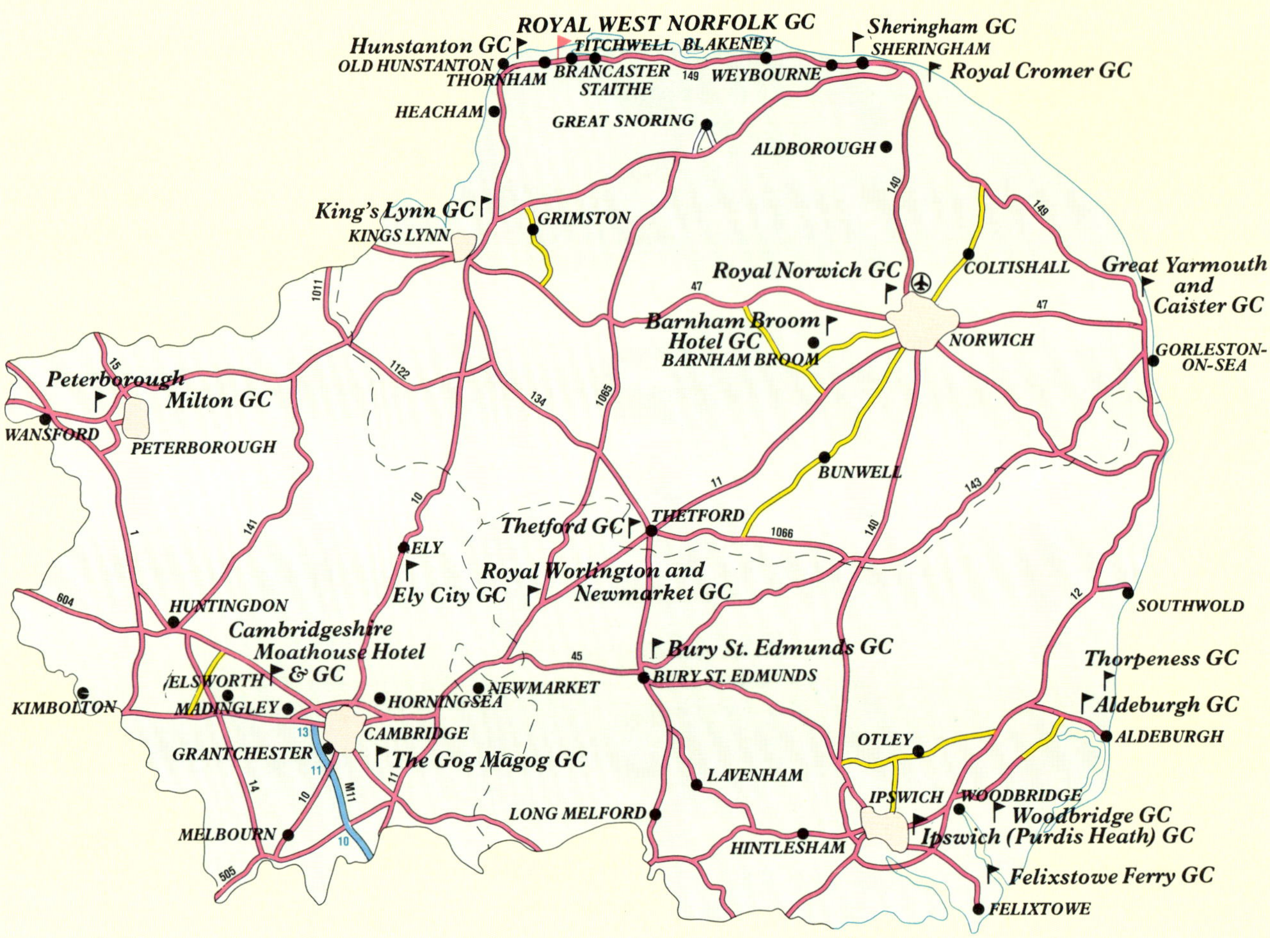

JULIAN BARROW *"Brancaster"* BURLINGTON GALLERY

EAST ANGLIA

CHOICE GOLF

NORFOLK

It is doubtful whether any county in England can surpass Norfolk's great range of outstanding courses. In short it offers a bit of everything. There are the magnificent links courses at **Hunstanton** and **Brancaster**, some terrifically scenic golf along the cliffs at **Sheringham** and **Cromer** and a number of superb inland courses of which **Thetford** and **Kings Lynn** are prime examples.

However, the title of 'Oldest Club' in Norfolk goes to **Great Yarmouth and Caister**, founded in 1882. A fine seaside links, it is located to the north of Great Yarmouth close to the old Roman town of Caister-on-Sea and near to the start of the **A149** coastal road. Punters may wish to note that the golf course is actually situated inside part of Great Yarmouth race course. Anyone who does think of combining the two might look to Gorleston-on-Sea for a night's rest and the **Cliff Hotel (0493) 662179** (apologies Yarmouth).

Cromer, some 25 miles north along the A149 is apparently famed for its crabs – the town, not the golf course I hasten to add – and also for its 150 year old lighthouse. The latter is a feature of **Royal Cromer's** attractive cliff top course. The 14th, the 'Lighthouse Hole', was played by Tony Jacklin during his '18 holes at 18 different courses helicopter round'. Several elevated tees and a generous spread of gorse make for an interesting game. The Club celebrated its centenary in 1988.

Sheringham is only five miles further along the coast and is Norfolk's other great cliff top course. Founded some three years after Cromer it is perhaps less exacting than its neighbour (though beware of the thick gorse and the adjoining railway line!) but certainly no less scenic. The view from the 5th hole is particularly stunning looking out across the rugged north Norfolk coastline – quite invigorating! Green fees at Sheringham are similar to those at Cromer – **£13** midweek, **£17** at weekends.

A glorious day's golf (followed perhaps by some early evening bird watching? – don't forget the binoculars) and time to relax. Well, in Sheringham **The Beacon (0263) 822019** and **The Beaumaris (0263) 822370** are handy and in nearby Weybourne **The Swiss Restaurant (0263) 70220** is a splendid restaurant, while **Maltings Hotel (026 370) 731** is a perfect base. On the road towards Brancaster (still the A149) the Blakeney area offers a glorious coastline and two beautifuly sited hotels, **The Manor (0263) 7403767** and **The Blakeney (0263) 740797**.

And so on to Brancaster and Hunstanton, an outstanding pair to put it mildly. Brancaster, or the **Royal West Norfolk Golf Club**, is featured later in this section but the Championship links at Hunstanton is certainly not short of admirers, and is famed for its beautiful and very slick greens. An amazing event happened at Hunstanton on the short 16th in 1974. One R.J. Taylor holed in one here on three consecutive days, once with a one iron and twice with a six iron. I suppose he was surprised when he missed on the fourth day. A day's golf at Hunstanton is priced at **£13** midweek, **£18** at the weekend.Once again, there's no shortage of places in which to relax and reflect on the day's golf. In Old Hunstanton, adjacent to the links, is the **Lodge Hotel (04853) 2896** and on Golfhouse Road **Le Strange Arms (04853) 34411** is highly thought of. The village of Thorham lies between Hunstanton and Brancaster and here one might consider **The Chequers Inn (048526) 229** or **The Kings Head (048526) 213**. To the south east of Brancaster **The Old Rectory (0328) 820597** at Great Snoring sounds like the perfect place for a particularly long rest and a little nearer at Brancaster Staithe **The Jolly Sailors (0485) 210314** is a good pub with an accompanying restaurant. Further accommodation can be found at Titchwell, the **Titchwell Manor (04951) 210221** and for a really homely Country House **The Holly Lodge (0485) 70790** at Heacham takes some beating.

Kings Lynn is our next port of call, and another very good golf course, one of the area's newest additions, although the **Kings Lynn Golf Club** was founded back in 1923. It has played at Castle Rising to the north of the town since 1975. An Alliss-Thomas creation, it's very heavily wooded and quite a demanding test of golf. At a cost of **£12.50** visitors can play on Mondays, Wednesdays, Thursdays and Fridays. Returning to the town itself suggestions for an overnight stay include **The Dukes Head Hotel (0553) 774996** and **The Riverside Rooms (0553) 773134**. A short journey to Grimston and one finds a real gem in **Congham Hall (0485) 600250**, an elegant and very well run Georgian Manor House.

The golfing visitor to Norwich, one of England's more attractive county towns, should have little difficulty in finding a game. For a fine combination of the old and the new try **Royal Norwich** and **Barnham Broom**. Both are parkland courses, fairly lengthy and at the latter there is a considerable amount of water to confront – in a nutshell the River Yare. Barnham Broom is part of an Hotel and Country Club Complex and has facilities to rival the Belfry. If Norwich is to be the base though, then **The Maids Head (0603) 76111** is most comfortable and among many good restaurants are **Marco's (0603) 624044** and **Greens Seafood (0603) 623733.**

Last but not least we must visit **Thetford**, right in the very heart of East Anglia and close to the the Norfolk-Cambridgeshire boundary. Thetford is surely one of England's most beautiful inland courses. Set amid glorious oaks, pines and silver birches it is also a great haven for wildlife (rather like Luffenham Heath). Golden pheasants abound and one can also sight red deer and even, I'm told, Chinese Water Deer (whatever they may be!).The green fee of **£12.50, (£15** at the weekends) is money well spent. The second place to invest the cash is at **The Bell Hotel (0842) 4455** in Thetford – a jolly good place to lie down the golf bag.

And so we've reached the end of our little trip. Looking back it appears we've travelled Felixstowe-Hunstanton-Thetford rather than Felixstowe-Thetford-Hunstanton. But I'm sure it doesn't matter – there's no doubting we'll be back!

The three counties of East Anglia stretch from 'Constable Country' in the south, through the Fens and the Broads to the tip of the Wash. For golfers this means it stretches from Felixstowe Ferry, through Thetford to Hunstanton. There are numerous other combinations capable of whetting the golfing appetite, for East Anglia is one of the games richest regions. In terms of actual numbers the area is relatively thin on the ground but for quality and variety it has few equals. It is also a corner of Britain where golf has long been a popular pastime.

SUFFOLK

Of the twenty or so Golf Clubs in Suffolk, about half were founded in the 19th Century and the **Felixstowe Golf Club** which dates from 1880 is the fifth oldest club in England. Given its location close to the boundary with Essex, and the fact that it was here that Bernard Darwin began to play his golf, Felixstowe Ferry is as good a place as any to begin a golfing tour of East Anglia.

EAST ANGLIA

CHOICE GOLF

The course lies about a mile to the north east of Felixstowe and is a classic test of traditional links golf. This part of Suffolk is fairly remote and at times it could easily be imagined that one was playing one of the better Scottish links courses. The greens are first class and the wind is often a major factor. Apart from early in the day on Saturdays and Sundays, visitors are welcome at all times at Felixstowe with a game priced at around **£10** during the week, **£12** at weekends. Those looking to spend some time in this area (the courses at Ipswich and Woodbridge are only a short drive away) should note the **Marlborough Hotel (0394) 285681** in Felixstowe.

The A45 links Felixstowe with Suffolk's largest town. The **Ipswich** Golf Club at Purdis Heath, (green fees **£12**) three miles east of Ipswich, was designed by James Braid and is possibly East Anglia's finest parkland layout. Always well-maintained the fairways wind their way between two large ponds and are bordered by an attractive assortment of hardwood trees and silver birches. Visitors are welcome at most times but a quick telephone call is probably advisable before setting off. **Woodbridge** provides an excellent contrast to Purdis Heath (and to Felixstowe for that matter). Like the Ipswich course it's beautifully mature but is much more undulating and is of the heather and gorse variety as opposed to parkland. Fees here are **£11** per round, **£15** day, but visitors are not received at weekends. The Golf Club is located two miles east of Woodbridge along the B1084 Orford road.

The Ipswich-Woodbridge area is blessed with some outstanding places to stay and the seafood served in these parts is some of the best in Britain. In Woodbridge, **Seckford Hall (0394) 385678** is superb while **Melton Grange (03943) 4147** also appeals. For those who enjoy their lobster Orford should be visited, more particularly the **Butley-Orford Oysterage (03945) 0277**. In Ipswich another **Marlborough Hotel (0473) 57677** both comfortable and good value and to the west of the town at Hintlesham is **Hintlesham Hall (047387) 268**, a glorious country house with an excellent restaurant.

Back to the golf though and a little further up the Suffolk coast lie two delightful holiday courses, **Thorpeness** and **Aldeburgh**. Although close to the sea both are again heath and gorse types. The town of Aldeburgh is of course famed for its annual music festival and Benjamin Britten once lived next to the 14th fairway. Thorpeness, another James Braid creation, is about two miles north of Aldeburgh and is especially scenic. On the 18th an unusual water tower (the 'House in the Clouds') and a restored windmill provide a unique background. A game on either course is priced at around **£10-£13**. Thorpeness Golf Club has its own **Golf Hotel (07285) 2176** which is naturally very convenient, but in Aldeburgh there are a number of alternatives, many of which specialise in golfing breaks. Ideas here include the **Wentworth (072885) 2312**, the **White Lion (072885) 2720** and the **Uplands Hotel (072885) 2420**. A final thought before moving inland is **The Crown** as Southwold to the north of Thorpeness – some pleasant rooms and some very good beer!

Over to the west of Suffolk the two courses that stand out are **Bury St. Edmunds** and **Royal Worlington** (green fees are around **£15**). The former is a fairly tough parkland course and the venue of the country's amateur championship in 1987. Royal Worlington and Newmarket, to give it its full title, is located two miles from Mildenhall, midway between Cambridge and Bury St. Edmunds. A marvellous heath and heather affair it was once described as 'the finest nine holes in the world'. Not surprisingly it's a popular course and visitors must contact the club before making any arrangements. They should also note that fourball matches are not permitted. An attractive market town, Bury St. Edmunds offers a first rate hotel in **The Angel (0284) 39216** while to the south of the town two cosy establishments are **The Bull** at Long Melford with its 15th Century frame and **The Swan (0787) 78494** at Lavenham.

CAMBRIDGESHIRE

Having ventured west it may be time to inspect the 'land of the fens' and the courses of Cambridgeshire. Not a county exactly renowned for its golf, the courses tending as one might expect, to be rather flat. One great exception though, is the **Gog Magog** Golf Club situated to the south east of Cambridge. The Club takes its name from the ridge of low hills on which it lies. Apparently taking a line due east from here the next range of hills one comes across is the Ural Mountains! A fine test of golf, visitors are welcome on weekdays, fees being **£15** per round or day. A second good course, close to the famous University City belongs to the **Cambridgeshire Moat House Hotel (0954) 80555**. Certainly a tough course when played from the back tees with a lake and several ditches providing the challenges. A preliminary telephone call is essential but generally golfers are welcome seven days a week, the cost of a game being slightly cheaper than at Gog Magog.

Cambridge with its magnificent colleges is a marvellous place to spend a day or two and the Moat House is just one of many fine hotels. Of the others **The Garden House Hotel (0223) 63421** perhaps takes pride of place and is particularly welcoming. It also possesses a first class restaurant. Another good eating place in town is **Jean Louis (0223) 315232**. Some notable hostelries in the area include **The Plough and Fleece** at Horningsea, **The Three Horse Shoes** at Madingley and **The Green Man** at Grantchester.

THE OLD RECTORY

The Old Rectory promises a peaceful retreat in the heart of rural Norfolk. Great Snoring is a small village 3 miles from Fakenham and within easy reach of the Heritage coast, nature reserves, coastal golf courses and areas of outstanding natural beauty.

Accommodation in this former manor house comprises six individually styled bedrooms, each with bathroom ensuite and direct dial telephone. There is a dining room, heavily beamed with a fine example of stone mullioned windows, where guests are able to enjoy breakfast and dinner (traditional English cooking complemented by fine wines).

BTA Commended. Egon Ronay. The Good Hotel Guide.

The Old Rectory,
Great Snoring,
Fakenham,
NR12 0HP
Tel: (032) 872) 597

ROYAL WEST NORFOLK (BRANCASTER)
CHAMPIONSHIP GOLF

Excluding those which have staged an Open Championship, there are perhaps two courses that exude a sense of tradition, history and character above all others. One is **Westward Ho!** and the other is **Brancaster** or, to give them their correct titles, **Royal North Devon** and **Royal West Norfolk**.

Apart from their rather geographical names, they have much in common; both enjoy a wonderously remote setting (particularly Brancaster), yet are fairly close to a superb Championship links (Saunton and Hunstanton); both have a unique hazard (sea rushes and tidal marshes) and both are particularly friendly Clubs, emphasising that tradition need not accompany aloofness.

Brancaster is something of a golfer's Camelot. Having reached the attractive little village, there is every possibility that a high tide will have flooded the road that leads to the course. Indeed, many choose to leave their car in the village and walk the remainder of the journey. (Don't worry, it's not that far!) The golf course lies in a range of sand hills between marshland and sea. There is a story that the course was laid out on the suggestion of the **Prince of Wales** (later King Edward V11), having conceived the idea while he was out shooting on the land. Certainly, it was he who bestowed patronage on the Club immediately on its foundation in **1891**. The 'Royal flavour' has continued and there have been no fewer than four Royal Captains, most recently the **Duke of Kent** in 1981.

Approaching centenary year, **Major N.A. Carrington Smith, M.B.I.M.** is the **Secretary** – a very pleasant man he is too, and can be contacted on **(0485) 210223**. The Club's full address is the **Royal West Norfolk Golf Club, Brancaster, Nr. King's Lynn, Norfolk, PE31 8AX**. There are no general restrictions on **visitors**, who may play at all times; the only restriction as such is that visitors must have handicap of 18 or less – given the challenge that lies ahead, this is entirely reasonable, generous even. Visiting parties of eight or more must make prior arrangement with the Secretary.

In 1989, the **green fee** was set at **£20** during the week and **£25** during the weekend and on Bank Holidays. The preferred days for golfing **societies** are Mondays, Wednesdays and Fridays, subject of course, to confirmation with the Club. The professional at Brancaster is **Mr. R.E. Kimber**, who can be contacted on **(0485) 210616**.

The problem of being 'wonderously remote' is that travelling to the course can be a lengthy journey. Brancaster is approximately eight miles from Hunstanton and twenty-five miles from Kings Lynn to the south and south west respectively, and about thirty miles from Cromer to the east. Linking each to the other is the **A149**.

Like our friend Westward Ho!, Brancaster has the traditional out and back links layout. A quick glance at the scorecard tells us that one nine is considerably shorter than the other, the outward half measuring **3369** yards to the inward's **2933** yards. However, as at every good seaside course, wind direction is all important and the back nine can play, or at least seem, much longer. In total, the **6302** yards, par **70** represents a considerable test of golf. From the ladies tees the course measures **5868** yards, par **75**.

As well as the tidal marshes which come into play around the **8th** and **9th**, Brancaster is famed for its great wooden sleepered bunkers. Many are cross bunkers, which, as Sir Peter Allen wrote: '... can be alarming to play over and frightening to play out of'. The course has received very few alterations over the years, although two greens were lost to the sea in 1939 and 1940. There is no gentle beginning: the first three holes all measure over 400 yards and the great cross bunkers are introduced on the **3rd** hole, one of the most difficult on the course. The bunker is fifty yards short of the green, which itself sits on a plateau. The **4th** is a short par three, but deceptively tricky, especially into the wind. The 8th and 9th have been mentioned, and the marshes must be carried twice on the 8th and from the tee on the dog-legged 9th, which has a cross bunker in front of the green. The **11th** and **12th** are played deep in the dunes, but the **14th** is perhaps the most difficult hole, with the **18th** close behind – a hole with sleepered bunkers both to the front and back of the green.

The Clubhouse which is only a year younger than the course, is decidedly comfortable and is separated from the sea only by a sea wall. There is a lovely verandah from which there are some glorious views. The setting really is something special. Nobody described it better than **Tom Scott**: 'It has a quiet and restful beauty, and when you leave the Clubhouse and drive across the marsh to the main road in the dusk of a summer evening, look back for a minute and perhaps you will be rewarded, as I have frequently been, with a view of the red sun setting over the sea with a golden glow. You will see too, the long shadows cast by the great sand hills, and you will hear the call of the many birds across the marshes, a sound to my mind typical of Norfolk'.

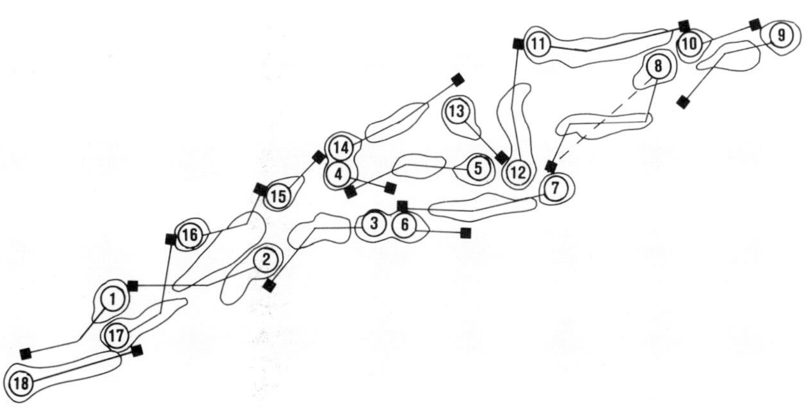

Hole	Yards	Par	Hole	Yards	Par
1	410	4	10	151	3
2	449	4	11	478	5
3	407	4	12	386	4
4	128	3	13	191	3
5	421	4	14	432	4
6	186	3	15	188	3
7	486	5	16	346	4
8	478	5	17	377	4
9	404	4	18	384	4
Out	3,369	36	In	2,933	34
			Out	3,369	36
			TOTALS	6,302	70

THE BLACK LION

Situated on the green, in this fully restored 17th century coaching inn, you will find a family run hotel where nothing is too much trouble. A veritable home form home, famed for its Countryman restaurant.

Classically influenced, mouthwatering dishes are freshly made to your order by Stephen, who trained at the Dorchester Hotel. He uses fresh locally grown Suffolk produce, seasoned with herbs cultivated in his own garden. There are two menus at lunch and dinner to stimulate your tastebuds, and these are changed each month. To compliment this epicural delight, Janet his wife, can offer you a selection from 150 carefully chosen wines. Apart from her long standing interest in the subject, she has been awarded several higher certificates in wine, to give you expert guidance in making the perfect choice. After an agonising decision of which luscious dessert to choose, comes the cheeseboard. Expect to find at least 14 different cheeses, a speciality of the house. Retire from the intimate dining room to relax in the informal and delightful surroundings of either of the two lounges, equipped with books, magazines and games. Perhaps even a sip of liqueur from a selection of over 100.

And so to bed. From this vantage point, there are panoramic views of the hamlet of Long Melford and you can be forgiven for thinking that you have stepped back in time a couple of centuries. Each of the 10 spacious bedrooms are equipped with its own private bathroom, direct dial telephone, colour TV, radio and tea and coffee facilities. If you are lucky you could be sleeping soundly in one of the two four poster beds or the mahogany half tester. There is a family suite, and well behaved children are catered for. Dogs are accepted by appointment.

Long Melford is famous for its quaint architecture and a wealth of antique shops. A stones throw away are two country houses, 15th century Kentwell Hall, restored lovingly to its original state and National Trust Melford Hall, the family seat of the Hyde-Parkers, who are still in residence. Other places of interest nearby are the wool villages of Lavenham, historic Bury St Edmunds, winner of 'England in Bloom', Sudbury, the home of Gainsborough, horse racing at Newmarket, a preserved steam railway at Castle Headingham and Constable country.

The Black Lion Hotel and Countryman Restaurant is featured in all recognised guides and the Errington family wish you a warm and pleasant stay.

The Black Lion Hotel
The Green
Long Melford
Suffolk CO10 9DN
Tel: (0787) 312356

EAST ANGLIA
COMPLETE GOLF

NORFOLK

Barnham Broom Hotel G. & C.C.
(18) 6603 yards
Norwich
(060545) 393

Dereham G.C.
(9) 6225 yards
Quebec Rd, Dereham
(0362) 693122

Diss G.C.
(9) 5900 yards
Stuston, Diss
(0379) 2679

Eaton G.C.
(18) 6074 yards
Newmarket Rd, Norwich
(0603) 51686

Fakenham G.C.
(9) 5879 yards
The Racecourse, Fakenham
(0328) 2867

Gorleston G.C.
(18) 6279 yards
Warren Rd, Gorleston
Great Yarmouth
(0493) 661911

Great Yarmouth & Caister G.C.
(18) 6235 yards
Beach House, Caister-on-Sea
(0493) 728699

Hunstanton G.C.
(18) 6670 yards
Golf Course Rd, Old Hunstanton
(04853) 2811

Kings Lynn G.C.
(18) 6552 yards
Castle Rising, Kings Lynn
(055387) 654

Links Country Park Hotel & G.C.
(9) 4814 yards
West Runton
(026375) 691

Mundesley G.C.
(9) 5376 yards
Mundesley, Norwich
(0263) 720095

Norwich Golf Centre
(9) 5154 yards
Long Lane, Bawburgh
((0603) 746390

Royal Cromer G.C.
(18) 6508 yards
Overstrand Rd, Cromer
(0263) 512884

Royal Norwich G.C.
(18) 6603 yards
Hellesdon, Norwich
(0603) 49928

Royal West Norfolk G.C.
(18) 6302 yards
Brancaster, Nr. Kings Lynn
(0485) 210233

Ryston Park G.C.
(9) 6292 yards
Denver, Downham Market
(0366) 382133

Sheringham G.C.
(18) 6430 yards
Weybourne Rd, Sheringham
(0263) 823488

Sprowston Park G.C.
(18) 5985 yards
Wroxham Rd, Sprowston,
Norwich
(0603) 410657

Swaffham G.C.
(9) 6252 yards
Clay Rd, Swaffham
(0760) 21611

Thetford G.C.
(18) 6504 yards
Brandon Rd, Thetford
(0842) 2169

SUFFOLK

Aldeburgh G.C.
(18) 6330 yards
Saxmundham Road, Aldeburgh
(072 885) 2890

Beccles G.C.
(9) 5392 yards
The Common, Beccles
(0502) 712244

Bungay &
Waveny Valley G.C.
(18) 5944 yards
Outney Common, Bungay
(0986) 2337

Bury St. Edmunds G.C.
(18) 6615 yards
Tuthill, Bury St. Edmunds
(0284) 5978

Felixstowe Ferry G.C.
(18) 6042 yards
Ferry Road, Felixstowe
(0394) 286834

Flempton G.C.
(9) 6050 yards
Flempton, Bury St. Edmunds
(028484) 291

Fornham Park G.C.
(18) 6212 yards
Fornham St. Martin, Bury St. Edmunds
(0284) 63426

Haverhill G.C.
(9) 5680 yards
Coupals Road, Haverhill
(0440) 61951

Ipswich G.C.
(18) 6405 yards
(9) 3860 yards
Purdis Heath, Ipswich
(0473) 78941

Newton Green G.C.
(9) 5442 yards
Newton Green, Sudbury
(0787) 77501

Rookery Park G.C.
(18) 6649 yards
Carlton Colville, Lowestoft
(0502) 60380

Royal Worlington
& Newmarket G.C.
(9) 6210 yards
Worlington, Bury St. Edmunds
(0638) 712216

Rushmere G.C.
(18) 6287 yards
Rushmere Heath, Ipswich
(0473) 75648

Southwold G.C.
(9) 6001 yards
The Common, Southwold
(0502) 723248

Stowmarket G.C.
(18) 6119 yards
Onehouse, Stowmarket
(04493) 473

Thorpeness G.C.
(18) 6241 yards
Thorpeness
(072885) 2176

Woodbridge G.C.
(18) 6314 yards
(9) 4486 yards
Bromeswell Heath, Woodbridge
(03943) 2038

CAMBRIDGESHIRE

Cambridgeshire Moat House Hotel G.C.
(18) 6734 yards
Bar Hill, Cambridge
(0954) 80555

Ely City G.C.
(18) 6686 yards
Cambridge Road, Ely
(0353) 2751

Eynesbury Hardwicke G.C.
(18) 6214 yards
Eynesbury Hardwicke, St. Neots
(0480) 215153

Girton G.C.
(18) 5927 yards
Dodford Lane, Cambridge
(0223) 276169

Gog Magog G.C.
(18) 6386 yards (Old)
(9) 5833 yards (New)
(0223) 247626

Links G.C.
(18) 6402 yards
Cambridge Rd, Newmarket
(0638) 663000

March G.C.
(9) 6278 yards
Grange Rd, March
(0354) 52364

Peterborough Milton G.C.
(18) 6431 yards
Milton Ferry, Peterborough
(073121) 489
(0733) 380489

Ramsey G.C.
(18) 6136 yards
Abbey Terrace, Ramsey
(0487) 812600

St. Ives G.C.
(9) 6052 yards
St. Ives, Huntingdon
(0480) 68392

St. Neots G.C.
(18) 6027 yards
Crosshall Rd, St. Neots
(0480) 72363

Thorpe Wood G.C.
(18) 6595 yards
Nene Parkway, Peterborough
(0733) 264150

***J. HORWOOD 'East Anglian Links'** BURLINGTON GALLERY*

DERBYSHIRE & NOTTINGHAMSHIRE

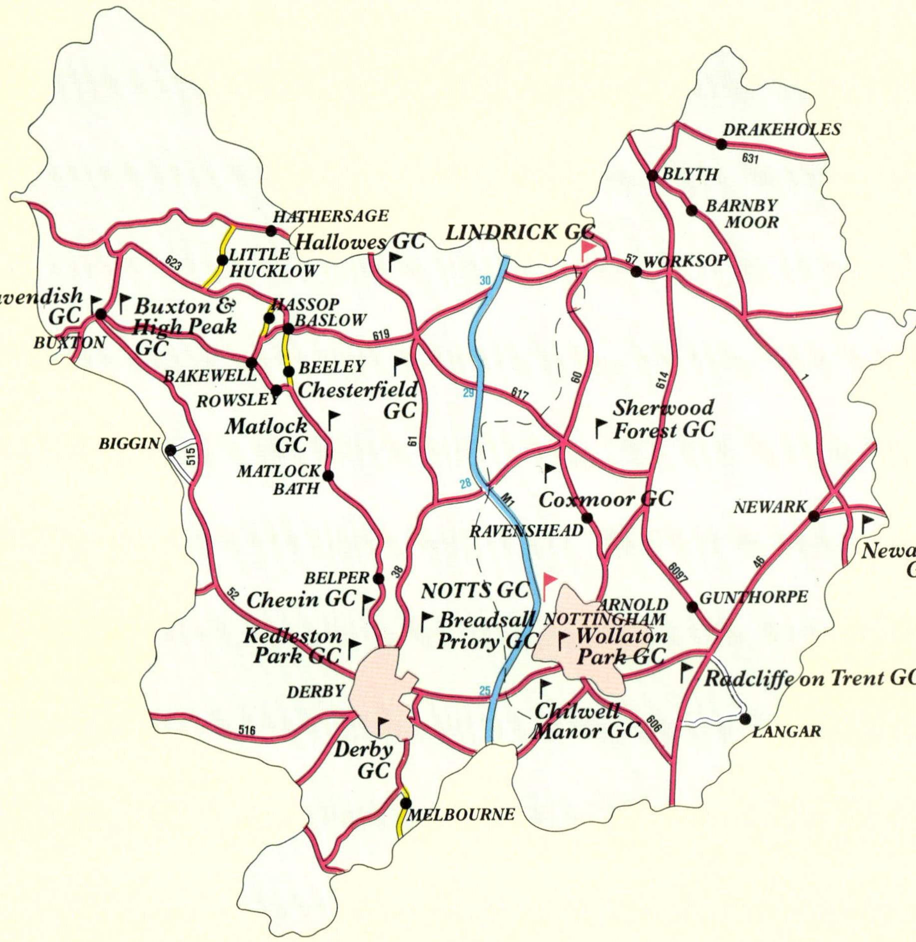

MICHAEL BROWN "Preparing to Play" BURLINGTON GALLERY

DERBYSHIRE & NOTTINGHAMSHIRE
CHOICE GOLF

Having earlier referred to the map of Berkshire as being 'cigar-shaped; I'm afraid I cannot resist describing the combination of Derbyshire and Nottinghamshire as 'heart-shaped'. Given their geography it doesn't seem too inappropriate although I don't sup pose the people of Nottinghamshire are all that happy being told that they inhabit the left ventricle of England, nor the Derbyshire folk that they live in the right ventricle – just put it down to the way some minds work!

Heart-shaped or otherwise, between them the two counties possess a number of very fine golf courses. While those of Nottinghamshire are perhaps more widely known, especially the Notts Golf Club at Hollinwell, Derbyshire too has plenty to interest the visiting golfer.

NOTTINGHAMSHIRE

Taking **Nottinghamshire** first, **Notts Golf Club** is featured separately on a later page. In addition to this rather splendid 'Nottingham gorse affair' those visiting the county town should strongly consider the merits of **Wollaton Park**, an attractive course set amidst the deer park of a stately home, close to the centre of Nottingham. Slightly further afield but well worth noting are the parkland courses at **Chilwell Manor (A6005)** and **Radcliffe on Trent (A52** East of the town). Green fees at Wollaton are approximately **£12**, at the other two perhaps slightly less.

Nottingham has no shortage of comfortable modern hotels and **The Albany (0602) 470131** and **The Royal (0602) 414444** are both first rate and centrally located. To the north of the city at Arnold. **The Bestwood Lodge (0602) 203011** is less stylish but good value while to the south, lovers of the country house scene should delight in Langar Hall at Langar (seems to have a golfing ring to it, don't you think?) The best known pub in town is probably the **Olde Trip to Jerusalem** – said to be the oldest in England.

Two of the county's finest courses lie fairly close to one another near the centre of Nottinghamshire, **Coxmoor** and **Sherwood Forest**. The former is a moorland type course situated just south of Mansfield at Sutton-in-Ashfield. The Sherwood Forest course is more of a heathland type, well wooded, (as one might expect given its name) with much tangling heather. Measuring over 6,700 yards it is quite a test too. Visitors (with handicaps) are welcome at both courses, green fees are around the **£12** mark.

Over towards the border with Lincolnshire is the attractive town of Newark with its twelfth century castle and cobbled market square. **Newark Golf Club** lies four miles east of the town off the **A17.** Reasonably flat and quite secluded the golf here is a little less testing than at some of the county's bigger clubs (fairly inexpensive too). The place to stay here is **The Clinton Arms (0636) 72299**, a charming Georgian listed building. Also in town **The Old Kings Arms** is a fine pub **(0636) 703416**.

Before inspecting Derbyshire, a brief word on **Lindrick** (green fees **£16** a round). Although it's postal address is in Nottinghamshire the majority of the course lies in South Yorkshire. In any event, like Notts it's featured ahead. If a nights rest is required 'this side' of the border, then **Ye Old Bell Hotel** at Barnby Moor **(0777) 705121** is a pleasant coaching inn and **The Angel (090976)213** Blyth is a friendly pub with some accomodation also.

DERBYSHIRE

Not wishing to be unkind but Derby, the town, isn't one of earth's more inspiring places – nor for that matter are most of the Midland's industrial sprawls but **Derbyshire** the county is a different matter altogether. **The Peak District** is without question one of the most scenic regions in Britain and commencing only a short distance north of Derby, it covers the greater part of the county – the Pennine Way of course starts in Derbyshire.

As well as being the beginning of all things beautiful, the area just north of Derby is where three of the county's leading golf courses are to be found: **Kedlestone Park, Breadsall Priory** and **Chevin**. Located approximately 4 miles from Derby off the **A111** (and well signposted) **Kedleston's** golf course occupies a beautiful situation and is the leading course in Derbyshire, it measures 6636 yards from the back tees (par 72) and has a variety of challenging holes. Eyeing the course from across a lake is the impressive Kedleston Hall, historic house of Lord Scarsdale. Visitors are welcome during the week, the cost of a game being **£11** although it is probably just as well to give the club a quick call before setting off. I'm not sure what the 13th century monks would have made of the **Breadsall Priory Golf and Country Club**, 3 miles north east of Derby off **A61**, but for us heathens of the 20th century it provides an ideal setting for one of the most enjoyable games in the Midlands. Golfwise, Breadsall Priory has only been on the map since 1976 but the undulating parkland course with its imported Cumberland turf greens has matured rapidly and for about **£10** per round is well worth a visit.

Chevin lies slightly further north off the **A6** at Duffield, it has an interesting layout, the first ten holes are a steady climb towards a spectacular vantage point after which holes eleven to eighteen gently bring you down to earth (or at least to Duffield!).

If Derby has to be one's base then **The Crest Hotel (0332) 514933** in Littleover is comfortable enough. In Belper **Remy's (077 382) 2246** is a very good French restaurant – a perfect place to celebrate one's closing birdie at Chevin. **Breadsall Priory (0332) 832235** itself offers a most satisfying 19th hole.

Moving 'up' country, the picturesque town of **Matlock** (green fees **£10**), has a fairly short but pleasant course situated north of the town of the Chesterfield road, and if heading in that direction **Chesterfield's** course at Walton is worth a visit. Two recommendations: **Riber Hall (0629) 2795** near Matlock (outstanding) and **The New Bath Hotel (0629) 3725** in Matlock Bath.

The town of Buxton lies in the heart of the Peak District and is for many people their idea of the perfect town. This may have something to do with the fact that some of the finest pubs in England are located round about, but it is also helped by the fact that there are two excellent golf courses either side of the town – **Buxton and High Peak** and **Cavendish**. Of similar length it is difficult to say which is the better, in any event both welcome visitors seven days a week at green fees that should leave a few pennies for celebrating nearby. Green fees at both are about **£8**. After a day on the fairways (not to mention an evening in a Buxton pub) a suitable hotel is required. Again there are two thoughts: **The Palace Hotel (0298) 2001** and **The Lee Wood Hotel (0298) 70421** which overlooks the cricket ground.

Having done my bit for the Buxton tourist board another suggestion for this delightful area include in Hassop, **Hassop Hall (062 987) 488**. Other good locals include **The Old Bulls Head**, Little Hucklow, in Hathersage, **The George** and in Beeley, **The Devonshire Arms**, is near to Chatsworth and no trip to the area would be complete without visiting this incredible stately home.

HOLLINWELL
CHAMPIONSHIP GOLF

For many people Nottinghamshire is simply mining country, part of the 'black country'. To more romantic souls, it's the land of Robin Hood, Little John and Friar Tuck, not of course forgetting Maid Marion. But for those of us who thrash a little white ball around the counties of the realm, talk of Nottingham will invariably invoke thoughts of **Hollinwell**, home of the **Notts Golf Club** and one of the finest inland courses in the Kingdom.

1987 was an important landmark for the Notts Golf Club, it being centenary year, although the Club's first home was in fact nearer to Nottingham itself at Bulwell Forest. Apparently the proposed move from Bulwell to Hollinwell which occurred around the turn of the century met with considerable opposition. However, still undeterred, the 'radicals' invited **Willie Park Jnr.** to design the new course and by the time **John H. Taylor** had added some finishing touches, not a squeak of discontent was to be heard. Park and Taylor had presented the members with a masterpiece.

The gentleman presently looking after the interests of the Notts golfers is the **Secretary, Mr. J.R. Walker. Visitors** seeking a game are advised to contact him some time in advance of intended play. Mr. Walker can be reached by telephone on **(0623) 753225** while the address for written correspondence is **The Notts Golf Club, Hollinwell, Derby Road, Kirkby-in-Ashfield, Nottinghamshire, NG17 7QR**.

As a general guide, visitors can play between Mondays and Fridays, although it should be noted that Friday morning is Ladies Day. The first tee is reserved for members on Wednesdays and Thursdays between 12.30pm and 2.30pm or 12pm and 1.30pm during the winter months. **Societies** are equally welcome with Mondays and Tuesdays the favoured days. In 1989, the **green fees** were set **£22** per round or **£25** per day.

Since the Club's move to Hollinwell in 1900, it has had somewhat remarkably only four professionals. The present incumbent is **Brian Waites** probably our best known 'club pro' and one who made history in 1983 by becoming the oldest British player to make his debut in the Ryder Cup. He and his staff may be contacted on **(0623) 753087**.

The course is located to the north west of Nottingham on the **A611**. Approaching from either the North of South of England, the **M1** is very convenient. The motorway should be left at junction **27** at which the **A608** should be followed until it joins the **A611**. The Club is then two miles away and is signposted off to the right.

From the Championship tees the course is something of a minor monster stretching to a shade over 7000 yards (**7020** yards, par **72**). Even from the forward tees, it represents a formidable test at **6609** yards. The ladies course measures **5882** yards, par **75**. If Hollinwell is a monster, then it's a pretty one (if there can be such a creature!), with a wealth of heather and gorse lining the fairways together with some superb oaks and silver birch trees; certainly a splendid setting in which to enjoy a day's golf.

Similar to Woodhall Spa the **1st** at Hollinwell is relatively straightforward and has been described as 'ideal for the early morning top!' – something to be avoided on the lengthy **2nd**, a hole famed for the huge rock which guards the back of the green known as Robin Hood's Chair. Another notable hole on the front nine is the **8th**, perhaps not so intimidating from the forward tees, but from the forward tees, it requires a very straight and solid drive to carry a lake. Half hidden by trees to the right of the tee is the 'holy well' from which the name Hollinwell derives. Whether its waters will give you divine inspiration to tackle the back nine is debatable but it's worth a look. Actually, a prayer or two, or at least a little luck may be required when the **13th** is confronted. One of only three short holes, although short is hardly apt, it was once called 'an absolute terror', having 'trouble everywhere'. The round ends with two good par fours which if achieved will certainly earn you drink at the club's comfortable nineteenth.

Championship golf regularly visits Hollinwell. Both **Sandy Lyle** and **Nick Faldo** have triumphed here, Lyle winning the 1975 Brabazon Trophy as a precocious seventeen year old and Faldo the European Tournament Players Championship of 1982. Arguably the most celebrated event was the 1970 John Player Classic when **Christy O'Connor** pocketed a cheque for £25,000, at the time a world record first prize – no doubt a few Irish eyes were smiling.

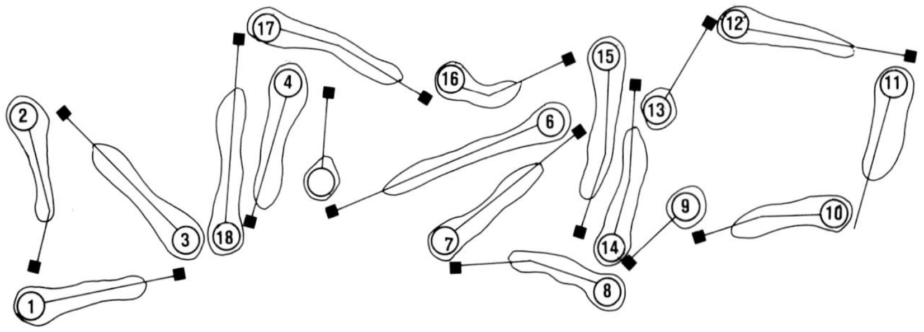

Hole	Yards	Par	Hole	Yards	Par
1	376	4	10	362	4
2	430	4	11	365	4
3	511	5	12	433	4
4	455	4	13	236	3
5	193	3	14	403	4
6	533	5	15	440	4
7	403	4	16	355	4
8	410	4	17	480	5
9	178	3	18	457	4
Out	**3,489**	**36**	**In**	**3,531**	**36**
			Out	**3,489**	**36**
			TOTALS	**7 020**	**72**

DERBYSHIRE & NOTTINGHAMSHIRE

COMPLETE GOLF

DERBYSHIRE

Alfreton G.C.
(9) 5012 yards
Wingfield Road, Oakesthorpe
(0773) 832070

Allestree Park G.C.
(18) 5749 yards
Allestree Hall, Derby
(0332) 550616

Ashbourne G.C.
(9) 5359 yards
Clifton, Ashbourne
(0335) 42077

Bakewell G.C.
(9) 4808 yards
Station Road, Bakewell
(062981) 2307

Breadsall Priory G. & C.C.
(9) 6402 yards
Moor Road, Morley, Derby
(0332) 832235

Burton-on-Trent G.C.
(18) 6555 yards
Ashby Road East, Burton-on-Trent
(0283) 44551

Buxton &
High Peak G.C.
(18) 5954 yards
Fairfield, Buxton
(0298) 6923

Cavendish G.C.
(18) 5815 yards
Gadley Lane, Buxton
(0298) 5052

Chesterfield G.C.
(18) 6326 yards
Walton, Chesterfield
(0246) 566032

Chesterfield
Municipal G.C.
(18) 6044 yards
Crow Lane, Chesterfield
(0246) 73887

Chevin G.C.
(18) 6043 yards
Golf Lane, Duffield
(0332) 841864

Craythorne G.C.
(18) 5164 yards
Stretton, Burton-on-Trent
(0283) 64329

Derby G.C.
(18) 6183 yards
Shakespeare Street, Sinfin, Derby
(0332) 766462

Erewash Valley G.C.
(18) 6444 yards
Stanton-by-Dale, Ilkeston
(0602) 322984

Glossop &
District G.C.
(11) 5726 yards
Sheffield Road, Glossop
(04574) 3117

Ilkeston Borough G.C.
(9) 4116 yards
West End Drive, Ilkeston
(0602) 320304

Kedleston Park G.C.
(18) 6636 yards
Kedleston, Quarndon, Derby
(0332) 840035

Matlock G.C.
(18) 5871 yards
Chesterfield Road, Matlock
(0629) 2191

Mickleover G.C.
(18) 5621 yards
Uttoxeter Road, Mickleover
(0332) 518662

Ormonde Fields G. & C.C.
(18) 6007 yards
Nottingham Road, Codnor, Ripley
(0773) 42987

Pastures G.C.
(9) 5005 yards
Pastures Hospital, Mickleover
(0332) 513921 (ext 348)

Renishaw Park G.C.
(18) 6253 yards
Station Road, Renishaw
(0245) 432044

Shirlands G. & S.C.
(18) 6021 yards
Lower Delves, Shirland
(0773) 834935

Sickleholme G.C.
(18) 6064 yards
Barnford
(0433) 51306

Stanedge G.C.
(9) 4867 yards
Walton, Chesterfield
(0246) 566156

NOTTINGHAMSHIRE

Beeston Fields G.C.
(18) 6404 yards
Beeston Fields, Nottingham
(0602) 254280

Bulwell Forest G.C.
(18) 5572 yards
Hucknall Road, Bulwell, Nottingham
(0602) 278008

Chilwell Manor G.C.
(18) 6379 yards
Meadow Lane, Chilwell, Nottingham
(0602) 257050

Coxmoor G.C.
(18) 6501 yards
Coxmoor Road, Sutton-in-Ashfield
(0623) 557359

Edwalton Municipal G.C.
(9) 6672 yards
Edwalton, Nottingham
(0602) 234775

Kilton Forest G.C.
(18) 6772 yards
Blyth Road, Worksop
(0909) 486563

Lindrick G.C.
(18) 6615 yards
Lindrick Common, Worksop
(0909) 475820

Mapperley G.C.
(18) 6224 yards
Mapperley Plains, Nottingham
(0602) 265611

Newark G.C.
(18) 6486 yards
Coddington, Newark
(063684) 282

Nottingham City G.C.
(18) 6120 yards
Lawton Drive, Bulwell, Nottingham
(0602) 278021

Notts G.C.
(18) 7020 yards
Hollinwell, Derby Road, Kirkby-in-Ashfield
(0623) 753225

Oxton G.C.
(18) 6630 yards
Oxton, Southwell
(0602) 653545

Radcliffe-on-Trent G.C.
(18) 6423 yards
Cropwell Road, Radcliffe-on-Trent
(06073) 3125

Retford G.C.
(9) 6230 yards
Ordsall, Retford
(0777) 703733

Sherwood Forest G.C.
(18) 6709 yards
Eakring Road, Mansfield
(0623) 26689

Stanton-on-the-Wolds G.C.
(18) 6379 yards
Stanton-on-the-Wolds, Keyworth
(06077) 2044

Wollaton Park G.C.
(18) 6494 yards
Wollaton Park, Nottingham
(0602) 787574

Chatsworth

LINCOLNSHIRE

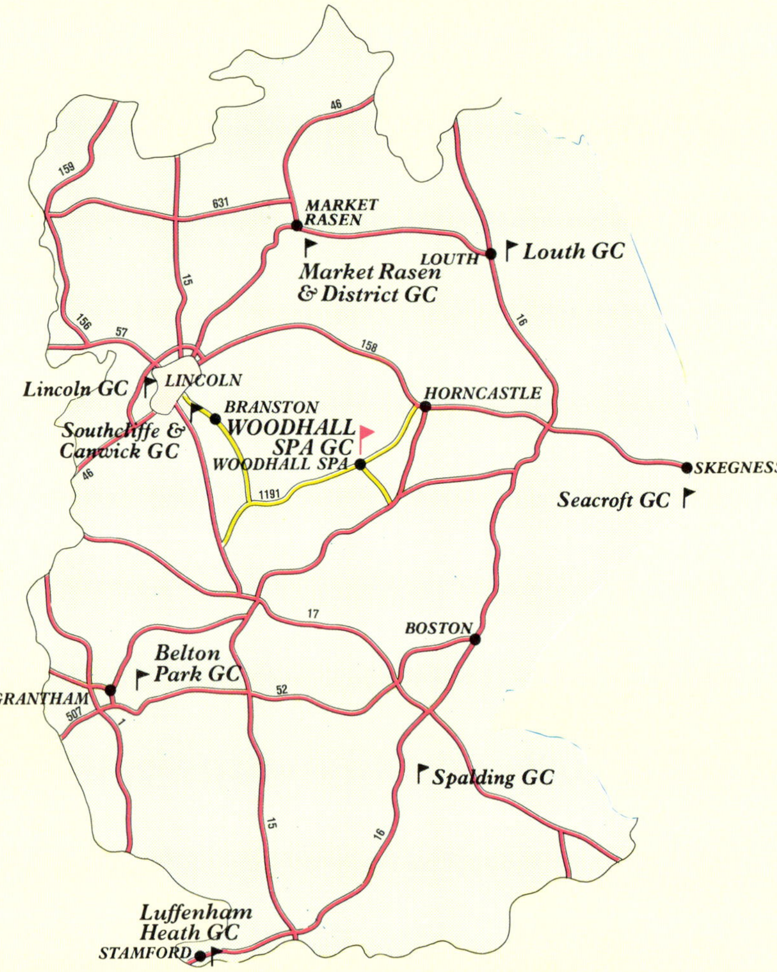

A.B. FROST "Temper" ROSENSTIELS

LINCOLNSHIRE
CHOICE GOLF

Lincolnshire is a large county. It used to be even larger before Grimsby, Scunthorpe and Cleethorpes were all snatched away by that upstart Humberside. Still, by my reckoning there are seventeen golf courses left. **Woodhall Spa** is of course head and shoulders above the rest but although the county as a whole is unlikely to be the venue for the many golfing holidays there are certainly a handful of courses well worthy of a game.

Woodhall Spa is featured ahead, for those fortunate enough to be able to spend a few days playing the course, here are some suggestions. The appropriately named **Golf Hotel (0526) 53535** is probably the most popular and convenient place in which to stay, but **The Abbey Lodge (0526) 52538** and **The Petwood (0526) 52411** are also recommended and **The Dower House (0526) 53535** is very pleasant. Lincoln of course may be a base and for those not minding a bit of a drive **The George (0780) 55171** at Stamford is quite excellent – a charming atmosphere with a very fine restaurant. Stamford is a delightful town: Burghley is found here, an outstandingly attractive Elizabethan House while just over the county boundary in Leicestershire lies **Luffenham Heath**, a truly splendid golf course, costing **£16** at the weekend, or **£10** mid-week.

Lincoln was briefly mentioned, it really is an attractive city – a beautiful cathedral, a castle and a wealth of history. The **White Hart (0525) 26222** is a noted hotel and there are some fine restaurants – one of the best is **Whites (0522) 24051**. Simpler food and a great pub can be found in the **Wig and Mitre (0522)b 35190**. Outside the city in Branston, **The Moor Lodge Hotel (0522) 791366** is good value. The best golf to be found in **Lincoln** is at Torksey just to the nort west of the city. It's a fairly sandy, heathland course with a lovely selection of trees. Green fees here are about **£10-£12**. A quick telephone call before visiting is recommended. **Southcliffe and Canwick**, on the opposite side of Lincoln is a shorter, parkland course but challenging in its own way.

Two courses of note towards the north of the county are at **Market Rasen** and **Louth**. Both are very welcoming, although visitors are only received during the week at the former. Market Rasen is a very good woodland type course and Lough has an attractive setting in a local beauty spot, the Hubbards Hills. Green fees at both are approximately **£8**. **The Limes Hotel (0673) 842357** is ideal for Market Rasen, and in Louth, **The Priory (0507) 602930** offers a comfortable stop-over. (There are some fine pubs in Louth too, note especially **The Wheatsheaf).**

Skegness is a famous resort, perhaps not everyone's cup of tea, but a game here is certainly recommended for those who like their links golf. **Seacroft** is the place, flattish, windy and plenty of sand dunes – (**£9** per round).

The south of the county comprises much rich agricultural land but little in the way of golf. **Spalding** is worth inspecting particularly when the famous bulbs have flourished. An 18 hole course here, and in the south west, **Belton Park** (27 holes), with green fees of **£11**, near Grantham and **Sleaford** are also worth a visit. But play Woodhall Spa and I can guarantee you'll leave Lincolnshire a happy man!

COUNTRY LIFE CIGARETTES

WOODHALL SPA
CHAMPIONSHIP GOLF

I've already remarked in the piece on Liphook in Hampshire how the golf-rich counties of Berkshire and Surrey don't possess the complete set of England's truly great heathland courses. Well, for what this humble opinion is worth, here's another thought. Between them **Sunningdale** and **Walton Heath** have seventy two holes, each with an 'Old' and a 'New'. Many may disagree but if a composite eighteen were created, taking the best eighteen holes from the four courses I still don't think we'd see a better course than the round offered at **Woodhall Spa** and I certainly don't view Sunningdale and Walton as anything less than outstanding.

Woodhall Spa Golf Club was founded in **1905**. The course itself was originally laid out by **Harry Vardon** although substantial alterations were made firstly by **Harry Colt** and later by **Colonel Hotchkin**.

As one of the country's greatest (and most beautiful) heathland courses Woodhall Spa is understandably extremely popular and **visitors** looking for a game must make prior arrangements with the Club's **Secretary**. (This applies to individual visitors and Golfing Societies alike). **Mr. S.R. Sharp** is the very helpful gentleman, and may be contacted via **The Woodhall Spa Golf Club, Woodhall Spa, Lincolnshire**, telephone **(0526) 52511**. The Club's professional, **Peter Fixter** can be reached on **(0526) 53229**.

The **Green fees** at Woodhall Spa for 1989 were set at **£16** per round during the week with **£20** payable for a full day's golf and **£18** per round at weekends, or **£22** for a full day. Reduced rates are available to junior golfers, but only if accompanied by a member.

Glancing at the map, Woodhall Spa looks fairly close to Lincoln. By road the distance is, in fact, at least twenty miles. Those approaching from the Cathedral city should take the **B1188** towards Sleaford, taking a left fork onto the **B1189** towards the village of Martin. At Martin the **B1191** road should be picked up and followed to Woodhall Spa, the Club being directly off this road. Those travelling from further north will probably need to use a combination of Motorways before joining the **A15** – this road linking Lincoln to the **M180** (juntion **4**). Persons motoring from the south may have to do even more map-reading! Anyway the following is hopefully of assistance: the **A1** is likely to be a starting point; it should be left just north of Colsterworth and the **B6403** taken towards Ancaster and R.A.F. Cranwell. Just beyond R A F Cranwell the **A15** can be joined. A right fork should be taken towards the wonderfully named hamlet of Ashby de la Launde on to the **B1191**. The **B1191** takes us to Martin – remember Martin? The **B1191** runs from Martin to Woodhall Spa.

The journey across Lincolnshire will have taken the traveller alongside many miles of flat agricultural land – hardly golfing country. Suddenly everything changes as Woodhall Spa looms on the horizon like a mirage. Often described as the great golfing oasis, Woodhall Spa has all the classic heathland characteristics; sandy subsoil, heather running riot and glorious tree lined fairways.

The course measures a lengthy **6866** yards, par **73** (from the ladies tees, **5771** yards par **73**). It is arguably most renowned for its vast cavernous bunkers and while it is almost impossible to select individual holes, perhaps those that particularly stand out are to be found towards the middle of the round, between the **9th** and the **13th**. Indeed the **11th** is quite possibly the finest par four in the country and certainly one of the prettiest. A plaque beside the **12th** tee records how in March 1982 two Members halved the hole in one.

Another feature of Woodhall Spa is the remarkable variety of wildlife that the golfer is likely to come across (especially the more wayward hitter!) One obviously dedicated individual claimed after hitting a rather poor drive to the **18th** that he was 'distracted by the merry gathering of partridges and pheasants to the right of the tee and by the squirrel who was chasing a magpie across the fairway'.

Although none of the major professional tournaments have visited the course (primarily a result of its isolation) numerous major amateur events have. These have included the **Youths Amateur Championship, the English Amateur Championship,** and the **English Ladies Amateur Championship**. **The English Amateur Championship** is again scheduled for 1990.

The Members are fortunate in having a wonderfully intimate Clubhouse. The atmosphere is both friendly and informal and there's an almost Colonial feel about the place – a Raffles in Lincolnshire?! A full complement of catering is offered throughout the week, with very reasonably priced meals. I referred earlier to the often alarmingly deep bunkers; apparently a competitor in the **1974 English Amateur Championship**, in his endeavours to find the entrance to the Club drove his car straight into a particularly huge bunker beside the 4th green.....one wonders whether this might have had a little to do with the aforementioned friendly atmosphere to be found at the 19th!

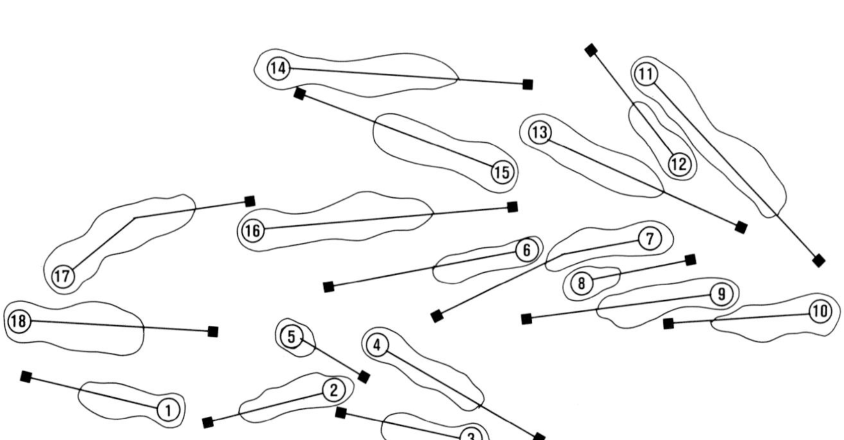

Hole	Yards	Par	Hole	Yards	Par
1	363	4	10	333	4
2	408	4	11	442	4
3	417	4	12	152	3
4	415	4	13	437	4
5	155	3	14	489	5
6	506	5	15	325	4
7	435	4	16	398	4
8	193	3	17	322	4
9	560	3	18	516	5
Out	**3,452**	**36**	**In**	**3,414**	**37**
			Out	**3,452**	**36**
			TOTALS	**6,866**	**73**

LINCOLNSHIRE
COMPLETE GOLF

Belton Park G.C.
(9) 6412 yards
(9) 6101 yards
(9) 5857 yards
Londonthorpe Road,
Grantham
(0476) 67399

Blankney G.C.
(18) 6232 yards
Blankney, Lincoln
(0526) 25272

Boston G.C.
(18) 5795 yards
Horncastle Rd,
Boston
(0205) 50589

Burghley Park G.C.
(18) 6236 yards
Stamford
(0780) 53789

Carholme G.C.
(18) 6086 yards
Carholme Road,
Lincoln
(0522) 23725

Lincoln G.C.
(18) 6400 yards
Torksey, Lincoln
(042771) 721

Louth G.C.
(18) 6502 yards
Crowtree Lane,
Louth
(0507) 603681

Market Rasen and District G.C.
(18) 6031 yards
Legsby Rd,
Market Rasen
(0673) 842416

North Shore G.C.
(18) 6010 yards
North Shore Rd,
Skegness
(0754) 3298

Sandilands G.C.
(18) 5995 yards
Sandilands,
Mablethorpe
(0521) 41617

Seacroft G.C.
(18) 6478 yards
Seacroft, Skegness
(0754) 3032

Sleaford G.C.
(18) 6443 yards
South Rauceby,
Sleaford
(05298) 273

Southcliffe and Canwick G.C.
(18) 6257 yards
Canwick Park,
Lincoln
(0522) 22166

Spalding G.C.
(18) 5782 yards
Surfleet,
Spalding
(077585) 386

Stoke Rochford G.C.
(18) 6204 yards
Stoke Rochford,
Grantham
(047683) 275

Sutton Bridge G.C.
(9) 5850 yards
Sutton Bridge,
Spalding
(0406) 350323

Thonock G.C.
(18) 5824 yards
Thonock,
Gainsborough
(0427) 3088

Woodhall Spa G.C.
(18) 6866 yards
The Broadway,
Woodhall Spa
(0526) 25211

CHARLES CROMBIE The Rules of Golf *ROSENSTIEL'S*

STAFFORDSHIRE & SHROPSHIRE

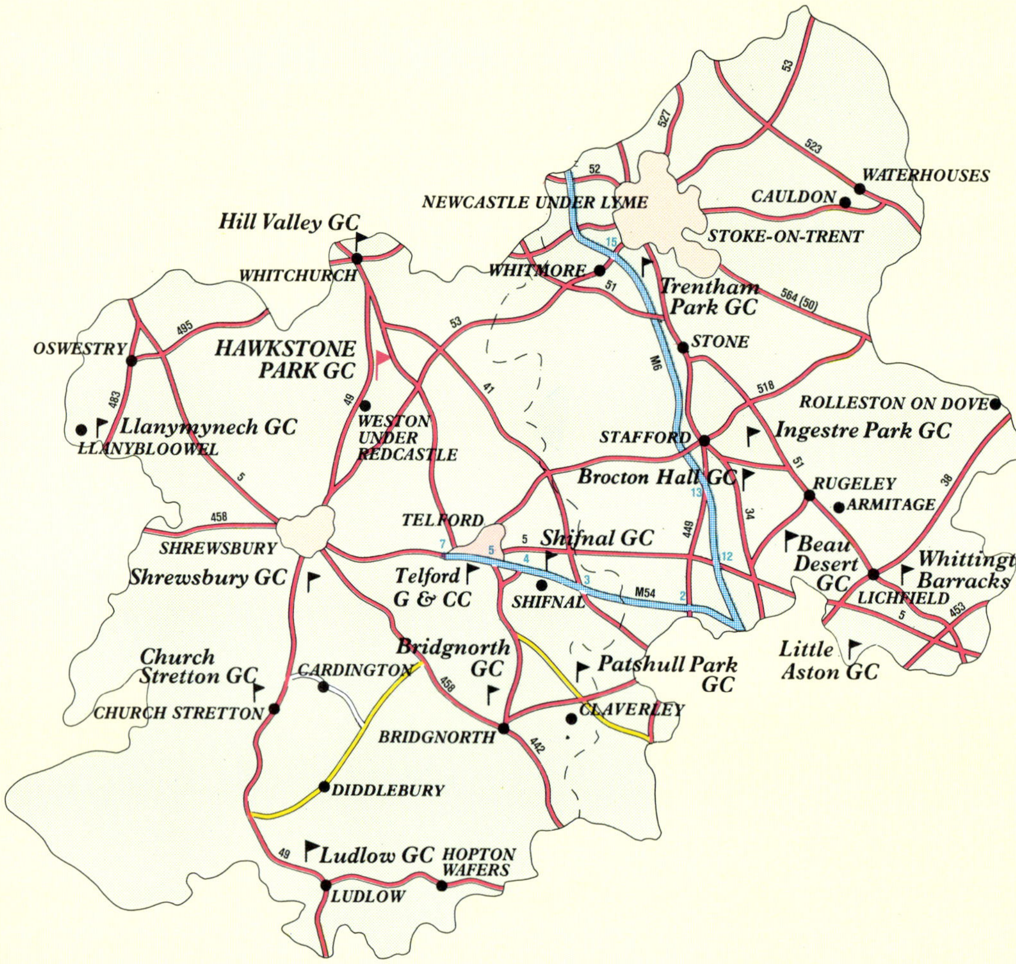

H. ROUNTREE "Perfectly Placed" BURLINGTON GALLERY

STAFFORDSHIRE & SHROPSHIRE

CHOICE GOLF

Staffordshire and Shropshire: two essentially rural counties. Staffordshire shares a boundary with the West Midlands and as for Shropshire, it enjoys a splendid peace, broken only perhaps by the mooing of cows and the yells of 'fore'! from the county's many fairways.

Both have a great deal to offer the visiting golfer: in Staffordshire **Beau Desert** and **Whittington Barracks** are two of the best courses in the Midlands (two of the prettiest too) while Shropshire in addition to providing the likes of Hawkstone Park can boast having produced 16.67% of the British and European Ryder Cup Team – both Sandy Lyle and Ian Woosnam were born and bred in the county.

STAFFORDSHIRE

Making a start in **Staffordshire, Whittington Barracks** and **Beau Desert** have already been mentioned. The former, located near Lichfield off the **A51** is a heathland type course with fine views towards the three spires of Lichfield Cathedral. Quite a testing course, visitors should be able to arrange a game between Mondays and Fridays. **Beau Desert Golf Club** near Hazel Slade occupies an unlikely setting in the middle of **Cannock Chase**. Surrounded by fir trees and spruces it is indeed quite a haven. Perhaps a mixture of heathland and woodland, and less testing than Whittington Barracks, it is nonetheless equally enjoyable. A day's golf on either course (weekdays only at Whittington Barracks) should set the visitor back about **£13**. Both can be very popular and prior telephoning is recommended.

In Lichfield **The Angel Croft (0543) 258737** is a comfortable hotel for a night's stay and **Thrales (0543) 255091** is a particularly good restaurant. After a round at Beau Desert, Rugeley may be the place to head for, here the **Cedar Tree Hotel (08894) 584241** is welcoming but if a restaurant is sought then Armitage may be the answer with **The Old Farm House**.

From the heart of Cannock Chase to the heart of the Potteries, there are a number of courses in and around Stoke-on-Trent. **Trentham, and Trentham Park** near neighbours to the south of the city, are both well worth a visit particularly perhaps the latter where visitors are welcome throughtout the week, fees being **£9** midweek, **£11** at weekends. The course is well-wooded and there are many delightful views. Perhaps the best hotel in Stoke is **The North Stafford (0782) 744477**, however as the recommended courses are south of the town Stone may be the most convenient place to spend a night. Two suggestions here **The Crown Hotel (0785) 813535** and **The Stone House (0785) 815531** both are comfortable. Also **The Star** is a good pub. East of Stoke **The Old Beams (05386) 254** in Waterhouses is an excellent restaurant while in nearby Cauldon **The Yew Tree** is a superb hostelry.

Stafford, the county town, is pretty much in the middle of things. Once again a pair of courses to note; to the south of Stafford is **Brocton Hall** (green fees **£12**) and to the north east, set in the grounds of the former home of the Earl of Shrewsbury is **Ingestre Park**. Both offer a very relaxing game. If a bed is needed then **Tillington Hall (0785) 53531** in Stafford is quite satisfactory and a bit of a drive perhaps, but Rolleston on Dove offers **The Brookhouse Inn (0283) 81488** a splendididly converted farmhouse.

SHROPSHIRE

Moving into **Shropshire**, many will wish to head straight for **Hawkstone Park** and given its two exceptionally attractive courses and fine **Hotel (093 924) 611** this is understandable. However, Shropshire has a lot more than Hawkstone Park on the menu. **Patshull Park** makes a marvellous starter, especially considering its closeness to the Midlands – an ideal retreat in fact. Like at Hawkstone golf is played amid very peaceful and picturesque surroundings and a **Hotel (0902) 700100** lies on the course's doorstep, so to speak. Company days are very popular here but individual visitors are equally welcome and tee times can be booked. **Ian Woosnam** is the touring professional attached to Patshull.

Shrewsbury is a pleasant county town with many charming half-timbered buildings. **Shrewsbury Golf Club** is situated about five miles from the town centre off the **A49**. It is a newish but interesting course with a railway track running through the middle. Fees are approximately **£10. The Prince Rupert Hotel (0743) 236400** in Shrewsbury itself is good value and the oak beams and sloping floors add character.

Travelling a little further down the **A49** into southern Shropshire, **Church Stretton**, (green fee **£6**) set amidst the Long Mynd Hills, is well worth a visit. Not the longest course in Britain but one that offers quite outstanding views. **The Stretton Hall Hotel (0694) 72322** is an obvious but comfortable base and those needing to quench their thirst might note the **Royal Oak** in Cardington (some pleasant accommodation also).

The largest town in Shropshire is Telford. It's a strange mixture of the old and the new: a modern centre yet surrounded by a considerable amount of history – the famous Ironbridge is here. **Telford Hotel Golf and Country Club (0952) 585642** is situated near to the Ironbridge Gorge, high above it in fact, and is easily accessible from the **M54 (junction 4 or 5)**. Visitors are welcome to play the course at all times (bookings required), green fees being **£12.50** midweek, **£17.50** at the weekend. Numerous leisure facilities are offered at the Hotel.

To the east of Telford, **Shifnal** is another popular place for societies. The course is set in a glorious park and an old manor house serves as an impressive Clubhouse. Green fees are slightly less than at Telford. **The Park House Hotel (0952) 460128** in Shifnal is an excellent place for a stop-over and the hotel's restaurant, The Idsall Rooms is particularly outstanding.

In the middle of Shropshire, **Bridgnorth** (green fees **£8**, midweek, **£12** at weekends), is one of the oldest and longest courses in the county (note the distinguished **Haywain (0746) 780404** restaurant in town), and in the far south is historic **Ludlow**. it's now a fairly quiet market town but in former times was the capital of the West Marches. The golf course takes you around the race course – or is it vice versa? – Anyway it's an interesting challenge and if a round of golf is being combined with a weekend's racing then **The Feathers (0584) 5261** in Ludlow provides an ideal place in which to relax – note the outstanding Jacobean facade. A day's golf is priced at around **£10**. Not too great a distance from Ludlow is Hopton Wafers where **The Crown** offers some first rate cooking and a fine drop of ale. To the north of Shropshire two courses are strongly recommended and they offer considerably contrasting golf. Close to the Welsh border, **Llanymynech** lies on high ground and is very 'up-and-down'. On the 4th hole you stand on the tee in Wales and drive into England (always good for the ego). Still high in the hills another 'Llany', this time Llanyblodwel is where excellent refreshment can be found – **The Horseshoe** with its spectacular setting. **Hill Valley** brings us down to earth. We may get wet as well – water affecting many holes on this fairly new American-styles course. As well as the water there are many challenges and at **£8** midweek, **£12** at the weekend, it's well worth inspecting. **Terrick Hall Hotel (0948) 3031** is practically adjacent to the course.

HAWKSTONE PARK
CHAMPIONSHIP GOLF

What is a man to do when his two daughters, his pride and joy, tell him that they wish to leave home? Well, such was the dilemma facing a certain **Sir William Gray** in **1921**. His solution you might think was an admirable one .... he promised to build them a golf course. For two young ladies much bitten by the bug it proved irresistible - clearly bribery of the highest calibre. In 1921 the ingenious Sir William owned **Hawkstone Park**, and the golf course, the subject of this tale, grew from an original nine holes to the present day Hawkstone course.

Today probably every golfer from Lands End to John O'Groats has heard of Hawkstone Park – nothing to do with the 'golfing Grays', of course, but one **Sandy Lyle**, Open Champion of 1985 and U.S. Tournament Players Champion of 1987. Sandy's association with Hawkstone Park has been life-long . Whilst there is probably no truth in the rumour that he was born adjacent to the first tee he certainly grew up nearby. For many years his father Alex served as professional and in every sense it was here that Sandy learnt his game. Hawkstone Park is, of course, much more than the 'birthplace' of Sandy Lyle. There are in fact two 18 hole courses, the **Hawkstone** and the **Weston** and both are set in the beautiful grounds of the Hawkstone Park Hotel. The hotel itself is certainly a grand affair. In a guide book of 1824 it was described as 'more like the seat of a nobleman than an hotel' and the grounds are not only exceptionally beautiful - exotic plants and flowers abound – but they are also steeped in history and legend.

The hotel runs the golf courses and other than an early morning tee reservation for residents there are no general restrictions on visitors, but starting times must be pre-booked. This can be done either by telephoning the Hotel on **(093924) 611** or by contacting the professional shop on **(093924) 209**. Parties of twelve or more are deemed to be golfing **societies**, subject again to making prior arrangements. They are equally welcome and written applications may be made in writing to the **Banqueting Manager, Hawkstone Park Hotel, Weston-under-Redcastle, Nr Shrewsbury SY4 5UY**.

In 1989 a **green fee** of **£21.50** midweek and **£26.50** at the weekend entitles the visitor to a day's golf over both courses, with a round obtainable over the Hawkstone course for **£16** during the week or **£20** at weekends. One can play a round over the Weston course for **£10** during the week, **£12** at weekends, whilst a day's golf will set you back **£16.50** between Monday and Friday, and **£19.50** on Saturday and Sunday. For the weary, golfing buggies are available for **£14** a round, and electric trolleys for **£4**. Those not playing in Societies should pay their green fee to the professional **Keith Williams**, who is also the Director of Golf at Hawkstone Park.

It has been said that one of the reasons for Hawkstone Park enjoying such a delightfully peaceful setting is that it is 'miles from anywhere' - not strictly true: it is only seven miles south of Whitchurch, or if you prefer, 12 miles north of Shrewsbury, and is easily accessible. The **A49** is the best route when approaching from either of these towns. Shrewsbury itself is linked to the West Midlands by way of the **M54** and the **A5**, while those motoring from the north will find the **M6** of assistance.

At **6465** yards (par **72**) from the medal tees, the Hawkstone course is 1,000 yards longer than the Weston (**5368** yards, par **66**); both courses, however, are maintained in superb condition and if possible a round over both should be attempted. It need hardly be added that Sandy Lyle holds the Hawkstone amateur course record with an impressive 65.

I have already referred to the outstanding 19th. However, as an alternative to the Hotel with its restaurant offering traditional cuisine (jacket and tie required for dinner), Hawkstone Park also possesses its own pub where real ale is served. The hotel and golf course complex combine well to provide the perfect facilities for golf meetings at a corporate or local level; the management and staff display an attitude of helpfulness and competence in a relaxed but busy country house atmosphere. It's all come a long way since Sir William Gray's golf-mad daughters, but I am sure they would be delighted with this Shropshire paradise.

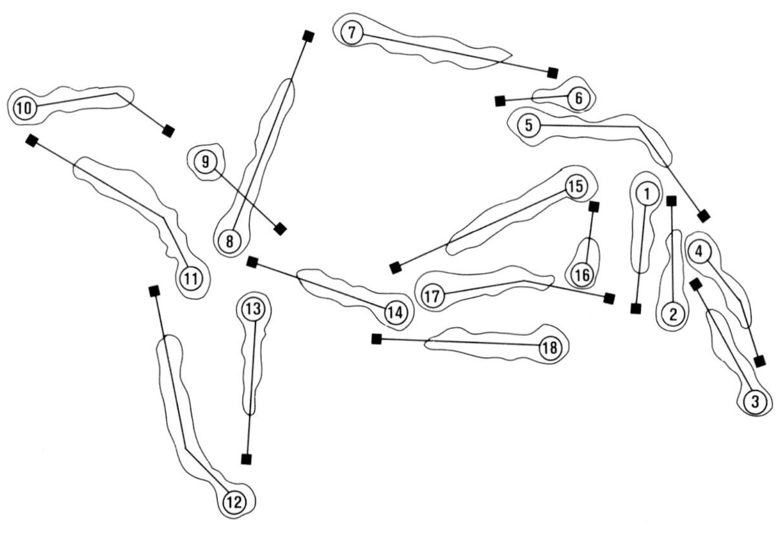

Hawkstone Course

Hole	Yards	Par	Hole	Yards	Par
1	322	4	10	373	4
2	367	4	11	476	5
3	362	4	12	317	4
4	436	4	13	255	4
5	481	5	14	386	4
6	188	3	15	398	4
7	525	5	16	217	3
8	441	4	17	364	4
9	147	3	18	410	4
Out	3,269	36	In	3,196	36
			Out	3,269	36
			TOTALS	6,465	72

STAFFORDSHIRE & SHROPSHIRE

COMPLETE GOLF

STAFFORDSHIRE
(See also West Midlands)

Alsager G. & C.C.
(18) 6192 yds
Alsager Rd, Alsager
(09363) 5700

Beau Desert G.C.
(18) 6285 yds
Hazel Slade, Cannock
(05438) 2492

Branston G.C.
(18) 6458 yds
Branston, Burton-on-Trent
(0283) 43207

Brocton Hall G.C.
(18) 6095 yds
Brocton, Stafford
(0785) 661901

Burslem G.C.
(11) 5813 yds
High Lane, Tunstall,
Stoke-on-Trent
(0782) 87006

Drayton Park G.C.
(18) 6414 yds
Drayton Park, Tamworth
(0827) 251139

Greenway Hall G.C.
(18) 5676 yds
Stockton Brook, Stoke-on-Trent
(0782) 503158

Ingestre Park G.C.
(18) 6376 yds
Ingestre, Weston, Stafford
(0889) 270845

Lakeside G. & C.C.
(18) 5800 yds
Meaford Rd, Barlaston, Stone
(08894) 3181

Leek G.C.
(18) 6229 yds
Cheadle Rd, Leek
(0538) 385889

Leek Westwood G.C.
(9) 5567 yds
Newcastle Rd, Leek
(0538) 382651

Newcastle-under-Lyme G.C.
(18) 6450 yds
Whitmore Rd, Newcastle
(0782) 617006

Newcastle Municipal G.C.
(18) 6301 yds
Keele Rd, Newcastle
(0782) 627596

Stafford Castle G.C.
(9) 6347 yds
Newport Rd, Stafford
(0785) 3821

Stone G.C.
(9) 6272 yds
Filleybrooks, Stone
(0785) 813103

Tamworth G.C.
(18) 6695 yds
Eagle Drive, Tamworth
(0827) 53850

Trentham G.C.
(18) 6523 yds
Barlaston Old Rd, Trentham,
Stoke-on-Trent
(0782) 658109

Trentham Park G.C.
(18) 6403 yds
Trentham Park, Trentham,
Stoke-on-Trent
(0782) 658800

Uttoxeter G.C.
(9) 5461 yds
Wood Lane, Uttoxeter
(08893) 4844

Whittington Barracks G.C.
(18) 6457 yds
Tamworth Rd, Lichfield
(0543) 432317

Wolstanton G.C.
(18) 5807 yds
Dimsdale Old Hall, Newcastle
(0782) 622413

SHROPSHIRE

Bridgnorth G.C.
(18) 6673 yards
Stanley Lane, Bridgenorth
(0742) 2400

Church Stretton G.C.
(18) 5008 yards
Trevor Hill, Church Stretton
(0694) 722281

Hawkstone Park Hotel & G.C.
(18) 6465 yards (Hawkstone)
(18) 5368 yards (Weston)
Weston-under-Redcastle,
Shrewsbury
(093924) 611

Hill Valley G & C.C.
(18) 6050 yards
Terrick Road, Whitchurch
(0948) 3584

Lilleshall Hall G.C.
(18) 5891 yards
Lilleshall, Newport
(0952) 604776

Llanymynech G.C.
(18) 6114 yards
Pant, Oswestry
(0691) 830542

Ludlow G.C.
(18) 6239 yards
Bromfield, Ludlow
(058477) 285

Market Drayton G.C.
(11) 6265 yards
Sutton, Market Drayton
(0630) 2266

Meole Brace G.C.
(9) 5830 yards
Meole Brace, Shewsbury
(0743) 64050

Oswestry G.C.
(18) 6046 yards
Aston Park, Oswestry
(069188) 535

Shifnal G.C.
(18) 6422 yards
Decker Hill, Shifnal
(0952) 460330

Shrewsbury G.C.
(18) 6229 yards
Condover, Shrewsbury
(074372) 2976

Telford Hotel G & C.C.
(18) 6228 yards
Greay Hay, Telford
(0952) 585642

Wrekin G.C.
(18) 5699 yards
Wellington, Telford
(0952) 44032

***CHARLES CROMBIE 'The Rules of Golf – Rule 14'** ROSENSTIEL'S*

CHESHIRE

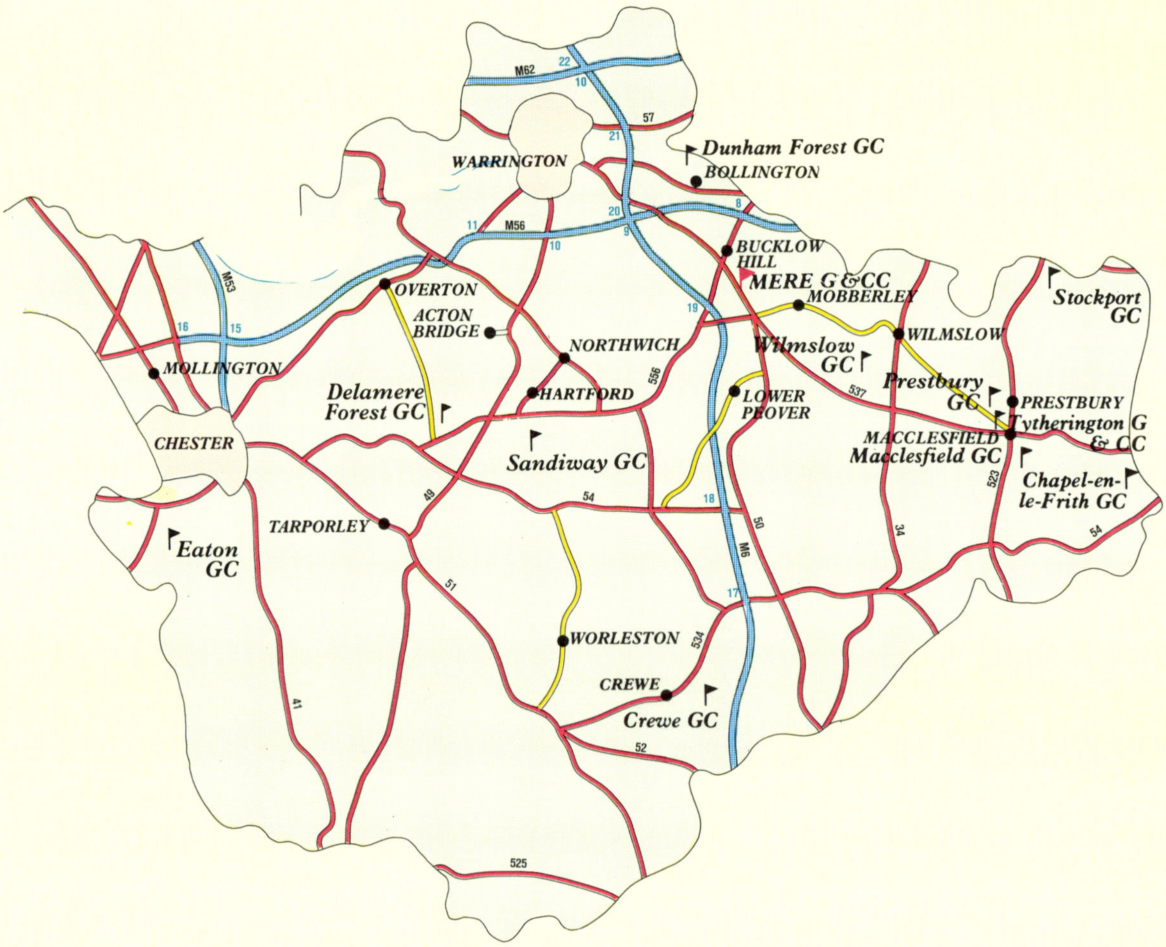

SPY "James Braid" BURLINGTON GALLERY

CHESHIRE
CHOICE GOLF

Cheshire could be described as the 'Surrey of the North'. In many parts it's decidedly affluent, with a great band of commuter towns lining its northern fringes. There's also a sand belt where heathland golf is found – no Sunningdale here perhaps but **Delamere Forest** and **Sandiway** would certainly be at home in either Surrey of Berkshire. Delamere is particularly good. A creation of Herbert Fowler who also designed Walton Heath and The Berkshire, it's a marvellous heather and gorse type course – some superb trees also. Visitors are always welcome at Delamere, although it's very popular; telephoning before setting off is recommended. Green fees are approximately **£12-£15**. The words 'temporary green' do not exist at Delamere Forest (something winter-golfers might wish to bear in mind) nor apparently does the word 'par' – the old fashioned term 'bogey' being preferred as a more realistic yardstick of a hole's difficulty – at least for the non-pro.

There are a number of excellent places in which to stay in the area but pride of place must go to **Rookery Hall (0270) 626866** in Worleston near Nantwich. Part Georgian, part Victorian, it's a wonderful hotel with a restaurant to match. Nearer to Sandiway in Hartford, **Hartford Hall (0606) 75711** is very pleasant while at Acton Bridge **The Rheingold Riverside Inn (0606) 852310** offers some really stylish food. Finally a good pub for Delamere is **The Ring of Bells** at Overton.

Mere is possibly the best course in Cheshire and is featured ahead along with Hawkstone Park. After eagling the 18th at Mere the perfect place for celebration is in Lower Peeover at **The Bells of Peover (05658) 2269** (pronounced 'Peever' I'm assured).

The area around Wilmslow is fairly thick with Clubs. **Wilmslow** itself and **Prestbury** have two of the better courses. For many years the former was the venue of The Greater Manchester Open. Both are very well kept parkland type courses. Visitors are generally welcome during the week although prior telephoning is essential. Fees are around the **£12** mark. Again there are many fine hotels to choose from, one thought though is **Mottram Hall (0625) 878135** at Mottram St Andrews – quite magnificent.

Stockport provides a dramatic contrast to rural Cheshire – not the prettiest of places perhaps but full of character (with a wonderful market). Offerton is where **Stockport Golf Club** is found. It's a good test and well worth the **£11** green fee. **Macclesfield** offers some extensive views (beware of hooking at the first!) and between Macclesfield and Prestbury **The Tytherington Club** is a very new creation which promises great things.

Over to the far east of Cheshire, close to the Derbyshire border is **Chapel-en-le-Frith**. A really friendly Club this and some very enjoyable golf too. There are many tremendous views towards the Derbyshire Peaks. A day's golf at Chapel is priced at **£8** midweek, **£12** at the weekend.

From the far east to the far west. **Chester** demands inspection – a fascinating Roman city with all manner of attractions. The best place to swing a club is at **Eaton**, (green fees **£8** during the week, **£10** at weekend), a parkland course to the south of the city. The best hotel by far is **The Chester Grosvenor (0244) 324024** (note the superb restaurant). An interesting alternative is **The Blossoms Hotel (0244) 323186** where Ghost Hunting and Murder Weekends are organised!

Fairly centrally in the county, **Crewe** offers a pleasant 18 holes but our final visit takes us to the end of a very leafy lane in Altrincham – the impressive **Dunham Forest Golf and Country Club**. Only two miles from the **M56 (junction 7)** and not all that far from the whirl of Manchester it nonetheless delights in an incredibly tranquil setting. The beautifully mature tree-lined fairways are a sheer delight to play on and if you cannot enjoy your golf here, well, let's just say you've got problems.

W.G. STEVENSON 'The Field' *BURLINGTON GALLERY*

MERE

CHAMPIONSHIP GOLF

On passing through the impressive Elizabethan styled entrance to the **Mere Golf and Country Club** one is entering historic grounds – not of the St Andrews nature but Mere itself and the Manor are mentioned in the Domesday Book when a gentleman by the name of **Gilbert Venables**, Baron of Kinderton, held the land. Golf, alas did not come to Mere until 1934.

A more modern gentleman by the name of **Mr Edgar W. Hart** founded the Club and obtained the impressive services of **George Duncan** as the first golf professional. Duncan, the Open Champion of **1920** and the Ryder Cup Captain of **1929** was responsible, together with **James Braid**, for the design of the new course. Nine holes were ready for play on New Years Day in **1935** with an official opening of the full eighteen holes taking place on **May 11th**. A challenge match was arranged for that day and the participants were **Duncan** and **Braid, Henry Cotton** and **J.J. Busson**. Mere quickly acquired a considerable reputation and today is regarded as one of, if not the finest inland course in the north west of England.

The present Golf Secretary at Mere is **Mr Alf Turner**,and he may be contacted at **The Mere Golf and Country Club, Mere, Knutsford, Cheshire WA16 6LJ**, telephone **(0565) 830155**. The Managing Director of the Country Club is **Mr Max Brown** who may also be contacted via the above telephone number.

Subject to making prior arrangements, **visitors** possessing an official handicap are welcome to play the course on Mondays, Tuesdays and Thursdays. Golfing Societies are equally welcome and tees can be reserved for numbers of up to 150. The **green fees** for a day's golf in **1989** were set at **£30**. The Club's professional is **Eddie Goodwin**, a former assistant to George Duncan; he has been the professional at Mere for more than 20 years.

Although set amidst extremely peaceful surroundings Mere is easily accessible from all directions and lies only a few minutes from two motorway junctions: the **M6** exit **19** and the **M56** exit **7**. For those approaching from Manchester motorways can be avoided if the **M56** is picked up – it runs from the city centre directly past the Club entrance (by which time though it has become the **A556**). The Club in fact lies adjacent to both the **A556** and the **A537** Warrington to Knutsford roads. The **M56** is likely to be most helpful for those motoring from the Chester and Wirral areas, while the **M6** should assist the northbound traveller and persons coming from north of Manchester.

The peaceful location referred to is the edge of the Cheshire sand belt. However, the course is more of a parkland nature than heathland (unlike the other outstanding sand belt courses of **Delamere** and **Sandiway**). Adding to the attractive setting are two lakes, 'The Mere' and 'The Little Mere'. Neither really comes into play (or at least shouldn't!) although a new green for the 18th has recently been built beside the lake's edge and when in play will turn the final hole into a spectacular par five. The closing stretch at Mere already contains some superb holes and those from the **15th** to the **18th** are known as the 'Famous Last Four'. A brook crosses the middle of the **15th** fairway; the **16th** is a sharp dog-leg left with trees lining one side of the fairway and an out of bounds the other, while the **17th** is a fairly short par four, but the second must be played to a well guarded plateau green.

From its back tees the course measures **6744** yards (par **70** S.S.S. **72**). The tees of the day shorten the length to **6367** yards, and the ladies play over **5811** yards, par **74**.

In addition to Braid, Cotton and of course Duncan, many of the games 'greats' have visited Mere. They have included **Harry Vardon, Gene Sarazen, Bobby Locke, Peter Thomson, Bernhard Langer** and **Gary Player**.

Mere Hall serves as an impressive nineteenth, and although it suffered much damage in 1973 when a terrible fire swept through the entire building, recovery has been remarkable. The catering facilities offered are first class and hot meals are available from 11am to 10pm. Many golfers will be keen to note that there are no fewer than five bars (there is also a bar beside the 11th green – clearly a well organised Club!)

A novel development at Mere has been the recent construction of a driving range where floating golf balls are struck into the Lake. Sounds great fun, but I can't for the life of me imagine quite what Gilbert Venables would have made of it all.

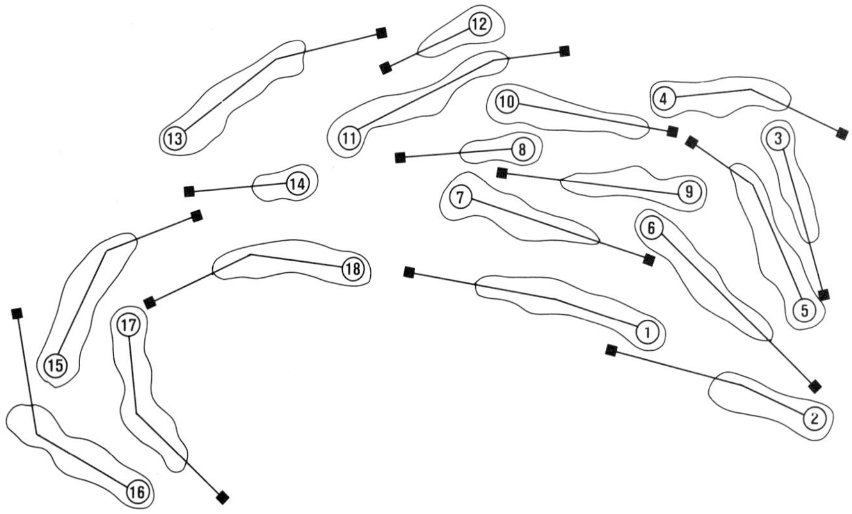

Hole	Yards	Par	Hole	Yards	Par
1	530	5	10	427	4
2	409	4	11	401	4
3	174	3	12	188	3
4	357	4	13	467	4
5	420	4	14	169	3
6	437	4	15	393	4
7	434	4	16	441	4
8	195	3	17	349	4
9	500	5	18	453	4
Out	3,456	36	In	3,288	34
			Out	3,456	36
			TOTALS	6,744	70

CHESHIRE
COMPLETE GOLF

CHESHIRE
(See also Gtr. Manchester)

Alderley Edge G.C.
(9) 5839 yards
Brook Lane, Alderley Edge
(0625) 585583

Astbury G.C.
(18) 6269 yards
Peel Lane, Astbury, Congleton
(0260) 272772

Birchwood G.C.
(18) 6666 yards
Kelvin Close,
Birchwood, Warrington
(0925) 818819

Chapel-en-le-Frith G.C.
(18) 6065 yards
The Cockyard, Manchester Road,
Chapel-en-le-Frith
(0298) 813943

Chester G.C.
(18) 6487 yards
Curzon Park, Chester
(0244) 677760

Congleton G.C.
(9) 5704 yards
Biddulph Road, Congleton
(0260) 273540

Crewe G.C.
(18) 6277 yards
Fields Road, Haslington, Crewe
(0270) 584099

Davenport G.C.
(18) 6006 yards
Worton Hall, Middlewood Road,
Higher Poynton
(0625) 877319

Delamere Forest G.C.
(18) 6287 yards
Station Road,
Delamere, Northwich
(0606) 882807

Eaton G.C.
(18) 6446 yards
Eaton Park, Eccleston, Chester
(0244) 680474

Ellesmere G.C.
(18) 5957 yards
Old Clough Lane, Worsley
(051) 339 7689

Helsby G.C.
(18) 6262 yards
Towers Lane, Helsby, Warrington
(09282) 2021

Knights Grange G.C.
(9) 6240 yards
Grange Lane, Winsford
(06065) 52780

Knutsford G.C.
(9) 6288 yards
Mercheath Lane, Knutsford
(0565) 3355

Leigh G.C.
(18) 5853 yards
Kenyon Hall,
Culcheth, Warrington
(092576) 2943

Lymm G.C.
(18) 6319 yards
Whitbarrow Road, Lymm
(092575) 5020

Macclesfield G.C.
(9) 5974 yards
The Hollins, Macclesfield
(0625) 23227

Malkins Bank G.C.
(18) 6071 yards
Betchton Road, Sandbach
(0270) 765931

Mere G. & C.C.
(18) 6788 yards
Mere, Knutsford
(0565) 830219

New Mills G.C.
(9) 5924 yards
Shaw Marsh, New Mills
(0663) 43816

Poulton Park G.C.
(9) 5512 yards
Cinnamon Brow, Warrington
(0925) 812034

Prestbury G.C.
(18) 6359 yards
Macclesfield Road, Prestbury
(0625) 828241

Runcorn G.C.
(18) 6012 yards
Clifton Road, Runcorn
(09285) 74214

Sandbach G.C.
(9) 5533 yards
Middlewich Road, Sandbach
(0270) 762117

Sandiway G.C.
(18) 6435 yards
Chester Road, Sandiway
(0606) 883247

Tytherington Club
(18) 6700 yards
Macclesfield
(0625) 34562

Upton-by-Chester G.C.
(18) 5875 yards
Upton Lane, Chester
(0244) 381183

Vicars Cross G.C.
(18) 5804 yards
Tarvin Road, Littleton, Chester
(0244) 335174

Walton Hall G.C.
(18) 6647 yards
Higher Walton, Warrington
(0925) 66775

Warrington G.C.
(18) 6217 yards
Appleton, Warrington
(0925) 61775

Widnes G.C.
(18) 5688 yards
Highfield Road, Widnes
(051) 424 2995

Widnes Municipal
(9) 5982 yards
Dundalk Road, Widnes
(051) 424 6230

Wilmslow G.C.
(18) 6500 yards
Great Warford,
Mobberley, Knutsford
(056587) 2148

CHARLES CROMBIE 'The Rules of Golf – Rule 13' *BURLINGTON GALLERY*

LANCASHIRE & THE ISLE OF MAN

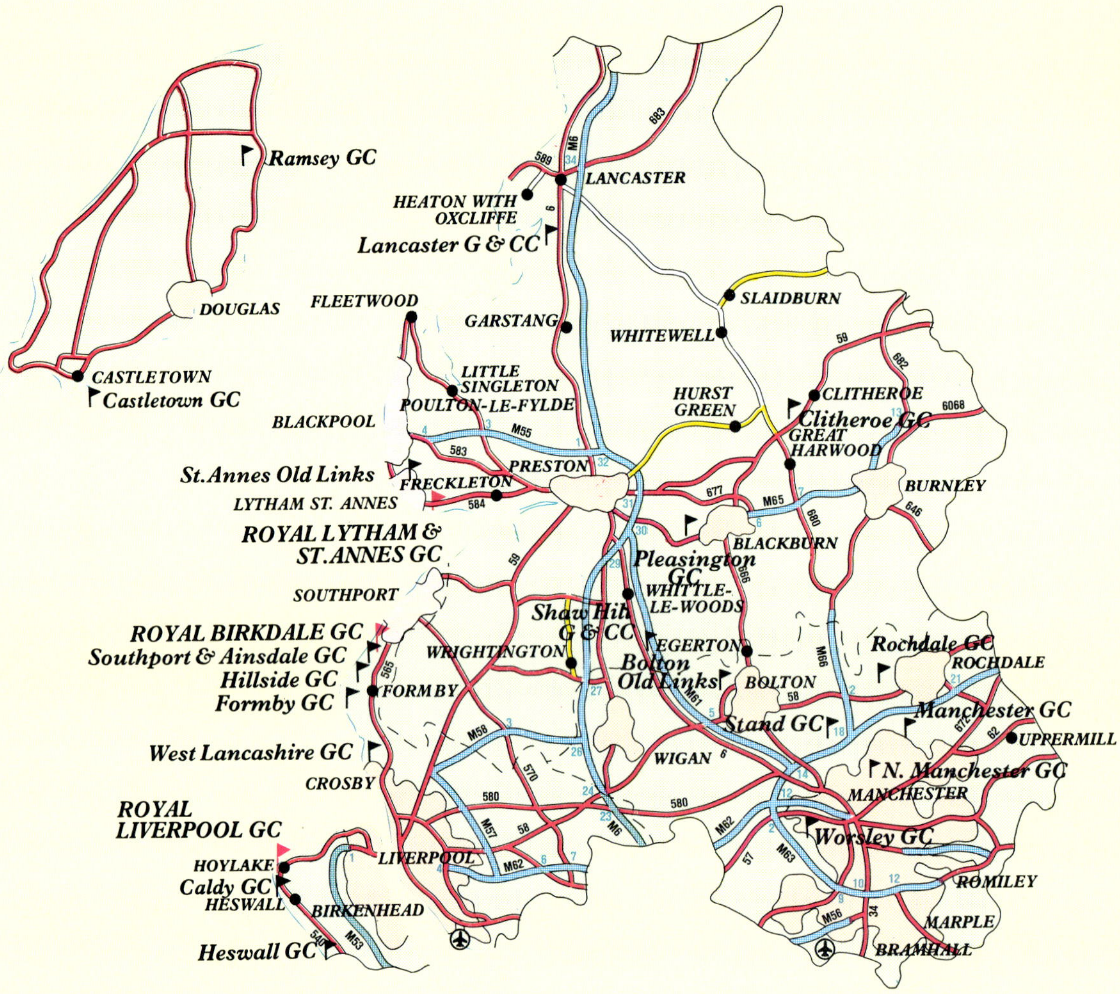

"Hoylake" SARAH BADDIEL'S BOOK GALLERY

LANCASHIRE & THE ISLE OF MAN

CHOICE GOLF

'Caddies are not allowed on the greens when wearing clogs' – recorded in the Minutes of a Lancashire Golf Club, 1984.

I don't suppose they appreciate it in the slightest but the many horses that race across the sands near Southport early each morning (and the donkeys that do their best to race across the same sands) are performing within a few yards of one of the greatest stretches of golfing country in the world. On the Lancashire coast between Liverpool and Blackpool lie a magnificent collection of natural golfing links. Being more specific, between **Hoylake** on the Wirral Peninsula and **Royal Lytham** (a distance of less than 40 miles) are to be found the likes of **West Lancashire, Formby, Southport and Ainsdale, Royal Birkdale, Hillside,** and **St Annes Old Links**. A truly formidable list, Hoylake, Birkdale and Lytham have, of course, each staged the Open Championship on a number of occasions, while the Amateur Championship has been played at both Hillside and Formby, and Southport and Ainsdale has twice hosted the Ryder Cup. When the wind hammers across from the Irish Sea any of the links mentioned can become treacherously difficult and the famous Lancashire sandhills rarely provide shelter from the elements.

The green fee for a day's golf in this part of the world tends to range between **£10** at the quieter Clubs and **£18** at the bigger Clubs. Visitors are welcome to play at any although weekdays are naturally the best times to try and arrange a visit. Telephoning in advance is normally preferred. Hoylake, Birkdale and Lytham are each featured on later pages but a visit to any of the above will certainly not meet with disappointment (though it may result in a little damaged pride!).

Having done battle with the elements, and perhaps after visiting the treacherous Gumbley's bunker at 'S and A' or the many pines at Formby a drink will be in order. A good meal and a comfy bed for the night may also be required. Here are some suggestions. In **Southport** there are a number of ideas: **The Scarisbrick Hotel (0704) 43000** and **The Prince of Wales (0704) 36688** are probably the pick of the hotels; accommodation here is plentiful. In Formby **The Tree Tops Motel (07048) 79651** is an ideal base as is **The Blundells Hotel (051) 924 6516**, only a mile from the West Lancashire links.

Lytham St. Annes is another golfer's paradise. It's a pleasant little town and again two hotels to note are **The Chadwick (0253) 720061** on the seafront and **The Clifton Arms Hotel (0253) 739898. Bennett's Bistro** is a well known fish restaurant in town. While we're on the subject of fish, Fleetwood to the north has to be mentioned and one of the best fish restaurants here is **The Trafalgar (03917) 2266**.

Blackpool, famed for its great tower and impressive funfair is more of a paradise for children than golfers, but then if games are being sneaked in on the family holiday it may be the best choice for a stay. On the North Promenade are two of the town's best hotels, **The Pembroke (0253) 23434** and **The Imperial (0253) 23981**. Comfort here is guaranteed but there are numerous, slightly cheaper alternatives and pot luck may be the order of the day.

It may well be that many people will have some business in **Liverpool** that has to be dealt with before one can put one's plus fours on and stride out onto the fairways. If you are staying in this Liver city then the **Britannia Adelphi 051 709 7200** and the **Atlantic Tower 051 227 4444** are both good, while excellent leisure facilities can be found in **The Liverpool Moat House 051 709 0181**. The city has a reputation for splendid Indian and Chinese food but two European establishments are our recommendations. On the one hand **The Armadillo 051 236 4123** and on the other **La Grande Bouffe 051 236 3375**. The nearest of the great links courses is **West Lancashire**, although **Formby** too is within easy reach. The **A565** is the road to take out of Liverpool.

For the purposes of this piece Liverpool and Manchester have been included in Lancashire, a county to which they both once belonged (and still do in spirit). As the whole of Merseyside has been included – it's here that Royal Birkdale and Royal Liverpool are now siuated – parts of former Cheshire are also included. Confused? Let's visit the Wirral. For such a relatively small area the peninsula is fairly thick with Golf Clubs. In addition to the links at Hoylake and Wallasey, **Heswall** offers a quite outstanding parkland challenge. Situated alongside the River Dee off the **A540**, it's a medium length course, beautifully maintained with views towards the distant Welsh hills. A strong word also for **Caldy** which is a parkland-cum-clifftop course, similarly well-kept and similarly scenic. Fees at both are approximately **£12** pe day. If an hotel and restaurant are sought on the Wirral then a quick pair of recommendations – for an hotel, the spendidly named **Bowler Hat Hotel 051 652 4931** at Birkenhead is most comfortable, while **Les Bougies 051 342 6673** at Heswall is a fine Frenchrestaurant.

Looking to play more centrally in Lancashire, **The Shaw Hill Golf and Country Club** is most definitely one to note if travelling along the **M6**. Located just north of Chorley it enjoys a very peaceful setting and is a particular favourite of golfing societies. Visitors are welcome seven days a week, fees being **£12** per day.

The other side of the **M6, Pleasington Golf Club** enjoys similarly secluded surroundings (and very scenic ones too). The course is situated three miles west of Blackburn along the **A59**. Visitors are welcome at most times though prior arrangement with the Secretary is essential. The cost of a day's golf is approximately **£12**.

Still moving 'up' the country, **Preston** welcomes visitors throughout the week; a pleasantly undulating course, just north of the town, it can easily be reached from the **M6 (junction 32)**. Green fees here are about **£10**.

Clitheroe Golf Club lies on the edge of the Forest of Bowland amidst superb countryside. The course lies approximately two miles south of the town with views across to the Pendle Hill. Visitors are welcome during the week and on Sundays. The fees in 1989 were **£11** midweek, **£13** on Sundays.

Lancashire wouldn't be complete without mentioning its county town. There are a number of Clubs at hand, perhaps the best being the **Lancaster Golf and Country Club** located three miles south of the city on the **A588** at Stodday. An attractive parkland course close to the River Lune estuary (can be breezy!).

A few ideas for the 19th now follow: The city of Lancaster lies west of some gorgeous moorland scenery. The **M6** carves its way through and near to **junction 34, The Post House Hotel (0524) 65999** is ideal for travellers. A little further north in Heaton with Oxcliffe a pub with a splendid riverside setting is **The Golden Ball** – well worth a visit when in these parts. Resist the temptation to travel further north and tie the knot in Gretna Green and instead travel to Morecambe where as well as some excellent shops **The Midland Hotel (0524) 417180** is welcoming.

LANCASHIRE & THE ISLE OF MAN

CHOICE GOLF

If you have time, do try and make tracks to Whitewell. Now here amid the delightful Forest of Bowland lies the charming **Inn at Whitewell (02008) 222**. Excellent bar snacks, a splendid restaurant and some charming bedrooms – ideal for hunting, shooting and fishing in between golf. People remaining on the **A6** or **M6** may select another pub – on this occasion **Th' Owd Tithebarn**, or further south and near **junction 32** and Broughton, this pub is entitled **The Plough** at Eaves.

If one has decided to play at Preston or Clitheroe a few thoughts for you. In Hurst Green **The Shireburn Arms Hotel (025486) 518** is well worth a visit. Not only can you enjoy the splendid Ribblesdale countryside but some fine cooking is also to be found. An alternative eating establishment, a restaurant on this occasion is **Tiffany (0254) 889528** at Great Harwood – a fine standard of cuisine where the fish is particularly good. In Clitheroe itself **The Swan and Royal Hotel (0200) 23130** is recommended while people wishing to have a quick tipple before hitting the tees should note the **Hodder Bridge Hotel** at Higher Hodder Bridge. Slaidburn is also convenient for the golf at Clitheroe and here **The Parrock Head Farm Hotel (02006) 614** is strongly recommended.

One place that really should be high on golfers' lists to visit is the **Shaw Hill Hotel (02572) 69221** near Chorley -an excellent golf course and an elegant mansion house in which to hang up one's clubs before ordering dinner. Splendid. Another tremendous place to settle down to first class fodder is **The High Moor (02575) 2364** at Wrightington. A pleasant atmosphere and some first rate cuisine. Ideal if your golf wasn't perhaps as wonderful as you had hoped.

And so to Greater Manchester. The city itself is famed the world over for the liberal amount of rain that falls. Mancunians will quickly tell you that this is pure poppy-cock (or something like that). Of course, the only time that rain can be guaranteed is during the five days of an Old Trafford Test Match. If you do happen to get caught in the rain, be it on the streets or the fairways, here are a few superior shelters. You ought to be able to find a room in **The Britannia Hotel 061 228 2288** for there are 365 (one for every day of the year?). An alternative is the **Hotel Piccadilly 061 236 8414**, which is massive and especially for the city centre. Outside the conurbation, there are several other options, to the North in Egerton. **The Egerton House (0204) 57171** is better value especially at weekends and a far better country setting can be enjoyed. The well respected restaurant adds appeal. Another thought is **The Last Drop Village Hotel (0204) 591131** with its many leisure facilities, while in Bramhall, a most attractive place, **The Bramhall Moat House 061 439 8116** is ideal for the businessman (note the two fine courses here). Altrincham has a trio to consider: **The Cresta Court 061 928 8017** is modern but well equipped, **The Bowdon 061 928 7121** is Victorian and comfortable, while the former coaching inn, the **George and Dragon 061 928 9933** has most appeal.

The number of restaurants is, as you'd expect, considerable. Some of the very best include **The Bonne Auberge 061 437 5701** in Heald Green (excellent French cooking), **Truffles 061 832 9393** in Bridge Street (handy for the Opera) and **The Waterside (0794) 517353** in Romiley. Ideal after a day's golf.

It is probably a fair assessment to say that for golf courses, Manchester, rather like London, gets top marks for quantity but is a little shaky on the quality score. Certainly it compares unfavourably with Liverpool and Leeds; it is a shame because historically Manchester was the scene of some of the earliest golf outside Scotland. The **Old Manchester Club** was founded back in **1818**. Its current status is 'temporarily without a course' – one can only hope that its Members have found somewhere else to play ... **North Manchester** perhaps? Only four miles from the city centre this Club welcomes visitors on Mondays, Wednesdays and Fridays, the green fees being **£7**. Societies are also welcome on the above days and for parties of eleven or more a package comprising a light lunch, green fees and three-course meal can be obtained for **£13**.

A close neighbour of North Manchester is the **Manchester Golf Club**. Visitors are similarly welcome with green fees moderately priced at **£10**. Elsewhere in Manchester, **Stand** (Whitefield) and **Worsley** (Eccles) are fine courses while to the north **Rochdale** is well worth travelling to. The area around Bolton boasts a number of courses of which **Bolton Old Links** (green fees **£10**), is probably the best. It is a tough and interesting moorland course at which visitors are always made welcome. As for the title 'Links' your guess is as good as mine – but there again, what are we to make of Wigan Pier?

ISLE OF MAN

A very brief word here for that tax haven the **Isle of Man**. Golf here is very good with the links at **Castletown and Ramsey** particularly standing out. With fairly modest green fees and plentiful places to stay it's an ideal place for a golf holiday – ask Nigel Mansell! For Castletown, Ballasalla is a convenient place to stay, and there are two excellent restaurants, **Silverburn Lodge (0624) 822343** and **La Rosette (0624) 822940**, whilst the **Castletown Golf Links Hotel (0624) 822201** is quite superb. In Ramsey, two gems spring to mind, namely the large **Grand Island Hotel (0624) 812455** and **The Harbour Bistro (0624) 814182**, an informal and friendly restaurant.

ROYAL LYTHAM & ST. ANNES

CHAMPIONSHIP GOLF

'There goes a hundred thousand bucks.....' the immortal words of **Al Waltrous** after having witnessed the most magnificently outrageous stroke in golfing history. Imagine yourself in his shoes, striding down the 17th fairway sharing the lead in the Open Championship; you have played two strokes and are safely on the edge of the green, your partner (and effectively opponent) has driven wildly into the rough and has found a small bunker – he faces a terrifying shot over sandhills, scrub and goodness-knows-what else, – a blind shot of fully 170 yards....seconds later the impossible happens and his ball is lying a few yards from the hole, well inside your second. Minutes later you walk from the green having taken five to your opponent's four.

The occasion was, of course, the **1926 Open Championship** at **Royal Lytham** and 'your opponent', the incomparable **Bobby Jones**.

In February 1986 Royal Lytham and St. Annes proudly celebrated its one hundredth birthday; few Golf Clubs in the world can have enjoyed such a rich and colourful history. Presently in charge of all administrative matters at Lytham is the Club's **Secretary, Major Stewart Craven**; he may be contacted by telephone on **(0253) 724206**. **Eddie Birchenough** is the Club's professional and he may be reached on **(0253) 720094**. Visitors wishing to tread the famous fairways are asked to provide a letter of introduction from their home Club but subject to this requirement they are welcome on any day between Mondays and Fridays, restrictions applying at the weekend. Whilst advance booking is not essential it is clearly advisable and those wishing to write to the Club should address correspondence to the Secretary at **Royal Lytham and St. Annes Golf Club, Links Gate, Lytham St. Annes, Lancashire FY8 3LQ**. The **green fees** at Lytham were priced at **£30** for a single round in 1989, or £40 for a full day's golf. In addition, gentlemen players can enjoy two rounds of golf, dinner and bed and breakfast for a fee of **£60**.

Motoring to the course is assisted greatly by the **M6** and the **M61**. Southbound travellers should leave the **M6** at junction **32**; here the **M55** can be picked up. The **M55** runs out of steam at junction **4** but a left turn will take you to Lytham St. Annes. Those travelling northwards along the **M6** have a number of choices, perhaps the best being to leave at exit **29** and thereafter follow a combination of the **A582, A583** and **A584** towards Lytham St. Annes. The **M61** links the Greater Manchester area to the outskirts of Preston. From Preston the **A583** can be joined and followed as above. The course is situated only a mile from the centre of the town close to the railway line.

The railway line is in fact a major feature of the opening holes at Lytham, forming a continuous boundary to the right. From the back markers the course measures **6673** yards par **71** (s.s.s.**73**) with the ladies playing over **5814** yards par **75** (s.s.s.**75**). Rather unusually Lytham opens with a par three, which at over 200 yards is quite a testing opener although the real threat of the railway looms on the **2nd** and **3rd**. Of the other par three holes at Lytham perhaps the **12th** stands out – normally played into a prevailing wind it calls for a searching tee shot towards a raised and heavily guarded green. The back nine is generally felt to be the more difficult of the two halves although the determining factor at Lytham, as on most links courses, will nearly always be the wind. The **17th** has been mentioned and a plaque marks the spot from where the Jones miracle recovery shot was played. As for the **18th** it of course invokes many 'Open memories': **Tony Jacklin's** arrow-straight drive en-route to winning the **1969** Championship; **Gary Player** putting left handed from up against the Clubhouse wall in **1974** and then the Championship in **1979** – the 22 year old **Ballesteros** storming to victory in cavalier fashion.

The nineteenth at Royal Lytham is a marvellous Victorian building, and the golfer can enjoy a full and excellent catering service which is offered throughout the day.

While there may be more than a hundred years of eventful history to look back upon, on the future for the Club looks equally exciting. In 1988 the **Open** returned for the eighth time. As history now relates, senor Ballesteros triumphed once again, his golf suitably matching the many tests of the Lytham Links. Who could forget the closing holes? Mr. Waltrous would, I feel, have been most impressed.

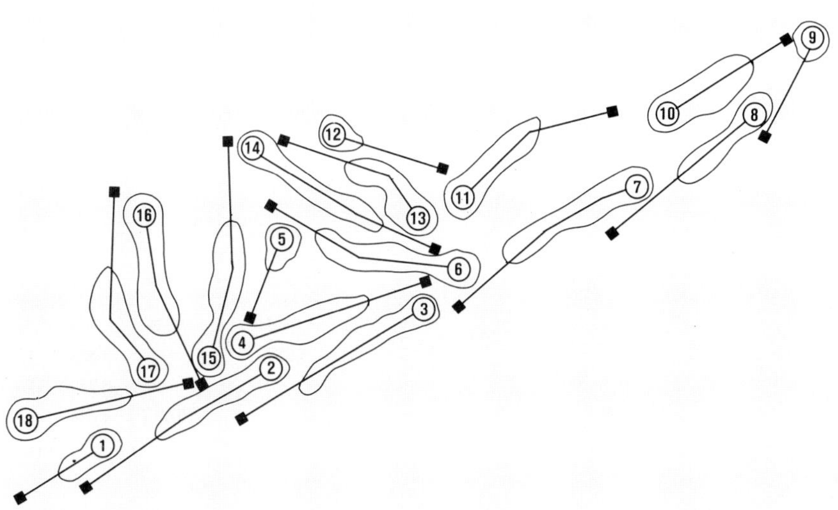

Hole	Yards	Par	Hole	Yards	Par
1	206	3	10	334	4
2	420	4	11	485	5
3	458	4	12	189	3
4	393	4	13	339	4
5	188	3	14	445	4
6	486	5	15	468	4
7	551	5	16	356	4
8	394	4	17	413	4
9	162	3	18	386	4
Out	3,258	35	In	3,415	36
			Out	3,258	35
			TOTALS	6,673	71

ROYAL BIRKDALE
CHAMPIONSHIP GOLF

Back in 1889 your average J.P. was probably not the most popular man in town; however, in a certain **Mr. J.C. Barrett,** Birkdale possessed a man of rare insight and one clearly cognisant of the finer things in life. Mr. Barrett was a golfer. On the 30th July, 1889, he invited eight fellow addicts to his home and together they resolved to form a Golf Club. One can imagine their enthusiasm as they formulated their plans, perhaps over a brandy and cigars, I know not; but very quickly a clubhouse was secured – a single room in a private residence at a four shilling per week rental! Land (at £5 per year rental) was acquired and soon a 9 hole course was laid out. It all sounds rather unsophisticated, but compared with todays problems of first finding a suitable site and then obtaining planning permission, I suppose it was relatively straightforward.

Whilst no one could question its present day status as one of the country's leading Championship courses, historically **Birkdale** set off rather like the proverbial tortoise. Forced eviction in 1897 led to the Club's rerooting in its present position where a full eighteen holes are available. During the 1930's a modern style Clubhouse was built and **John H. Taylor** and **Fred Hawtree** were commissioned to redesign the course. As one would expect they made a splendid job of it and it was only a question of time (and the small matter of a world war) that prevented Birkdale from staging an Open Championship.

Since the war our golfing tortoise has left many of the hares behind. No fewer than six Open Championships have now been held at Birkdale in addition to numerous other major events.

Golfers wishing to play at Birkdale must be able to provide a letter of introduction from their home club and possess a handicap. Before setting off such persons are advised to contact the **Secretary, Mr. Norman N.T. Crewe**. This applies to individual visitors as well as those hoping to organise a Society game. Mr. Crewe can be contacted at **The Royal Birkdale Golf Club, Waterloo Road, Birkdale, Southport, Merseyside PR8 2LX. Tel. (0704) 67920**. Golf clubs may be hired from the professional, **Mr. R.N. Bradbeer, (0704) 68857** and it may also be possible to obtain the services of a caddy. Individual visitors may play from Monday to Friday, **green fees** being **£30** per round, or **£45** per day, whilst Societies are welcome on Wednesdays and Thursdays.

The Club is situated approximately **2 miles** from the centre of **Southport** close to the main **A565** road. From the **North** this road can be reached via the **A59**, leaving the **M6** at Preston and from the **South** via the **M62** and **M57** or alternatively, as when travelling from Manchester and the **East**, by taking the **A580** and then following the **A570** into Southport.

Mention has been made of Birkdale's strikingly modern looking **Clubhouse**. Within, the catering has a high reputation and there are three bars. However, hungry golfers should note that dinner is only available to parties of 21 and over. A jacket and tie must be worn in the lounge. Whilst the course possesses many of the towering sandhills so familiar with links golf, the holes tend to wind their way between and beneath the dunes along fairly flat and narrow valleys. From the lush fairways the awkward stance and blind shot are the product of poor golf, not poor fortune. Fair it may be, but easy it certainly is not. From the medal tees the course measures **6711** yards and is a stiff par **72**. Anyone playing from the Championship tees (6968 yards) can be forgiven for scratching his head and wondering how on earth **Craig Stadler** managed a score of **64**. From the red tees, the ladies course is **5777 yards** and has a par of **75**.

With its three par 5's the back nine is probably the easier half – at least to the longer hitter – although with the menacingly thick, rough and narrow strategically bunkered fairways the wild long hitter will be severely penalised. A journey into the rough on the 16th, however, is recommended, although only to visit **Arnold Palmer's** plaque – placed in memory of the great man's miraculous 6 iron shot with which he somehow contrived to find the green.

Birkdale may have a relatively short history as an 'Open course', but her list of Champions is as impressive a list as can be found anywhere: **Thomson (twice), Palmer, Trevino, Miller** and most recently **Tom Watson**, who claimed his fifth title in nine years when winning in 1983. The course has also thrown up more than its fair share of drama. Perhaps most notably in **1969** when **Jack Nicklaus**, ever the sportsman, conceded **Tony Jacklin's** very missable putt on the 18th green, so tying the **Ryder Cup**. In **1961,** Palmer's Open, an almighty gale threatened to blow the tented village and all inside far out into the sea. In stark contrast was the **1976** Open when fire engines were close at hand as Birkdale (and all of Britain come to that) suffered in the drought. That 1976 Championship saw the mercurial **Johnny Miller** at his brilliant best as he shook off first the challenge of Jack Nicklaus and then of an inexperienced and unknown 19 year old who had a name no one at the time could pronounce ...... **Severiano Ballesteros**.

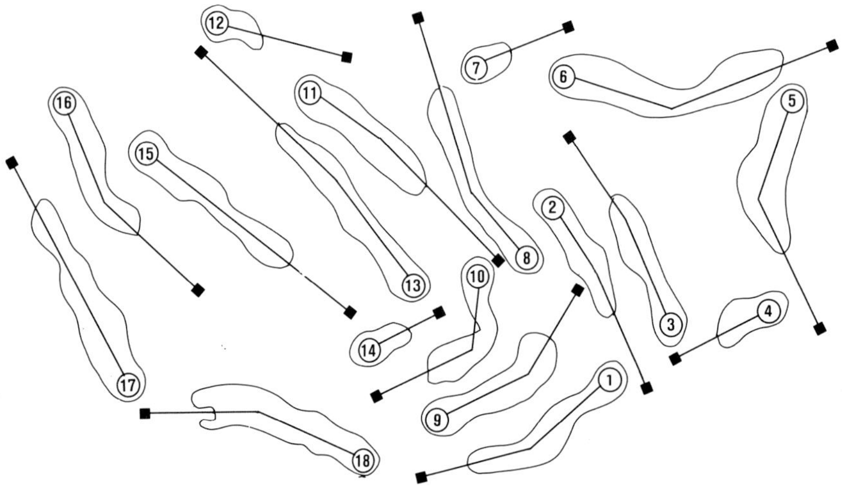

Hole	Yards	Par	Hole	Yards	Par
1	450	4	10	384	4
2	423	4	11	411	4
3	410	4	12	184	3
4	206	3	13	505	5
5	343	4	14	198	3
6	468	4	15	542	5
7	150	3	16	415	4
8	470	4	17	526	5
9	410	4	18	473	4
Out	**3,330**	**34**	**In**	**3,638**	**37**
			Out	**3,330**	**34**
			TOTALS	**6,968**	**71**

ROYAL LIVERPOOL (HOYLAKE)
CHAMPIONSHIP GOLF

The **Royal Hotel** at **Hoylake** (alas no longer with us) played a starring role in the early history of the **Royal Liverpool Golf Club**. In **1869** a meeting was held there which led to the famous Club's formation. Perhaps of great significance that day, with no disrespect whatsoever to those founding Members, was the presence in the Hotel of a seven year old boy. **John Ball** whose father was the Hotel proprietor grew to become not only Hoylake's favourite son, but also the finest amateur golfer Britain has ever produced.

In the early days, golf at Hoylake must have been at times a trifle frustrating, for the Club shared the links with a racecourse and hoof prints on the fairways were a fairly common hazard. However, by **1876** the horses (doubtless equally frustrated), had found elsewhere to gallop and the golf course quickly developed into England's premier Championship test. The **1869** birthdate in fact makes Hoylake England's second oldest links course, just four years younger than Westward Ho!

Ten **Open Championships** and sixteen **Amateur Championships** later the **Secretary** at Royal Liverpool is **Mr. J.R. Davidson**. Mr. Davidson can be contacted by telephone on **(051) 632 3101. Visitors** are welcome to play at Hoylake, subject to proof of handicap or letter of introduction from their home Club, between Mondays and Fridays; visitors cannot play at Hoylake over the weekend.

The **green fees** as set in April 1989 are **£25** during the week (**£20** for ladies). Golfing **Societies** are equally welcome, and those organising should address written applications to the Secretary, care of **Royal Liverpool Golf Club, Meols Drive, Hoylake, Wirral, Merseyside. John Heggarty** is the Club's professional and sets of golf clubs can be hired from him. It may also be possible to arrange for the services of a caddy. Mr. Heggarty can be reached on **(051) 632 5868**.

Hoylake is located at the tip of the Wirral peninsula, approximately ten miles west of Liverpool and fifteen miles north of Chester. The north west of England is particularly well-served by motorway connections and finding the course shouldn't be a problem. Approaching from either the north or south the **M6** is likely to be of assistance; it passes midway between Manchester and Liverpool and should be left at junction **19A**. Thereafter the **M56** can be followed towards Chester joining the **M53** at junction **15**. The **M53** will then take you to the far end of the Wirral where the **A553** Hoylake road should be picked up. (In a nutshell: **M6**–**M56**–**M53** –**A553**).

The course occupies fairly flat ground and is very exposed to the elements. It is most unusual for the wind not to blow. (You have been warned!) It was his mastery of the wind, a skill acquired playing at Hoylake that enabled John Ball to win many of his record eight Amateur Championships. His victories were achieved between **1888** and **1912**. Ball's great rival during those years, both remarkably and ironically was a fellow Hoylake man, **Harold Hilton**. Hilton himself won four Amateur Championships. In addition both Hilton and Ball won the Open Championship, Ball in **1890** and Hilton twice in **1892** and **1897**. The immortal Bobby Jones is the only other Amateur golfer to have won the Open title.

Even on those very rare occasions when all is calm, Hoylake is still an exceptionally difficult test. From the medal tees the course measures **6804** yards, par **72**, and it can play every inch of its length. It is helpful to strike the ball, in the words of the Club's motto, 'far and sure'. Rather like Carnoustie, Hoylake is renowned for its exacting final stretch. It contains two par fives and three par fours any of which is capable of wrecking a potentially good score. The **16th** in particular can be cruelly punishing with its out of bounds to the right of the fairway.

The ten Opens held at Hoylake have produced ten different Champions and among them some of the games greatest names: **Harold Hilton, John H. Taylor, Walter Hagen** and **Bobby Jones**. The latter's victory in **1930** was the second leg of the historic **grand slam**. The sole reason for the course being presently off the 'Open rota' (the last staging was in **1967**) is that the course cannot accommodate the vast crowds that the event now attracts. Unfortunately, it is the same enthusiastic public who suffer most, for there are many who maintain that Hoylake remains the greatest of all England's Championship links.

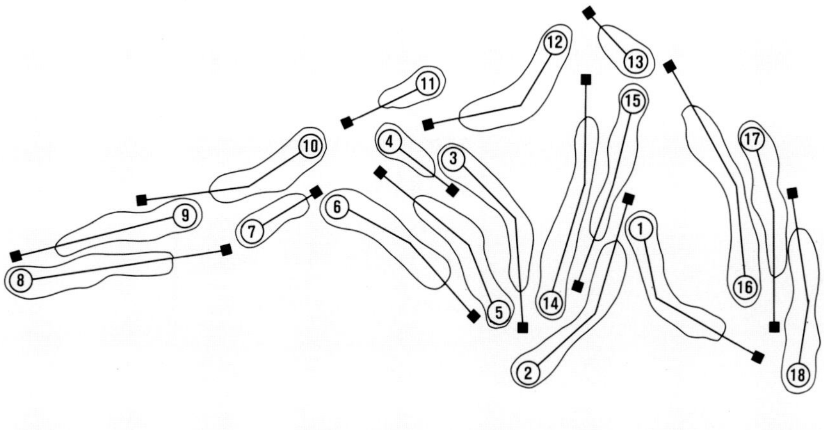

Hole	Yards	Par	Hole	Yards	Par
1	428	4	10	409	4
2	369	4	11	200	3
3	505	5	12	395	4
4	184	3	13	157	3
5	407	4	14	516	5
6	383	4	15	460	4
7	200	3	16	509	5
8	479	5	17	391	4
9	393	4	18	395	4
Out	3,348	36	In	3,432	36
			Out	3,348	36
			TOTALS	6,780	72

LANCASHIRE & THE ISLE OF MAN
COMPLETE GOLF

GREATER MANCHESTER

Altrincham G.C.
(18) 6162 yards
Stockport Road, Timperley, Altrincham
(061) 928 0761

Ashton-in-Makerfield G.C.
(18) 6160 yards
Gardwood Park, Liverpool Road, Ashton-in-Makerfield
(0942 727745

Ashton-on-Mersey G.C.
(9) 6242 yards
Church Lane, Sale
(061) 973 3220

Ashton-under-Lyne G.C.
(18) 6157 yards
Kings Road, Ashton-under-Lyne
(061) 330 1537

Blackley G.C.
(18) 6235 yards
Victoria Avenue East, Blackley
(061) 643 3912

Bolton G.C.
(18) 6215 yards
Lostock Park, Bolton
(0204) 43067

Bolton Municipal
(18) 6012 yards
Links Road, Lostock, Bolton
(0204) 42336

Bolton Old Links
(18) 6406 yards
Chorley Old Road, Bolton
(0204) 42307

Brackley G.C.
(9) 6006 yards
Bullows Road, Little Hulton, Worsley
(061) 790 6076

Bramhall G.C.
(18) 6300 yards
Ladythorn Road, Bramhall
(061) 766 2213

Bramhall Park G.C.
(18) 6214 yards
20 Manor Road, Bramhall
(061) 485 3119

Breightmet G.C.
(9) 6407 yards
Redbridge, Ainsworth, Bolton
(0204) 27381

Brookdale G.C.
(18) 5878 yards
Woodhouses, Failsworth
(061) 681 8996

Bury G.C.
(18) 5953 yards
Blackford Bridge, Bury
(061) 766 4897

Castle Hawk G.C.
(18) 6316 yards
Castleton, Rochdale
(0706) 40841

Cheadle G.C.
(9) 5006 yards
Shiers Drive, Cheadle
(061) 485 2160

Chorlton-Cum-Hardy G.C.
(18) 6004 yards
Barlow Hall Road, Chorlton, M21
(061) 881 5830

Crompton & Royton G.C.
(18) 6187 yards
High Barn, Royton, Oldham
(061) 624 2154

Davyhulme Park G.C.
(18) 6237 yards
Gleneagles Road, Davyhulme
(061) 748 2260

Deane G.C.
(18) 5511 yards
Junction Road, Deane, Bolton
(0204) 651808

Denton G.C.
(18) 6290 yards
Manchester Road, Denton, M34
(061) 336 3218

Didsbury G.C.
(18) 6230 yards
Ford Lane, Northenden, M22
(061) 998 2811

Disley G.C.
(18) 5977 yards
Jackson's Edge, Disley
(06632) 2071

Dukinfield G.C.
(18) 5544 yards
Yew Tree Lane, Dukinfield
(061) 338 2669

Dunham Forest G. & C.C.
(18) 6636 yards
Oldfield Lane, Altrincham
(061) 928 2605

Dunscar G.C.
(18) 5995 yards
Bromley Cross, Bolton
(0204) 53321

Ellesmere G.C.
(18) 5957 yards
Old Clough Lane, Worsley
(061) 790 2122

Fairfield G. & S.C.
(18) 5664 yards
Booth Road, Andenshaw, M34
(061) 370 2292

Flixton G.C.
(9) 6441 yards
Church Road, Flixton, Urmston
(061) 748 2116

Gathurst G.C.
(9) 6308 yards
Sherington, Wigan
(02575) 2432

Gatley G.C.
(9) 5934 yards
Styal Road, Heald Green
(061) 437 2830

Great Lever & Farnworth G.C.
(18) 5859 yards
Lever Edge Lane, Bolton
(0204) 62582

Greenmount G.C.
(9) 4915 yards
Greenmount, Bury
(020488) 3712

Hale G.C.
(9) 5734 yards
Rappax Road, Hale
(061) 980 4225

Harwood G.C.
(9) 6028 yards
Harwood, Bolton
(0204) 28028

Hazel Grove G.C.
(18) 6300 yards
Buxton Road, Hazel Grove
(061) 483 7272

Heaton Moor G.C.
(18) 5876 yards
Heaton Mersey, Stockport
(061) 432 6458

Heaton Park G.C.
(18) 5849 yards
Heaton Park, Prestwich
(061) 798 0295

Hindley Hall G.C.
(18) 5875 yards
Hall Lane, Hindley, Wigan
(0942) 55991

Horwich G.C.
(9) 5404 yards
Horwich, Bolton
(0204) 696298

Houldsworth G.C.
(18) 6078 yards
Wingate House, Levenshulme, M19
(061) 224 8108

CHARLES CROMBIE 'The Rules of Golf – Rule 23' *ROSENSTIEL'S*

LANCASHIRE & THE ISLE OF MAN

COMPLETE GOLF

Lobden G.C.
5750 yards
Whitworth, Rochdale
(070685) 49000

Lowes Park G.C.
(9) 6003 yards
Walmersley, Bury
(061) 764 1231

Manchester G.C.
(18) 6554 yards
Rochdale Road, Middleton, M24
(061) 643 3202

Marple G.C.
(18) 5506 yards
Hawk Green, Marple, Stockport
(061) 427 5989

Mellor & Townscliffe G.C.
(18) 5925 yards
Mellor, Stockport
(061) 427 2208

Mirrlees G.C.
(9) 6102 yards
Bramhall Moor Lane, Hazel Grove
(061) 483 1000

North Manchester G.C.
(18) 67542 yards
Manchester Old Road,
Middleton M24
(061) 643 9033

Northenden G.C.
(18) 6435 yards
Palatine Road, Northenden M22
(061) 998 4738

Oldham G.C.
(18) 5045 yards
Lees New Road, Oldham
(061) 624 4305

Pike Fold G.C.
(9) 5789 yards
Cooper Lane, Victoria Avenue,
Blackley M9
(061) 740 1136

Prestwich G.C.
(18) 4712 yards
Hilton Lane, Prestwich M25
(061) 773 2544

Reddish Vale G.C.
(18) 6048 yards
Southcliffe Road,
Reddish, Stockport
(061) 480 2359

Ringway G.C.
(18) 6494 yards
Hale Barns, Altrincham
(061) 980 2630

Rochdale G.C.
(18) 5981 yards
Bagslate, Rochdale
(0706) 46024

Romiley G.C.
(18) 6357 yards
Goosehouse Green,
Romiley, Stockport
(061) 430 72757

Saddleworth G.C.
(18) 5961 yards
Uppermill, Oldham
(04577) 2059

Sale G.C.
(18) 6351 yards
Golf Road, Sale M33
(061) 973 1638

Springfield Park G.C.
(18) 5209 yards
Marland, Rochdale
(0706) 49801

Stamford G.C.
(18) 5619 yards
Huddersfield Road, Stalybridge
(04575) 4829

Stand G.C.
(18) 6411 yards
Ashbourne Grove, Whitefield M25
(061) 766 2214

Stockport G.C.
(18) 6319 yards
Offerton Road, Offerton, Stockport
(061) 427 4425

Swinton Park G.C.
(18) 6628 yards
East Lanes Road, Swinton M27
(061) 794 0861

Tunshill G.C.
(9) 5812 yards
Milnrow, Rochdale
(0706) 342095

Turton G.C.
(9) 5805 yards
Bromley Cross, Bolton
(0204) 852235

Walmersley G.C.
(9) 6114 yards
Garretts Close, Walmersley, Bury
(061) 764 0018

Werneth G.C.
(18) 5296 yards
Garden Suburb, Oldham
(061) 624 1190

Werneth Low G.C.
(9) 5734 yards
Werneth Low, Hyde
(061) 366 0054

Westhoughton G.C.
(9) 5834 yards
Westhoughton, Bolton
(0942) 811085

Whitefield G.C.
(18) 6106 yards
Higher Lane, Whitefield M25
(061) 766 2904

Wigan G.C.
(9) 6058 yards
Arley Hall, Haigh, Wigan
(0257) 421360

Wigan Metropolitan
(18) 6423 yards
Haigh Hall Park, Wigan
(0942) 401107

William Wroe G.C.
(18) 4395 yards
Pennybridge Lane, Flixton M31
(061) 748 8680

Withington G.C.
(18) 6411 yards
243 Palatine Road,
West Didsbury M20
(061) 445 9544

Worsley G.C.
(18) 6217 yards
Monton Green, Eccles M30
(061) 789 4202

LANCASHIRE

Accrington & District G.C.
(18) 5954 yards
West End, Oswaldtwistle,
Accrington
(0254) 32734

Ashton & Lea G.C.
(18) 6286 yards
Blackpool Road, Lea, Preston
(0772) 735282

Bacup G.C.
(9) 5652 yards
Maden Road, Bacup
(0706) 873170

Baxenden & District G.C.
(9) 5740 yards
Top o' th' Meadow, Baxenden,
Accrington
(0254) 34555

Beacon Park G.C.
(18) 5996 yards
Dalton, Up Holland, Wigan
(0695) 622700

CHARLES CROMBIE 'The Rules of Golf – Rule 18' *ROSENSTIEL'S*

LANCASHIRE AND THE ISLE OF MAN

COMPLETE GOLF

Blackburn G.C.
(18) 6099 yards
Beardwood Brow, Blackburn
(0254) 51122

Blackpool North Shore G.C.
(18) 6440 yards
Devonshire Road, Blackpool
(0253) 52054

Blackpool Park G.C.
(18) 6060 yards
North Park Drive, Blackpool
(0253) 53382

Burnley G.C.
(18) 5891 yards
Glen View, Burnley
(0282) 22032

Chorley G.C.
(18) 6311 yards
Whalley Road, Clitheroe
(025 72) 63024

Colne G.C.
(9) 5961 yards
Skipton Old Road, Colne
(0282) 67158

Darwen G.C.
(18) 5752 yards
Winter Hill, Darwen
(0254) 75613

Dean Wood G.C.
(18) 6097 yards
Lafford Lane, Up Holland,
Skelmersdale
(0695) 622219

Duxbury Park G.C.
(18) 6390 yards
Duxbury Park, Chorley
(02572) 65380

Fairhaven G.C.
(18) 6810 yards
Lytham Hall Park, Ansdell,
Lytham St Annes
(0253) 736976

Fishwick Hall G.C.
(18) 6203 yards
Farringdon Park, Preston
(0772) 798300

Fleetwood G.C.
(18) 6437 yards
Princes Way, Fleetwood
(03917) 3661

Green Haworth G.C.
(9) 5513 yards
Green Haworth, Accrington
(0254) 37580

Heysham G.C.
(18) 6224 yards
Trumacar Park, Heysham
(0524) 51011

Ingol G. & S.C.
(18) 6345 yards
Ingol, Preston
(0772) 734556

Knott End G.C.
(18) 5852 yards
Wyreside, Knott End on Sea,
Blackpool
(0253) 810576

Lancaster G. & C.C.
(18) 6442 yards
Ashton-with-Stodday, Lancaster
(0524) 751247

Lansil G.C.
(9) 5608 yards
Caton Road, Lancaster
(0524) 67143

Leyland G.C.
(18) 6067 yards
Wigan Road, Leyland
(0772) 436457

Longridge G.C.
(18) 5678 yards
Jeffrey Hill, Longridge
(077478) 3291

Lytham Green Drive G.C.
(18) 6043 yards
Ballam Road, Lytham
(0253) 737390

Marsden Park G.C.
(18) 5806 yards
Townhouse Road, Nelson
(0282) 67525

Morecambe G.C.
(18) 5766 yards
Bare, Morecambe
(0524) 412841

Nelson G.C.
(18) 5961 yards
Brierfield, Nelson
(0282) 64583

Ormskirk G.C.
(18) 6333 yards
Lathom, Ormskirk
(0695) 72227

Penwortham G.C.
(18) 5915 yards
Penwortham, Preston
(0772) 744630

Pleasington G.C.
(18) 6417 yards
Pleasington, Blackburn
(0254) 22177

Poulton-le-Fylde G.C.
(9) 5752 yards
Breck Road, Poulton-le-Fylde
(0253) 892444

Preston G.C.
(18) 6249 yards
Fulwood, Preston
(0772) 700011

Rishton G.C.
(9) 6094 yards
Eachill Links, Rishton
(0254) 884442

Rossendale G.C.
(18) 6267 yards
Haslinden, Rossendale
(0706) 213056

Royal Lytham & St Annes G.C.
(18) 6673 yards
Links Gate, Lytham St Annes
(0253) 724206

St Annes Old Links
(18) 6616 yards
Highbury Road, St Annes, Lytham
(0253) 723597

Shaw Hill G. & C.C.
(18) 6467 yards
Whittle-le-Woods, Chorley
(02572) 69221

Silverdale G.C.
(9) 5262 yards
Redbridge Lane, Silverdale,
Carnworth
(0524) 701300

Todmorden G.C.
(9) 5818 yards
Stone Road, Todmorden
(070681

Towneley G.C.
(9) 5840 yards
Towneley Park, Burnley
(0282) 38473

Whalley G.C.
(9) 5953 yards
Whalley, Blackburn
(025482) 2236

Whittaker G.C.
(9) 5636 yards
Whittaker Lane, Littleborough
(0706) 78310

Wilpshire G.C.
(18) 5991 yards
Wilpshire, Blackburn
(0254) 48276

MERSEYSIDE

Allerton Municipal
(18) 5081 yards
Allerton, Liverpool 18
(051) 428 1046

CHARLES CROMBIE 'The Rules of Golf – Rule 32' *ROSENSTIEL'S*

LANCASHIRE & THE ISLE OF MAN

COMPLETE GOLF

Alt G.C.
(18) 5939 yards
Park Road West, Southport
(0704) 35268

Arrowe Park G.C.
(18) 6377 yards
Arrow Park, Woodchurch, Birkenhead
(051) 677 1527

Bidston G.C.
(18) 6207 yards
Leasowe, Wirral
(051) 638 8685

Bootle G.C.
(18) 6362 yards
Dunningsbridge Road, Bootle
(051) 928 1371

Bowring G.C.
(9) 5580 yards
Roby Road, Huyton
(051) 489 1901

Brackenwood G.C.
(18) 6285 yards
Bebington, Wirral
(051) 608 3093

Bromborough G.C.
(18) 6650 yards
Raby Hall Road, Bromborough
(051) 334 2978

Caldy G.C.
(18) 6665 yards
Links Hey Road, Caldy, Wirral
(051) 625 5660

Childwall G.C.
(18) 6425 yards
Naylor's Road, Liverpool 27
(051) 487 9871

Eastham Lodge G.C.
(15) 5826 yards
Ferry Road, Eastham, Wirral
(051) 327 3003

Ellesmere Port G.C.
(18) 6432 yards
Chester Road, Hooton, S. Wirral
(051) 339 7689

Formby G.C.
(18) 6871 yards
Golf Road, Formby
(07048) 72164

Grange Park G.C.
(18) 6480 yards
Prescot Road, St. Helens
(0744) 26318

Haydock Park G.C.
(18) 6014 yards
Golborne Park, Newton-le-Willows
(09252) 6944

Hesketh G.C.
(18) 6478 yards
Cambridge Road, Southport
(0704) 36897

Heswall G.C.
(18) 6472 yards
Cottage Lane, Heswall, Wirral
(051) 342 1237

Hillside G.C.
(18) 6850 yards
Hastings Road, Southport
(0704) 67169

Hoylake Municipal
(18) 6312 yards
Carr Lane, Hoylake
(051) 632 2956

Huyton & Prescot G.C.
(18) 5738 yards
Hurst Park, Huyton
(051) 489 3948

Leasowe G.C.
(18) 6204 yards
Leasowe Road, Moreton, Wirral
(051) 677 5852

Lee Park G.C.
(18) 6024 yards
Childwall Valley Road, Liverpool 27
(051) 487 3882

Liverpool Municipal
(18) 6588 yards
Ingoe Lane, Kirkby
(051) 546 5435

Prenton G.C.
(18) 6379 yards
Golf Links Road, Prenton, Birkenhead
(051) 608 1053

Royal Birkdale G.C.
(18) 6968 yards
Waterloo Road, Southport
(0704) 67920

Royal Liverpool G.C.
(18) 6780 yards
Meols Drive, Hoylake, Wirral
(051) 632 3101

Sherdley Park G.C.
(18) 5941 yards
Elton Road, St. Helens
(0744) 813149

Southport & Ainsdale G.C.
(18) 6603 yards
Bradshaws Lane, Ainsdale, Southport
(0704) 78000

Southport Municipal
(18) 5939 yards
Park Road West, Southport
(0704) 35286

Southport Old Links
(9) 6486 yards
Moors Lane, Southport
(0704 24294

Wallasey G.C.
(18) 6607 yards
Bayswater Road, Wallasey
(051) 639 3700

Warren G.C.
(9) 5914 yards
Grove Road, Wallasey
(051) 639 5730

West Derby G.C.
(18) 6333 yards
Yew Tree Lane, West Derby, Liverpool 12
(051) 228 3420

West Lancashire G.C.
(18) 6756 yards
Hall Road West, Blundellsands, Liverpool 23
(051) 924 1076

Wirral Ladies G.C.
(18) 4967 yards
Budston Road, Oxton, Birkenhead
(051) 652 1255

Woolton G.C.
(18) 5712 yards
Doe Park, Woolton, Liverpool 25
(051) 486 2298

ISLE OF MAN

Castletown G.C.
(18) 6804 yards
Fort Island, Castletown
(0624) 822125

Douglas G.C.
(18) 6080 yards
Pulrose Road, Douglas
(0624) 75952

Howstrake G.C.
(18) 5243 yards
Grondle Road, Onchan
(0624) 20430

Peel G.C.
(18) 5914 yards
Rheast Lane, Peel
(0624) 843456

Ramsey G.C.
(18) 6019 yards
Brookfield Avenue, Ramsey
(0624) 812244

Rowany G.C.
(18) 5813 yards
Rowany Drive, Port Erin
(0624) 834108

Artist : ***Charles Crombie THE RULES OF GOLF-RULE 33*** *Courtesy of : ROSENSTIEL'S*

SOUTH & WEST YORKSHIRE

H. ROUNTREE "Cassiobury Park" *SARAH BADDIEL'S BOOK GALLERY*

SOUTH & WEST YORKSHIRE

CHOICE GOLF

While many consider the delights of Yorkshire to be exclusive to its northernmost area this is totally wrong. The small villages that nestle amid the wild Pennines or the Moors are delightful. The river Wharfe carves its way through the area revealing howls of Haworth and from the Bronte country to the jovial singing in a pub on Ilkley Moor, there is a rich tradition – reserve your best golf for the eighteenth fairway.

A glance at the map tells you that the two counties of South and West Yorkshire are fairly littered with golf courses: the major towns of Leeds and Sheffield are exceptionally well served while Bradford, Huddersfield and Rotherham all have much to offer. In fact wherever you happen to be in Southern Yorkshire there is always a golf course around the corner (well almost!)

SOUTH YORKSHIRE

Perhaps the pick of the courses in the Sheffield area are the moor land course at **Hallamshire,** (green fees **£12**) three miles west of the city off the **A57, Abbeydale**, a fine wooded parkland test to the south west and **Lees Hall,** (green fees **£7**) a mix of parkland and meadowland, south of the town centre, and occupying a lofty situation with marvellous views over the city. Visitors are welcome at Hallamshire during the week and while it may be possible to arrange a game at the other two for the weekend, prior telephoning is essential.

Having saved our best golf for the 18th fairway a few thoughts now emerge for the 19th. Perhaps the best hotel in Sheffield is **The Grosvenor House (0742) 720041** while **The Hallam Tower Post House (0742) 670067** is particularly convenient for the Hallamshire course. Top class restaurants are few but for lovers of Indian food, **Nirmal's Tandoori (0742) 724054** is first rate. One major landmark not to be missed in these parts is **The Crucible Theatre (0742) 24054**, one of Britain's leading repertory companies producing shows of the highest quality – some pretty good snooker here too! Finally we ought to recommend a good pub, the area is riddled with them, the **Cross Keys** in Handsworth Road is the selection.

Before noting some of the other courses in South Yorkshire a brief word on **Lindrick**. We've featured the course in this section although it properly belongs in Nottinghamshire. True, its administrative ties lie with Yorkshire and a great number of members live in the Sheffield area. Anyway, whichever side of the fence it's on (and the larger part lies in Yorkshire) it is quite superb and well worth making the short journey.

Rotherham's course is at Thrybergh Park, two miles north of the town on the **A630**. It can be visited most days of the week although prior arrangement with the secretary is essential. Green fees are **£12** – good value. Crossing the **A1** we arrive at Doncaster. The **Doncaster Town Moor Golf Club** is situated very close to the famous racetrack on the **A638**. Like Rotherham it's a parkland type course though not as testing. Apart from Sunday mornings visitors are welcome here at all times.

In Doncaster aside from a classic racecourse **The Danum (0302) 342261** and **The Grand St Ledger (03029 64111** are the recommended establishments. In the countryside surrounding the busy railway town Cadeby offers a pleasant establishment in **The Cadeby Inn**, while in Hatfield Woodhouse **The Green Tree** offers a warm welcome and some good snacks. The hotel with the most character in the area is **The Crown** at Bawtry **(0302) 710341** – a pleasant High Street inn. In contrast people seeking what are commonly known as leisure facilities ie. gym, sauna, etc will find Rotherham's modern **Moat House (0709) 364902** to their liking.

WEST YORKSHIRE

It is in **West Yorkshire** that the greater number of golf courses are to be found. Quantity is certainly matched by quality with the area just to the north of **Leeds** being particularly outstanding. Within a short distance to one another are **Moortown** (feature with Lindrick on a later page), **Alwoodley, Sand Moor** and **Moor Allerton** all of which are of Championship standard and indeed all enjoy the most superb settings.

Whilst Alwoodley and Sand Moor are predominantly moorland in character, Moor Allerton, where there are 27 holes, is more strictly parkland. When travelling to any of the four Clubs, the **A61** should be taken out of Leeds. Prior telephoning at each is strongly recommended. Moortown and Moor Allerton are probably the most widely known courses in southern Yorkshire (if one excludes Lindrick). Moortown is remembered for its British Ryder Cup victory back in 1929 and Moor Allerton for its associations with Peter Alliss and Howard Clark. However, many consider Alwoodley and Sand Moor to be at least their equal. Play all four if you can! Fees are around the **£16** mark.

Sustenance will now be in order. As one would expect there are a number of hotels in Leeds. **The Queen's Hotel (0532) 431323** is the best of the older school while **The Hilton (0532) 442000** is a more modern but extremely comfortable place to stay. For restaurants, as in Sheffield it may be a case of pot-luck unless you happen to have been directed by a knowledgeable local. One recommendation though is **La Grillarde (0532) 459707**. Before we leave Leeds a quick note for one of the courses to the south of the town. **Howley Hall** is the choice, a fine parkland course near Morley (Saturdays should be avoided).

Following the Wharfe into the east of West Yorkshire – if you see what I mean, one finds some superb countryside. This is the land of the Brontes – quite delightful. In Bramhope there is an hotel, a far cry from the romance of the Brontes but a particularly popular hotel for businessmen visiting Leeds. It is the **Leeds Wharfedale Post House (0532) 842911**. In contrast, the delightul **Harewood House** is well worth visiting between Easter and October. The gem in this area is however a restaurant with rooms – **The Pool Court (0532) 842288** in Pool-in-Wharfedale. Delightfully pleasant rooms are complemented by some of the most excellent cooking in the country.

Another concentration of good golf courses is to be found to the north of Bradford, more particularly **Northcliffe, Keighley** and **Shipley**. Northcliffe is probably the pick with some outstanding views of the nearby moors, but each is well worth a game. Green fees are **£8** during the week, or **£10** at the week-end at Northcliffe.

Yet another trio encircles Huddersfield, with **Bradley Park** to the north, **Woodsome Hall** to the south and **Huddersfield Golf Club** to the west. It was over the latter course that **Sandy Herd** learnt his game. The Open Champion of 1902, Herd finished in the first five in the Championship on no fewer than twelve occasions; he would have doubtless won on several of those, but for a fellow from Ganton across the way.

Two courses remain to be visited, the first is **Ilkley** and the second is **Otley**. They are without question two of the most attract-

SOUTH & WEST YORKSHIRE

ive courses in Yorkshire. The River Wharfe winds its way through much of the Ilkley course and is a major hazard on several of the early holes. The course at Otley nestles majestically in the Wharfe Valley. Both courses receive visitors throughout the week although weekends are naturally busy and prior telephoning is advisable. A day's golf on either is priced at around **£10-£14**.

Beyond the fairways and the rough the gourmet golfer is superbly well catered for. Here are some suggestions. In Ilkley the 'Edwardian Breakfast' at **Rombald's (0943) 603201** is legendary but the hotel itself and the restaurant are both thoroughly recommended. Elsewhere in Ilkley, a town where delightful antique shops clutter the street one finds **The Craiglands Hotel (0943) 607676,** this has a setting adjoining that famous moor, the hotel is most comfortable. Another good value establishment is **The Cow and Calf (0943) 607335** one of the country's finest restaurants – book well in advance!

Continuing in the tradition of quality and class one need go no further than Kildwick, for here **Kildwick Hall (0535) 32444** is a gorgeous Jacobean manor house which provides an outstanding place to stay and an excellent restaurant. Bingley, Otley, all this area is riddled with enthusiastic cricket and rugby sides as well as golfers – popular pubs for one and all include **The Fox** at Menston, **The Malt Shovel** at Harden and in Ryburn where there would seem to be a focal point; here **The Old Bridge** and **The Over the Bridge** (both provide excellent lunches). For a splendid restaurant visit Golcar – **The Weavers Shed (0484) 515444** with its superb setting. Finally two more hotels – in Huddersfield **The George (0484) 25444** and in Holdsworth near Halifax, **The Holdsworth House (0422) 240024** is very highly thought of. Here endeth the 19th hole.

H. ROUNTREE 'Casual Water' *BURLINGTON GALLERY*

POOL COURT

Pool Court was converted into a small, exclusive restaurant in 1966. It is conveniently situated in a fine Georgian mansion at Pool-in-Wharfedale in West Yorkshire, approximately nine miles from Leeds, Bradford and Harrogate.

Since opening Hanni and Michael Gill have striven to achieve the very highest standards of food in the restaurant and unparalleled elegance and comfort in the bedrooms.

The very special rooms all have en-suite bathrooms, of course, and each one is decorated in its own distinctive style. There are the facilities you would expect, including direct dial telephone, individual bar/fridge, private wall safe and colour television.

The reputation has been built on the restaurant and care has been taken not to become an 'hotel', but rather a restaurant with rooms. Top accolades have been received from The Good Food Guide, Egon Ronay, A.A. and Michelin, and it is therefore not surprising that booking well in advance is advised.

Should you choose to gather for a business or a family affair, The Georgian Cellar Rooms provide a small, intimate area available to private parties of up to 30 guests. The restaurant is available for the exclusive use of parties of 80 for a sit-down or buffet meal. We feel sure you will enjoy your visit.

Pool Court Restaurant with Rooms,
Pool-in-Wharfedale,
Otley, West Yorkshire,
Tel: (0532) 842288
Fax: (0532) 843115

LINDRICK
CHAMPIONSHIP GOLF

There are two golf courses in England whose names will be forever linked with the Ryder Cup: one is **The Belfry**, the other is **Lindrick** – and they couldn't be more different. The Belfry (perhaps one should be precise and say the Brabazon Course) is a big strapping youngster of not much more than ten years in age, immature in some ways though agreeable in others. Lindrick is the seasoned campaigner; it's seen a lot in its ninety odd years (and in fact is due for a telegram in 1991); it is no giant but it is charming, subtle and full of challenge.

Before the Ryder Cup came to Lindrick in **1957**, many golfing enthusiasts knew very little of the Yorkshire course, indeed some knew nothing at all; by the end of that heady, wind-swept week in October, none would ever forget it. It was the last time an exclusively British and Irish team would ever beat the mighty men from across the sea.

Lindrick lies close to the boundaries of Yorkshire, Nottinghamshire and Derbyshire. Indeed in places, it actually forms the boundary. The majority of the course lies in Yorkshire, but some holes are in Nottinghamshire, and to the considerable annoyance of every Yorkshireman, the postal address is Lindrick, Notts!

The golf course occupies the best part of 200 acres of common-land – Lindrick Common, and is essentially heathland in nature, lying on top of limestone rock. There is a mass of gorse which when in bloom adds great colour, (though can be a devil if you land in it!) and a wealth of pine, oak and silver birch – a delightful setting to be sure.

Visitors are very welcome to test their skills in this splendid environment, although prior arrangement with the Club is required. The new Secretary is **Mr. G. Bywater**, who may be contacted by telephone on **(0909) 475282**. Written correspondence should be addressed to **The Secretary, Lindrick Golf Club, Lindrick Common, Worksop, Notts, S81 8BH**. All bookings should be made through the Secretary's office, but and as a general guide, visitors are not permitted to play on Tuesday mornings and the first tee is normally reserved for Members for an hour around lunch time, but again it's best to check.

The **green fees** at Lindrick vary according to the season and the following are the figures for 1989: in the summer, **£20** per day during the week, or **£25** for a round during the weekend; in the winter, **£15** per day during the week or **£20** at the weekend. Reductions of 50% are available to junior golfers if accompanied by an adult.

Although Lindrick Common may look a little isolated on the map, strangers shouldn't have too much difficulty in locating the course. Those coming from the south should find the **M1** and the **A1** of great assistance. The Club is actually situated just off the **A57** Worksop to Sheffield road, to the west of the former and is well signposted.

From the medal tees, the course measures **6377** yards, with the par a fairly tight **69**. Quite refreshingly, it is not a long hitter's course, the fairway shots to the green being what Lindrick is all about, and there are some excellent par fours. The **2nd**, with its uphill second and the **10th**, where there is a potentially punishing cross bunker, are two noted holes, but perhaps the best known is the **4th**. This requires a blind approach to a low lying green backed by trees and behind which the River Ryton flows. The green has a stage- like setting and it was here that the boundaries of Yorkshire, Derbyshire and Nottinghamshire once emerged. In days of old, the 'stage' was used for bare fist-fighting and cockfighting, contestants and spectators being able to step into a convenient county whenever the unfriendly law authorities showed up. The round concludes with some very testing holes and the par three **18th** provides a particularly good finish.

The Clubhouse of Linrick provides golfers with a fine view of the 18th green and many a drama will have been witnessed; but I don't suppose there will ever be anything to equal the scenes of 1957 and the time when Dai Rees and his boys made the old campaigner smile.

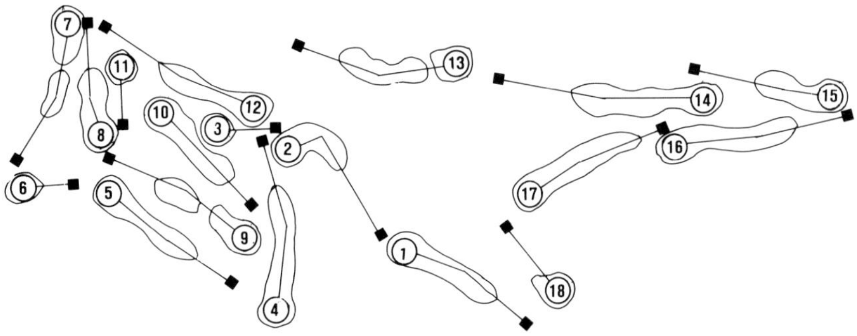

Hole	Yards	Par	Hole	Yards	Par
1	396	4	10	361	4
2	344	4	11	154	3
3	151	3	12	445	4
4	464	4	13	418	4
5	424	4	14	541	5
6	131	3	15	351	4
7	425	4	16	467	4
8	300	4	17	393	4
9	423	4	18	189	3
Out	3,058	34	In	3,319	35
			Out	3,058	34
			TOTALS	6,377	69

MOORTOWN
CHAMPIONSHIP GOLF

Moortown enjoys an enviable situation. It lies within minutes of the town centre of Leeds, yet it also lies within minutes of the Pennines and the beauty of the Yorkshire Moors. The Club was founded in the autumn of **1909** with the course being laid out by **Alister Mackenzie**. Less than twenty years after its formation Moortown was selected to host the first ever **Ryder Cup** to be played on British soil. It proved a momentous occasion. The American side was virtually identical to the one that had crushed the British team 9-2 in the inaugural staging at Worcester, Massachusetts two years previously.

It included the likes of **Walter Hagen**, then reigning British Open Champion, **Gene Sarazen, Johnny Farrel** the US Open Champion, **Leo Diegel** the U.S.P.G.A. Champion and **Al** (there goes a hundred thousand bucks) **Waltrous**. To cut a long story short the British side won by six matches to four. On the final day **George Duncan** defeated Walter Hagen by 10 and 8 and **Archie Compston** defeated Gene Sarazen 6 and 4. Well whatever it may have done to American pride, and I note that Wall Street collapsed later that summer, it certainly put Moortown on the map!

Stepping forward nearly sixty years, **Mr. R.H. Brown** is the **Secretary** at Moortown. He may be contacted by telephone on **(0532) 686521**, while the Club's professional **Bryon Hutchinson** can be reached on **(0532) 683636**. Visitors are welcome at Moortown between Mondays and Fridays. Golfing **Societies** are also welcome during the week although prior arrangement with the secretary is essential. All written correspondence should be addressed to Mr Brown at **The Moortown Golf Club, Harrogate Road, Alwoodley, Leeds LS17 7DB**. In 1989 the **green fees** were **£20** for a single round with **£25** payable for a full day's golf during the week, and weekend golf costing **£25** for a round, or **£30** for the day.

Moortown's aforementioned enviable situation is a product of the **A61** – the Leeds to Harrogate Road which runs from the heart of the city to within yards of Moortown's front door. For those travelling from the city centre, if you reach Eccup Reservoir you'll have gone too far! Leeds itself is well served by motorway connections, the **M62** linking Leeds to Greater Manchester and the **M1** joining Sheffield to Leeds. Some roads which may prove helpful include the **A64** (York to Leeds) and the **A65** (Skipton to Leeds). Our friend the **A61** approaches from the north via Ripon, Ripley and Harrogate.

With its spread of heather and gorse Moortown can properly be described as heathland, although occasionally it is classed as a moorland type course. Either way, it is always beautifully maintained and has the fine combination of being sufficiently testing yet not too severe.

From its medal tees, the course measures **6412** yards, par **69** (s.s.s. **72**). The forward tees reduce the length to **6,200** yards while for the ladies, Moortown measures **5743** yards par **74** (s.s.s. **74**). The generally held view is that the front nine is the easier of the two halves; this may have something to do with the fact that it begins with what golfers usually term a 'birdiable hole', being a short par five to a fairly open green. Perhaps Moortown's finest hole is the **8th**, a par three hole named **Gibraltar**; measuring **176** yards it calls for a shot to a plateau green built on a foundation of rock. The **10th** is an excellent par five, aptly titled 'The Long' for it stretches to **559** yards. **Archie Compston** once holed out here in two strokes.

Over the years Moortown has been the venue for several major events, both amateur and professional. Three **English Amateur Championships** have been held at Moortown, and also the English **Ladies Amateur** and the **Ladies British Amateur**. In recent years the Car Care professional tournament has also been played over the course.

Being situated directly behind the 18th green, Moortown's Club house is very much a nineteenth hole. Lunches are served daily (excepting Mondays) and both breakfast and dinner can be arranged with prior notice.

In concluding it seems appropriate to return to the course. The **18th** hole at Moortown seems to have an alarming affect on certain people. Countless numbers, including Severiano Ballesteros, have been known to overclub and fire the ball over the green into the Clubhouse area.

In the **1929** Ryder Cup during one of the foursomes matches, Joe Turnesa hooked his second behind the marquee adjoining the Clubhouse whereupon his partner promptly sailed it back over the marquee to within a yard of the hole. In the **1974** English Amateur Stroke Play tournament one player actually put his second into the Men's Bar. Opening the Clubhouse windows he played his third out onto the green. The Clubhouse certainly has a welcoming atmosphere but this would seem to be taking things a little too far!

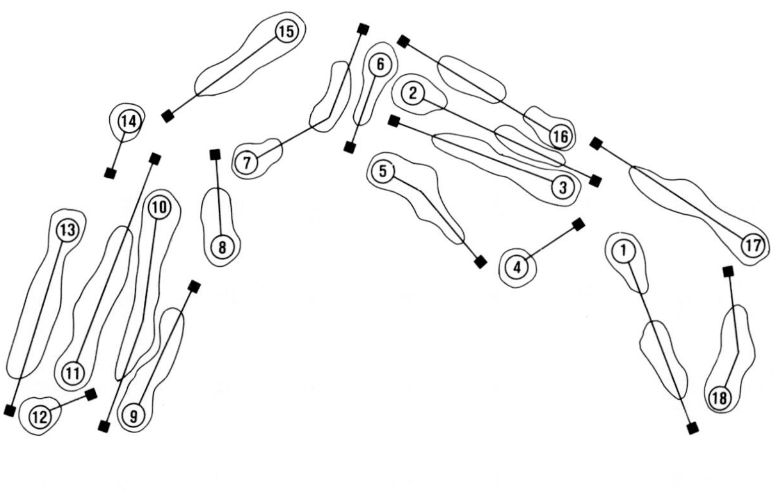

Hole	Yards	Par	Hole	Yards	Par
1	492	5	10	559	5
2	457	4	11	443	4
3	448	4	12	134	3
4	176	3	13	425	4
5	374	4	14	162	3
6	221	3	15	396	4
7	450	4	16	423	4
8	176	3	17	356	4
9	369	4	18	442	4
Out	**3,163**	**34**	**In**	**3,340**	**35**
			Out	**3,163**	**34**
			TOTALS	**6,503**	**69**

SOUTH & WEST YORKSHIRE
COMPLETE GOLF

SOUTH YORKSHIRE

Abbeydale G.C.
(18) 6419 yards
Twentywell Lane,
Dore, Sheffield
(0742) 360763

Austerfield Park G.C.
(18) 6824 yards
Cross Lane,
Austerfield
(0302) 710850

Barnsley G.C.
(18) 6048 yards
Staincross,
Barnsley
(0226) 382856

Beauchief G.C.
(18) 5428 yards
Abbey Lane,
Sheffield
(0742) 620648

Birley Wood G.C.
(18) 6275 yards
Birley Lane,
Sheffield
(0742) 390099

Concord Park G.C.
(18) 4280 yards
Shiregreen Lane,
Sheffield
(0742) 613605

Crookhill Park G.C.
(18) 5846 yards
Conisbrough,
Doncaster
(0709) 863466

Doncaster G.C.
(18) 6230 yards
Bescarr,
Doncaster
(0302) 868404

Doncaster Town Moor G.C.
(18) 6081 yards
Belle Vue,
Doncaster
(0302) 535286

Dore & Totley G.C.
(18) 6301 yards
Broadway Rd,
Sheffield
(0742) 369872

Grange Park G.C.
(18) 6461 yards
Upper Wortley Rd,
Rotherham
(0709) 559497

Hallamshire G.C.
(18) 6396 yards
Sandygate,
Sheffield
(0742) 302153

Hallowes G.C.
(18) 6366 yards
Hallowes Lane,
Dronfield,
Sheffield
(0246) 413734

Hickleton G.C.
(18) 6401 yards
Hickleton,
Doncaster
(0709) 892496

Hillsborough G.C.
(18) 6100 yards
Worrall Rd,
Sheffield
(0742) 349151

Lees Hall G.C.
(18) 6137 yards
Hemsworth Rd,
Norton,
Sheffield
(0742) 552900

Lindrick G.C.
(see Nottinghamshire)

hoenix G.C.
(18) 6145 yards
Brinsworth,
Rotherham
(0709) 370759

Rotherham G.C.
(18) 6324 yards
Thrybergh Park,
Rotherham
(0709) 850812

Serlby Park G.C.
(18) 5325 yards
Serlby,
Doncaster
0777) 818268

Silkstone G.C.
(18) 6045 yards
Field Head,
Silkstone,
Barnsley
(0226) 790328

Sitwell Park G.C.
(18) 6203 yards
Shrogswood Rd,
Rotherham
(0709) 541046

Stocksbridge & District G.C.
(15) 5055 yards
Royd Lane,
Townead,
Deepcar,
Sheffield
(0742) 882408

Tankersley Park G.C.
(18) 6241 yards
High Green,
Sheffield
(0742) 468247

Tinsley Park G.C.
(18) 6045 yards
Darnall, Sheffield
(0742) 560237

Wath G.C.
(9) 5606 yards
Abdy Rawmarsh, Rotherham
(0709) 878677

Wheatley G.C.
(18) 6345 yards
Armthorpe Rd, Doncaster
(0302) 831655

Wortley G.C.
(18) 5960 yards
Hermit Hill Lane, Wortley
Sheffield
(0742) 885294

WEST YORKSHIRE

Alwoodley G.C.
(18) 6301 yards
Wigton Lane, Alwoodley
Leeds 17
(0532) 681680

Baildon G.C.
(18) 6178 yards
Baildon, Shipley
(0274) 584266

Ben Rhydding G.C.
(9) 4711 yards
Ben Rhydding, Ilkley
(0943) 608759

Bingley St. Ives G.C.
(18) 6480 yards
Harden, Bingley
(0274) 562506

Bradford G.C.
(18) 6259 yards
Hawksworth Lane, Guisley,
Leeds
(0943) 75570

Bradford Moor G.C.
(9) 5854 yards
Pollard Lane, Bradford
(0274) 638313

Bradley Park G.C.
(18) 6100 yards
Bradley Rd, Huddersfield
(0484) 39988

Branshaw G.C.
(18) 5790 yards
Oakworth, Keighley
(0535) 43235

City of Wakefield G.C.
(18) 6405 yards
Luspet Park, Wakefield
(0924) 376214

Clayton G.C.
(9) 5527 yards
Thornton View Rd, Clayton,
Bradford
(0724) 880047

Cleckheaton & District G.C.
(18) 5994 yards
Bradford Rd, Cleckheaton
(0274) 877851

Crosland Heath G.C.
(18) 5962 yards
Crosland Heath, Huddersfield
(0484) 653262

Dewsbury District G.C.
(18) 6226 yards
Sands Lane, Mirfield
(0924) 492399

East Bierley G.C.
(9) 4308 yards
South View Rd, Bierley,
Bradford
(0274) 681023

Elland G.C.
(9) 5526 yards
Leach Lane, Elland
(0422) 73276

Fulneck G.C.
(9) 5432 yards
Pudsey
(0532) 565191

Garforth G.C.
(18) 6296 yards
Long Lane, Garforth, Leeds
(0532) 863308

Gott's Park G.C.
(18) 4449 yards
Armley Ridge Rd, Leeds
(0532) 684865

Halifax G.C.
(18) 6038 yards
Union Lane, Ogden, Halifax
(0422) 244171

Halifax Bradley Hall G.C.
(18) 6213 yards
Holywell Green, Halifax
(0422) 70231

Hanging Heaton G.C.
(9) 5874 yards
Bennett Lane, Dewsbury
(0924) 461729

Headingley G.C.
(18) 6238 yards
Back Church Lane, Adel,
Leeds
(0532) 679573

Headley G.C.
(9) 4918 yards
Thornton, Bradford
(0274) 833481

Horsforth G.C.
(18) 6243 yards
Horsforth, Leeds
(0532) 585200

Howley Hall G.C.
(18) 6446 yards
Scotchman Lane, Morley, Leeds
(0924) 478417

Huddersfield G.C.
(18) 6437 yards
Fixby Hall, Huddersfield
(0484) 26203

Ilkley G.C.
(18) 6249 yards
Myddleton, Ilkley
(0943) 600214

Keighley G.C.
(18) 6139 yards
Howden Park, Keighley
(0535) 604778

Leeds G.C.
(18) 6097 yards
Elmete Lane, Leeds
(0532) 658775

Lightcliffe G.C.
(9) 5888 yards
Knowle Top Rd, Lightcliffe
(0422) 202459

Longley Park G.C.
(9) 5269 yards
Maple St, Huddersfield
(0484) 22304

Low Laithes G.C.
(18) 6440 yards
Flushdyke, Ossett
(0924) 274667

Marsden G.C.
(9) 5702 yards
Hemplow, Marsden
(0484) 844253

Meltham G.C.
(18) 6145 yards
Meltham, Huddersfield
(0484) 850227

Middleton Park G.C.
(18) 5233 yards
Middleton Park, Leeds
(0532) 700449

Moor Allerton G.C.
(9) 3242 yards
(9) 3138 yards
(9) 3441 yards
Coal Rd, Wike, Leeds
(0532) 661154

Moortown G.C.
(18) 6503 yards
Harrogate Rd, Leeds
(0532) 686521

SOUTH & WEST YORKSHIRE

Mount Skip G.C.
(9) 5114 yards
Wadsworth, Hebden Bridge
(0422) 842896

Normanton G.C.
(9) 5284 yards
Syndale Rd, Normanton
(0924) 892943

Northcliffe G.C.
(18) 6093 yards
High Bank Lane
(0274) 596731

Otley G.C.
(18) 6225 yards
West Busk Lane, Otley
(0943) 463403

Outlane G.C.
(18) 5590 yards
Outlane, Huddersfield
(0422) 74762

Painthorpe G.C.
(9) 4108 yards
Crigglestone, Wakefield
(0924) 255083

Phoenix Park G.C.
(9) 4776 yards
Phoenix Park, Thornbury
(0274) 667178

Pontefract & District G.C.
(18) 6227 yards
Park Lane, Pontefract
(0977) 792115

Queensbury G.C.
(9) 5102 yards
Brighouse Rd, Queensbury
(0274) 882155

Rawdon G.C.
(9) 5964 yards
Rawdon, Leeds
(0532) 506040

Riddlesden G.C.
(18) 4247 yards
Riddleston, Keighley
(0535) 602148

Roundhay G.C.
(9) 5166 yards
Park Lane, Leeds
(0532) 661686

Sand Moor G.C.
(18) 6429 yards
Alwoodley Lane, Leeds
(0532) 681685

Scarcroft G.C.
(18) 6426 yards
Skye Lane, Leeds
(0532) 892311

Shipley G.C.
(18) 6203 yards
Cottingley Bridge, Bingley
(0274) 568652

Silsden G.C.
(14) 4780 yards
Silsden, Keighley
(0535) 52998

South Bradford G.C.
(9) 6004 yards
Odsal, Bradford
(0274) 676911

South Leeds G.C.
(18) 5835 yards
Gipsy Lane, Leeds
(0532) 771676

Temple Newsam G.C.
(18) 6448 yards
(18) 6029 yards
Temple Newsam Rd, Leeds
(0532) 645624

Wakefield G.C.
(18) 6626 yards
Sandal, Wakefield
(0924) 250287

West Bowling G.C.
(18) 5756 yards
Rooley Lane, Bradford
(0274) 724449

West Bradford G.C.
(18) 5752 yards
Haworth Rd, Bradford
(0274) 42767

West End G.C.
(18) 6003 yards
Highroad Well, Halifax
(0422) 53068

Wetherby G.C.
(18) 6244 yards
Linton Lane, Wetherby
(0937) 63375

Woodhall Hills G.C.
(18) 6102 yards
Calverley, Rudsey
(0532) 554594

Woodsome Hall G.C.
(18) 6068 yards
Fenay Bridge, Huddersfield
(0484) 602971

*Artist **J. C. Dollman THE STYMIE, NORTH BERWICK** Courtesy of : BURLINGTON GALLERY*

NORTH YORKSHIRE & HUMBERSIDE

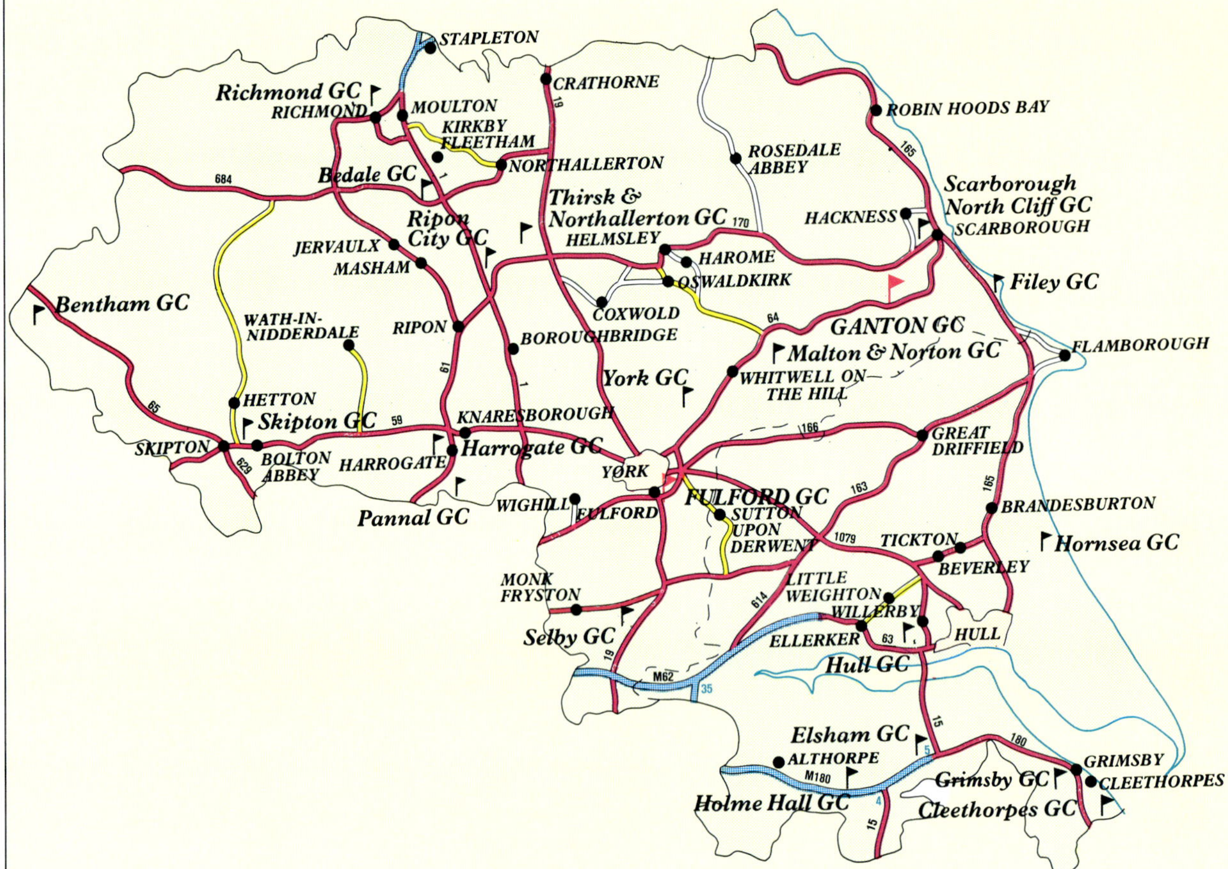

WILL HENDERSON "Teeing Up" BURLINGTON GALLERY

NORTH YORKSHIRE & HUMBERSIDE
CHOICE GOLF

To the south and west the Yorkshire Dales; to the north and east the Yorkshire Moors. North Yorkshire is England's largest county and quite possibly England's most beautiful.

The Dales and the Moors may not sound like great golfing country and indeed by far the greater number of Yorkshire's golf courses lie in the more populated and industrial regions of South and West Yorkshire. However, visitors to North Yorkshire will not be disappointed; not only does the county boast the likes of **Ganton and Fulford**, two of England's greatest inland courses, but there are twenty five or so others, the majority of which are set in quite glorious surroundings and welcome visitors throughout the week.

HUMBERSIDE

To North Yorkshire we must tag on Humberside, much of which once belonged to Yorkshire anyway. It has been a much maligned county and it's not fair to compare Scunthorpe and Grimsby with the likes of Harrogate and York. It has its treasures like any other, a forty mile stretch of sand: pretty villages nestling in the Wolds and the Holderness countryside; it would be difficult to imagine a more pleasant market town than Beverley and then there's the spectacular Humber Bridge and dramatic Flamborough Head.

Unfortunately try as I may I cannot trot off a list of wonderful golf courses. There are enough of them, a handy eighteen in fact, but there's no Ganton or Fulford here, alas. The best in the county is arguably at **Hornsea**, famed, of course for its pottery. It is a beautiful heathland course with particularly outstanding greens. One tip – try not to kill the ducks on the 11th! A day's golf at Hornsea is good value at **£8** midweek, **£12** at the weekend.

Beverley is no great distance from Hornsea and **The Beverley Arms (0482) 869241** is a superb place for a night's rest. Tickton offers the excellent **Tickton Grange (0964) 543666** and for a pleasant drink visit **The White Horse** in Brandesburton.

If one has crossed all 1,542 yards of the Humber Bridge to reach the county's largest town then the **Hull Golf Club** at Kirk Ella is probably the best choice for a game while **The Waterfront (0482) 227222** is the most attractive hotel. The seafood ought to be sampled and **Cerutti's (0482) 28501** is one of the best places to do so.

Across the Humber, **Elsham** is well thought of (an old haunt of Tony Jacklin's this) and slightly nearer to Scunthorpe, **Holme Hall** at Bottesford is a championship length parkland course. Green fees at either are approximately **£8**.

Finally over to the Humberside coast – both **Grimsby and Cleethorpes** are worth a game. Both towns are full of character – characters as well and if you do play don't miss out on the local fish and chips – they're the best in Britain!

NORTH YORKSHIRE

York, they say is a city everyone should visit at least once. I recommend at least twice for there are two outstanding golf courses within 3 miles of York Minster: **Fulford** to the south and **York Golf Club** at Strensall to the north. Fulford (see feature page) is perhaps the better known, but **York** is also a Championship course and has many admirers. It is a fine woodland course laid out to the edge of Strensall Common. Visitors are welcome to play at York on any day of the week although as it is popular, it is essential to telephone the Club in advance. Green fees are priced at **£12** midweek, **£15** at weekends.

Staying in York really is a delight, there is a wealth of attractions – Shambles has some gorgeous shops, the Minster itself is sensational, museums galore and some excellent hostels. The star of the show is **Middlethorpe Hall (0904) 640241**, a beautiful mansion house and an exquisite restaurant, a delight to visit. **The Mount Royale (0904) 6288565** is another well run hotel and is less expensive, while closer to the centre of town **The Judges Lodging (0904) 38733** is particularly elegant. The town centre has many tea shops and small restaurants as well as some pleasant pubs, note **The Olde Starr** in Stonegate. (**The Ten Green Bottles** is also good fun). A fine pub outside the city can be found in Wighill – **The White Swan** – good value bar snacks. In Fulford village two pubs very handy for the course are **The Saddle** and **The Plough.**

Next to York, **Harrogate** probably offers most to both sightseer and golfer. **Pannal and Harrogate** are the pick of the courses in the area, the former being a fairly lengthy championship challenge. It is moorland in nature and heavily wooded. Harrogate is possibly the more attractive with its lovely setting at Starbeck near Knaresborough. Green fees at either course are about **£15** per day. While again there are no specific restriction on visitors a quick phone call before setting off is recommended.

Harrogate is renowned for its many fine restaurants. They include **The Drum and Monkey (0423) 502650** (superb seafood) and **Number Six (0423) 530585**. The restaurants in the hotels are also particularly good notably **The Hotel Majestic (0423) 68972, The Russell (0423) 509866 and The Studley (0423) 60425**. In Knaresborough, **The Dower House Hotel (0423) 863302** offers a very pleasant stay and **Schwallers (0423) 863899** is a well thought of Swiss restaurant.

Before heading towards the Dales and Moors it is worth noting **Selby** in the south of the county. Laid out over fairly sandy sub-soil the course could be described as part links, part parkland. The Club welcomes visitors throughout the week, with prior telephoning required at weekends. Green fees at Selby are **£9** midweek, **£11** at weekends. A day's golf might be followed by a visit to Monk Fryston and its hotel, **The Monk Fryston Hall (0977) 682369**.

Skipton is known as the 'Gateway to the Dales'. The ancient market town has a fine parkland course only a mile or so from the town centre. Green fees here are **£8** a week or **£10** at weekends. The views are magnificent and a mountain stream runs through the course adding to the many challenges. Visitors are welcome throughout the week. An appetite created, dinner is recommended at **The Devonshire Arms (075671) 441** in Bolton Abbey. If simply a good drink is all that's required then **The Angel** at Helton may be preferable.

Ripon is a very charming place; there are only nine holes here (at **Ripon City**) though they offer great variety nonetheless. The surrounding countryside is quite stupendous. Jervaulx Abbey, founded in 1156 is well worth inspecting (note the outstanding **Jervaulx Hall Hotel (0677) 60235**, as is Fountains Abbey. For accommodation, Ripon has **The Ripon Spa Hotel (0765) 2172** and in nearby Boroughbridge, **The Crown (0423) 322328** is a comfortable old inn. Lovers of Theakston's should make a pilgrimage to **The White Bear** at Masham.

NORTH YORKSHIRE & HUMBERSIDE
CHOICE GOLF

Two of North Yorkshire's most beautiful courses are situtated fairly close to one another in the centre of the county: **Thirsk & Northallerton** and **Bedale**. The former lies very close to Thirsk racetrack. The views here are towards the Cleveland Hills on one side and the Hambleton Hills on another. **Bedale Golf Club** can be found off the **A684** and is known for its beautiful spread of trees. At each course visitors are welcome between Mondays and Saturdays, fees being approximately **£8** per day.

In the north of the county, **Richmond** (green fees **£8**) is another course that enjoys glorious surroundings. The town itself has a strange mixture of medieval, Georgian and Victorian architecture and is dominated of course by the Castle. Fine restaurants once again abound – in Moulton **The Black Bull Inn (032577) 289** is excellent as is **The Bridge Inn (0325) 50106** at Stapleton. Firmly recommended also is **The Miller's House (0969) 22630** at Middleham – a small but superb hotel.

Dropping back down in the county, **Malton and Norton** shouldn't be overlooked. It is also paricularly convenient for those heading towards **Ganton** on the **A64**. Ganton, thought by many to be the finest inland course in the North of England, boasts a superb setting on the edge of the Vale of Pickering, and along with Fulford is featured on a later page.

Yorkshire's coast contrasts greatly with that of Lancashire, with spectacular cliffs rather than dunes dominating the coastline. Not surprisingly there are no links courses to be found here. However, visitors to the resorts of **Filey** and **Scarborough** will be able to enjoy a game with views over sea and sand (hopefully avoiding both!) Green fees at these clubs are **£9**.

The splendid **Royal Hotel (0723) 364353** in Scarborough caters for all tastes and **The Hotel St. Nicholas (0723) 364101** offers fine views. Slightly inland at Hackness, **The Hackness Grange Country Hotel (0723) 82345** enjoys a beautiful setting and makes for a pleasant stay (there's also a pitch and putt course to sneak in some early morning practice).

I cannot leave North Yorkshire without quoting one of the Secretaries who kindly sent us information. It's probably best that he remains anonymous for when asked if anything of particular note had occurred in his Club's long history he duly replied: 'Nothing really other than Births, Deaths, Marriages and a few holes in one'!

BURLINGTON GALLERY

ENGLISH ROSE HOTELS

ENGLISH ROSE HOTELS SCARBOROUGH

During your stay at an English Rose Hotel you will be more than welcome to visit any of the others and take advantage of the facilities available to our guests.

HOLBECK HALL HOTEL

Holbeck Hall is a 4 Star Country House Hotel, set in 3 acres of lawns, gardens and woodlands overlooking Scarborough's South Bay and Harbour. Located at the most southerly point of South Cliff this magnificent mansion is in close proximity to Scarborough's South Cliff. In recent years the hotel has been extensively renovated and modernised to cater especially for those who seek excellence in cuisine and comfort, without sacrificing the original charm and character of this splendid country house. The moment you step into the magnificent oak panelled reception hall with its impressive pine stairway, imposing baronial fireplace and intriguing minstrels'gallery you'll be captivated by the elegance of Holbeck Hall

Holbeck Hall
South Cliff,
Scarborough YO11 2XX
Tel: (0723) 374374

WREA HEAD COUNTRY HOTEL

Wrea Head Country Hotel, built in 1881, retains all the character and charm of a family country house and is ideally situated for both countryside and coast. The hotel stands in 14 acres of woodland and landscaped grounds, once part of a large deer park dating back to the 13th century. The cellars are well stocked with fine wines and the cuisine is predominantly English with much of the produce fresh from the kitchen gardens. The hotel is open all the year round, has full central heating, and in winter a blazing log fire in the Ingle Nook fireplace adds a cheerful welcome. It is even possible to bring your horse with special facilities for stabling and grazing adjoining the grounds.

Wrea Head Country,
Scalby, Scarborough
YL13 0PB
Tel: (0723) 378 211

HACKNESS GRANGE

Hackness Grange Country Hotel is a 19th Century Country House of style and character set in 11 acres of beautiful parkland on the banks of the River Derwent, amid the lush scenery of the Forge Valley in the spectacular North York Moors National Park. Originally built in 1840 the property was later enlarged in 1890 to be occupied by the second Lord Derwent and subsequently by the Earl of Listowel. Hackness Grange offers something for everyone. We have our own indoor heated swimming pool, a pitch and putt golf course, all weather tennis court and 11 miles of trout fishing on the Derwent. In more recent years extensive renovation and modernisation to the house and stable block has provided the present luxury accommodation in an idyllic setting whilst still retaining its overall charm.

Hackness Grange Hotel,
North Yorkshire Moors National Park,
Near Scarborough,
YO13 0JW.
Tel: (0723) 82 345

FULFORD
CHAMPIONSHIP GOLF

These days golf is not only played in every foreign field but it is also played in the most unlikely of places. In **1971** American astronaut **Captain Alan Shepherd** struck two golf shots from the surface of the moon, becoming in the process the only man able to shank a ball 200 yards. Not to be outdone, as ever, **Arnold Palmer** in **1977** hit three golf balls from off the second stage of the Eiffel Tower, while in **1981** at Fulford, York, **Bernhard Langer** decided to take golf into further alien territory by shinning up a rather large tree and playing his chip shot to the 17th green from amidst its spreading branches.

Fulford Golf Club was founded soon after the turn of the century, but it was only as recently as **1985** that the club celebrated fifty years of playing over the present course. The televised **Benson and Hedges International** open tournament has undoubtedly turned the North Yorkshire Club into a 'golfing household name', but in golf's more discerning circles it has for a long time possessed the reputation of having one of the country's finest inland courses.

Golfers wishing to visit Fulford must make prior arrangements with the Club's **Secretary, John Gledhill**. Individuals and Society Members alike are required to belong to recognised Golf Clubs and be able to provide proof of handicap. Mr. Gledhill can be contacted by writing to the club, the full address being, **Fulford Golf Club, Heslington Lane, Fulford, York,** or by telephoning on **(0904) 413579.**

Fulford is situated about a mile to the south of York, just off the **A19.** For persons travelling from the south of England the **A1** and **M1** can assist as far as the Leeds area from where the **A64** runs straight through to Fulford. Perhaps a more direct route through, is to join the **A19** near Doncaster. Those approaching York from the north should find their route a little more scenic, the most helpful roads again probably being the **A19** (via Thirsk) and the **A64** (via Malton – which incidentally passes Ganton further to the north east). Those journeying from easterly directions should either use the **A1099** or the **A166** before joining the **A64** east of York. The famous city is well served by rail connections and finally the Leeds/Bradford Airport is located approximately 30 miles to the west of York.

On arriving at the Club a **green fee** of **£18** entitles the visitor to either a single round or a full day's golf during the week, but at weekends, Fulford is not open to the visiting golfer. **Bryan Hessay** is the resident professional at Fulford, he can be reached by telephone on **(0904) 412882.**

Fulford's homely looking Clubhouse is quite spacious inside with a comfortable Lounge and Dining Room. A full catering service is provided throughout the week with the exception of Mondays. Jackets and ties should be worn in the Clubhouse after 6pm.

Measuring just a little under **6800** yards from the back tees, (par **72,** s.s.s. **72**) Fulford provides quite a stern test for the club golfer, but it is no more than a medium length course for the professionals. Much of the prodigiously low scoring achieved at Fulford during the **Benson and Hedges** tournament has, however, precious little to do with the length of the course. As the Members will quickly tell you it simply reflects the superb condition in which the fairways and the putting surfaces are maintained. Fulford is renowned for its fast and very true greens. Certainly Welsh Ryder Cup player **Ian Woosnam** found them much to his liking as he holed putt after putt during an extraordinary sequence of eight successive birdies during his final round in the **1985** Championship. Woosnam's score of **62** that day set a new course record but unfortunately it wasn't quite good enough to prevent **Sandy Lyle** from adding the Benson and Hedges title to the British Open Championship he had won earlier that year.

The Scotsman, (or Anglo-Scot as many south of the border prefer to call him) joined an already impressive list of winners at Fulford, including four Open Champions: **Tony Jacklin** (1971); **Lee Trevino** (1978); **Tom Weiskopf** (1981); and **Greg Norman** (1982). The young **Peter Baker** won the competition in 1988 – a most exciting win.

The more mortal golfer probably won't be leaving Fulford with a 62 under his belt – nor one presumes will he have been shinning up the trees – but he ought to be heading home a contented soul having spent a day on what is unquestionably one of the country's most pleasurable golf courses.

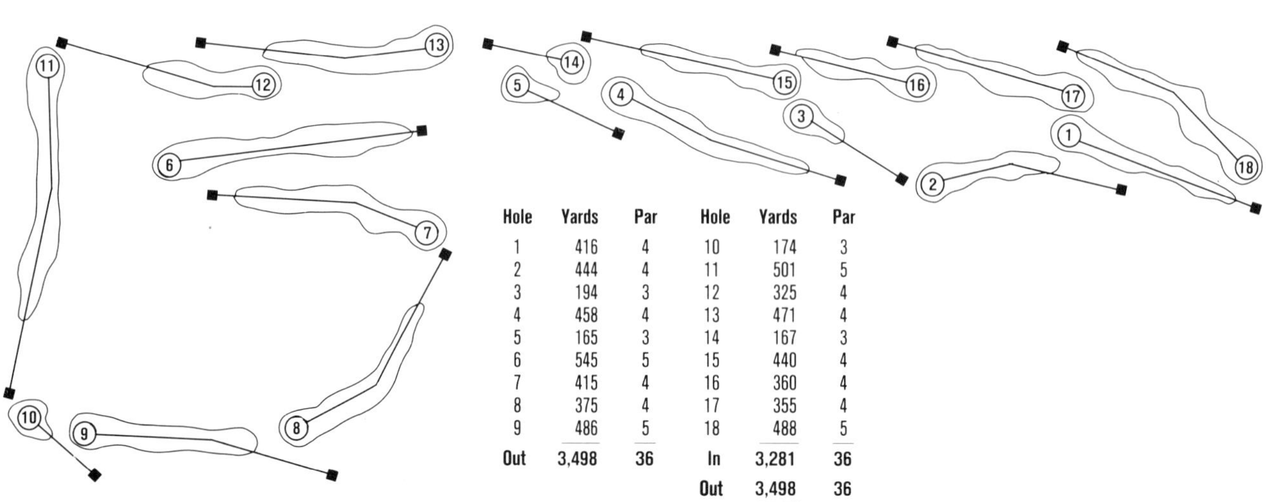

Hole	Yards	Par	Hole	Yards	Par
1	416	4	10	174	3
2	444	4	11	501	5
3	194	3	12	325	4
4	458	4	13	471	4
5	165	3	14	167	3
6	545	5	15	440	4
7	415	4	16	360	4
8	375	4	17	355	4
9	486	5	18	488	5
Out	3,498	36	In	3,281	36
			Out	3,498	36
			TOTALS	6,779	72

GANTON
CHAMPIONSHIP GOLF

They used to say at **Ganton** that when **Harry Vardon** played the course twice in the same day, in his afternoon round he'd often hit his tee shots into the very divots he'd created in the morning. The chances are that this was a little bit of Yorkshire bluff but then the Members at Ganton were fortunate to witness what were probably the very finest years of Britain's greatest ever golfer.

Vardon came to Ganton in **1896**, just five years after the Club's formation. Within a few weeks of his appointment he won his first **Open Championship** at Muirfield defeating the then hat-trick-seeking John H. Taylor in a play-off. In **1900** Vardon returned from America with the **U.S. Open** trophy, by which time he'd added two more Open Championships and was half way towards his record number of **six** victories in that event. By the time that Vardon left in 1903 the name of Ganton had been firmly put on the golfing map.

Located approximately nine miles from the sea, Ganton could hardly be called a 'golf links' in the strict sense but it is often said that it has many of the features of links golf with crisp seaside turf and sandy sub-soil. Indeed whenever new bunkers are cut, sea-shells are often discovered lying beneath the surface – it appears that the whole of the surrounding area was once an arm of the sea.

Golfers wishing to play at Ganton must make prior arrangements with the Club's **Secretary, Air Vice Marshal Price** who may be contacted via the **Ganton Golf Club, Ganton, Scarborough, North Yorkshire YO12 4PA**, telephone **(0944) 70329**. The Club's professional, **Gary Brown**, can be reached on **(0944) 70260**. Subject to proof of handicap and prior arrangement, visitors are made most welcome and it is possible to pre-book starting times. The **green fees** for 1989 were set at **£20** for a day's golf during the week with **£30** payable at the weekend. The above rates are halved for those teeing off after 4pm. Golfing **Societies** are equally welcome, although those organising should note that no societies are received at weekends.

Although in a non-golfing sense Ganton is a fairly small dot on the map, travelling to the course is made straightforward by the **A64**. This road links the village directly with Scarborough to the north east (12 miles) and to both York (30 miles) and Leeds (60 miles) to the south west. If approaching from the Humberside region a combination of the **A164** to Great Driffield and the **B1249** will take you to within 2 miles of the course, while travellers from further north can avoid the city of York by heading for Thirsk and thereafter heading for Malton by way of the **A170** and the **B1257**. Malton lies on the **A64** road and like Scarborough is approximately 12 miles from Ganton.

Ganton enjoys a beautifully peaceful setting nestling on the edge of the Vale of Pickering and the Yorkshire Moors. While the golf course is indeed beautiful, particularly when the gorse is in full bloom, it is very rarely 'peaceful' and when the winds sweep across it can become fearsomely difficult and there are few inland courses with such cavernous bunkers – 105 of them in all. In addition to the many bunkers and the great spread of gorse, there are numerous fir trees and pines which can come into play following the wayward shot, the dog-leg **18th** being a notable example and one that provides a very testing finishing hole. The finest hole on the course is thought by many to be the **4th** where the second has to be played across a plunging valley towards a plateau green that is heavily bunkered to the right. In total the course measures **6693** yards, par **72**, from the medal tees, with the club tees reducing the length to **6371** yards, par **71**. The ladies play over **6052** yards, par **75**.

The nineteenth at Ganton has a most welcoming atmosphere and offers an extensive range of catering. Lunches are served daily between 12pm and 2.30pm and both breakfast and dinner can be arranged with some forewarning. Dress is informal in the men's bar until 6pm Mondays to Saturdays, though a jacket and tie should be worn in all other public rooms.

Inevitably Ganton's name will always be linked with Vardon's. But another great player also developed his talents on the Yorkshire course – **Ted Ray**, the famed long hitter who found fortune in America winning their Open in **1920**. In so doing he ironically held off the challenge of the then 50 year old Vardon. The greatest event in Ganton's distinguised history was undoubtedly the great **Ryder Cup** match of **1949** when the home team led by three matches to one at the end of the first day only to lose eventually by seven to five. **Ben Hogan**, convalescing from his near fatal accident, led the American side as non-playing captain.

Twice since the War the **Amateur Championship** has been staged at Ganton, in **1964** and **1977**; it is due to be held here again in **1991**, the Centenary Year for the Club. In addition the **English Amateur**, the **Youths Amateur** and the **British Ladies Championship** have each been held at Ganton while the professionals have also visited in recent years with the **Dunlop Masters** of **1975**, won by **Bernard Gallacher** and in **1981** the **P.G.A. Championship**, resulting in a third victory in four years for **Nick Faldo**.

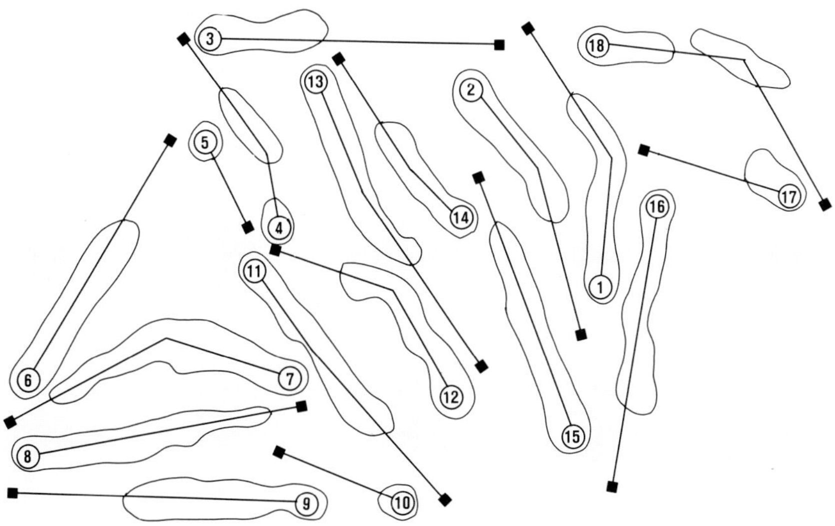

Hole	Yards	Par	Hole	Yards	Par
1	375	4	10	169	3
2	416	4	11	403	4
3	334	4	12	364	4
4	406	4	13	498	5
5	157	3	14	283	4
6	447	4	15	437	4
7	430	4	16	448	4
8	392	4	17	251	4
9	494	5	18	389	4
Out	3,451	36	In	3,242	36
			Out	3,451	36
			TOTALS	6,693	72

MIDDLETHORPE HALL

Middlethorpe stands in twenty-six acres of parkland to the south of York, overlooking the Knavesmire Racecourse. Built in 1699 in Queen Anne style, it is now an elegant hotel restored to its full 18th Century splendour by Historic House Hotels.

A magnificent carved oak staircase leads the visiting guests to the first of eleven beautifully furnished bedrooms in the house. The remainder of the thirty one rooms are in the adjacent classical courtyard and all have an Edwardian style bathroom as well as a colour television, an electric trouser-press and a direct-dial telephone.

There are two restaurants at Middlethorpe giving a choice of dining in th oak-panelled Dining Room overlooking the gardens or the informal Grill Room where a pianist plays most evenings. The award winning Dining Room provides the best of British contemporary cooking created by chef Kevin Francksen, while the Grill Room is more traditional and uses local recipes and ingredients.

After dinner, guests can admire the house, the antiques and fine paintings or stroll through the traditional English gardens, all of which make up the excellence of Country house hospitality.

Middlethorpe Hall,
Bishopthorpe Road,
York YO2 1QB.
Tel: (0904) 641241

NORTH YORKSHIRE & HUMBERSIDE

COMPLETE GOLF

NORTH YORKSHIRE

Aldwark Manor G.C.
(18) 5172 yards
Alne, York
(03473) 8146

Bedale G.C.
(18) 5857 yards
Leyburn Rd, Bedale
(0677) 22451

Bentham G.C.
(9) 5752 yards
Robin Lane, Bentham
(0468) 61018

Catterick Garrison G.C.
(18) 6332 yards
Leyburn Rd, Catterick Garrison
(0748) 833268

Easingwold G.C.
(18) 6222 yards
Stillington Rd, Easingwold
(0347) 21486

Filey G.C.
(18) 6030 yards
West Ave, Filey
(0723) 513293

Fulford G.C.
(18) 6779 yards
Heslington Lane, Fulford, York
(0904) 412882

Ganton G.C.
(18) 6693 yards
Ganton, Scarborough
(0944) 70329

Ghyll G.C.
(9) 5738 yards
Ghyll Brow, Barnoldswick
(0282) 842466

Harrogate G.C.
(18) 6204 yards
Starbeck, Harrogate
(0423) 862999

Heworth G.C.
(11) 6078 yards
Mancastergate, York
(0904) 424618

Kirkbymoorside G.C.
(18) 5958 yards
Manor Vale, Kirkbymoorside
(0751) 31525

Knaresborough G.C.
(18) 6281 yards
Boroughbridge Rd,
Knaresborough
(0423) 862690

Malton & Norton G.C.
(18) 6411 yards
Norton, Malton
(0653) 692959

Masham G.C.
(9) 5338 yards
Masham, Ripon
(0765) 89379

Oakdale G.C.
(18) 6456 yards
Oakdale, Harrogate
(0423) 67162

Pannal G.C.
(18) 6594 yards
Follifoot Rd, Pannal, Harrogate
(0423) 872628

Pike Hills G.C.
(18) 6048 yards
Copmanthorpe, York
(0904) 708756

Richmond G.C.
(18) 5704 yards
Bend Hagg, Richmond
(0748) 2568

Ripon City G.C.
(9) 5752 yards
Palace Rd, Ripon
(0765) 700411

Scarborough North Cliff G.C.
(18) 6425 yards
Burniston Rd, Scarborough
(0723) 360786

Scarborough South Cliff G.C.
(18) 6085 yards
Deepdale Ave, Scarborough
(0723) 374737

Selby G.C.
(18) 6246 yards
Mill Lane, Selby
(075782) 622

Settle G.C.
(9) 4900 yards
Giggleswick, Settle
(07292) 3921

Skipton G.C.
(18) 6191 yards
Grassington Rd, Skipton
(0756) 3257

Thirsk & Northallerton G.C.
(9) 6087 yards
Thornton-le-Street, Thirsk
(0845) 22170

Whitby G.C.
(18) 5710 yards
Low Straggleton, Whitby
(0947) 600660

York G.C.
(18) 6275 yards
Lords Manor Lane, Strensall,
York
(0904) 490304

HUMBERSIDE

Beverley & East Riding G.C.
(18) 5414 yards
The Westwood, Beverley
(0482) 869519

Boothferry G.C.
(18) 6651 yards
Howle, Goole
(0430) 430364

Bridlington G.C.
(18) 6320 yards
Belvedere Rd, Bridlington
(0262) 672561

Brough G.C.
(18) 6012 yards
Cave Rd, Brough
(0482) 667374

Cleethorpes G.C.
(18) 6015 yards
Kings Rd, Cleethorpes
(0472) 812059

Driffield G.C.
(9) 6225 yards
Sunderlandwick, Driffield
(0377) 43116

Elsham G.C.
(18) 6420 yards
Barton Rd, Elsham
(0652) 680291

Flamborough Head G.C.
(18) 5438 yards
Flamborough, Bridlington
(0262) 850333

Ganstead G.C.
(9) 5769 yards
Coniston, Hull
(0482) 811121

Grimsby G.C.
(18) 6058 yards
Littlecoates Rd, Grimsby
(0472) 42630

Hainsworth Park G.C.
(9) 5350 yards
Driffield
(0401) 42362

Hessle G.C.
(18) 6638 yards
Cottingham, Hull
(0482) 650171

Holme Hall G.C.
(18) 6475 yards
Bottesford, Sainthorpe
(0724) 862078

Hornsea G.C.
(18) 6470 yards
Rolston Rd, Hornsea
(04012) 2020

Hull G.C.
(18) 6242 yards
Packman Lane, Kirk Ella,
Hull
(0482) 658919

Normanby Hall G.C.
(18) 6398 yards
Normanby Park, Scunthorpe
(0724) 720226

Scunthorpe G.C.
(18) 6281 yards
Burringham Rd, Scunthorpe
(0724) 866561

Sutton Park G.C.
(18) 6251 yards
Holderness Rd, Hull
(0482) 74242

Withernsea G.C.
(9) 5112 yards
Chesnut Ave, Withernsea
(0964) 612258

BURLINGTON GALLERY

CUMBRIA & THE NORTH EAST

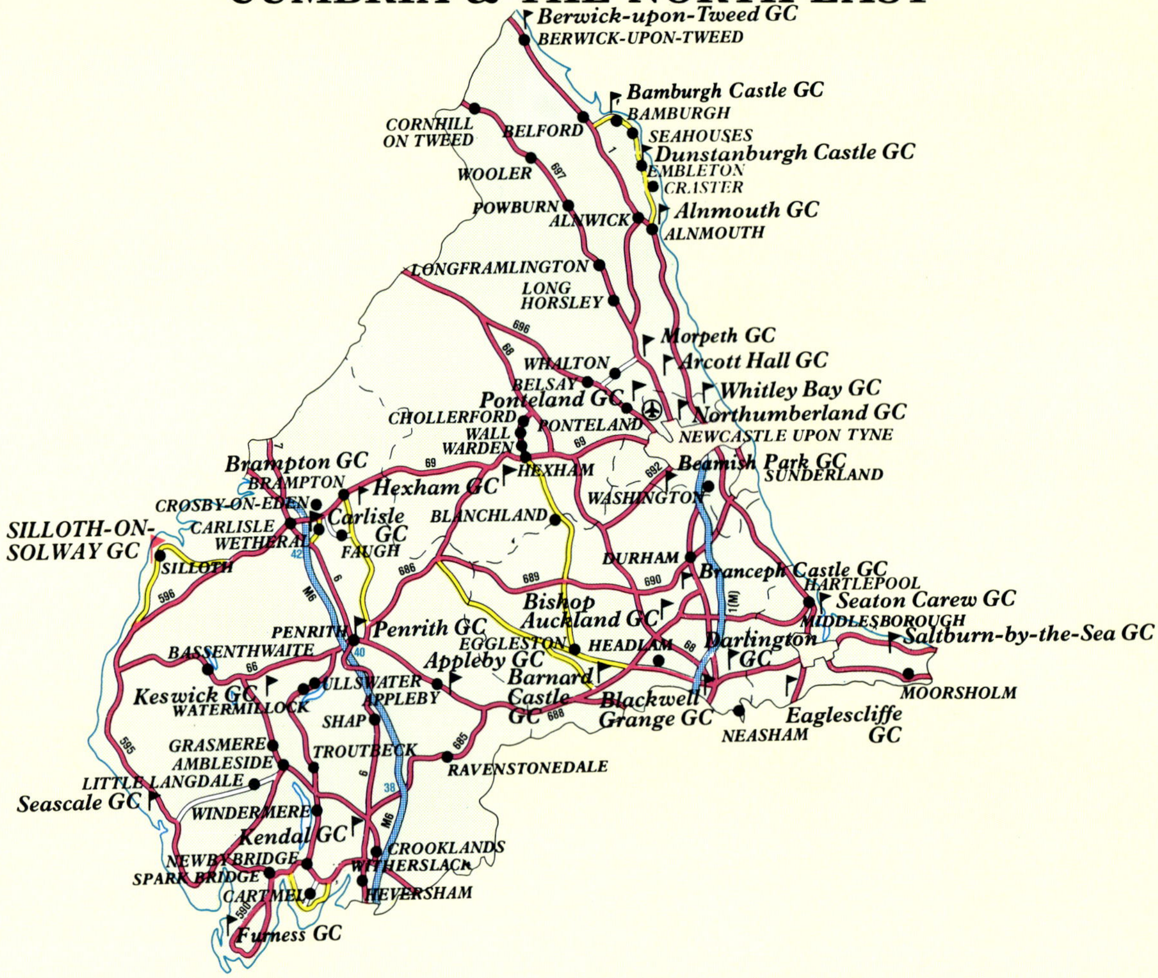

H. ROUNTREE *"It's A One"* BURLINGTON GALLERY

CUMBRIA & THE NORTH EAST

CHOICE GOLF

Just as Devon is often viewed by 'holiday-makers' as a mere stepping stone to Cornwall (which as a Devonian pleases me greatly!) so the far north of England is often viewed by golfers as a mere pretty pathway to the delights of Scotland – Turnberry, Gleneagles etc. Indeed some even believe that north of Lytham there's nothing much in the way of golfing challenges until the 'Bonny Land' is reached. To those I simply say, 'shame on you!'

Our region covers **Cumbria** as well as the **North East**. Now admittedly Cumbria is hardly golfing territory. A Sunningdale in the middle of the Lake District is hard to imagine (although some spectacular holes are clearly possible!) But there are a number of golf courses in between the fells and the lakes, and furthermore Cumbria comprises more than just the Lake District. Before the counties were rearranged and renamed in the early seventies, Cumberland was the most northerly county in the West of England, and home not only to the famous sausage but to the **Silloth-on-Solway Golf Club**, which is, dare I say it, as good a links as you'll find anywhere in England. As for the North East, **Seaton Carew** near Hartlepool offers championship golf of a very high calibre while even further north along the Northumberland coast lie a string of golfing pearls – **Alnmouth, Dunstanburgh, Bamburgh and Goswick** – uncrowded courses with breathtaking scenery.

CUMBRIA

Let us make a start in the **Lake District** with the hope that in addition to the picnic hamper and the climbing boots, we've left room in the back of the car for the golf clubs.

The Lake District is the land of the poets. 'Where breezes are soft and skies are fair' (W.C. Bryant), and 'Where nature reveals herself in all her wildness, all her majesty' (S. Roger).

At Keswick the golfer can meet the poet. **Keswick Golf Club** lies 4 miles east of the lakeland town via the **A66**. Whilst the course now measures well over 6,000 yards it once held a rather dubious claim to being the shortest course in Britain – in 1976 there was a splendid Clubhouse but only five holes – no doubt some remarkable scores were returned! These days scoring is a little more difficult with several streams and some dense woodland to be avoided. As one might imagine the views are quite breathtaking and a visit will not disappoint. A day's golf is priced at around **£7**.

Still in the Lakes, we find **Kendal** a fine parkland course, just three-quarters of a mile from the town centre and only 2 miles from the **M6** linkroad. Although a fair bit shorter than Keswick its first hole is often considered to be the toughest opener in Britain – 231 yards, uphill all the way, out of bounds to the left and woods to the right! Should one make it to the 2nd the holes get much easier; however there is an infamous quarry on the right of the 15th fairway which has been known to receive more than golf balls. One frustrated chap after firing ball after ball into its murky depths decided to throw in his bag for good measure. Fortunately he didn't throw himself in as well but word is he never played golf again. Who said it was only a game! Anyway a proper day's golf should again be possible for **£5**.

The other notable course within the National Park boundary is at **Penrith** (Green fees **£8**). Close to the **A6** but a lovely setting near Ullswater and several challenging holes. Fees here are a shade dearer than at Kendal or Keswick, but then it's probably the pick of the three.

Recommending superior establishments in the area is a difficult task to put it mildly simply because there are so many. But hopefully the following suggestions will prove of assistance. Grasmere is a personal favourite and here **Michael's Nook (09665) 496** is an outstanding country hotel with an excellent restaurant.

The Wordsworth (09665) 592 is another grand hotel while at **White Moss House (09665) 295** – the poet's former residence – another superb restaurant can be found. Slightly nearer to Keswick, **Armathwaite Hall (059681) 551** in Bassenthwaite is charming, while for a really relaxing country inn **The Pheasant Inn (059681) 234** in Bassenthwaite Lake can have few equals. In Keswick itself there is **The Woolpack (07687) 72775** and **The Underscar Country House (07687) 72469.**

Penrith is a bustling town with numerous hotels. As an alternative to staying in town Ullswater naturally attracts and here the **Sharrow Bay Hotel (08536) 301** and its restaurant are particularly stylish. Cheaper accommodation is available nearby in one of the areas best pubs, **The Queen's Head** at Askham, while **The Old Church Hotel** at Watermillock offers spectacular views **(085 36) 204**.

Oh-so-popular Windermere is convenient for Kendal and the town offers a wealth of good hotels. Two certainly meriting attention are **The Miller Howe (09662) 2536** and the **Langdale Chase (05394) 3201. Rogers (09662) 4954** in the High Street is a first class restaurant. Other ideas for Kendal must include **The Old Vicarage (04484) 381** at Witherslack. **The Mortal Man (0966) 33193** at Troutbeck (wake up to a glorious setting), **The Wild Boar** in Crook and for a really popular pub try the **Masons Arms** in Cartmel Fell.

To the south of Cumbria the **Furness Golf Club** lays claim to being the oldest in the county. A true links and being quite exposed is often more difficult than the card suggests. However, visitors should have little trouble organising a game. Green fees here are about **£6**. An after-golf thought here is **Bridge House (022985) 239** at Spark Bridge.

Travelling along Cumbria's coast, **Seascale** is soon reached. Another links, and somewhat under-rated. One shouldn't be put off by the thought of being close to the Seascale nuclear installations (and jokes about the balls glowing in the dark are uncalled for): it's an excellent test of golf and good value at **£7** midweek, **£9** at weekends. Some tremendous views too towards the Wasdale Screes and the Scafell Range. There is doubtless some convenient accommodation nearby but I'll recommend a trip to another personal favourite, Buttermere, one of the more westerly lakes, and where **The Bridge Hotel (059685) 252** is superb.

Silloth-on-Solway has already been referred to and is featured separately on a later page. The course certainly deserves more than a fleeting visit and two handy hotels in the town are **The Queens Hotel (0965) 31373** and **The Golf Hotel (0965) 31438**. Both are very comfortable and specialise in golf packages, as does **The Skinburness Hotel (06973) 32332** – perhaps the pick of the bunch – an excellent hotel, with good facilities.

Returning inland we find Carlisle, an attractive county town with a particularly striking cathedral. Golfers are well catered for her with two good courses in the area, **Carlisle and Brampton**.

The latter is located to the east of Carlisle off the **B6413** and is a beautifully kept course, laid out four hundred feet above sea-level with extensive views towards the nearby hills. It is probably best described as moorland whereas Carlisle, equally well maintained, is more of a parkland type. Both receive visitors throughout the week, fees ranging from **£8** to **£9**. For an overnight stop in Carlisle the **Crown and Mitre (0228) 25491** is welcoming while in Brampton **Farlam Hall (06976) 234** is an excellent hotel and **The Hare and Hounds (06977) 3456** a comfortable inn. **Fantails (0228) 60239** in Wetheral is possibly the best restaurant in the area; for pleasant water setting Crosby-on-Eden and **The Crosby Lodge (022873) 618** is recommended.

Before leaving Cumbria a quick mention for the somewhat isolated **Appleby Golf Club**. If you are in the vicinity it's strongly worth a visit. A splendid combination of moorland and heathland – very colourful, and cheap, at **£4.50** a round.

Remote, perhaps but in nearby Appleby-in-Westmoreland the **Appleby Manor (07683) 51571** awaits while for a friendly inn note the **Black Swan** at Ravenstondale.

And so to the North East and what a mix! **Durham, Cleveland, Tyne & Wear and Northumberland**. An area encompassing Tyneside, Teeside and Wearside, it also includes the Cleveland Hills, the Cheviots and the wild spectacular coast of ancient Northumbria. The four modern-day counties stretch from the far end of the Yorkshire Pennines and intrude into the Scottish Borders, the greater part of Northumberland lying north of Hadrian's Wall.

The appeal of any golf course can naturally be affected greatly by its surroundings; nowhere in Britain does the accompanying landscape seem to dictate the enjoyment of a game as much as in this part of the world. The contrast between the industrial and rural North East is dramatic to put it mildly. The golf courses in the former tend towards the uninspiring – **Seaton Carew** being one great exception – whilst the likes of **Bamburgh and Hexham** offer such magnificent scenery that the quality of the golf can often be relegated to a secondary consideration.

CLEVELAND

Beginning in the south of the region, **Cleveland** is one of the smallest counties in England and not surprisingly has very few courses. **Seaton Carew**, already referred to, is far and away the best in the county. It is located approximately 3 miles south of Hartlepool and has a skyline dominated by far-off chimneys which at night appear like giant torches. Golf here is played amidst the dunes with gorse and devilishly thick rough lining the fairways. In recent years several important Championships have been held here, including the Boys Amateur in 1978 and 1986. Visitors are received at most times although prior telephoning is wise. Fees are approximately **£12**.

South of the Tees, despite its name, the golf course at **Saltburn** isn't by the sea, it's about a mile west of the town and is a well-wooded meadowland course. Quite a contrast to Seaton Carew: a trifle easier, but certainly worth a visit. Around Teeside itself there are courses at Middlesborough and Billingham but perhaps the best in the area is found at **Eaglescliff**. A hilly course, there are some marvellous views of the Cleveland Hills. Visitors should be able to arrange a game during the week, for about **£10**.

There are a number of hotels in the county but the majority are modern and unfortunately rather characterless. An exception to this is **The Crathorne Hall Hotel (0642) 700398** at Yarm. Most handy for Seaton Carew is probably **The Grand (0429) 266345** in Hartlepool. At Saltburn an excellent pub can be recommended, namely **The Ship** with its splendid sea views, while a little inland at Moorsholm **The Jolly Sailor** offers some very good food. Those playing at Eaglescliff can enjoy mid-day sustenance (or evening celebration) at **The Blue Bell**.

DURHAM

Crossing into **Durham**, people often talk of (some even whistle about) 'Old Durham Town', but of course it's very much a city with a catherdral that was recently adjudged the most beautiful building in the world. Withouth doubt the course to visit here is **Brancepeth Castle**, 4 miles south west of the city in very beautiful surroundings. Rather like St. Pierre at Chepstow the course occupies land that was formerly a deer park and a 13th Century church and castle provide a magnificent backcloth. The time to organise a game is mid-week and the fees are **£10**.

Perhaps the most convenient place to stay is at Croxdale, **The Bridge Hotel (0385) 3780524** but there are a number of hotels in Durham itself including **The Royal County (0385) 3866821**.

Further north, **Beamish Park** near Stanley is another laid out in a former deer park (belonging to Beamish Hall) and well worth a detour if heading up the A1. Fees are approximately **£7**. **Bishop Auckland** in the centre of the county is a pleasant parkland course. The land here belongs to the Church of England and one of the terms of the lease is that the course has to close on Good Friday and Christmas Day. Play at your peril! A day's golf at Bishop Auckland is priced at **£10** midweek, **£10** at the weekend.

Travelling south, **Barnard Castle** enjoys another delightful setting. More of a moorland course than anything else with a stream that must be crossed seventeen times during a round! At about **£7** per day it's a bargain and there are some fine establishments nearby in which to celebrate (or perhaps even dry out?) In Barnard Castle itself **The Jersey Farm Hotel (0833) 38223** is excellent value for a night's stay while those just looking for a bar snack and a drink might visit the nearby villages of Cotherstone **The Fox and Hounds** and Ronaldkirk **The Rose and Crown**. A slightly longer drive to Eggleston, also possible from Bishop Auckland and one finds **The Three Tuns** – famed for its lunches.

Darlington is the largest town in the county. It may not have the appeal of Durham but for golfers there's a twin attraction. To the north, **Haughton Grange** with its great selection of McKenzie greens and to the south, **Blackwell Grange** with its variety of trees. Both courses are parkland and always superbly maintained. For an ideal base one doesn't really have to look further than the 17th Century **Blackwell Grange Moat House (0325) 380888**. However, a good French restaurant to note in the town is **The Bishop's House (0325) 286666** and for a drink visit **The Kings Head (0325) 380222**.

TYNE & WEAR

Tyneside is essentially a tale of two cities, Newcastle and Sunderland, home of the Geordies and where the welcome is second to none. There are plenty of golf courses in the area but the really attractive golf lies further north along the coast. The **Northumberland Golf Club** and **Ponteland** probably have the best two courses. The former is situated alongside Gosforth Park racecourse and like Seaton Carew has staged several national championships. However the visitor may find it easier to arrange a game at Ponteland (at least during the week) – a particularly well-kept course this and very convenient if you happen to be flying to or from Newcastle Airport. **Whitley Bay** is another that welcomes visitors mid-week (fairly inexpensive too). It is quite a long windswept course with very large greens and a wide stream that can make scoring pretty difficult.

If there's one large town in England that could really do with a good golf challenge it's Sunderland, a place of great character – golf architects please note! Staying in and around Newcastle the leading hotels are **The Gosforth Park Thistle (091) 236411** and the **Holiday Inn (091) 2363432**. Both offer all the mod-cons and some first class leisure facilities. Good restaurants abound; in Jesmond, **Francesca's (0632) 281586** is superb value while more pricey but excellent cooking is found in either **The Fisherman's Lodge (091) 2813281** or **The Fisherman's Wharf (091) 2321057**. In Chinatown **The Ming Dynasty (0632) 2615785** also has a fine reputation. Ponteland possesses two inns of note, namely **The Wagon** and **The Rendezvous**.

NORTHUMBERLAND

Finally then a look at **Northumberland**, a county with a splendid, almost mythical history. First on the way up, as it were, is **Arcot Hall**, 6 miles north of Newcastle and a most tranquil setting. A James Braid creation, Arcot Hall is a heathland course with a many trees and a lake. The 9th here is a particularly good hole. Green fees are about **£10** with visitors welcome at weekends – something to note if stuck for a game in Newcastle. A sumptious Clubhouse but beware of The Grey Lady who ghosts in and out from time to time! If thoroughly frightened many peaceful villages are at hand and some very good pubs. The **Highlander** at Belsay is such a place and equally convenient after a day's golf at Ponteland.

Trekking northwards again **Morpeth** should be next on the agenda. Another pleasant course designed this time by one of James Braid's old rivals – Mr. Vardon no less. One of England's finest Georgian Country Houses lies only a short distance away at Longhorsley, **Linden Hall (0670) 516611** – very relaxing. Also nearby is **The Besom Barn (066570) 627** at Longframlington – a good place for a drink with some splendid English cooking. **Embleton Hall (066570) 249** at Longframlington is also excellent.

Along the rugged coast some tremendous golf lies ahead. **Alnmouth** is very pleasing and in the village is the comfortable **Marine House Hotel (0665) 830349**. Just a little beyond are the magnificent 'Castle courses' of **Dunstanburgh** (at Embleton) and **Bamburgh** (green fees **£7**). The golf is glorious, the scenery spectacularly superb. Dunstanburgh Castle, the ruins of which were immortalised in water colour by Turner, occupies a wonderously remote setting. The course is a genuine links, hugging close to the shore and staring out across miles of deserted beach. Visitors are welcome to play at all times. Bamburgh Castle is perhaps even more special, sometimes called England's most beautiful course. Not long by any means – but the setting! Holy Island and Lindisfarne, the Cheviot Hills and a majestic watching castle. Furthermore the fairways are bordered by a blaze of colour, with gorse, purple heather and numerous wild orchids.

Having placated the golfing soul a few suggestions for the body include **The Dunstanburgh Castle Hotel (0665) 76203** – as its name suggests, very handy for the golf course, **The Lord Crewe Arms (06684) 243** in Bamburgh – good for a drink with some accommodation also. A further good resting place is to be found in Belford, **The Blue Bell Hotel (06683) 543**. Among several good pubs are the **Tankerville Arms** in Wooler, **The Olde Ship** in Seahouses and the **Jolly Fisherman** in Craster.

For centuries the town of Berwick-upon-Tweed didn't know whether it was 'coming or going', passing between England and Scotland like the proverbial shuttlecock. However disorientated, it has a fine links course at **Goswick**, 3 miles south of the town. Visitors are always welcome with fees only **£6-£8**. Two thoughts for what may be one's last night in England – maybe one's first? Anyway **The Kings Arms Hotel (0289) 307454** and **The Turret House Hotel (0289) 307344**, are both good.

Having sent the golfer north of Newcastle I am aware of having neglected **Hexham**. It's only a short drive west of the city, along either the A69 or the A695. The journey is well worth making, the course has a gorgeous setting and the nearby villages with their many inns – note the **Hadrian** (at would you believe) Wall and **The Boat** at Warden – cry out for inspection.

A golfing holiday I believe is in order – who needs Scotland!

BURLINGTON GALLERY

Welcome to Cumbria's Golf Coast where exciting things are happening!

Just a mile from the challenging championship course at Silloth-on-Solway, a newly developed complex offers every golfing facility and our own 9 hole course

Features include:

- GOLF DRIVING RANGE — superb 300 yard range with optional covered bays, flood-lighting and video. Open seven days a week throughout the year.
- INCLUSIVE GOLF PACKAGES — for groups and individuals, including choice of accommodation, green fees and tuition.
- INDOOR SIMULATED GOLF — an intriguing all-weather opportunity to "enjoy a round on the Pebble Beach" on the Par-T golf machine. No wind, no rain and refreshment available at every tee!

The Skinburness Hotel

- ACCOMMODATION CHOICE

The Skinburness Hotel — just half a mile from Solway Village — a superbly restored and refurbished Victorian hotel, offering exceptional comfort and sensational cuisine, with in-house fitness centre, sauna and sunbed and splendid billiard room. Late bar facilities and a warm welcome for individuals and groups.

Solway Village

SILLOTH-ON-SOLWAY

For full details write to:
"Cumbria's Golf Coast",
The Solway Village, Silloth,
Cumbria CA5 4QY or telephone:
Silloth (06973) 31236

The Solway Village — attractive self-catering lodges, fully equipped for families of 2-6 people with excellent on-site amenities — licensed club, sports facilities, teenage disco, bistro and coffee shop, superb indoor leisure pool and beauty salon.

Enthusiasts of other sports will find sea fishing and windsurfing on the beautiful Solway Firth, plus breathtaking coastal walks, birdwatching havens and delightful views.

Far from the madding crowd, yet in an Area of Outstanding Natural beauty, Cumbria's Golf Coast offers the perfect setting for golfing breaks and family holidays.

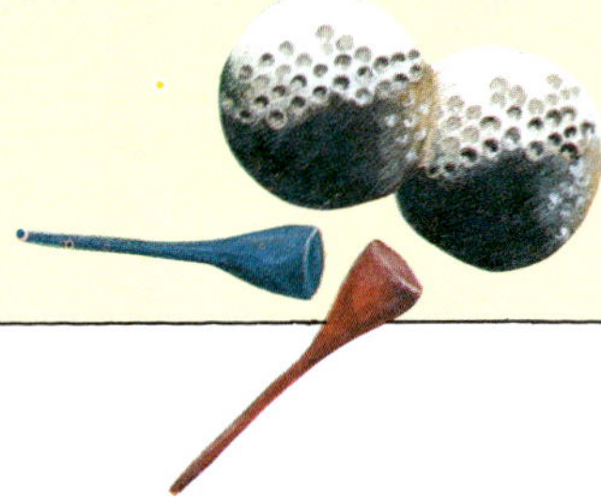

SILLOTH-ON-SOLWAY

CHAMPIONSHIP GOLF

One of the greatest ever lady golfers, **Miss Cecil Leitch** once said: 'If you can play Silloth you can play anywhere'. The four times British Ladies Champion and the great rival of Joyce Wethered knew better than most for she grew up in Silloth and it was on Silloth's Championship links that she and her four golfing sisters learnt to play.

Silloth-on-Solway Golf Club has a mischievous date of foundation somewhere between **1892** when the first holes were laid out and **1903** when the Club together with its 'new' Clubhouse was formally opened by the Speaker of the House of Commons, **The Rt. Hon. Edward Gully**.

Today Silloth is perhaps one of Britain's lesser known Championship links, this doubtless a result of its somewhat remote situation lying some 23 miles north west of Carlisle. Remote it may be but it is a journey decidedly worth making, for not only is this one of Britain's greatest tests of golf but the Silloth Club is just about the most friendly one is likely to come across.

Most responsible for the welcoming atmosphere is the Club's affable **Secretary, Mr. Geoff Hartley**, who may be contacted by telephone on **(0965) 31304**. There are no restrictions on visiting golfers and they may play at all times. Prior telephoning is however advisable during the summer as Silloth is becoming increasingly popular with Societies. Indeed the Secretary informs me that on one occasion, three separate parties made bookings from Kuala Lumpur!

The cost of a day's golf at Silloth in 1989 was priced at **£10** during the week and **£15** at weekends – for such a splendid Championship course surely excellent value. The fees for juniors were half the above rates. In 1989 a **weekly** ticket (Monday to Friday) could also be purchased for the sum of **£40**. Golfing Societies must book starting times either by telephoning the Club or by writing to the Secretary at **The Silloth-on-Solway Golf Club, Silloth-on-Solway, Carlisle, Cumbria CA5 4BL**. Should the need arise, sets of clubs may be hired from the professional, **David Forsythe**. Tel: **(0965) 31304**.

With the **M6** running to Carlisle, Silloth isn't actually quite as remote as it may appear on the map. Those travelling from the south should leave the M6 at junction **41** and thereafter take the **B5305** to Wigton. At Wigton the **B5302** should be picked up and followed to Silloth. Those who have been sensible enough to take their golf clubs to the Lake District may find the **B5300** road helpful; it runs along the coast from Maryport to Silloth. Finally those approaching from Scotland should head for Carlisle and thereafter follow a combination of the **B5307** and the **B5302** to Silloth.

Measuring **6343** yards, par **72** (**5780** yards, par **75** for Ladies). Silloth may not sound particularly frightening, and you may just be wondering what all the fuss is about. Standing on the 1st tee with the wind hammering into your face you'll know exactly what all the fuss is about. Humbling is perhaps the best way to describe the sensation. Two shots later (hopefully!) you'll also discover why the large greens at Silloth have acquired such a reputation. Of the many great holes perhaps the par five **13th** stands out. Appropriately named 'Hogs Back' it has an exceptionally narrow fairway that is heather lined on either side and a plateau green – miss it and you're in trouble!

The Clubhouse at Silloth offers full catering until 9pm after which light snacks may be obtained from the Bar. The lunchtime menu is quite outstanding and provided some warning is given, a full Cumberland breakfast can be arranged (sounds like an excellent idea).

The Club is understandably proud of the fact that twice in the last ten years it has been selected to host the British Ladies Open Championship. However, it can also be proud of the courage some of its members displayed back in 1912; for this information I am indebted to the Secretary. On behalf of all the Clubs in the British Isles Silloth appealed against the assessment to income tax on green fees. Unfortunately for the Golf Clubs the learned judge found in favour of the Inland Revenue; this left Silloth with the task of finding **£433-12-9** pence for legal expenses. 81 Clubs promised subscriptions to help towards the debt and they eventually raised **£140-11** shillings leaving a deficiency of almost £300. One very famous Club I am told subscribed one shilling!

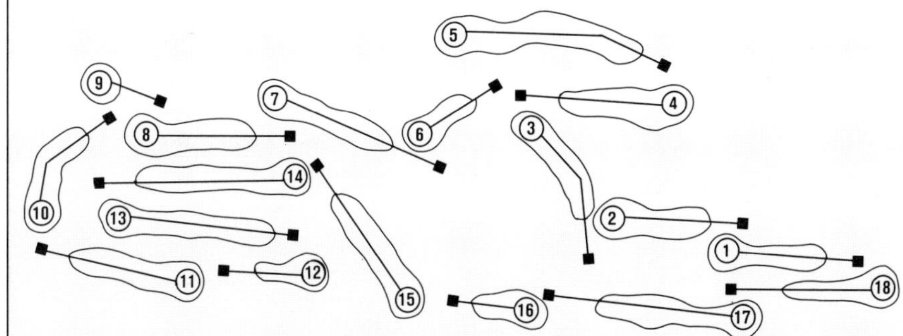

Hole	Yards	Par	Hole	Yards	Par
1	380	4	10	308	4
2	325	4	11	389	4
3	362	4	12	192	3
4	377	4	13	482	5
5	486	5	14	484	5
6	184	3	15	417	4
7	408	4	16	179	3
8	370	4	17	486	5
9	127	3	18	387	4
Out	3,019	35	In	3,324	37
			Out	3,019	35
			TOTALS	6,343	72

BAMBURGH
CHAMPIONSHIP GOLF

In an earlier piece I quoted one of Henry Longhurst's most celebrated comments, namely 'What a lovely place to die' (referring to the 18th hole at Killarney). The golf course at Bamburgh merits another from the great man, 'Golf takes you to such beautiful places.' The setting is quite stunning. A number of Britain's golf courses are gazed over by castles; Royal St David's and Harlech Castle are perhaps the best known, Cruden Bay and Dunstanburgh are another pair but none is dominated quite the way that Bamburgh is. Standing 150 feet high on a rocky crag and covering eight acres, Bamburgh is one of Britain's most majestic castles, towering over both the village and of course the adjoining 18 hole golf links. Apparently we have to thank the Normans for the splendid keep; it was they who built it, having acquired the original castle from Matilda, Countess of Northumberland, after threatening to take out the eyes of her captive husband – (charming times!)

Turning to less gory subjects, **Mr. T.C. Osborne** is the Secretary of Bamburgh Golf Club; he may be contacted by telephone on **(06684) 321**. The Club has no golf professional but should you turn up without any balls, fear not, a supply can be purchased from behind the bar.

Visitors are made exremely welcome at Bamburgh, the only times they are restricted is on major Club competition days and on Public Holidays when visitors must be accompanied by a Member.

The green fees at Bamburgh vary according to the season. The summer fees, applicable between the 24th March and the 21st October, are as follows: **£12** per day for a round during the week (**£6** for juniors) and **£12** per round, **£16** per day at weekends (**£10** and **£8** respectively for juniors). For Autumn and Winter visitors the fees set in 1989 are **£6** during the week and **£8** at weekends. Finally, seven day 'temporary Membership' can be purchased for **£45** during the Summer (**£30** for juniors). Golfing **Societies** are equally welcome at Bamburgh, though pre-booking with the Secretary is essential. All written enquiries should be addressed to Mr Osborne at **The Bamburgh Castle Golf Club, The Club House, Bamburgh, Northumberland**.

Bamburgh has what might be described as an 'invigorating climate'. Situated on the north eastern coast of Northumberland, only Berwick-upon-Tweed lies further north in England and Bamburgh is a shade closer to the North Pole than either Prestwick, Turnberry or Troon. Despite its remoteness, the journey is a fairly straightforward one and furthermore it is one that is decidedly worth making. Both northbound and southbound travellers should pick up the **A1** which runs between **Berwick and Alnwick**, passing Bamburgh midway. It doesn't, however, pass through Bamburgh. Those approaching from the north should exit left on the **B3142** at **Belford**, while those approaching from the south are best leaving the **A1** just north of **Warenford** and following the **B3141** to Bamburgh. Anyone motoring across the glorious Northumberland countryside may find **Wooler** a useful place to head for: the **B6348** joins Wooler to the A1 just north of the **B1341** turn off.

By any standards Bamburgh is a short course, measuring **5465** yards (par **68**) from the men's tees and **5064** yards from the ladies tees (par **70**). Short it may be but it isn't without its tests; there are many whin bushes and several of the fairways are flanked with much tangling heather. As with every seaside course the moods of the wind must always be considered. In any event the golfer will not have come to Bamburgh to seek golf's toughest challenge, it is the splendour of the unique setting that is to be enjoyed. The Castle isn't the only sight that demands attention: there are magnificent views across to nearby Holy Island and Lindisfarne Castle and the Cheviot Hills provide a glorious backdrop. As for the course itself, in addition to the great spread of heather, a number of fairways are lined with rare wild orchids. It is hardly surprising that Bamburgh is often described as Britain's most beautiful course.

What about the 19th? In short, exceptionally friendly (as one comes to expect in this part of England). There are no formal dress requirements and lunches and dinners are offered daily in addition to light snacks.

There is a saying used in many sports that 'a good big 'un' is always better than 'a good little'un'; the golf course at Bamburgh provides the clearest possible evidence that the phrase has no meaning in golf.

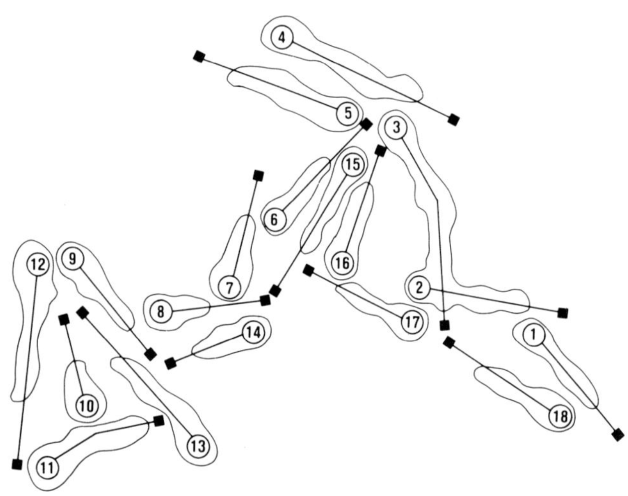

Hole	Yards	Par	Hole	Yards	Par
1	182	3	10	196	3
2	213	3	11	334	4
3	510	5	12	413	4
4	476	5	13	406	4
5	314	4	14	149	3
6	224	3	15	404	4
7	279	4	16	268	4
8	162	3	17	260	4
9	361	4	18	314	4
Out	2,721	34	In	2,744	34
			Out	2,721	34
			TOTALS	5,465	68

CUMBRIA & THE NORTH EAST

COMPLETE GOLF

CUMBRIA

Alston Moor G.C.
(9) 5010 yards
The Hermitage, Alston
(0498) 81675

Appleby G.C.
(18) 5895 yards
Blackenber Moor, Appelby in Westmoreland
(0930) 51432

Barrow G.C.
(18) 6209 yards
Hawcoat, Barrow-in-Furness
(0229) 25444

Brampton G.C.
(18) 6426 yards
Talkin Tarn, Brampton
(06977) 2255

Carlisle G.C.
(18) 6278 yards
Aglionby, Carlisle
(022872) 303

Cockermouth G.C.
(18) 5496 yards
Embleton, Cockermouth
(059681) 223

Dunnerholme G.C.
(10) 6105 yards
Duddon Road, Askam-in-Furness
(0229) 62675

Furness G.C.
(18) 6374 yards
Central Drive, Barrow-in-Furness
(0229) 41232

Grange Fell G.C.
(9) 5278 yards
Fell Road, Grange-over-Sands
(04484) 2536

Grange-over-Sands G.C.
(18) 5660 yards
Meathop Road, Grange-over-Sands
(04484) 3180

Kendal G.C.
(18) 5550 yards
The Heights, Kendal
(0539) 24079

Keswick G.C.
(18) 6175 yards
Threlkeld Hall, Keswick
(07687) 72147

Kirkby Lonsdale G.C.
(9) 4058 yards
Casterton Road, Kirkby Lonsdale
(0468) 71483

Maryport G.C.
(18) 6272 yards
Bank End, Maryport
(0900) 812605

Penrith G.C.
(18) 6026 yards
Salkeld Road, Penrith
(0768) 62217

St. Bees School G.C.
(9) 5082 yards
Station Road, St. Bees
(0946) 822695

Seascale G.C.
(18) 6372 yards
The Banks, Seascale
(094 67) 28202

Sedbergh G.C.
(9) 4134 yards
Millthrop, Sedburgh
(0587) 20993

Silecroft G.C.
(9) 5627 yards
Silecroft
(0657) 4250

Silloth-on-Solway G.C.
(18) 6343 yards
Silloth-on-Solway, Carlisle
(0965) 31304

Stonyholme Municipal G.C.
(18) 5600 yards
St. Aidans Road, Carlisle
(0228) 34856

Ulverston G.C.
(18) 6092 yards
Bardsea Park, Ulverston
(0229) 52824

Windemere G.C.
(18) 5002 yards
Cleabarrow, Windemere
(09662) 3123

Workington G.C.
(18) 6202 yards
Branthwaite Road, Workington
(0900) 3460

DURHAM

Barnard Castle G.C.
(18) 5838 yards
Marmire Road, Barnard Castle
(0833) 38355

Beamish Park G.C.
(18) 6205 yards
Beamish, Stanley
(091) 3701133

Birtley G.C.
(9) 5154 yards
Portobello Road, Birtley
(091) 402207

Bishop Auckland G.C.
(18) 6420 yards
Durham Road, Bishop Auckland
(0388) 663648

Blackwell Grange G.C.
(18) 5587 yards
Briar Close, Blackwell, Darlington
(0325) 464464

Brancepeth Castle G.C.
(18) 6300 yards
Brancepeth Village, Durham
(091) 3780075

Chester-le-Street G.C.
(18) 6269 yards
Lumley Park, Chester-le-Street
(091) 3883218

Consett & District G.C.
(18) 6001 yards
Elemfield Road, Consett
(0207) 502186

Crook G.C.
(18) 6089 yards
Low Job's Hill, Crook
(0388) 762429

Darlington G.C.
(18) 6032 yards
Haughton Grange, Darlington
(0325) 484555

Dinsdale Spa G.C.
(18) 6078 yards
Middleton St. George, Darlington
(0325) 332297

Durham City G.C.
(18) 6118 yards
Langley Moor, Durham
(091) 3780069

Mount Oswald G.C.
(18) 6009 yards
South Road, Durham
(0385) 386 7527

Seaham G.C.
(18) 5972 yards
Dawdon, Seaham
(091) 5812354

South Moor G.C.
(18) 6445 yards
The Middles, Craghead, Stanley
(0207) 232848

Stressholme G.C.
(18) 6511 yards
Snipe Lane, Darlington
(0325) 461002

TYNE AND WEAR

Backworth G.C.
(9) 5930 yards
Backworth, Shiremoor
(091) 2681048

Boldon G.C.
(18) 6319 yards
Dipe Lane, East Boldon
(0783) 364182

City Of Newcastle G.C.
(18) 6492 yards
Three Mile Bridge, Gosforth
(091) 2851775

Garesfield G.C.
(18) 6610 yards
Chopwell
(0207) 561278

Gosforth G.C.
(18) 6030 yards
Broadway East, Gosforth
(091) 285 3495

Heworth G.C.
(18) 6442 yards
Heworth, Gateshead
(026785) 692137

Hobson Municipal G.C.
(18) 6502 yards
Hobson, Burneyfield
(0207) 70941

Houghton-le-Spring G.C.
(18) 6248 yards
Copt Hill, Houghton-le-Spring
(091) 584 1198

Newcastle United G.C.
(18) 6498 yards
Ponteland Road, Cowgate, Newcastle
(0632) 864693

Northumberland G.C.
(18) 6640 yards
High Gosforth Park, Newcastle
(0632) 362498

Ponteland G.C.
(18) 6512 yards
Bell Villas, Ponteland, Newcastle
(0661) 22689

Ravensworth G.C.
(18) 5872 yards
Wrekenton, Gateshead
(091) 487 2843

Ryton G.C.
(18) 6034 yards
Clara Vale, Ryton
(091) 413 3737

South Shields G.C.
(18) 6264 yards
Cleadon Hills, South Shields
(091) 456 0475

Tynemouth G.C.
(18) 6351 yards
Spital Dean, Tynemouth, North Shields
(091) 413 2177

Tyneside G.C.
(18) 6055 yards
Westfield Lane, Ryton
(091) 413 2742

Wallsend G.C.
(18) 6601 yards
Bigges Main, Wallsend-on-Tyne
(091) 262 1973

Washington G.C.
(18) 6528 yards
Cellar Road, Washington
(091) 417 2626

Wearside G.C.
(18) 6204 yards
Coxgreen, Sunderland
(091) 5342518

Westerhope G.C.
(18) 6468 yards
Westerhope, Newcastle
(091) 2869125

Whickham G.C.
(18) 6129 yards
Hollinside Park, Newcastle
(091) 488 7309

Whitburn G.C.
(18) 6035 yards
Lizard Lane, South Shields
(091) 5294210

Whitley Bay G.C.
(18) 6712 yards
Claremount Road, Whitley Bay
(091) 252 0180

FARLAM HALL

Farlam Hall has been personally owned and run by the Quinion and Stevenson families since 1975 and has been lovingly restored over the years to the high standards now offered.

Set in mature gardens, this elegant border manor house offers a haven of peace and calm.

Downstairs spacious lounges, filled with antiques and flowers complement the airy dining room with its views over the gardens. Open fires add to the year-round appeal of Farlam Hall, inviting you to relax and unwind.

The 13 bedrooms, two of which are on the ground floor, are all totally different in size and style, ranging from the smaller 17th century rooms at the centre of the house to the high ceilinged Victorian ones on the two wings. All rooms have private facilities, colour television and direct-dial telephones.

Barry Quinion heads a team of English chefs with international experience, and they have a reputation, gained over many years, for producing the best of country house food. The menu includes light dishes as well as hearty ones, so welcome after a day enjoying the local scenery.

Farlam Hall is ideally situated, not just for Brampton and Carlisle golf courses, but also as a base from which to enjoy the other numerous and varied courses. These range from simple country ones to coastal courses, all beautifully maintained, with friendly and helpful staff. Also if heading north to play in Scotland, the hotel's proximity to major routes makes it a perfect overnight resting place.

Farlam Hall Hotel,
Brampton,
Cumbria CA8 2NG.
Tel: (06976) 234/357

CUMBRIA & THE NORTH EAST
COMPLETE GOLF

NORTHUMBERLAND

Allendale G.C.
(9) 4580 yards
Allendale, Hexham
(043483) 412

Alnmouth G.C.
(18) 6414 yards
Foxton Hall, Alnmouth
(0665) 830368

Alnmouth Village G.C.
(9) 6078 yards
Marine Road, Alnmouth
(0665) 830370

Alnwick G.C.
(9) 5379 yards
Swansfield Park, Alnwick
(0665) 602499

Arcot Hall G.C.
(18) 6389 yards
Dudley, Cramlington
(091) 236 2794

Bamburgh Castle G.C.
(18) 5465 yards
Bamburgh
(06684) 321

Bedlingtonshire G.C.
(18) 6825 yards
Acorn Bank, Bedlington
(0670) 822457

Bellingham G.C.
(9) 5226 yards
Boggle Hole, Bellingham
(0660) 20530

Berwick-upon-Tweed G.C.
(18) 6399 yards
Goswick, Berwick-upon-Tweed
(0289) 87348

Blyth G.C.
(18) 6533 yards
New Delaval, Blyth
(067) 367728

Dunstanburgh Castle G.C.
(18) 5817 yards
Embleton, Alnwick
(0665) 67276

Hexham G.C.
(18) 6026 yards
Spital Park, Hexham
(0434) 603072

Magdalene Fields G.C.
(18) 6551 yards
Berwick-upon-Tweed
(0289) 306384

Morpeth G.C.
(18) 6215 yards
The Common, Morpeth
(0670) 519980

Newbiggin-by-the-Sea G.C.
(18) 6444 yards
Newbiggin-by-the-Sea
(0670) 817344

Prudhoe G.C.
(18) 5812 yards
Eastwood Park, Prudhoe
(0661) 32466

Rothbury G.C.
(9) 5650 yards
Old Race Course, Rothbury
(0669) 20718

Seahouses G.C.
(18) 5399 yards
Bednell Road, Seahouses
(0665) 720794

Stocksfield G.C.
(18) 6037 yards
New Ridley, Stocksfield
(0661) 843041

Tynedale G.C.
(9) 5706 yards
Tyne Green, Hexham
(0434) 605701

Warkworth G.C.
(9) 5856 yards
Warkworth
(0665) 711596

CLEVELAND

Billingham G.C.
(18) 6430 yards
Sandy Lane, Billingham
(0642) 554494

Castle Eden & Peterlee G.C.
(18) 6297 yards
Castle Eden, Hartlepool
(0429) 836220

Cleveland G.C.
(18) 6707 yards
Queen Street, Redcar
(0642) 483693

Eaglescliffe G.C.
(18) 6275 yards
Yarm Road, Eaglescliffe
(0642) 780098

Hartlepool G.C.
(18) 6325 yards
Hart Warren, Hartlepool
(0429) 274398

Middlesborough G.C.
(18) 6106 yards
Marton, Middlesborough
(0642) 311515

Middlesborough Municipal
(18) 6314 yards
Ladgate Lane, Middleborough
(0642) 315533

Saltburn-by-the-Sea G.C.
(18) 5803 yards
Hob Hill, Saltburn-by-the-Sea
(0287) 22312

Seaton Carew G.C.
(18) 6604 yards
Tees Road, Seaton Carew
(0429) 266249

Teeside G.C.
(18) 6472 yards
Acklam Road, Thornaby
(0642) 616516

MAJOR HOPKINS "Crookham" *BURLINGTON GALLERY*

SOUTH & MID WALES

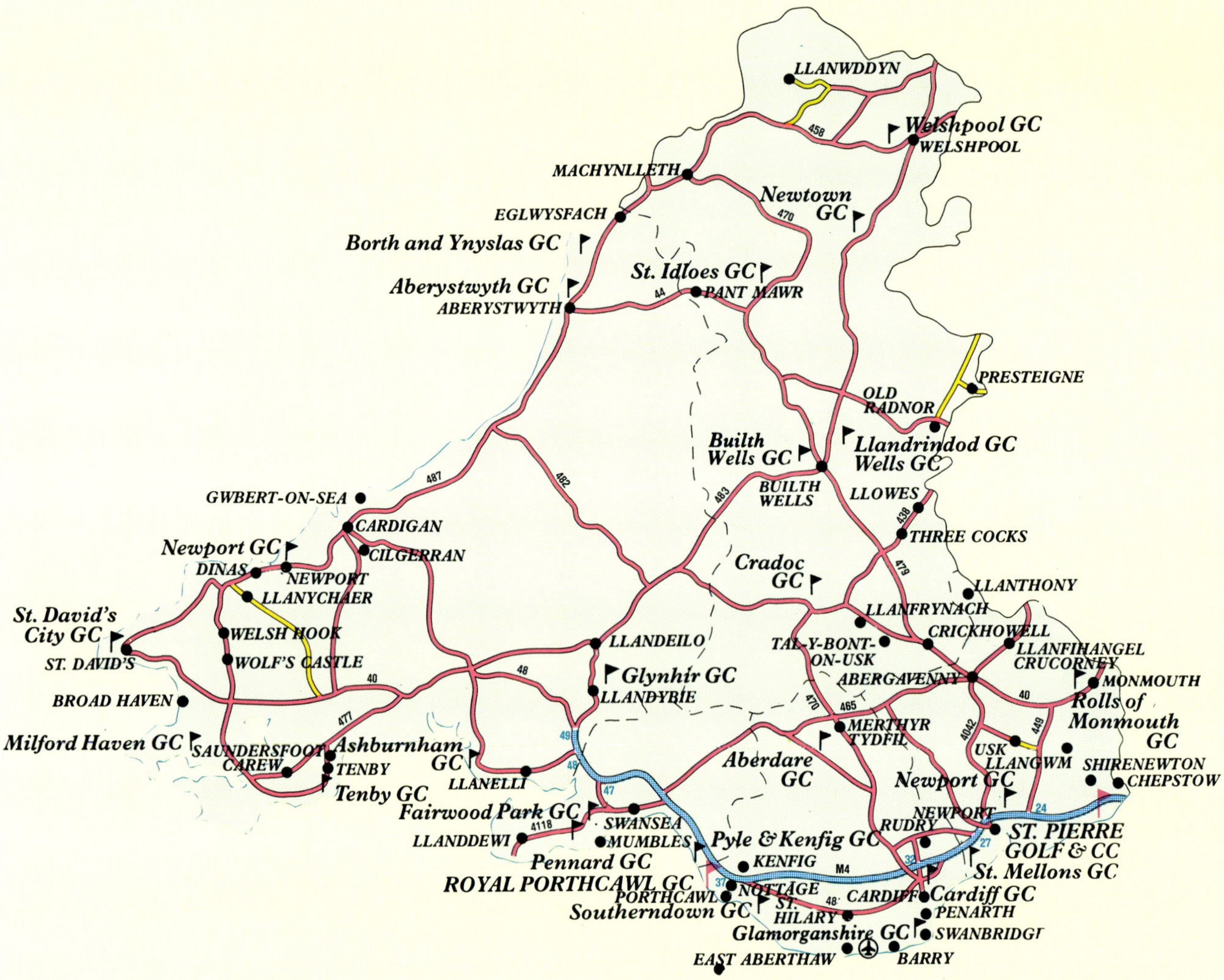

H. ROUNTREE *"Porthcawl"* SARAH BADDIEL'S BOOK GALLERY

SOUTH & MID WALES

CHOICE GOLF

Balls in South Wales are often large, oval-shaped and made of leather. However, those belonging to the much smaller dimpled breed – usually white, though these days sometimes shocking yellow – are to be found in some particularly pleasant spots, and in a great variety of places between the Wye Valley and the Gower Peninsula.

In addition to 'The Glamorgans' and Gwent our region takes in Mid Wales as well, that is the larger, less inhabited counties of Dyfed and Powys – the 'real Wales', they'll tell you there.

GWENT

For many travellers their first sample of golf in South Wales will be the impressive **St Pierre Golf and Country Club** at Chepstow (see feature page). Unfortunately far too great a number make St Pierre their one and only stop. Futher up the Wye Valley both **Monmouthshire** and **The Rolls of Monmouth** offer an outstanding game in delightful surroundings. Bounded by the River Usk the Monmouthshire Golf Club lies half a mile west of Abergavenny at Llanfoist. The club will soon celebrate one hundred years of golf – quite an achievement when one considers its unusual beginnings. Laid out on ground formerly used for polo and later for horseracing, golf was started here in 1892, as the Club handbook tells you, 'the result of a bet as to whether such a venture could be run successfully at Abergavenny'! Clearly the golfers backed a winner. Visitors are welcome to play the course during the week at a cost of **£10**, proof of handicap being required. Societies are also catered for on Mondays and Fridays. Golf at 'The Rolls' is played around a spectacular mansion house, the Hendre, country seat of the Rolls family since 1767. A new Club founded in 1982, it provides quite a tough test, but an immensely enjoyable one. The course is located some 3 miles west of Monmouth on the **B4233**. St Pierre itself is a likely base while golfing in the area. **The Hotel (02912) 5261** is a 14th Century mansion providing a whole range of facilities. However, those not wishing to wake up next to the 18th green should note the **Castle View Hotel (02912) 70349**, also in Chepstow and very comfortable. In Abergavenny, **The Crowfield Hotel (0873) 5048** offers a splendid nest both for the nearby golf course and the delights of the Brecon Beacons and **The Walnut Tree (0873) 2792** is without doubt one of the finest restaurants in Wales. Monmouth provides **The Kings Head Hotel (0600) 2177** and if after a day's golf on the lengthy Rolls course you have any energy left, a drive north to Llanthony is strongly recommended – the **Abbey Hotel (087 38) 894087** is superb and enjoys a most spectacular setting.

The other golf course in Gwent which is well worth a visit is **Newport** at Rogerstone. It is a very fine downland course and decidedly handy when travelling along the M4 (junction 27). Green fees here are approximately **£12**; prior telephoning is preferred.

GLAMORGAN

Golfers in Cardiff (or Caerdydd) are quite fortunate having a number of well-established courses close at hand. Not surprisingly they tend to be busier than the majority of Welsh courses and therefore before setting off it is probably wise to contact the particular Club in question. The **Cardiff Golf Club** is a superior parkland course situated some 3 miles from the city centred at Cyncoed. Visitors must accompany Members at the weekends, but a game can be enjoyed there on weekdays, for approximately **£10**. **St Mellons**, north east of the City, within easy access of the **M4**, is another popular parkland course. Quite challenging, with several interesting holes. To the south of Cardiff, **Wenvoe Castle**, one of the more hilly courses in South Glamorgan, should be good for a game, during midweek, as should the **Glamorganshire** course, located to the west of Penrith.

Perhaps the best three hotels in Cardiff are the **Park Hotel (0222) 383471**, and **Angel Hotel (0222) 32633** and the very modern **Stakis Inn on the Avenue (0222) 732520**. Among the better restaurants, **Gibsons (0222) 41264** in Romilly Crescent is very well thought of, while the **Blas-Ar Cymru (0222) 382132** offers a delightful taste of Wales. Another good eating place is found in Penarth, **The Caprice (0222) 702424** – excellent sea food accompanies fine views over the Bristol Channel. Also in Penarth **The Captain's Wife** is recommended (a pub it should be added). More pubs, and to the north and south of Cardiff are **The Maenllwyd** at Rudry and the beautifully thatched **Bush at St Hilary**. Still further south is the excellent **Blue Anchor** at East Aberthan (superb lunches).

Before heading off to the glorious coastal strip around Porthcawl a course certainly deserving a mention is **Aberdare** – and not merely because the professional goes by the impressive name of Mr A Palmer! Aberdare is an excellent woodland course, the finest in 'the Valleys' and where golf can be enjoyed for the modest fee **£6** during the week, **£7** at weekends.

One would have to travel many a mile to find a course the equal of **Royal Porthcawl** (also featured later this chapter) but its near neighbour to the east, **Southerndown** gets closer than most. Situated on high ground it is an outstandingly scenic downland course measuring a little over **6600** yards (par 70). Visitors are welcome between Mondays and Saturdays, fees being **£10** midweek, **£13** on Saturdays. Even closer to Porthcawl is the fine links of **Pyle and Kenfig**, on more than one occasion the venue of the Welsh Amateur Stroke Play Championship. Fairly testing, being open to the elements, visitors are able to play on weekdays at a cost of **£10**.

Some ideas for a well-earned night's rest in the area include: in Porthcawl, **The Atlantic Hotel (065 671) 5011** and **The Fairways (065 671) 2095**. In Nottage, **The Rose and Crown (065 671) 4850** is an excellent pub serving good food and with some accommodation and another notable drinking establishment is **The Prince of Wales** in Kenfig.

Beyond Pyle and Kenfig the M4 heads into West Glamorgan passing through Port Talbot towards Swansea, and beyond Swansea is the beautifully secluded Gower Peninsula. If you are fortunate enough to be visiting these parts, two courses that can be strongly recommended are **Fairwood Park** and **Pennard**. The former, situated close to Swansea Airport, is a second course over which racehorses once galloped. A recent change of ownership has seen a rapid improvement in both the course and the facilities offered. Visitors are received at all times, the cost of a weekday round being **£7** with **£10** payable at weekends and Bank Holidays. Several long par fours are the feature of this attractive course. From Pennard's cliff-top course there are some splendid views out across the Bristol Channel. Again visitors can play on any day of the week, fees here being **£8** Mondays to Fridays, **£9** at weekends.

A hotel for the area? In Swansea, the **Dragon Hotel (0792) 51074** is very good and in nearby Mumbles **The Norton House Hotel (0792) 404891** is most pleasant. On the Gower **Fairyhill Country House (0792) 390139** is recommended, especially for its cuisine. As for a drink there are numerous pubs, here are two: **The Joiners Arms** in Bishopston and the **Welcome to Town** in Llanrhidian.

SOUTH & MID WALES

CHOICE GOLF

For every person in New Zealand there are 23.8 sheep. Regrettably I don't have the figures for **Dyfed** and **Powys** but I suspect they're fairly similar. The 'bad news' is that the lack of human beings is unfortunately reflected by a low number of top class golf courses (unlike in New Zealand it should be said). However, the 'good news' is that even during the summer months most of the courses remain relatively uncrowded and the green fees tend to be cheaper than in most parts of Britain.

DYFED

The two Championship courses in this area lie on Dyfed's southern coast, some 30 miles apart. Both **Ashburnham and Tenby** were founded before the turn of the century and each has staged more than one **Welsh Amateur Championship**, Ashburnham in fact being a regular venue.

Located one mile west of Burry Port, Ashburnham's links is fairly close to industrial South Wales which I suppose extends as far as Llanelli, or at least to where the **M4** from London fizzles out. The course measures 7,000 yards from the Championship tees and 6,686 yards from the medal tees – certainly not a course for the inexperienced. Connoisseurs of the game, however, should find it an excellent challenge and for approximately **£12** the Club offers a warm welcome to visitors.

There are more glorious sandy beaches around **Tenby** than one could care to count. There is a story of one five year old boy who raced on to one of these golden stretches arms aloft shouting, 'This is the sixth beach I've been on today!' Anyway as well as being a haven for the bucket and spade it is also a wonderful place for a round of golf. Tenby is a true links course with natural sand hazards. A day's golf here can be enjoyed for **£8.50** during the week and for **£10** at weekends.

In Llanelli, **The Diplomat (0554) 758171** is comfortable enough, however, golfers may prefer to stay in Tenby, here **The Imperial (0834) 3737** and the less grand, but friendly **Richmond Hotel (0834) 2533** are recommended. A local favourite is the **St Brides Hotel (0834) 812304** which enjoys superb views of Carmarthen Bay and its restaurant makes the best use of locally captured lobster. Another good hotel which also offers excellent sea food can be found in Broadhaven – **The Druidstone Hotel (0437) 781221**. Crab here is the order of the day.

Moving westwards along the Dyfed coast the next 18 holes are to be found at **Milford Haven**, a medium-length parkland course to the west of the town. In days of old the former whaling town may well have been a 'haven' but the present day 'landscape in oils' isn't everyone's cup of tea. More attractive is **St Davids** with its beautiful Cathedral making it the smallest city in Britain. Unfortunately for golfing visitors there is only a modest 9 hole golf course. 20 miles away at **Newport**, although again only a 9-holer, there is a very fine golf course, and one which offers some tremendous sea views. The Club welcomes visitors at all times.

St Davids has many pleasing hotels, and **Warpool Court (0437) 720300** is particularly good. Should one strangely tire of the coast then **The Wolfscastle Country Hotel (043 787) 225**, in Wolfscastle is tremendously welcoming (even though it may not sound like it).

Perhaps the place for golfers who have played somewhat waywardly is the village of Welsh Hook. **Stone Hall (0348) 840212** is the establishment – a small number of bedrooms and an excellent restaurant. Good places for a drink include the contradictory **Sailors Safety** and **The Ship Aground** at Dinas and **The Golden Lion** in Newport. If you are still hungry then the best tip is to visit Cardigan and **The Pantry (0239) 820420**. Failing the Pantry, try The Kitchen – **The Castle Kitchen (0239) 615055**, an informal but well-run restaurant. I have one last thought on the restauarants in the area and that's Cobblers, but before you take offence, try out **The Cobblers (0269) 850540** – a friendly restaurant making the best of some delightfully fresh produce. Leaving 'Little England beyond Wales' and heading still further up the coast, the University town of **Aberystwyth** (green fees **£7**), has an 18 hole course that looks out over Cardigan Bay. More impressive though is **Borth and Ynyslas** (green fees **£8**), one of the oldest Clubs in Wales. Borth is a superbly-maintained seaside links. A road, the **B4353**, runs right alongside much of the course and is often peppered by golf balls. Taking out insurance before playing Borth is to be recommended.

The **Cliff Haven Hotel (097 871) 871** in Borth may be the most convenient place for a good sleep but further north at Eglwysfach, 16th Century **Ynyshir Hall (065 474) 209** is well worth inspecting (note the nearby bird sanctuary) and in Machynlleth, **The Wynnstay Arms (0654) 2941** is a cosy former coaching inn. Back in Borth, the **Victoria Inn** is a good pub.

Inland there is precious little to speak of in Dyfed, though there is a fairly testing hilltop course at **Carmarthen** – one which is decidedly better in summer than in winter and an attractive parkland course at **Glynhir**, near the foothills of the Black Mountain Range. The latter is a particularly friendly club situated close to the Glynhir Mansion where the first news of Wellington's victory at Waterloo is reputed to have been received by carrier pigeon (must have been a pretty sharp pigeon!). Green fees at Glynhir are good value at **£6** midweek, **£8** at the weekend. One doesn't have to look far for a night's stay either; in Llandybie, the excellent **Mill at Glynhir (0269) 850672** overlooks the 14th green.

POWYS

The golf courses in Powys are few and far between, but those that there are tend to be set amidst some splendid scenery. There is an 18 hole course at **Welshpool** up in the hills near the English border and two interesting 9 hole courses at Newton (**St Giles**) and at Llanidloes (**St Idloes**) in the quiet of the Cambrian Mountains (note the very fine **Glansevern Arms (05515) 240** in Pant Mawr). Two of the best courses are situated right in the centre of Wales, **Llandrindod Wells** and **Builth Wells**. Both are attractive courses, Llandrindod in particular offers spectacular views situated as it is on a plateau 1,000 feet above sea level. Green fees at either course are only about **£7**. In Builth Wells, **The Lion Hotel (0982) 553670** is an historic inn in the centre of town, very pleasant too, while in Llandrindod the large **Metropole Hotel (0597) 2881** is very convenient (and comfortable). **The Harp** at Old Radnor is an ideal place for a drink and a snack.

One final course to mention and one good enough to have held the Welsh Amateur Stroke Play Championship is **Cradock**. A lovely course this, very scenic being within the Brecon Beacons National Park. Green fees are **£6** midweek, **£9** at the weekend. This may be one's last night in Wales; if so here's a tip; a drink at **The White Swan** in Llanfrynach followed by dinner and a relaxing stay at **Gliffaes (0874) 730371** in Crickhowell – marvellous!

GLIFFAES

A thoroughly charming Victorian country house hotel, Gliffaes boasts fine gardens and parkland, situated in the National Park yet only one mile off the main A40 road. It offers peace and tranquillity as well as being easily accessible.

The house, which faces due south, stands in its own 29 acres in the beautiful valley of the River Usk, midway between the Brecon Beacons and the Black Mountains. Built in 1885 as a private residence, it has been ideally adapted to provide spacious comfort in the country house tradition. There are nineteen bedrooms with private bathrooms or showers and all are individual in decor and furnishings.

The downstairs rooms include a large, comfortable, panelled sitting-room which leads into an elegant regency style drawing-room. From here, french windows open into a glass-fronted sun-room and on to the terrace. The dining-room and comfortable bar also open on to the terrace, with the glorious views of the surrounding hills and River Usk one hundred and fifty feet below. The billiard room has a full sized table and provides an additional sitting-room with something of a club atmosphere.

Breakfast is served from a sideboard, lunch is a cold buffet with soup and a hot dish. Dinner is either table d'hote or a la carte. In fact, country house standards of the old order are carefully maintained by the resident owners; the Brabner family have held sway here since 1948.

External facilities include fishing for salmon and trout in the part of the Usk which the hotel overlooks, tennis, bowls, putting and croquet. There is an extensive range of short walks in the vicinity and a nearby riding and pony trekking establishment where horses and ponies can be hired.

The hotel is justly proud of its in-house cooking and remains open from the middle of March to the end of the year.

Gliffaes,
Crickhowell,
Powys,
Wales.
Tel: (0874) 730371

ST. PIERRE
CHAMPIONSHIP GOLF

One of the first jokes that an English Schoolboy learns is 'how do you get two whales in a mini?' (Answer) – 'Cross the Severn Bridge'. For golfers the act of crossing the famous bridge usually means one thing – **The St Pierre Golf and Country Club** at **Chepstow**.

St. Pierre has been in existence for a little over a quarter of a century. **Mr. Bill Graham** founded the Club in **1961** with the **Ken Cotton** designed **Old Course** opening the following May. The first thing to strike one at St. Pierre is the setting: quite simply magnificent. The golf course occupies land that was originally a deer park and it has an abundance of mature trees. There is also a lake covering eleven acres situated in the heart of the course. Whilst the 'Old' Course is understandably St. Pierre's 'pride and joy', there are of course 36 holes, with a second eighteen, the **New Course** opened in **1975**.

Mr. Terry Cleary is the **Golf Secretary** at St. Pierre, he may be contacted by telephone on **(0291) 625261**. All written correspondence should be addressed to **The Secretary, St. Pierre Golf and Country Club, St. Pierre Park, Chepstow, Gwent NP6 6YA**. The Club's professional, **Renton Doig**, can also be contacted via the above telephone number.

Visitors wishing to arrange a game at St. Pierre must book starting times in advance. Other than proof of handicap there are no general restrictions on times of play. The **green fees** as set in 1989 are as follows: **£20** for a round over the **Old Course** during the week, **£24** at the weekend, with **£14** and **£16** payable for a game on the New Course at similar periods. For those wishing to play a round over both courses the fees are **£27.50** between Monday and Friday, or **£32** at the weekend. For junior golfers a single round on the Old Course is priced at **£12** with **£10** purchasing a game on the New. Both courses are extremely popular with Golfing Societies and prior arrangements can be made with the Secretary. Societies are normally only received during the week unless they are resident at the hotel, in which case they may also play at week-ends.

Travelling to St. Pierre ought to present few problems. The Golf Club is located to the South of Chepstow off the **A48**. The **M4** links Chepstow to Cardiff and Swansea in the west and to London and Bristol in the east. The M4 should be left at exit **22**, the **A446** then taken into Chepstow where the **A48** can be joined and followed to St. Pierre. The best route for those approaching from Birmingham and the north of England is probably to travel south on the **M5** leaving at exit **8**, thereafter picking up the **M50** to Ross-on-Wye. From Ross-on-Wye a combination of the **A40** and **A466** provides a pleasant drive through the Wye Valley to Chepstow.

The Old and the New Course differ quite considerably in length. The Old is the Championship Course and from the back tees it measures **6700** yards,(par **71**). The forward tees reduced the length to **6285** yards, while for the ladies it measures **5718** yards, (par**73**). The respective distances for the New course are **5762** yards (par **68**), **5593** yards and **5214** yards (par **70**). Despite its relative youth as a Championship course, the Old Course has been the venue for a remarkable number of professional events. The **Dunlop Masters** and **Silk Cut Masters** were staged regularly here; illustrious winners included **Tony Jacklin, Bernhard Langer** and **Greg Norman**. The latter on his way to victory in 1982 drove the 362 yard 10th with a three wood. In recent years the **Epson Grand Prix of Europe** matchplay tournament has chosen St. Pierre to begin its life. The first two events bringing first tour successes for two Swedes, **Ove Selberg** winning in **1986** and **Mats Lanner** in **1987**. In June **1980** St. Pierre hosted the **Curtis Cup**.

Perhaps the most famous hole on the Old Course is the 18th, surely one of the most dramatic finishing holes in golf. A par 3 of 237 yards, it requires a brave tee shot across the edge of the lake with large trees lining the left hand side of the fairway. Standing proudly behind the green is the beautiful **St. Pierre Hotel**.

The Hotel is in fact a former 14th century country mansion and it serves the golfer as a particularly impressive 19th. In addition to an excellent restaurant which offers breakfast, lunch and dinner, there are four bars. Celebrating at the end of a round is always to be recommended – particularly if the 18th hole has been tackled successfully. Spare a thought though for a person by the name of Arwyn Griffiths who came to the 18th needing a three for a gross 63. A few minutes later he walked off the green having taken eleven strokes – even he celebrated though, for he still won the competition!

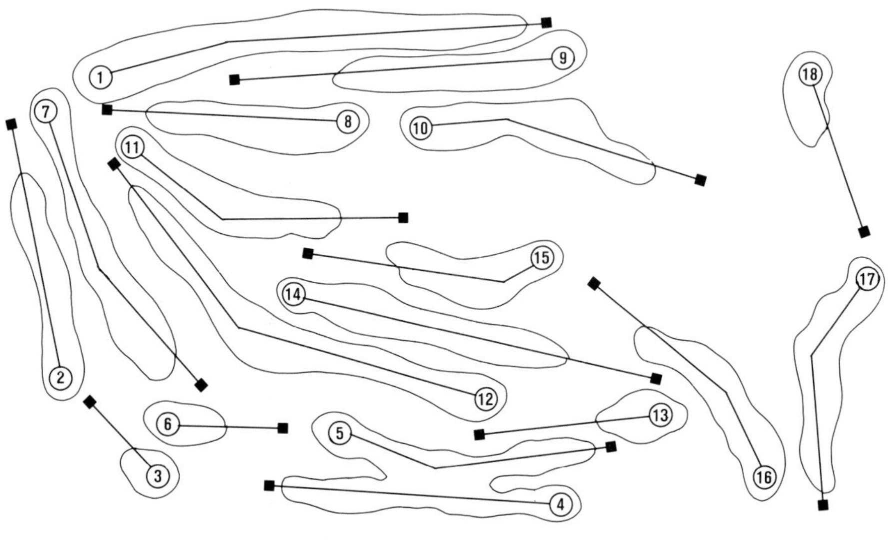

Old Course

Hole	Yards	Par	Hole	Yards	Par
1	576	5	10	362	4
2	364	4	11	369	4
3	135	3	12	545	5
4	379	4	13	219	3
5	420	4	14	521	5
6	165	3	15	375	4
7	442	4	16	426	4
8	309	4	17	412	4
9	444	4	18	237	3
Out	3,234	35	In	3,466	36
			Out	3,234	35
			TOTALS	6,700	71

ROYAL PORTHCAWL
CHAMPIONSHIP GOLF

By common consent **Royal Porthcawl** is not only the finest course in Wales, it is also one of the greatest Championship links in the British Isles. Like many famous Clubs, Porthcawl's beginnings were rather humble. The Club was founded in June **1891** and the following year a nine hole course was laid out on a patch of common land known as **Lock's Common**, consent having been given by the local parish vestry. Having to share the 'course' with, amongst other things cattle,soon frustrated the Members and a second nine holes were sought. These they found on the present site closer to the shore. By **1898** Locks Common was abandoned altogether and the 'favoured' second nine holes were extended to a full eighteen. Once settled the Club prospered and in **1909** patronage was bestowed upon the Club. Royal Porthcawl had well and truly arrived.

The Members were extremely fortunate in finding this new home, for today Royal Porthcawl is not only considered to be one of Britain's finest golfing challenges but also one of the most beautifully situated. Every hole on the course provides a sight of the sea, and from many points there are spectacular views across the Bristol Channel to the distant hills of Somerset and North Devon.

Presently presiding over the Royal domain is the Club's helpful **Secretary, Mr. Tony Woolcott**; he may be contacted by telephone on**(065671) 2251**. The professional **Graham Poor** can be reached on **(065671) 6984**. Golfers wishing to visit Royal Porthcawl can expect a warm welcome. Subject to possessing a Golf Club handicap there are no general restrictions; however, being an understandably popular Club prior telephoning is advisable. Those wishing to organise Golfing Society Meetings should either telephone or preferably address a written application to the Secretary at **The Royal Porthcawl Golf Club, Porthcawl, Mid Glamorgan, Wales, CF36 3UW**. Tuesdays and Thursdays are the usual Society days.

The **green fees** at Royal Porthcawl for 1989 were set at **£18** per day during the week with **£23** payable at weekends. A rather novel and most encouraging policy is adopted towards junior golfers. Junior Members of the Club can introduce an 'outside' junior during the week for a green fee of **£1** during weekdays.

The course is situated approximately 15 miles east of Swansea and about 20 miles west of Cardiff. The **M4** makes travelling to Porthcawl fairly straightforward. Approaching from either east or west the motorway should be left at junction **37**; thereafter the **A4229** can be followed into Porthcawl. The course's precise location is towards the northern end of the town.

In the opening paragraph Porthcawl was described as a 'links'. This isn't perhaps entirely accurate for although much of the course is certainly of a links nature, some parts are more strictly downland and heathland in character. Certainly there aren't the massive sandhills that feature so prominently on the great Championship links of Lancashire, and which are indeed to be found at neighbouring Pyle and Kenfig. The absence of sandhills means there is no real protection from the elements on stormy days and when the winds blow fiercely Porthcawl can be as tough a challenge as one is likely to meet.

From its Championship tees the course stretches to **6605** yards (par **72** s.s.s.**74**) while from the medal tees it measures **6409** yards (par **72**) with the ladies playing over **5682** yards (par **75**). Good scores at Porthcawl (the course record stands at **65**) are likely to be fashioned on the first ten holes; from the tough par 3 11th inwards there are some very difficult holes. The second shot from the fairway on the dog-leg 13th is one not to be hurried, the views out across the course are quite breathtaking. The 15th and 16th are two quite lengthy par fours and the round ends with a glorious downhill finishing hole.

In 1987 the **Welsh Amateur Championship** was once again played for at Porthcawl while in 1988 the Club staged the **Amateur Championship** for the fifth time since the last war.

As for its 19th Porthcawl has a splendid Clubhouse. There is an informal Men's Bar where spikes may be worn, a mixed lounge (jacket and tie after 7pm) and a Dining Room (jacket and tie at all times). Both lunches and dinners can be arranged with prior notice, and light snacks are offered at all times excepting Sundays.

One final thought for those wishing to explore the delights of Royal Porthcawl, I beg you to consider carefully before deciding to visit late on a November's afternoon: as the light fades and a mist starts to descend upon the links the ghost of the Maid of Sker walks the 17th fairway – don't say you haven't been warned!

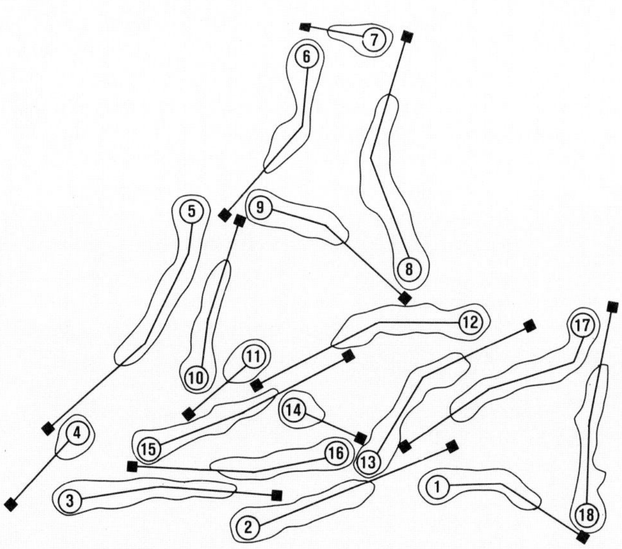

Hole	Yards	Par	Hole	Yards	Par
1	326	4	10	337	4
2	436	4	11	187	3
3	420	4	12	476	5
4	197	3	13	426	4
5	485	5	14	152	3
6	394	4	15	421	4
7	116	3	16	420	4
8	480	5	17	489	5
9	371	4	18	385	4
Out	**3,225**	**36**	**In**	**3,380**	**36**
			Out	**3,225**	**36**
			TOTALS	**6,605**	**72**

THE METROPOLE HOTEL

The Metropole Hotel has witnessed many changes in Llandrindod Wells during the last 116 years; motor cars have come on the market, guests' eating habits have changed, health crazes have come and gone. One thing has remained constant – the Hotel, despite changes of ownership and name, has always remained very much a family affair with Justin and Sarah, son and daughter of the current owner David Baird-Murray, being the fifth generation in the same hotel, a claim made by no other hotelier in the country.

The closure of the old Spa Treatment Centre in 1972 recognised the changing consumer tastes. Today's guests can still sample the water drawn from the Chalybeate Spring, but are happier with Brecon Water to drink, hairdryers in every room and an altogther different kind of Health Spa, one with an indoor swimming pool, rowing machines and modern beauty treatments.

Following a major refurbishment programme, The Metropole Hotel has, over the past 18 months become the most luxurious hotel set peacefully on the border of Wales.

All 121 guest rooms have been raised to international standard; light now floods through 15 ft glass skylights over banks of poinsettias, dusky pink wallpapering and modern grey paintwork in the open plan reception area.

Beyond the skylights, through double doors, is the stress-free environment of the Francis Leisure Centre where a sauna, steam room and sunbeds lead to the piece de resistance – a kidney shaped 54 ft x6 ft 6 in, blue mosaic tiled, jet stream swimming pool. Swimming or just relaxing in the whirlpool is a pleasure under the 63 panel Victorian style glass conservatory, which envelops you in facials and body massage.

At the tiled poolside, conference delegates and holiday makers alike can work-out on the computerised rowing and cycling machines or opt for either a strenuous or relaxed 'toning' dance class. Guests can book from a wide range of beauty treatments including facials and body massage.

Whatever your level of golf, a professional or a Sunday hacker, you will enjoy a game or two on one of the three superb courses nearby. Llandrindod Wells is a moorland course with easy walking and panoramic views. The second course is set in beautiful parkland just outside the centre of the town of Builth Wells, while Kington is the highest course in England and Wales with views over seven counties.

The Metropole
Llandrindod Wells,
Powys LD1 5DY.
Tel: (0597) 2881/2
Fax: (0597) 4828

SOUTH & MID WALES
COMPLETE GOLF

GWENT

Blackwood G.C.
(9) 5304 yards
Cwmgelli, Blackwood
(0495) 223152

Caerleon G.C.
(9) 6184 yards
Caerleon, Nr. Newport
(0633) 420342

Greenmeadow G.C.
(9) 6128 yards
Treherbert Road, Cwmbran
(06333) 69321

Llanwern G.C.
(18) 6202 yards
(9) 5674 yards
Tennyson Avenue, Llanwern
(0633) 412380

Monmouth G.C.
(9) 5434 yards
Leasebrook Lane, Monmouth
(0600) 2212

Monmouthshire G.C.
(18) 6045 yards
Llanfoist, Abergavenny
(0873) 2606

Newport G.C.
(18) 6370 yards
Great Oak, Rogerstone, Newport
(0633) 892683

Pontnewydd G.C.
(10) 5340 yards
West Pontnewydd, Cwmbran
(06333) 67185

Pontypool G.C.
(18) 6070 yards
Trevethyn, Pontypool
(04955) 3655

Rolls of Monmouth G.C.
(18) 6723 yards
The Hendre, Monmouth
(0600) 5353

St. Mellons G.C.
(18) 6225 yards
St. Mellons, Nr. Cardiff
(0633) 680401

St. Pierre G. & C.C.
(18) 6700 yards (Old)
(18) 5762 yards (New)
St. Pierre Park, Chepstow
(02912) 5261

Tredegar Park G.C.
(18) 6044 yards
Bassaleg Road, Newoport
(0633) 894433

Tredegar and Rhymney G.C.
(9) 5730 yards
Cwmtysswg, Rhymney
(0685) 840743

West Monmouthshire G.C.
(18) 6097 yards
Pond Road, Nantyglo
(0495) 310233

SOUTH GLAMORGAN

Brynhill G.C.
(18) 6000 yards
Port Road, Barry
(0446) 720277

Cardiff G.C.
(18) 6015 yards
Sherborne Ave, Cyncoed, Cardiff
(0222) 753320

Creigiau G.C.
(18) 5736 yards
Criegiau, Cardiff
(0222) 890263

Dinas Powis G.C.
(18) 5377 yards
Old High Walls, Dinas Powis
(0222) 512157

Glamorganshire G.C.
(18) 6342 yards
Lavernock Road, Penarth
(0222) 701185

Llanishen G.C.
(18) 5296 yards
Cwm-Lisvane, Cardiff
(0222) 752205

Radyr G.C.
(18) 6031 yards
Drysgol Road, Radyr, Cardiff
(0222) 842408

RAF St Aihan G.C.
(9) 5957 yards
RAF St. Aithan, Barry
(0446) 751043

Wenvoe Castle G.C.
(18) 6411 yards
Wenvoe Castle, Cardiff
(0222) 594371

Whitchurch G.C.
(18) 6245 yards
Pantmawr Road, Whitchurch, Cardiff
(0222) 591094

MID GLAMORGAN

Aberdare G.C.
(18) 5875 yards
Abernant, Aberdare
(0685) 873387

Bargoed G.C.
(18) 6012 yards
Hoelddu, Bargoed
(0443) 830143

Bryn Meadows G. & C.C.
(18) 5963 yards
The Bryn, Nr. Hengoed
(0495) 225590

Caerphilly G.C.
(14) 6063 yards
Mountain Rd, Caerphilly
(0222) 863441

Llantrisant and Pontyclun G.C.
(12) 5712 yards
Talbot Green, Llantrisant
(0443) 222148

Maesteg G.C.
(18) 5845 yards
Mount Pleasant, Maesteg
(0656) 732037

Merthyr Tidfil G.C.
(9) 5794 yards
Cilsanws Mountain, Cefn Coed, Merthyr Tydfil
(0685) 3063

Morlais Castle G.C.
(9) 6356 yards
Pant, Dowlais, Merthyr Tydfil
(0685) 2822

Mountain Ash G.C.
(18) 5535 yards
Cefnpennar
(0443) 472265

Pontypridd G.C.
(18) 5650 yards
Tygwyn Road, Pontypridd
(0443) 402359

Pyle and Kenfig G.C.
(18) 6655 yards
Kenfig
(065671) 3093

Rhondda G.C.
(18) 6428 yards
Pontygwaith, Rhondda
(0443) 433204

Royal Porthcawl G.C.
(18) 6605 yards
Porthcawl
(065671) 2251

Southerndown G.C.
(18) 6615 yards
Ewenny, Bridgend
(0656) 880476

Whitehall G.C.
(9) 5750 yards
Nelson, Treharris
(0443) 740245

WEST GLAMORGAN

Clyne G.C.
(18) 6267 yards
118, Owls Lodge Lane, Mayals, Swansea
(0792) 401989

Fairwood Park G. & C.C.
(18) 6606 yards
Upper Killay, Swansea
(0792) 203648

Glynneath G.C.
(9) 5742 yards
Pontneathvaughan, Neath
(0639) 720679

Langland Bay G.C.
(18) 5812 yards
Langland Bay, Swansea
(0792) 66023

Morriston G.C.
(18) 5722 yards
Claremont Rd, Morriston, Swansea
(0792) 796528

Neath G.C.
(18) 6460 yards
Cadoxton, Neath
(0639) 3615

Palleg G.C.
(9) 3209 yards
Lower Cwmtwrch, Swansea
(0639) 842524

Pennard G.C.
(18) 6266 yards
Southgate Road, Southgate, Swansea
(044128) 3131

Pontardawe G.C.
(18) 6061 yards
Cefn Llan, Pontardawe
(0792) 863118

Swansea Bay G.C.
(18) 6302 yards
Jersey Marine, Neath
(0792) 814153

DYFED

Aberystwyth G.C.
(18) 5868 yards
Bryn-y-Mor, Aberystwyth
(0970) 615104

Ashburnham G.C.
(18) 7016 yards
Cliff Terrace, Burry Port
(05546) 2269

Borth and Ynyslas G.C.
(18) 6094 yards
Borth
(097081) 202

Cardigan G.C.
(18) 6207 yards
Gwbert-on-Sea
(0239) 612035

Carmarthen G.C.
(18) 6212 yards
Blaenycoed Road, Carmarthen
(0267) 87214

Glynhir G.C.
(18) 6090 yards
Glynhir Rd, Llandybie, Nr. Ammanford
(0269) 850571

Haverfordwest G.C.
(18) 5945 yards
Arnolds Down, Haverfordwest
(0437) 68409

Lampeter G.C.
(9) 5318 yards
Cilgwyn, Llangbyi, Lampeter
(057045) 286

Milford Haven G.C.
(18) 6235 yards
Hubberton, Milford Haven
(06462) 2521

Newport (Pembs) G.C.
(9) 6178 yards
Newport
(0239) 820244

St. David's City G.C.
(9) 2587 yards
Whitesands Bay Hotel,
St. Davids
(0437) 720403

South Pembrokeshire G.C.
(9) 5804 yards
Defensible Barracks, Pembroke Dock
(0646) 682035

Tenby G.C.
(18) 6232 yards
The Burrows, Tenby
(0834) 2978

POWYS

Brecon G.C.
(9) 5218 yards
Llanfaes, Brecon
(0874) 2004

Builth Wells G.C.
(9) 5458 yards
Builth Wells
(0982) 553296

Cradoc G.C.
(18) 6318 yards
Penoyre Park, Cradoc, Brecon
(0874) 3658

Llandrindod Wells G.C.
(18) 5748 yards
Llandrindod Wells
(0597) 2059

Machynlleth G.C.
(9) 5734 yards
Machynlleth
(0654) 2000

St. Giles G.C.
(9) 5864 yards
Pool Rd, Newtown
(0686) 25844

St. Idloes G.C.
(9) 5210 yards
Penrhalt, Llanidloes
(05512) 2205

Welshpool G.C.
(18) 5708 yards
Golfa Hill, Welshpool
(0938) 3377

NORTH WALES

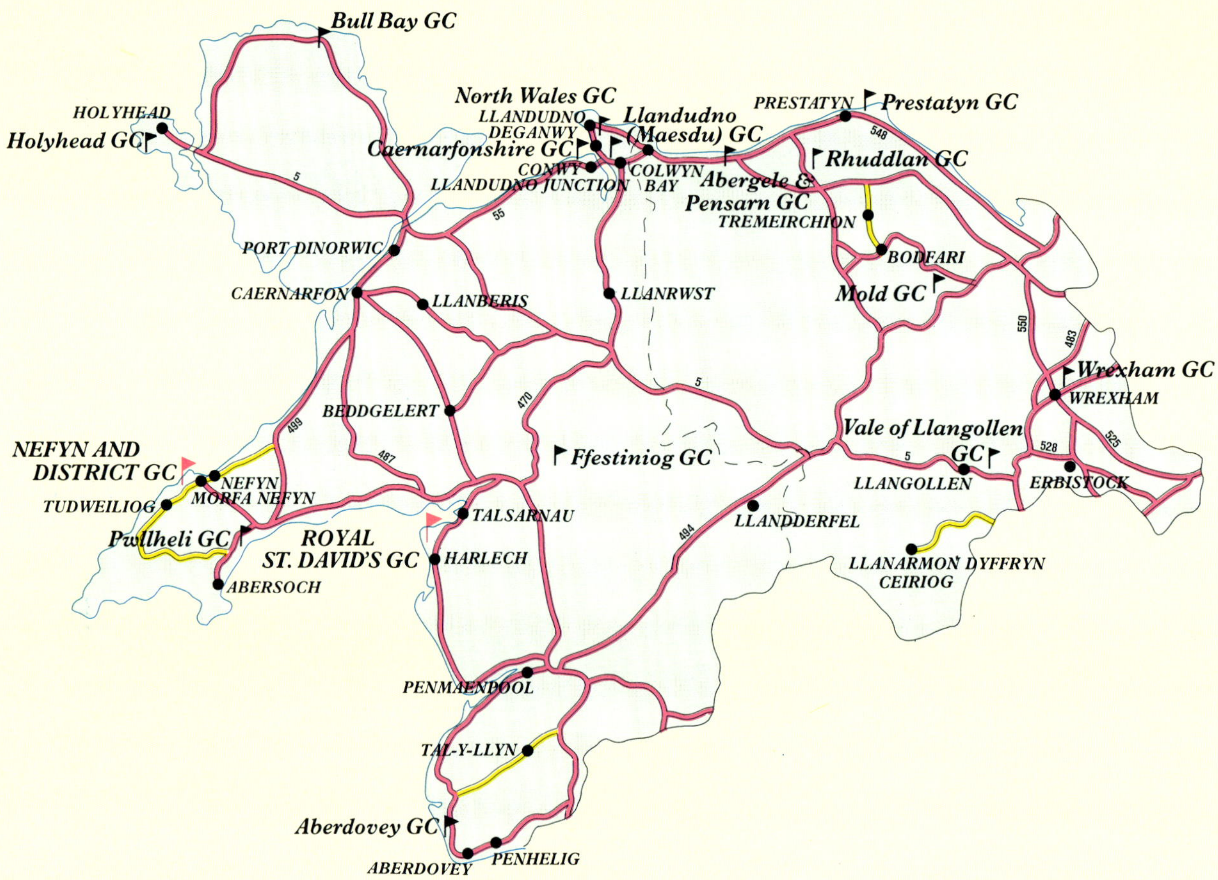

C.E. BROCK "The Bunker" SOTHEBY'S

NORTH WALES
CHOICE GOLF

One's first thoughts of North Wales are often of lakes, great castles and even greater mountains, or as a fine fellow by the name of **Hywell ap Owain**, 12th Century **Prince of Gwynedd**, put it (I offer it in translation):

'I love its sea-marsh and its mountains, And its fortress by its forest and its bright lands, And its meadows and its water and its valleys, And its white seagulls and its lovely women'.

A man who had obviously seen much of the world! Of course in the 12th Century the Welsh didn't play golf, or at least if they did they kept it pretty quiet and in any case you can be pretty confident that Hywell ap Owain would have told us about it. Well, what about the golf in North Wales then? In a word, 'marvellous'. Inland it tends to get hilly to put it mildly, and should you wish to venture up into 'them thar hills' as well as the climbing gear, don't forget to bring the waterproofs! But there again, leave room for the camera (hope you've got a large golf bag).

In the main though, it is to the coast that the travelling golfer will wish to head. Between Flint to the east of Clwyd and Aberdovey in southern Gwynedd are the impressive Championship links of **Prestatyn, Maesdu, North Wales, Conwy, Royal St Davids** and of course **Aberdovey** itself. In addition there are several with spectacular locations, **Nefyn** on the Lleyn Peninsular and **Bull Bay** on Anglesey being two outstanding examples.

CLWYD

Before journeying around the coast though, a brief mention for some of the inland courses, with a few thoughts as to where one might stop off in order to eat, drink or simply rest the weary golf clubs. Away from the sea and sand probably the best two challenges are to be found at **Wrexham** and **Llangollen**. The former, located just off the **A53**, is fairly close to the English border and indeed the views here are across the Cheshire Plain. Two good holes to look out for are the 4th and 14th. Wrexham is a regualr venue for the major Welsh Championships. LLangollen's splendid course, **The Vale of Llangollen**, is set out alongside the banks of the River Dee. There are some truly excellent holes, notably the 9th. Appropriately named the River Hole it is a really tough par four of 425 yards. The golfer who likes a spot of fishing (or perhaps even the golfing fisherman) would be in his element here and on a good day he should see a few of the famous Dee Salmon being landed – probably easier than netting a birdie. Green fees at both courses are around the **£7-£9** mark.

As host to the famous International Eisteddfod Festival Llangollen has long been a popular tourist centre and there are a number of fine hotels in the town including the **Hand (0978) 860303** and the **Royal (0978) 860202**. Also in Llangollen **Gales Wine Bar** is well recommended as is **Caesar's** restaurant **(0978) 860133** with its enterprising menu. Practically midway between Llangollen and Wrexham with a beautiful Deeside setting is the **Boat Inn (0978) 780143** at Erbistock – not quite the first (or is it the last) inn in Wales, but one of the best – especially appealing when floodlit at night. In Wrexham itself, the **Crest Hotel** offers a comfortable forty winks.

Remaining in Clwyd and the unfortunately named town of **Mold**. A pleasant parkland challenge this time and more reaching views, while still further north and getting nearer the coast is the **Rhuddlan Golf Club**. They say you should never rush a round a Rhuddlan. If you are heading for the tougher links courses on the coast then this is the ideal place to 'groove the swing'. The course is laid out in the grounds of Bodrhydden estate and overlooks the Vale of Clwyd. As at Mold visitors should have little trouble arranging a game with the cost of a days golf in the **£8** bracket. Just a couple of thoughts for golfers wishing to wet the whistle; **The Dinorben Arms** at Bodfari and the **Salisbury Arms** at Tremeirchion – two fine hostelries.

Golfwise there is not a great deal more in the deeper realms of North Wales. **Ffestiniog** famed for its mountain railway, has a short nine holes of the moorland variety but the scenery in these parts may prove a little too distracting. Ffestiniog nestles in the heart of Snowdonia and the encircling mountains are quite awe-inspiring. Exploring the countryside is a delight and there is a plentiful supply of country houses and inns to entice the traveller. Somewhat isolated, though quite outstanding, is **Pale Hall (06783) 285** at Llandderfel near Bala (off the **B4401**). Lake Bala is actually not that far away and those who enjoy watersports should take note. Another charming place to rest is the 16th Century **Hand Hotel (069176) 666** at Llanarmon Dyffryn Ceiriog – all wooden beams and roaring fires – wonderful! Time to tear oneself away; the coast beckons and it's time to put that grooved swing into practise.

Prestatyn warrants first attention. Closer to Pontin's holiday camp (or is it village nowadays?) it is a genuine links and when the prevailing westerly blows, can play very long (the Championship tees stretch the course to 6714 yards). Visitors are welcome at Prestatyn though Tuesdays and weekdays can be busy. Fees are **£7** during the week, **£9** at weekends. If a day at Pontin's isn't your cup of tea then the **Sands Hotel (07456) 6471** located in the town is convenient. Thirsty golfers might also find the time to drive 'over the hill' to the village of Gwaenysgor and the **Eagle and Child** pub – good food and good ale.

The **A55** is the coastal road that should be followed to find our next port of call, the **Abergele and Pensarn Golf Club**, just west of Abergele. This course is a fairly new parkland layout (the bulldozer having removed the former) and it lies beneath the walls of Gwyrch Castle. Games are often won or lost on the last three holes at Abergele. The round is supposed to finish five, three, five – but not many scorecards seem to! Again visitors are very welcome, with a days golf priced at **£8** midweek, **£10** at weekends.

GWYNEDD

A trio of Championship courses are to be found a little further along the coast and just over the county border is Gwynedd. Golfers in Llandudno are more fortunate than most, having two fine courses to choose from: **North Wales and Llandudno (Maesdu).** The latter is perhaps the better known of the two but both are of a high standard and each offers superb views across the Conway estuary towards Anglesey. Green fees are approximately **£8-£9**.

The **Caernarvonshire Golf Club** (**£10** at weekends, **£8** midweek), lies the other side of the estuary close to the old walled town of Conway – yet another spectacular siting between the sea and mountains and another course where the wind can blow fiercely. A regular venue of the Welsh Championships, Conwy is generally considered second only to Royal St. Davids in terms of golfing challenges in North Wales. It possesses everything that makes links golf so difficult – gorse, rushes, sandhills and more gorse, rushes and sandhills – quite frightening! Fees are similar to those at the Llandudno courses and although no general restrictions apply, weekdays are inevitably the best times for a visit.

NORTH WALES

CHOICE GOLF

The Llandudno-Conway-Colwyn Bay area is riddled with places of interest and places to stay; indeed it offers a veritable feast for the golfing gourmet. Here are a few thoughts. In Llandudno, famed for its Great Orme, are three excellent hotels, the **Empire (0492) 79955, St Tudno (0492) 74411 and St. George's (0492) 77544** while slightly inland at Deganwy is the renowned 17th Century **Bodysgallen Hall (0492) 84466**. Set amid quite idyllic grounds, the hotel offers great style as well as sumptuous cuisine. Less expensive accomodation can be found at the **Bryn Cregin Garden Hotel (0492) 85266** also in Deganwy and highly recommended. Returning to Llandudno the **Floral** restaurant **(0492) 7573775** has a gregarious atmoshpere and is most pleasing while a pair of pubs whose names you should have little difficulty in remembering are the **Kings Head** and **The Queens Head** the latter a little to the south of the town at Llandudno Junction. Nearby in Conway **The Castle Bank Hotel (0492) 593888** and its restaurant are well thought of and a liquid round can be enjoyed at **The Liverpool Arms** on the quay. There are many attractions in the area;: the great castle of course and the town walls, Bodnant Gardens in the Conwy Valley and even the smallest house in Great Britain. Finally in Colwyn Bay among the many hotels two that merit attention are **The Norfolk House Motel (0492) 531757** and the interestingly named **Hotel Seventy Degrees (0492) 516555**.

Heading for the golf courses of the Lleyn Peninsular, many may wish to break their journey at Caernafon. The castle is splendid and well worth inspecting. Those staying in the area might note that one of the best restaurants in Wales is to be found here – **The Seahorse (0248) 670546** at Port Dinorwic.

I suppose every golfer has at one time or another drawn up a mental listing of his favourite golf courses. Anyone who has made the trip to **Nefyn** is almost certain to have the course high on his list. A sheer delight to play on (See the feature page), Nefyn was a regular haunt of **Lloyd George** as was neighbouring **Pwllheli**, which was in fact opened by him in 1909 when he was the Chancellor of the Exchequer. A true seaside course the fees at Pwllheli are **£7** midweek, **£8** at the weekend.

Handy stop offs for the Nefyn include the **Linksway (0758) 720258, Woodland Hall (0758) 720425** and the **Caeau Capel Hotel (0758) 720240** There are numerous pubs, including the **Ty Coch Inn** on the course itself, and the **Sportsman**. Close by situated right on the cliffs is the provocatively named **Dive Inn (0758) 7246** at Tudweilog, an excellent restaurant. Another pleasant establishment is the lively **Bryncyann Inn (0758) 720879** in Morfa Nefyn. In Pwllheli **The Tower Hotel (0758) 612822** and the **Bel-Air Restaurant (0758) 613198** can be recommended.

A trip to the north west of Wales wouldn't be complete without a visit to Harlech, another great castle and certainly a great golf course, home of course, of the **Royal St. Davids Golf Club**. It is featured on a later page. On the culinary side in Harlech there are two good restaurants, the **Castle Cottage (0766) 780479** (some accommodation) and the **Cemlyn (0766) 780425**, while not far off in Talsarnau is the excellent **Maes-u-Neuadd (0766) 780200** Hotel and restaurant. It enjoys a gloriously peaceful setting with views towards Snowdonia.

Heading further south and passing the friendly **George III Hotel (0341) 4225285** at Penmaenpool, **Aberdovey** is soon reached. The subject of favourite courses has been raised and Aberdovey was the choice of the celebrated golf writer **Bernard Darwin**, 'the course that my soul loves best of all the courses in the world'. It has an interesting layout, sandwiched between the sand dunes on the one side and a railway line on the other, (the railway line in fact links Aberdovey to Harlech and is an excellent service). Golfers ending their journey in Aberdovey will find that the superb **Trefeddian Hotel (065472) 213** is exceptionally convenient for the course.

As an alternative there is the attractive **Hotel Plas Penhelig (065 472) 676** which overlooks the Dovey estuary. In 1992 Aberdovey Golf Club will celebrate its centenary – big celebrations are planned. Already some peculiar things have been taking place involving flower pots and periscopes – I shall say no more other than that visitors are most welcome to come and investigate!

ISLE OF ANGLESEY

The Isle of Anglesey is linked by a road bridge to the mainland across the Menai Straits. There is a choice of four golf courses with perhaps the best two games to be found at **Bull Bay**, near Amlwch, and at **Holyhead** on Holy Island. Both courses are very scenic, especially Bull Bay with its fairly remote location on the northern coast of the island. Bull Bay is a hilly course and with much gorse and several rocks to confront, it can be very tricky. The Club handbook tells how in an exhibition match to mark the opening of the course, featuring John H. Taylor and James Braid, the latter tangled with the gorse on the short third hole and finished up with an eight! The fees at both Bull Bay and Holyhead are fairly inexpensive at around **£5-£7**. Two convenient resting places are the **Bull Bay Hotel (0407) 830223** at Amlwch and the impressive **Trearddur Bay Hotel (0407) 860301** which lies adjacent to the Holyhead Golf Club.

THE BRYN CREGIN GARDEN HOTEL

The Bryn Cregin Garden Hotel was originally built in the 1890's as a fine house for a retiring ship's captain. The good fellow obviously knew what he was doing as he set his home in its own beautiful gardens with panoramic views over the Conwy Estuary, Conwy Castle and the Snowdonia mountains.

We must assume that he was also a keen golfer as the hotel is within two miles of three of North Wales' finest championship courses. Llandudno (Maesdu) and North Wales are on the east shore of the estuary and are kept to a very high standard. Both offer superb views over the water to Anglesea. Opposite, on the West shore, is the famous and sometimes daunting Caernarvonshire course (Conwy). A classic links course with an ample supply of gorse and rushes. Leave your woods in the bag on a windy day!

Today, after extensions in the 30's and a complete refurbishment in the mid 80's, the Bryn Cregin is one of the most finely appointed and comfortable hotels in the area. The hotel has 16 bedrooms all with private bath or shower. Each room has remote control colour TV, direct dial telephone, radio and tea and coffee making facilities. All rooms are individually furnished and decorated to a very high standard and most overlook the estuary and garden.

After a testing day on the course what better than to sit on the terrace, drink in hand, and watch the sun set over Anglesea and Puffin Island. Then bath and change and down to a splendid dinner in our intimate restaurant. A bottle of fine wine from the cellar to accompany the meal and a snifter or two with coffee afterwards why not!

The opening of the North Wales expressway (A55) as dual carriageway as far as Conwy has made getting to this beautiful part of the world very much easier. Well under 2 hours from most parts of Cheshire, Lancashire, the West Midlands and the Yorkshires. Journey time from the home counties is about 4 hours.

At the Bryn Cregin we welcome golfers all year round and can cater for parties up to 25. Our basic package is for two nights dinner, bed and full breakfast and three glorious days of golf. The three courses are featured so you can try them all or master just one. If you want to stay longer that's no problem and you will find welcome reductions for extended holidays.

For long suffering nongolfers there is ample to do and see in the local area. Riding, Hill walking visiting the wealth of National Trust properties and gardens or just taking in the wonderful scenery.

Please write or call for a free illustrated brochure.

The Bryn Cregin Garden Hotel
Ty Mawr Road
Deganwy
Nr Conwy
Gwynedd Ll31 9UR
Tel: (0492) 85266 & 83402

ROYAL ST. DAVIDS

CHAMPIONSHIP GOLF

With a St. Andrews in Scotland and a **St. Georges** in England, it seems only right that there should be a **St. David's** in Wales. Along with Royal Porthcawl in the South, the **Royal St. David's Golf Club** at **Harlech** is one of the Principality's two greatest Championship links.

The Club was founded in **1894** by **the Hon. Harold Finch-Hatton** together with **Mr. W.H. More** who for twenty years acted as Honorary Secretary. The course itself was open for play at the end of 1894 and the opening competition was fittingly won by the greatest golfer of the day, and the then reigning Amateur Champion, **John Ball**. St. David's became 'Royal' St David's early this century and in 1935 **The Duke of Windsor** (then Prince of Wales), became the Club's captain.

Of its many attributes St David's is perhaps best known for its glorious setting: on the one side stretch the blue waters of Tremedog Bay, and on the other the imperious Snowdon and the other great mountains of Snowdonia National Park; while surveying all from its lofty perch is the almost forbidding presence of Harlech Castle. The massive fortress built by Edward I has known a particularly turbulent past. It played a prominent role in the War of the Roses when a great seige took place eventually ending in surrender. The seige is commemorated in the song 'Men of Harlech'.

The present 'Men of Harlech' to whom I should introduce you are the Secretary, **Mr Harry Fairbrother** and the Club's professional **John Barnett**. Both may be contacted by telephone on **(0766) 780361**. The Club has the simple address of **Royal St David's Golf Club, Harlech, Gwynedd, LL46 2UB** (very simple by Welsh standards!)

St David's has a reputation for being one of Britain's friendliest Clubs; subject to being Members of Golf Clubs **visitors** and Golfing **Societies** are welcome at all times although those wishing to make party bookings must do so by written application to the Secretary. The cost of a day's golf in 1989 was set at **£12** during the week with **£14** payable at the weekend and on Bank Holidays. For junior golfers, the corresponding figures were **£6** and **£7** respectively.

The setting is indeed superb but the journey to get there can be a lengthy one – Harlech alas isn't like the proverbial Rome and there is one road that travellers must join, namely the **A496**. From the North this road approaches from **Blaenau Ffestiniog** via **Maentwrog (east of Porthmadog)** and from the South via **Dolgellau** and **Barmouth**. Those coming from further afield may find **Bala** (if travelling from the north) and **Welshpool** (if motoring from the south) useful towns to head for. Bala links with Maentwrog by way of the **A4212** and the **A487**, while the **A458** and **A470** link Welshpool to Barmouth. Finally, for those without horsepower, the train station at Harlech may prove of assistance.

Measuring **6495** yards from the Championship tees (**6427** yards from the medal tees) St David's may not at first glance seem overly testing. However the general consensus is that the course, to adopt golfers' terminology, plays long. Par is a very tight **69** and there are only two par fives on the card. Furthermore the rough can be very punishing (not to mention frustrating) and it is very rare for there not to be a stiff wind. It is interesting to note that despite countless Championships the course record stands at only three under par.

Perhaps the most difficult holes on the course are the **10th**, a long par four into the prevailing wind, and the **15th** which requires quite a lengthy carry. The round finishes with, to adopt another curious golfing expression, 'a nasty long short hole.'

As one might imagine, each of the major Welsh Championships is staged regularly at St David's; in addition the **Ladies British Open Amateur Championship** and both Mens and Ladies **Home International Matches** have also been played at Harlech.

The nineteenth at St David's matches the high standards set by the previous eighteen. There is an excellent bar (for celebration or recuperation) and light snacks, lunches and dinners are all offered. With prior warning a full English (or should one say Welsh?) breakfast can also be arranged.

The friendliness of the Club has already been mentioned; unfortunately there are some English who consider the Welsh a little insular – a visit to Royal St David's can make one realise that the Welsh Golf Clubs could teach many of their English counterparts a thing or two...and on that controversial note, I wish you good golfing!

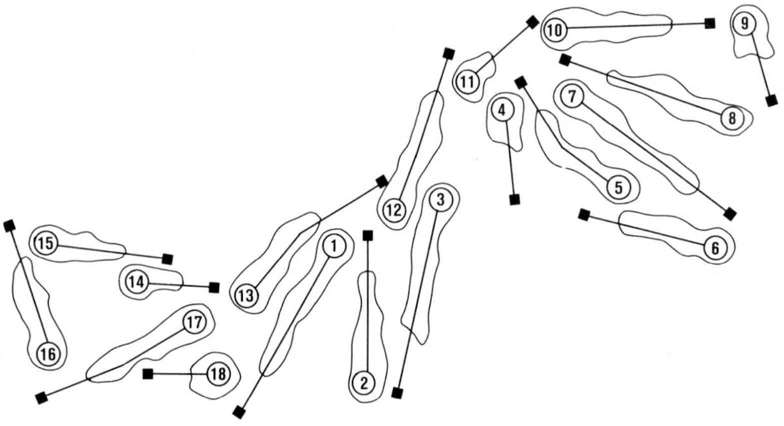

Hole	Yards	Par	Hole	Yards	Par
1	436	4	10	458	4
2	373	4	11	144	3
3	463	4	12	437	4
4	188	3	13	451	4
5	393	4	14	218	3
6	371	4	15	427	4
7	481	5	16	354	4
8	499	5	17	427	4
9	173	3	18	202	3
Out	3,377	36	In	3,118	33
			Out	3,377	36
			TOTALS	6,495	69

NEFYN
CHAMPIONSHIP GOLF

We golfers in Britain are doubly fortunate – not only do we have an infinite variety of courses to play upon (contrast for instance the Surrey heathland with the Scottish links), but we also possess a wealth of outstandingly scenic courses. Perhaps one of our lesser known treasures is perched on the cliffs of North Wales' western tip. Nefyn, or more precisely **Nefyn and District**, was founded in **1907**, although the course really came into its own in **1920** when an extension was opened by **James Braid and John H. Taylor** (where was Harry you ask!)

I suppose Nefyn could be described as a 'classic holiday course'; there is a very pleasant drive to the Club (which is probably just as well as it is quite a way off the beaten track). The course is always well maintained with particularly pleasing fairways; whilst the golf is by no means easy, it is never too severe or unfair (indeed, unless the wind blows fiercely, good scores should definitely appear on the cards); the views as mentioned are quite stupendous and Good Lord to cap it all, there is even a pub two thirds of the way round! Well, what more could a golfer ask for?

Visitors to Nefyn must be prepared to produce a handicap certificate and be a member of a recognised Club. Should there be a wish to contact the Club before setting off then the **Secretary, Lt. Col. R.W. Parry** can be contacted via **The Nefyn & District Golf Club, MorfaNefyn, Pwllheli, N. Wales, tel. (0758) 720966** and the **professional, John Pilkington** on **(0758) 720218. Green fees** for**1989** were very reasonably priced at **£10** for **weekdays** with **£12** payable at **weekends** and **Bank Holidays**. Those holidaying close by may well be interested in a **weekly** ticket. In **1989** this cost **£50** – particularly attractive to the serious connoisseur who has a little time onhis hands. Keen competitors may well wish to note that the Club stages**open events** annually during the first fortnight in **August**. **Societies** are welcome at Nefyn although prior arrangement with the secretaryis necessary.

A glance at the map tells you that this part of the world is not particularly well served with major roads (although this doubtless contibutes to the area's natural beauty). Visitors from afar are more than likely to have planned some kind of golfing holiday and so it is to be assumed that the traveller is already in North Wales. Coming from the Colwyn Bay, Llandudno area one should take the **A55** towards Bangor. Then from Bangor head for Caernafon on the **A487** and just beyond Caernafon take the **A499** and the **B4417** roads through Nefyn to Morfa Nefyn. From the South the **A497** connects Pwllheli with Nefyn.

From the back markers Nefyn stretches to **6335 yards** and has a par of **72**. Ian Woosnam, the Welsh Ryder Cup player, holds the professional course record of **67**. I am reliably informed that another model of Welsh consistency, **Lloyd-George**, was a frequent visitor to Nefyn and that this trend was in turn followed up by **Clement Attlee** – who doubtless found the golf here a welcome diversion from the pressures of No. 10.

During the high season it is possible to acquire the services of a caddy. The course is hardly an endurance test, but perhaps this might be the place to spoil yourself and let some healthy young lad take the weight off your shoulders as you delight in the splendid surroundings.

After a lengthy opener which certainly invites a hearty belt from the tee (sorry, controlled power) the course moves out along by the cliff edges for a number of spectacular holes. It then turns back on itself before heading in a different direction out on to a headland where holes **11** to **18** are found. There is no real place on the course where you lose sight of the sea and you may just encounter the occasional sunbather who has lost his or her way. If the holiday mood really takes you, then down in a cove by the **12th green** is the **Ty Coch Inn**. Yes, it is accessible from the course and on a really hot summer's day can doubtless be mistaken for a heavenly mirage. One cannot help wondering how many steady score cards have suddenly taken on erratic proportions from the 13th hole in!

Returning to the Clubhouse you will find that full catering facilities are offered. There is a snooker room and a genuinely pleasant atmosphere in which to relax and reflect on your day. Well, if you have not enjoyed your golf at Nefyn then I must venture to suggest that you are a very difficult person to please!

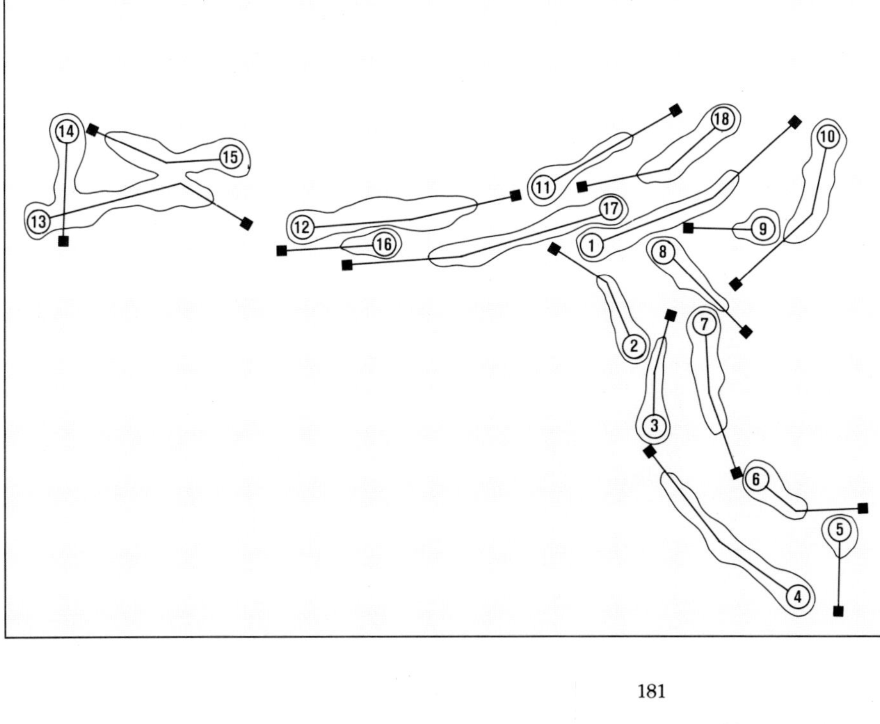

Hole	Yards	Par	Hole	Yards	Par
1	458	4	10	415	4
2	361	4	11	323	4
3	380	4	12	478	5
4	486	5	13	415	4
5	156	3	14	165	3
6	330	4	15	328	4
7	532	5	16	172	3
8	322	4	17	526	5
9	163	3	18	325	4
Out	3,188	36	In	3,147	36
			Out	3,188	36
			TOTALS	6,335	72

PALE HALL

Built in 1870 for a wealthy railway engineer, Pale Hall has recently been converted to a luxurious and exquisite hotel. It has however, retained all its finest original Victorian features.

The most interesting of all these must surely be the original barn and adjoining bedroom used by Queen Victoria during her stay at Pale Hall for a short time after Prince Albert's death. Then there is the 'boudoir', a beautiful interior boasts a magnificent hand painted dome ceiling and the Corwen Bar where one can see the unusual bar made from the marble firplaces that have been removed from the bedrooms.

Each of the seventeen bedrooms are individually designed and finished to compliment their own particular features. It is this fine attention to detail that makes Pale Hall so interestingly unique. Despite its strong historical identity, however, it still provides all the home comforts of the present day subtly blended into this fine regal setting.

The restaurant and its cuisine is also of an exceptionally high standard. Interestingly, breakfast and morning coffee is served in the Bala Kitchen, which is still enhanced by its original cooking range from the late nineteenth century.

From the building and its grounds, spectacular views can be enjoyed. Here you can walk in solitude, sail serene waters, shoot, fish or enjoy a round of golf. Whatever your interests the Welsh hospitality will ensure a relaxing visit.

Pale Hall
Llandderfel
Nr Bala
Gwynedd
Tel: (06783) 285

NORTH WALES
COMPLETE GOLF

CLWYD

Abergele & Pensarn G.C.
(18) 6086 yards
Tan-y-Goppa Rd, Abergele
(0745) 824034

Denbigh G.C.
(9) 5650 yards
Henllan Rd, Denbigh
(074571) 4159

Flint G.C.
(9) 5829 yards
Cornist Park, Flint
(03526) 2327

Hawarden G.C.
(9) 5735 yards
Groomsdale Lane, Hawarden
(0244) 531447

Holywell G.C.
(9) 6484 yards
Brynford, Holywell
(0352) 710040

Mold G.C.
(18) 5521 yards
Pantmywyn, Nr. Mold
(0352) 740318

Old Colwyn G.C.
(9) 5268 yards
Old Colwyn, Colwyn Bay
(0492) 515581

Old Padeswood G.C.
(18) 6728 yards
Station Rd, Padeswood, Mold
(0244) 547401

Padeswood & Buckley G.C.
(18) 5746 yards
Station Lane, Padeswood, Mold
(0244) 542537

Prestatyn G.C.
(18) 6714 yards
Marine Rd. East, Prestatyn
(07456) 88353

Rhuddlan G.C.
(18) 6038 yards
Rhuddlan, Rhyl
(0745) 590675

Rhyl G.C.
(9) 6057 yards
Coast Rd, Rhyl
(0745) 53171

Ruthin-Pwllglas G.C.
(9) 5306 yards
Ruthin-Pwllglas, Ruthin
(08242) 4658

St. Melyd G.C.
(9) 5805 yards
Melyden Rd, Prestatyn
(07456) 88858

Vale of Llangollen G.C.
(18) 6617 yards
Holyhead Rd, Llangollen
(0978) 860050

Wrexham G.C.
(18) 5868 yards
Holt Rd, Wrexham
(0978) 364268

GWYNEDD

Aberdovey G.C.
(18) 6421 yards
Aberdovey
(065472) 493

Abersoch G.C.
(9) 5722 yards
Pwllheli, Abersoch
(075881) 2622

Bala G.C.
(10) 4934 yards
Penlan, Bala
(0678) 520359

Betws-y-Coed G.C.
(9) 4996 yards
Betws-y-Coed
(06902) 556

Caernarfon G.C.
(18) 5859 yards
Llanfaglan, Caernarfon
(0286) 3555

Caernarfonshire G.C.
(18) 6723 yards
Conway
(0492) 592423

Criccieth G.C.
(18) 5755 yards
Ednyfed Hill, Criccieth
(076671) 2154

Dolgellau G.C.
(9) 4662 yards
Pencefn Rd, Dolgellau
(0341) 422603

Ffestiniog G.C.
(9) 4536 yards
Blaenau Ffestiniog
(076) 676 2612

Llandudno (Maesdu) G.C.
(18) 6513 yards
Hospital Rd, Llandudno
(0492) 76450

Llanfairfechan G.C.
(9) 3119 yards
Llanfairfechan
(0248) 680144

Nefyn and District G.C.
(18) 6335 yards
Morfa Nefyn
(0758) 720966

North Wales G.C.
(18) 6132 yards
Bryniau Rd, West Shore, Llandudno
(0492) 75325

Penmaenmawr G.C.
(9) 5031 yards
Conway Old Road, Penmaenmawr
(0492) 622085

Portmadoc G.C.
(18) 5728 yards
Morfa Bychan, Portmadoc
(0766) 2037

Pwllheli G.C.
(18) 6110 yards
Golf Rd, Pwllheli
(0758) 612520

Royal St. David's G.C.
(18) 6495 yards
Harlech
(0766) 780361

St. Deiniol G.C.
(18) 5545 yards
Bangor
(0248) 353098

ISLE OF ANGLESEY

Anglesey G.C.
(18) 6204 yards
Rhosneigr
(0407) 810219

Baron Hill G.C.
(9) 5564 yards
Beaumaris
(0248) 810231

Bull Bay G.C.
(18) 6160 yards
Almwch
(0407) 830960

Holyhead G.C.
(18) 6090 yards
Trearddur Bay
(0407) 3279

Artist : ***Spelter FIGURE OF A GOLFER*** *Courtesy of : The Burlington Gallery*

DUMFRIES & GALLOWAY AND BORDERS

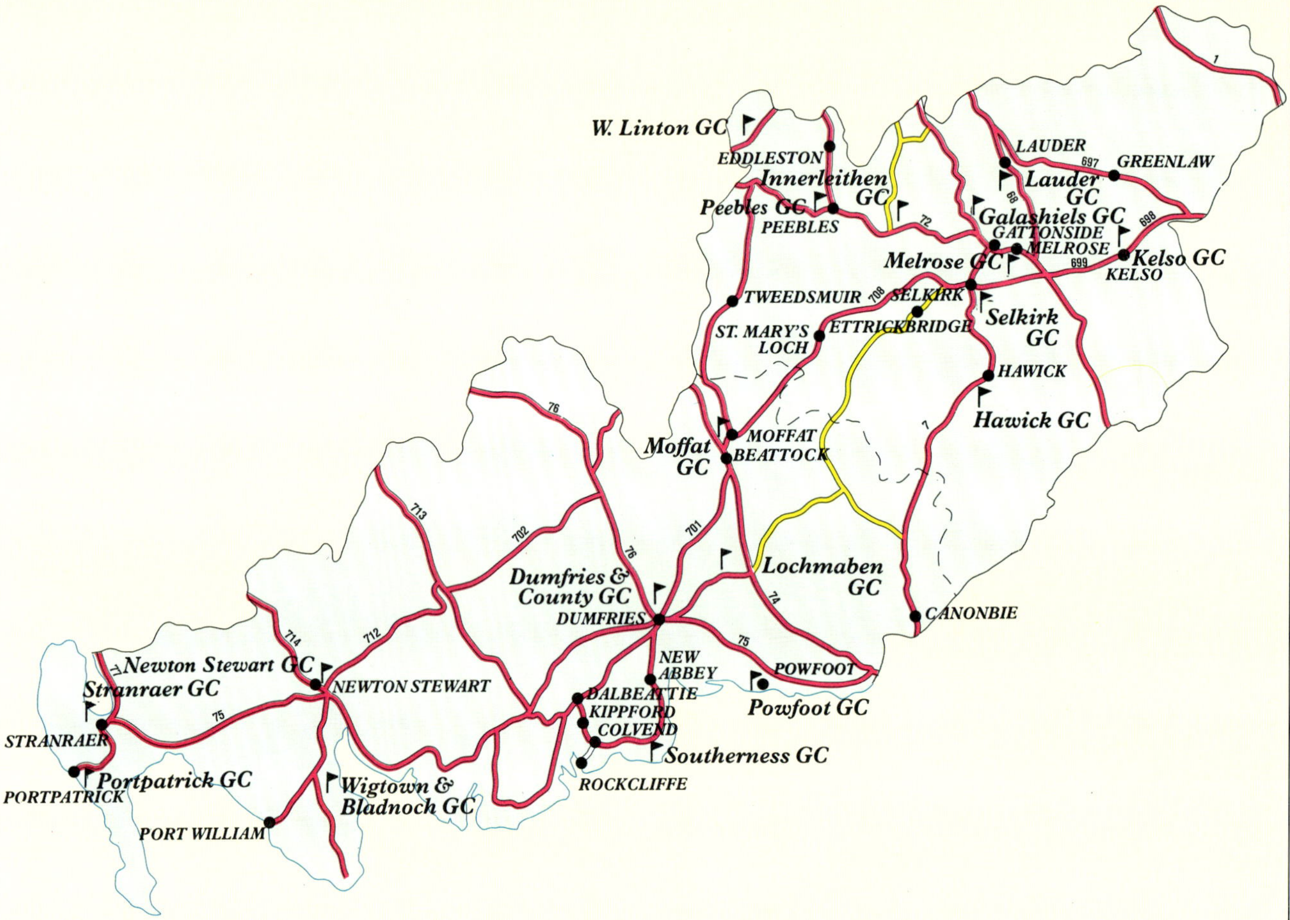

SAM GARRATT "Peebles" BURLINGTON GALLERY

DUMFRIES & GALLOWAY AND BORDERS

CHOICE GOLF

Two of Britain's greatest (and least explored) links courses stare at one another across the Solway Firth – one is on the 'English side' at Silloth and the other lies north of the border at Southerness. As close as they appear on the map, the only way of travelling from one to the other is by a fairly lengthy drive around the coast via Gretna Green. Before the War, a bridge crossed the Solway, but before the **War Southerness** didn't have a golf course.

The two modern counties of Dumfries and Galloway and Borders (bit of a mouthful? – try the old Dumfrieshire, Kirkudbrightshire, Wigtwonshire, Berwickshire, Peebleshire, Roxburghshire and Selkirkshire) encompass most of the Scottish Lowlands. A beautiful area of Britain – as of course is most of Scotland – but not one terribly renowned for its golf. However, even excluding Southerness there are a number of superb courses, many are outstandingly scenic and because the great hordes head for Turnberry, Gleneagles and St Andrews, wonderfully uncrowded.

DUMFRIES & GALLOWAY

Situated 16 miles south of Dumfries off the **A710 Southerness** is the only Championship links in Great Britain to have been built since 1945. Not only is it the finest course in the far South of Scotland, but it has also quickly acquired a reputation that is the envy of many of the country's more famous Championship courses. Very much a natural links, designed by Mackenzie Ross (architect of Turnberry) it stretches to **6,548** yards from the medal tees making it a very tough par **69**. Visitors are always welcome (societies also by arrangement with the Secretary) the green fees being **£10** per day during the week, **£10** at weekends and **£40** for a full week's golf.

Two convenient resting places after a game at Southerness are in Rockliffe, **The Baron's Craig Hotel (055663) 225** and a little closer in Colvend, **The Clonyard House (055663) 372**. Good eating places include, **The Abbey Arms** and **The Griffel Inn**, both in New Abbey, and **The Pheasant** in Dalbeattie. Powfoot has **The Golf Hotel (04617) 254** while not too close, but a splendid place to visit all the same is Canonbie, here the restaurant at the **Riverside Inn (05415) 512** is exceptional and some reasonable bedrooms are also available.

Powfoot is a fairly close neighbour of Southerness (though again not by road) the course lying 5 miles west of Annan off the **B724**. A 'semi-links', measuring **6,283** yards, the course is quite undulating and provides extensive views towards the Cumberland Hills to the south and the Galloway Hills to the West. Visitors should be able to get a game here most days, the only general restriction being at weekends before 10-30am and between 12.30pm and 2.45pm. Fees at Powfoot are **£8** per round, **£10** per day.

Nearby there are two eighteen hole courses at Dumfries, **Dumfries and County**, to the north of the town perhaps being the pick of the two, but golfers travelling north would do well to pay **Lochmaben** a visit. It is a very friendly Club with an interesting 9 hole course designed by James Braid. The setting around the Kirk Loch is most picturesque, and the course is famed for its many beautiful old trees. A days golf at Lochmaben can be enjoyed for just **£5**.

When inspecting any of the above courses Dumfries is a likely base, here **The Cairndale Hotel (0387) 54111** is most pleasant. Other recommended establishments nearby include **The Dryfesdale (05762) 2427** in Lockerbie and **The Lockerbie House Country Hotel (05762) 2610**. Also note the **Barjarg Tower (0848) 31545** at Auldgirth, an excellent 16th century country house hotel.

Towards the western corner of Dumfries and Galloway there is some more marvellous golf. Two nine hole courses well worth playing are at Wigtown, **Wigtown and Bladnoch** to be precise, and at **Newton Stewart**. Still further west, **Stranraer**, the ferry terminal for Larne, has a fine parkland course north of the town at **Portpatrick**, rated by many to be one of the most beautiful courses in Britain. Gretna Green was mentioned in the opening paragraph, apparently Portpatrick was for many years in the last century Ireland's Gretna Green – couples sailing across the Irish Sea to get 'hitched' in Portpatrick's tiny church. The golf course provides some breathtaking scenery, particularly outstanding is the view from the 13th fairway. It can often get quite breezy and although only 5,644 yards in length, the course is certainly no pushover. Visitors are always welcome, fees being **£8** weekdays, **£10** at weekends.

Superb golf is accompanied by an exceptional number of first rate hotels. In Newton Stewart, the **Kirroughtree Hotel (0671) 2141** is outstanding, while more modest but still welcoming is **The Bruce (0671) 2294**. Port William offers the very fine **Corsemalzie House Hotel (09886) 254** while a number of alternatives are found at Portpatrick. Pick of an excellent bunch is **The Knockinaam Lodge Hotel (077681) 471** a glorious setting and a really tremendous restaurant. Others to note here are **The Fernhill (0877681) 220** and **The Portpatrick Hotel (077681) 333**. Word has it **The Crown** is the place for a pint.

BORDERS

Having sampled the delights of the coast of Southern Scotland one may head inland to the delights of the Border towns. En route, **Moffat** is an excellent golfcourse which has a gorgeous setting in the valley of Allandale and **The Black Bull** is well worth a visit. People wishing to stay in the area may wish to consider **The Auchen Castle Hotel (068 33) 407** in Beattock (good value and a pleasant setting). The Border towns offer castles aplenty, some superb woollens and some excellent rugby. Golfwise, no course here could claim to be of Championship proportions, however, the majority can boast spectacular settings, visitors are always welcome and the green fees in these parts are just about the cheapest in Britain – a full day's golf normally possible for less than **£7**.

A cluster of courses are to be found in the centre of the County. The town of **Melrose** is famed for its ruined Abbey where the heart of Robert The Bruce is said to have been buried (gruesome stuff!) It has a fine nine hole course and there are others equally pleasant at **Selkirk, Harwick, Lauder and Innerliethan.** The 18 hole course at **Kelso** has an interesting layout being inside Kelso racecourse. Finally well worth noting are **Peebles and Galashiels** – both are public courses, very well maintained and true to form set amidst some magnificent countryside.

Walter Scott's land really does deserve a lengthy inspection. This alas isn't the place but whether one is golfing in the Borders or simply breaking a journey, here are some ideas. In Peebles, two excellent hotels, **Cringletie House Hotel (0721) 3233** and **The Peebles Hotel Hydro (0721) 20602**. Golfers who like a spot of fishing should also note **The Tweed Valley Hotel (089687) 220** in nearby Walkerburn. St Mary's Loch offers **The Tiblie Meils Inn (0750) 42231** and Tweedsmuir the cosy **Crook Inn (03997) 272. Ettrickshaws (0759) 52229** In Ettrickbridge is first class as is **The Sun Laws House Hotel (05735) 331** in Kelso on the banks of the Teviot. In Melrose a notable small hotel is **Barts (089682) 2285** while that other historic town Selkirk offers **The Philipburn Hotel (0759) 20747**.

*Artist : **J. Reid TOM MORRIS** Courtesy of : The Burlington Gallery*

BARJARG TOWER

Bajarg Tower means 'The Red Hill Top Fort'. The original Peel Tower, which now forms the north east corner of the house was built in the 16th century. Barjarg Tower has been converted by its present owners, Mary and Archie Donaldson, into a small but lavishly appointed hotel, where guests are offered personal service and fine food in a tranquil and luxurious setting.

Standing in grounds of some 40 acres, the hotel contains several gracious public rooms, ideal for those who seek a degree of privacy and excellent for small conferences and meetings. In the handsome oak panelled dining room the emphasis is on fine food, good wine and personal, friendly service. The cooking is classic in style, with all dishes being prepared in the hotel's own kitchen using mostly local produce, such as game from the Barjarg Estate, salmon from the River Nith, Galloway beef and, whenever possible, locally grown vegetables. There is an extensive and carefully chosen wine list, with a particularly good selection of chateau-bottled claret. Selected to suit all tastes, it ranges from simple table wines to famous vintages. Since the daughter of the house is a vegetarian, guests who prefer not to eat meat or fish can, provided reasonable notice is given, be catered for.

Each of the 8 beautifully appointed double bedrooms has a spacious private bathroom, while all bedrooms offer such facilities as direct-dial telephone, colour television, trouser presses and hairdryers.

The hotel is surrounded by beautiful Dumfriesshire, which offers a wide variety of places of interest for visitors, such as Drumlanrig Castle, the ancestral home of the Duke of Buccleuch, and the home of Robert Burns, as well as a fair number of excellent golf courses. Barjarg Tower makes a ideal setting for an extremely comfortable and enjoyable holiday.

Barjarg Tower Country House Hotel
Auldgirth
Dumfriesshire
DG2 0TN
Tel: 0848 31545 Fax: 0848 30918

KNOCKINAAM LODGE HOTEL

KNOCKINAAM
LODGE
HOTEL

Knockinaam was built as a holiday house for Lady Hunter Blair in 1869 and enlarged in 1901. The house stands in a secluded enclave at the foot of a deep and thickly wooded glen, surrounded on three sides by sheltering cliffs and looking out to sea. A beautiful garden with wide lawns runs down to a private sandy beach where guests can enjoy magnificent views of the distant Irish coastline, the changing moods of sea and sky, and stupendous sunsets. Indeed, such is the timeless traquility of this extraordinary place, that Sir Winston Churchill chose it during the Second World War for a secret meeting with General Eisenhower and their Chiefs of Staff.

In 1971, the house was bought by a French chef, who converted it into a 'restaurant avec chambres' and quickly established a reputation for the finest cooking in the south of Scotland. This reputation has been assiduously maintained and today, you can sit in the attractive dining room with the sea breaking over the rocks at the end of the lawn and dine on the tender Galloway beef – surely the best in the world? – fresh lobsters, scallops, scampi, and many other locally produced delicacies, including home grown vegetables. In cooler weather, log fires burn in the public rooms and there is full central heating throughout the house. Small business meetings can be accommodated during the autumn.

Knockinaam is an ideal base for exploring this little known and unspoiled corner of Scotland. Quaint villages, early Christian sites, ruined and still inhabited castles, standing stones dot an undulating green landscpae, dissected by rough, dry stone walls and twisting single track roads. The unusually mild climate engendered by the Gulf Stream can support almost every species of tropical plant and there are many famous gardens within easy reach. There are two excellent golf courses close to the hotel, and world famous Turnberry is less than an hour's drive. Further inland, forests of spruce and larch lead into vast tracts of wild country, easily accessible by car or on foot, where a wonderful variety of wild game abounds amongst lochs, rivers and tawny hills.

Knockinaam offers its visitors the chance to escape from the pressures of the outside world, to shed cares and restore neglected values. The passage of time has left the holiday house atmosphere intact, and those romantic qualities that Sir Winston Churchill appreciated, remain unchanged.

The resident owners, Marcel and Corina Frichot and their attentive young staff, look forward to welcoming you to this unique and unforgettable place.

Knockinaam Lodge Hotel
Portpatrick
Wigtownshire
Scotland DG9 9AD
Tel: (077681) 471

DUMFRIES & GALLOWAY AND BORDERS

COMPLETE GOLF

BORDERS

Duns G.C.
(9) 5826 yards
Hardens Road, Duns
(0361) 83327

Eyemouth G.C.
(9) 5446 yards
Gunsgreen House, Eyemouth
(08907) 50551

Galashiels G.C.
(18) 5309 yards
Ladhope Recreation Ground, Lalashiels
(0896) 3724

Hawick G.C.
(18) 5929 yards
Vertish Hill, Hawick
(0450) 72293

Innerliethen G.C.
(9) 5802 yards
Innerliethen Water
(0896) 830951

Jedburgh G.C.
(9) 5520 yards
Dunion Road, Jedburgh
(0835) 63770

Kelso G.C.
(18) 6066 yards
Racecourse Road, Kelso
(0573) 23009

Lauder G.C.
(9) 6002 yards
Galashiels Road, Lauder
(05782) 381

Melrose G.C.
(9) 5464 yards
Dingleton, Melrose
(089682) 2811

Minto G.C.
(18) 5460 yards
Minto Village, Denholm, Hawick
(0450) 72267

Peebles G.C.
(18) 6137 yards
Kirkland Street, Peebles
(0721) 20153

St. Boswells G.C.
(9) 5054 yards
St. Boswells
(0835) 22359

Selkirk G.C.
(9) 5560 yards
The Hill, Selkirk
(0750) 20621

West Linton G.C.
(18) 5835 yards
West Linton
(0968) 60256

DUMFRIES & GALLOWAY

Castle Douglas G.C.
(9) 5408 yards
Abercromby Road, Castle Douglas
(0556) 2801

Colvend G.C.
(9) 4208 yards
Sandyhills, Dalbeattie
(055663) 398

Dumfries & County G.C.
(18) 5914 yards
Edinburgh Road, Dunfries
(0387) 62045

Dumfries & Galloway G.C.
(18) 5782 yards
Laurieston Avenue, Dumfries
(0387) 63848

Kirkcudbright G.C.
(18) 5598 yards
Stirling Crescent, Kirkcudbright
(0557) 30542

Lochmaben G.C.
(9) 5338 yards
Castlehill Gate, Lochmaben
(038781) 0552

Lockerbie G.C.
(9) 5228 yards
Currie Road, Lockerbie
(05762) 2165

Moffatt G.C.
(18) 5218 yards
Coateshill, Moffatt
(06833) 20020

Newton Stewart G.C.
(9) 5512 yards
Newton Stewart
(0671) 2172

Portpatrick (Dunskey) G.C.
(18) 5644 yards + (9) 1442 yards
Portpatrick, Stranraer
(0776) 83215

Powfoot G.C.
(18) 6283 yards
Cummertrees, Annan
(04612) 2866

Sanquhar G.C.
(9) 5144 yards
Old Barr Road, Sanquhar
(06592) 577

Southerness G.C.
(18) 6548 yards
Southerness
(038766) 677

Stranraer G.C.
(18) 6300 yards
Creachmore, Stranraer
(0776) 87245

Thornhill G.C.
(18) 6011 yards
Blacknest, Thornhill
(0848) 30546

Wigtown & Bladnoch G.C.
(9) 5462 yards
Lighhands Avenue, Wigtown
(09884) 3354

Wigtownshire County G.C.
(9) 5826 yards
Mains of Park, Glenluce
(05813) 420

N. ARTHUR LORRAINE "A Mixed Foursome" *BURLINGTON GALLERY*

LOTHIAN

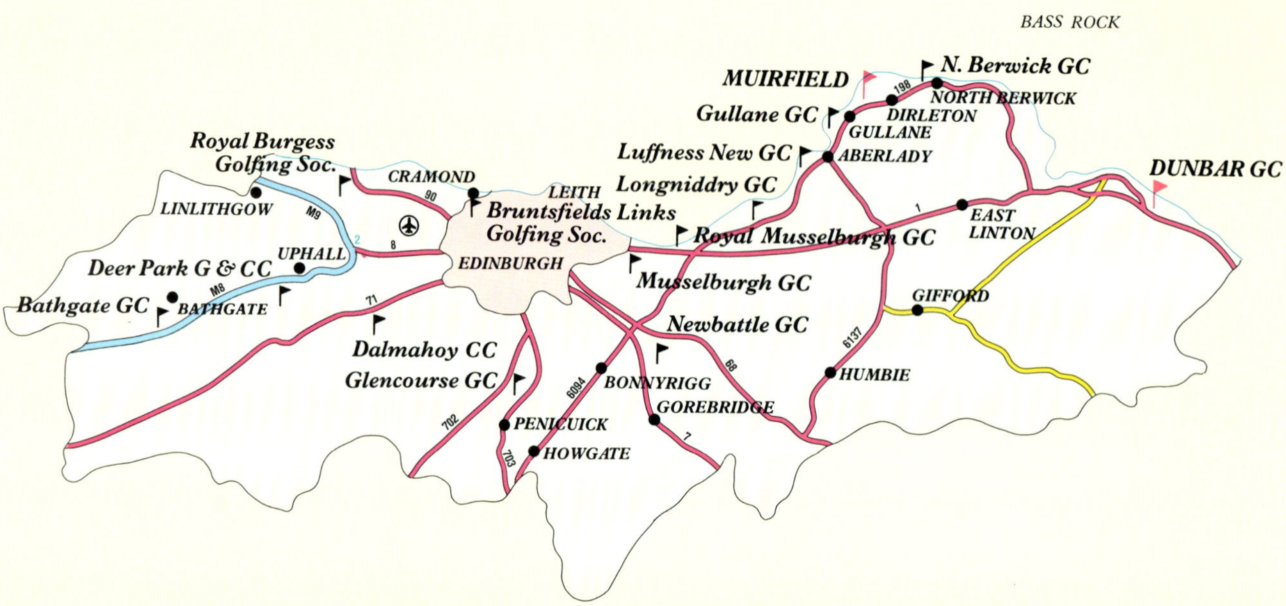

SCOTTISH SCHOOL "Leith Links" BURLINGTON GALLERY

LOTHIAN

CHOICE GOLF

'Hard by in the fields called the links, the citizens of Edinburgh divert themselves at a game called golf, in which they use a curious kind of bat tipt with horn and a small elastic ball of leather stuffed with feathers rather less than tennis balls, but out of a much harder consistency and this they strike with such force and dexterity that it will fly to an incredible distance'.

When a gentleman by the name of **Tobias Smollett** wrote these words in **1771** golf had already been played in the 'fields' around Edinburgh for at least three hundred years. The seemingly harmless pastime wasn't always popular with the authorities. In 1593 the Town Council of Edinburgh deplored the fact that a great number of its inhabitants chose to spend the Sabbath in the town of Leith where 'in tyme of sermons' many were 'sene in the streets, drynking in taverns, or otherwise at Golf'. Shame on them!

Visitors to the beautiful City of Edinburgh, the so called 'Athens of the North', should have little trouble getting a game on one of the many nearby courses. Quite in contrast it must be said to the problems the stranger is likely to encounter when turning up in Glasgow. To the west of the City lie a particularly historic pair – **Bruntsfield Links** and **Royal Burgess**: between them they have witnessed nearly 500 years of golfing history. Both receive visitors although prior telephoning is essential as a number of restrictions apply. Weekday afternoons are likely to be the best times for arranging a game, with fees approximatley **£18**.

The **Dalmahoy Country Club** situated to the west of the City nestles at the base of the Pentland Hills and has two excellent 18 hole courses. The East Course which measures close to 6,700 yards has been the venue for many important Championships. Visitors are welcome here on any day of the week, green fees being **£10** midweek, **£12** at weekends. (Note the excellent **hotel** here **(031) 333 1845**.

Spending a few days in Edinburgh is a real treat whether one is a golfer or not. There is a wealth of things to do and places to see. The solemn castle looks down but one is forced to admire the outstanding fortress – home of the Military Tattoo, The National Gallery, Holyrood Palace, the bustle of Princes Street and its excellent shopping and in summer the Edinburgh Festival, the whole city seems to become a theatre – contrasting with the morning of the rugby international at Murrayfield, theatricals of another kind but no less marvellous to be a part of. The city's most outstanding hotel is **The Caledonian 031-225 2433** situated at the west end of Princes Street. The hotel's **Pompadour Restaurant** is quite superb. Although the hotel is most distinguished it does organise weekend breaks – excellent value. Among the many other hotels **The Sheraton 031-229 9131** is superbly relaxing albeit modern while **The George 031-225 1251** is another most impressive edifice. The city is as well blessed with restaurants as it is with hotels. These are some of the many to consider: **Aye 031-320 1238** is an outstanding Japanese restaurant (visting golfers from the Orient who have become a touch homesick please note); **La Caveau 031-556 5707** and **L'auberge 031 556 5888** will delight lovers of French food, while those who prefer pasta should sample **Cosmo 031 226 6743**.

The courses of West Lothian are not as well known as their 'Eastern Counterparts', however, two are particularly worth considering, **Bathgate** and the **Deer Park Golf and Country Club** at Livingston. Both lie within easy access of Edinburgh and welcome visitors seven days of the week. The Bathgate Club which recently celebrated its centenary can lay claim to having produced two Ryder Cup players – Eric Brown and Bernard Gallagher, both of whom were members of the 1969 and 1971 sides. While Bathgate is moorland in nature, Deer Park is more parkland (suprise, suprise!) and is surrounded by beautiful countryside. Fees at Deer Park are about **£12**, at Bathgate they're about **£7**. As for hotels, one thought here is **The Golden Circle (0506) 53771** very comfortable.

Travellers wishing to explore the delights of the East Coast should aim to pick up the **A198** at Prestonpans near Musselburgh. Before it reaches Longniddry the road passes through Seton, where **Mary Queen of Scots** is known to have sharpened up her golf swing more than 400 years ago. 13 miles East of Edinburgh, **Longniddry** ought not to be considered as merely a stopping place en route to **Muirfield**. It is a superb course, part links part parkland with every hole having a view of the sea. A former venue of the P.G.A. Seniors Championship it is regularly used as a qualyifying course for the British Open. Green fees are approximately **£15**.

Luffness New and the three neighbouring courses of **Gullane**, lie only a short distance further along the coast. Each is outstanding in its way though if you only have time to play two then Luffness New and Gullane Number One are probably the pick. The panoramic view from the top of Gullane Hill on the latter's 7th hole is one of the most famous in golf. Visitors are welcome at both Gullane and Luffness though prior telephoning is again essential.

Most golfers will probably want to play a game at **Muirfield** (see feature page) but travelling on to **North Berwick** and **Dunbar** is strongly recommended – besides it may be much easier to arrange a visit. Green fees at Dunbar are about **£11**, at North Berwick, **£13**.

Both courses are outstanding in their own way. The West Links at North Berwick perhaps has the more charm and tradition, two of its holes, the 14th 'Perfection' and the 15th 'Redan' have been imitated all over the world. Dunbar is more of a true championship test with a number of potential disaster holes. Both are very scenic with splendid views across to Bass Rock.

Time for a 19th hole and many thoughts emerge. Hotels are numerous, as indeed are good restaurants, here are some ideas. In Gullane, **Greywalls (0620) 842144** is quite exceptional and superbly convenient for Muirfield and Gullane, while **La Potiniere (0620) 843214** is a restaurant to savour while in these parts. In Aberlady the **Kilspindie House Hotel (08757) 682** and **The Wagon (08757) 319** are both welcoming as is clearly **The Open Arms (062085) 241** in Dirleton. **The Marine Hotel (0620) 2406** is convenient for North Berwick while other well priced alternatives include **The Mallard (0620) 843228, The Royal (0620) 2401** and **The Point Garry Hotel (0620) 2380. The Folly (0629) 3622** is a fine restaurant. Excellent in Uphall, for touring the whole Lothian area is **Houstoun House (0506) 853831**.

Towards Dunbar, in the town itself, **The Bellevue (0368) 62322** and **The Bayswell (0368) 62225** are both comfortable hotels, while many super establishments are found a little inland. Note especially **The Harvesters Hotel (0620) 860395** at East Linton, **The Tweedale Arms (0620) 81240** at Gifford and the 17th Century **John Stounbourn House (087 533) 696** at Humbie. Travelling back westwards and still further through the ages to Gorebridge, here the **Borthwick Castle (0875) 20514** – a 15th Century castle and a fine hotel as well. For the touring golfer in Scotland, a country cottage is recommended as a good base; both **Blakes Country Cottages (0603) 783227** and **Mackay's 031-225 3539** offer a varied range of self-catering accommodation to rent at reasonable prices.

MUIRFIELD

CHAMPIONSHIP GOLF

Muirfield is of course much more than one of the world's greatest golf links; It is also the home of the world's oldest Golf Club. **The Honourable Company of Edinburgh Golfers** are the direct descendants of the 'Gentlemen Golfers' who played at **Leith Links** from at least as early as the fifteenth century. On **7th March 1744** 'several Gentlemen of Honour skilful in the ancient and healthful exercise of Golf' petitioned the city fathers of Edinburgh to provide a silver cup to be played for annually on the links at Leith. The winner of this competition became 'Captain of Golf' and the club was paraded through the city. In 1744 the Edinburgh Golfers formulated the game's first code of rules, The Thirteen Articles, which were adopted almost word for word ten years later by the Royal and Ancient Club at St Andrews when it formed its first rules.

The Company played over the five holes at Leith for almost a hundred years before overcrowding forced the decision to move to the nine hole course at **Musselburgh**, to the east of the city. Long before they had left Leith the Members had begun to dine and play in the famous red uniform; failure to wear this usually resulted in a fine. A minute from the 1830's records how one member was fined 'two tappit hens' for playing golf without his red coat. The **Open Championship** first came to Musselburgh in **1874** and was held there every third year until 1889. Meanwhile Musselburgh, like Leith, had become terribly crowded and the Company decided that the time had come for a second move. Again they looked to the east and almost twenty miles from Edinburgh, under the lee of Gullane Hill, they discovered Muirfield. The course was designed by **Old Tom Morris** and opened for play on **3rd May 1891**. In its early years the course received much criticism, one professional described it as 'nothing but an auld watter meddie' but it appears that this had more to do with the fact that when the Honourable Company left Musselburgh they took the Open Championship with them. It was held at Muirfield in **1892** (the first 72 hole tournament) and it never again returned to Musselburgh. Following the success of the 1892 Championship Muirfield's reputation grew rapidly and today it is widely considered to be fairest, if not the finest test in golf.

Visitors wishing to play at Muirfield must make prior arrangements with the Secretary, **Major J. G. Vanreenen**, who may be contacted by telephone on **(0620) 842123**. For **gentlemen** golfers there is a requirement that they belong to a recognised Golf Club and carry a handicap of 18 or less, while for **lady golfers** (who may only play if accompanied by a gentleman player) the handicap limit is 24. A letter of introduction from the visitor's home Club is helpful. The days on which visitors are welcome are Tuesdays, Thursdays and on Friday mornings. It should also be noted that by tradition foursome matches are strongly favoured at Muirfield and four ball games will only be permitted in the mornings. Golfing Societies (limited to 40 players) are also received on the usual visiting days and arrangements may be made with Major Vanreenen. All written correspondence should be addressed to **The Secretary, The Honourable Company of Edinburgh Golfers, Muirfield, Gullane, East Lothian, EH31 2EG.**

The **green fees** for 1989 were set at **£30** for a single round with **£40** entitling the visitor to a full day's golf. All fees should be paid to the cashier in the Clubhouse Dining Room.

There is no professional shop at Muirfield but the services of a caddie may be arranged if requested in advance (via the above telephone number), and golf trolleys can be hired from the Caddie Master. In the Clubhouse a jacket and tie should be worn in all public rooms, lunches being served between 12.30pm and 2pm and afternoon tea until 5.30pm.

Travelling to Muirfield (or Gullane) will often be by way of **Edinburgh**. Gullane is connected to the capital city by the **A198**. Northbound travellers can avoid Edinburgh by approaching on the **A1** which runs to **Dunbar** to the east of Gullane. From Dunbar the **A198** can be picked up. Those coming from the north and west of Scotland will need to travel via Edinburgh. The **M8** links Glasgow to Edinburgh, whilst the **M9** should be taken from **Stirling** and the **M90** will assist from **Perth**.

One of the unique features of Muirfield (or at least unique in terms of Scottish Championship links) is its layout of two separate loops, an outer and an inner. This ensures that the golfer will not have to play several successive holes into or against the same wind direction. Although quite undulating the course doesn't (or at least shouldn't) require blind shots as at St Andrews, St Georges and Prestwick and this contributes much to Muirfield's 'fairness' tag. From the Championship tees the course stretches to **6941** yards, and with the often prodigiously thick rough, it can be a very severe test of golf. From the Medal tees Muirfield still measures a fairly lengthy **6601** yards, par **70**.

Since 1892 the **Open Championship** has been played at Muirfield on **11** occasions. Before the last War winners included **Harry Vardon, James Braid** and **Walter Hagen**. The first Open to be held at Muirfield after the War was in 1948, when **Henry Cotton** won his third title. Cotton's second round of 66 was achieved in front of the watching **King George VI**. **Gary Player** won in **1959** and **Jack Nicklaus** in **1966**. Perhaps the most dramatic Open in Muirfield's history came in **1972** when **Lee Trevino** holed his famous chip shot from the edge of the 17th green and in the process 'stole' the title from **Tony Jacklin**. The Open was last played at Muirfield in **1987, Nick Faldo** securing a memorable victory for Britain.

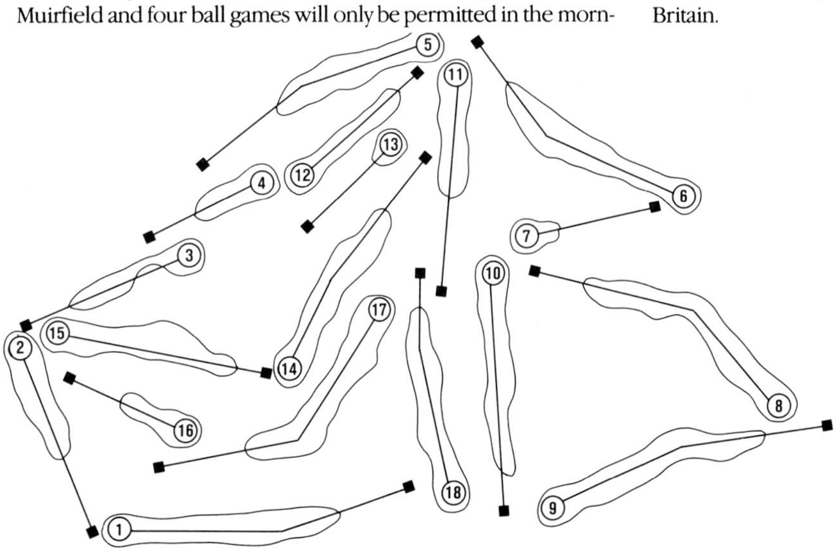

Hole	Yards	Par	Hole	Yards	Par
1	449	4	10	475	5
2	349	4	11	386	4
3	379	4	12	381	4
4	181	3	13	153	3
5	558	5	14	447	4
6	471	4	15	396	4
7	185	3	16	188	3
8	444	4	17	542	5
9	510	5	18	447	4
Out	3,526	36	In	3,415	36
			Out	3,526	36
			TOTALS	6,941	72

DUNBAR

CHAMPIONSHIP GOLF

In common with much of Eastern Scotland it isn't entirely clear when golf was first played at Dunbar. Whilst the **Dunbar Golf Club** was founded in **1856** following a meeting in the Town Hall, **The Dunbar Golfing Society** had been instituted in **1794**. Furthermore, records suggest that some cruder form of golf had been played at least as early as the beginning of the 17th century. In **1616** two men of the parish of Tyninghame were censured by the Kirk Session for 'playing at ye nyneholis' on the Lord's Day and in **1640** an Assistant Minister of Dunbar was disgraced 'for playing at gouff'.

Times, as they say, change and three hundred years later 'gouff' is still played at Dunbar, although none are likely to be censured or disgraced for doing so and there are now eighteen splendid holes.

Presently 'in charge' of the famous links is the Club's **Secretary, Mr. Arnold Poole**. He may be contacted on **(0368) 62317**. Very much a welcoming golf club, Dunbar receives visitors at all times. Societies are equally catered for although pre-booking is not surprisingly required. Those organising Societies should write to Mr. Poole at **The Dunbar Golf Club, East Links, Dunbar, East Lothian.** In 1989 the **green fees** for either a single round or a full day's golf was priced at **£12** during the week and **£20** at weekends. One final introduction; **Derek Small** is the Club's Professional, he may be reached on **(0368) 62086**.

Having spent countless hours poring over maps trying to work out the best routes to a particular Golf Club it is with great pleasure that I turn to Dunbar: from the west, approach via the **A1**; from the south east approach via the **A1**! Less flippantly, the A1 runs from Berwick upon-Tweed to Edinburgh and passes through Dunbar. Those travelling from the Borders region of Melrose and Galashiels may find helpful a combination of the **A68** and the **A6137** to Haddington, thereafter picking up the A1 to Dunbar.

Dunbar is very much a natural links, laid out on a fairly narrow tract of land closely following the contours of the shoreline. It is bounded by a stone wall which runs the full length of the course. Whilst Dunbar is by no means the longest of Scottish links, when the winds blow it can prove to be one of the most difficult – this may have something to do with the fact that there is an 'out of bounds' on the **3rd, 4th, 5th, 6th, 7th, 8th, 9th, 16th 17th** and **18th** holes, and the beach can come in to play on the **4th, 5th, 6th, 7th, 12th, 14th, 15th, 16th** and **17th!** (straight hitting would appear to be called for).

Dunbar is without doubt one of the East Coast's most attractive links with some splendid views out across the sea towards **Bass Rock**. The first three holes are played fairly close to the Clubhouse, the opening two being relatively tame par fives and the third a spectacular short hole played from an elevated tee. The fourth then takes you alongside the beach as the course begins to move away from the Clubhouse. Perhaps the most testing holes on the course occur around the turn, the ninth to the twelfth, and there is no let-up either on the closing stretch with the beach readily receiving the mildest of slices. The eighteenth can also be a card-wrecker with the stone wall out of bounds running the length of the fairway to the right.

All the major Scottish Championships have been played at Dunbar, including the **Scottish Amateur** and **Scottish Professional Championships**. The Club has also staged the **British Boys** Championship and has become something of a home in recent years for the Scottish Boys title. The course record stands at an impressive **66**.

Dunbar's 19th is a comfortable building with views from the lounge across much of the course. Lunches and snacks are available seven days a week and with prior arrangement both breakfasts and dinners are also offered. A jacket and tie should be worn after 7.30pm. One final thought as you relax in the Clubhouse – one of the Regulations of the Dunbar Golfing Society dated 1794 reads as follows: 'When the expense of each Member for dinner amounts to two shillings and sixpence, the Club shall be dissolved' – times, as they say, change!

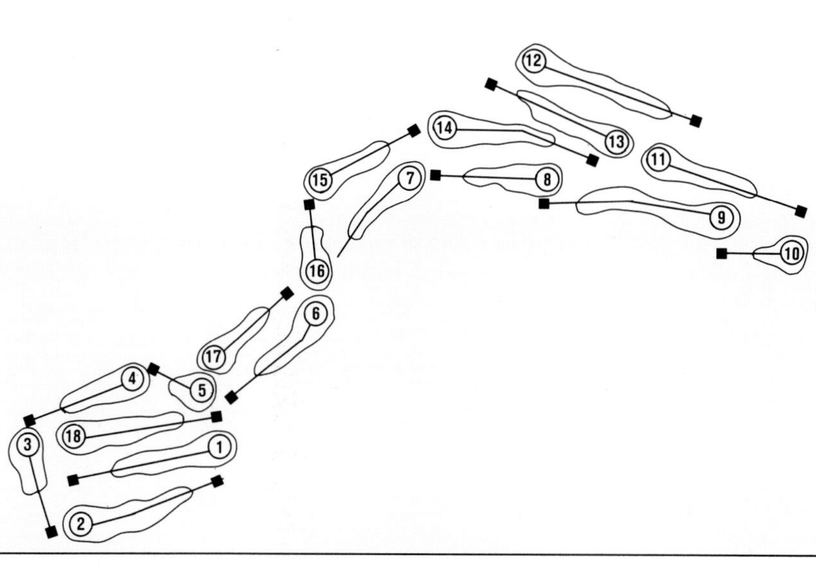

Hole	Yards	Par	Hole	Yards	Par
1	477	5	10	202	3
2	494	5	11	417	4
3	172	3	12	459	4
4	349	4	13	378	4
5	148	3	14	433	4
6	350	4	15	343	4
7	386	4	16	166	3
8	369	4	17	339	4
9	507	5	18	437	4
Out	3,252	37	In	3,174	34
			Out	3,252	37
			TOTALS	6,426	71

GREYWALLS

Greywalls is a Country House Hotel close to Edinburgh, but it is a hotel with a difference – originally it was designed as an Edwardian home. The Weaver family, who used to live in the house, have since converted it to an hotel and still live there today.

Although Greywalls was opened as an hotel in 1948, it retains the look and feel of the house that was designed in 1901 by the renowned Edwardian architect Sir Edwin Lutyens. The gardens were laid out by his imaginative partner, Gretrude Jekyll, so the complete arrangement of house and garden fulfills the Edwardian aspirations of a 'Lutyens house with a Jekyll garden'.

King Edward V11 used to stay at Greywalls and admire the views across the south to the Lammermuir Hills, immortalised by Sir Walter Scott. Today most bedrooms are still furnished with period pieces and all have their own bathroom. The panelled library, perhaps the most inviting room in Greywalls, offers the guest the warmth and comfort of real fires and discreet first-class service. The cuisine, now served in a dining room that was once a courtyard, is of the highest standard, using the finest fresh ingredients for both traditional menus and house specialities. Greywalls offers the atmosphere of home, but with the amenities and service of one of the country's leading hotels.

For the sportsman, Greywalls and the Lothians offer a wealth of activity. The house itself looks over the immaculate 9th and 18th greens of Muirfield golf course, where the Open Championship is played regularly. Accordingly the guests at such times reflect the proximity of such a course – Nicklaus, Watson, Trevino and Palmer are just a few of the famous visitors. There are 10 golf courses within 5 miles and a hard tennis court and a croquet lawn within the grounds, while there is also fine shooting and fishing nearby.

For the sightseer Edinburgh is only 40 minutes drive away and the Scottish Border country is less than an hour away. Closer to hand are ancient castles such as Tantallon and and the famous bird sanctuary on the Bass Rock. The Lammermuirs offer delightful walks as do the endless sandy beaches along the coast. Even for the businessman, Greywalls can offer the prospect of countryside comfort, peace and quiet and the promise of good food at the end of a hard day's work in the city.

Greywalls provides, for the golfer or gourmet, businessman of holidaymaker, the highest standards of comfort and cooking in an Edwardian house that has been both home and hotel for the same family for over 35 years.

Greywalls Hotel
Muirfield
Gullane
East Lothian EH31 2EG
Tel: (0620) 842144

LOTHIAN
COMPLETE GOLF

LOTHIAN

Baberton G.C.
(18) 6140 yards
Juniper Green, Edinburgh
(031453) 4911

Bathgate G.C.
(18) 6326 yards
Edinburgh Road, Bathgate
(0506) 630505

Braids United G.C.
(18) 5731 yards (No. 1)
(18) 4832 yards (No. 2)
Braids Hill Approach,
Edinburgh
(031447) 3327

Broomieknowe G.C.
(18) 6046 yards
Golf Course Road, Bonnyrigg
(031663) 9317

Bruntsfield Links Golfing
Society
(18) 6407 yards
32, Barnton Avenue, Davidsons,
Mains, Edinburgh
(031336) 1479

Craigmillar Park G.C.
(18) 5846 yards
Observatory Road, Edinburgh
(031667) 2837

Dalmahoy C.C.
(18) 6664 yards (East)
(18) 5212 yards (West)
Dalmahoy, Kirknewton
(031333) 2055

Deer Park G. & C.C.
(18) 6636 yards
Livingston
(0506) 38843

Duddingston G.C.
(18) 6647 yards
Duddingston Road, Edinburgh
(031661) 7688

Dunbar G.C.
(18) 6426 yards
East Links, Dunbar
(0368) 62317

Dundas Park G.C.
(9) 6026 yards
South Queensferry
(031331) 3090

East Links
(18) 6079 yards
East Links, North Berwick
(0620) 2340

Gifford G.C.
(9) 6138 yards
Station Road, Gifford
(062081) 267

Glencorse G.C.
(18) 5205 yards
Milton Bridge, Penicuik
(0968) 77189

Greenburn G.C.
(18) 6210 yards
Bridge Street, Fauldhouse
(0501) 70292

Gullane G.C.
(18) 6479 yards (No. 1)
(18) 6127 yards (No. 2)
(18) 5035 yards (No. 3)
Gullane
(0620) 842255

Honourable Company of
Edinburgh Golfers
(18) 6941 yards
Muirfield, Gullane
(0620) 842123

Kilspindie G.C.
(18) 5410 yards
Aberlady
(0875) 358

Kingsknowe G.C.
(18) 5979 yards
Lanark Road, Edinburgh
(031441) 1145

Linlithgow G.C.
(18) 5858 yards
Braehead, Linlithgow
(0506) 842585

Longniddry G.C.
(18) 6210 yards
Links Road, Longniddry
(0875) 52141

Lothianburn G.C.
(18) 5671 yards
Biggar Road, Edinburgh
(031445) 2288

Luffness New G.C.
(18) 6085 yards
Aberlady
(0620) 843336

Merchants of Edinburgh G.C.
(18) 4889 yards
Craighill Gardens, Edinburgh
(031447) 1219

Mortonhall G.C.
(18) 6557 yards
Braid Road, Edinburgh
(031447) 6974

Murrayfield G.C.
(18) 5727 yards
Murrayfield Road, Edinburgh
(031337) 3478

Musselburgh G.C.
(18) 6623 yards
Monktonhall, Mussellburgh
(031665) 2005

Newbattle G.C.
(18) 6012 yards
Abbey Road, Dalkeith
(031663) 2123

North Berwick G.C.
(18) 6317 yards
West Links, Beach Road,
North Berwick
(0620) 2135

Prestonfield G.C.
(18) 6216 yards
6, Piestfield Road North,
Edinburgh
(031667) 9665

Ratho Park G.C.
(18) 6028 yards
Ratho, Newbridge
(031333) 1752

Royal Burgess Golfing Society
(18) 6604 yards
Whitehouse Road, Barton,
Edinburgh
(031339) 2075

Royal Musselburgh G.C.
(18) 6204 yards
Prestongrange House, Pretonpans
(0875) 810276

Silverknowes G.C.
(18) 6210 yards
Silverknowes, Parkway,
Edinburgh
(031336) 5359

Swanston G.C.
(18) 5024 yards
111, Swanston Road, Edinburgh
(031445) 2239

Torphin Hill G.C.
(18) 5030 yards
Torphin Road, Colinton,
Edinburgh
(031441) 1100

Turnhouse G.C.
(18) 6171 yards
154, Turnhouse Road,
Edinburgh
(031339) 7701

Uphall G.C.
(18) 5567 yards
Uphall
(0506) 856404

West Lothian G.C.
(18) 6629 yards
Airngath Hill, Linlithgow
(0506) 826030

Winterfield G.C.
(18) 5220 yards
North Road, Dunbar
(0368) 62564

STRATHCLYDE

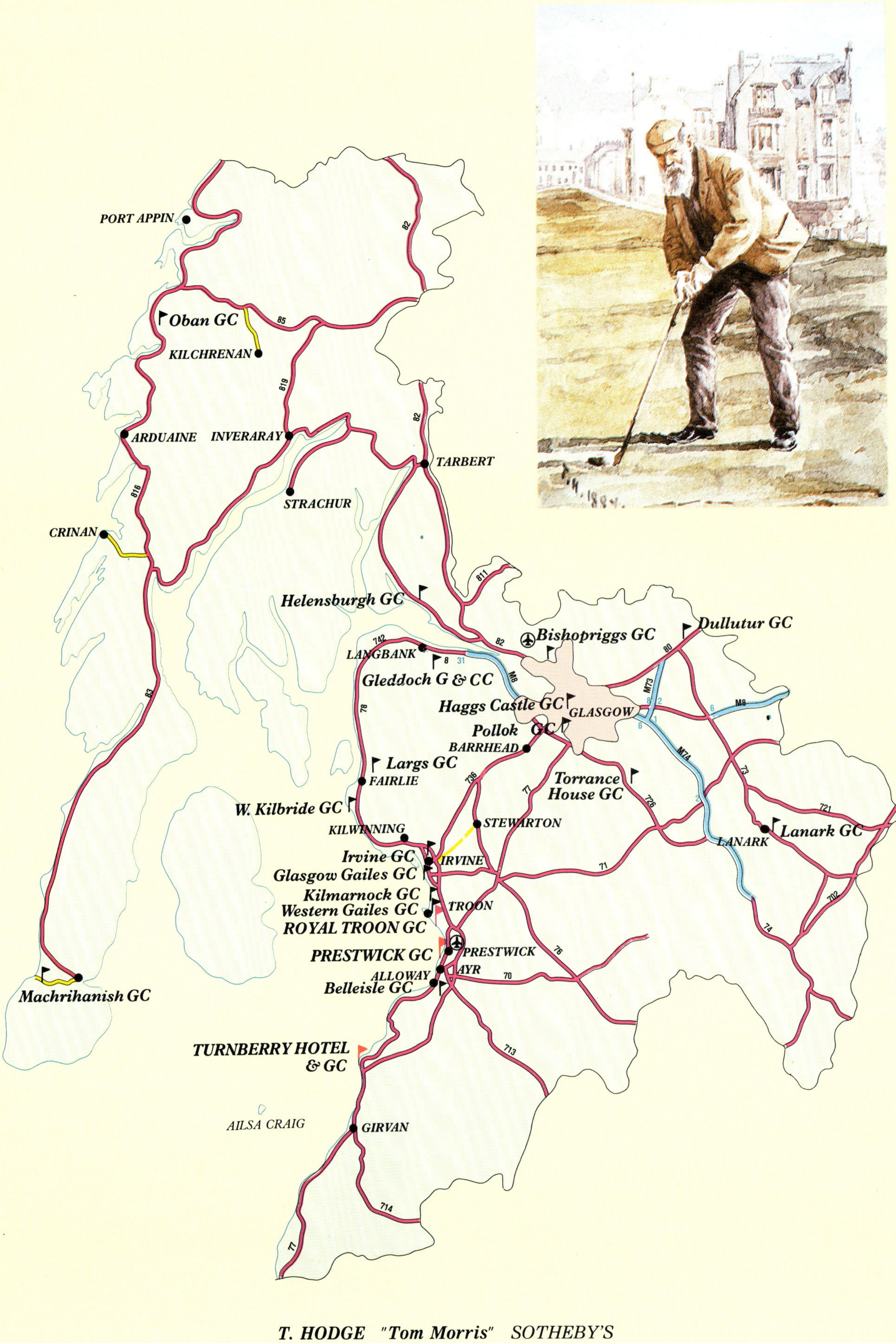

T. HODGE "Tom Morris" SOTHEBY'S

STRATHCLYDE
CHOICE GOLF

An ancient golfing rhyme from the land of Burns runs:

'Troon and Prestwick, old and classy,
Bogside, Dundonald, Glasgow Gailes, Barassie,
Prestwick St. Nicholas, Weston Gailes,
St. Cuthbert, Portland – memory fails,
Troon Municipal (three links there)
Prestwick Municipal, Irvine, Ayr,
They faced the lists with delighted smiles –
Sixteen courses within ten miles.

Even without **Turnberry** some fifteen miles south of Ayr, an extradorinarily impressive list, and little wonder that this small region of Scotland's coast has become nothing short of a mecca for golfers the world over.

Prestwick, Troon and **Turnberry** have of course each staged the Open Championship. Prestwick was the birth-place of the event back in 1860 and is probably the most classical examination of links golf; penal the American architects would describe it on account of the many blind shots. The Open is no longer held at Prestwick but the history of the place is overwhelming and quite magnetic. Troon and Turnberry are both firmly on the 'Open' rota. It was played over the latter's Ailsa course in 1986 (Norman's great victory) and was held at Troon in 1989. Understandably the golfer making a pilgrimage to the Ayrshire coast will be drawn towards this famous trio. However, if time isn't, as they say, of the essence it would be bordering on a disgrace not to sample as many of the nearby delights as possible. As the old rhyme relates, within short distance of one another lie a number of outstanding courses and at any of which it may be easier to arrange a game.

While not all roads lead to Ayr, as the largest town on the coast, it's probably as good a starting point as any. Here we find a belle – **Belleisle** to be precise and a most attractive parkland course. Considered by many to be the finest public course outside of St Andrews and Carnoustie and being somewhat sheltered it's an admirable retreat from the more windswept links nearby. Furthermore as a municipal course the green fees are less expensive at about **£8** a round.

Just north of Ayr lie a series of outstanding links courses, all within a mile or two of one another. Prestwick and Troon are featured on later pages (as is Turnberry) but also in this area one finds **Barrassie, Western Gailes, Glasgow (Gailes) and Irvine** (also known somewhat unfortunately as **Bogside**). Each warmly welcome visitors and although less busy than the 'big three' prior telephoning is advisable, especially during the peak summer months. Week-days are invariably the best times for a visit with fees for a day's golf tending to range around the **£12** to **£18** mark.

Just as there is a proliferation of golf courses so the area is inundated with all manner of hotels, guest houses, pubs and restaurants. A few thoughts follow: To start at a pinnacle **The Turnberry Hotel (0655) 3100**, the first ever purpose built Hotel and Golf Course. Both Hotel and restaurant are outstandingly luxurious in every way. Guests enjoy reduced green fees and more importantly have priority on the golf courses. If staying in this area, **Culzean Castle** (open between April and October) is well worth a visit and in nearby Girvan an excellent place for liquid refreshment is the **King's Arms (0465) 3322** (specialists in golfing cocktails like the 'Perfect Slice'!). Perhaps the most popular, and certainly the most convenient hotel for Royal Troon is **The Marine Highland (0292) 314414**. It proudly overlooks the championship links as well as the sea beyond. A second splendid hotel in Troon is **Piersland House (0292) 314747**. The two best known hotels in Ayr are **The Caledonian (0292) 269331** and **The Pickwick (0292) 260111** while close by in Alloway is the excellent **Balgarth Hotel (0292) 42441**. On to Prestwick, which if you've arrived by plane may well by your first port of call, and here **The Carlton (0292) 76811** and **The Parkstone (0292) 77286** stand out. Kilmarnock is now a busy industrial centre. It was here that Robbie Burns' first collection of poems was published. Just to the north of the town at Irvine is **The Hospitality Inn (0924) 74272**: Like its name, most welcoming. If an escape to the countryside is sought then a trip to Stewarton is highly recommended. Set in glorius surroundings is the redoubtable **Chapeltoun House (0560) 82696**. Quiet, and very comfortable with a first class restaurant. Kilwinning is a final recommendation for this area; somewhat off the beaten track but the **Montgreenan Mansion House (0294) 57733** is superbly comfortable.

To the north of the famous golfing stretch there is plenty of less testing golf to be found. This may well be necessary in order to restore battered pride! **West Kilbride** (another links type) and **Largs**(a well-wooded parkland course) should suit admirably. Both also offer some magnificient views across to Argyle and the Isle of Arran. Again weekdays is the preferred time for inspection with the fees approximately**£12**.

Glasgow is Britian's third largest city after London and Birmingham and being Scottish-to-boot has not surprisingly a huge number of golf courses. Indeed some wag once said of Glasgow that there was a pub in every street with a Golf Club around each corner. Unfortunately the problem for the golfing stranger to Glasgow is that the majority of the city's leading Clubs only permit visitors to play if accompanied by a Member; **Haggs Castle** perhaps being an outstanding example. A game however is possible at **Pollok**, one of the city's finest parkland courses. Gentleman visitors are welcome here on Mondays, Wednesdays, Thursdays and Fridays, fees being **£15**. The course is situated to the south west of the town centre off the **A736**. There are a number of public courses in Glasgow so the golfer confined to the city need not get too depressed. The pick of the municipals is probably **Lethamhill and Little Hill** – a game on either is remarkably inexpensive.

Forgetting the golf for a moment, it may surprise many south of the border to hear that Glasgow has been named as European City of Culture for 1990, in succession to Athens and Paris, among other cities. It really is ever-improving. **The Burrell Collection** in Pollock Park has become Scotland's most visited Art Museum and is quite outstanding. Hotels are not as prolific as golf courses but a list of the best might include **The Holiday Inn (041) 226 5577**, the **Hospitality Inn (041) 332 3311** and the less modern (and with a more attractive exterior) **Stakis Grosvenor (041) 339 8811**. For good value **The White House (041) 339 9375** is highly recommended. As for restaurants, fish lovers will adore **Rogano's Oyster Bar (041) 248 4055** in Exchange Square while those seeking first class French cuisine should head for **The Buttery (041) 221 8188** on Argyle Street. For a spot of culture the **Theatre Royal (041) 331 1234** offers distinguished ballet, opera and drama.

Time for a spot more golf, **The Gleddoch House Hotel Golf and Country Club (047554) 711** (**£8** a round **£12** a day), provides the solution. Located at Langbank it is close to the Clyde Estuary and offers views of the Lombard Hills. It is easily accessible from Glasgow by way of the **M8** and in a nutshell could be described as a darn good hotel with a darn good restaurant and a darn good golf course!

From Glasgow Troon, Turnberry and Prestwick lie to the south west (the **A77** is incidentally the most convenient route), but

STRATHCLYDE

CHOICE GOLF

Championship golf can also be found to the north and east. **Dullatur** is one such venue, **Lanark** another. The former is a parkland course whereas Lanark is essentially moorland. Visitors are welcome at both during the week although prior telephoning is preferred. For Dullatur a notel to note is **Crow Wood House (041779) 3861** and an excellent restaurant, **La Campagnola (041 779) 3405** – both are in Muirhead. **The Cartland Bridge Hotel (0555) 4426** is recommended for the course at Lanark. Before heading for the more distant corners of Strathclyde a quick mention for two courses lying due south of the city. **Torrance House** and **Strathaven** are the pair in question. Both are very easily reached by way of the **A726**, although Strathaven is quite a bit away from the city and by the time you arrive at the course you'll have climbed 700 feet above sea level. A lovely setting here and a most convenient hotel, **The Strathaven (0357) 21778** awaits on Hamilton Road. A sneak preview here for the forthcoming complex, the **Westerwood Hotel, Country Club and Golf Course (0860) 263746** near Cumbernauld to the east of Glasgow – looks promising.

What of the more remote outposts then? Strathclyde is a vast region extending well into the Highlands and beyond Oban. There's not a great deal in the way of golf challenges here – the landscape precludes it – but the countyrside is quite glorious and there are some extremely fine hotels and country houses nestling in and around the hills, all making splendid bases for exploring the delightful surroundings. North of Loch Lomond one finds **The Stonefield Castle (08802) 207** at Tarbet alongside Loch Fyne. If inspecting the delights of Oban a detour to Kilchrenan is highly recommended. **The Ardanaiseig (08663) 333** is the place – outstandingly relaxing. Still nearer to Oban at Knipoch, **The Knipoch Hotel (085 26) 251** offers great comfort together with all manner of country pursuits.

Two great courses still remain to be viewed – those magical 'M's' – **Machrie and Machrihanish**. Each enjoys a kind of splendid isolation and both are superb tests of golf. Machrie (**£8** a round, **£10** a day) is to be found on the distant Isle of Islay at Port Ellen. As it can now be reached by plane from Glasgow there can be no excuse for not making the trip; besides right on the course is the excellent **Machrie Hotel (0496)2085.** Many have already made the pilgrimage to **Machrihanish** and as it too is reachable by air a large number are certain to follow. It is easy to see why. A classic links, which **Tom Morris** is reputed to have described as 'designed by the Almighty for playing golf'. The very first hole has the golfer teeing off across the waters of the Atlantic – death or glory! Marvellous stuff and for **£9.50** per day midweek **£10** at weekends it's exceptionally good value. There are a number of hotels nearby both in Machrihanish itself and in Campbeltown, and it's well worth spending a few days here. Before you leave the area a mellow tune may come to mind. It actually sold more copies than any other – Mull of Kintyre by one Paul McCartney. The music inspired millions, the golf course and its surrounds will almost certainly give you equal satisfaction.

*Artist **Macbeth-Raeburn ROYAL DORNOCH** Courtesy of : The Burlington Gallery*

TURNBERRY

The world-renowned Turnberry Hotel is well-situated, overlooking Scotland's south west Ayrshire coast. Within its 360 acres are a luxury hotel, golf course and leisure resort with few equals in the world.

Two famous championship links courses, owned and managed by the hotel make it a year round Mecca for golfers. The Ailsa course hosts great golfing events which include the British Open. It is complemented by the slightly shorter Arran course, and there are putting greens and a pitch and putt course. The hotel has all-weather tennis courts and a swimming pool. Nearby are riding stables and the hotel can also arrange for guests to enjoy sea and river fishing, rough shooting, stalking and trap shooting. Culzean Castle, Robert Burns country and the Burrell Collection are some of the major nearby attractions.

The hotel was built at the turn of the century and the tradition of elegance and comfort is retained in the bedrooms. At Turnberry the living is indeed comfortable and relaxed. Every bedroom has its individual character and offers both comfort and style. Indoor amenities also include a sauna, solarium, exercise area, billiards room, table tennis, a boutique and a hairdressing salon.

The anticipation of culinary treats in store fills the restaurant with an atmosphere of excitement and sparkle. Every day master chef Stewart Cameron creates different menus to delight you, using the very best local produce. And what a splendid setting for dinner; Edwardian elegance and gracious service combined with the most magical views. There can be few more memorable sights than the sun setting slowly over the islands of Arran and Ailsa Craig, as you dine superbly to the accompaniment of resident musicians.

Staying at Turnberry is like being a guest in a grand country house. You will appreciate the warm hospitality, the constant concern and those little formalities and gracious touches that make all the difference. Perhaps it is because of this that so many guests and their families choose to return year after year.

The Turnberry Hotel and Golf Courses,
Turnberry,
Ayrshire,
SCOTLAND KA26 9LT

Tel: (0655) 31000
Telex: 777779 Fax: (0655) 31706

TURNBERRY
CHAMPIONSHIP GOLF

Not so many years ago it was said that the golfing visitor to Scotland journeyed to **St. Andrews** for the history and to **Turnberry** for the beauty. Incomparable is a word often used to describe Turnberry's setting, magnificent and majestic are two others. Quite what causes **Ailsa Craig** to be so mesmerising is a mystery, but mesmerising it is and the views towards the distant **Isle of Arran** and the **Mull of Kintyre** can be equally captivating and enchanting. Since **1977** Turnberry has possessed history as well as beauty.

The **Open Championship** of **1977**, Turnberry's first, is generally considered to have been the greatest of all Championships. **Nicklaus** and **Watson**, the two finest golfers of the day turned the tournament into a titanic, head-to-head confrontation. On the final day, both having pulled a long way clear of the field, Nicklaus held a two stroke advantage as they left the 12th green. 'Who in the world can give Jack Nicklaus two shots over six holes and beat him?' asked Peter Alliss – the rest, as they say, is indeed history.

There are two Championship courses at Turnberry; the better known **Ailsa Course** and the **Arran Course**. Both are owned and run by the **Turnberry Hotel. Visitors** with handicaps are welcome to play on either course although prior arrangements must be made with the **Golf Club Manager Mr. R. Hamblett.** Mr. Hamblett can be contacted via **The Turnberry Hotel, Turnberry, Strathclyde, KA26 9LT**, telephone **(0655) 31000 Ext. 376**.

In 1989 the **green fees** were set at **£31** for a day's golf consisting of one round on each course, (**£36** at weekends), or alternatively **£24** for two rounds on any day of the week on the Arran. A single round on the Arran is priced at **£19**. Reduced rates are available to Hotel residents. Turnberry's professional **Bob Jamieson** can also be contacted on **(0655) 31000**. Caddies and hire of clubs are best arranged by telephone.

The Clubhouse facilities are first class at Turnberry, with a Golf Club restaurant that is open from 8am to 8pm. The bar is open daily from 11am and there are no specific dress requirements.

The Hotel and golf courses lie approximately 13 miles south of the town of **Ayr** off the **A77**. For those travelling from the Glasgow region, the **A77** runs direct from Glasgow to Turnberry and is dual carriageway for much of the journey. Motoring from Edinburgh the **A71** is the best route, picking up the **A77** at Kilmarnock and following it as above, skirting around Ayr. Approaching from England, Carlisle is likely to be a starting point (**M6** to Carlisle). The distance from Carlisle to Turnberry is one of just under 120 miles, and although there are two choices, the quickest route is to head north on the **A74** leaving (in what appears to be no man's land) and joining the **A70** towards Ayr. Finally, **Prestwick Airport** is situated just to the north of Ayr.

From its elevated perch the red-roofed Turnberry Hotel enjoys a commanding view over both courses. It will have witnessed much of Turnberry's rather turbulent past. During the War the rolling expanse of links had been used as an air base and a vast runway had been constructed. Much levelling of the ground had also taken place and in 1945 the last thing Turnberry must have looked was the setting for two Championship courses. **Mackenzie Ross** is the architect we all have to thank.

From its medal tees the **Ailsa** course isn't a great deal longer than the **Arran**, their respective distances being **6408** yards, par **70**, and **6276** yards, par **69**. The same from the ladies tees are **5836** yards, par **75** and **5732 yards**, par **73**. When the **Open Championship** returned to Turnberry in **1986** the Ailsa course weighed in at **6950** yards, par **70** and the fairways had been narrowed to alarming proportions. **Greg Norman's** second round **63** achieved in far from perfect weather conditions was a remarkable feat. The weather can, of course, be Turnberry's devil and for many the outstanding memory of the 1986 Championship is of the torrential storm that struck at the end of the third day capturing Norman and a handful of others as they struggled to complete their rounds.

After three holes 'inland' as it were, the Ailsa course hugs the shore tightly for a series of dramatic holes between the **4th** and the **11th**. The **6th**, named **'Tappie Toorie'** is possibly the most difficult par three on the course (although the **15th** can be pretty treacherous) the shot is to a heavily guarded green across a valley. The **9th** and the **10th** though are the holes most likely to be remembered. The **9th 'Bruce's Castle'**, is played alongside the famous Turnberry lighthouse built over the remains of Turnberry Castle, birthplace of Robert the Bruce, King of the Scots. The Championship tee for this hole is one of the most spectacularly sited in the world perched on a pinnacle of rock with the sea crashing below. The **10th 'Dinna Fouter'** calls for a daring drive across the bay; parallels have often been drawn here with the famous 18th at Pebble Beach. Following the par three **11th** the holes turn inland and if the scenery is a little less spectacular the challenge in no way diminishes. The closing holes will invariably invoke thoughts of the Nicklaus-Watson battle. To complete 'the history' Nicklaus played the final six holes in one under par yet was still beaten. The end of an era cried many – they should have known better!

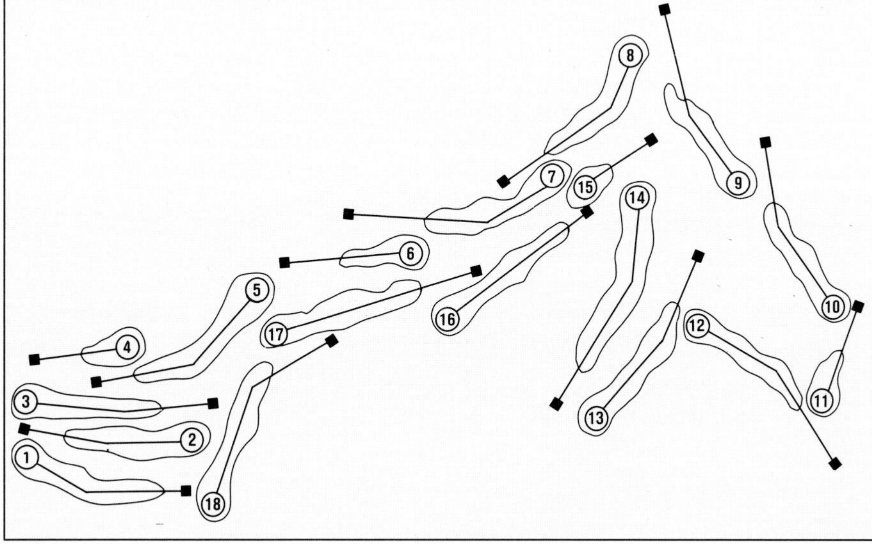

Ailsa Course

Hole	Yards	Par	Hole	Yards	Par
1	350	4	10	452	4
2	428	4	11	177	3
3	462	4	12	448	4
4	167	3	13	411	4
5	441	4	14	440	4
6	222	3	15	209	3
7	528	5	16	409	4
8	427	4	17	500	5
9	455	4	18	431	4
Out	3,480	35	In	3,477	35
			Out	3,480	35
			TOTALS	6,957	70

Ardanaiseig

Ardanaiseig is in Argyll in the heart of the mountainous region over which the Clan Campbell held undisputed sway for centuries. Built in 1834 for a member of that clan, this gracious mansion was until recently a family home.

The first owner was so inspired by the setting of his new house on the shores of Loch Awe, beneath Cruachan's mighty peaks, that he began planting a great garden. A number of conifers and other rare trees he planted stand today, loftily surveying the acres of woodland and shrub laid out by subsequent owners.

Rhododendrons, Azaleas and Embothriums flourish in the soft West Coast climate and give Ardanaiseig a unique position among Scotland's Country House Hotels. The rooms are of sensible proportions and have been tastefully decorated and comfortably furnished with big chintzy chairs, polished tables and fresh flowers. The house is warm and the atmosphere relaxed, a combination of elegance and most caring hosts. The bedrooms are quite charming, centrally heated with their own private bathrooms, and enjoy utter peace.

The service is unobtrusive yet attentive, and a recent award for cuisine highlights the importance attached to the kitchen where talented young chefs have, by their flair and skilful use of all the fresh produce for which Scotland is famed, made dining at Ardanaiseig a memorable experience.

Most of the pleasures of a Highland holiday are provided. The Hotel has its own private pier on Loch Awe and boats from which to fish or explore and picnic on the many Islands not too far away from the shore. There is a beat on the River and various hill Lochs for the more serious fisherman. There is excellent walking and wildlife observation and carefully mapped woodland trails have been created over much of this rugged estate. There is Highland Croquet, a Tennis Court and a Clay Pigeon Trap.

Whether it is to relax after following the fairway or to inspire beforehand, we shall extend a warm welcome, sympathy and encouragement in equal measures!

Ardanaiseig
Kilchrenan by Taynuilt
Argyll
Scotland
Tel: (08663) 333

ROYAL TROON
CHAMPIONSHIP GOLF

'O'a the links where i hae golfed Frae Ayr to Aberdeen, On Prestwick or Carnoustie and mony mair I ween What tho' the bents are rough and bunkers yawn aroun' I dearly lo'e the breezy links, the breezy links o'Troon.' (Gilmour) When the golfing mind focuses on **Troon** it invariably thinks of the **Postage Stamp,** the par three **8th** on the **Old Course,** unquestionably the world's most celebrated short hole. During the **1973** Open Championship **Gene Sarazen**, then at the mature age of 71, holed out with his punched five iron shot in front of the watching television cameras. Sarazen declared that he would take with him to heaven a copy of the film to show to Walter Hagen and Co. Legend has it that on hearing of Sarazen's feat an American flew to Britain and travelled to Troon. He strode to the 8th tee and proceded to strike 500 balls in succession towards the green. Not suprisingly he failed to equal Sarazen's achievement whereupon he left the course and duly flew home to America. Who said it was only mad dogs and Englishmen?

Anyone contemplating the above ought at least to consult the **Secretary** first, **Mr. J.D. Montgomerie** being the gentleman in question. he can be contacted at the **Royal Troon Golf Club, Craigend Road, Troon, Strathclyde. Tel. (0292) 311555**.

The Royal Troon Club possesses two 18 hole courses, **'The Old'** and **'The Portland'. Gentlemen** visitors are welcome to play both courses between Mondays and Thursdays provided prior arrangement is made with the Secretary. **Lady** golfers are also welcome, although on Tuesdays and Thursdays they are limited to playing on the Portland Course. All visitors must be members of a recognised club and be able to produce a certificate of handicap. **Society** games may be arranged, but organisers should note that their numbers must not exceed forty. In **1989** a **green fee** of **£30** entitled the visitor to a round on each course, while a fee of **£20** secured a full day's golf on the Portland Course. There are no concessionary rates for junior golfers, who in any event must have attained the age of eighteen before they will be permitted to play over the Old Course. Sets of clubs and trolleys may be hired from the Club's **professional, Brian Anderson (tel. 0292 313281)**. A caddy can also be obtained – provided you can speak the local dialect, something to be seriously considered.

The town of Troon lies just to the north of Prestwick and Ayr. Apparently, its name derives from the Old Welsh word 'trwyn' meaning nose, describing the rocky promontory that forms part of the coastline around Troon. The town can be reached from Glasgow and the north via the **A77**, which also runs from near Stranraer in the south. The **A78** is the coastal road, running from Largs through Irvine to Loans, just east of Troon. Travelling from Edinburgh, the **A71** should be taken, whilst from the North of England the best route is probably via the **A74** and the **A71**. Finally, **Prestwick Airport** is no more than two miles away. Located as it is, bordering the Firth of Clyde, the wind often blows very fiercely across the links and Troon is hardly a place for the faint-hearted golfer.

The Club is proud of its great history. When it was founded in **1878** by twenty-four local enthusiasts there were originally only five holes -by **1923** it had staged its first **Open Championship**. Since then the Club has held four further Opens, in **1950, 1962** (when a rampant **Palmer** stormed to a six stroke victory), **1973** and most recently in **1982** when **Tom Watson** won the fourth of his five titles to date. **1989** also sees the Open staged at Troon for the sixth time. In addition, Troon has played host to four **Amateur Championships** as well as being the venue for several other important events.

The **Old Course** at Troon has both the longest hole of any Open Championship course – the **6th** at **577 yards** and the shortest – the Postage Stamp, which measures a mere **126 yards**. In the **11th** it also possesses one of the toughest, with its railway out-of-bounds, thick gorse and painfully narrow fairway. The great **Jack Nicklaus** once took a 10 at this hole (there's hope for us all yet!). At **6274 yards** the **Portland Course** represents a more modest test, but it is none the less a very fine course and it has all the challenges of traditional links golf.

If you have played all 36 holes at Troon and waged a successful war against the elements you will have earned your drink at the 19th. The Clubhouse provides all the usual facilities and the catering has a very good reputation. When you leave you will probably not have a film to take to heaven, but you will at least know that you have visited one of the earth's greatest golfing shrines.

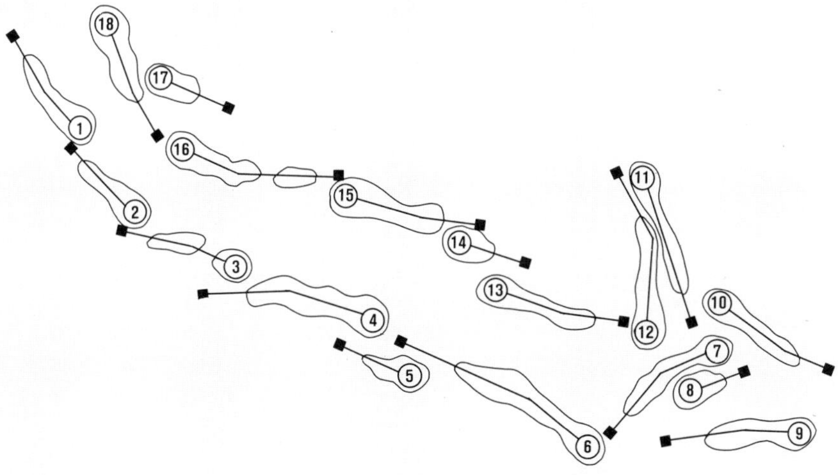

Old Course

Hole	Yards	Par	Hole	Yards	Par
1	362	4	10	437	4
2	391	4	11	481	5
3	381	4	12	432	4
4	556	5	13	468	4
5	210	3	14	180	3
6	577	5	15	457	4
7	400	4	16	542	5
8	126	3	17	223	3
9	419	4	18	425	4
Out	3,422	36	In	3,645	36
			Out	3,422	36
			TOTALS	7,067	72

PRESTWICK
CHAMPIONSHIP GOLF

One could be forgiven for thinking that they take their golf a little too seriously at **Prestwick** – at least when one hears of such stories as the monk from a nearby monastery who once played a match against the Lord of Culzean to settle a deadly feud: at stake was the monk's nose!

The truth more likely is that Prestwick folk are a competitive breed. Only nine years after the formation of their Club in **1851** the Members got together and decided to stage an annual Open competition. The winner of the event was to receive an elegant red belt subscribed for by the Members. Whilst there may have been only eight entrants, the **1860 Open** marks the birth of the world's most prestigious Championship.

Willie Park of Musselburgh (a 'foreigner from the east coast') won the 1860 Open and it was decided that if anyone won the event three years in succession they would win the Belt outright. **Young Tom Morris** (somehow Tom Morris Junior doesn't seem quite appropriate) was the greatest player of his day and fittingly enough in 1870 won his third title in as many years. Whereas Tom may have kept the Belt, Prestwick didn't keep the Open, or at least not the sole rights, as St. Andrews and Muirfield now joined Prestwick in the dawning of a new era.

In those early days the combatants played over a twelve hole course; today there are eighteen holes though the distinctive flavour remains, (in fact seven of the original greens are in the same place). The modern day golfer must still play over the humps and hillocks, face blind shots and tackle the numerous deep sleeper-faced bunkers.

Visitors wishing to play the historic course are advised to approach **Mr. J.A. Reid**, the Club's **Secretary**, in order to book a starting time. Mr. Reid can be contacted at **The Prestwick Golf Club, 2 Links Road, Prestwick, Ayrshire, KA9 1QG, Tel. (0292) 77404.** Visitors should note that they will not be permitted to play at weekends, or after 11am on Thursdays, and that the first tee will usually be reserved for Members between the hours of 9am-10am and 12.30pm and 2.45pm. Furthermore prior to 9am three ball and four ball matches are not generally allowed.

In **1989** the summer **green fee** was set at **£30** per day; however, for those arriving after 2.45pm the green fee is reduced to **£20**. The winter green fee is set at **£20** per day. Sets of golf clubs and caddies can be hired through the professional, **Frank Rennie, Tel. (0292) 79483.**

I suppose like most things at Prestwick, the Clubhouse could be described as having a traditional atmosphere. Ladies are not permitted in the Dining and Smoking Rooms where jackets and ties must be worn at all times, but all may enter the Cardinal Room where some fine light lunches are offered. Dinners can also be arranged though some prior warning is necessary.

At one time Prestwick was a fairly remote place. However, the opening of an **International Airport** has made the area much more accessible from all directions (including overseas). More immediately the **A77** runs directly from Glasgow in the North and along the coast from Stranraer in the South. Those travelling from Edinburgh should use the **A71**, joining the **A77** at Kilmarnock.

From the back markers Prestwick measures **6544 yards** and has a par of **71**. Perhaps not overly long by modern Championship standards it is nonetheless extremely challenging and local knowledge (not to mention rub of the green) can make a considerable difference. At 346 yards the opening hole is as small beer in comparison to the first on the original twelve hole layout – that one measured a lengthy 578 yards and in an age of hickory shafts and gutty balls no doubt proved a stiff bogey six. One can only wonder as to how in the 1870 Open, en route to his aforementioned hat trick, Young Tom Morris managed to hole out in three strokes! Another of Tom's notable achievements at Prestwick occurred in the 1868 Open when he recorded the first known hole in one.

The **3rd** hole at Prestwick is probably the most famous; here the golfer must carry the vast **Cardinal Bunker** which stretches the width of the fairway. Later on in his round he must also confront the legendary **'Himalayas' (5th)** and the **'Alps' (17th)**. The course is not actually quite so mountainous as some of the names suggest and the American who arrived at the Airport saying he was going to take thirteen clubs and a pick-axe was himself going a little 'over the top'. If the golfer does find himself getting frustrated with his game he should at least enjoy the marvellous views of Ailsa Craig and Arran.

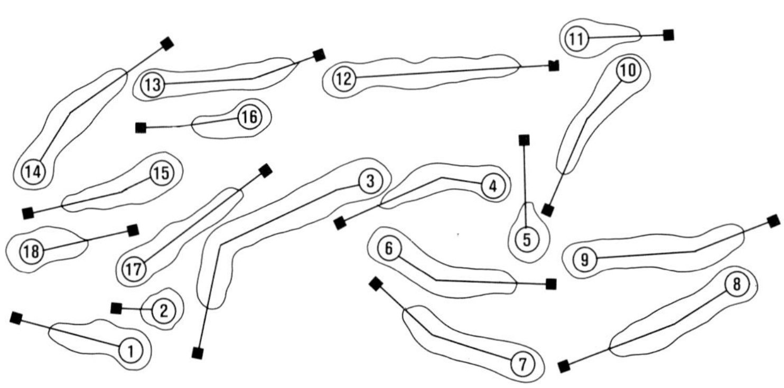

Hole	Yards	Par	Hole	Yards	Par
1	346	4	10	454	4
2	167	3	11	195	3
3	482	5	12	513	5
4	382	4	13	460	4
5	206	3	14	362	4
6	362	4	15	347	4
7	430	4	16	288	4
8	431	4	17	391	4
9	444	4	18	284	4
Out	**3,250**	**35**	**In**	**3,294**	**36**
			Out	**3,250**	**35**
			TOTALS	**6,544**	**71**

STRATHCLYDE
COMPLETE GOLF

STRATHCLYDE

Airdrie G.C.
(18) 6004 yards
Rochsoles, Airdrie
(02364) 62195

Alexandra Park Municipal
(9) 4562 yards
Alexandra Parade, Glasgow
(041) 556 3711

Annanhill G.C.
(18) 6269 yards
Irvine Road, Kilmarnock
(0563) 21644

Ardeer G.C.
(18) 6630 yards
Greenhead, Stevenston
(0294) 64542

Ayr Belleisle G.C.
(18) 6540 yards (Belleisle)
(18) 5244 yards (Seafield)
Belleisle Park, Ayr
(0292) 41258

Ayr Dalmilling G.C.
(18) 5401 yards
Westwood Avenue, Ayr
(0292) 263893

Ballochmyle G.C.
(18) 5952 yards
Ballochmyle, Mauchline
(0290) 50469

Balmore G.C.
(18) 5516 yards
Balmore, Torrance
(03602) 0240

Barshaw G.C.
(18) 5703 yards
Barshaw Park, Paisley
(041) 884 2533

Bearsden G.C.
(9) 5977 yards
Thorn Road, Bearsden
Glasgow
(041) 942 2351

Beith G.C.
(9) 5488 yards
Bigholm, Beith
(05055) 2011

Bellshill G.C.
(18) 6607 yards
Orbiston, Bellshill
(0698) 745124

Biggar G.C.
(18) 5256 yards
Broughton Road, Biggar
(0899) 20618

Bishopbriggs G.C.
(18) 6041 yards
Brackenbrae Road, Bishopbriggs,
Glasgow
(041) 772 1810

Blairbeth G.C.
(18) 5448 yards
Rutherglen, Glasgow
(041) 634 3355

Blairmore & Strone G.C.
(9) 4224 yards
Blairmore, Argyll
(036984) 217

Bonnyton G.C.
(18) 6252 yards
Eaglesham, Glasgow
(03553) 2781

Bothwell Castle G.C.
(18) 6432 yards
Blantyre Road, Bothwell,
Glasgow
(0698) 853177

Brodick G.C.
(18) 4404 yards
Brodick, Isle of Arran
(0770) 2349

Bute G.C.
(9) 5594 yards
Killchattan Bay, Bute
(0700) 83242

Calderbraes G.C.
(9)5186 yards
57, Roundknowe Road,
Uddingston
(0698) 813425

Caldwell G.C.
(18) 6102 yards
Uplawnmoor
(050585) 329

Cambuslang G.C.
(9) 6072 yards
Westburn Drive, Cambuslang,
Glasgow
(041) 641 3130

Campsie G.C.
(18) 5517 yards
Crow Road, Lennoxtown,
Glasgow
(0360) 0244

Caprington G.C.
(18) 5718 yards
Ayr Road, Kilmarnock
(0563) 23702

Cardross G.C.
(18) 6466 yards
Main Road, Cardross,
Dumbarton
(0389) 841754

Carluke G.C.
(18) 5805 yards
Hallcraig, Carluke
(0555) 71070

Carnwath G.C.
(18) 5860 yards
Main Street, Carnwath
(0555) 840251

Carradale G.C.
(9) 4774 yards
Carradale, Argyll
(05833) 624

Cathcart Castle G.C.
(18) 5832 yards
Mearns Road, Clarkston,
Glasgow
(041) 638 9449

Cathkin Braes G.C.
(18) 6266 yards
Cathkin Road, Rutherglen,
Glasgow
(041) 634 6605

Cawder G.C.
(18) 6229 yards (Cawder)
(18) 5877 yards (Keir)
Cadder Road, Bishopbriggs,
Glasgow
(041) 772 7101

Clober G.C.
(18) 5068 yards
Craigton Road, Milngauie
(041) 956 1685

Clydebank & District G.C.
(18) 5815 yards
Hardgate, Clydebank
(0389) 73289

Clydebank Municipal G.C.
(18) 5349 yards
Overtoun Road, Clydebank
(041) 952 6372

Cochrane Castle G.C.
(18) 6226 yards
Craigston, Johnstone
(0505) 20146

Colonsay G.C.
(18) 4775 yards
Isle of Colonsay
(09512) 316

Colville Park G.C.
(18) 6208 yards
Jerviston Estate, Motherwell
(0698) 63017

Corrie G.C.
(9) 3896 yards
Corrie, Isle of Arran
(077081) 223

Cowal G.C.
(18) 5820 yards
Ardenslate Road, Kirn, Dunoon
(0396) 5673

Cowglen G.C.
(18) 5976 yards
301, Barhead Road, Glasgow
(041) 632 0556

Crow Wood G.C.
(18) 6209 yards
Muirhead, Chryston
(041) 779 1943

BURLINGTON GALLERY

STRATHCLYDE

COMPLETE GOLF

Cumbernauld Municipal
(18) 6412 yards
Cumbernauld
(02367) 28138

Dougalston G.C.
(18) 6683 yards
Milngauie, Glasgow
(041) 956 5750

Douglas Park G.C.
(18) 5957 yards
Hiilfoot, Bearsden, Glasgow
(041) 942 2220

Douglas Water G.C.
(9) 5832 yards
Ayr Road, Rigside,
Lanark
(0555) 2295

Drumpellier G.C.
(18) 6205 yards
Drumpellier, Coatbridge
(0236) 24139

Dullatur G.C.
(18) 6253 yards
Dullatur, Glasgow
(02367) 27847

Dumbarton G.C.
(18) 5981 yards
Broadmeadow, Dumbarton
(0389) 32830

Dunaverty G.C.
(18) 4597 yards
Southend, Campbelltown,
Argyll

Easter Moffat G.C.
(18) 6221 yards
Mansion House, Plains,
Airdrie
(0236) 842289

East Kilbride G.C.
(18) 6419 yards
Chapelside Road, Nerston,
East Kilbride
(03552) 47728

East Renfrewshire G.C.
(18) 6097 yards
Pilmuir, Newton Mearns,
Glasgow
(03555) 258

Eastwood G.C.
(18) 5864 yards
Muirshield, Newton Mearns,
Glasgow
(03555) 280

Elderslie G.C.
(18) 6004 yards
Main Road, Elderslie
(0505) 23956

Erskine G.C.
(18) 6287 yards
Bishopston
(0505) 2302

Fereneze G.C.
(18) 5821 yards
Fereneze Avenue, Barrhead,
Glasgow
(041) 881 1519

Girvan G.C.
(18) 5075 yards
Golf Course Road, Girvan
(0465) 4272

Glasgow Gailes G.C.
(18) 6447 yards
Gailes, Irvine
(0294) 311247

Glasgow Killermont G.C.
(18) 5968 yards
Killermont, Glasgow
(041) 942 2011

Gleddoch G. & C.C.
(18) 6200 yards
Langbank
(047554) 304

Glencruitten G.C.
(18) 4452 yards
Glencruitten, Oban
(0631) 62868

Gourock G.C.
(18) 6492 yards
Cowal View, Gourock
(0475) 31001

Greenock G.C.
(27) 5838 yards
Forsyth Street, Greenock
(0475) 20793

Greenock Whinhill G.C.
(18) 5454 yards
Beith Road, Greenock
(0475) 24694

Haggs Castle G.C.
(18) 6464 yards
70, Drumbreck Road,
Glasgow
(041) 427 1157

Hamilton G.C.
(18) 6264 yards
Riccarton, Ferniegair,
Hamilton
(0698) 282872

Hayston G.C.
(18) 6042 yards
Campsie Road, Kirkintilloch,
Glasgow
(041) 775 0882

Helensburgh G.C.
(18) 6058 yards
East Abercromby Street,
Helensburgh
(0436) 4173

Hilton Park G.C.
(18) 6021 yards (Hilton)
(18) 5409 yards (Alexander)
Stockiemuir Road, Milngavie,
Glasgow
(041) 956 4657

Hollandbush G.C.
(18) 6110 yards
Lesmahagow, Coalburn
(0555) 893484

Innellan G.C.
(9) 4878 yards
Innellan, Argyll
(0369) 3546

Irvine G.C.
(18) 6454 yards
Bogside, Irvine
(0294) 75979

Irvine Ravenspark G.C.
(18) 6429 yards
Kidsneuk Road, Irvine
(0294) 79550

Kilbirnie Place G.C.
(18) 5479 yards
Largs Road, Kilbirnie
(050582) 683398

Kilmacolm G.C.
(18) 5964 yards
Porterfield, Kilmacolm
(050587) 2695

Kilmarnock (Barassie) G.C.
(18) 6460 yards
Hillhouse Road, Barassie,
Troon
(0292) 311077

Kilsyth Lennox G.C.
(9) 5944 yards
Tak-Ma-Doon Road, Kilsyth,
Glasgow
(0236) 822190

Kirkhill G.C.
(18) 5889 yards
Greenlees Road, Cambuslang,
Glasgow
(041) 641 8499

Kirkintilloch G.C.
(18) 5269 yards
Todhill, Campsie Road,
Kirkintilloch
(041) 776 1256

Knightswood G.C.
(9) 2717 yards
Lincoln Avenue, Knightswood,
Glasgow
(041) 959 2131

Kyles of Bute G.C.
(9) 4758 yards
Tighnabruaich, Argyll
(0700) 811355

Lamlash G.C.
(18) 4681 yards
Lamlash, Isle of Arran
(07706) 296

Lanark G.C.
(18) 6416 yards
The Moor, Lanark
(0555) 3219

Landoun G.C.
(18) 5824 yards
Edinburgh Road, Galston
(0563) 821993

Largs G.C.
(18) 6257 yards
Irvine Road, Largs
(0475) 673594

Larkhall G.C.
(9) 6236 yards
Burnhead Road, Larkhall
(0698) 881113

Leadhills G.C.
(9) 4062 yards
Leadhills, Biggar
(06594) 222

Lenzie G.C.
(18) 5982 yards
Crosshill Road, Lenzie,
Glagow
(041) 776 1535

Lethamhill G.C.
(18) 6073 yards
Cumbernauld Road, Glasgow
(041) 770 6220

Linn Park G.C.
(18) 4832 yards
Simshill Road, Glasgow
(041) 637 5871

Littlehill G.C.
(18) 6199 yards
Auchinairn Road, Bishopbriggs,
Glasgow
(041) 772 1916

Lochranza G.C.
(9) 3580 yards
Brodick, Isle of Arran
(077083) 273

Lochwinnoch G.C.
(18) 6223 yards
Burnfoot Road, Lochwinnoch
(0505) 842153

Machrie Hotel and G.C.
(18) 6226 yards
Machrie Hotel, Port Ellen,
Isle of Islay
(0496) 2310

Machrie Bay G.C.
(9) 4246 yards
Machrie Bay, Isle of Arran
(077084) 258

Machrihanish G.C.
(18) 6228 yards
Machrinhanish, Campbeltown,
Argyll
(0586) 81213

Maybole G.C.
(9) 5270 yards
Memorial Park, Maybole
Maybole 82454

Millport G.C.
(18) 5831 yards
Golf Road, Millport,
Isle of Cumbrae
(0475) 530485

Milgavie G.C.
(18) 5818 yards
Laigh Park, Milngavie,
Glasgow
(041) 956 1619

Mount Ellen G.C.
(18) 5525 yards
Johnston House, Gartcosh,
Glasgow
(0236) 782277

Old Ranfurly G.C.
(18) 6266 yards
Ranfurly Place, Bridge of Weir
(0505) 613612

Paisley G.C.
(18) 6424 yards
Braehead, Paisley
(041) 884 2292

Pollok G.C.
(18) 6257 yards
90, Barrhead Road, Glasgow
(041) 632 4351

Port Bannatyne G.C.
(13) 4654 yards
Port Bannatyne, Isle of Bute
(0700) 2009

Port Glasgow G.C.
(18) 5712 yards
Port Glasgow
(0475) 704181

Prestwick G.C.
(18) 6544 yards
2, Links Road, Prestwick
(0292) 77404

Prestwick St. Cuthbert G.C.
(18) 6470 yards
East Road, Prestwick
(0292) 79120

Prestwick St. Nicholas G.C.
(18) 5864 yards
Grangemuir Road, Prestwick
(0292) 77608

Raiston G.C.
(18) 6100 yards
Raiston, Paisley
(041) 882 1349

STRATHCLYDE
COMPLETE GOLF

Ranfurly Castle G.C.
(18) 6284 yards
Golf Road, Bridge of Weir
(0505) 612609

Renfew G.C.
(18) 6818 yards
Blythswood Estate,
Inchinan Road,
Renfrew
(041) 886 6692

Rothesay G.C.
(18) 5358 yards
Rothesay, Isle of Bute
(0700) 2244

Routenburn G.C.
(18) 5650 yards
Largs
(0475) 674289

Royal Troon G.C.
(18) 6641 yards (Old)
(18) 6274 yards (Portland)
Criagend Road, Troon
(0292) 311555

Sandyhills G.C.
(18) 6253 yards
223, Sandyhills Road, Glasgow
(041) 778 1179

Shiskine G.C.
(12) 3000 yards
Blackwaterfoot, Isle of Arran
(077086) 293

Shotts G.C.
(18) 6125 yards
Blairhead, Shotts
(0501) 20431

Skelmorlie G.C.
(13) 5056 yards
Skelmorlie
(0475) 520152

Strathaven G.C.
(18) 6226 yards
Overton Avenue, Glasgow Road,
Strathhaven
(0357) 20421

Strathclyde Park G.C.
(9) 6294 yards
Motel Hill, Hamilton
(0698) 66155

Tarbert G.C.
(9) 4460 yards
Kilberry Road, Tarbert,
Argyll
(08802) 565

Torrence House G.C.
(18) 6640 yards
Strathaven Road, E. Kilbride,
Glasgow
(03552) 33451

Troon Municipal G.C.
(18) 6687 yards (Lochgreen)
(18) 6327 yards (Darley)
(18) 4784 yards (Fullarton)
Harling Drive, Troon
(0292) 312464

Turnberry Hotel
(18) 6956 yards (Ailsa)
(18) 6276 yards (Arran)
Turnberry Hotel, Turnberry
(06553) 1000

Vaul G.C.
(9) 6246 yards
Scarinish, Isle of Tiree,
Argyll
(08792) 566

Western Gailes G.C.
(18) 6833 yards
Gailes, by Irvine,
Ayrshire
(0294) 311649

Western Isles G.C.
(9) 4920 yards
Tobermory, Isle of Mull
(0688) 2020

West Kilbridge G.C.
(18) 6348 yards
Fullerton Drive, West Kilbride
(0294) 823911

Whitecraigs G.C.
(18) 6230 yards
72, Ayr Road, Giffnock,
Glasgow
(041) 639 4530

Whiting Bay G.C.
(18) 4405 yards
Whiting Bay, Isle of Arran
(07707) 487

Williamwood G.C.
(18) 5878 yards
Clarkeston Road, Netherlee,
Glasgow
(041) 637 2715

Windyhill G.C.
(18) 6254 yards
Baljaffray Road, Bearsden,
Glasgow
(041) 942 7157

Wishaw G.C.
(18) 6134 yards
Cleland Road, Wishaw
(0698) 3782869

PIMM 'Putting' *ROSENSTIEL'S*

FIFE

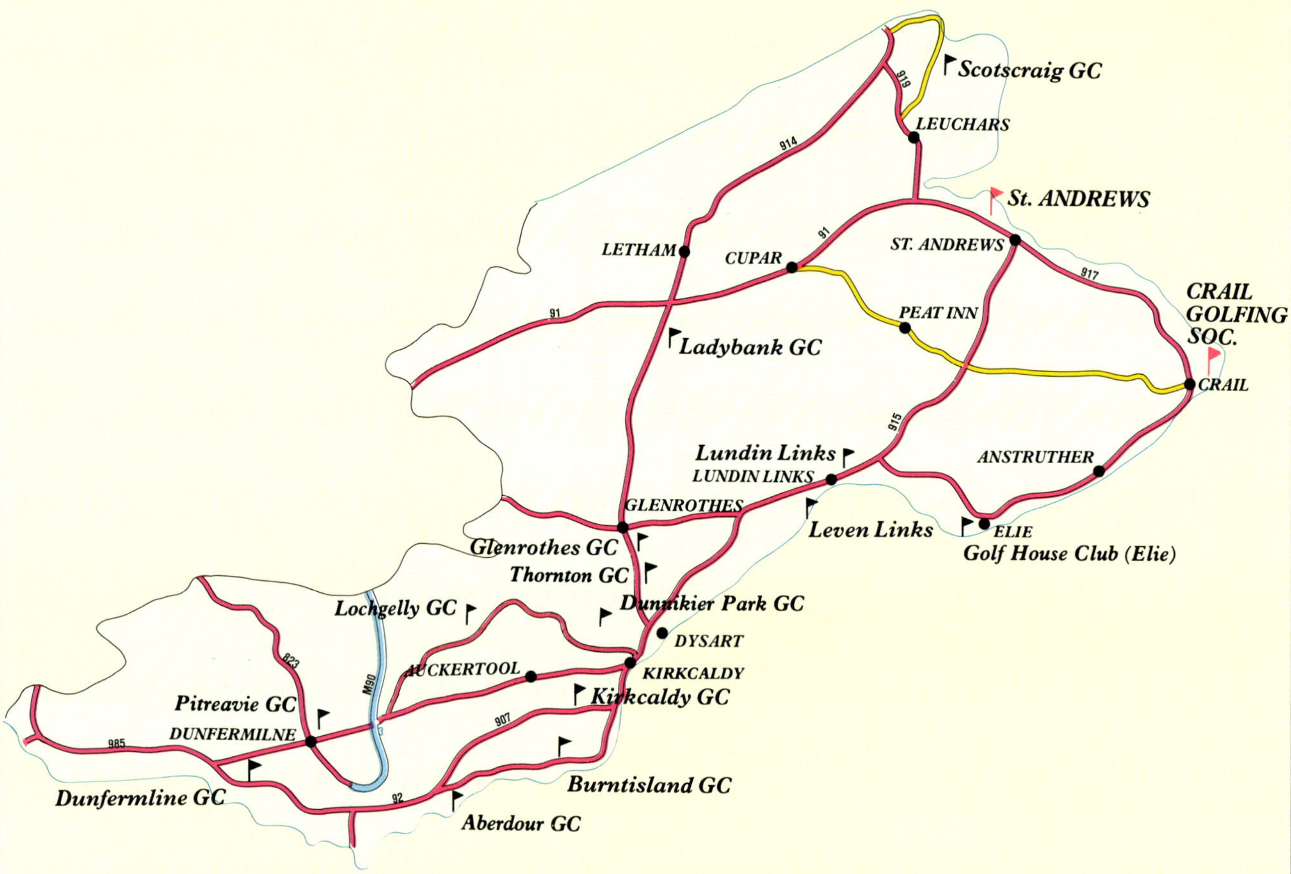

CHARLES WAGSTAFF "The Golfers" ROSENSTIELS

FIFE

CHOICE GOLF

Many years ago watching an England versus Scotland soccer game at Wembley I remember being amused by one of the banners caried by a group of Scottish supporters which boldly declared, 'Remember Bannockburn'. Being a pigheaded Englishman I thought to myself they ought to remember it – it was just about the only battle they won in centuries. Of course, all is now abundantly clear – the Scots were far too busy priming their golfing skills to bother themselves fighting the Sassenachs.

As long ago as **1457** the Scottish Parliament, unimpressed at the performance of their sharp shooters, felt that too much golf and football was to blame for the lack-lustre performances on the battlefields. An Act was passed stating that because of their interference with the practice of archery 'the fute-ball and golf be utterly cryit down and nocht usit'. History would seem to suggest that the Scots didn't take a blind bit of notice and golf steadily grew in popularity. Juggle the figures that make up 1457 and we have **1754**, perhaps the most significant date in golf's history – the year the Society of St Andrews golfers drew up the first written rules of golf.

Today **St Andrews** deep in the 'Kingdom of Fife', is the place every golfer in the world wants to visit. Even if he's only swung a club at the local municipal he'll be itching to do the same at St Andrews. However, for those contemplating a pilgrimage to the centre of the golfing world if should be said that St Andrews has several near neighbours that warrant the most discerning attention of any intrepid traveller. Between Dunfermline, to the west of Fife, and St Andrews, lie what are undoubtedly some of the finest courses in Scotland.

For six hundred years Dunfermline was the country's capital and the body of its most famous king, Robert the Bruce, lies buried in Dunfermline Abbey (minus his heart which is in Melrose Abbey). The town has two courses, **Dunfermline** and **Pitreavie**. Both are parkland courses at which visitors are welcome provided some prior arrangement is made. Neither is unduly hard on the pocket. For those wishing to spend a day or two in the old royal town, the appropriately named **King Malcolm Thistle Hotel (0383) 722611** provides convenient comfort.

East of Dunfermline there is a testing links at **Burntisland** with fine views over the Firth of Forth and there are again two courses in Kirkcaldy, the **Dunnikier Park** and **Kirkcaldy** Golf Clubs, the latter welcoming visitors during the week (Tuesdays excluded) and on Sundays; Dunniker Park is a public course and so a game is much cheaper there . At the other two a days golf should still be possible for less than **£10**. One other course to note in the area is **Aberdour** – more pleasant views. For a good night's rest the **Camilla Hotel (0592) 780590** in nearby Auchtertool can be recommended while in Dysart the **Old Rectory Inn (0592) 51211** is a most pleasant pub-cum-restaurant.

Beyond Kirkcaldy along a glorious stretch of spectacular coast lie Fife's famous five – **Leven Links, Lundin Links, Elie, Balcomie** and of course **St Andrews**. The first two are often considered as a pair probably on account of there being very little land in between. Two clubs share the 6,433 yards links at Leven, the **Leven Golfing Society** and **Leven Thistle**. Visitors looking for a game should book in advance and whilst there is no similar requirement at **Lundin** (6,377 yards) being equally popular prior telephoning would seem advisable, especially during the summer. Fees at both are approximately **£12** per day.

Elie, or the **Golf House Club**, lies a short distance from the two across Largo Bay, the **A917** linking the town with Leven. Elie is famed for its unique periscope by the first tee and for the fact that it was here that **James Braid** fashioned many of the skills that won him five Open Championships. A charming and very natural links measuring 6,241 yars, several of the holes are laid out right alongside a rocky shoreline. A ballot system operates at Elie during the months of July and August but otherwise there are not general restrictions on times visitors can play. The cost of a day's golf is **£12** during the week, **£15** at weekends.

Following the **A917** eastwards from Elie the town of Crail is soon reached. Just beyond the town at Fife Ness is the magnicifent **Balcomie** links, the home of the two hundred year old **Crail Golfing Society**. Together with St Andrews it is featured a few pages on. Beyond St Andrews the A917 joins the **A91** and heads off towards Dundee.

Apart from a few large hotels in St Andrews, accommodation near to the great links courses of Fife is generally inexpensive. A great number are geared almost solely towards the interests of the golfing community and are situated within pitching distance of the nearest fairway. Here are a few thoughts; In Lundin links, the **Old Manor Hotel (0333) 320368** is highly thought of with a particularly good restaurant while less expensive accommodation can be enjoyed at the **Lundin Links Hotel (0333) 330207**. The **Golf Hotel (0333) 330209** in Elie is self explanatory, and just a short distance away in Anstruther is the **Craws Nest Hotel (0333) 310691** – midway between Elie and Crail it's an excellent base. In Anstruther one might also visit the **Smugglers Inn**, a cosy 300 year old tavern. Crail is a delightful fishing village and here the **Golf Hotel (0333) 50206** is another obvious choice, it's a place of great character and is one of Scotland's oldest licensed inns. Still in Crail, the **Caiplie Guest House (0333) 50564** is great value. Two restaurants that can be strongly recommended are **Ostlers Close (0334) 55574** at Cupar and the exceptional **Peat Inn (0334) 84206** on the road to Cupar – be sure to look.

It isn't an overstatement to say that **St Andrews** is the centre of the golfing world. As early as 1691 it was described as the 'Metropolis of Golfing'. With pilgrims making the trip from all corners of the globe (and especially from America and Japan) the number of hotels and guest houses is understandably considerable. The **Old Course Hotel (0334) 74371** stand alongside the 17th fairway and its combination of leisure pursuits headed, of course, by the golf itself makes for a really tremendous time. The **Eden Restaurant** has an excellent reputation and what a place to celebrate a birdie at the seventeenth. St Andrews does have several other hotels of note; they are also less expensive than the Old Course. **Rufflets Hotel (0334) 72594** just outside the town is an excellent base while another room with a view can be booked at the **Rusacks Marine Hotel (0334) 74321**; formerly the Golf Inn, the restaurant is also good and rather appropriately named the **Niblick**. The other hotels which might just hint at a round of the good old game include the **St Andrews Golf Hotel (0334) 72611** and the **Scores Hotel (0334) 72451**, both good value and pleasant. While golf clearly takes centre stage one should not forget the pleasant coastline nearby, the twelfth century Cathedral or Scotland's oldest university. One final thought is the popular **Grange Inn (0334) 72670** in Grange Village – an excellent place. The varied menu includes both French and local specialities making particularly good use of fish and game.

Just as the leading courses of Surrey aren't all heathland and heather neither are those of Fife all seaviews and sandhills. **Ladybank and Glenrothes** both in the heart of Fife are two of Scotland's greatest inland courses. **Ladybank** is situated only a few miles north of Leven but is completely different in character with heathland fairways and much pine and heather – a very beautiful course. Golf can be enjoyed at Ladybank for around the **£10** to **£15** mark, weekend mornings are best avoided.

In an area steeped in history **Glenrothes** is a relative newcomer to the scene being founded less than twenty years ago. Young, perhaps, but an excellent course nonetheless. Situated to the west of the town it is a fairly hilly parkland type offering many superb views. Visitors are always made welcome though pre-booking (one day before intended play) is advisable. The green fees here are outstandingly good value, **£2.65** per round midweek, **£3.75** at weekends. The names of two of the holes, however, worry me a little – the 11th, titled 'Satan's Gateway' and the 18th, 'Hell's End'!

A restful 19th is clearly in order. In Glenrothes quality places abound. The **Balgeddie House (0592) 742511** is superbly secluded and most relaxing, while the **Rescobie Hotel (0592) 742143** and the **Rothes Arms (0592) 753701** should also placate the soul. Letham is only a short distance from Ladybank and here the **Fernie Castle (033781) 381** is recommended.

Two other courses that are well worth visiting if journeying inland are at **Thornton (£4 to £6** per round where the River Ore makes for some challenging holes) and at **Lochgelly** – convenient if travelling between Dunfermline and Kirkcaldy. The final mention though goes to **Scotscraig**, an Open Championship qualifying course at Tayport. Although close to the sea it's actually a downland type course rather than a links. Green fees are around **£10 to £12**.

Following a game at Scotscraig one is likely to be left with a difficult decision. To the north **Carnoustie** and many other great challenges await; but then no golfer who experienced the pleasures of the Kingdom of Fife ever left easily.

N. ARTHUR LORRAINE "Tom Morris Putting" *BURLINGTON GALLERY*

ST. ANDREWS
CHAMPIONSHIP GOLF

If there is such a thing as a truly global sport then it has to be golf. From its parochial beginnings on the east coast of Scotland it is now played on every continent, in every conceivable corner. Not only are there golf courses on the exotic islands of Tahiti and Bali but there is one in the Himalayas and there is one in the Arctic; golf has even been played on the moon. For all this there remains but one home – **St. Andrews**.

Whilst we will never be able to put an exact date on the time golf was first played on the famous links, several documents refer to a crude form of the game being played as early as the mid 1400s. Whether it was called gowf, goff or gouffe matters not, it was played on land close to the sea with a club and a small ball which was struck towards a distant hole cut in the ground, the object being to 'hole out' in as few strokes as possible. As for the right to play at St Andrews, which of course, the whole world enjoys, the origins are embodied in a licence dated **1552** drawn up by the **Archbishop** of **St. Andrews**. It permitted the community to breed rabbits on the links and to 'play at golf,futeball, schueting, at all gamis with all uther, as ever they pleis and in ony time'. Furthermore the proprieter was bound 'not to plough up any part of said golf links in all time coming.'

Organised golf came to St. Andrews in **1754** when twenty-two 'Noblemen and Gentlemen' formed the **St. Andrews Society of Golfers**. In **1834** the Society became the **Royal and Ancient Golf Club**.

Not only can all the world play at St. Andrews, but all the world wants to and arranging a game on th Old Course can be a little difficult. **The St. Andrews Links Management Committee** handles all matters relating to times of play and they should be contacted will in advance. The summer months are naturally the busiest period and it is best to write to the Committee two to three months prior to intended play, offering if possible a number of alternative dates. The address to write to is **The St. Andrews Links Management Committee, Golf Place, St. Andrews, Fife, KY16 9JA**. The Secretary, **Mr. Alec Beveridge** and his staff can be contacted by telephone on **(0334) 75757**. There are no handicap limits to play over the Old Course. However a handicap certificate or letter of introduction is required. It should also be noted that there is no Sunday golf on the Old Course. In 1989 the **green fee** for a round was priced at **£20**.

In addition to the Old Course there are four other links at St. Andrews, the **New Course**, which dates from 1896, **the Jubilee** (1897), **the Eden** (1914) and **the Balgove** (1972), the latter being a 9 hole course. No handicap certificate is required to play over any of the above four and the **green fees** for 1989 on each were **£10, £7, £8** and **£1.50** respectively. It should also be noted that a new Museum should be open at St. Andrews in time for the 1990 Open.

St. Andrews is situated 57 miles north east of Edinburgh. For northbound travellers the most direct route to take is the **M90** after crossing the Forth Road Bridge. The **A91** should be joined at junction **8**. This road can be followed to St. Andrews. Southbound travellers should head for Perth which is linked in turn to Dundee by the **A85** and to the north of Scotland by the **A9**. From Perth a combination of the **A90** and the **A913** takes one to Cupar where the **A91** can be picked up. Finally, the nearest train station is at Leuchars, approximately six miles from the centre of the town.

It was nature that fashioned St. Andrews and over the centuries the Old Course has seen little change. Its myriad of tiny pot bunkers remain both a fascination and a frustration – providing just enough room as **Bernard Darwin** put it 'for an angry man and his niblick'. Laid out on a narrow strip of land ranging from 50 to 100 yards in width, St. Andrews is famed for its enormous double greens. There are seven in all and some are more than an acre in size. With little definition between the fairways there tends to be no standard way of playing a particular hole and as a rule the wind direction will determine the preferred line. Individual holes are not likely to be easily remembered the first time of playing, especially as one will probably be walking the course in a semi-trance. History is everywhere and on the first hole as you cross the bridge over the **Swilcan Burn** a voice from somewhere says 'they've all walked this bridge' – and of course they have,just as they've all passed through the **Elysian Fields**, tackled **Hell's Bunker**, **the Beardies** and the **Principal's Nose**. And then of course they've all faced the **Road Hole** with its desperate drive and even more desperate approach and then finally strolled over the great expanse of the **18th** fairway towards the **Valley of Sin**.

It isn't always love at first sight with St. Andrews and **Bobby Jones** tore up his card on the 11th when he first played. Jones went on to meet great triumph at St. Andrews and it is perhaps fitting to end with a few words from the great man: 'the more I studied the Old Course the more I loved it, and the more I loved it the more I studied it, so that I came to feel that it was for me the most favourable meeting ground possible for an important contest.'

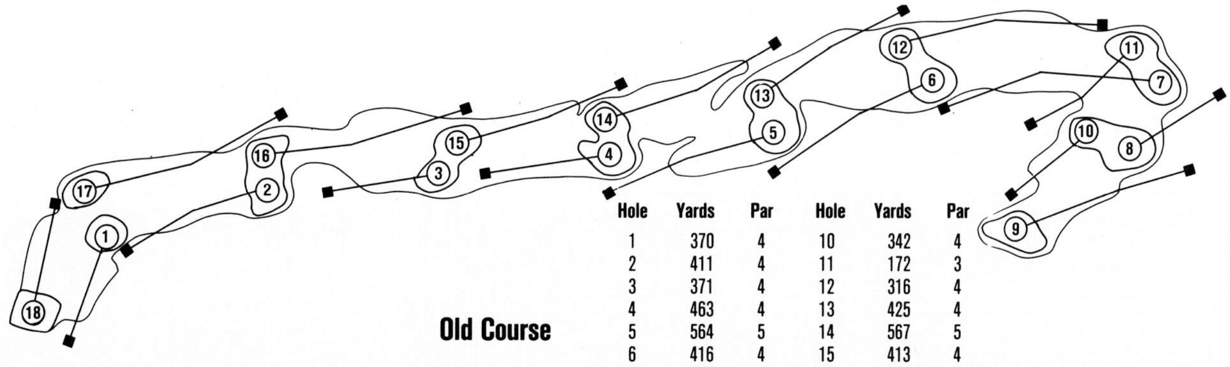

Old Course

Hole	Yards	Par	Hole	Yards	Par
1	370	4	10	342	4
2	411	4	11	172	3
3	371	4	12	316	4
4	463	4	13	425	4
5	564	5	14	567	5
6	416	4	15	413	4
7	372	4	16	382	4
8	178	3	17	461	4
9	356	4	18	354	4
Out	3,501	36	In	3,432	36
			Out	3,501	36
			TOTALS	6,933	72

CRAIL GOLFING SOCIETY

CHAMPIONSHIP GOLF

On **23rd February 1986** the seventh oldest Golf Club in the world celebrated its bicentenary. Some three years before the Bastille was stormed a group of eleven gentlemen met at the **Golf Inn** in Crail and together formed the **Crail Golfing Society**. The records of that historic day are still preserved; indeed remarkably the Society possesses a complete set of minutes from the date of its inception. In those early days the Society members wore scarlet jackets with yellow buttons and dined at the Golf Inn after a day on the links. The local punch flowed and a good time was doubtless had by all – now those were the days!

Since 1895 the Club has played over the **Balcomie Links** which is located approximately two miles north east of Crail at Fifeness. Earlier the Society had used a narrow strip of land at **Sauchope**, slightly closer to Crail (and of course to the Golf Inn).

The atmosphere is still jovial and visitors are made most welcome. With the exception of a few competition days there are no general restrictions on times of play. However, individual visitors are advised to telephone the Starter one day before playing. The Starter can be contacted on **(0333) 50686**. Societies, or golfing parties, are equally welcome and advance bookings can be made at all times excepting the very peak summer period. Written enquiries should be addressed to the **Secretary, Crail Golfing Society, Balcomie Clubhouse, Crail, Fife.** The Secretary, **Mr G.B.Thomson M.B.E.**, can be reached by telephone on **(0333) 50960**.

The **green fees** for **1989** were pitched at **£8** per round, **£12** per day during weekdays or **£10** per round, and **£15** per day at weekends. Juniors can obtain a weekday round for **£3.50** though at other times full fees are charged. In addition short Temporary Membership is offered: examples from 1988 included **£24** for 3 consecutive weekdays, **£40** for a weekly ticket (excluding Sundays) and **£64** for a fortnightly ticket (again excluding Sundays).

The Balcomie Links in in fact ideal for 'holiday golf'. Without being overly long **(5,720** yards, **par 69)** – though the wind can affect it greatly – it offers some exceptionally spectacular scenery and similar to Cruden Bay further North, a nearby Castle casts a watchful eye. **Balcomie Castle**, where Mary of Guies, mother-to-be of Mary Queen of Scots, spent her first few days in Scotland, comes complete with ghost. The course is always well maintained and the holes have been laid out so that each provides a view of the sea. They possess some rather interesting names too: 'Fluke Dub' **(4th)** 'Hell's Hole' **(5th)** 'Castle Yetts' **(9th)** and 'Lang Wang' **(11th)** – the latter fuelling the belief that Scotland and Taiwan once had closer ties.

From all points south travelling to Crail will be by way of the Forth Road Bridge and thereafter following a combination of 'A roads'. However, the M90 may also be used if St Andrews is to be taken in en route. The **A915/A917** approaches Crail from along the coast via Lundin Links and Elie, while from Cupar and St Andrews the **A91/A917** should be taken. As stated the course is situated two miles from Crail in the direction of Fifeness and is well-signposted.

The 19th at Crail is as it should be, right next to the 18th green and provides commanding views over much of the course. Smart casual dress is acceptable in the Clubhouse, though presumably today if you strolled in wearing a bright scarlet jacket you might raise a few eyebrows. A full complement of catering is offered at all times but for those wishing to make advanced arrangements, a quick telephone call to the Steward is never a bad idea. **Mr New** is the gentleman in question and can be contacted on **(0333) 50278**.

The temptation for many on crossing the Forth Road Bridge is of course to head straight for the Royal and Ancient. Although St Andrews may be the undisputed sovereign in the so-called 'Kingdom of Fife', there are also a number of handsome Princes. Balcomie stands comparison with the best and is a course of which the two hundred year old Society can justifiably be proud.

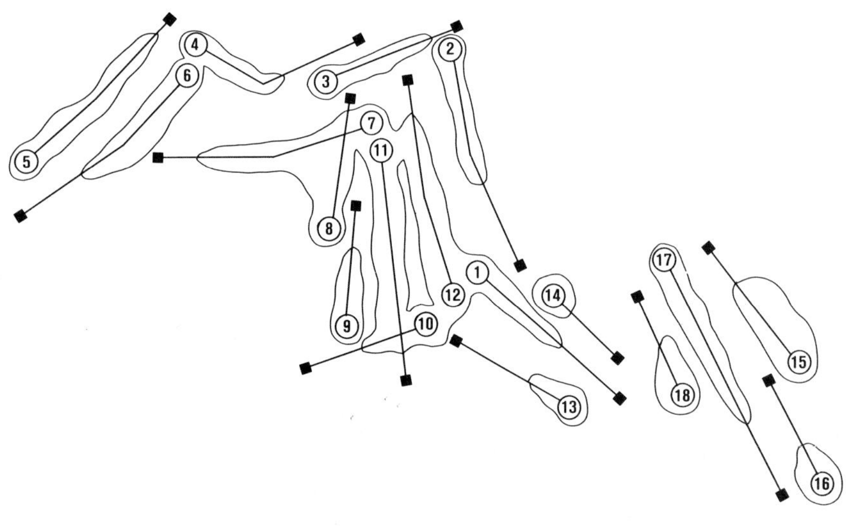

Hole	Yards	Par	Hole	Yards	Par
1	312	4	10	209	3
2	480	5	11	500	5
3	179	3	12	489	5
4	348	4	13	215	3
5	346	4	14	149	3
6	334	4	15	265	4
7	421	4	16	163	3
8	306	4	17	461	4
9	334	4	18	209	3
Out	3,060	36	In	2,660	33
			Out	3,060	36
			TOTALS	5,720	69

FIFE

COMPLETE GOLF

FIFE

Aberdour G.C.
(18) 5432 yards
Seaside Place, Aberdour
(0383) 860688

Anstruther G.C.
(9) 4504 yards
Anstruther
(0333) 310224

Auchterderran G.C.
(9) 5250 yards
Woodend Road, Cardenden
(0592) 721579

Balbirnie Park (1983)
(18) 6444 yards
Balbirnie Park, Markinch,
Glenrothes
(0592) 752006

Ballingry G.C.
(9) 6244 yards
Crosshill, Lochgelly
(0592) 860086

Burntisland Golf House Club
(18) 5871 yards
Dodhead, Burntisland
(0592) 874093

Canmore G.C.
(18) 5474 yards
Venturefair Avenue, Dunfermline
(0383) 724969

Crail Golfing Society
(18) 5720 yards
Balcomie Clubhouse, Fifeness,
Crail
(0333) 50278

Cupar G.C.
(9) 5074 yards
Hilltarvit, Cupar
(0334) 53549

Dunfermline G.C.
(18) 6271 yards
Pitfirrane, Crossford,
Dunfermline
(0383) 723534

Dunnukier Park G.C.
(18) 6601 yards
Dunnikier Way, Kirkcaldy
(0592) 261599

Glenrothes G.C.
(18) 6444 yards
Golf Course Road, Glenrothes
(0592) 758686

Golf House Club (Elie)
(18) 6241 yards
Elie, Leven
(0333) 330301

Kinghorn G.C.
(18) 5269 yards
Macduff Crescent, Kinghorn
(0592) 890345

Kirkcaldy G.C.
(18) 6007 yards
Balwearie Road, Kirkcaldy
(0592) 203258

Ladybank G.C.
(18) 6617 yards
Annsmuir, Ladybank
(0337) 30814

Leslie G.C.
(9) 4686 yards
Balsillie Laws, Leslie
Leslie 741449

Leven Links
(18) 6434 yards
Links Road, Leven
(0333) 23509

Leven Municipal
(18) 5403 yards
Adjoins Leven Links

Lochgelly G.C.
(18) 5491 yards
Cartmore Road, Lochgelly
(0592) 780174

Lundin Links
(18) 6377 yards
Golf Road, Lundin Links
(0333) 320202

Lundin Ladies G.C.
(18) 4730 yards
Woodiela Road, Lundin Links
(0333) 320022

Pitreavie G.C.
(18) 6086 yards
Queensferry Road, Dunfermline
(0383) 722591

St Andrews
(18) 6933 yards (Old)
(18) 6604 yards (New)
(18) 6284 yards (Jubilee)
(18) 5971 yards (Eden)
(9) (Balgove)
St Andrews
(0334) 75757

St Michaels G.C.
(9) 5510 yards
Leuchars
(033483) 365

Saline G.C.
(9) 5302 yards
Kineddar Hill, Saline
(0383) 591

Scotscraig G.C.
(18) 6486 yards
Golf Road, Tayport
(0382) 552515

Thornton G.C.
(18) 6177 yards
Station Road, Thornton
(0592) 771111

SHORTSPOON "In the Burn" *BURLINGTON GALLERY*

TAYSIDE & CENTRAL

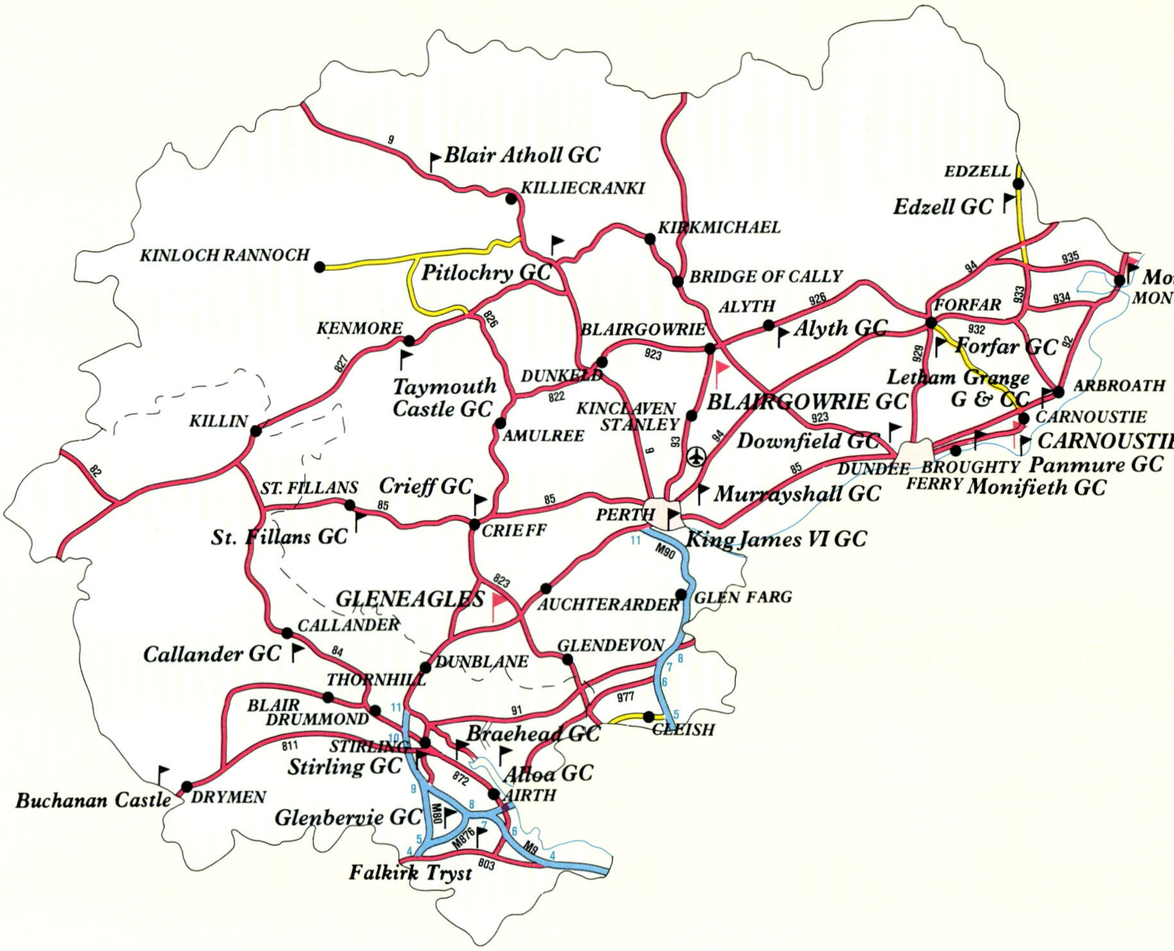

ARTHUR WEAVER "Gleneagles" BURLINGTON GALLERY

TAYSIDE & CENTRAL
CHOICE GOLF

TAYSIDE

After Gleneagles, **Blairgowrie** is probably the best known course in this part of Scotland and it too is featured on a later page. However, the golfer should undoubtedly pay a visit to the 'fair city of Perth'. **The King James VI Club** (green fees **£8.50**), on Moncrieffe Island is steeped in history while nearby at Scone – former crowning place of Kings – is **The Murrayshall House Hotel** and its superb golf course. A round over each is strongly recommended, green fees are around the **£9** mark and **Murrayshall House (0738) 51171** naturally provides a splendidly convenient (and very comfortable) base. An excellent eating place within Perth is the **Coach House (0738) 27950** and just to the south at Glenfarg is the pleasant **Bein Inn (05733) 216.**

Golfers wishing to stay close to Blairgowrie should note the **Rosemount Golf Hotel (0250) 2604** (very handy). A little distance to the west of Perth there is more fine golf at **Crieff** (note the **Crieff Hydro (0764) 2401**) and a very pretty nine hole course even further west at **St Fillans** and where **The Four Seasons (076485) 333** is a charming place to stay. **Dalmunzie House (025 085) 224** should not be forgotten either; situated at Spittal O'Glenshee, it is quite superb.

If a game cannot be arranged at Blairgowrie the heathland course at **Alyth** is very nearby and certainly won't disappoint. Perth's delights as mentioned are at hand to the south, while to the west is **Taymouth Castle** and to the north along the **A9** stands **Pitlochry**. The latter is another course many will choose to play, for this is one of the most attractive in Britain – a veritable 'theatre in the hills'. Green fees here are approximately **£8-£10**. Still further north **Blair Atholl** is also worth a visit.

More ideas for a relaxing stay include the **Kenmore Hotel (08873) 205** in Kenmore, Scotland's oldest inn, and very near Taymouth Castle, the amusingly named **Killiecrankie Hotel (0796 3220** in Killiecrankie (north of Pitlochry), **The Lands of Loyal Hotel (088283) 3151**, at Alyth; the sporty **Ballathie House (025083) 268** at Kinclave by Stanley, **Kinloch House (025084) 237** at Kinloch Rannoch and **The Log Cabin (025081) 288** at Kirkmichael. Indeed, the list is almost endless such is the magnificence of this area. However, let us return to the fairways.

Some of Scotland's greatest links courses are to be found between **Dundee** and **Montrose** on the Tayside coast. However, to the north west of Dundee lies **Downfield** one of the country's finest inland courses. It is said that Downfield is very popular with American visitors because it reminds them of some of their courses 'back home'. No one though would have found it particularly popular in 1938 when a whirlwind struck the course tossing a wooden shelter fifty feet in the air and causing untold damage! Today things are a little quieter and golf can be enjoyed for **£10** per day midweek and for **£15** per day at weekends (prior telephoning is preferred).

East of Dundee **Monifieth** (**£8** a round), staged the **Scottish Amateur Championship** in 1986, while **Panmure** at Barry has in the past staged the **Seniors Championship**. Both are outstanding links courses and fairly inexpensive to play over. **Carnoustie** is, of course, one of Scotland's greatest golfing shrines and along with Gleneagles and Blairgowrie is featured ahead. **Montrose** (**£8.50** a day), like Monifeith is a public links (two courses at each in fact) and when the winds blow can be extremely difficult. Montrose has one of those par fours (the 17th) which requires, as a caddy once put it, 'three damned good shots to get up in two!' As noted, fees along this great coastal stretch are relatively cheap and provided some forward planning is done a game is possible at most times.

A brief word on staying in the area. In Carnoustie, **The Links Hotel** is very convenient, as is **The Park Hotel (0674) 73415** in Montrose. Perhaps the pick of the many hotels in Dundee is **The Angus Thistle Hotel (0382) 26874** while in nearby Broughty Ferry **L'Auberge (0382) 730890** is a fine restaurant.

Finally, two inland courses to the north east of Tayside which strongly merit attention are **Edzell**, and **Letham Grange**. The former just north of Brechin and in a charming village is a beautiful heathland course. Some marvellous mountain views can be enjoyed. Green fees are **£10** and **The Glenesk Hotel (03564) 319** is but a par four away.

Letham Grange is in fact a **Hotel and Country Club (024189) 373** and is situated at Colliston near Arbroath. The hotel is a splendidly restored Victorian Mansion, while the course is brand new (**£9.50** a day), officially opened in 1987 by Henry Cotton, but equally splendid. Water, water everywhere – an Augusta in Scotland? See for yourself, you'll be made most welcome.

If, as the song says, the streams of the mountains please you more than the sea then it is to the likes of **Gleneagles, Pitlochry and Callander** you will head; if you are one of the diehards who think there is but one form of the golf then you will probably set course for **Carnoustie, Monifieth and Montrose**, but then again if it is felt that variety is the spice of golf a nice combination of the two can be devised. The heart of Scotland has much to offer of everything.

CENTRAL

Before **Gleneagles** is reached some excellent golf is to be found at **Falkirk Tryst, Glenbervie** (Larbert), **Braehead** and **Alloa**, while over to the west of the Central region picturesque **Buchanan Castle** is well worth the drive. The town of **Stirling** is know as the 'Gateway to the Highlands' and Stirling's golf course has a beautiful setting beneath the Ochil Hills. **Callander** is one of Scotland's lesser known courses (green fees **£8** a day), and is quite glorious. At Callander in early Spring the deer come down from the Perthshire hills to forage – a wonderful sight.

The world renowned **Gleneagles Hotel (07646) 2231** near Auchterarder is a superb base, not only when playing its own four courses (see feature page) but also for exploring the many fine golf courses nearby. However, there is certainly no shortage of very good alternatives. Three miles away **The Auchterarder House Hotel (07646) 63646** is excellent and is set amid beautiful gardens. In Cleish, **Nigingston House (05575) 216** is a small, very pleasant family-run hotel – ideal for the **M90 (exit 5)**, while at Dunblane set in its own 5,000 acre estate is the redoubtable **Cromlix House (0786) 822125** (note especially the marvellous restaurant). Stirling, with its splendid castle offers **The Park Lodge (0786) 74862**, Callander, **The Roman Camp Hotel (0877) 3003** and Drymen **The Buchanan Arms (0360) 60588** (perfect for The Buchanan Castle course). Finally near Falkirk **Airth Castle (032483) 411** at Airth is wonderfully relaxing.

MURRAYSHALL

The Murrayshall Country House Hotel and Golf Course is only 4 miles from Perth, set in 300 acres of parkland. Deer stroll the wooded hillside, pheasants and peacocks call from the greens. The natural beauty and splashes of colour in the garden are complemented by the mellow stone of the main house with its crow stepped gables.

The hotel, completely refurbished in 1987, is elegantly furnished in a traditional style but with the use of the wonderful fabric designs available today. The bedrooms all have ensuite facilities, self dial telephone and colour television.

The aptly named Old Masters Restaurant has walls hung with Dutch masters and table settings befitting the artistry of master chef, Bruce Sangster. The restaurant has received the accolade of Taste of Scotland Best Restaurant of the Year 1988 and Bruce Sangster currently holds the Scottish Chef of the Year Title. Vegetables and herbs from the hotel's walled garden and an abundance of local produce form the basis of the menus which have a Scottish flavour with a hint of modern French cuisine. A well balanced wine list is complemented by the finest of rare malt whiskies.

The 6420 yard, 18 hole, par 73 course is interspersed with magnificent specimen trees lining the fairway, water hazards and white sanded bunkers to offer a challenge to all golfers. Buggies and sets of clubs are available for hire. Neil Mackintosh, our resident professional, is pleased to give tuition, from half an hour to a week's course. Perth is ideally situated for Scotland's major golf courses. Golfers can relax in the newly refurbished club house which overlooks the course. This can make an ideal venue for a company golfing event.

Other sporting activities include tennis, croquet and bowls. The hotel offers a selection of activity weekends which include ballooning and skirmish. Perth is famous for its published walks. A moderate 6 mile walk starts from the Murrayshall estate or you can just stroll in the varied countryside with its rivers, heaths and hills.

Private dining and conference facilities are available in both the hotel and club house. Conference organisers, requiring the best of service and attention for their senior delegates, will find Murrayshall the ideal venue.

Murrayshall Country House Hotel and Golf Course
Scone
Perthshire PH2 7PH
Tel: (0738) 51171
Fax: (0738) 52595

GLENEAGLES
CHAMPIONSHIP GOLF

There is a vast oil painting that hangs in the Tate Gallery in London, the artist is John Martin and the painting is titled 'The Plains Of Heaven'. Some may know it well, others will wonder what on earth I'm jibbering on about – suffice to say that it depicts in the most vivid colours imaginable the artist's impression of paradise. I suspect that John Martin wasn't a golfer. Blasphemy isn't intended but for many of us who stalk the fairways of the world, **Gleneagles** is just about our best idea of how heaven might look – give or take a couple of angels.

Gleneagles is set in the heart of some of the most glorious Perthshire countryside. Surrounded by the foothills of the Grampian Mountain range everywhere one turns there is a shock of colour. The mountains themselves often appear wrapped in purples and blues. Heather, silver birch and rowan cover the crisp moorland turf. With so much around one could be forgiven for losing a little concentration, yet the golf too is glorious and there are now four eighteen hole courses – there really is nothing quite like Gleneagles. The land was first surveyed with a view to designing one or more golf courses before the first World War and **James Braid** was called in to direct affairs. By **1919** the **Kings** and **Queens** courses were both open for play. Braid's work met with instant acclaim and in **1921** the forerunner of the Ryder Cup was staged at Gleneagles, when a team of British Professionals played a team from America. The **Princes** and **Glendevon** courses are fairly recent additions being opened in **1974** and **1980** respectively.

The four courses are efficiently managed and maintained by the **Gleaneagles Hotel. Visitors** are welcome to play on any, seven days a week and they need not possess a certificate of handicap. However, Gleneagles is understandably extremely popular and prior arrangements must be made in advance. The gentleman to contact is the **Golf Manager, Tom Younger**, either by telephoning on **(07646) 3543** (**telex 76105**) or by writing to **The Golf Office, Gleneagles Hotel, Auchterarder, Perthshire PH3 1NF**. The only specific restrictions on teeing times apply to the Kings and Queens courses where before 10.30am and between 1.30pm and 2.30pm, the tees are reserved for hotel residents and members.

In 1989 the **green fees** for non-residents at Gleneagles were **£32** for a day's golf on either the **Kings** or **Queens** and **£13** for a game on the **Princes** or **Glendevon** courses. For hotel residents a day ticket for the **Kings** and **Queens** courses was priced at **£20** with a day's golf on the **Princes** and **Glendevon** courses costing **£12**. Golfers wishing to hire sets of clubs and trolleys can do so through the professional **Ian Marchbank** who can be reached on **(07646) 2231**.

Located approximately midway between Perth and Stirling and half a mile west of Auchterarder,Gleneagles is easily reached by road. The **A9** which in fact links Perth to Stirling is likely to prove of most assistance. Travelling from the Glasgow region a combination of the **A80** and the **M80** should be taken to Stirling. Those approaching from further south can avoid Glasgow by following the **A74** and the **M74/M73** joiningthe **A80** below Stirling. Motoring from Edinburgh the best route is to cross the Forth Road Bridge via the **A90** heading for Dunfermline and thereafter taking the **A823** road to Auchterarder. Southbound travellers will find the **A9** helpful if coming from the Highlands via Blair Atholl and Pitlochry. Motoring from Aberdeen and the North East of Scotland, the**A92** links Aberdeen to Dundee and Dundee is in turn linked to Perth by the **A85** (dual carriageway all the way). Gleneagles can also be reached by rail, with a bus meeting trains from Gleneagles Station. Measuring **6452** yards, par **71**, the **Kings Course** is the longest of the four, the distance of the others being the **Queens, 5964** yards, par **69**, the **Princes, 4664** yards, par **64**, and the **Glendevon, 5719** yards, par **68**. Perhaps the best known hole at Gleneagles is **Braid's Brawest**, the **13th** on the Kings Course – a tough par four which requires a long straight drive to carry a ridge and a second to a raised and heavily guarded sloping green. Each of the 72 holes at Gleneagles is named, and someone has obviously enjoyed themselves: on the Glendevon Course we have, **Muckle Skelp** (9th), **Wimplin Wyne**, **Pass O'Pinkie** and **Dinkie Slap**.

The **Gleneagles Dormy House** is the golfers 19th. It provides superb catering and is open throughout the day. The Player's Bar serves bar snacks and basket suppers which are available between 6pm and 9pm. A luncheon buffet is served in the main restaurant between 11.30 and 3.00pm and an a la carte menu is offered between 7.45pm and 10pm.

Many will have viewed the glories of Gleneagles through the medium of television – the BBC Pro-Celebrity series being staged on several occasions over the Kings Course. The most warming thought of all is that each one of us is able to view its glories first hand. The fairways of Gleneagles might not be Paradise itself, but for many golfers it's pretty close.

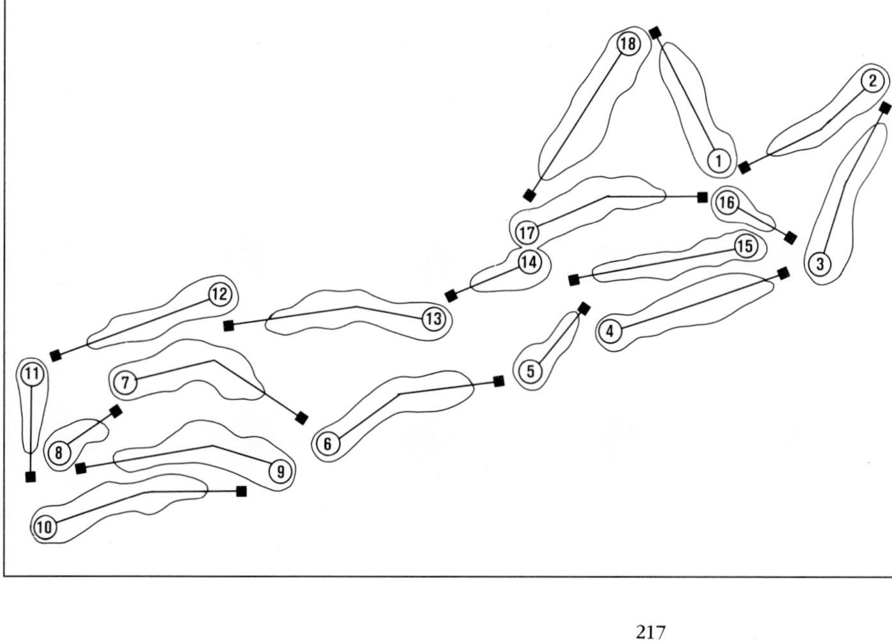

King's Course

Hole	Yards	Par	Hole	Yards	Par
1	362	4	10	445	4
2	405	4	11	230	3
3	377	4	12	387	4
4	465	4	13	446	4
5	160	3	14	260	4
6	476	5	15	457	4
7	439	4	16	133	3
8	158	3	17	376	4
9	351	4	18	525	5
Out	3,193	35	In	3,259	35
			Out	3,193	35
			TOTALS	6,452	70

THE PARK HOTEL

The Park Hotel is situated on the Mid Links in the seaside town of Montrose, a few minutes walk from the Town centre, the beach, and the famous Montrose Links courses.

The Park Hotel is privately owned and makes an ideal base for your holiday. The Hotel which combines modern style with traditional charm has been recently modernised and extended, but still retains the friendly and comfortable atmosphere of a family run hotel.

The Park Hotel has 59 tastefully furnished bedrooms, all with tea and coffee making facilities and most with en suite shower or bath. The spacious restaurant features 'Taste of Scotland' dishes, all freshly prepared by our Chef.

Alternatively, you may wish to relax and have a bar lunch or supper, or drink in the main cocktail lounge.

The Park Hotel has facilities for conferences or seminars for 10-150 delegates. Any package can be designed to meet your requirements.

Special golf breaks can be arranged in conjunction with the Montrose Links Trust.

Whatever your reason to visit the Park Hotel, you will be sure of a welcome change.

Park Hotel
John Street
Montrose
DD10 8RJ
Tel: 0674-73415
Fax: 0674-77091

MONTROSE
CHAMPIONSHIP GOLF

Perhaps there are two things that strike you most when you arrive at one of the famous golfing links on the east coast of Scotland: the first will almost certainly be the thought 'So this is where it all started' – a feeling that can often leave one slightly numb; the second and equally numbing is likely to be the thought 'Will this wretched wind ever die down?' The famous links at Montrose is just such a place.

Golf has been played on Montrose links since the 16th century and according to the best records it is the fifth oldest course in the world. By 'course' is meant the **Medal Course**, for there are two 18 hole links at Montrose, the Medal and the shorter **Broomfield Course**, the former having altered very little since it was first laid out. In common with St Andrews and Carnoustie, Montrose is a public links and although four Golf Clubs play over the two courses, namely, the **Royal Albert, Victoria, Caledonia** and **Mercantile** Clubs, both are run by the Montrose Links Trust who handle all administrative matters. Any written correspondence should be addressed to this body care of **The Secretrary, The Starters Box, Traill Drive, Montrose, Angus D10 8SW. Mrs Margaret Stewart** is in fact the Secretary and she may be contacted by telephone on **(0674) 72634**. Also most helpful is the professional **Alastair Webster**; he can be reached on the same telephone number. Being a public links there are very few restrictions on the times **visitors** can play. Indeed the only one as such is that visitors cannot tee off before 10.30am on Saturdays and Sundays. The **green fees** are remarkably good value. In 1989 a day ticket to play on the **Medal Course** was priced at **£10** during the week and **£11.50** at weekends with a single round costing **£7** midweek and **£8.50** at weekends. To play a round over the **Broomfield Course**, the fee is **£4.50** or **£5** for midweek and weekend respectively, with a day ticket available for **£5** (**£7** at weekends). Those staying in the area might consider a weekly ticket; in 1989 these were priced at **£27.50** for the **Medal** course and **£21** for the **Broomfield** Course. Reductions of up to fifty per cent are usually available to junior golfers.

Apart from their length, the **Medal** course measures **6451** yards (par **71**) and the **Broomfield 4815** yards (par **66**). The two courses also differ in other respects. The Broomfield is in fact laid out on the landward side of the Medal and is considerably flatter. With its many undulations the Medal is by far the more testing and it is not surprisingly over this links that the major Championships are held; (these have included the **Scottish Amateur Championship**) with **British Boys International Championship** due to be played in 1991.

For twelve of its eighteen holes, the course follows closely the line of the dunes, though some of its best holes appear at the end of the round: the **16th** ('Gully') being a particularly long par 3 and the **17th** ('Rashes') with its raised green, one of those par fours requiring, as a caddy once put it, 'three damned good shots to get up in two'!

As the crow flies Montrose lies approximately midway between St Andrews and Aberdeen. For those of us without wings the **A92** is likely to be of most assistance. Those travelling from the St Andrews region, or indeed from all points south, should head for **Dundee**. The **A92** runs from Dundee to Aberdeen passing though the centre of Montrose. Montrose links lies to the north of the town, east off the **A92** and is well signposted. Anyone approaching from the west (including **Blairgowrie**) can avoid Dundee by heading for **Brechin** and thereafter following the **A935** into Montrose passing Montrose Basin (where in winter you may sight a few pink-footed Arctic geese – quite possibly the only birdies you'll see all day).

As for its 19th hole, the catering requirements of visitors are more than adequately met by the Golf Clubs mentioned earlier, each being adjacent to the links.

There are no airs and graces about Montrose; it is what might be described as a 'good honest links'. But if you've come to Scotland to admire the golf, Montrose is clearly one that shouldn't be missed.

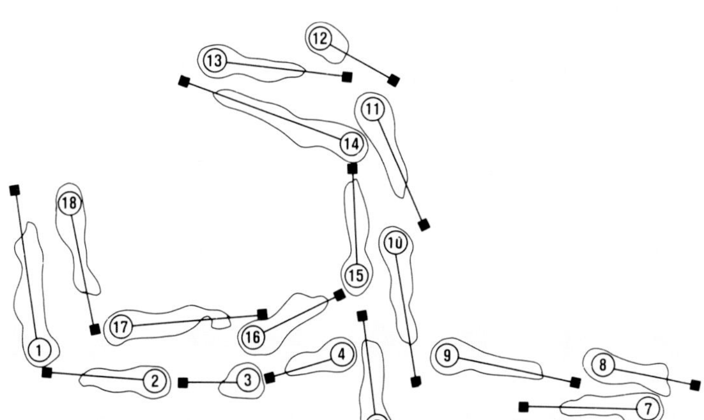

Medal Course

Hole	Yards	Par	Hole	Yards	Par
1	393	4	10	382	4
2	390	4	11	440	4
3	156	3	12	153	3
4	363	4	13	323	4
5	288	4	14	416	4
6	478	5	15	524	5
7	372	4	16	234	3
8	331	4	17	415	4
9	444	4	18	349	4
Out	3.215	36	In	3,236	35
			Out	3,215	36
			TOTALS	6,451	71

DALMUNZIE HOUSE

Dalmunzie House enjoys a glorious position in the mountains of the Scottish Highlands. The hotel stands in its own 6,000 acre mountain estate. It is owned and run by the Winton family who have been in the glen for a number of decades and have many years' experience looking after guests. Exacting attention to detail and unobtrusive service ensure a comfortable stay at all times.

In the magnificent dining room, guests can enjoy a cuisine which satisfies the most discerning of palates. The finest of ingredients, many of them produced locally, are cooked with delicacy, skill and flair, and complemented with wines from the hotel's superbly stocked cellar.

Most of the bedrooms have ensuite facilities. Many are of individual character and all are centrally heated. Their charming decor, restful tranquility and beautiful arrangements of fresh flowers reflect the ambience found elsewhere at Dalmunzie.

Many activities can be pursued here. The hotel has its own private golf course, and in addition there is a tennis court and games room for the family complete with bar billiard table. River and loch fishing as well as shooting and stalking can all be easily arranged. Some of Scotland's finest mountains surround the hotel and for cross country and alpine skiers the Glenshee Ski Centre is only a few minutes' drive away.

Dalmunzie House Hotel,
Spittal o'Glenshee,
Blairgowrie, Perthshire
Scotland, PH10 7QG.
Tel: (025 085) 224

ROSEMOUNT, BLAIRGOWRIE
CHAMPIONSHIP GOLF

With so many outstanding courses to choose from, all within fairly close proximity of one another, even the most blinkered of diehard Englishmen would be forced to concede that Scotland is the finest place on earth for a week's golfing holiday. Given seven precious days a large number of would-be travellers on opening their maps of Scotland are likely to plan a trip thus: three days on the west coast playing Prestwick, Turnberry and Troon; a day 'in the middle' visiting Gleneagles, finishing with three on the east coast taking in Carnoustie, St Andrews and Muirfield. Marvellous stuff of course, but many of the golfing sages hold the opinion that such an itinerary misses out the greatest gem of all – the **Rosemount** course at **Blairgowrie**.

There are in fact two 18 hole courses at Blairgowrie, the older and more celebrated **Rosemount**, designed by **James Braid** and the **Lansdowne** course, a fairly recent addition, the work of **Peter Alliss** and **Dave Thomas**. On each, golf is played over beautiful moorland fairways, lined by forests of pine and silver birch. A liberal sprinkling of purple heather and gorse add considerable colour to an already majestic setting – as one observer put it, 'somebody seems to have gone mad with a paint brush!'

Persons wishing to sample the delights of either course are advised to book starting times through the Club's Professional, **Gordon Kinnock**, tel **(0250) 3116**. **Visitors** are welcome at Blairgowrie on Mondays, Tuesdays, Thursdays and, to a limited extent, on Fridays. Fourball matches, it should be noted, are not normally allowed before 10 a.m. on the Rosemount course. Furthermore all visitors must be able to provide proof of handicap. Golfing parties are also welcome on the above days though teeing off will not be permitted between 12pm and 2pm nor after 4 pm. Those wishing to organise golfing parties should address written applications to the Club's **Secretary, Mr. Kirkland**, the Club's full address being, **Blairgowrie Golf Club, Rosemount, Blairgowrie, Perthshire**. Mr. Kirkland can be contacted by telephone on **(0250) 2622**. In **1989** the **green fee** for a single round on either course was set at **£15**, while for the sum of **£22** a full day's golf can be enjoyed. These prices apply during the week only, as a day ticket is not available at weekends, though the price for a round is **£20**.

Having metaphorically chastised the golfer who doesn't make Blairgowrie a 'must' on any golfing tour I had better detail the best routes to reach it. Hopefully the following will prove of assistance: approaching from the south the **A93** Braemar road runs directly from Perth, Perth being linked to Edinburgh by the **A90/M90**. From easterly directions, Blairgowrie (Rosemount is just south of the town) is connected to Dundee by the **A923** and to Forfar by the **A926**. Anyone motoring down from the north will probably travel either on the **A9** (via Aviemore and Pitlochry) or on the **A93** passing through Ballater and Braemar. Blairgowrie is 15 miles from Perth and 18 miles from Dundee. Gleneagles (via Perth) and Carnoustie and St Andrews (both via Dundee) are all approximately 30 miles away.

Measuring around the **6600** yard mark, the Rosemount course could be described as having the classic formula: both the front nine and the back nine comprise five par 4's, two par 3's and two par 5's – 36 out and 36 back, making the par a traditional 'level fours'. The official course record at Rosemount stands at 66, though in **1973**, during a practice round for the Sumrie Better-Ball tournament, Professional **Lionel Platts** achieved a world record ten consecutive birdies between the **8th** and **17th** – quite obscene don't you think?!

The Lansdowne course is slightly longer than its older brother, and many would say a much sterner test – either way a game on each is strongly recommended.

It need hardly be added that Blairgowrie with its two courses – three if one includes the aptly named Wee Course, a short nine-holer – has a more than adequate 19th. Lunches, high teas, dinners and light snacks are all offered. There are also two bars, comfortable places where many will choose to go and celebrate a magnificent day's golfing in one of the most glorious settings the game has to offer. Planning a week's golf?

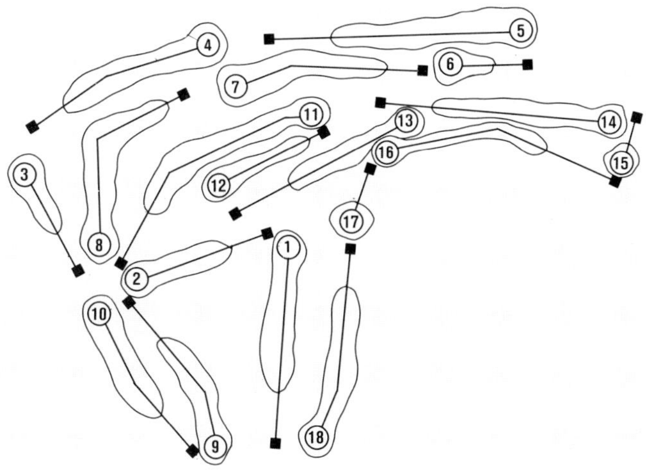

Rosemount Course

Hole	Yards	Par	Hole	Yards	Par
1	446	4	10	425	4
2	335	4	11	498	5
3	218	3	12	291	4
4	408	4	13	402	4
5	536	5	14	513	5
6	160	3	15	128	3
7	327	4	16	468	4
8	501	5	17	168	3
9	380	4	18	388	4
Out	3,311	36	In	3,281	36
			Out	3,311	36
			TOTALS	6,592	72

CARNOUSTIE
CHAMPIONSHIP GOLF

Walter Hagen – a shrewd judge you might think – once described **Carnoustie** as 'the greatest course in the British Isles'. There are many who would agree with the great man, though doubtless the disciples of **St. Andrews** and several honourable gentlemen at **Muirfield** would beg to differ. Greatest or not, very few would dispute that when the winds blow – as they invariably do in these parts - Carnoustie is the toughest of all our Championship links.

In the days when the Campbells and the MacDonalds were busy slaughtering each other up in the Highlands, down at Carnoustie more civilised pursuits were taking place. Records suggest that golf (or gowf) was being played on the adjoining Barry Links, as early as the **16th** century. The first 'official Club' at Carnoustie – today there are six - was founded in 1842 and golf was played over a ten hole course laid out by **Allan Robertson. 'Old' Tom Morris** came on the scene and extended the links to a full 18 holes, but the present Championship course didn't really begin to take shape until **James Braid** made several alterations in 1926. By 1931 Carnoustie was ready to stage its first **Open Championship**.

As previously mentioned there are presently six Clubs at Carnoustie and play is now over three courses, all of which are publicly owned. Administrative matters are in the hands of the **Carnoustie Golf Links Management Committee** and persons wishing to visit Carnoustie should direct correspondence to the Committee's **Secretary, Mr. E.J.C. Smith**. The full address to write to is The **Carnoustie Golf Links Management Committee, Links Parade, Carnoustie, Tayside, DD7 7SE**. Contact by telephone can be made on **(0241) 53789**. Starting times must be booked in advance and the above telephone number should also be used to acquire the services of a caddy.

In **1989** the **green fees** to play over the Championship Links were fixed as follows: **£19** for a single round with **£28** payable for a full day's golf; these prices are applicable both during the week and at weekends. A weekly ticket is also available – priced at **£80**.

The cluster of Clubs that go to make up Carnoustie's permanent golfing village provide all the ususal amenities for the visiting golfer – golf shops for clothing, equipment and club hire and of course a more than adequate 19th hole. Travelling to Carnoustie shouldn't present too many problems. For large numbers it will simply be a case of getting over the Firth of Tay and turning right. The Forth Road Bridge and the **M90** link the Edinburgh region with Perth; Perth in turn is linked to Dundee by the **A85** (dual carriageway all the way) and Dundee to Carnoustie by the **A390**. Those on golfing tours will quite likely be coming via St. Andrews: the **A91 (A919)** runs from St. Andrews towards Dundee; it picks up the **A92** just before the Tay Road Bridge and on crossing the Bridge the **A930** should immediately be joined. Approaching from northerly directions, the **A92** runs from Aberdeen (and beyond) to within a couple of miles of Carnoustie at Muirdrum, while the **A958** links the town with Forfar. Carnoustie can also be reached by train with connections from Perth, Dundee and Aberdeen.

It isn't only the wind of course that makes Carnoustie such a difficult test. When the Championship tees are in use – or the **Ben Hogan tees** as they are sometimes known – the course stretches close to **7200** yards making it the longest of our 'Open Courses'. From the Club medal tees, **6931** yards is still a formidable proposition. Many courses in America are of similar proportions but anyone expecting the ball to fly through the air as sweetly as it does at Palm Springs or Augusta is in for quite a shock!

Scotland is the land of Burns. It is also the land of 'burns' – streams or rivers anywhere else in the English-speaking world – and Carnoustie is famous for them. The ubiquitous **Barry Burn** and its wee brother **Jocky's Burn** traverse the fairways in the most unfriendly of places, often in front of greens and across the spot you'd ideally like to drive to. More than anything else though, Carnoustie is renowned for its incredibly tough finishing stretch. The **16th** is an exceptionally long 'short hole' and **Jack Nicklaus** is said to have once needed a driver followed by an 8 iron to get up! The **17th** has the Barry Burn meandering across its fairway, making it a particularly difficult driving hole and at the **18th** the Burn crosses in front of the green necessitating one of the most exciting (or nerve-racking) closing shots in golf.

Each of the five Opens held at Carnoustie has produced great Champions – **Tommy Armour** (1931), **Henry Cotton** (1937), **Ben Hogan** (1953), **Gary Player** (1968) and **Tom Watson** (1975). Many consider Hogan's victory in 1953 – he won by four strokes with rounds of 73-71-70-68 – to be the greatest ever performance in a major Championship. There are also those who feel that his final round of 68 represents the true course record. The wind blew that day and Carnoustie's teeth were gnashing. Twenty two years later when **Jack Newton** scored his 65 Carnoustie was smiling. It was the only Open Hogan ever played in.

Hand on their hearts, no one could describe Carnoustie as picturesque – in fact it's pretty bleak in parts, but on stepping out on to the first tee the sense of history is quite awe-inspiring. Those yet to do battle over the famous links have missed out on a unique experience, and, if Walter Hagen was right, the greatest course in the British Isles.

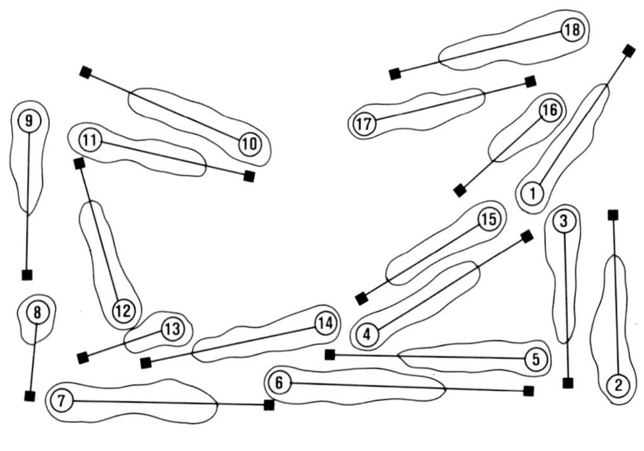

Hole	Yards	Par	Hole	Yards	Par
1	395	4	10	426	4
2	432	4	11	370	4
3	345	4	12	476	5
4	381	4	13	161	3
5	376	4	14	482	5
6	529	5	15	460	4
7	384	4	16	248	3
8	169	3	17	432	4
9	425	4	18	440	4
Out	3,436	36	In	3,495	36
			Out	3,436	36
			TOTALS	6,931	72

TAYSIDE & CENTRAL

COMPLETE GOLF

CENTRAL

Aberfoyle G.C.
(18) 5205 yards
Braval, Aberfoyle, Stirling
(087 72) 441

Alloa G.C.
(18) 6230 yards
Schawpark, Sauchie, Alloa
(0259) 722745

Alva G.C.
(9) 4574 yards
Beauclerc Street, Alva
(0259) 60431

Bonnybridge G.C.
(9) 6058 yards
Larbert Road, Bonnybridge
(0324) 812645

Braehead G.C.
(18) 6013 yards
Cambus, Alloa
(0259) 722078

Bridge of Allan G.C.
(9) 4932 yards
Sunnylaw, Bridge of Allan
(0786) 2332

Buchanan Castle G.C.
(18) 6032 yards
Drymen
(0360) 60307

Callander G.C.
(18) 5125 yards
Aveland Road, Callander
(0877) 30090

Dollar G.C.
(18) 5144 yards
Brewlands House, Dollar
(02594) 400

Dunblane New G.C.
(18) 5878 yards
Perth Road, Dunblane
(0786) 823711

Falkirk G.C.
(18) 6090 yards
Stirling Road, Falkirk
(0324) 611061

Falkirk Tryst G.C.
(18) 6053 yards
Burnhead Road, Larbert
(0324) 562091

Glenbervie G.C.
(18) 6452 yards
Stirling Road, Larbert
(0324) 562605

Grangemouth G.C.
(18) 6339 yards
Polmont, Falkirk
(0324) 711500

Muckhart G.C.
(18) 6115 yards
Dramburn Road, Muckhart, Dollar
(025981) 423

Polmont G.C.
(9) 6088 yards
Maddison, Falkirk
(0324) 711277

Stirling G.C.
(18) 6409 yards
Queens Road, Stirling
(0786) 64098

Tillicoultry G.C.
(9) 5256 yards
Alva Road, Tillicoultry
(0259) 50741

Tulliallan G.C.
(18) 5982 yards
Alloa Road, Kincardine, Alloa
(0259) 30897

TAYSIDE

Aberfeldy G.C.
(9) 5466 yards
Taybridge Road, Aberfeldy
(0887) 20535

Alyth G.C.
(18) 6226 yards
Pitcrocknie, Alyth
(08283) 2411

Arbroath G.C.
(18) 6078 yards
Ellito, Arbroath
(0241) 72666

Auchterader G.C.
(18) 5741 yards
Orchil Road, Auchterader
(07646) 2804

Bishopshire G.C.
(9) 4360 yards
Kinnesswood
(059284) 860379

Blair Atholl G.C.
(9) 5710 yards
Blair Atholl
(079681) 274

Blairgowrie G.C.
(18) 6592 yards (Rosemount)
(18) 6865 yards (Lansdowne)
(9) 4614 yards (Wee)
Rosemount, Blairgowrie
(0250) 3116

Brechin G.C.
(18) 5267 yards
Trinity, Brechin
(03562) 2383

Caird Park G.C.
(18) 6303 yards
Mains Loan, Dundee
(0382) 453606

Camperdown (Municipal) G.C.
(18) 6561 yards
Camperdown Park, Dundee
(0382) 2715

Carnoustie Courses
(18) 6931 yards (Championship)
(18) 5935 yards (Burnside)
(18) 6445 yards (Buddon Links)
Links Parade, Carnoustie
(0241) 53749

Comrie G.C.
(9) 5966 yards
Polinard, Comrie
(0764) 70544

Craigie Hill G.C.
(18) 5379 yards
Cherrybank, Perth
(0738) 22644

Crieff G.C.
(18) 6363 yards (Ferntower)
(9) 4772 yards (Dornock)
(0764) 2909

Dalmunzie G.C.
(9) 4458 yards or 2035
Spittal of Glenshee, Blairgowrie
(025085) 226

Downfield G.C.
(18) 6899 yards
Turnberry Avenue, Dundee
(0382) 825595

Dunkeld & Birnam G.C.
(9) 5264 yards
Fungarth, Dunkeld
(03502) 524

Dunning G.C.
(9) 4836 yards
Rollo Park, Dunning
(076484) 398

Edzell G.C.
(18) 6299 yards
High Street, Edzell, Brechin
(03564) 7283

Forfar G.C.
(18) 6255 yards
Cunninghill, Arbroath Road, Forfar
(0307) 62120

Glenalmond G.C.
(9) 5812 yards
Trinity College, Glenalmond
(073888) 270

Gleneagles Hotel
(18) 6452 yards (King's)
(18) 5964 yards (Queen's)
(18) 5719 yards (Glendevon)
(18) 4664 yards (Prince's)
Gleneagles Hotel, Auchterarder
(07646) 3543

Green Hotel G.C.
(18) 6339 yards
Green Hotel, Kinrose
(0577) 63467

Killin G.C.
(9) 5016 yards
Killin
(05672) 312

King James VI G.C.
(18) 6037 yards
Moncrieffe Island, Perth
(0738) 32460

Kirriemuir G.C.
(18) 5591 yards
23 Bank Street, Kirriemuir, Angus
(0575) 73317

Letham Grange G. & C.C.
(18) 6290 yards
Letham Grange, Colliston, Arbroath
(0241) 89373

Milnathort G.C.
(9) 5918 yards
South Street, Milnathort
(0577) 64069

Monifieth Golf Links
(18) 6657 yards (Medal)
(18) 5123 yards (Ashludie)
45 Ferry Road, Monifieth
(0382) 532767

Montrose Links Trust
(18) 6451 yards (Medal)
(18) 4815 yards (Broomfield)
Trail Drive, Montrose
(0674) 72932

Murrayshall G.C.
(18) 6416 yards
Murrayshall, New Scone
(0738) 52784

Muthill G.C.
(9) 4742 yards
Peat Road, Muthill, Crieff
(0764) 3319

Panmure G.C.
(18) 6302 yards
Burnside Road, Barry
(0241) 53120

Pitlochry G.C.
(18) 5811 yards
Golf Course Road, Pitlochry
(0796) 2792

Royal Perth Golfing Society
(18) 5141 yards
Atholl Crescent, Perth
(0738) 22265

St. Fillans G.C.
(9) 5268 yards
St. Fillans
(076485) 312

Taymouth Castle G.C.
(18) 6066 yards
Kenmore, Aberfeldy
(08873) 228

GRAMPIAN & HIGHLAND

"Maghie" BURLINGTON GALLERY

GRAMPIAN & HIGHLAND

CHOICE GOLF

Mist-covered mountains and bottomless lochs, bagpipes, whisky and haggis. I doubt whether there is a more romantic place in the world than the Highlands of Scotland. I doubt also that there is a place quite so shatteringly beautiful.

For our purposes 'the Highlands' covers the administrative regions of Grampian and Highland. The latter extends from the Cairngorms northwards, encompassing the Great Glen and the Western Isles. Grampian covers a similarly vast area, the entirety of north eastern Scotland. The area was at one time covered by a dense forest of pine broken only by the soaring granite peaks of the Grampian mountain range. It was the home of the savage Caledonian tribe, a land where wolves hunted in packs. Nowadays very little of the forest remains. As for the wolves, most of them were killed by the Caledonians, but then unfortunately most of the Caledonians were killed by the Romans. No wonder they called life 'nasty, brutish and short'!

GRAMPIAN

Let us make a start in Grampian. Forgetting the wolves, the savages and the Romans, what we see is a good 18 holes – and, of course, a suitable 19th. Aberdeen is a fine place to begin. **Balgownie** and **Murcar** (green fees **£12** a day) lie right on the town's doorstep and are unquestionably two of the finest courses in Scotland. Balgownie links is the home of the **Royal Aberdeen Golf Club** and is featured ahead but Murcar is certainly not overshadowed and is a true Championship test. It should be possible to arrange a game at Murcar on most days of the week but it's a good idea to phone the club before making plans. Fees are approximately **£15** per day.

There are numerous hotels in Aberdeen but a large number are modern and somewhat unattractive, indeed many may prefer to stay outside the town. Anyway some of the best include **The Holiday Inn (0224) 770011** (note the particularly good restaurant), **The Skean Dhu Hotel (0224) 725252** and the unfortunately named **Bucksburn Moat House (0224) 713911**. Two other hotels strongly recommended by the golfing fraternity are **The Atholl (0224) 323505** in Kings Gate and **The New Marcliffe (0224) 321371** in Queens Road. An excellent seafood restaurant to visit is the **Atlantis (0224) 591403** while **Gerrard's (0224) 639500** is also highly thought of.

North of Aberdeen **The Udny Arms (03586) 444** at Newburgh enjoys a splendid situation overlooking the Ythan Estuary and is a total contrast to the modern hotels of Aberdeen. Due west of the latter another striking location is found at Kildrummy by Alford. Here **The Kildrummy Castle (03365) 288** is excellent. Finally to the north west **The Pittodrie House Hotel (04676) 444** at Pitcaple enjoys glorious surroundings while in Old Meldrum one finds the similarly splendid **Meldrum House Hotel (06512) 2294** – convenient for Aberdeen but also needless to say for the **Old Meldrum** course.

Looking to play outside Aberdeen, the golfer is faced with two equally appealing choices – he can either head north along the coast towards Cruden Bay, or alternatively head inland along the **A93**. The latter choice broadly involves following the path of the River Dee and will take the traveller through some truly magnificent scenery. The 18 hole courses at **Banchory, Aboyne, Ballater** and **Braemar** all lie along this road and not surprisingly boast spectacular settings. Each welcomes visitors seven days a week at green fees representing excellent value, a day's golf costing around the **£5-£9** mark.

There are several superb places in which to stay as you golf your way along the Dee. In Banchory, **Raemoir House (03302) 48184** is outstanding and the **Tor-na-Coille (03302) 2242** has excellent facilities, as does the **Banchory Lodge Hotel (03302) 2625** at Banchory. Aboyne offers the **Birse Lodge Hotel (0339) 2253** while Ballater boasts a number of fine establishments. **Tullich Lodge (0338) 55406** is one of the finest mansion houses in Scotland but also note **the Craigendarroch Hotel (0338) 55858** and its excellent restaurant. Should you, of course, time it right then Braemar boasts that magnificent spectacle, **The Highland Games** gathering.

Journeying northwards, **Cruden Bay** is clearly the first stopping point. A truly splendid golf links this, situated some 23 miles north of Aberdeen on Scotland's Buchan Coast. The location is a dramatic one with nearby Slains Castle providing an eerie backdrop. Bram Stoker who spent some time in these parts is reputed to have been inspired by the castle when writing his Dracula stories. For golfers the course should prove equally inspiring. Green fees are **£9** midweek, **£12** at the weekend.

The old fishing town of **Peterhead** has an interesting seaside course where sea winds can make scoring tricky. Green fees are **£4.50**. A restaurant worth noting here is **The Waterside Inn (0779) 71121** while in nearby Mintlaw, **Saplinbrae House (0771) 23515** is an excellent hotel.

From fishing port to Georgian elegance – **The Duff House Royal Golf Club** at Macduff is looked over by an impressive baroque-style mansion. The course too has a touch of class being designed by the Mackenzie brothers immediately prior to their constructing the legendary Augusta National course in America – note the many two-tiered greens. **Royal Tarlair** at Banff is also well worth a visit and like Duff House is always beautifully maintained. To the south of Banff, long the **A947, Turriff** is a pleasant alternative to the seaside courses – very pretty too. While visitors are most welcome in the summer as they can get very popular and at Duff House a booking sheet system is often used. Fees are agin good value at around **£7-£8**.

In Macduff the **Fire Arms Hotel (0261) 32408** is recommended and in Banff's High Street, **The Country Hotel (02612) 5353**. Also, in Cullen the **Seafield Arms Hotel (0542) 40791** is comfortable.

Crossing the salmon-filled River Spey at Fochabers the City of **Elgin** is soon reached. There aren't too many cathedrals in this part of the world but Elgin, the capital of Morayshire, has a beautiful one that dates from the 13th Century. It also possesses one of the finest inland golf courses in the north of Scotland. A mile or so south of the city and some distance away from the often fierce coast winds, the course is sheltered by many pines and silver birch trees. Inevitably, it occupies a glorious setting with distant purple hills forming a spectacular horizon. A day's golf at Elgin is priced at about **£9**.

Returning one final time to the coast and Lossiemouth the **Moray Golf Club** has two outstanding links courses, the 'Old Course' which is approaching its centenary, and the 'New Course', less than ten years old. Whilst the fighter aircraft from neaby RAF Lossiemouth may occasionally irritate, it would be difficult to find a finer combination of superb natural golf and scenic splendour. Green fees are similar to those at Elgin.

GRAMPIAN & HIGHLAND

CHOICE GOLF

In Elgin, two hotels, **The Mansion House (0343) 48811** and **The Eight Acres (0343) 3077** and in Rothes, **The Rothes Glen (03403) 254** is superbly relaxing. Finally in Findhorn **The Crown and Anchor** is ideal for a post match beverage.

HIGHLAND

And so to the Highland region. In Scotland where there is land there is golf and though this be a wild and somewhat remote part of the country it nonetheless has its share of golfing gems – and more than that, in the minds of many, it has in **Royal Dornoch** the finest of them all.

As well as its gems, the region has a number of golf's genuine outposts, none more so than the **Gairloch Golf Club** situated in the far west of Scotland with views across to the Isle of Skye. There are 9 holes at Gairloch, each wonderfully named. The 6th, however, baffles me – 'Westward Ho!' is its title?! The 9th though has more of a Celtic ring to it – 'Mo Dhachaidh'. There is no Sunday golf at Gairloch though visitors can play at all other times, **£5** being the cost of a day's golf. Others in the 'lonely category' include **Fort Augustus** (green fees **£4**) on the edge of Loch Ness and **Fort William**, a moorland course, laid out in the shadows of Ben Nevis.

In the south of Highland, the area around Aviemore has become an increasingly popular holiday retreat, particularly for winter sports enthusiasts. However, whilst the skis must go on the roof, the golf clubs can fit in the boot, and there are five or six courses at hand each of which possess a truly glorious setting. Picking two of them the **Kingussie** and **Boat of Garten** Golf Clubs lie either side of Aviemore close to the **A9**. Both have spectacular courses at which visitors are always welcome, fees being around the **£6** mark. Neither is particularly long, though the hills at Kingussie and the narrow fairways and small greens at Boat of Garten can make scoring extremely difficult and you are more likely to see eagles than score one. At Boat of Garten you may also catch a glimpse of one of the famous ospreys.

Some thoughts for the 19th include in the Newtonmore-Kingussie area, **The Highlander (05403) 341** and **The Osprey (05402) 510** both pleasant hotels, and **The Cross (05402) 762**, an outstanding restaurant in Kingussie. In Fort William one finds **The Inverlochy Castle (0397) 2177**, one of the country's finest hotels and restaurants, while two other gems are the remote **Arisaig House (06875) 622** in Arisaig on the western coast and in Ballachulish, **The Ballachulish Hotel (08552) 606** which enjoys a superb lochside setting.

In Boat of Garten, **The Boat (047983) 258** is exceptionally convenient overlooking the golf course (note the special golf weeks). **The Grant Arms Hotel (0479) 2526** in Grantown-on-Spey is comfortable and good value and nearer the coast at Advie is the extremely gracious **Tulchan Lodge (08075) 200**.

Inverness as the so-called 'Capital of the Highlands' is where many may choose to spend a day or two – the Loch Ness monster lives nearby and the famous 'fields of destruction' at Culloden Moor are only a few miles to the east. Golfers may wish to note the town's 18 hole course situated just south of the town centre – green fees are **£10** a day. However, the magnificent Championship links at **Nairn** is just 16 miles away along the **A96** – a journey many will wish to make. The famous Club celebrated its centenary in 1987 by hosting both the men's and ladies' Scottish Amateur Championships. It's a great place for the more humble golf too – the welcome is a warm one, the green fees are excellent value at around **£12** and the setting really is superb.

Both Inverness and Nairn have many places in which to stay. In the former, **The Dunain Park Hotel (0463) 230512** and the 18th Century **Kingsmills (0463) 237166** are ideal, and near to the famous battlefield is the impressive **Culloden House Hotel (0463) 790461** where a portrait of the Bonnie Prince will welcome you. **The Golf View Hotel (0667) 52301** is situated right alongside the famous Nairn course but strong recommendations also for **The Newton Hotel (0667) 53144** and **The Clifton Hotel (0667) 53119** also in Nairn.

On the Chanonry Peninsula linked to Inverness by way of the Kessock Bridge, the **A9** and the **A832**, is the flattish links course of **Fortrose and Rosemarkie** – well worth a visit, although lunchtime and early evenings are best avoided. **Strathpeffer Spa**,(green fees **£5**) a moorland course, is the prettiest of stepping stones for those heading north of Inverness along the **A9**. This road passes through **Tain** – and another 18 holes – but by now most will be itching to reach Dornoch.

Royal Dornoch's course is featured ahead. For those wishing to reflect on their day's golf **The Dornoch Castle (0862) 810216** is genuinely splendid. Other hotels to try are **The Royal Golf Hotel (0862) 810283** and **The Burghfield House (0862) 810212**.

Having played **Royal Dornoch**, many, Tom Watson included, find it difficult to tear themselves away, but there are two excellent courses a short distance to the north, **Golspie** and **Brora** that are decidedly worth visiting. Both are testing links courses set in the most majestic surroundings with views to distant hills and along a spectacular coast. Brora in fact stretches out right alongside three miles of deserted sandy beach. Being so far north golf can be played at absurdly late hours and at both, the fees are a mere **£6**.

In Brora, **The Royal Marine (048) 21252** and **The Links (0408) 21225** hotels are both strategically placed on the aptly named Golf Road, while another well titled hotel can be found at Golspie, **The Golf Links Hotel (04083) 3408**; all three are recommended.

Beyond Brora we really are getting remote! However, the **A9** makes it all the way to John O'Groats. There are 18 hole courses at **Wick** and **Reay**, where the fees are only **£5** per day. But the furthest north is **Thurso**, not too far from the Dounreay Power Station. I should imagine it gets pretty cold up there, but if you do make it, and are looking for fresh challenges then there is always the golf club in the Arctic – fittingly called the **'Polar Bear Club'** – and which, I suppose it goes without saying, was founded by Scotsmen!

MELDRUM HOUSE

Meldrum House has been the home of the family which still owns it since the thirteenth century. For the past thirty years Robin Duff of Meldrum, the present Laird, has opened the house as an hotel. Furniture collected over the centuries, and many fine pictures, combine to give the impression that guests are visitors in a fine pre-war country house.

Set in several hundred acres of fields and gardens, and beside a small lake, Meldrum is the ideal place for a golfing holiday – for golfers, and for others who may want to visit castles and gardens, walk in the beautiful countryside, or, for that matter, just laze about. The hotel is internationally known for its cuisine – the best of Scottish food with a slight French accent, and there is an excellent cellar.

The aim is to maintain a country house atmosphere, and to make guests feel thoroughly at home. Mealtimes are flexible, and, if you so wish, breakfast is served in your room without extra charge.

Recently a very distinguished visitor from the United States wrote – 'Your staff at Meldrum were simply wonderful. I can't say enough about their courtesy and efficiency and kindness during our stay.'

A group of golfers from Florida, who previously toured Scotland to play golf, have now decided that in future, they will spend their whole visit at Meldrum and play from there!

The people of Old Meldrum have in recent years become keen golfers and some years ago, they created a good nine hole golf course. Now they are proceeding towards an eighteen hole course. But, more importantly, Meldrum is very well situated for visits to many top-class course with Cruden Bay and Royal Aberdeen to the East, and Royal Tarlair, Duff House Royal and Elgin all within striking distance to the North of the hotel. A slightly longer journey which takes in some delightful Scottish scenery, will allow visitors to reach Nairn or even Dornoch. In the evening your return to Meldrum House, will be as welcoming as ever and our staff eager to hear of your achievements on the links.

Meldrum House Hotel
Old Meldrum
Grampian AB5 0AE
Tel: (065 12) 2294

PITTODRIE HOUSE

Pittodrie House dates back to 1490 when it was originally owned by the Erskine Family. The house and estate was originally bought by the Grandfather of the present owner in 1896 and was converted by his Grandson Theo Smith to a Hotel in 1977.

The house was extensively modernised internally to bring it up to a high standard of comfort. A lot of time has been spent trying to retain the atmosphere of a Country House. All the rooms abound in antiques, paintings and family portraits.

A 5 course dinner is served nightly in the restaurant with the emphasis on fresh local produce. The menu changes daily. We have an impressive wine list with over 200 wines from 19 different countries. The bar is also well stocked with over 80 different malt whiskies and over 50 liqueurs.

We offer people at Pittodrie a chance to relax in comfortable surroundings. It is possible to take leisurely strolls in the 3 acre walled garden or a more energetic walk up Bennachie – the hill behind the house. There are also 2 squash courts, tennis court, snooker table, croquet, table tennis and clay-pigeon shooting.

The Pittodrie House Hotel
Pitcaple
Aberdeenshire AB5 9HS
Tel: (04676) 444

ROYAL ABERDEEN
CHAMPIONSHIP GOLF

Founded in **1780, Royal Aberdeen** is the sixth oldest Golf Club in the world. For the first thirty five years of its existence the Club was known as **The Society of Golfers at Aberdeen** with membership of the Society being determined by ballot. They were clearly a meticulous group of gentlemen, for in **1783** they became the first to introduce the five minute limit on searching for golf balls. A sensible idea you may think, but one that has caused the modern day Aberdeen Golfer much distress – a subject to which I shall return in due course.

In **1815** on the eve of the Battle of Waterloo the Society changed its name to the Aberdeen Golf Club and in 1903 the 'Royal' prefix was bestowed on the Club. Originally the members played over a strip of common land between the Rivers Don and Dee but in the second half of the 19th century the Club acquired its own course at **Balgownie** on the northern side of the River. Today Balgownie Links is regarded as one of Scotland's greatest Championship courses.

Mr. A.W. Baird is the **Secretary** at Royal Aberdeen, he may be contacted by telephone on **(0224) 648797**. All written correspondence should be addressed to the Secretary at **The Royal Aberdeen Golf Club, Balgownie, Bridge of Don, Aberdeen. Mr Ron MacAskill** is the Club's professional and he may be reached on **(0224) 702221**.

Visitors are made extremely welcome at Royal Aberdeen and they may play at Balgownie on any week day. Visitors are not permitted to play at weekends. The **green fees** for 1989 were set at **£18** per day during the week with a **£15** fee for a single round. Travelling to Aberdeen is made fairly straightforward by the **A92**. From the south this road passes along the coast from **Dundee via Arbroath, Montrose** and **Stonehaven** to Aberdeen. It also connects the town to **Fraserburgh** in the North. Those approaching from the north west should find the **A96** helpful (it in fact runs directly from **Inverness**). Other roads which may prove of assistance are the **A947** from **Oldmeldrum** and the **A93** which links Aberdeen to **Perth** and passes through **Blairgowrie**. The links itself is situated 2 miles north of Aberdeen and can be sighted immediately to the right after crossing the River Don.

From its medal tees Balgownie measures **6372** yards, par **70** with the forward tees reducing the length to **6104** yards, par **69**. Although perhaps not overly long the course is fairly open to the elements and the wind can often make a mockery of some of the distances. There is also a considerable spread of gorse and the rough can be very punishing. It should be added that there are no fewer than ninety-two bunkers – ten of which appear on the par three 8th! Balgownie has the traditional 'out and back' links layout, the front nine hugging the shore and the back nine returning on the landside towards the Clubhouse. The outward nine is perhaps the more interesting of the two halves; the eminent golf writer **Sam McKinlay** was moved to say: 'There are few courses in these islands with a better, more testing, more picturesque outward nine than Balgownie.' However, the most difficult hole on the course is possibly the last hole, a lengthy par four, well bunkered and usually played into the teeth of the prevailing wind.

The **Balgownie Short Course** is also worth a look; this second 18 hole course measures **4033** yards, par **60**. Green fees in **1989** were **£9** per day, or **£7.50** per round.

Royal Aberdeen has played host to a number of major events. Both the **Scottish Amateur** and the **Northern Open Championship** are regularly played over Balgownie Links. Numerous exhibition matches have also taken place; participants have included Tom Morris Junior, Harold Vardon, James Braid, John H. Taylor, Walter Hagen and Henry Cotton.

I now return to the matter of the five minute rule. In the opening paragraph, I mentioned how in 1783 the Aberdeen Golfers had introduced the five minute limit on searching for lost balls. Well somebody somewhere it seems didn't approve and 200 years later a plague of crows was sent to deliver retribution. Throughout the long summers of 1983 and 1984 the crows determined that no one should search for his ball. They descended on the links stealing Titleists and Top-Flites, Pinnacles and Penfolds. Several Members had more than one ball stolen in a round. Use of the larger American ball was encouraged but alas to no avail. Even a crow trap was built but still they plundered. Then just as suddenly as they came, they left, never it is presumed to return. Sanity restored, Balgownie became once more one of Britain's friendliest links.

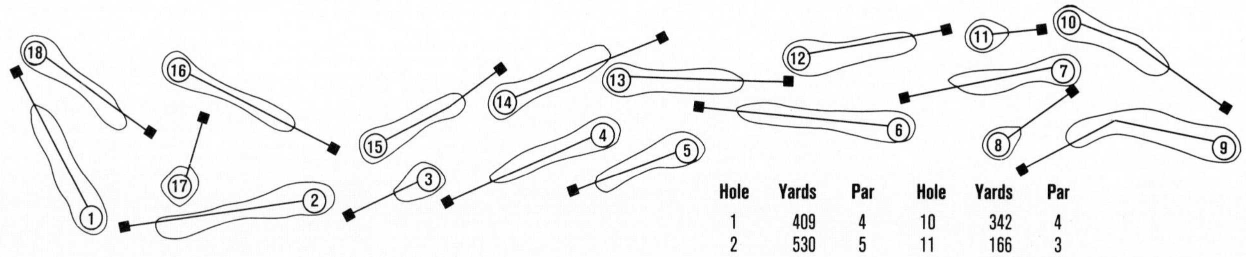

Hole	Yards	Par	Hole	Yards	Par
1	409	4	10	342	4
2	530	5	11	166	3
3	223	3	12	383	4
4	423	4	13	375	4
5	326	4	14	390	4
6	486	5	15	341	4
7	375	4	16	389	4
8	147	3	17	180	3
9	453	4	18	434	4
Out	3,372	36	In	3,000	34
			Out	3,372	36
			TOTALS	6,372	70

CRUDEN BAY

CHAMPIONSHIP GOLF

One often reads of famous Golf Clubs having been founded in local hostelries – **Deal** (The Black Horse), **Crail** (The Golf Inn) and **Hoylake** (The Royal) to name but three; well the birth of **Cruden Bay** apparently took place during a meeting in the North of Scotland Bank – one presumes a much more sober affair! The precise date of the meeting was **16th June 1898** and in March the following year the Cruden Bay Hotel and Golf Course were opened.

The Hotel (alas long since demolished) and the 18 hole golf course were originally both owned by the Great North of Scotland Railway Company. Within a month of their opening the company staged a professional tournament which attracted many of the day's leading players including **Harry Vardon** (then Open Champion), **James Braid** and **Ben Sayers**. The event proved an outstanding success with Vardon taking the first prize of **£30**. Cruden Bay was firmly on the golfing map.

The Club's full title is the **Cruden Bay Golf Club** with its full address being **Aulton Road, Cruden Bay, Peterhead, Aberdeenshire**. In addition to the 18 hole Championship Course there is also a well-kept 9 hole short course, the **St Olaf**, opened in 1968.

The present Secretary (or Golf Manager) is **Mr Ian McPherson**. He may be contacted via the above address and by telephone on **(0779) 812285**. The Club's professional, **David Symington**, can be reached on **(0779) 812285**. Casual **visitors** are welcome at Cruden Bay, although not surprisingly certain restrictions apply during Saturdays and Sundays. It is generally advisable to telephone the Club at weekends to check whether the tees have been reserved for any competition or, as may be the case during holiday periods, a starting sheet system is being operated. Visitors should also note that they are not permitted to play the 18 hole course between 4.30 pm and 6.30 pm on Wednesdays and that at weekends, unless accompanied by a Member, handicap certificates must be provided. No specific restrictions relate to the St Olaf course.

In **1989** the **green fee** to play on the Championship course was priced at **£12** for a weekday ticket, with **£15** payable at weekends. A week's golf could be purchased for **£50** and a full fortnight for **£75**. For juniors (under 18) the respective rates were **£5, £7, £30** and **£45**. A day's golf on the St Olaf course could be obtained for **£6** during the week and **£8** at weekends (£4 and £5 for juniors). Further reductions were also available to juniors aged under 14.

Cruden Bay is situated on Scotland's Buchan Coast, some 23 miles north east of Aberdeen and seven miles south of the old whaling port of Peterhead. The Golf Course itself has a dramatic setting with nearby **Slains Castle** providing a rather eerie backdrop. **Bram Stoker** who spent some time in these parts is reputed to have been inspired by the castle when writing his **Dracula** stories.

Fortunately the rest of the surrounding countryside bears little resemblance to Transylvania (wherever it may be) and strangers should find travelling in the area a pleasant experience. The best route when journeying from the south is probably by way of the **A92** coastal road which runs from **Dundee** via **Montrose** and through **Aberdeen.** One should leave the **A92** near **Newburgh** and follow the **A975** direct to Cruden Bay. The **A92** approaches from the North via **Fraserburgh** and **Peterhead**.

Originally laid out by **Thomas Simpson**, Cruden Bay is very much a traditional Scottish links of fairly medium length, being around the **6400** yards mark (or as the score card will tell you, a little over **5800 metres**). Par is a fairly tight **70** (s.s.s. 71) with the amateur course record standing at 67. From the ladies tees the course measures **5761** yards (par being **74)**. A good old Scottish Burn is a predominant feature of the course affecting several of the holes while the beach too (if one is a little wayward) can come into play around the **14th** and **15th**. The two par fives on the course are genuine fives and as a rule, accurate approach play as opposed to sheer length is likely to determine the quality of scoring. As one might expect given its geography the wind is often a major factor and the golfer that can master the low run-up shot to the subtly contoured greens will be on to a winner. The magnificent views over the Bay of Cruden naturally add to the pleasure of the round. The professional course record was broken in May 1989 by Colin Brooks with a round of 64, whilst the amateur record of 66 is held jointly by Peter McLeod and Stuart Bannerman; the latter is the son of Harry Bannerman, who until recently served as the distinguished professional at Cruden Bay.

The Clubhouse at Cruden Bay has the kind of atmosphere one comes to expect in this part of the world – friendly, and casual dress may be worn at all times. Meals are served throughout the day with lunches, high teas, dinners and some delightful steak suppers being offered in addition to bar snacks.

South of Hadrian's Wall Cruden Bay is probably not as well known as it ought to be. The legions who arrange their golfing trips around the more traditional favourites often miss out on some of Scotland's finest courses. Cruden Bay should be included in anyone's itinerary – it is a magnificent course and perhaps of equal importance, a place where the warmest of welcomes can be guaranteed.

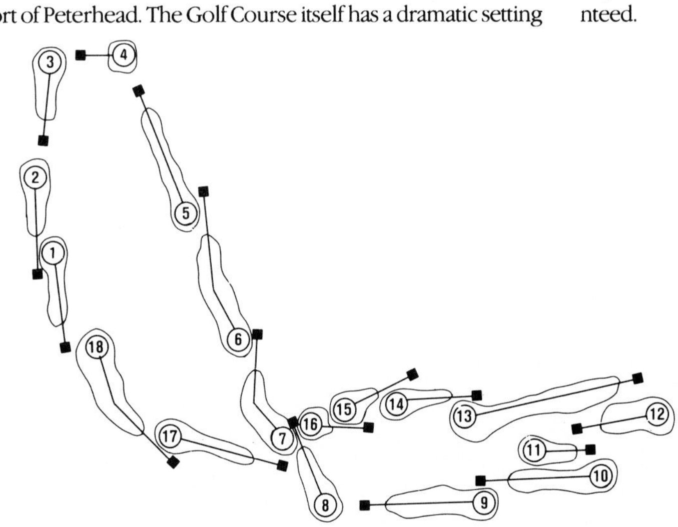

Hole	Yards	Par	Hole	Yards	Par
1	416	4	10	380	4
2	339	4	11	158	3
3	286	4	12	320	4
4	193	3	13	550	5
5	454	4	14	372	4
6	521	5	15	239	3
7	392	4	16	215	3
8	260	4	17	428	4
9	462	4	18	416	4
Out	3,323	36	In	3,078	34
			Out	3,323	36
			TOTALS	6,401	70

DORNOCH
CHAMPIONSHIP GOLF

Usually when a person describes his first visit to a golf course as 'the most fun I've had playing golf in my whole life,' very little is thought of it; however when that person happens to be **Tom Watson**, five times Open Champion, one tends to sit up and take notice. Like countless others before who have made the pilgrimage Watson was enchanted by the 'Star of the North'.

There are two words that are normally associated with **Royal Dornoch,** one is 'greatness' and the other is 'remoteness'. Situated sixty miles north of Inverness, Dornoch enjoys a kind of splendid isolation. It is the course every golfer wants to play but the one that very few actually do.

So what is the charm of Dornoch? Firstly there's the setting; (this is when people forgive its remoteness!) Bordered by the Dornoch Firth and a glorious stretch of sand, distant hills with their ever-changing moods fill the horizon creating a feeling that one is playing on a stage. And then of course there's the history: although the **Royal Dornoch Golf Club** dates from **1877** mention is made of golf being played on the links at least as early as **1616**. Writing in the 17th century **Sir Robert Gordon** wrote of Dornoch: 'About this town are the fairest and largest links on any part of Scotland, fitt for Archery, Golfing, Ryding and all other exercises; they doe surpasse the fields of Montrose and St Andrews.' Finally, and most importantly, there's the very links itself, described on more than one occasion as the most natural golf course in the world.

As the pen runs away, time for a few introductions. The **Secretary** at Royal Dornoch is **Mr. Kinnear**, who may be contacted by telephone on **(0862) 810219**. All written correspondence should be addressed to **The Secretary, Royal Dornoch Golf Club, Golf Road, Dornoch IV25 3LW Sutherland. William Skinner** is the Club's helpful professional; he may be reached on **(0862) 810902**.

Visitors are welcome at Royal Dornoch seven days a week. However it is probably wise to telephone the Club prior to setting off to check if any tee reservations have been made – an ever-growing number of people are now 'making the trip' and during the months of July and August the links can get busy. The cost of a day's golf in 1989 was priced at **£20** with a single round fee (if after 11am) at **£15** (only during weekdays). There is also an additional eighteen hole course at Dornoch, (the Struie course) measuring **5242** yards, par **68**; a day ticket for this course could be purchased for **£6** in 1989.

Travelling to Dornoch gets ever easier. The **A9** runs from Perth to John O'Groats, Perth being linked to Edinburgh by the **M90**. There are regular flights from London and other parts of the country to **Inverness Airport** and the links itself has an adjacent landing strip for light aircraft (which may interest some!)

By today's standards Dornoch could probably be described as medium length, the links measuring **6577** yards, par **70** (s.s.s. **72**) and possibly even short by Championship standards – Turnberry, Troon and St. Andrews all stretching close to 7,000 yards for the major events. However, the last thing in the world that Dornoch is, is an easy course. It has been said that the prevailing wind at Dornoch comes from every direction but even when the winds don't thunder in from across the Firth or down from the hills the links can be the proverbial smiler with the knife.

Although formed in **1877**, when **Old Tom Morris** was brought from St. Andrews ten years later to survey the links there was still only a rather crude nine hole layout. The master craftsman set to work and not only completely redesigned the nine but extended the course to a full eighteen holes. By using the natural contours of the terrain many magnificent plateau greens were created and despite major alterations made to the links by **John Sutherland** thirty years later, it is the plateau greens that remain the hallmark of Dornoch, the classic example perhaps being the celebrated **14th, 'Foxy'**, a double dog-leg hole. **Donald Ross**, considered by many to be the greatest of all golf architects was for many years the professional and head green keeper at Dornoch and several of the great American courses he later designed incorporate many of Dornoch's features.

Today there are signs that Dornoch is at last shedding its 'remoteness' tag. In **1985 the Club staged the Amateur Championship** for the first time in its history – this being in the minds of many alarmingly overdue. It may be to indulge in pure fantasy but one cannot resist wondering what it would be like if the hallowed links were ever visited by the greatest of all compliments.

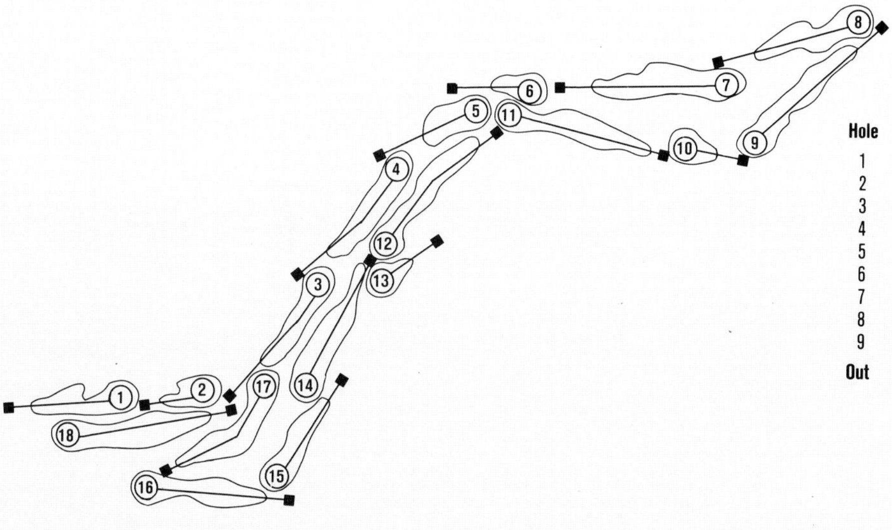

Hole	Yards	Par	Hole	Yards	Par
1	336	4	10	148	3
2	179	3	11	445	4
3	414	4	12	504	5
4	418	4	13	168	3
5	361	4	14	448	4
6	165	3	15	322	4
7	465	4	16	405	4
8	437	4	17	406	4
9	499	5	18	457	4
Out	3,274	35	In	3,303	35
			Out	3,274	35
			TOTALS	6,577	70

NAIRN
CHAMPIONSHIP GOLF

A glorious setting, a superb Championship course and a warm welcome to visiting golfers – that, in a nutshell, is Nairn. In **1987** the Club celebrated its **centenary** and played host to both men's and ladies' **Scottish Amateur Championships.**

Originally designed by **Archie Simpson** and modified two years later by **Old Tom Morris**, the present layout owes much to the work of **James Braid**, arguably the greatest of all golf architects.

Nairn is very much a traditional Scottish links with the opening holes stretching out along the shoreline. At the **10th** comes the inevitable about-turn, and the head for home. It is a fine test of golf and with the abundant heather, gorse and the distant mountains providing a spectacular backdrop, this is a veritable haven.

Being so far north on the golfing map Nairn has probably not received the recognition it must surely deserve – at least in terms of sponsored Championships. Yet with an airport (Inverness) a mere 8 miles away and an adequate road and rail network Nairn ought not to be considered too remote in the way that Royal Dornoch generally is.

A refreshingly relaxed atmosphere prevails. **Visitors** to the area are actively encouraged to play on the links and there is no requirement for a handicap certificate. Except during peak hours at weekends visitors may play when they choose, though early starters should note that fourballs are not permitted before 9.30am.

For a Championship course the **green fees** at Nairn are very reasonable. In 1989 the Club is charging **£14** for a weekday round with **£17** payable at weekends. For only £3 extra a day ticket can be purchased (surely worth considering?), whilst **junior** golfers should find Nairn something of a golfing paradise – In 1989 their green fee is a mere **£7**.

The Club's Secretary is **Mr. David Patrick**; anyone wishing to arrange a **Society** game should contact him via **Nairn Golf Club, Seabank Road, Nairn, Highland IV12 4HB. Tel. (0667) 53208**. Both clubs and caddy carts can be hired from the professional, **Robin Fyfe**, who can be reached on **(0667) 52787**.

Unless the traveller has made use of **Inverness airport** (80 minutes flying time from **London** and 40 minutes from **Glasgow**) he is sure to have taken in some wonderfully spectacular scenery. Motoring from the south the **A9** runs from Perth to Inverness via Pitlochry, Blair Atholl and Aviemore - over the mountains, through the valleys, beside forests and lochs – breathtaking stuff! The **A96** links Inverness with Nairn, a journey of some 25 miles passing **Culloden Forest**- scene of that rather nasty skirmish. An alternative route from Glasgow is to follow the **A82** which runs to the west of Loch Lomond, through Glencoe and along the shores of Loch Ness all the way to Inverness, an equally beautiful road. From the east, the **A96** is the main Aberdeen to Inverness road, passing through Nairn. The golf course is located on the town's West shore.

From the medal tees the course measures **6436** yards and has a par of **71** (the Championship tees extend the course by a further 100 yards) whilst the ladies play over **5755** yards, par being **75**. Nairn is certainly no monster and accuracy rather than length should determine the quality of scoring. The front nine is the shorter of the two although the prevailing south-westerly may well cause this to be the tougher half. Anyone suffering a bout of the dreaded sliced tee-shot is likely to find himself doing battle with the Moray Firth and throughout the round careful placing of shots will be necessary to avoid the many well-positioned bunkers. Notwithstanding the abundant hazards, provided the wind doesn't blow too strongly, a reasonable score is always a strong possibility.

And so, as they say, to the nineteenth. The distinct feeling of welcome has already been mentioned. The Club is not a stickler for the jacket and tie and casual dress may be worn at all times. In mid-September 1989, the Clubhouse is due to be demolished, and portacabins will be put up instead. Thankfully this is only a temporary measure, as a magnificent new Clubhouse costing £650,000 is to be constructed. During the summer months a full range of catering is offered on all days except Thursday. Special menus can be prepared by prior arrangement.

The Club has staged a number of open competitions in previous years, and this is expected to be repeated in 1990. For those who enjoy their golf in pleasant surroundings, and who feel the urge to 'get away from it all', there can surely be no finer place to visit than Nairn.

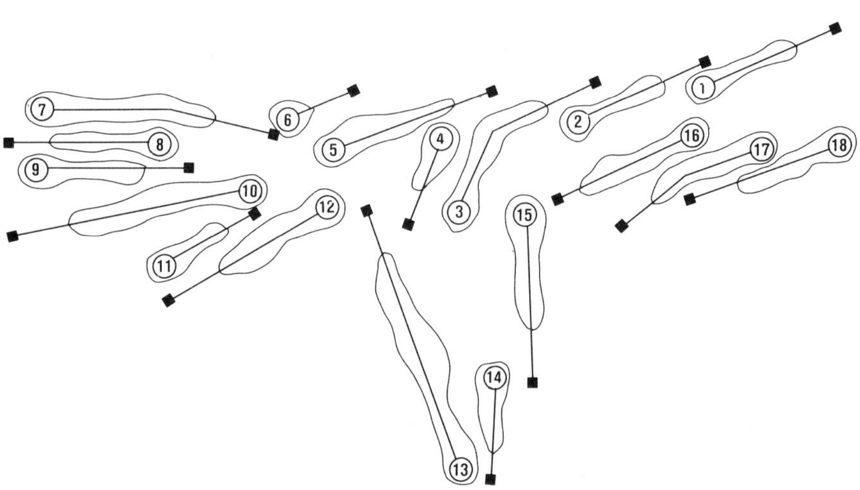

Hole	Yards	Par	Hole	Yards	Par
1	400	4	10	500	5
2	474	4	11	161	3
3	377	4	12	445	4
4	145	3	13	430	4
5	378	4	14	206	3
6	183	3	15	309	4
7	494	5	16	418	4
8	330	4	17	361	4
9	325	4	18	500	5
Out	**3,106**	**35**	**In**	**3,330**	**36**
			Out	**3,106**	**35**
			TOTALS	**6,436**	**71**

CULLODEN HOUSE

Culloden House is a handsome Georgian mansion with a tradition of lavish hospitality stretching back hundreds of years. Among its famous visitors was Bonnie Prince Charlie who fought his last battle by the park walls. The house stands in forty acres of elegant lawns and parkland, enhanced by stately oaks and beech trees.

The resident proprietors, Ian and Marjory McKenzie, extend a warm welcome to all visitors to their hotel. Culloden House is decorated to the highest standard, particularly the comfortable drawing room, which is decorated with magnificent Adam-style plaster work.

Every bedroom is individually decorated and has direct dial telephone, television, trouser press, bath and shower. Guests can choose from four-poster bedrooms, standard rooms, or rooms with a Jacuzzi. Dining is also a memorable experience at Culloden House; the emphasis in the Adam Dining room is on friendly and unobtrusive service, matched by the highest standards of cuisine. The wine cellars hold a superb range of wines from the great vineyards of the world, and there is a wide selection of aged malt whiskies.

Leisure facilities include a hard tennis court, sauna and solarium. There is also much to visit in the surrounding area – golfing, fishing and shooting can be arranged, and the Highlands, Loch Ness and Inverness are just waiting to be explored. Also nearby are Cawdor Castle, the Clava Cairns and Culloden Battlefield.

Situated three miles from the centre of Inverness, off the A96 Inverness – Nairn Road, Culloden House extends the best of Scottish hospitality to all its guests.

Culloden House,
Inverness,
Scotland,
IV1 2NZ.
Tel: (0463) 790461
Fax: (0463) 792181

THE UDNY ARMS

The Udny Arms Hotel on the beautiful Aberdeenshire coast offers you everything you need to make your golfing holiday one to remember.

There are three championship courses within 10 minutes' drive of the hotel or alternatively you'll find one of the finest 9-hole links courses in Scotland just at the bottom of our garden.

The Victorian charm, friendly atmosphere and excellent facilities of the hotel have drawn visitors to Newburgh for over 100 years. With menus changing daily you will find lots of variety in both the Dining Room and the less formal Bistro with special emphasis on local produce.

Udny Arms Hotel
Newburgh, Ellon,
Aberdeenshire AB4 0BL.
Tel: (03586) 89444
Fax: (03586) 89012

BANCHORY LODGE

The Banchory Lodge Hotel, enlarged and improved first by General William Burnett in the 18th century and then by the Jaffrays since 1966 combines Georgian charm with the distinctive leisured atmosphere of a country house.

There is ample opportunity for sport and relaxation, with local golf courses, tennis courts, putting and bowling, forest walks and nature trails nearby. Salmon fishing on the River Dee can be arranged through the hotel.

The public rooms, including the dining room, where cuisine of a very high standard is served, offer superb views of the River Dee. All the 24 bedrooms are individually furnished and have private bathrooms, colour television and tea-making equipment.

The traditional hospitality of the Lodge ensures an enjoyable and comfortable stay.

Banchory Lodge Hotel,
Banchory,
Banchory on Royal Deeside,
Aberdeen,
Scotland
Tel: (03302) 2625

GRAMPIAN & HIGHLAND

GRAMPIAN

Aboyne G.C.
(18) 5330 yards
Formaston Park, Aboyne
(0339) 2328

Auchinbale G.C.
(9) 4748 yards
Auchinblae
(0569) 407

Auchmill G.C.
(9) 5500 yards
Auchmill, Aberdeen
(0224) 642121

Ballater G.C.
(18) 6106 yards
Ballater
(0338) 55567

Balnagesk G.C.
(18) 5975 yards
St. Fittick's Road, Aberdeen
(0224) 867697

Banchory G.C.
(18) 5271 yards
Kinneskie, Banchory
(03302) 2365

Braemar G.C.
(18) 5011 yards
Cluniebank, Braemar
(033083) 618

Buckpool G.C.
(18) 6257 yards
Barhill Road, Buckie
(0542) 32236

Cruden Bay G.C.
(18) 6401 yards (Championship)
(9) 4710 yards (St. Olaf)
Aulton Road, Cruden Bay
(0779) 812285

Cullen G.C.
(18) 4610 yards
The Links, Cullen
(0542) 40685

Deeside G.C.
(18) 5972 yards
Bieldside, Aberdeen
(0224) 86797

Duff House Royal G.C.
(18) 6161 yards
Barnyards, Banff
(02612) 2062

Dufftown G.C.
(9) 4556 yards
Dufftown
(0340) 20325

Elgin G.C.
(18) 6401 yards
Birnie Road, Elgin
(0343) 2338

Fraserburgh G.C.
(18) 6217 yards
Philarth, Fraserburgh
(0346) 28287

Hazelhead
(18) 6045 yards
(18) 5205 yards
Hazelhead Park, Aberdeen
(0224) 317336

Huntly G.C.
(18) 5399 yards
Cooper Park, Huntly
(0466) 2643

Inch G.C.
(9) 5488 yards
Golf Terrace, Insch
(04642) 0363

Inverallochy G.C.
(18) 5137 yards
Inverlallochy, Fraserburgh
(03465) 2324

Inverurie G.C.
(18) 5703 yards
Blackhall Road, Inverurie
(0467) 24080

Keith G.C.
(18) 5745 yards
Fife Park, Keith
(05422) 2469

Kings Links
(18) 6520 yards
Kings Links, Aberdeen
(0224) 632269

Kintore G.C.
(9) 5240 yards
Kintore, Inverurie
(0467) 32631

McDonald G.C.
(18) 5986 yards
Hospital Road, Ellon
(0358) 20576

Moray G.C.
(18) 6258 yards (New)
(18) 6643 yards (Old)
Stotfield Road, Lossiemouth
(034381) 2018

Murcar G.C.
(18) 6226 yards
Bridge of Don, Aberdeen
(0224) 704370

Newburgh-on-Ythan G.C.
(9) 6404 yards
Millend, Newburgh
(03586) 389

Old Meldrum G.C.
(9) 5252 yards
Old Meldrum
(06512) 2212

Peterhead G.C.
(18) 6070 yards
Craigewan Links, Peterhead
(0779) 72149

Royal Aberdeen G.C.
(18) 6372 yards
(18) 4003 yards
Balgownie, Bridge of Don, Aberdeen
(0224) 702221

Royal Tarlair G.C.
(18) 5866 yards
Buchan Street, Macduff
(0261) 32897

Spey Bay G.C.
(18) 6059 yards
Spey Bay, Fochabers
(0343) 820424

Stonehaven G.C.
(18) 5103 yards
Cowie, Stonehaven
(0569) 62124

Strathiene G.C.
(18) 5957 yards
Buckie
(0542) 31798

Tarland G.C.
(9) 5812 yards
Tarland, Aboyne
(033981) 413

Torphine G.C.
(9) 2330 yards
Golf Road, Torphine
(033982) 493

Turriff G.C.
(18) 6105 yards
Rosehall, Turriff
(0888) 62745

Westhill G.C.
(18) 5866 yards
Westhill, Skene
(0224) 740159

HIGHLAND

Abernethy G.C.
(9) 2484 yards
Nethybridge
(047982) 377

Alness G.C.
(9) 4718 yards
Ardross Road, Alness
(0349) 883877

Boat-of-Garten G.C.
(18) 5690 yards
Boat-of-Garten
(047983) 282

Bonar Bridge G.C.
(9) 4616 yards
Bonar Bridge
(054982) 248

Brora G.C.
(18) 6110 yards
Golf Road, Brora
(0408) 21475

Carrabridge G.C.
(9) 5250 yards
Barrbridge
(047986) 674

Forres G.C.
(18) 6141 yards
Muiryshade, Forres
(0309) 72949

Fort Augustus G.C.
(9) 5454 yards
Markethill, Fort Augustus
(0320) 6460

Fortrose & Rosemarkie G.C.
(18) 5964 yards
Ness Road East, Fortrose
(0381) 20529

Fort William G.C.
(18) 5640 yards
North Road, Fort William
(0397) 4464

Gairloch G.C.
(9) 4186 yards
Gairloch
(0445) 2407

Garmouth & Kingston G.C.
(18) 5649 yards
Garmouth Road, Fochabers
(034387) 388

Golspie G.C.
(18) 5763 yards
Ferry Road, Golspie
(04083) 3266

Grantown-on-Spey G.C.
(18) 5700 yards
Golf Course Road, Grantown-on-Spey
(0479) 2079

Hopeman G.C.
(18) 5439 yards
Hopeman
(0348) 830578

Invergordon G.C.
(9) 6028 yards
Cromlet Drive, Invergordon
(0349) 852116

Inverness G.C.
(18) 6226 yards
Culcabock Road, Inverness
(0463) 239882

Kingussie G.C.
(18) 5466 yards
Bynack Road, Kingussie
(05402) 374

Lybster G.C.
(9) 3770 yards
Main Street, Lybster
(05932) 359

Muir of Ord G.C.
(18) 5022 yards
Great Northern Road, Muir of Ord
(0463) 870825

Nairn G.C.
(18) 6436 yards
Seabank Road, Nairn
(0667) 53208

Nairn Dunbar G.C.
(18) 6431 yards
Lochloy Road, Nairn
(0667) 52741

Newtonmore G.C.
(18) 5890 yards
Golf Course Road
Newtonmore
(05403) 328

Orkney G.C.
(18) 5406 yards
Grainbank, Kirkwall, Orkney
(0856) 2457

Reay G.C.
(18) 5876 yards
Reay, Thurso
(084781) 288

Royal Dornoch G.C.
(18) 6577 yards
(9) 2485 yards
Golf Road, Dornoch
(0862) 810219

Sconser G.C.
(9) 4796 yards
Sconser, Isle of Skye
(0478) 2364

Shetland G.C.
(18) 5791 yards
Dale, Shetland
(059584) 369

Stornoway G.C.
(18) 5119 yards
Lady Lever Park, Stornoway, Isle of Lewis
(0851) 2240

Strathpeffer Spa G.C.
(18) 4813 yards
Strathpeffer
(0997) 21219

Stromness G.C.
(18) 4665 yards
Ness, Stromness, Orkney
(0856) 850772

Tain G.C.
(18) 6222 yards
Tain
(0862) 2314

Tarbat G.C.
(9) 4656 yards
Portmahomack
(086287) 519

Thurso G.C.
(18) 5818 yards
Newlands of Geise, Thurso
(0847) 63807

Torvean G.C.
(18) 4308 yards
Glenurquart Road, Inverness
(0463) 237543

Western Isles G.C.
(9) 4920 yards
Stronsaule, Tobermory, Isle of Mull
(0688) 2020

Wick G.C.
(18) 5976 yards
Reiss, Wick
(0955) 2726

NORTHERN IRELAND

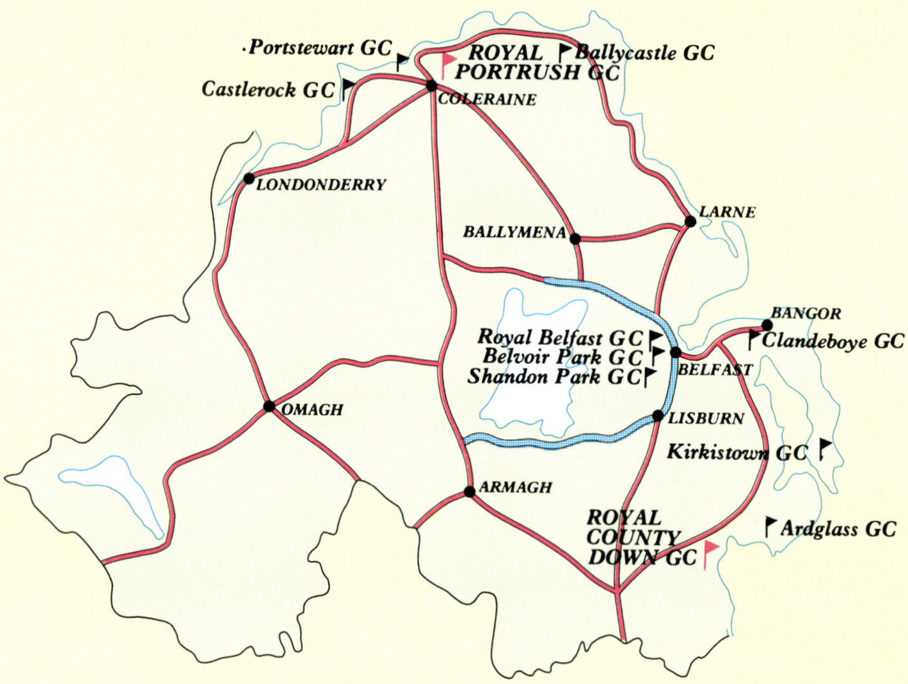

H. ROUNTREE "Portrush" SARAH BADDIEL'S BOOK GALLERY

NORTHERN IRELAND

CHOICE GOLF

It is no secret that Northern Ireland has lived through a turbulent history; what is less widely known, however, is that it is a stunningly beautiful place. It is a land of forests and lakes, of mountains and glens . It boasts the most spectacular coastal scenery in the British Isles and where else can you view the handiwork of a giant? So much in a country no larger than Yorkshire.

The quality of golf is equally outstanding. There are approximately sixty courses in all, a large number of which are to be found close to the aforementioned coast enjoying some quite splendid isolation. Belfast, which is about the size of Bristol, has no shortage of good courses and not just parkland types either, and then, of course, there are the two jewels in the crown – Portrush and Newcastle, or if you prefer, **Royal Portrush** and **Royal County Down**.

COUNTY DOWN

Belfast is a likely starting point and getting there should be fairly straightforward. Approaching from Dublin it is a case of following the **N1** and the **A1**, while from Britain car ferries run regularly from Liverpool and travelling by air is even simpler should you be thinking of hiring a car when you arrive.

Having declared nothing but your urge to break 80, resist at all costs the temptation to zoom off northwards to Portrush or southwards to Newcastle; Belfast offers much more than you probably imagine. The best golf course immediately at hand is the appropriately named **Royal Belfast**. It is situated just outside the city on the north coast alongside Belfast Lough. A number of holes here are very scenic particularly around the turn and there is considerable challenge to combine with the charm. Royal Belfast is the oldest Golf Club in Ireland having been founded in 1881. It is therefore older than either Royal Lytham or Royal Birkdale just across the Irish Sea. The course is understandably very popular but with a little forward planning the visitor should have little difficulty arranging a game; fees are currently **£10** midweek, **£15** at the weekend.

Remaining in Belfast two 'Parks' are decidedly worth inspecting. The first is Belvoir (pronounce it Beever) and the second is **Shandon. Belvoir Park** lies about five miles south of the city centre, **Shandon Park** just to the north; both are Championship courses. The former is possibly the pick of the two with its magnificent tree-lined fairways. Fees at Belvoir are approximately **£10**. Shandon has the advantage of being slightly cheaper; it also offers a view of Stormount where the ill-fated Parliament sat. **Clandeboye Golf Club** not too far from Royal Belfast along the Bangor Road offers a different test of golf. Clandeboye is more wooded and 'heathy' with a considerable splash of gorse. There are two courses; the more difficult Ava and the Dufferin. Both are attractive, quite tricky and, on the Ava course, some very precise shots are called for. The green fees are good value at approximately **£8-£10**.

A good base is required. In Belfast itself the **Europa Hotel (0232) 327000** is both modern and very comfortable but the most popular choice will probably be the **Culloden Hotel (02317) 5223** at Holywood (very convenient for Royal Belfast). The Culloden is an exceptionally impressive looking building, a Baronial styled Victorian mansion. Its restaurant is particularly highly recommended. Another good eating place in Hollywood is the **Iona Restaurant (0237) 5655** and on the subject of sumptuous fare, Belfast offers **The Strand (0232) 682266** and **Restaurant 44 (0232) 244844**. Whatever you do don't forget to sample one or two of the local pubs; in most the atmosphere is tremendous. For a really cosy inn, however, the best bet is to head east from Royal Belfast and Clandeboyne towards Bangor to Crawfordsburn where **The Old Inn (0247) 853255** is the place to find, a superb hostelry and some delightful bedrooms (which is probably just as well!)

Relaxed, well fed, well lubricated and swing nicely grooved, the next golf course to play is **Kirkistown Castle**. It lies near the foot of the Ards Peninsula (once described somewhat alarmingly a the proboscis of Ulster!). Kirkistown is a real gem. James Braid assisted in the design of the course and is reputed to have commented wistfully 'If only I had this within 50 miles of London'. There are some glorious views over the Irish Sea from the course and some equally glorious holes too, about 18 of them, all of which can be enjoyed for a green fee of just **£5** during the week **£8** at weekends (something else which would be welcome in Greater London). The town of Portaferry is no great distance away and the **Portaferry Hotel (02477) 28231** is a marvellous place to spend the night. It is another of those cosy inns (note the splendid seafood here).

If you're not is a rush it is worth spending some time on a Peninsula. It is a remote and very beautiful corner of Ireland and Lough Strangford is a great bird sactuary and wild life reserve.

From Portaferry, a ferry can be taken to Strangford and from here a short drive will take you to **Ardglass** on the coast. Perched on craggy rocks the layout is reminiscent of some of the better seaside courses in Cornwall and the green fees are again very reasonable.

Beyond St John's Point and around Dundrum Bay – or a journey of approximately twelve miles lies Newcastle: an attractive seaside town and where, as the famous song tells you, 'the mountains O'Mourne sweep down to the sea'. For golfers it is a paradise. **Royal County Down Golf Club** is quite simply one of the greatest courses in the world and is featured on a later page. For those lucky people who are able to enjoy a few days here, the **Burrendale Hotel (03967) 22599** is very popular (and only about a five minute drive from the golf course), and it has a fine seafood restaurant. Also recommended is **The Slieve Donard Hotel (03967) 23681** which practically adjoins the famous links. If one is staying in the area some sight seeing is strongly advised. To the south and west the mountain scenery is quite magnificent while the southern coastal road takes in some very different but beautiful views. It is an area where smuggling was once notorious.

CO ANTRIM

Our journey now takes us back northwards, past Belfast to the Antrim coast. Here there is perhaps the most spectacular scenery of all and, equally important, yet more glorious golf.

Now, what kind of being can pick thorns out of his heels whilst running and can rip up a vast chunk of rock and hurl it fifty miles into the sea? Who on earth could perform such staggering feats? The answer is Finn McCool (who, alas is not eligible for Ryder Cup selection). Finn was the great Warrior Giant who commanded the armies of the King of all Ireland. He inhabited an Antrim headland, probably not far from Portrush in fact. Having fallen madly in love with a lady giant who lived on the Hebridian Island of Staffa, Finn began building a giant bridge to bring Her across the water. Either Finn grew fickle or the lady blew him out but the bridge was never completed; still the **Giants Causeway** remains a great monument to one Finn McCool.

NORTHERN IRELAND

CHOICE GOLF

Royal Portrush is a monument to the Royal and Ancient game. Like County Down it is featured separately. However, there are three eighteen hole courses nearby which clearly merit inspection. To the east of Portrush, **Ballycastle** has a superb links overlooking an inviting stretch of sand and, if it didn't look so cold, the sea would be equally inviting. It is nothing like as tough as Portrush, more of a holiday course really, but tremendously enjoyable all the same, and great value at about **£7** per round.

Midway between Ballycastle and Portrush there is a pleasant nine holes at Bushfoot in Portballintrae where the **Bayview Hotel (02657) 31453** provides an ideal base for golfing in the area. One should visit the famous Bushmills Distillery nearby. It is the oldest distillery in the world and whisky has been produced here since 1608 – just think what Finn might have done after a magnum of Black Bush.

One mustn't play golf (never mind drink whisky) on an empty stomach and in Portrush, **Ramore (0265) 824313** is an excellent little restaurant.

Four miles west of Portrush and further along the coast is the quaint fishing town of **Portstewart**. It has another very fine golf course. The first nine holes are particularly good and the opening hole is considered to be one of the best in Ireland. A day's golf is priced at around **£10. The Edgewater Hotel (026583) 3314** in town is most pleasant and offers, as golfers will have come to expect, a very friendly welcome.

One final course remains to be played on this splendid Causeway coast and that is **Castlerock**, (green fees **£8** midweek, **£11** at week-ends), just a few miles across the River Bann from Portstewart. Excluding Portrush this is probably the most difficult of the four courses and it has staged a number of important championships. Once again it is a classic links set amid towering sand dunes and there are many marvellous and far-reaching views. There are many golfing delights that we have not explored, however; should this be your last port of call you'll have no excuses for not leaving Ireland a very contented soul. What's more, if this has been a first visit you'll probably have a very different view of the place from the one you had when you arrived. This really is a charming land.

*Artist : **Michael Brown COUNTY DOWN** Courtesy of : The Burlington Gallery*

ROYAL COUNTY DOWN
CHAMPIONSHIP GOLF

Approximately thirty miles to the south of Belfast and beneath the spectacular gaze of the Mountains of Mourne there lies the most beautiful golf course in the world. A daring statement perhaps, but then who is likely to disagree?

Royal County Down is situated in Newcastle and the course stretches out along the shores of Dundrum Bay. It was laid out in **1889** by **'Old' Tom Morris** from St. Andrews, who for his labours we are told was paid the princely sum of four pounds. In a way though, there was little that Old Tom had to do; for Royal County Down is also one of the world's most natural golfing links.

Within four years of the first ball being struck the course was considered good enough to stage the **Irish Open Amateur Championship** which was duly won by the greatest amateur of the day, John Ball. Before the 20th century had dawned County Down was already being considered as the finest course in all Ireland and some were even extending the accolade further.

Beautiful and natural, what next? Degree of difficulty. 'It was in fact the sternest examination in golf I had ever taken', the words of the very knowledgeable and well travelled golf writer **Herbert Warren Wind**. From its Championship tees County Down measures **6968** yards, par **71**. The fairways are often desperately narrow, the greens small, slick and not easy to hold; there are a number of blind shots amid the dunes and the rough can be, as someone once put it, 'knee-high to a giant'. Imagine what it's like in a fierce wind! Royal County Down is one of the toughest courses in the world.

Those wishing to pay homage should telephone the Club well in advance of intended play. **Visitors** are certainly welcome, but the course can naturally only accommodate so many. Weekends are best avoided as indeed are Wednesdays, but Mondays, Tuesdays and Fridays are relatively easy for visitors; a letter of intoduction form the golfer's home Club is helpful. The **Secretary, Mr. A.S. Foster**, can be approached by telephone on **(03967) 23314** while the address to write to is **Royal County Down Golf Club, Newcastle, Co. Down. BT33 0AN**. The Club's professional, **Mr. E.T. Jones**, can be contacted on **(03967) 22419**. In 1989, the **green fees** were set at **£18** per day during the week with **£20** at the weekend.

Visitors should also take note of the **No. 2** Course at Royal County Down, measuring **4087** yards, par **65**; this course is open to visiting golfers all week, with **green fees** set at **£7.50**.

The thirty mile journey from Belfast is via Ballynahinch along the **A24** and the **A2**. The road is a good one and it should take less than an hour. From Dublin to the south the distance is about ninety miles and here the route to follow is the **N1** to Newry and then again the A24, this time approaching Newcastle from the west. On a very clear day the Mountains of Mourne are visible from Portmarnock's Championship links. Unlike many of the great natural links courses, County Down doesn't have the traditional out and back type of layout; rather there are two distinct loops of nine. The outward loop, or half, is closer to the sea and hence is more sandy in nature and the dunes are consistently larger; it probably offers the greater challenge. Among the finest holes on the front nine are the short **4th**, where the tee shot must carry over a sea of gorse directly towards the majestic peak of Slieve Donard, the dog-legged **5th**, and the **9th** with its blind uphill drive over the dunes followed by a second to a well guarded plateau green – a particularly tough hole.

The back nine may not have so many great sandhills, but there are some and there is a plentiful supply of heather and gorse. Of the better holes perhaps the **13th** stands out: the fairway curves its way through a heather lined valley and the second is again played blind towards a smallish putting suface.

Given its rather remote situation and the lack of facilities or space to cope with a vast crowd of spectators the Open could never be staged at Royal County Down – sadly. The Amateur Championship has been played here though, **Michael Bonallack** completing a hatrick of victories in 1970. The Irish Amateur Championship visits County Down regularly and there have been some truly memorable finals. In 1933, **Eric Fiddian** playing against Jack McLean, holed in one at the **7th** in the morning round and them again at the **14th** in the afternoon. A magical moment in a magical setting – and I don't suppose he felt too sore when McLean eventually won the match.

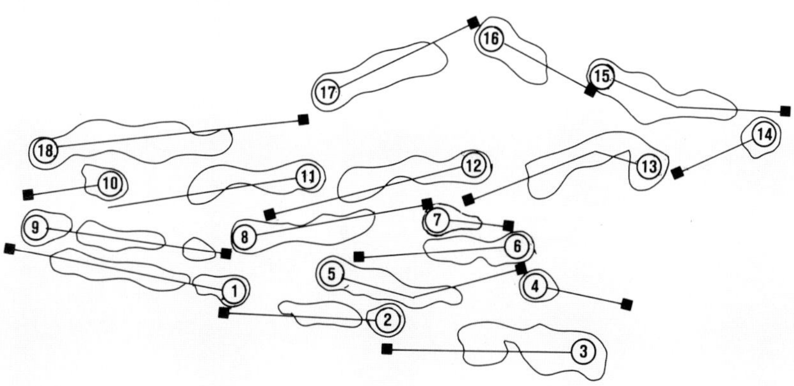

Hole	Yards	Par	Hole	Yards	Par
1	500	5	10	200	3
2	374	4	11	429	4
3	473	4	12	476	5
4	217	3	13	422	4
5	418	4	14	213	3
6	368	4	15	445	4
7	129	3	16	265	4
8	428	4	17	376	4
9	431	4	18	528	5
Out	3,338	35	In	3,354	36
			Out	3,338	35
			TOTALS	6,692	71

ROYAL PORTRUSH
CHAMPIONSHIP GOLF

In May 1988, **Royal Portrush** celebrated its one hundredth birthday. One could say that this famous Club was born with a golfing spoon in its mouth. Within four years of its foundation patronage was bestowed and there could never be a finer natural setting for a Championship links. The course is laid out amid huge sand dunes which occupy slightly elevated ground providing commanding views over the Atlantic. And what views! The Antrim coast is at its most spectacular between **The Giants Causeway** and Portrush and adjoining the links are the proud ruins of a magnificent castle, **Dunluce**, from which the Championship Course takes its name. The first professional the Club employed was **Sandy Herd**, who went on to win the Open Championship in 1902, and as if by way of a final blessing, in **1951**, Portrush became the first (and to this day the only) Club in Ireland to stage **The Open Championship**.

There are in fact two Championship Courses at Portrush. When people talk of the Championship links they are invariably referring to the **Dunluce** links, but there is also **The Valley** links which can stretch to **6278** yards and is used for many important events; somewhat surprisingly it has only twenty bunkers. **Visitors** are made very welcome at Portrush and can play either links on any day of the week excepting Wednesday afternoons; the Valley course is also closed to visitors on Sunday mornings. It is always wise to telephone the Club in advance as tees may have been reserved and Portrush is extremely popular.

In 1989 the **green fees** to play over the **Dunluce** links were set at **£14** per round between Monday and Friday, **£20** on weekends and Bank Holidays (when available) and **£9** for the **Valley** course during the week (**£12** at the weekend). Fees differ for those living outside Ireland, and are a little more expensive; however for the cost conscious golfer, there are substantial reductions for those teeing off after 4.30pm. On both courses, weekly tickets are available and are excellent value for those staying in the area (Dunluce links: **£63**, Valley: **£49**). Golfing **Societies** are equally welcome, subject of course to prior arrangement with the Secretary.

The Golf Club lies about half a mile from Portrush town. Portrush itself is easily accessible. It is linked by coastal road to Portstewart and Ballycastle and to Belfast by major road, a distance of approximately sixty miles. Londonderry is about thirty-five miles to the west. The Club is immediately off Bushmills Road and don't forget to visit the famouse distillery when you're in the area – it'll do wonders for your golf!

Although the game has now been played at Portrush for a hundred years, the Dunluce links in fact bears little resemblance to the original Championship course. **Harry Colt** is responsible for the present layout and we all owe him a great debt. Work was carried out between 1929 and 1932 and on completion he is said to have considered it his masterpiece – and Harry Colt built many a great course. **Bernard Darwin** wrote in 'The Times' after viewing the links during the 1951 Open: 'It is truly magnificent and Mr. H.S. Colt, who designed it in its present form, has thereby built himself a monument more enduring than brass'.

Portrush's most celebrated holes are the **5th** and the **14th**. The 5th (**White Rocks**) is one of the most exhilerating two-shot holes in golf. From the tee, there is a splendid view of the Antrim Coast towards The White Rocks and The Giant's Causeway beyond. However spellbound, considerable care is required with both the drive and the approach. The hole is properly a dog-leg although a brave drive can cut the angle, failure resulting in a trip into the deep, deep rough; over- hit your second and you're in the Atlantic. The green here nearly fell into the sea some years ago, but a retaining wall was built and it has been saved. The 14th is titled **Calamity Corner**, and not without good reason – a par three of over 200 yards in length, the direct line to the pin requires a very precise shot to carry an enormous ravine – mis-hit this one and you can be playing your next shot from at least fifty feet below the hole.

As with most of the great links courses, the greens at Portrush are very large and the bunkers often deep. The course poses a considerable challenge but it's a fair one nonetheless. In the 1951 Open only twice during the entire tournament did a player break 70. Silverspoon or not, you can be sure my good friend Finn McCool would have been mightily impressed.

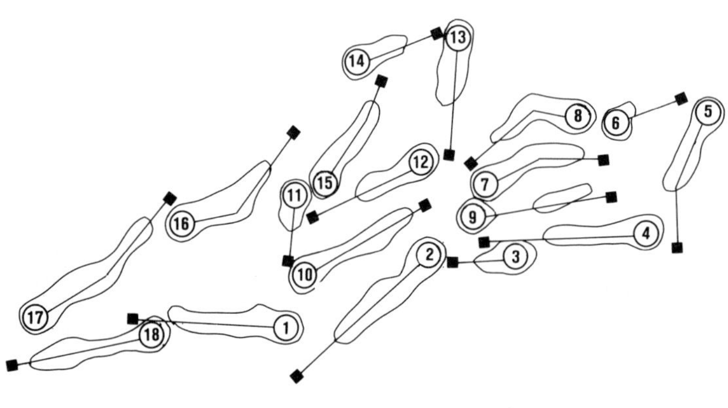

Hole	Yards	Par	Hole	Yards	Par
1	381	4	10	477	5
2	493	5	11	166	3
3	150	3	12	389	4
4	454	4	13	366	4
5	380	4	14	205	3
6	187	3	15	361	4
7	420	4	16	415	4
8	365	4	17	508	5
9	476	5	18	477	5
Out	3,306	36	In	3,364	37
			Out	3,306	36
			TOTALS	6,670	73

NORTHERN IRELAND
COMPLETE GOLF

CO. ANTRIM

Ballycastle G.C.
(18) 5902 yards
Ballycastle
(026) 5762536

Ballyclare G.C.
(9) 6708 yards
Springvale Road, Ballyclare
(096) 0322696

Ballymena G.C.
(18) 5168 yards
128 Raceview Road, Ballymena
(026) 6861487

Bushfoot G.C.
(9) 5572 yards
Portballintrae, Bushmills
(026) 5731317

Cairndhu G.C.
(18) 6112 yards
Coast Road, Ballygally, Larne
(0574) 83324

Carrickfergus G.C.
(18) 5789 yards
North Road, Carrickfergus
(096) 0363713

Cushendall G.C.
(9) 4678 yards
Shore Road, Cushendall
(026) 6771318

Dunmurry G.C.
(18) 5832 yards
Dunmurry Lane, Dunmurry, Belfast
(0232) 621402

Greenisland G.C.
(9) 5951 yards
Upper Road, Greenisland
(023) 862236

Larne G.C.
(9) 6114 yards
Ferris Bay, Islandmagee, Larne
(096) 0361217

Lisburn G.C.
(18) 6255 yards
Eglantine Road, Lisburn
(08462) 77216

Massereene G.C.
(18) 6554 yards
Lough Road, Antrim
(08494) 62096

Royal Portrush G.C.
(18) 6810 yards (Dunluce)
(18) 6259 yards (Valley)
(9) 1187 yards
Bushmills Road, Portrush
(0265) 822311

Whitehead G.C.
(18) 6412 yards
McCrae's Brae, Whitehead
(09603) 72792

CO. ARMAGH

County Armagh G.C.
(18) 6184 yards
Newry Road, Armagh
(0861) 522501

Craigavon Golf & Ski Centre
(18) 6496 yards
Silverwood, Lurgan
(0762) 6606

Lurgan G.C.
(18) 6380 yards
Lurgan
(0762) 322087

Portadown G.C.
(18) 6119 yards
Carrickblacker, Portadown
(0762) 335356

Trandragee G.C.
(18) 6084 yards
Trandragee, Craigavon
(0762) 840727

BELFAST

Balmoral G.C.
(18) 6250 yards
Lisburn Road, Belfast
(0232) 381514

Belvoir Park G.C.
(18) 6476 yards
Newtown, Breda, Belfast
(0232) 643693

Cliftonville G.C.
(9) 6240 yards
Westland Road, Belfast
(0232) 744158

Fortwilliam G.C.
(18) 5642 yards
Downview Avenue, Belfast
(0232) 771770

The Knock G.C.
(18) 6292 metres
Summerfield, Dundonald, Belfast
(02318) 3251

Malone G.C.
(18) 6433 yards
Upper Malone Road, Dunmurry
(0232) 612695

Ormeau G.C.
(9) 5306 yards
Ravenhill Road, Belfast
(0232) 641069

Shandon Park G.C.
(18) 6252 yards
73 Shandon Park, Belfast
(0232) 794856

CO. DOWN

Ardglass G.C.
(18) 6500 yards
Castle Place, Ardglass
(0396) 841219

Banbridge G.C.
(12) 5879 yards
Huntly Road, Banbridge
(08206) 22342

Bangor G.C.
(18) 6450 yards
Broadway, Bangor
(0247) 270922

Carnalea G.C.
(18) 5513 yards
Carnalea
(0247) 270368

Clandeboye G.C.
(18) 6650 yards (Dufferin)
(18) 5634 yards (Ava)
Conlig, Newtownards
(0247) 271767

Donaghadee G.C.
(18) 6099 yards
Warren Road, Donaghadee
(0237) 883624

Downpatrick G.C.
(18) 6196 yards
Saul Road, Downpatrick
(0396) 2152

Helen's Bay G.C.
(9) 5638 yards
Helen's Bay, Bangor
(0247) 852601

Holywood G.C.
(18) 5885 yards
Nuns Walk, Demesne Road, Holywood
(02317) 2138

Kilkeel G.C.
(9) 5623 metres
Mourne Park, Ballyardle
(069) 3762296

Kirkistown Castle G.C.
(18) 6157 yards
Cloughey, Newtownards
(02477) 71233

Mahee Island G.C.
(9) 5580 yards
Comber, Belfast
(0238) 541234

Royal Belfast G.C.
(18) 6205 yards
Holywood, Craigavad
(0232) 428165

Royal County Down G.C.
(18) 6968 yards
(18) 4100 yards
Newcastle
(039) 6723314

Scrabo G.C.
(18) 6000 yards
Scrabo Road, Newtownards
(0247) 812355

The Spa G.C.
(9) 5770 yards
Grove Road, Ballynahinch
(0238) 562365

Warrenpoint G.C.
(18) 6215 yards
Lower Dromore Road, Warrenpoint
(069) 3772219

CO. FERMANAGH

Enniskillen G.C.
(9) 5476 yards
Enniskillen
(0365) 25250

CO LONDONDERRY

Castlerock G.C.
(18) 6694 yards
Circular Road, Castlerock
(0265) 848314

City of Derry G.C.
(18) 6362 yards (Prehen)
(9) 4708 yards (Dunhugh)
Victoria Road, Londonderry
(0504) 46369

Kilrea G.C.
(9) 4326 yards
Drumagarner Road, Kilrea
(026) 653 397

Moyola Park G.C.
(18) 6517 yards
Shanemullagh, Castledawson
(0648) 68392

Portstewart G.C.
(18) 6784 yards (Strand)
(18) 4733 yards (Town)
117, Strand Road, Portstewart
(026) 583 2015

CO TYRONE

Dungannon G.C.
(18) 5914 yards
Mullaghmore, Dungannon
(08687) 22098

Fintona G.C.
(9) 6250 yards
Fintona
(0662) 841480

Killymoon G.C.
(18) 6000 yards
Killymoon, Cookstown
(06487) 62254

Newtownstewart G.C.
(18) 6100 yards
Golf Course Road, Newtownstewart
(06626) 61466

Omagh G.C.
(18) 5800 yards
Dublin Road, Omagh
(0662) 3160

Strabane G.C.
(18) 6100 yards
Ballycolman, Strabane
(0504) 882271

IRELAND

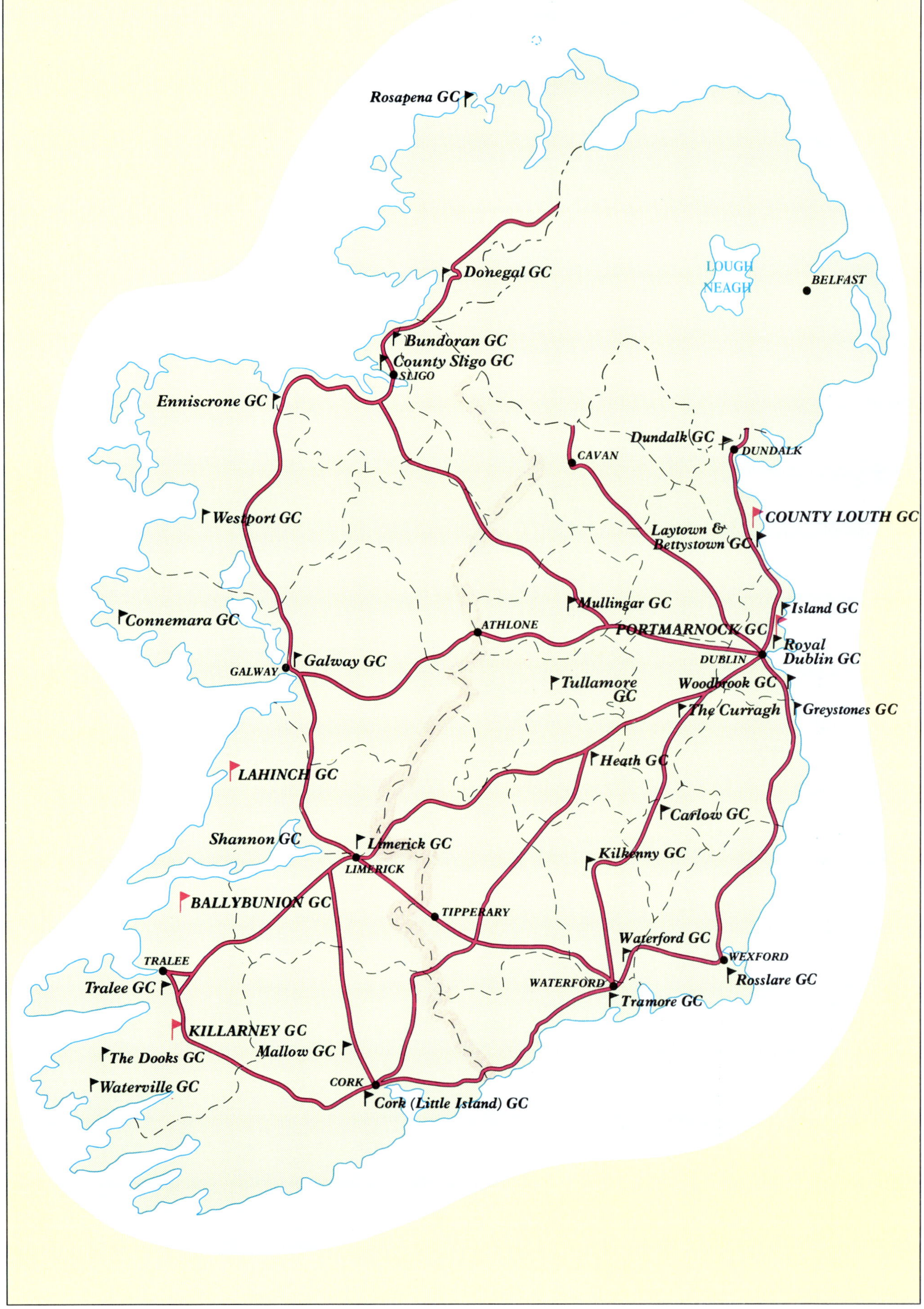
Rosapena GC
Donegal GC
LOUGH NEAGH
BELFAST
Bundoran GC
County Sligo GC
SLIGO
Enniscrone GC
Dundalk GC
DUNDALK
CAVAN
COUNTY LOUTH GC
Westport GC
Laytown & Bettystown GC
Mullingar GC
Island GC
Connemara GC
ATHLONE
PORTMARNOCK GC
Royal Dublin GC
DUBLIN
Galway GC
GALWAY
Tullamore GC
Woodbrook GC
The Curragh
Greystones GC
Heath GC
LAHINCH GC
Carlow GC
Shannon GC
Limerick GC
LIMERICK
Kilkenny GC
BALLYBUNION GC
TIPPERARY
Waterford GC
WEXFORD
TRALEE
WATERFORD
Rosslare GC
Tralee GC
Tramore GC
KILLARNEY GC
Mallow GC
The Dooks GC
CORK
Waterville GC
Cork (Little Island) GC

IRELAND

CHOICE GOLF

Without any shadow of doubt some of the greatest golf courses in the world are to be found in the south west of Ireland. For many years **Ballybunion, Killarney and Lahinch** were known as the 'big three'. To this list we must now add **Tralee** and **Waterville**, and with the recent completion of a second course at Ballybunion there is a growing consensus that this is the richest of all golfing areas, surpassing California's Monteray Peninsula, where Pebble Beach and Cypress Point are found, and the Ayrshire coast of Scotland, Turnberry, Troon and all.

Now as any Irishman worth his Guinness will tell you, great golf in the west of Ireland certainly isn't confined to the south western corner – it starts from County Donegal downwards. Apart from its magnificent golf, the south west is renowned for its beautiful scenery; majestic Killarney and the glorious Ring of Kerry in particular, stunning for sure but the north can be equally spectacular. This is what W.M. Thackeray had to say of the area around Westport: 'It forms an event in one's life to have seen the place, so beautiful is it, and so unlike all other beauties that I know of'. Clearly inspired, he continued: 'But the Bay – and the Reek which sweeps down to the sea – and a hundred islands in it, were dressed up in gold and purple and crimson, with the whole cloudy West in a flame'. Marvellous!

CO. DONEGAL

I don't suppose many golfers are likely to begin a tour in the very far north and head all the way downwards but we shall have a go all the same. **Rosapenna** is our first port of call – almost a John O'Groats of Ireland – on the northern coast of County Donegal. Somewhat isolated one could say but a fine eighteen hole course, nonetheless, it was laid out in 1893 by Old Tom Morris and is part-links, part-inland in nature. There are said to be more rabbits on this course than on any other – not a description of the members I might add! The place has a bleak beauty, rather in the way that Dartmoor has. Green fees are about **£7**. **The Rosapenna Golf Hotel (074) 55301** provides a comfortable and convenient base while those looking for grander accommodation might consider **Rathmullan House (0741) 58188** in Rathmullan, a Georgian building with splendid gardens.

Donegal, famed for its tweeds and wool has one of the longest courses in Ireland measuring 7,200 yards (try playing it in a fierce wind!). The course is actually outside of the county town at Murvagh. At **£6** a round it's probably the cheapest per yard in the country. There are a number of hotels in Donegal, but perhaps the best in the area is to be found at Rossnowlagh, here the **Sand House Hotel (072) 517774** enjoys superb views over Donegal Bay, and there is a short nine hole golf course within the hotel grounds. A little south of Rossnowlagh is **Bundoran**, another tough championship links. Right in the middle of the course is the **Great Northern Hotel** which has 150 rooms. Green fees at Bundoran are about **£8**.

CO. SLIGO

Our next visit is a real gem. County Sligo, or **Rosses Point** as it is commonly known, is certainly among the top ten courses in Ireland and is the home of the prestigious West of Ireland Amateur Championship. Laid out right alongside the Atalntic coast it is a true links and can be greatly affected by the elements. County Sligo is another charming part of Ireland; it is the counry of W.B. Yeats and the landscape is dominated by the formidable Ben Bulben mountain. A game at Rosses Point should cost around **£10** which represents excellent value. An outstanding seafood restaurant is located in Rosses Point – **The Moorings (098) 25874**. The **Sligo Park Hotel (071) 60291** is very convenient for the course while in Dromahir another Georgian country house is found, the **Drumlease Glebe House (071) 64141**.

Speeding down the coast, and noting the links at **Innescrone** (green fees **£7**) which is laid out on the shores of Killala Bay, we reach **Westport**, Thackeray's paradise. The town nestles in the shadows of the massive Croagh Patrick mountain. It was on its peak that St. Patrick is said to have fasted and prayed for 40 days. The golf course is another on the grand scale – 7,000 yards when fully stretched. It's a fairly new course having been designed by Fred Hawtree in 1973. Although some holes run spectacularly along the shoreline, Westport is more of an inland course than a links. The Irish Amateur Championship has been played here twice in recent years. Once again the green fees are tremendous value at just **£8**. There is no shortage of good accommodation in Westport and some hotels provide free golf. Approximately twenty miles away at Cong stands the redoubtable **Ashford Castle (094) 46003** a place fit for a king and probably the finest hotel in Ireland. Its setting on the edge of Lough Corrib is quite breathtaking.

CO. GALWAY

Connemara is located about thirty miles south of Westport amid very rugged country. It is wild, remote and incrediby beautiful. the course must be one of the toughest links that one is ever likely to meet. Green fees are in the **£8-£10** bracket. Despite the remoteness there are several first class establishments at hand. The best places for a night's stay are the **Rock Glen Country House Hotel (095) 21035** and the **Abbeyglen Castle Hotel (095) 21201**. Both are in Clifden and both have very good restaurants. Another of Ireland's leading country houses is to be found in Cashel, the **Cashel House Hotel (095) 31001**.

Galway is a delightful place to visit and the town has a very enjoyable course overlooking Galway Bay. It was here that Christy O'Connor developed many of his skills. Fees are approximately **£12**. The **Great Southern Hotel (091) 55281** in the town provides an ideal base, and in Spiddal the **Bridge House (091) 83118** is a cosy inn in a charming little village.

CO. CLARE

Leaving County Galway we move into County Clare where **Lahinch** is found. To the north of the county is Ballyvaughan. **Gregans Castle Hotel (065) 77005** offers a wonderfully relaxing stay, perfect for collecting ones thoughts before tackling Lahinch. The famous links is featured on a later page but an idea for staying in the area might include the **Aberdeen Arms Hotel (065) 81100**. Back in Liscannor a visit to **Joseph McHugh's** pub is recommended – not until you've played the course though! Slightly nearer Limerick in Newmarket-on-Fergus, **Dromoland Castle (061) 71144** is for the true connoiseur. The person who stayed at Ashford Castle will probably be staying here.

Both **Limerick** and **Shannon** have pleasant inland courses, the latter is very close to Shannon's International Airport. Fees at both are about **£10-£12**. **Jury's Hotel (061) 55266** in Limerick is comfortable but most golfers here will be itching to head-off to the delights of County Kerry.

CO. KERRY

Ballybunion is the first course we come across in County Kerry. Like Lahinch, and Killarney for that matter, it's featured ahead. Those wishing to stay in Ballybunion should note the large

IRELAND
CHOICE GOLF

Ambassador Hotel (068) 27111 and the more cosy **Marine Hotel (068) 27139** with its fine seafood restaurant. **Killarney** provides a more central base and as an enormously popular tourist destination has numerous hotels. Among the best are the **Great Southern (064) 31262**, the very attractive **Cahernane (064) 31895**, and the **Castlerosse (064) 31144**. A restaurant to note in Killarney is **Gahy's (064) 32519**, and **Laurel's** is a recommended pub. To the south of Killarney, the **Park Hotel Kenmare (064) 41200** is where our friends from Dromoland Castle will now be heading.

Tralee is thirty miles northwest from Killarney. The links is actually some seven miles from the town itself and occupies a narrow peninsula at Barrow. Although still an exceptionally young course it has already gained an outstanding reputation. It was designed by the legendary Arnold Palmer, his first assignment in Europe. Stunningly spectacular is the only phrase to describe his creation. Several holes run right alongside the cliff edges and a number of daring shots are called for. It seems to cry out for a swashbuckling approach; an Arnold Palmer golf course indeed. The green fees are about **£12-£14**.

Waterville is the other great course in County Kerry, and green fees here are about **£15**. It is difficult to imagine a course with a more remote setting. Waterville is for the big man, one of the longest in Europe in fact, when played from the back tees. It has it's charm as well though and Sam Snead described it as 'the beautiful monster'. Some suggestions for a 19th in Tralee include the **Brandon Hotel (066) 23333** and the small **White Sands Hotel (066) 33102** and in Waterville, the **Waterville Lake Hotel (0667) 4183** and the **Butler Arms Hotel (0667) 4144**. A quick note here for **Shamrock Cottages (0749) 76715**; anyone considering a fine selection of cottages in most scenic locations, will be delighted.

CO. CORK

Coming down from rather dizzy heights County Cork deserves a brief inspection. In the city itself, the Cork Golf Club on **little Island** is decidedly worth a visit. Approximately five miles east of the town centre the course overlooks Cork Harbour. It was at Little Island that Jimmy Bruen learnt his game. For the visitor, a days golf will cost around **£10**. A delightful place to stay in Cork is the **Arbutus Lodge Hotel (021) 501237** while just outside in Shanagarry is **Ballymaloe House (021) 652531**, where the restaurant is particularly outstanding. Finally to **Mallow** and the order of the day is an enjoyable round of golf followed by a stay at **Longueville House (022) 47156**. And I think we've earned a good rest!

CO. DUBLIN

From the time you arrive in Ireland and crack your first drive straight down the middle, to the time you leave having holed that tricky putt on the final green (and then drained your last drop of Guinness at the 19th), you cannot fail to be impressed by the natural charm and helpfulness of the Irish people. Nowhere is it more noticeable than in **Dublin** – what a contrast to many of the world's capital cities. Nothing seems rushed and nothing seems too much trouble. You see, the welcome from these folk is quite simply second to none.

You may have come by rail and sea or you may have flown (both methods are surprisingly inexpensive); either way you'll be itching to play some golf. In Dublin, as indeed throughout Ireland, the only real problem is deciding where to start.

Within ten miles of the city centre there are two great championship links and at least twenty other courses, the majority of which are of a very high standard. **Portmarnock** is the most celebrated course, and indeed is one of the great golf links of the world. It is featured on a later page. **Royal Dublin** is said to be the only Championship course located within the boundaries of a capital city. It lies just to the north of Dublin's centre on Bull Island in the charmingly named area of Dollymount. It is generally less severe than Portmarnock, not as long and the rough isn't quite so punishing. It makes an ideal place for us to crack that one straight down the middle.

The two best known holes on the course are probably the 5th and the 18th. The former is one of the most frighteningly difficult holes to be found anywhere. There is a story that when Danny Kaye visited the course he took one look at the 5th and turned to his caddy and asked for a rifle! The 18th is a shortish par five, reachable with two good hits but only if the second is carried over a dog-leg out of bounds – an all or nothing finish. The Irish Open Championship has been played here on a number of occasions. In 1966 Christy O'Connor who was then and still is attached to the Club came to the 16th needing three birdies to tie Eric Brown – he finished eagle-birdie-eagle. Another memorable finish was in 1982 when Seve Ballesteros defeated Bernhard Langer in a thrilling play-off to win his second Irish title. For we lesser mortals the green fees at Royal Dublin are **£18** during the week and **£20** at the weekend. Prior arrangement with the Secretary is advisable.

Portmarnock lies to the north of Royal Dublin, and a short distance to the north of Portmarnock on a tiny peninsula is the **Island** golf links (green fees **£10**). Until the mid 1970's the course could only be reached by rowing boat from the village of Malahide and the fare paid was included within the green fee. It is a delightful course, not overly long, but deceptively tough with a number of blind holes – something of a mini Prestwick perhaps.

In Malahide **The Grand Hotel (01) 450633** provides a perfect place to base oneself when playing the Dublin courses. It is particularly handy for the Island and Royal Dublin and is less expensive (and certainly more attractive) than the majority of the capital's more centrally located hotels. However, if one does wish to be more in the middle of things then among the better hotels in Dublin are **The Shelbourne (01) 766471, The Burlington (01) 605222** and **Jury's (01) 605000**. In Howth, **The King Sitric (01) 325235** is an excellent seafood restaurant, and again convenient for the courses to the north of Dublin. Good restaurants abound in the centre of Dublin and suggestions could include **The Grey Door (01) 763286, Le Coq Hardi (01) 689070** and **Locks (01) 543391**. Visiting a Dublin bar is an experience in itself and ought not to be missed. Take your pick but when you do venture in, be prepared for a good sing-song.

The leading course to the south of Dublin is **Woodbrook**. It too has played host to the Irish Open, in addition to many other important tournaments. Woodbrook is a mixture of links and parkland golf. It is always immaculately kept and a green will cost approximately **£15**. A few miles further down the coast and into County Wicklow is the pleasant course at **Greystones**. It's a bit of a drive from Dublin, but well worth it. The course is probably best described as heathland and while the front nine is relatively flat the second takes in a few climbs and offers some glorious views of the Wicklow Mountains and the Irish Sea. A very friendly Club, visitors are welcomed for **£8** during the week, **£9** at the weekend.

Following a round at Woodbrook, the **Parks (01) 886177** restaurant in Blackrock Village is highly recommended and in Bray, not far from Greystones an evening spent at **The Tree of Idleness (01) 863498** should be extremely relaxing.

CO. LOUTH

Thirty miles north of Dublin in the charming village of Baltray near Drogheda is the **County Louth Golf Club**. In the opinion of many this is the most attractive links on the east coast. **Baltray**, as the course is known, enjoys a wonderfully remote setting, but while it may be a peaceful place the course will test your game to the full and it measures a lengthy 6,729 yards. A day's golf at Baltray will set you back **£11** during the week and **£15** at the weekend – it's money very well spent. One needn't look far for a bed as the Club offers its own accommodation (telephone **041 22329** for details) however, if there's no room at the 19th the best bet is **The Neptune (041) 27107** in nearby Bettystown. The hotel is very close to the **Laytown and Bettystown** links which while not in the same class as Baltray certainly poses enough problems. It is the home club of the Ryder Cup player Des Smyth. Those in search of a good restaurant at Dunderry should investigate the **Dunderry Lodge (046) 31671** near Navan – it's one of the best in Ireland. Before we head inland **Dundalk** deserves a brief mention. Again it's not in the same league as Baltray, but then very few are. Still, it's definitely worth visiting if only for the tremendous scenery it offers. The course is set out alongside the shores of Dundalk Bay with the Mountains of Mourne and the Cooley Mountains providing a spectacular backdrop. A game at Dundalk should cost about **£8** and **The Ballymascanlon Hotel (042) 71124** in Dundalk is very good value if a night's stopover is required.

CO. KILDARE

For those who enjoy horseracing as well as golf (this must include near enough every Irishman), a good route to take out of Dublin is the **N7**. Given a clear road The Curragh is little more than half an hour's drive away. This is the Epsom of Ireland. Golf has been played on the great stretch of heathland since the 1950's and the **Curragh Golf Club** was founded in 1883 making it the oldest Golf Club in the Republic. Rather like England's senior links, Westward Ho!, the fairways are shared with the local farmers' sheep. There's also a nearby army range – one presumes golf is rarely uneventful at the Curragh! It's actually a very good course and the green fees are fairly modest, at **£5** midweek, **£7** at week-ends.

Baberstown Castle (01) 288206 at Celbridge is an excellent place to head for after a day on the heath, especially if a game of golf has been combined with a day at the races. The **Hotel Keadeen (045) 31666** at Newbridge is also strongly recommended and is in fact a little closer to the Curragh.

CO. WESTMEATH

Venturing further inland, **Mullingar** in County Westmeath is one of the country's best parkland courses, green fees are about **£10** and in County Ofaly, **Tullamore** is of a similar nature although it perhaps has a little more variety. Both enjoy delightful locations. Mullingar is close to the beautiful Loughs Ennel, Owel and Derravargh while Tullamore is not too far from the romantic Slieve Bloom Mountain range.

CO. LAOIS AND CO. CARLOW

Continuing our wander down through the counties of Southern Ireland, County Laois is the next we come across. There's only one eighteen hole course, **The Heath** and no guesses as to the type of golf offered. The course is laid out on common land and rather like The Curragh, there's a fair chance that you'll spot more sheep than golfers. Still, with green fees only **£5** it makes for a very pleasant day. Stumbling into County Carlow we find probably the best inland course in south east Ireland. **Carlow** is a superb parkland course; well-bunkered and well-wooded, it presents a considerable test of golf but a very fair one nonetheless. There are a number of convenient hotels in Carlow itself but for a real treat stay in Castledermot at **Kilkea Castle (0503) 45100**, a converted 12th century castle. A very popular restaurant is also found in Castledermot, **The Doyles School House (0503) 44282** (some accommodation also).

CO. KILKENNY

Kilkenny is one of those places that has to be visited. It's a town steeped in Irish history. In medieval times it housed the Irish Parliament, then there's the famous Kilkenny Castle and Kytelers Inn. The golf course is a bit of a youngster in comparison, but it's a fine parkland course, very typical of Ireland's better inland courses. **The Newpark Hotel (056) 22122** is just one of several comfortable establishments in the town.

CO. TIPPERARY

From Kilkenny it's certainly not a long way to Tipperary. Visitors to the county with the famous name should slip a game in at **Clonmel** (green fees **£6**). This is a fairly isolated part of Ireland and you may just have the course to yourself. A good place to put the feet up after a game is the **Clonmel Arms Hotel (052) 21333** and not too far away in Cashel, **The Cashel Palace Hotel (062) 61411** and its restaurant, **The Four Seasons** are quite outstanding.

CO WATERFORD

Nearing the south coast there is a pretty good course at Waterford, famous of course for its magnificent crystal, and an even better one at **Tramore**, a popular seaside resort. The golf course lies a little inland and is parkland in nature. It is good enough to have hosted the Irish Amateur Championship in 1987. There are many hotels in the Waterford – Tranmore region, one of the best is the **Granville Hotel (051) 55111** in Waterford. (Do inspect the glass factory if you can).

CO WEXFORD

We end our journey at **Rosslare** in the far south east corner of the county. Having started on a links, we end on a links, and here is where that tricky putt on the last green is made. It may not be a Royal Dublin but for lovers of the traditional game – rolling sand dunes and a hammering wind – it will do perfectly.

KILKEA CASTLE

Kilkea Castle is the oldest inhabited castle in Ireland, built in 1180 by Hugh de Lacy, one of the most distinguished of the Anglo-Norman invaders of Ireland.

From as early as the 13th century Kilkea had connections with one of Ireland's most prominent families, the Fitzgeralds of Leinster, until it was sold in 1960 by the Marquis of Kildare.

It has recently been renovated to offer today's traveller all the modern comforts while retaining all the splendour of the past.

At Kilkea, we use the word 'guest' in its fullest sense. We have no formula applicable to everyone, because everyone is an individual, each demanding different needs and different priorities. This is our challenge and your pleasure.

Kilkea offers sport and relaxation on a grand scale. The Castle is situated on the bank of the river Greese which has been carefully restored to its former splendour and the ardent fisherman has a treat in store.

An indoor pool ensures that even on the coldest of days, you can enjoy a refreshing swim.

Beyond the formal gardens, you'll find two flood-lit hard tennis courts, while the surrounding area provides no less than five challenging golf courses with which the hotel can make advance bookings for guests staying at Kilkea Castle.

Clay pigeon shooting, horse riding and rough-shooting are also available.

After your day of taking the freshest of Irish air, you can return to the Castle's dining room where you can enjoy the true spirit of creativity and imagination at work. The finest ingredients the season can offer are prepared in a fresh and imaginative way. Throughout the Castle, you will be struck with the enthusiasm of the staff – never settling for second best, never giving less than their all.

But all the words in the world can't capture the Kilkea Castle experience.

We look forward to welcoming you to Kilkea Castle – the Castle with an air.

Kilkea Castle is situated only forty miles from Dublin on the Dublin to Carlow Road, offering 48 rooms (all en-suite), an a la carte restaurant, banqueting and conference facilities.

Kilkea Castle
Castledermot
County Kildare
Tel: (0503) 45156/45100
Fax: (0503) 45187

PORTMARNOCK
CHAMPIONSHIP GOLF

One day in 1893 a Scot domiciled in Dublin named W.C. Pickman was riding his bicycle along the road from Baldoyle to Portmarnock when looking across the estuary, it occurred to him that he was looking at magnificent golfing terrain ....Portmarnock is located to the North of Dublin and lying on a peninsula is surrounded by water on three sides. It can be as tough a challenge as any in the world – more than 7,000 yards from the back tees with the rough often mercilessly punishing (knee-high in parts!) But Portmarnock, rather like Muirfield, offers a genuinely fair challenge. There are no blind shots, no hidden traps and the greens are among the most true in the world. As for that rough, well, as an obviously straight-hitter once remarked, 'you've no business being there in the first place' and you cannot really argue with that! Portmarnock has its beauty too: to the South, the Hill of Howth and the great sweep of Dublin Bay and to the West, Drogheda and the distant Mountains of Mourne. All in all it's a magnificent place to pursue the Royal and Ancient game.

The **Secretary** at Portmarnock is the very helpful **Mr. Wally Bornemann**. He may be contacted by writing to **The Secretary, Portmarnock Golf Club, Portmarnock, Co. Dublin** and by telephone on **(01) 323082** (the code is **(0001)** from the U.K.) The Club's professional is the former tournament player, **Peter Townsend**, he can be reached on **(01) 323157**.

Providing **visitors** possess a handicap of 24 or less they are very welcome to play the famous links; however, ladies cannot play this famous course at weekends or over Bank Holidays. It seems that half of Dublin wants to play Portmarnock (not to mention you and me) and the course can be extremely popular. The wisest move is to telephone the Club before you set off. The **green fees** as set in 1989 are for gentleman **£25** midweek, **£30** at the weekend, and for lady visitors, **£10** midweek. As a bit of a tip, Monday and Tuesdays are the quietest days. Golfing Societies are equally welcome subject to prior arrangement with the Secretary.

It is far easier to travel to Portmarnock than to any of the country's other great golfing attractions. The Capital is very well served by international flights and Dublin's airport is only six miles from the links. From Britain, Sealink offer a very cheap return to Dublin. As mentioned, Portmarnock lies to the north of the Capital, a distance of about eight miles. By road it's essentially a case of heading for Portmarnock village and then looking out for signs off to the right; as one would imagine the Club is very clearly signposted.

The casual visitor will not have to attempt the full 7000 yards plus, but he's still likely to be facing a good 6600 yards so he'd better have his game in fine fettle! Happily there is a relatively gentle break-in with three holes measuring less than 400 yards. The course then changes direction and the stroke one hole confronts you. Normally, the wind will be with you, but don't bank on it! A number of second shots will be played to plateau greens which can be very difficult to hold and a good Irish pitch-and-run may be needed frequently. The most celebrated holes are probably the **14th** and the **15th**, the former has been discribed by Henry Cotton as one of the greatest par fours in golf and it's easy to see why. The hole is played towards the sea along a gently curving fairway; the green sits on a plateau and is protected by two bunkers set into the rise of the green with many humps and hillocks surrounding the putting surface – nothing but a precise second shot will do. The 15th is a tricky short hole played close to the shore; once again the green is difficult to find. Even then there is no let up and the five-four-four-finish is one of the toughest around. The gentle wind down of course begins at the 19th. Portmarnock has a splendid Clubhouse, though not the original, which unfortunately burned down. The atmosphere is tremendous and some excellent snacks are offered daily with dinner also possible during the week.

Portmarnock has staged many great Championships including, somewhat surprisingly, the (British) **Amateur Championship** which was won – it goes without saying – by an Irishman. The World Cup has been played here and on several occasions recently the Irish Open. In 1989, **Ian Woosnam** won this splendid Championship - a great course which produces great champions.

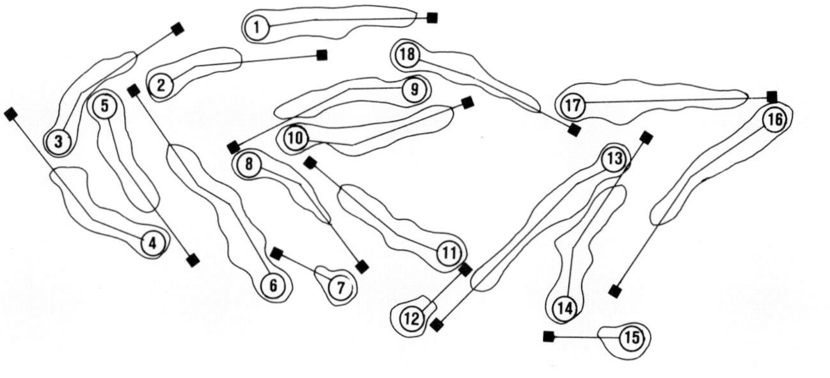

Hole	Yards	Par	Hole	Yards	Par
1	388	4	10	380	4
2	368	4	11	445	4
3	388	4	12	144	3
4	460	4	13	565	5
5	407	4	14	385	4
6	586	5	15	192	3
7	180	3	16	527	5
8	370	4	17	466	4
9	444	4	18	408	4
Out	3,591	36	In	3,512	36
			Out	3,591	36
			TOTALS	7,103	72

KILLARNEY
CHAMPIONSHIP GOLF

Killarney is often described as 'paradise on earth', and not merely by we blasphemous golfers. This is Ireland's most famous beauty spot; somehow the lakes here seem a deeper and clearer blue and the mountains a more delicate shade of purple. It is a place where even the most miserable of wretches would be forced to smile.

The two golf courses of the **Killarney Golf and Fishing Club** take full advantage of the majestic surroundings. A Gleneagles afloat perhaps? Not really. The golf at Killarney is parkland rather than heathland, but it can generate a similar degree of pleasure and, like Gleneagles, can be a welcome retreat from the tremendously testing links courses nearby. A place to sooth one's damaged pride.

Killarney has lived through through a somewhat chequered history. Golf has been played here since the late 19th century. The first course was nothing grand, laid out in an old deer park owned by the Earl of Kenmare. However, in 1936 the Earl's very keen golfing heir, and a great character of of his time, **Lord Castlerosse**, decided that Killarney deserved a course that would reflect the glorious setting. Eighteen holes were laid out by **Sir Guy Campbell** and the new course opened in 1939. Castlerosse, who had played a very active role in the design, was very pleased with the creation but continued to suggest imaginative improvements, unfortunately, not all of which were carried through following his untimely death in 1943. In the 1970's a second eighteen holes were built and the two present courses, **Mahoney's Point** and **Killeen** are each a combination of the old holes and the new. Basking beside the shores of Lough Leane and encircled by the splendour of the Macgillicuddy Reeks and the Carrauntoohill mountains, Killarney really is a golfer's dream.

The present **Secretary** at Killarney is **Tom Prendergast**, who may be contacted by telephone on **(064) 31034** (from the U.K. **(01035364) 31034**). Any written correspondence should be addressed to **The Secretary, Killarney Golf and Fishing Club, Mahoney's Point, Killarney, Co. Kerry, Ireland.** The Club's professional, **Mr. T. Coveney** can be reached on **(064) 31615**. As seems to be the case with all of Ireland's great courses, **visitors** are warmly greeted. There are no specific restrictions on playing during the week, although some do exist at the weekend, and as Saturdays are particularly popular with golfing societies, it's as well to telephone the Club before making any firm arrangements. The daily **green fee** at Killarney for 1989 was set at **£18** for the first round, with **£5** payable for the next round. At weekends, each round costs **£18**. If possible the day ticket should always be taken advantage of, at **£23** during the week, and **£56** at weekends.

Killarney is the most accessible of Kerry's golfing delights, the town being linked to both Limerick (seventy miles) and Cork (six miles) by road. The Golf Club lies about three miles west of the town off Killorglin Road and is well signposted. Those staying in the area might note that Killarney is the starting point of the famous one hundred mile Ring of Kerry road, which takes in surely some of the most marvellous scenery to be enjoyed anywhere in the world.

In such a setting, inspired golf is clearly on the cards (or so one hopes!) **Mahoney's Point** is the better known of the two courses, largely on account of its spectacular finishing holes, but when Championships are staged here, a composite course is always used. Both offer considerable variety and challenge, not of course to mention overwhelming charm. **The Killeen** is in fact the longer of the two measuring **6246** metres, par **73**, compared with **Mahoneys' Point**, which measures **6138** metres, par **72**. Among the better holes on the Killeen Course are the dog-legged **1st**, which follows the curve of Lough Leane's shore, the **3rd**, also alongside the water's edge and the exacting **13th** – one of Castlerosse's favourites from the Campbell layout – a long par four which has a stream crossing the fairway to catch the mis-hit second.

Mahoney's Point's celebrated finish begns at the par five **16th** where the course returns toward Lough Leane. The **18th** is the hole that everyone remembers. It's a par three hole, which in itself is fairly unusual at the end of a round, and the tee shot is played across the edge of the lake, practically all carry. Rhododendron bushes and trees surround the green; very beautiful, yet potentially very treacherous. 'The best short hole in the world' enthused Henry Longhurst. He also suggested that it might be a fitting place to end one's days. With the spectacular course and the new Clubhouse recently completed at a cost of £1 million, Killarney truly is a Paradise indeed.

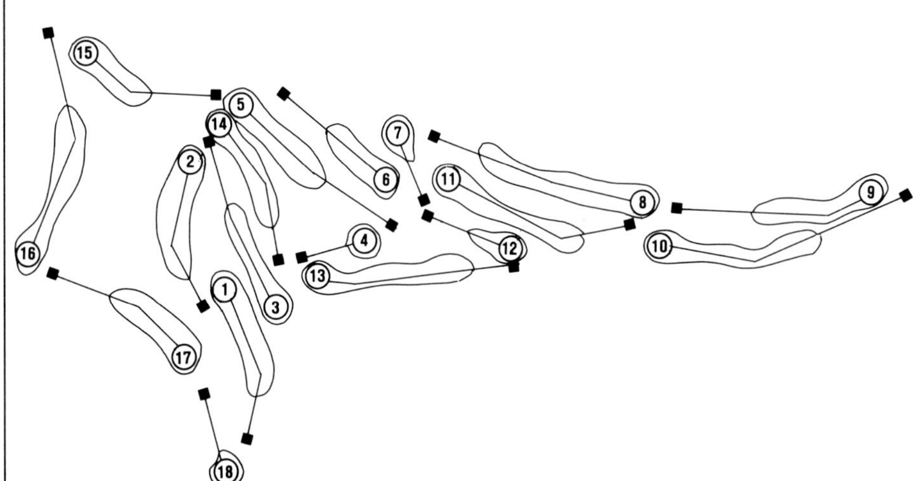

Mahony's Point Course

Hole	Metres	Par	Hole	Metres	Par
1	333	4	10	365	4
2	409	4	11	433	4
3	426	4	12	168	3
4	127	3	13	437	5
5	454	5	14	346	4
6	357	4	15	257	4
7	168	3	16	474	5
8	531	5	17	370	4
9	298	4	18	185	3
Out	3,103	36	In	3,035	36
			Out	3,103	36
			TOTALS	6,138	72

BALLYBUNION
CHAMPIONSHIP GOLF

Ballybunion is a place of true pilgrimage. To golfers this is where gold has been struck, not once, but twice with two of the greatest golf courses in the world lying side by side. The **Old Course** at Ballybunion has long been regarded as the ultimate test in links golf. It lies in a very remote corner of County Kerry close to the Shannon estuary amid the most massive sand hills in the British Isles. It has a very wild beauty; no course could be closer to the sea and a number of the holes run right along the cliff edges. It's incredibly spectacular stuff and when the wind lashes in from the Atlantic, it is not a place for faint hearts.

The Old Course was begun in **1896** although a full eighteen holes were not completed until thirty years later. The renowned American writer **Herbert Warren Wind** said of the creation: 'It is the finest sea-side course I have ever seen.' When **Tom Watson** first visited in 1981 (and he has returned on several occasions), he instantly supported Wind's contention and he went on to tell the members as much in a personal letter of thanks to the Club. What then of the **New Course**, just five or so years young? Architect **Robert Trent Jones** had this to say: 'When I first saw the piece of land chosen for the new course at Ballybunion, I was thrilled beyond words. I said it was the finest piece of linksland I had ever seen. I feel totally confident that everyone who comes to play at Ballybunion will be as thrilled as I was by the unique majesty of this truly unforgettable course'.

Happily, Ballybunion isn't jealous of its treasures and **visitors** are welcome at all times. About 15,000 play each year with well over fifty per cent making the trip from across the Atlantic. The above figure will tell you that the two courses are nothing like as crowded as say St. Andrews and Gleneagles and only during the weekend is it necessary to book a starting time – not that a prior telephone call ever hurt. The Golf **Secretary** at Ballybunion is **Mr. Sean Walsh**. He can be contacted by telephone on **(068) 27146** or from the U.K. on **(01035368) 27146**. The professional at Ballybunion is **Mr. Ted Higgins**, who can be rung on **(068) 27209**. A full day's **green fee** in 1989 was priced at **£18** for members of other Irish golf clubs or **£25** if not. This entitles the visitor to a round over both the Old and New – not of course compulsory, but if the body can take it, and it's likely to receive a fair battering en route, it would be a tragedy not to play the pair.

The nearest airport to Ballybunion is at Shannon, a distance of approximately sixty miles to the north east, while Cork's airport is about eighty miles to the south east. The cross country journey can take about an hour and a half but there cannot be a soul on earth who didn't enjoy a trek through the south west of Ireland. From Shannon, travel via Limerick and from Cork via Mallow and Listowel; from Ballybunion the course is about a mile's drive along the L106.

There is certainly no shortage of land at Ballybunion and both courses can be stretched to 7,000 yards – an alarming prospect! From the medal tees the two are of fairly similar length, the **Old** measuring **6529** yards, par **72**, the **New, 6477** yards, par **72**. But don't be fooled by the scorecard, each can be a monster when the mood takes it. The truly great holes on the Old Course begin at the **6th** which has a frighteningly narrow entrance to a plateau green. The **7th** runs its entire length along the shore – one of the most spectacular par fours one is likely to play. The **8th** is a shortish downhill par three, but if you miss the green, you can be in serious trouble. And so it continues with the **11th** being perhaps the most famous hole on the course. The sight from the tee is intimidating to put it mildly; the Atlantic waves are beneath you to the right, with some enormous sand dunes to the left.

The **New Course** is arguably even more dramatic! The sand hills are even more massive, and some of the carries required from the tee are prodigious. Of the **10th** hole, architect Robert Trent Jones waxed lyrical: 'There is no more natural golf hole in the world, an outrageously beautiful stretch of God-given terrain'. The round finishes with two lengthy par fives, one in fact measuring 612 yards – it may just be a classic case of four good shots needed to get up in three.

The 19th at Ballybunion is a grand place for recuperation. It is conveniently situated midway between nature's two masterpieces. Nowhere are stories swapped so enthusiastically and perhaps nowhere will you hear so often the phrase, 'Just wait 'til next time!' Gold diggers them all.

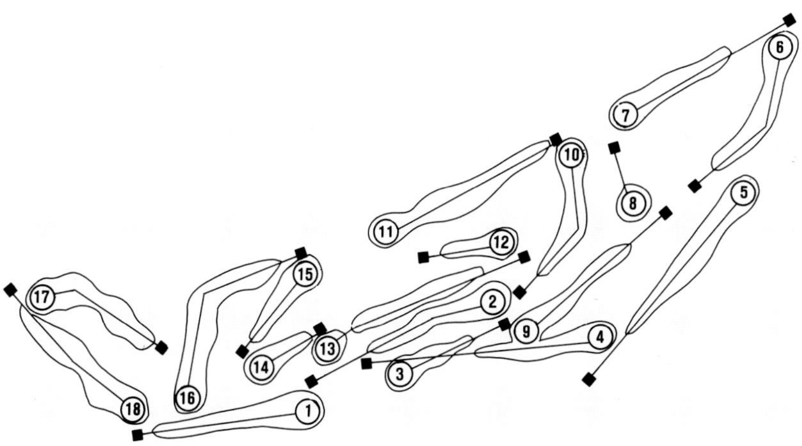

Old Course

Hole	Yards	Par	Hole	Yards	Par
1	377	4	10	356	4
2	434	4	11	443	4
3	217	3	12	185	3
4	504	5	13	485	5
5	508	5	14	136	3
6	364	4	15	228	3
7	417	4	16	483	5
8	151	3	17	379	4
9	455	4	18	381	4
Out	3,427	36	In	3,076	35
			Out	3,427	36
			TOTALS	6,503	71

LAHINCH
CHAMPIONSHIP GOLF

On the rugged coast of County Clare, two miles from the spectacular Cliffs of Moher lies the 'St. Andrews of Ireland'.

In 1892, officers of the famous Black Watch Regiment stationed in Limerick discovered a vast wilderness of duneland. Being good Scotsmen, they knew at once that this was the perfect terrain for a golf links. On Good Friday **1893, Lahinch** was duly founded. The obvious choice of person to design the course was **'Old' Tom Morris** of St. Andrews. Tom accepted but then other than laying out the tees and greens, he felt there was little he could do. He said: 'I consider the links is as fine a natural course as it has ever been my good fortune to play over'. More praise was to follow. In 1928, **Dr. Alister Mackenzie** was invited to make a number of adjustments to the links. On completion he suggested that 'Lahinch will make the finest and most popular course that I, or I believe anyone else, ever constructed'. Not perhaps the most modest statement, but coming from a man who had just designed Cypress Point and was soon to construct Augusta, it can hardly be taken lightly.

Visitors wishing to play at Lahinch will find the Club extremely welcoming. There are no restrictions at all on times of play. However, as it is so popular, advance booking is required. The present **Secretary** is **Mr. Alan Reardon**, who can be contacted by telephone on **(065) 81003** (from the U.K. (010 353 65) 81003. The club's professional is **Robert McCavery**, and he can be reached on **(065) 81408**.

Since Dr. Mackenzie's alteration, there have been two eighteen hole courses: the Championship **Old Course** and the shorter **Castle Course**, the latter having been extended from nine holes to eighteen in 1975. **Green fees** in 1989 to play on the Old Course were set at **£16** per day, whilst a day's golf on the Castle Course was priced at **£10**. During the off-peak season, certain discounts are available to those staying in local hotels. Golfing **Societies** are equally welcome and bookings can be made for any day other than Sunday.

Unfortunately, Lahinch wins no prizes for accessibility, but then if a course is good enough, a bit of a hike never put a keen golfer off. Unless one happens to live in the Emerald Isle, it is likely to be a case of flying to **Shannon International Airport** and picking up a car, but then again, I suppose one may have brought the wheels over. Anyway, flights to Shannon are frequent and Lahinch is located approximately thirty miles to the north west of the airport. On leaving Shannon, Ennis is the town to head for, and thereafter, Ennistimon, just two miles from Lahinch. One consolation is that you will journey through some marvellous countryside, and incidentallly, do visit the Cliffs of Moher – in places they rise to a sheer drop of over six hundred feet, the highest in Europe.

Lahinch is not as tough as a Portmarnock or a Ballybunion; it doesn't have the length for a start, but then it's anything but straightforward. A premium is placed on accurate tee shots and the slightest straying puts you amongst the dunes. Many greens sit on plateaus and can be tricky to hit. The most famous holes are undoubtedly the **5th** and **6th**, both of which Mackenzie was forbidden to touch. Having won for Open Championships at Prestwick, 'Old Tom' clearly relished the blind shot and this is what is called for at both the **5th** (Klondyke) and the **6th** (Dell). Not too many quibble with the 5th; it is a par five, although the blind second shot is over a prodigious sand hill and the green is a further two hundred yards on. The 6th however, is a par three! The green nestling between two steep sand dunes, all the player sees from the tee is a white marker-stone placed on the fronting hill to indicate the current position – 'hit and hope' perhaps but charming all the same.

The Castle Course is literally over the road from the Old and occupies much more level ground. The fairways wind their way around the remains of O'Brien's Castle. It may not be as challenging, but it's still a good honest links and is just as superbly maintained.

The Clubhouse at Lahinch is fairly small, but marvellously intimate; an excellent place to adjourn to should the heavens open. And you'll have ample warning of the impending doom for the goats that graze on the dunes will make their way towards the shelter of the 19th. A bit of Irish blarney? Try telling that to the Members!

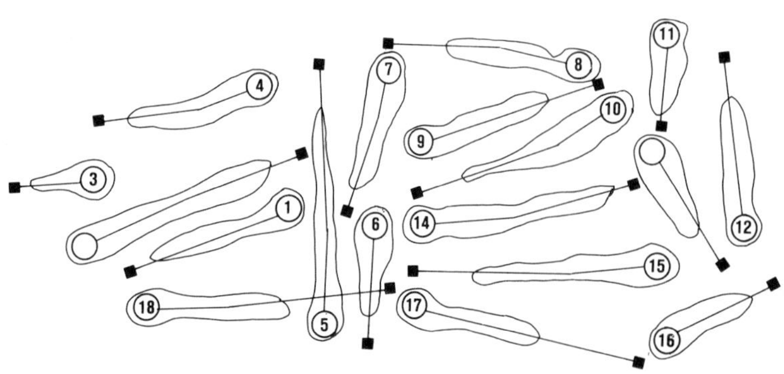

Hole	Yards	Par	Hole	Yards	Par
1	387	4	10	453	4
2	515	5	11	139	3
3	157	3	12	353	4
4	424	4	13	274	4
5	488	5	14	486	5
6	156	3	15	456	4
7	376	4	16	196	3
8	341	4	17	435	4
9	348	4	18	520	5
Out	3,192	36	In	3,312	36
			Out	3,192	36
			TOTALS	6,504	72

IRELAND
COMPLETE GOLF

WESTERN IRELAND

CO CLARE

Dromoland Castle G.C.
(9) 6560 yards
Newmarket on Fergus
(061) 71144

Ennis G.C.
(18) 5714 yards
Drumbiggle Road, Ennis
(065) 24074

Kilkee G.C.
(9) 6058 yards
East End, Kilkee
Kilkee 48

Kilrush G.C.
(9) 5478 yards
Parknamoney, Kilrush
Kilrush 138

Lahinch G.C.
(18) 6515 yards (Champion)
(18) 5450 yards (No. 2)
Lahinch
(065) 81003

Shannon G.C.
(18) 6480 yards
Shannon Airport
(061) 61020

Spanish Point G.C.
(9) 6248 yards
Miltown, Malbay
(065) 84198

CO CORK

Bandon G.C.
(18) 6101 yards
Castlebernard, Bandon
(023) 41111

Bantry G.C.
(9) 6436 yards
Donemark, Bantry
(027) 50579

Charleville G.C.
(18) 6380 yards
Charleville
(063) 257

Cork G.C.
(18) 6065 metres
Little Island
(021) 353451

Doneraile G.C.
(9) 5528 yards
Doneraile
(022) 24137

Douglas G.C.
(18) 5651 yards
Douglas
(021) 291086

Dunmore G.C.
(9) 4180 yards
Clonakilty, Dunmore
(023) 33352

East Cork G.C.
(18) 5602 yards
Gortacrue, Midleton
(021) 631687

Fermoy G.C.
(18) 5884 yards
Fermoy
(025) 31472

Glengarriff G.C.
(9) 4328 yards
Glengarriff
Glengarriff 150

Kanturk G.C.
(9) 5918 yards
Fairy Hill, Kanturk
(029) 50181

Kinsale G.C.
(9) 5580 yards
Ringnanean, Belgooly,
Kinsale
(021) 772197

Macroom G.C.
(9) 5850 yards
Lackaduve, Macroom
(026) 41072

Mallow G.C.
(18) 6559 yards
Balleyellis, Mallow
(022) 21145

Mitchelstown G.C.
(9) 5550 yards
Gurrane, Mitchelstown
(025) 24072

Monkstown G.C.
(18) 6000 yards
Parkgarriffe, Monkstown
(021) 841225

Muskerry G.C.
(18) 6350 yards
Carrigrohane
(021) 85297

Skibbereen G.C.
(9) 5890 yards
Skibbereen
(028) 21227

Youghal G.C.
(18) 6206 yards
Knockaverry, Youghal
(024) 2787

CO DONEGAL

Ballybofey & Stranoriar G.C.
(18) 5913 yards
Ballybofey
(074) 31093

Ballyliffin G.C.
(18) 6611 yards
Ballyliffin, Clonmany
Clonmany 19

Buncrana G.C.
(9) 2020 yards
Buncrana
Buncrana 1

Bundoran G.C.
(18) 6328 yards
Bundoran
(072) 41302

Donegal G.C.
(18) 6842 yards
Murvagh, Donegal
(073) 34054

Dunfanaghy G.C.
(18) 5450 yards
Dunfanaghy
(074) 36238

Greencastle G.C.
(9) 2693 yards
Greencastle
Greencastle 13

Gweedore G.C.
(9) 6234 yards
Derrybeg, Letterkenny
(075) 31140

Letterkenny G.C.
(18) 6299 yards
Barnhill, Letterkenny
(074) 21150

Nairn & Portnoo G.C.
(18) 5950 yards
Nairn & Portnoo
Clooney 7

North West G.C.
(18) 5895 yards
Lisfannon, Fahan
(077) 61027

Otway G.C.
(9) 4134 yards
Saltpans, Rathmullen
(074) 58319

Portsalon G.C.
(18) 5949 yards
Portsalon
Portsalon 11

Rosapenna G.C.
(18) 6254 yards
Rosapenna
(074) 55301

CO GALWAY

Athenry G.C.
(9) 5448 yards
Derrydonnell, Oranmore
(091) 94466

Ballinasloe G.C.
(9) 5844 yards
Ballinasloe
(0905) 42126

Connemara G.C.
(18) 7100 yards
Ballyconneely, nr. Clifden
(095) 21153

Galway G.C.
(18) 6193 yards
Blackrock, Salthill
(091) 22169

Gort G.C.
(9) 5688 yards
Gort
(091) 31336

Loughrea G.C.
(9) 5798 yards
Loughrea
(091) 41049

Mount Bellew G.C.
(9) 5564 yards
Mount Bellew
(0905) 79259

Oughterard G.C.
(9) 6356 yards
Gurteeva, Oughterard
(091) 82131

Portumna G.C.
(9) 5776 yards
Portumn
(0509) 41059

Tuam G.C.
(18) 6321 yards
Barnacurrahg, Tuam
(093) 24354

CO KERRY

Ballybunion G.C.
(18) 6542 yards (Old)
(18) 6477 yards (New)
Ballybunion
(068) 27146

Ceann Sibeal G.C.
(9) 6222 yards
Ballyferriter, Tralee
(066) 51657

Dooks G.C.
(18) 5850 yards
Glenbeigh, Dooks
(066) 68205

Kenmare G.C.
(9) 5900 yards
Kenmare
(064) 41291

Killarney Golf
& Fishing Club
(18) 6677 yards (Mahoney's Point)
(18) 6798 yards (Killeen)
Mahoney's Point, Killarney
(064) 31034

Parknasilla G.C.
(9) 5000 yards
Parknasilla
(064) 45122

Tralee G.C.
(18) 6800 yards
West Barrow, Ardfert
(066) 36379

Waterville G.C.
(18) 7146 yards
Waterville
(0667) 4102

CO. LEITRIM

Ballinamore G.C.
(9) 5680 yards
Ballinamore
(078) 44346

Carrick-on-Shannon G.C.
(9) 5922 yards
Carrick-on-Shannon
(078) 20157

CO LIMERICK

Adare Manor
(9) 5430 yards
Adare
(061) 86204

Castletroy G.C.
(18) 6089 yards
Castletroy
(061) 335753

Limerick G.C.
(18) 5767 yards
Ballyclough, Limerick
(061) 44083

Newcastle West G.C.
(9) 5482 yards
Newcastle West
Newcastle West 76

CO MAYO

Achill Island G.C.
(9) 5420 yards
Keel, Achill Island
(098) 43202

Ballina G.C.
(9) 5182 yards
Mosgrove, Shanaghy, Ballina
(096) 21050

Ballinrobe G.C.
(9) 2895 yards
Ballinrobe
Ballinrobe 52

Ballyhaunis G.C.
(9) 5852 yards
Coolnaha, Ballyhaunis
(0907) 30014

Belmullet G.C.
(9) 5714 yards
Belmullet, Balhina
(097) 81093

Castlebar G.C.
(18) 6109 yards
Rocklands, Castlebar
(094) 21649

Claremorris G.C.
(9) 5898 yards
Claremorris
(094) 71527

Mulrany G.C.
(9) 6380 yards
Mulrany, Westport
(098) 36185

Swinford G.C.
(9) 5230 yards
Swinford
(094) 51378

Westport G.C.
(18) 6706 yards
Carrowholly, Westport
Westport 547

CO. ROSCOMMON

Athlone G.C.
(18) 6000 yards
Hodson Bay, Athlone
(0902) 2073

Ballaghaderreen G.C.
(9) 5686 yards
Ballaghaderreen

Boyle G.C.
(9) 5728 yards
Roscommon Road, Boyle
(079) 62594

Castlerea G.C.
(9) 5466 yards
Clonalis, Castlerea
(0907) 20068

Roscommon G.C.
(9) 6215 yards
Mote Park, Roscommon
(0903) 6382

CO SLIGO

Ballymote G.C.
(9) 5032 yards
Ballymote
Ballymote 3460

County Sligo G.C.
(18) 6011 yards
Rosses Point
(071) 77186

Enniscrone G.C.
(18) 6511 yards
Enniscrone
(096) 36297

Strandhill G.C.
(18) 5523 yards
Standhill
(071) 68188

SOUTH EAST IRELAND

CO. CARLOW

Borris G.C.
(9) 6026 yards
Borris
(0503) 73143

Carlow G.C.
(18) 6347 yards
Deerpark, Carlow
(0503) 31695

CO. CAVAN

Belturbet G.C.
(9) 5180 yards
Ernie Hill, Belturbet
(049) 22287

Blacklion G.C.
(9) 6000 yards
Toam, Blacklion
(0017) 53024

County Cavan G.C.
(18) 6037 yards
Drumelis
(049) 31283

Virginia G.C.
(9) 4520 yards
Virginia
Virginia 35

CO. DUBLIN

Balbriggan G.C.
(9) 5952 yards
Blackhall, Balbriggan
(01) 412173

Ballinascorney G.C.
(9) 5322 yards
Ballinascorney
(01) 512516

Beech Park G.C.
(18) 5600 yards
Johnstown, Rathcoole
(01) 580522

Corballis G.C.
(18) 4898 yards
Donabate
(01) 450583

Carrickmines G.C.
(9) 6044 yards
Carrickmines, Dublin
(01) 895 676

Castle G.C.
(18) 6240 yards
Rathfarnham, Dublin
(01) 904207

Clontarf G.C.
(18) 5608 yards
Malahide Road, Dublin
(01) 315085

Deerpark G.C.
(18) 6647 yards
Deerpark Hotel, Howith
(01) 322624

Donabate G.C.
(18) 6187 yards
Balcarrick, Donabate
(01) 436059

Dublin Sport G.C.
(18) 5413 yards
Kilternan, Dublin
(01) 895418

Dun Laoghaire G.C.
(18) 5950 yards
Eglinton Park, Dun Laoghaire, Dublin
(01) 801055

Edmonstown G.C.
(18) 6177 yards
Rathfarnham, Dublin
(01) 931082

Elm Park G.C.
(18) 5485 yards
Donnybrook, Dublin
(01) 693014

Forrest Little G.C.
(18) 6400 yards
Cloghran
(01) 401183

Foxrock G.C.
(9) 5699 metres
Foxrock, Torquay Road, Dublin
(01) 895668

Grange G.C.
(18) 5517 yards
Whitechurch, Rathfarnham, Dublin
(01) 932832

Hermitage G.C.
(18) 6000 yards
Lucan
(01) 264549

Howth G.C.
(18) 6168 yards
Carrickbrack Road, Sutton, Dublin
(01) 323055

The Island G.C.
(18) 6227 yards
Corballis, Donabate
(01) 452205

Killiney G.C.
(9) 6201 yards
Killiney
(01) 851983

Lucan G.C.
(9) 6287 yards
Lucan
(01) 280246

Malahide G.C.
(9) 5568 yards
Coast Road, Malahide
(01) 450248

Milltown G.C.
(18) 6275 yards
Lower Churchtown Road, Dublin
(01) 976090

Newlands G.C.
(18) 6184 yards
Clondalkin, Dublin
(01) 593157

Portmarnock G.C.
(18) 6489 yards
(9) 3378 yards
Portmarnock
(01) 323082

Rathfarnham G.C.
(9) 6250 yards
Newtown, Dublin
(01) 931201

Royal Dublin G.C.
(18) 6810 yards
Bull Island, Dollymont, Dublin
(01) 331262

Rush G.C.
(9) 5655 yards
Rush
(01) 437548

St. Anne's G.C.
(9) 6104 yards
North Bull Island, Dublin
(01) 336471

Skerries G.C.
(18) 6300 yards
Skerries
(01) 491204

Slade Valley G.C.
(18) 5800 yards
Lynch Park, Brittas
(01) 582207

Woodbrook G.C.
(18) 6541 yards
Bray
(01) 824799

CO. KILDARE

Athy G.C.
(9) 6158 yards
Geraldine, Athy
(0607) 31727

Bodenstown G.C.
(18) 7031 yards
Bodenstown, Sallins
(045) 97096

Cill Dara G.C.
(9) 6196 yards
Cilldara, Kildare Town
(045) 21433

IRELAND
COMPLETE GOLF

Clongowes G.C.
(9) 5743 yards
Clongowes Wood, College Naas
(045) 68202

Curragh G.C.
(18) 6565 yards
Curragh
(045) 41238

Naas G.C.
(9) 6233 yards
Kerdiffstown, Naas
(045) 97509

CO. KILKENNY

Callan G.C.
(9) 5844 yards
Geraldine, Callan
(056) 25136

Castlecomer G.C.
(9) 6985 yards
Castlecomer
(056) 41139

Kilkenny G.C.
(18) 6374 yards
Glendine, Kilkenny
(056) 22125

CO. LAOIS

Abbey Leix G.C.
(9) 5680 yards
Abbey Leix, Portlaoise
(0502) 31450

Heath G.C.
(18) 6247 yards
Portlaoise
(0502) 26533

Mountrath G.C.
(9) 5492 yards
(0502) 32558

Portarlington G.C.
(9) 5294 metres
Garryhinch, Portarlington
(0502) 23115

Rathdowney G.C.
(9) 5416 yards
Rathdowney
(0505) 46170

CO. LONGFORD

Co. Longford G.C.
(18) 6028 yards
Dublin Road, Longford
(043) 46310

CO. LOUTH

Ardee G.C.
(9) 6074 yards
Town Parks, Ardee
(041) 53227

County Louth G.C.
(18) 6800 yards
Baltray, Drogheda
(041) 22329

Dundalk G.C.
(18) 6740 yards
Blackrock, Dundalk
(042) 21731

Greenore G.C.
(18) 6150 yards
Greenore
(042) 73212

CO. MEATH

Headfort G.C.
(18) 6393 yards
Kells
(046) 40148

Laytown & Bettystown G.C.
(18) 6254 yards
Bettystown, Drogheda
(041) 27534

Royal Tara G.C.
(18) 6343 yards
Bellinter, Navan
(046) 25244

Trim G.C.
(9) 6266 yards
Newtownmoynagh, Trim
(046) 31463

CO. MONAGHAN

Clones G.C.
(9) 550 yards
Hiton Park, Clone
Scotshouse 17

Nuremore G.C.
(9) 6032 yards
Nuremore, Carrickmacross
(042) 61438

Rossmore G.C.
(9) 5859 yards
Rossmore Park, Monaghan
(047) 81316

CO. OFFALY

Birr G.C.
(18) 6216 yards
The Glenns, Birr
(0509) 20082

Edenberry G.C.
(9) 5791 yards
Boherbree, Edenderry
(0405) 31072

Tullamore G.C.
(18) 6314 yards
Brookfield, Tullamore
(0506) 21439

CO. TIPPERARY

Cahir Park
(9) 6262 yards
Kilcommon, Cahir
(062) 41474

Carrick-on-Suir G.C.
(9) 5948 yards
Garravoone, Garrick-on-Suir
(051) 40047

Clonmel G.C.
(18) 6330 yards
Lyreanearla, Clonmel
(052) 21138

Nenagh G.C.
(18) 5911 yards
Beechwood, Nenagh
(067) 31476

Roscrea G.C.
(9) 6059 yards
Roscrea
(0505) 21130

Templemore G.C.
(9) 5194 yards
Templemore
Templemore 53

Thurles G.C.
(18) 6230 yards
Thurnes
(0504) 21983

Tipperary G.C.
(9) 6074 yards
Rathanny, Tipperary
(062) 51119

CO. WATERFORD

Dungarvon G.C.
(9) 6282 yards
Ballinacourty, Dungarvan
(058) 41605

Lismore G.C.
(9) 5460 yards
Lismore
(058) 54026

Tranmore G.C.
(18) 6408 yards
Tranmore
(051) 81247

Waterford G.C.
(18) 6237 yards
Newrath, Waterford
(051) 74182

CO. WESTMEATH

Moate G.C.
(9) 5348 yards
Moate
(0902) 31271

Mullingar G.C.
(18) 6370 yards
Belvedere, Mullingar
Mullingar 8366

CO. WEXFORD

Courtown G.C.
(18) 6398 yards
Courtown Harbour, Gorey
(055) 25166

Enniscorthy G.C.
(9) 6220 yards
Knockmarshall, Enniscorthy
(055) 33191

New Ross G.C.
(9) 6102 yards
Tinneranny, New Ross
(051) 21433

Rossclare G.C.
(18) 6485 yards
Strand, Rosslare
(053) 32113

Wexford G.C.
(9) 6038 yards
Mulgannon, Wexford
(053) 42238

CO. WICKLOW

Arklow G.C.
(18) 5770 yards
Arklow
(0402) 32492

Baltinglass G.C.
(9) 6070 yards
Baltinglass
(0508) 81350

Blainroe G.C.
(18) 6681 yards
Blainroe
(0404) 68168

Bray G.C.
(9) 6250 yards
Ravenswell Road, Bray
(01) 862484

Coollattin G.C.
(9) 5966 yards
Coollattin, Shillelagh
(055) 29125

Delgany G.C.
(18) 5249 yards
Delgany
(404) 874536

Greystones G.C.
(18) 5900 yards
Greystones
(01) 876624

Wicklow G.C.
(9) 5536 yards
Dunbar Road, Wicklow
(0404) 67379

Woodenbridge G.C.
(9) 5790 yards
Arklow
(0402) 5202

DRIVING RANGES

ENGLAND

Ascot
Lavender Park Golf Centre,
Swinley Road,
Ascot,
Berkshire.
Tel: (0344) 4074

Blackpool
Phoenix Sporting and
Leisure Centre,
Fleetwood Road,
Norbeck,
Blackpool,
Lancs.
Tel: (0253) 854846

Bolton
Kearsley Golf Range,
Moss Lane,
Kearley,
Bolton,
Greater Manchester
Tel: (0204) 75726

Chatham
Chatham Golf Centre,
Street-End Road,
Chatham,
Kent.
Tel: (0634) 48925

Chingford
Chingford Golf Range,
Waltham Way,
Chingford,
Essex.
Tel: 01-524 2409

Cobham
Fairmile Hotel,
Portsmouth Road,
Cobham,
Surrey.
Tel: (0932) 64419

Colchester
Ardleigh Golf Range,
Ipswich Road,
Ardleigh,
Colchester,
Essex.
Tel: (0206) 230211

Colnbrook
Colnbrooke Golf Driving Range,
Gallymead Road,
Colnbrook,
Slough,
Bucks.
Tel: (0753) 682670

Coventy
Coventry Golf Drive Centre,
Sandpits Lane,
Keresley,
Coventry,
West Midlands.
Tel: (020333) 3405

Croydon
Croydon Golf Centre,
175 Long Lane,
Addiscombe,
Surrey.
Tel: 01-656 1690

Ealing
Ealing Driving Range,
Rowdell Road,
Northolt,
Middlesex.
Tel: 01-845 4967

Finchley
Finchley Driving Range,
High Road,
Finchley,
London N12.
Tel: 01-445 0411

Gloucester
Gloucester Hotel and
Country Club,
Robinswood Hill,
Gloucester.
Tel: (0452) 25653

Horam
Easterfields Golf Complex,
Chiddingly Road,
Horam,
Nr. Heathfield,
East Sussex.
Tel: (0435) 3355

Ipswich
Ipswich Golf Range,
Suffolk Show Ground,
Bucklesham Road,
Ipswich,
Suffolk.
Tel: (0473) 76821

Kingston-on-Hull
National Avenue,
Hull,
Humberside.
Tel: (0482) 492720

Leatherhead
Riverside Driving Range,
River Lane,
Fetcham,
Leatherhead,
Surrey.
Tel: (0372) 5713

Leicester
Range Inn Golf Range,
Melton Road,
Leicester.
Tel: (0533) 664400

Newcastle
Gosforth Park Golf Centre,
High Gosforth Park,
Newcatle-upon-Tyne.
Tel: (0632) 4867

Northampton
Delapre Golf Complex,
Eagle Valley Way,
Northampton.
Tel: (0604) 64036

Norwich
Norwich Golf Centre,
Long Lane,
Bawburgh,
Norwich,
Norfolk.
Tel: (0603) 746390

Nottingham
Carlton Forum Golf Target Range,
Foxhill Road,
Carlton,
Nottingham.
Tel: (0602) 612949

Old Woking
Hoebridge Golf Centre,
Old Woking,
Surrey.
Tel: (04862) 22611/2

Orpington
Ruxley Golf Centre,
Sandy lane,
St. Paul's Crag,
Orpington,
Kent.
Tel: (0689) 71490

Pease Pottage
Fairways Golf Driving Range,
Horsham Road,
Pease Pottage,
Sussex.
Tel: (0293) 33000

Portsmouth
Portsmouth Golf Centre,
Eastern Road,
Portsmouth,
Hampshire.
Tel: (0705) 664549

Reading
Sindlesham Driving Range,
Mole Road,
Wokingham,
Berkshire.
Tel: (0734) 788494

Richmond
Richmond Driving Range,
Richmond Athletic Sports Ground,
Twickenham Road,
Surrey.
Tel: 01-940 5570

Saffron Walden
Saffron Walden Driving Range,
Little Walden Road,
Saffron Walden,
Essex.
Tel: (0799) 23339

St. Neots
St. Neots Leisure Centre,
Eynesbury Hardwicke Golf Club,
Eyesbury Hardwicke,
St. Neots,
Cambs.
Tel: (0480) 217951

Swindon
Broome Manor Golf Complex,
Pipers Way,
Swindon,
Wiltshire.
Tel: (0793) 32403

Tilsworth
Broad Range Golf and
Leisure Centre,
Dunstable Road,
Tilsworth,
Beds.
Tel: (0525) 210721/2

Warwick
Warwick Golf Centre,
The Racecourse,
Warwick.
Tel: (0926) 494316

Washington
George Washington Hotel,
Stone Cellar Road,
Washington,
Tyne & Wear.
Tel: (091417) 2626

Watford
Watford Driving Range,
Sheeptcot Lane,
Garston,
Watford,
Herts.
Tel: (0923) 75560

Welwyn Garden City
Welwyn Hatfield Sports Centre,
Gosling Stadium Driving Range,
Stanborough Road,
Welwyn Garden City,
Herts.
Tel: (0707) 331056

Windlemere
Windlemere Golf Course,
Windlesham Road,
West End,
Woking,
Surrey.
Tel: (09905) 8727

Wolverhampton
Three Hammers Golf Centre,
Coven,
Nr. Wolverhampton,
West Midlands.
Tel: (0902) 790428

Wokingham
Downshire Golf Club,
Easthampstead Park,
Wokingham,
Berkshire.
Tel: (0344) 424066

SCOTLAND

Edinburgh
Port Royal Golf Range,
Ingliston,
Lothian.
Tel: (031) 333 4377

Hamilton
Strathclyde Country Park
Golf Range,
Mote Hill,
Hamilton,
Strahtclyde.
Tel: (0698) 286505

Uddingston
Clydeway Golf Centre,
Blantye Farm Road,
Uddingston,
Strathclyde.
Tel: (041 641) 8899

CHANNEL ISLANDS

Jersey
Western Golf Range,
St. Ouen Bay,
Jersey.
Tel: (0534) 82787

NORTHERN IRELAND

Belfast
Knock Bracken Golf Centre,
Ballymaconaghy Road,
Befast.
Tel: (0232) 643554

Newtownards
Bradshaw's Brae Golf Centre Ltd.,
115 Belfast Road,
Killarn,
Newtownards,
Co. Down.
Tel: (0247) 813484

EIRE

Bishopswood
Ward Driving Range,
Bishopswood,
Ashbourne Road,
County Dublin.
Tel: (0001) 348711

Celbridge,
Celbridge Golf Range,
Dublin Road,
Celbridge,
County Kildare.
Tel: (0001) 288833

Dundalk
Paddock Wood Golf
Driving Range,
Green Gates,
Dublin Road,
Dundalk,
County Louth.
Tel: (042) 38108

Leopardstown
Leopardstown Golf Centre,
Leopardstown,
County Dublin.
Tel: (0001) 895341

Tallaght,
Spawell Driving Range,
Tallaght,
County Dublin.
Tel: (0001) 907990

PLAY GOLF AND GO RACING WITH KENSINGTON WEST PRODUCTIONS

FOLLOWING THE FAIRWAYS

"Personally I have been lucky enough to play on many courses, old and new, links by the sea, heathland and park courses inland. Like many golfers I have very happy memories of these visits and indeed of the hotels closely associated with the courses. Following the Fairways will remind me of them. I still share also the enjoyment of those who look forward to playing on a course for the first time. Again the book will be especially valuable."

Foreword to 3rd Edition — THE RT. HON. VISCOUNT WHITELAW, C.H., M.C.

— 2,000 golfcourses in the British Isles and Ireland

— 600 featured Golf courses

— Recommended Inns

— Hotels

— Restaurants

— Pubs

— 60 In-depth articles on Britain's leading Championship Courses including their course cards

— 80 Fine Art illustrations from the 18th Century to the Present

— 256 Pages full colour

THE HOLIDAY GOLF GUIDE 1990

The most up to date and informative guide to golf in Europe.
Includes information on:

— Hotels, Restaurants

— Tour operators, Airlines, Villa Hire, Car Hire, Local Information.

— Over 1200 golfing Holiday ideas in:

— France
— Ireland
— Spain
— England
— Portugal
— Wales
— Scotland

— Exotic golfing locations:

— Golf on Safari, Golf in the Far East Florida, and many more

— Interests for the non-golfing partner

— In-depth features on courses around the world

— 45 course cards of Europe's best

— Travel information and property articles

— Specially commissioned Holiday golf Guide listings for short breaks and special tours

— Specially commissioned fine art and maps

— 242 pages full colour

TRAVELLING THE TURF 1990

"I must admit I only recently came across Travelling The Turf but already I have found it invaluable. Although I spend a great deal of my time travelling I only know the areas by the racecourse so it is always a problem knowing where to stay and eat when the necessity arises during my travels. This publication offers all the information I need not only for here but Ireland as well."

PETER SCUDAMORE — Foreword to Travelling the Turf 1990

— Articles on Racehorse ownership

— Diversions for the non-racegoer

— In-depth features on all 59 Racecourses

— Recommended Inns

— Hotels

— Restaurants

— Pubs

— Other attractions near the racecourses

— Beautifully illustrated with over 120 colour plates

— 272 pages full colour

SEE PAGE 256 TO ORDER